Lecture Notes in Computer Science 14907

The series Lecture Notes in Computer Science (LNCS), including its subseries Lecture Notes in Artificial Intelligence (LNAI) and Lecture Notes in Bioinformatics (LNBI), has established itself as a medium for the publication of new developments in computer science and information technology research, teaching, and education.

LNCS enjoys close cooperation with the computer science R & D community, the series counts many renowned academics among its volume editors and paper authors, and collaborates with prestigious societies. Its mission is to serve this international community by providing an invaluable service, mainly focused on the publication of conference and workshop proceedings and postproceedings. LNCS commenced publication in 1973.

Rogier van de Wetering · Remko Helms ·
Ben Roelens · Samaneh Bagheri ·
Yogesh K. Dwivedi · Ilias O. Pappas ·
Matti Mäntymäki
Editors

Disruptive Innovation in a Digitally Connected Healthy World

23rd IFIP WG 6.11 Conference
on e-Business, e-Services and e-Society, I3E 2024
Heerlen, The Netherlands, September 11–13, 2024
Proceedings

Springer

Editors
Rogier van de Wetering
Open Universiteit
Heerlen, The Netherlands

Remko Helms
Open Universiteit
Heerlen, The Netherlands

Ben Roelens
Open Universiteit
Heerlen, The Netherlands

Samaneh Bagheri
Open Universiteit
Heerlen, The Netherlands

Yogesh K. Dwivedi
Swansea University
Swansea, UK

Ilias O. Pappas
University of Agder
Kristiansand, Norway

Matti Mäntymäki
University of Turku
Turku, Finland

ISSN 0302-9743 ISSN 1611-3349 (electronic)
Lecture Notes in Computer Science
ISBN 978-3-031-72233-2 ISBN 978-3-031-72234-9 (eBook)
https://doi.org/10.1007/978-3-031-72234-9

This Springer imprint is published by the registered company Springer Nature Switzerland AG
The registered company address is: Gewerbestrasse 11, 6330 Cham, Switzerland

Preface

The 23rd IFIP Conference e-Business, e-Services, and e-Society (I3E 2024) brought together contributions from various perspectives, disciplines, and communities to advance knowledge regarding disruptive innovation in a digitally connected, healthy world.

The advent of generative AI has significantly impacted businesses, societies, and countries globally. This technology, along with other disruptive innovations such as big data analytics, blockchain, robotics, IoT, online healthcare, and remote work solutions, has fundamentally transformed how organizations and societies address the evolving demands of customers and citizens in an increasingly intricate business landscape. Both scholarly research and practical observations indicate that integrating these digital advancements has witnessed a substantial leap forward at multiple tiers, from organizational to societal and national levels. The challenges of implementing these technologies are anticipated to persist in the long term, underscoring the enduring impact of generative AI and its counterparts on post-COVID economies and societies.

The rapid adoption of disruptive technologies presents substantial challenges and reshapes the world, businesses, and societies. It also offers opportunities to foster prosperity, human well-being, and sustainability of business ecosystems. Therefore, digital connectivity and skills will become even more critical as foundations to enable the adoption of broader disruptive technologies and maintain the viability, adaptiveness, and competitiveness of industries in this new ecosystem and economic environment. One particular industry that has seen increased investment in digital infrastructure and digital skills is healthcare. Globally, many healthcare systems struggled in the earliest stages of the COVID-19 pandemic. Also, in the post-COVID-19 era, healthcare organizations and systems are addressing key challenges of providing high-quality, efficient, and accessible care while facilitating the (tele)monitoring and management of exponentially increasing chronic diseases such as obesity, chronic obstructive pulmonary disease, and diabetes using digital technologies.

While the disruptive innovations reshape individual work behavior, organizational structures, and collaborations, many theoretical perspectives fall short of understanding the new reality. Moreover, rapid expansion and adoption of digital innovation provide many opportunities to discuss and rethink the theoretical and methodological underpinnings to understand how these innovations are used in practice. Digital innovation can be crucial in creating a sustainable, inclusive, and interconnected world. Therefore, this conference elucidated the opportunities for digital-driven disruptive innovations and reflected on how the research community can address the challenges of innovations.

The call for papers invited both full and short paper formats under the theme "Disruptive innovation in a digitally connected healthy world". In total 77 submissions were submitted to I3E 2024. All submissions underwent a single-blind peer-review process, with a minimum of three reviewers per submission. Reviewers were able to indicate their preferences for papers within their specific domain of expertise. Additionally, any conflicts of interest with colleagues and/or former collaborators were managed to ensure the objectivity of the reviews. This volume contains 36 articles, comprising 28 full papers and 8 short papers, resulting in an acceptance rate of 46.8%. The review process was completed in 31 days, thanks to the contribution of 41 Program Committee members and 32 additional reviewers. The conference also featured keynote sessions with academic and practitioner experts.

The papers included in this volume have been grouped according to the following topics:

- Artificial Intelligence Adoption and Impact
- Digital Transformation and Organizational Innovation
- Healthcare, Social Well-Being, and Ethics

I3E 2024 was hosted by the Open Universiteit in Heerlen, The Netherlands from 11th until 13th September 2024. The Open Universiteit is a public university with a unique mission to develop, innovate, and offer open higher education. The Open Universiteit contributes to innovation in Dutch higher education through educational research. It has thus developed into the leading expert in the field of learning and teaching in a technology-enhanced environment. Additionally, research is conducted in various other scientific fields. Within the National Science Agenda, the Open Universiteit focuses on three themes: 'digital learning,' 'criminal law,' and 'learning, resilience, and innovation.'

We would like to show deep appreciation to the Program Committee members and additional reviewers for their efforts in evaluating the submitted papers. Our thanks also go to the local organizers for their hard work in ensuring the conference's success. We hope this volume will contribute to the progress of new academic research.

September 2024

Rogier van de Wetering
Remko Helms
Ben Roelens
Samaneh Bagheri
Yogesh K. Dwivedi
Ilias O. Pappas
Matti Mäntymäki

Organization

Conference Chairs

Rogier van de Wetering	Open Universiteit, The Netherlands
Remko Helms	Open Universiteit, The Netherlands

Conference Co-chairs

Yogesh K. Dwivedi	Swansea University, UK
Ilias O. Pappas	University of Agder & NTNU, Norway
Matti Mäntymäki	University of Turku, Finland

Program Committee Chairs

Rogier van de Wetering	Open Universiteit, The Netherlands
Remko Helms	Open Universiteit, The Netherlands
Ben Roelens	Open Universiteit, The Netherlands
Samaneh Bagheri	Open Universiteit, The Netherlands
Yogesh K. Dwivedi	Swansea University, UK
Ilias O. Pappas	University of Agder & NTNU, Norway
Matti Mäntymäki	University of Turku, Finland

Program Committee

Jeroen Baijens	Zuyd University, The Netherlands
Edward Bernroider	WU Wien, Austria
Laury Bollen	Open Universiteit, The Netherlands
Stefano Bromuri	Open Universiteit, The Netherlands
Jocelyn Cranefield	Victoria University of Wellington, New Zealand
Joshua Doe	Open Universiteit, The Netherlands
Sunet Eybers	University of South Africa (UNISA), South Africa
Gilbert Fridgen	University of Luxembourg, Luxembourg
Shang Gao	Örebro University, Sweden
Frank Grave	Open Universiteit, The Netherlands
Karan Gupta	SunPower Corporation, USA
Shengnan Han	Stockholm University, Sweden

Arjen Hommersom	Open Universiteit, The Netherlands
Ben Honyenuga	Ho Technical University, Ghana
Luminita Hurbean	West University of Timisoara, Romania
Tim Huygh	Open Universiteit, The Netherlands
Christian Janiesch	TU Dortmund University, Germany
Gustaf Juell-Skielse	University of Borås, Sweden
Arpan Kar	Indian Institute of Technology Delhi, India
Yashoda Karki	University of South-Eastern Norway, Norway
Laleh Kasraian	De Montfort University, UK
Karlheinz Kautz	Royal Melbourne Institute of Technology University, College of Business, School of Business IT & Logistics, Australia
John Krogstie	Norwegian University of Science and Technology, Norway
Hongxiu Li	Turku School of Economics, Finland
Emanuele Gabriel Margherita	Tuscia University, Italy
Machdel Matthee	University of Pretoria, South Africa
Mohammad Merhi	Indiana University South Bend, USA
Patrick Mikalef	Norwegian University of Science and Technology, Norway
Sietse Overbeek	Utrecht University, The Netherlands
Patrick Cheong-Iao Pang	Macao Polytechnic University, Macao
Niki Panteli	Lancaster University, UK
Savvas Papagiannidis	Newcastle University, UK
Sofia Papavlasopoulou	Norwegian University of Science and Technology, Norway
Douglas Parry	Stellenbosch University, South Africa
Maurice Pattij	Open Universiteit, The Netherlands
Hanlie Smuts	University of Pretoria, South Africa
Tuure Tuunanen	University of Jyväskylä, Finland
Inge van de Weerd	Utrecht University, The Netherlands
Ronald van den Heuvel	Open Universiteit, The Netherlands
Hans Weigand	Tilburg University, The Netherlands
Hans-Dieter Zimmermann	OST Eastern Switzerland University of University of Applied Sciences, Switzerland

Additional Reviewers

Brennecke, Martin
Chan, Ka Ian
Ciftci, Seyyid
Davlembayeva, Dinara
Forsgren, Emma
Gritt, Emma
Guner, Evrim
He, Zhenni

Human, Soheil
Iannacci, Federico
Kim, Song-Kyoo
Lautenschlager, Jonathan
Li, Jiaxuan
Lima Baima, Renan
Limaj, Everist
Liu, Ting
Lu, Haiyan
Luo, Yiming
Mao, Chao
Marikyan, Davit
Marxen, Hanna
Nebel, Maximilian
Neumannova, Anita
Papageorgiou, Orestis
Roth, Tamara
Tan, Chekfoung
Tchappi, Igor
Tseloni, Evgenia Yvonni
van der Staay, Alexander
Zhang, Yaozhi
Zhao, Guoqing
Zheng, Dashun

Contents

Artificial Intelligence Adoption and Impact

Public Value-Driven Assessment of Trustworthy AI in the Public Sector: A Review

Samaneh Bagheri(✉) and Vanessa Dirksen

Open University of the Netherlands, Heerlen, The Netherlands
{samaneh.bagheri,vanessa.dirksen}@ou.nl

Abstract. Despite the potential benefits of Artificial Intelligence (AI) to enhance public services, the implementation of AI in the public sector is still limited. In this work, we review the trustworthy AI literature in the public sector and provide insights into the prevailing challenges of creating and sustaining public value with AI. Findings show that research on public value-driven AI assessment is still in its infancy. It lacks an overall critical perspective on human-centric AI in general and citizen engagement in particular. Recommendations are given for future research on conducting in-depth empirical studies geared towards measuring and operationalizing ethical and societal components of AI assessment frameworks in the public sector, specifically aiming at the creation of public value.

Keywords: Trustworthy AI · Public Value · Impact Assessment · Literature Review · Public Sector

1 Introduction

The number of AI applications in the public sector is rapidly growing, transforming various aspects of public administration and service delivery. Examples of AI applications in the public sector include AI being used in tax agencies to categorize taxpayers which helps tailor services and prevent fraud; public labor organizations profiling unemployed individuals to identify suitable support programs; and immigration authorities using predictive AI to recommend applications [1–3].

Applications of AI in the public sector often come with promises to enhance the efficiency, accuracy, and responsiveness of public services. However, these applications also face criticism regarding bias and discrimination. For instance, the Dutch government's fraud detection system was found to violate citizens' rights due to a lack of transparency and privacy concerns [2]. Integrating AI into public sector decision-making promises significant benefits but also poses challenges that necessitate careful consideration. Issues such as job displacement, bias in data and algorithms, and the digital divide must be addressed to harness AI's full potential in the public sector [4].

The deployment of AI in the public sector faces unique challenges that set it apart from the private sector. It must address complex policy, societal, legal, and economic factors that private companies might avoid. Public organizations have a mandate to

Published by Springer Nature Switzerland AG 2024
R. van de Wetering et al. (Eds.): I3E 2024, LNCS 14907, pp. 3–13, 2024.
https://doi.org/10.1007/978-3-031-72234-9_1

promote the public good and, therefore must safeguard and create public values with AI, going beyond merely cost and efficiency improvements and addressing the needs of diverse stakeholders [5]. Moreover, establishing a solid foundation for developing trustworthy AI systems is a challenge, for instance, government agencies often lack well-curated data resources [6]. Trustworthy AI is "a framework to ensure that a system is worthy of being trusted based on the evidence concerning its stated requirements. It makes sure that the users' and stakeholders' expectations are met in a verifiable way" [7]. In addition to these challenges, given that trustworthy AI in the public domain is specifically aimed at creating public value and societal benefit [8], AI Impact assessment in the public sector cannot simply borrow from assessment tools and methods developed for the private sector. AI Impact assessment is best understood as a tool to identify positive and negative impacts early on to safeguard AI's benefits and avoid its drawbacks [9].

Against this background, the main purpose of this study is to identify and summarize (1) the requirements associated with trustworthy AI in the public sector; and (2) the challenges of AI applications for public value creation; with the ultimate aim of defining their implications for AI impact assessment for public value creation, by conducting a systematic literature review.

In the following sections, we will first discuss the literature review method of the study. Next, we will present the results of the review and, finally, we will conclude the paper with suggestions for future research.

2 Methodology

To achieve the research objective, we performed a systematic literature review (SLR), according to the guideline of [10]. The SLR methodology was chosen for our study due to its rigorous and structured approach to identifying, evaluating, and synthesizing existing research. We conducted the search strings using the key terms *artificial intelligence, AI, impact assessment, audit, trustworthy, socially responsible, ethical issue, social issue, public value, public values analysis, public sector, public administration, and government* that were connected by AND, OR Boolean operators. The search strings were applied to the Web of Science database to identify peer-reviewed journal articles with relevant terms related to *trustworthy AI* and *public value creation with AI in the public sector* in their title, abstract, and keywords. The Web of Science database was chosen for its extensive coverage of high-quality, peer-reviewed literature across various disciplines.

We excluded editorials and papers whose primary focus is not on AI in the public sector, and those in languages other than English. We searched in April 2024 which yielded 97 hits. We then reviewed the titles and abstracts of these papers followed by skimming their content. Through the screening process, we selected 47 final papers (of which 19 papers on trustworthy AI and 28 papers on public value creation with AI (short: AI4PV) in the public sector) from which we extracted relevant data. Data extraction was done by means of a combination of top-down and bottom-up coding in Atlas.ti. Top-down included the following predefined coding categories: methods, key findings and limitations of the study; ethical principles and/or public values under investigation; assessment measures, process, and output; AI lifecycle and mitigation of risks.

3 Results

The findings from this literature review study indicate that the empirical landscape regarding AI's impact assessment in the public sector is currently in its infancy. Survey experiments are conducted representing mostly studies on the perceived impact [11], perceived impact [12], perceived fairness [13], perceived importance of ethics [14], and perceived trustworthiness of AI [15]. In-depth case studies and primary qualitative research are scarce. The few qualitative studies are mostly based on expert interviews [16–19]. Furthermore, existing studies predominantly rely on secondary data analysis, such as content analysis of policy documents [20] and government websites [21], national and regional AI strategies [22–24], desktop research of existing case material [18], and management practices [25], limiting the depth of understanding. The absence of comprehensive case studies and qualitative analysis hinders the identification of specific impacts and challenges faced by AI implementations in the public sector.

The thematic analysis of the selected papers identified two main themes: trustworthy AI in the public sector, and AI4PV. The following sub-sections provide a detailed discussion of these themes and the related requirements and challenges of trustworthy AI in the public sector and of AI4PV respectively.

3.1 Trustworthy AI in the Public Sector

Integration of AI in the public sector holds substantial promise for improving efficiency, accuracy, and responsiveness in public services. However, it is crucial to ensure that these AI systems are trustworthy [1].

Focusing on trustworthy AI requirements, Berman et al. [1] conducted a case study on the use of AI in the Swedish Public Employment Service. The study identified a significant gap between the theoretical ambitions of trustworthy AI for public services and practical outcomes. To enhance trustworthy AI systems in the public sector, they recommend more active involvement of end-users in the AI development and evaluation process, continuously monitoring and evaluating AI systems for ethical principles and societal values, and the use of professional judgment alongside AI recommendations. Additionally, their findings underscore the importance of transparently communicating the performance and accuracy of AI systems to all stakeholders.

Table 1 summarizes our identified requirements for trustworthy AI and the challenges associated with these systems in the public sector. A more comprehensive overview of AI challenges in the public sector is provided by [3, 26].

Although we followed the SLR methodology, we do not claim that the above list is exhaustive. In addition, this list does not highlight any specific challenges faced by the public sector in AI deployment, as distinct from those in the private sector. This opens avenues for future study to better understand the complexities of AI implementation in the public sector.

In addition, it should be noted that building trust in AI systems in the public sector requires a long-term perspective rather than short-term, project-based efforts. Kleizen et al., [15] by conducting surveys with participants from the general public, suggests that – at least in the short-term – it is difficult to influence the citizens' perceived trustworthiness of AI systems. Citizens' attitudes toward AI applications in the public sector

Table 1. Trustworthy AI requirements and challenges

Trustworthy AI requirements	Description	References
Fairness	Ensuring equitable treatment and preventing biases in AI systems	[1, 7, 27]
Transparency and Explainability	Making AI decisions understandable and transparent	[1, 7]
Accountability	Defining responsibility and mechanisms for contesting AI decisions	[1, 27]
Data Security and Privacy	Protecting data from unauthorized access and ensuring privacy in AI systems	[6, 7, 27]
Robustness and Reliability	The ability of an AI system to maintain its performance despite variations. It focuses on the AI system's resilience to errors	[27]
Human Agency and Oversight	Maintaining human oversight over AI decisions	[1, 27]
Accuracy	How well the AI system performs to produce correct and reliable outputs	[1, 27]
Acceptance	The user's willingness to use AI system. It is achieved by carefully evaluating the system through specific mechanisms that assess AI systems based on the expectations of the users	[1, 7, 27]
Challenges	**Description**	**References**
Bias and discrimination	Preventing AI from perpetuating societal biases	[1, 27]
Lack of transparency and opacity	Refers to the black-box nature of AI algorithms	[1, 7]
Data quality and integrity issue	Ensuring high-quality, complete, and up-to-date data is challenging in AI systems	[6]
Ethical and legal concerns	Involve fairness, accountability, data privacy, liability, and regulatory compliance issues	[26]
Technical limitations	Developing secure, reliable, and robust AI systems is challenging	[1, 27]

largely be shaped by their pre-existing attitudes towards government. They recommend ethical AI measures should be implemented government-wide to gradually allow society to build positive experiences with AI and prevent major trust breaches, fostering trust in AI over time.

AI Ethics and Human-Centric AI in the Public Sector

Given the government's societal mandate and its crucial role in regulating AI use, ensuring accountability and ethical standards are essential in the public sector [8]. Various ethical AI guidelines have been developed worldwide, such as the EU's AI Ethics Guidelines for Trustworthy AI [28], AI4People [29]. Bélisle et al., [30], in their review of 47 AI ethical guidelines, identify common tensions among ethical principles, such as transparency versus privacy, human oversight versus algorithm explainability, and the common good versus profit-driven objectives. Also, Wirtz and Müller [31] emphasize the importance of ethical AI standards in the public sector. They suggest developing a public AI code of ethics and recommend ongoing monitoring and evaluation of its implementation.

A human-centric approach and stakeholder engagement are essential for AI development and use in the public sector to ensure that AI systems are aligned with human values and societal needs. Human-centric AI emphasizes designing and deploying AI systems that prioritize human well-being, ethical values, and societal benefits [29, 30]. Effective stakeholder engagement ensures that the development and deployment of AI systems in the public sector are inclusive, democratic, and reflective of diverse perspectives [30, 32, 33]. Engaging a broad range of stakeholders, including citizens, civil society organizations, industry experts, and policymakers, in the AI development process helps to capture diverse viewpoints and address the needs and concerns of different groups.

Schmager et. al. [2], by developing a prototype of AI systems in public welfare services and interviewing participants (citizens) about their stances on AI, identified three factors contributing to their positive attitude toward these systems: a high level of trust in government; the clear value proposition of AI benefiting both collective and individual needs; and, reassurance provided by having humans in the loop and transparency in AI processes and data usage. However, human-centered AI is difficult to achieve in practice. In this regard, Henriksen and Blond [32], through a field study on AI implementation in public sector accounting and healthcare, reveal that it is challenging to envision a complementary partnership between human professionals and AI systems with long-term benefits if these systems prioritize managerial objectives of efficiency and cost reduction, and are imposed on professionals in a top-down manner. Furthermore, identifying potential conflicts between stakeholders' interests, especially when the interests of citizens differ from those of industry and regulators is a crucial consideration in the development and use of AI in the public sector [30].

The next section will explore how the assessment of trustworthy AI may depart from the existing body of knowledge on evaluating AI applications for public value creation in the public sector.

3.2 AI4PV

Public Value Creation with AI: Instrumental over Intrinsic Values

As is common for rather uncharted territories to do with applications of 'newly emerging' technologies, prior research on public value creation with AI (AI4PV) seems to be characterized by predominantly optimistic views on the opportunities and benefits of AI for the public sector [21, 34, 35]. Only a few publications direct attention towards the prospective social costs of governmental employment of AI [16], the extent to which public values are in jeopardy [36], or possibly even disrupted [12].

Not surprisingly then, in the PV-oriented publications of this review, we see a predominant focus on instrumental values over the more intrinsic ones. Accordingly, the synthesized PV themes, (cf. Rose et. al. [37]) 'enhancement of service' and 'duty', are well represented in the publications while socially oriented public values are hardly dealt with.

First, concerning the enhancement of service, most of the research efforts revolve around the efficiency and effectiveness of public values (see [13]). Papers in this PV cluster evaluate AI deployment in terms of improvement of speed, reduction of costs, and heightened responsiveness of public services [21, 34, 36] as well as in terms of doing away with government inefficiencies [38]. Emphasis on the effectiveness and efficiency of public values in the service domain is not surprising, seeing as most AI applications, to date, pertain to the level of internal processes (cf. [39]). Attention is paid to operational and strategic matters [34, 40] and common research topics include task replacement by AI (Ingrams et al., 2020) and organizational AI capability [18, 36].

Second, and concerning the duty-based PV cluster, referring to notions of 'good government' [41] and including procedural justice and citizen trust in government [42] attention is paid to values such as transparency and fairness of governmental deployment of AI [12, 13, 17, 43]. Noteworthy here, and rather typical for the PV-oriented strand of the literature, is the work done on the allocation of discretion to AI at the expense of the autonomy of the civil servant [20, 39, 43]. A rather underrepresented topic belonging to the duty-based PV cluster is public engagement and citizen participation (cf. [23, 24, 44, 45]), except for the work of Couture et al. [46] on the governance of AI in health.

Last, and concerning the third PV cluster, scant attention is paid to socially oriented public values by way of AI (except for [47]). This cluster refers to notions of 'public good' and collective preferences [41] and includes intrinsic values such as equality and a 'just society' [45]. In this category, only conceptual work was found. Examples include the work of Fatima et al. [16] on the inclusion of the component 'social costs' in their public value AI canvas, and Hjaltalin et al. [23] calling for AI's impact on democratic values from the perspective of excluded individuals. Notable, furthermore, is the underexposure of trade-off analyses between values of the three PV clusters (cf. [48]), except for Saldanha et al. [17] on public authorities' concern for offering faster and more efficient services at the expense of transparency and accountability and Ingrams et al. [38] on instrumental versus social-political implications.

Public Value Creation with AI: For Whom?

In our quest to understand what AI impact assessment in the public sector should abide to, and which factors should be taken into consideration, we have to delve deeper into the prevailing challenges of AI4PV. To begin with, the literature shows that understanding AI4PV entails asking the question: *public value creation for whom?* and; *as considered from which perspective?* Interestingly enough, these two questions do not seem to coincide with the reviewed studies on public value creation by means of AI in the public sector. On the one hand, we observe a disregard for the people who may *use*, and hence, influence AI systems in the public sector such as public sector IT professionals and data scientists, and other civil servant user groups. The exception to date includes the study of Criado et al. [43] on service inspectors as end-users of the public administration fraud detection system.

On the other hand, there is the underexposure of stakeholders' perspectives, i.e., the experiences and perspectives of people who are directly or indirectly *affected by* the deployment of AI systems by public administration, including civil servants and citizens. This, despite the fact that in the PV literature in general and with respect to PV creation with AI in government in particular, there is a lot to do about the citizen perspective [12, 40, 45, 46]. Yet, at the time of writing this review, empirical work highlighting the actual perspective of citizens as both end-users and/or affected stakeholders is if not scarce then flawed.

The small number of studies that specifically revolve around public value creation *for* citizens are based on survey designs. First, in the bulk of these studies, respondents are government representatives *representing the citizens' perspective* as it were. In the study of Saldanha et al. [17], for instance, the evaluation of transparency and accountability provided to citizens in digital public services is done on the basis of the opinions of the experts and managers of those services. Similarly, the study of Chatterjee et al. [40], concerned with the extent to which AI-enabled services generate public value for citizens, was done amongst representatives of Indian governmental agencies. Questions such as "I believe that citizens can easily use AI-enabled public services" and "Applications of predictive analytics for the public services could improve the citizens' experience" are quite common in those surveys.

Second, some surveys on public value creation for citizens are done with citizen respondents, however, not as actual but as hypothetical end-users of the AI systems under investigation. Respondents are in these instances drawn from users of Mechanical Turk and other social media platforms [12, 13, 38, 46]. Survey questions are defined on hypothetical vignettes of AI use cases, e.g. on child welfare [12] and Automated Decision-Making (ADM) for task performance on quarantining residents via the Health Code app [13].

When PV-driven AI assessment methods, measures, and procedures of evaluation are concerned, it is safe to say that scholarship is still in its infancy. With this respect, we observe a clear emphasis on normative over descriptive analyses. Whereas the former studies are merely conceptual [21, 25], the few studies of the descriptive kind are most commonly based on empirical research. Examples include the work of [16], based on design science research, and of [17], based on qualitative expert interviews. Important to note, however, is that these studies do not go beyond the level of identification and determination of the components of PV assessment frameworks and that the operationalization of the frameworks as well as the measurement of their components are lagging behind (e.g., [47]). Hence, the scant number of publications on PV-driven assessment remains on the level of AI readiness or 'promotion tools' for PV creation with AI, rather than attempting to measure the actual impact of AI on public values.

Altogether, it may be said that the scholarship on PV creation with AI in the public sector does not show an overly critical perspective. First, we showed how prior studies on PV creation with AI lack empirical research in general, and the analysis of primary empirical material and qualitative and in-depth case studies in particular. Second, we showed how the deliberation of opportunities and benefits in terms of, most of all, efficiency and effectiveness gains, prevails over taking into account the potential negative consequences of AI deployment in the public sector. Third, and concerning the prevailing key public values under investigation, we observed a focus on instrumental public values and a disregard for the more intrinsic values in general and the underexposure to societal consequences of AI deployment in particular. Fourth, and in line with prior observation, we pointed to the absence of direct experiences of civil servants and citizens on PV creation with AI. The relative lack of critical perspective is daunting, especially when looking at the kinds of cases and types of settings analyzed in the literature, such as fraud detection [20, 43]; tax services [38]; policing [13] and crime control [35].

4 Discussion and Conclusion

This review offers an overview of the current stage of research in trustworthy AI and AI's impact on public value in the public sector. Our literature analysis indicates that although there is broad interest in AI within the public sector, research in this area is still in its early stages. With the ultimate aim of developing a framework for AI impact assessment in the public sector, we highlight three key areas that should be the focus of future research.

First, there is a pressing need for empirical studies to identify the requirements of AI systems for public value creation and to assess the associated ethical risks across different stakeholder groups such as government policymakers, AI developers, and citizens. Given the substantial potential and risks of AI systems, it is essential to evaluate them from the perspective of public value [4]. To enhance the transparency and accountability of AI systems and foster trust and acceptance among stakeholders we recommend that future research focus on developing methodologies to assess AI impacts from a public value-based perspective. These methods should prioritize public values and ethical principles alongside technical and efficiency considerations, enhancing transparency, accountability, and stakeholder trust and acceptance of AI systems in the public sector whilst ensuring alignment with societal needs and values. Research on the public-value-driven AI impact assessment in the public sector needs to build on the emerging research streams on AI impact assessment [9] and be directed at the empirical development of procedures as well as measures of evaluation to not remain at the level of normative analyses but assess the actual impact and consequences of AI in the public sector.

Second, the critical perspective essential for assessing AI's societal implications is notably lacking in many publications. While strategic goals and operational achievements are often scrutinized [45], there is a lack of analysis regarding the ethical principles and intrinsic values underlying AI applications. Addressing this requires a two-fold approach. Firstly, there is a need for a more robust and critical examination of AI's impact on public values, moving beyond instrumental values to intrinsic ones. This includes assessing the unintended consequences of AI deployment and its effects on citizen participation and engagement. Secondly, a social impact assessment (SIA) framework is imperative for evaluating AI's broader societal implications in the public sector. Drawing from existing research on digitalization and e-government, such assessments should prioritize factors like accessibility, legitimacy, and the common good.

Third, future research should focus on understanding how various user and stakeholder groups, including both civil servants and citizens, experience and perceive the public value of AI (cf. [11]) and how their perspectives on AI ethical issues may differ within the public sector. This will provide insights into the diverse framings of ethical considerations and help in developing human-centric AI systems that address the concerns of different stakeholders in the public domain.

References

1. Berman, A., de Fine Licht, K., et al.: Trustworthy AI in the public sector: an empirical analysis of a Swedish labor market decision-support system. Technol. Soc. **76**, 102471 (2024)
2. Schmager, S., Grøder, C.H., et al.: Exploring citizens' stances on AI in public services: a social contract perspective. Data Policy **6**, e19 (2024)
3. Wirtz, B.W., Weyerer, J.C., et al.: Artificial intelligence and the public sector – applications and challenges. Int. J. Public Adm. **42**(7), 596–615 (2019)
4. Medaglia, R., Gil-Garcia, J.R., et al.: Artificial intelligence in government: taking stock and moving forward. Soc. Sci. Comput. Rev. **41**(1), 123–140 (2023)
5. Desouza, K.C., Dawson, G.S., et al.: Designing, developing, and deploying artificial intelligence systems: lessons from and for the public sector. Bus. Horiz. **63**(2), 205–213 (2020)
6. Harrison, T.M., Luna-Reyes, L.F.: Cultivating trustworthy artificial intelligence in digital government. Soc. Sci. Comput. Rev. **40**(2), 494–511 (2022)
7. Kaur, D., Uslu, S., et al.: Trustworthy artificial intelligence: a review. ACM Comput. Surveys **55**(2), 1–38 (2022)
8. Chen, Y.-C., Ahn, M.J., et al.: Artificial intelligence and public values: value impacts and governance in the public sector. Sustainability **15**(6), 4796 (2023)
9. Stahl, B.C., Antoniou, J., et al.: A systematic review of artificial intelligence impact assessments. Artif. Intell. Rev. **56**(11), 12799–12831 (2023)
10. Okoli, C., Schabram, K.: A guide to conducting a systematic literature review of information systems research (2010)
11. Falco, G., Viswanathan, A., et al.: A master attack methodology for an AI-based automated attack planner for smart cities. IEEE Access **6**, 48360–48373 (2018)
12. Schiff, D.S., Schiff, K.J., et al.: Assessing public value failure in government adoption of artificial intelligence. Public Admin. **100**(3), 653–673 (2022)
13. Wang, G., Guo, Y., et al.: What type of algorithm is perceived as fairer and more acceptable? A comparative analysis of rule-driven versus data-driven algorithmic decision-making in public affairs'. Gov. Inf. Q. **40**(2), 101803 (2023)
14. David, P., Choung, H., et al.: Who is responsible? US Public perceptions of AI governance through the lenses of trust and ethics. Public Understand. Sci. p. 09636625231224592 (2024)
15. Kleizen, B., Van Dooren, W., et al.: Do citizens trust trustworthy artificial intelligence? Experimental evidence on the limits of ethical AI measures in government. Gov. Inf. Q. **40**(4), 101834 (2023)
16. Fatima, S., Desouza, K.C., et al.: Public AI canvas for AI-enabled public value: a design science approach. Gov. Inf. Q. **39**(4), 101722 (2022)
17. Saldanha, D.M.F., Dias, C.N., et al.: Transparency and accountability in digital public services: learning from the Brazilian cases. Gov. Inf. Q. **39**(2), 101680 (2022)
18. van Noordt, C., Tangi, L.: 'The dynamics of AI capability and its influence on public value creation of AI within public administration. Gov. Inf. Q. **40**(4), 101860 (2023)
19. Alexander, C.S., Yarborough, M., et al.: Who is responsible for 'responsible AI'? Navigating challenges to build trust in AI agriculture and food system technology. Precis. Agric. **25**(1), 146–185 (2024)

20. Bullock, J., Young, M.M., et al.: Artificial intelligence, bureaucratic form, and discretion in public service. Inf. Polity **25**(4), 491–506 (2020)
21. Li, Y., Fan, Y., et al.: Making governance agile: exploring the role of artificial intelligence in China's local governance. Public Policy Admin, p. 09520767231188229 (2023)
22. Foffano, F., Scantamburlo, T., et al.: Investing in AI for social good: an analysis of European national strategies. AI Soc. **38**(2), 479–500 (2023)
23. Hjaltalin, I.T., Sigurdarson, H.T.: The strategic use of AI in the public sector: a public values analysis of national AI strategies. Gov. Inf. Q. **41**(1), 101914 (2024)
24. Wilson, C.: Public engagement and AI: a values analysis of national strategies. Gov. Inf. Q. **39**(1), 101652 (2022)
25. Makasi, T., Tate, M., et al.: Value-based guiding principles for managing cognitive computing systems in the public sector. Public Perform. Manag. Rev. **44**(4), 929–959 (2021)
26. Wirtz, B.W., Langer, P.F., et al.: Artificial intelligence in the public sector-a research agenda. Int. J. Public Adm. **44**(13), 1103–1128 (2021)
27. Alzubaidi, L., Al-Sabaawi, A., et al.: Towards risk-free trustworthy artificial intelligence: significance and requirements. Int. J. Intell. Syst. **2023**(1), 4459198 (2023)
28. Kaur, D., Uslu, S., et al.: Requirements for trustworthy artificial intelligence – a review. In: Book Requirements for Trustworthy Artificial Intelligence – A Review, pp. 105–115. Springer (2021)
29. Floridi, L., Cowls, J., et al.: AI4People – an ethical framework for a good AI society: opportunities, risks, principles, and recommendations. Mind. Mach. **28**, 689–707 (2018)
30. Bélisle-Pipon, J.-C., Monteferrante, E., et al.: Artificial intelligence ethics has a black box problem. AI Soc. 1–16 (2022)
31. Wirtz, B.W., Müller, W.M.: An integrated artificial intelligence framework for public management. Public Manag. Rev. **21**(7), 1076–1100 (2019)
32. Henriksen, A., Blond, L.: Executive-centered AI? Designing predictive systems for the public sector. Soc. Stud. Sci. **53**(5), 738–760 (2023)
33. Jobin, A., Ienca, M., et al.: The global landscape of AI ethics guidelines. Nat. Mach. Intell. **1**(9), 389–399 (2019)
34. Ishengoma, F.R., Shao, D., et al.: Integration of artificial intelligence of things (AIoT) in the public sector: drivers, barriers and future research agenda. Digit. Policy Regul. Govern. **24**(5), 449–462 (2022)
35. Serey, J., Quezada, L., et al.: Methodological proposals for the development of services in a smart city: a literature review. Sustainability **12**(24), 10249 (2020)
36. Bolton, M., Mintrom, M.: RegTech and creating public value: opportunities and challenges. Policy Des. Pract. **6**(3), 266–282 (2023)
37. Rose, J., Persson, J.S., et al.: Managing e-Government: value positions and relationships. Inf. Syst. J. **25**(5), 531–571 (2015)
38. Ingrams, A., Kaufmann, W., et al.: In AI we trust? Citizen perceptions of AI in government decision making. Policy Internet **14**(2), 390–409 (2022)
39. Zajko, M.: Automated government benefits and welfare surveillance. Surveill. Soc. **21**(3), 246–258 (2023)
40. Chatterjee, S., Khorana, S., et al.: Harnessing the potential of artificial intelligence to foster citizens' satisfaction: an empirical study on India. Gov. Inf. Q. **39**(4), 101621 (2022)
41. Madan, R., Ashok, M.: AI adoption and diffusion in public administration: a systematic literature review and future research agenda. Gov. Inf. Q. **40**(1), 101774 (2023)
42. Wang, C., Teo, T.S., et al.: Public and private value creation using artificial intelligence: an empirical study of AI voice robot users in Chinese public sector. Int. J. Inf. Manage. **61**, 102401 (2021)
43. Criado, J.I., Valero, J., et al.: Algorithmic transparency and bureaucratic discretion: the case of SALER early warning system. Inf. Polity **25**(4), 449–470 (2020)

44. Distel, B., Lindgren, I.: A matter of perspective: conceptualizing the role of citizens in E-government based on value positions. Gov. Inf. Q. **40**(4), 101837 (2023)
45. Soe, R.-M., Drechsler, W.: Agile local governments: experimentation before implementation. Gov. Inf. Q. **35**(2), 323–335 (2018)
46. Couture, V., Roy, M.-C., et al.: Ethical implications of artificial intelligence in population health and the public's role in its governance: perspectives from a citizen and expert panel. J. Med. Internet Res. **25**, e44357 (2023)
47. Jeong, J.: Introduction of the first AI impact assessment and future tasks: South Korea discussion. Laws **11**(5), 73 (2022)
48. Selten, F., Meijer, A.: Managing algorithms for public value. Int. J. Public Admin. Digit. Age **8**(1), 1–16 (2021)

RPA Ready? Unlocking Organizational RPA Readiness

Samaneh Bagheri(✉) and Rogier van de Wetering

Faculty of Science, Open University, Heerlen, The Netherlands
{samaneh.bagheri,rogier.vandewetering}@ou.nl

Abstract. Robotic Process Automation (RPA) is a relatively new digital technology in business process automation that is getting more widely adopted by many organizations in various industries. However, the promised benefits of RPA are not experienced by all organizations mainly because of a lack of organizational readiness. In this study, based on a literature review and in-depth interviews with sixteen RPA experts from eight industries, we identify 17 organizational readiness factors for RPA adoption. These factors are classified under five categories: change valence, change efficacy, technology context, organizational context, and environmental context, as outlined within our organizational RPA readiness framework. Our findings suggest a need to reassess and expand the existing list of organizational readiness factors typically applied to other digital technologies to better fit with the unique context of RPA. Notably, four factors have been identified as specifically tailored to RPA: exception handling, RPA strategy, RPA governance, and RPA Process fit. Moreover, some factors may hold greater importance in achieving organizational readiness for successful RPA adoption. Among these, RPA process fit, RPA governance, and top management support emerged as the most prominent, as highlighted by 15 out of 16 experts.

The proposed organizational RPA readiness framework can help managers better prepare for the planning, prioritizing, and decision-making regarding RPA adoption initiatives.

Keywords: Robotic Process Automation (RPA) · Organizational Readiness Factors · RPA Adoption · Digital Technology

1 Introduction

While Robotic Process Automation (RPA) is a relatively new digital technology in business process automation [1–5], this technology has received substantial business attention and is regarded as "the fastest-growing segment of the global enterprise software market" [6]. RPA is defined as a low-code process automation technology that consists of software bots with the capability to mimic human behavior when performing certain tasks in a business process [4, 7, 8]. The tasks that bots perform are typically rule-based, well-structured, and repetitive [3]. RPA benefits for organizations include employee relief, improved process performance, and improved service quality while implemented

Published by Springer Nature Switzerland AG 2024
R. van de Wetering et al. (Eds.): I3E 2024, LNCS 14907, pp. 14–28, 2024.
https://doi.org/10.1007/978-3-031-72234-9_2

at a relatively low cost compared to other forms of process automation [3, 9, 10]. The global RPA market volume is forecast to grow to reach USD 6.81 billion by 2026 [8]. RPA applications can be found in various industries such as banking, and Telecom [8, 10, 11]. Examples of routine tasks that RPA can handle include reading and extracting data from different systems, automated email query processing, collation of payroll data from various sources, and invoice processing [2, 10, 12].

However, RPA adoption presents challenges such as selecting suitable processes as the basis for automation. Furthermore, RPA demands additional consideration compared to conventional process automation. For instance, detailed bot rules are essential, as bots may overlook suspicious patterns that can be easily detectable by humans [3]. Managing bot access, data privacy, and security is also crucial [5, 12]. While traditionally, humans manage data access, software bots can mimic humans and may mishandle sensitive data, especially when bots have wide access rights, posing security risks [13]. Therefore, new measures are needed to regulate the bots' access to sensitive data. Moreover, in contrast to traditional business process automation technologies, RPA is often characterized as a more lightweight technology targeting the front-end user interface rather than a company's information infrastructure [3, 7, 9]. This lower complexity in RPA implementation might encourage organizations to take a more relaxed approach and be less prepared, potentially resulting in unsuccessfully adopting RPA [5]. Consequently, the novelty of the bots and lack of organizational readiness pose further challenges to successful RPA adoption by organizations.

To obtain the promised benefits of RPA, organizations must be adequately prepared for RPA adoption [3, 10, 14]. Therefore, identifying organizational readiness factors for RPA adoption is crucial as it enables organizations to better plan, and make informed decisions, thus increasing the likelihood of a successful RPA adoption and implementation. In this context, organizational readiness refers to an organization's assessment of its preparedness to effectively adopt, and use this technology to take advantage of it [15]. Nevertheless, organizational RPA readiness has not been subject to theoretical development or empirical study yet [6]. While organizational readiness for RPA adoption stems from prior research on digital technology adoption, unique characteristics of RPA (e.g., its low-code nature), call for a focused investigation to pinpoint specific readiness factors [3, 4, 15, 16]. This emphasis is essential because "readiness models require context-specific consideration and need to be tailored to the related domain, i.e. a specific technology" [15]. In response to this gap, in this study, we develop a theoretically grounded and empirically validated framework of organizational RPA readiness factors at the organizational level. In particular, this paper addresses the following research question: *What factors determine organizational readiness for Robotic Process Automation adoption?*

To answer the research question, we carried out a two-step research study. First, to identify organizational readiness factors for RPA, we conducted a literature review that resulted in an initial list of readiness factors. Second, to validate, refine, and supplement the identified factors we conducted 16 interviews with RPA experts from eight different industries that substantially invest in RPA.

The remainder of this paper is structured as follows: First, we provide the background of our study. Next, we present our research method, followed by the presentation and discussion of our findings. We conclude by summarizing the study's findings and limitations.

2 Theoretical Foundation

Despite the growing interest in RPA as an emerging research field [3, 10], a well-defined theoretical framework addressing organizational readiness for its adoption is still lacking. To establish a solid theoretical basis for our study, we rely on two well-established research areas: organizational technology readiness [15] and digital technology adoption, acknowledging RPA as an advanced cutting-edge digital technology [9, 10, 17]. This approach enables us to identify a more comprehensive list of readiness factors from these two literature streams.

Organizational technology readiness refers to "understanding whether an organization is prepared to change and embrace new technologies" [18]. Several studies have emphasized the importance of organization readiness as an essential prerequisite for the adoption and successful implementation of new technology [14, 15, 19]. At the organizational level, readiness entails the commitment of members to change (change valence) and their collective capability to implement it effectively (change efficacy) [14, 20]. In addition, scholars have emphasized the importance of contextual factors, like organizational structure and culture, in shaping organizational readiness for change [14, 15, 19, 20]. However, these studies typically focus on specific contextual factors and often lack a structured overview of the various contextual factors.

We use the TOE (Technology-Organization-Environment) framework to address these shortcomings. This framework is widely recognized for its applicability in studying technology adoption at the organizational level and provides a comprehensive understanding of contextual factors [10, 16, 21]. It covers three categories of contextual factors: the technological context, the organizational context, and the environmental context. The technological context encompasses both internal and external technologies relevant to the organization including IT infrastructure, and IT human resources. In this study, as our focus is on identifying the organizational factors related to IT adoption, only the internal technological context is considered. Organizational context relates to the characteristics and resources of the organization itself. This includes factors such as top management support, financial resources, and organizational structure. Environmental context refers to external business elements, like supplier relations [10, 16].

By integrating organizational technology readiness theory with the TOE framework, we develop an integrative framework consisting of five categories: change valence, change efficacy, technology context, organization context, and environment context. Within this framework (Table 1), we classify a range of organizational readiness factors identified in the literature on digital technology adoption.

While these theoretical factors offer valuable insights into organizational RPA readiness, their specific relevance in the context of RPA remains unclear and requires further investigation.

Tablel. Initial list of organizational readiness for digital technology adoption

Category	Organizational readiness factors for digital technology adoption	References
Change valence	Employees' motivation and willingness	[14, 19, 21]
Change efficacy	Resource readiness (financial resources, human resources, IT infrastructure)	[10, 14, 15, 19, 22–24]
	Cognitive readiness: knowledge (awareness, upskilling)	[14, 15, 19, 25]
Technological context	IT infrastructure	[14, 19, 21, 22]
Organizational context	Top management support	[10, 15, 22, 23]
	Communication	[4, 10, 14]
	Organizational culture (innovativeness, collaborative work)	[14, 15, 19, 23, 24]
	Organizational structure	[10, 19]
Environmental context	Vendor selection & relationship	[14, 19]

3 Methodology

This study aims to identify readiness factors for RPA adoption at the organizational level. Given the exploratory nature of this investigation, a cross-industry expert interview approach seems suitable [4, 15, 26]. This method allows for an in-depth understanding of the factors affecting organizational readiness for RPA, drawing on the insights and experiences of experts across different industries and organizations.

We conducted semi-structured interviews, incorporating a combination of open-ended and theoretically-driven questions [27]. Initially, opening questions encouraged participants to share their industry experiences and foster rapport with the interviewer. Subsequent interview questions were thematically structured, informed by the integration of the organizational technology readiness with the TOE framework as illustrated in Table 1. This approach facilitates the effective analysis of collected data using the theoretical construct applied in this study [21]. Each question targeted specific readiness factors within the initial framework, evaluating their relevance in the context of RPA. To gain rich contextual insights from interviewees they were encouraged to provide the rationale behind their responses by asking "why" questions.

To identify eligible participants for the study, we adopted a purposeful sampling strategy that involved defining participant selection criteria [28]. First, individuals considered RPA experts should have at least two years of experience actively engaging in RPA initiatives, ensuring they have a solid understanding of the subject. Given the relatively recent emergence of RPA in the market, this level of experience was considered sufficient. Second, participants should hold managerial positions such as senior managers, IT directors, project managers, or RPA implementation leads, as they play a crucial role in decision-making processes related to RPA adoption. Third, participants were selected from various industries, such as finance, and manufacturing, to capture diverse perspectives from a wide range of organizational contexts. Fourth, participants should have higher education as it provides enhanced analytical skills, critical thinking, a broad knowledge base. This can contribute to more nuanced discussions on RPA readiness factors.

We identified and enlisted 16 experts across different industries based on these criteria. These industries include telecom, insurance, retail, energy, manufacturing, banking & finance, and utilities, which are known for their substantial investments in RPA [29]. Our sample size of 16 experts adheres to the guideline proposed by [30] which suggests sample sizes ranging from 15 to 30 participants for qualitative studies. Table 2 outlines a summary of these experts.

Table 2. Overview of the Interviewees

ID	Industrial sector	Function	RPA Experience
A	Banking & Finance	Manager	3 years
B	RPA consultancy service	COO & co-founder	3.5 years
C	Banking & Finance	Senior RPA manager	4 years
D	Retail	IT datacenter & robotics manager	3 years
E	RPA consultancy service	Managing director	2.5
F	Telecom	Product owner RPA	2 years
G	Banking & Finance	RPA project manager	3 years
H	Retail	IT manager – RPA	4.5 years
I	Telecom	Product owner RPA	4
J	Banking & Finance	RPA project manager	3.5
K	Retail	Director BPI & RPA	3 years
L	Manufacturing	Corporate RPA lead	4 years
M	Banking & Finance	Global lead RPA	7 years
N	Banking & Finance	Senior RPA project manager	6 years
O	Insurance	Process & innovation manager	4.5 years
P	Utilities	RPA program and system manager	3.5 years

Most of the 16 participants in our study are affiliated with multinational organizations based in the Netherlands. The interviews were conducted virtually via Microsoft Teams over two months. Each interview took approximately 60–90 min and was recorded.

Following the transcription of all interviews, we proceeded with data analysis. Each interview transcript was reviewed and coded according to the readiness factors and main categories outlined in Table 1. Initially, one researcher conducted the coding process. To enhance the reliability of the results and minimize researcher bias, a second researcher independently coded four randomly selected transcripts. The research team then compared the coding results to identify, discuss, and resolve any inconsistencies. Additionally, we aimed to identify any additional readiness factors. The research team engaged in discussions regarding these newly identified readiness factors, aiming to decide whether they should be integrated into the existing factors or considered as distinct readiness factors specific to RPA adoption.

4 Results and Discussion

In this section, we present our findings derived from the analysis of interview data. In total 16 interviews were held with RPA experts from eight different industries. The participants highlighted the importance of organizations being prepared for RPA adoption and implementation, and they don't believe that all organizations are ready to implement RPA. For instance, Expert O stated, "*The ease of use of RPA was introduced within our company, caused us to overestimate our organizational readiness. It is more complex than expected*".

The relevance of readiness factors for RPA adoption (Table 1) was discussed with the participants. Moreover, during the interview, additional readiness factors for RPA were proposed by the participants which are discussed in this section. A total of 17 organizational RPA readiness factors are confirmed or proposed by the participants. These factors are classified into five categories following the structure of Table 1. A proposed framework for organizational RPA readiness factors is illustrated in Table 3.

Through data analysis of expert interviews, we confirmed all readiness factors outlined in the literature. Notably, among these factors, **top management support** emerged as paramount for successful organizational RPA adoption, as highlighted by 15 out of 16 participants. "*Everywhere I see RPA succeed, they have top management support*" (expert B). The top management support ensures that the resources are made available for RPA (experts A and G).

Additionally, RPA awareness, IT infrastructure, communication, and organizational structure were identified by 13 participants as relevant organizational RPA readiness factors. The experts indicated that **RPA awareness** is important for creating a clear understanding of what RPA is and its capabilities. Expert N noted "*it is very important for two reasons 1) demystifying because people find everything that has to do with robots quite scary, and (2), the more people know what RPA is, the easier it is to identify processes for automation.*" Organizations use various methods to raise RPA awareness among employees, including workshops, and inspirational sessions (Expert P).

Our experts highlighted the critical role of a stable **IT infrastructure** for ensuring the reliability and effectiveness of RPA applications (experts I and M). For instance, expert K stated, "*Every bot you build uses IT systems, so you need to coordinate that. Otherwise it will be difficult to run a robot*". They also indicated the crucial role of IT infrastructure for data security, bot onboarding, and maintenance.

The experts emphasized the importance of effective **communication** with stakeholders throughout the RPA adoption and implementation process. This includes sharing plans, activities, and results related to RPA initiatives. For example, expert N highlighted "*the effectiveness of communicating success stories from satisfied employees can improve a positive perception of RPA within the organization*". In line with this, expert D stated "*No matter what change you make within the organization, communication is important, without it people don't know it exists which may lead to potential misunderstandings*".

In addition, the majority of participants (13 out of 16) indicated the importance of establishing a clear **organizational structure** for RPA initiatives. This suggests that organizations must define roles and responsibilities, establish Centers of Excellence (CoEs), and adopt agile methodologies to drive successful automation projects. For example, expert B pointed out a common misstep in RPA implementation: "*Organizations often neglect to assign dedicated roles*". In line with this, expert E mentioned that "*four primary roles come into play in RPA initiatives: bot developers, project managers, process re-engineers, and domain experts.*" Our experts also emphasized the significance of CoE in guiding the success of RPA initiatives by centralizing expertise and resources (Expert C, E, and I). Moreover, many RPA teams opt for specific working methodologies such as agile, scrum, and DevOps. For instance, participant L emphasized the significance of *flexible and iterative project management practices in RPA development by adopting the agile approach.*

In contrast, the factor of **vendor selection & relationship** was perceived, by nine out of sixteen participants, to have minimal impact on RPA adoption. This is largely attributed to the fact that, as stated by Experts A, D, and P, "*the leading RPA vendors—Blue Prism, UiPath, and Automation Anywhere—offer comparable services, with minimal differences between them.*"

Besides confirmation of the factors outlined in Table 1, participants introduced four new readiness factors specific to RPA within the organizational context: exception handling, RPA strategy, RPA governance, and RPA Process fit. In the subsequent discussion, we delved into these unique factors.

Exception handling: Six participants highlighted the importance of incorporating exception-handling mechanisms in RPA projects. This underscores the need for proactive measures to address process inconsistencies and unexpected events to ensure the smooth execution of automated tasks. Participants C and H highlighted that failure to adequately manage exceptions can lead to increased maintenance efforts and potential automation failures. It should be noted that RPA has a limited capacity for exception handling, therefore, processes targeted for RPA should ideally have minimal encounters with exceptional behaviors to prevent interruptions in automation efforts. Previous studies have highlighted RPA's suitability for tasks characterized by standardized processes and minimal exception handling [3, 10, 25, 31]. Furthermore, while RPA is effective for rule-based tasks, the integration of AI into RPA can enhance its capacity for handling exceptions, as suggested by [31]. This presents promising avenues for future research.

RPA Strategy: Eleven participants underscored the importance of aligning RPA initiatives with organizational strategy. For example, expert B raised the question "*how do you want to implement RPA in your organization, so it is in line with the corporate strategy*". Similarly, expert C noted that "*our organization's strategy is clearly oriented towards process automation*". Moreover, participants E and N highlighted the importance of measuring the results and performance of RPA initiatives. This highlights the importance of having a clear vision and roadmap for RPA adoption, as well as establishing KPIs to measure RPA success, ensure alignment with business objectives, and maximize the value derived from RPA investments [4, 10].

Table 3. Organizational RPA Readiness Factors Framework

Readiness factor	Num.	Participant argument – Example quotes
Change Valence		
Motivation & Willingness	9	**H:** Unless the people are willing to automate their process, you cannot get near their work. You cannot robotize processes without consent from them. **I:** Forced upskilling doesn't work for RPA success. You need high potentials who enjoy working with RPA, people who are enthusiastic about it, and start working on it **K:** For our first bot we did not choose the best bot or the one with the most value, but what is the most enthusiasm [...]. you need to create that wow factor and have a certain energy showing. People need to get enthusiastic about RPA and then you will see more opportunities in your firm
Change Efficacy		
Financial resource	8	**F:** Automation is not cheap. It is an investment, especially in the beginning, but you can start small and you can grow big **K:** RPA is not free, so you need to have a budget for it. But, the RPA business case is so good, that it has a rapid return on investment
Human resource	10	**D:** The success of RPA relies on selecting the right individuals who fit within the right organizational structure and possess the requisite skills **J:** Introducing RPA within an organization often introduces a completely new line of work that differs from the company's existing expertise. And that must be taken into account **O:** You need the right people from the business and from IT, and certainly from the business to properly set up a process that you want to robotize

(*continued*)

Table 3. (*continued*)

Readiness factor		Num.	Participant argument – Example quotes
Cognitive Readiness	Upskilling	9	**B:** Success with RPA doesn't happen overnight. Upskilling plays a key role in shaping the entire pipeline of tasks within your organization. Especially on the business analyst side, it is very useful. You need people from the business who understand the processes well **O:** I think upskilling is conditional for implementing RPA sustainably. That your (software) robots can be flexible for a longer period of time
	RPA awareness	13	**G:** Very important because otherwise, you will not get the right processes in the RPA projects **J:** It plays an important role in RPA adoption because it addresses people's concerns without downplaying them
Technological Context			
Compatible IT Infrastructure		13	**I:** It has a lot of impact, as it supports the stability of your entire RPA landscape. If IT infrastructure is not arranged properly, RPA security also falls. **M:** It is important because you have to have a proper infrastructure when you want to scale RPA across your company and remain compliant.
Data security, privacy, and access control		11	**A:** The (software) robots that you build have access to different systems, so how you are going to grant the robot access to your systems? **F:** A robot can do a lot of things you may not want. Do we have the right security checks in place? How are you making it traceable? **M:** Since robots process privacy-sensitive information, then compliance with rules and regulations, like GDPR, is very important.

(*continued*)

Table 3. (*continued*)

Readiness factor		Num.	Participant argument – Example quotes
*Exception Handling		6	**C:** Build a robot in such a way that whenever things break, there is an automatic notification to humans to take action. **H:** Processes may run inconsistently with each execution, resulting in fluctuating performance. Also, RPA may face difficulties in handling exceptions effectively as robots struggle to understand and adapt to them. **F:** Robots are very sensitive to process changes.
Organizational context			
Top Management Support		15	**C:** If your top leaders don't believe in RPA technology and its power, then you have a real problem with its implementation. **G:** You need top management commitment to free up time and resources so that people can start RPA initiatives. **N:** Without top management support RPA won't work. You may build a few bots, but you can never scale it towards a large-scale here-to-stay initiative.
Communication		13	**A:** It is important otherwise you will lose people along the RPA journey. **H:** Effective communication is paramount, ensuring that employees perceive RPA as a valuable aid rather than a threat. **L:** Usually unfamiliarity with RPA is a challenge, so removing this unfamiliarity through communication. **N:** From the beginning of RPA adoption it's essential to ensure open communication between IT and the business side.
Culture	Innovative culture	8	**C:** For the successful RPA implementation you need to have a culture of innovation where people are incentivized to do it. **E:** Having a culture of innovation in your firm, accelerates RPA adoption and intelligent automation.

(*continued*)

Table 3. (*continued*)

Readiness factor		Num.	Participant argument – Example quotes
	Collaborative work	12	**B:** You cannot set up RPA in all separate units, there are many different departments involved, so collaboration is key. **C:** Without good collaboration with the Automation Center of Excellence (CoE), your bots may break as systems and processes change. **E:** RPA is business-led but the IT department plays a crucial role because they control all the systems that bots interact with. So, close collaboration between the business and IT departments is crucial for RPA.
Organizational Structure		13	**B:** You have different ways to set up a CoE (Center of Excellence) for RPA, like central decentral. We have chosen a hybrid model. **C:** Establishing a CoE for RPA is crucial for guiding the success of RPA. **L:** For RPA bot development, we adopt the agile approach, like Scrum. Every two weeks we have a demo where everyone is invited to provide feedback for further development. **O:** When it comes to (software) robot sourcing, we have a small group of internal RPA developers to develop bots in-house, and combine it with some external expertise as needed.
*RPA strategy		11	**E:** As you develop your RPA strategy, it is important to determine how you will calculate return on investment and assess the success of the RPA program in your company. **I:** You must have an architectural vision about how you will roll out RPA. **N:** Our company's RPA strategy outlines our objectives for RPA projects which are reflected in the KPIs determined in our RPA strategy.

(*continued*)

Table 3. (*continued*)

Readiness factor	Num.	Participant argument – Example quotes
*RPA Governance	15	**D:** The RPA governance needs to prevent robot misuse by individuals. **J:** It is needed to address crucial questions: How will the setup and arrangement of robots be managed? Who is responsible for what? And who has the authority to initiate processes and handle data? that makes a difference **K:** Every robot has a certain task that needs to be compliant with the segregation of tasks **M:** For each process, continuous risk assessment is essential. Having mechanisms to identify and assess process risks is a part of RPA governance.
*RPA Process Fit	16	**B:** You never successfully implement RPA if choose the wrong processes. You need to test the RPA suitability, selecting the right processes is key. **C:** Our company has certain criteria, like rule-based, representative, high volume, and low complexity, to identify process fit for RPA. **K:** That is really conditional. If the process does not fit for RPA, then you really should not apply RPA to it.
Environmental Context		
Vendor Selection	7	**D:** I noticed that vendors such as Blue Prism, UiPath, and Automation Anywhere, actually have comparable services. **J:** In terms of functionality, all those platforms are so hard working on RPA, all can do the same. **N:** Nowadays all leading vendors can do so much. The difference between vendors has become little

(**Num:** the number of participants who consider a readiness factor relevant for RPA; ***:** a new readiness factor proposed by participants).

RPA Governance: Fifteen participants emphasized the need for robust governance frameworks to govern RPA initiatives. RPA governance involves the establishment of clear policies, procedures, and controls to manage risks and ensure compliance with regulations (e.g., GDPR), while effectively using automation technologies. For instance, experts H and K emphasized the role of RPA governance in preventing potential misuse and ensuring accountability within RPA environments through the segregation of duties. In addition, expert P pointed out that "*the establishment of design standards, as a part of RPA governance, ensures uniformity in the development of robots across the organization*". Moreover, RPA governance facilitates the identification, assessment, and mitigation of risks associated with RPA implementations (Expert C and M). However, concrete guidance on how such governance should be structured remains a gap in current research [4]. This opens up new avenues for future studies.

RPA Process Fit: The selection of the right processes for RPA was considered to play a crucial role during RPA adoption and implementation with every participant emphasizing its significance for organizational RPA readiness. They stressed certain criteria, including rule-based, high-volume process, human effort, and cost (experts C, and L) as key factors for assessing a process's suitability for RPA. Having a set of criteria and procedures to evaluate a process's suitability ensures that the most appropriate tasks are automated through RPA. This suitability reduces complexity and has the potential to result in faster and greater returns on investment. Recent studies have also highlighted the importance of selecting the most appropriate processes for RPA. For instance, [1] outlined a detailed set of 32 criteria, while [3] identified 13 criteria to assess the suitability of process activities for RPA.

5 Conclusion

Introducing RPA into an organization is often more complex than portrayed by RPA vendors, potentially resulting in organizations adopting RPA without being organizationally ready. Based on the literature review and cross-industry qualitative study, with a purposeful sample of sixteen RPA experts from eight industries that are substantially active in RPA, we have identified a set of 17 organizational readiness for RPA adoption and classified them into five categories of change valence, change efficacy, technology context, organization context, and environment context. As a result, we have developed a structured framework for organizational RPA readiness factors (see Table 3). Comparing this framework to other frameworks that focus on organizational readiness for digital technology, such as those cited in [14, 15, 19, 22], reveals that integrating the theory of organizational technology readiness with the TOE framework, allows us to offer a more comprehensive perspective on the relevant factors. For instance, Lokuge et al. [14], based on the theory of organizational readiness for change, identify a set of readiness factors for digital innovation but lack a structured overview of the various contextual factors. Some other studies focus solely on contextual factors, for example [22] consider organizational, technological, and environmental contextual factors for digital financial innovations, while [15] focus on organizational factors for AI adoption and classify them into five categories.

The suggested framework provides organizations with a valuable tool to assess whether they have considered all readiness factors for RPA implementation. This enables them to evaluate their organizational readiness for RPA adoption effectively. Thus, it provides a basis for organizations to conduct self-assessments regarding their preparedness for introducing RPA within their organization. Our findings suggest that the existing list of organizational readiness factors, commonly used for other digital technologies, needs to be revisited and expanded to suit the unique context of RPA better. Notably, four new RPA-specific factors have been identified: exception handling, RPA strategy, RPA governance, and RPA Process fit. Moreover, some factors may hold greater importance in achieving organizational readiness for successful RPA adoption. Among these, RPA process fit, RPA governance, and top management support emerged as the most prominent, as highlighted by 15 out of 16 experts. Prior studies on organizational readiness for digital technology adoption also emphasize the significance of top management support as a crucial readiness factor [15, 18, 22].

Our study, like any other research, has its limitations. First, while we consider the insights gained from interviews with 16 RPA experts across various industries providing a solid foundation it is important to acknowledge that the list of organizational RPA readiness factors provided in this paper may not be exhaustive. Thus, while these factors serve as a valuable starting point for further exploration of RPA adoption at the organizational level, we recognize the potential for identifying additional factors in future research. Second, by involving 16 experts selected through purposeful sampling from eight industries, our findings are generalizable to similar contexts. However, to enhance the generalizability of our findings, it is crucial to test the framework in other settings. Third, we have discussed organizational RPA readiness factors individually in this paper, exploring the interrelationships between these factors requires investigation in future studies. Finally, in this paper, our focus is primarily on the early phase of RPA adoption. However, a more comprehensive understanding could be achieved by prioritizing these factors across different adoption and implementation stages. Therefore, future research should aim to explore these aspects further.

Acknowledgments. The author wishes to thank Manon Kromwijk for her invaluable input and assistance throughout this study.

References

1. Farinha, D., Pereira, R., et al.: A framework to support robotic process automation. J. Inf. Technol. **39**(1), 149–166 (2024)
2. Ivančić, L., Suša Vugec, D., et al.: Robotic process automation: systematic literature review. In: Business Process Management: Blockchain and Central and Eastern Europe Forum (2019)
3. Syed, R., Suriadi, S., et al.: Robotic process automation: contemporary themes and challenges. Comput. Ind. **115**, 103162 (2020)
4. Plattfaut, R., Borghoff, V., et al.: The critical success factors for robotic process automation. Comput. Ind. **138**, 130646 (2022)
5. Eulerich, M., Waddoups, N., et al.: The dark side of robotic process automation (RPA): understanding risks and challenges with RPA. Account. Horiz. 1–10 (2023)
6. Hofmann, P., Samp, C., Urbach, N.: Robotic process automation. Electron. Mark. **30**(1), 99–106 (2019). https://doi.org/10.1007/s12525-019-00365-8
7. Herm, L.-V., Janiesch, C., et al.: A framework for implementing robotic process automation projects. Inf. Syst. e-Bus. Manage. **21**(1), 1–35 (2023)

8. Fernandez, D., Dastane, O., et al.: Robotic process automation: bibliometric reflection and future opportunities. Eur. J. Innov. Manage. **27**(2), 692–712 (2024)
9. Hofmann, P., Samp, C., et al.: Robotic process automation. Electron. Mark. **30**(1), 99–106 (2020)
10. Flechsig, C., Anslinger, F., et al.: Robotic process automation in purchasing and supply management: a multiple case study on potentials, barriers, and implementation. J. Purchas. Supply Manage. **28**(1), 100718 (2022)
11. Pramod, D.: Robotic process automation for industry: adoption status, benefits, challenges and research agenda. Benchmark. Int. J. **29**(5), 1562–1586 (2021)
12. Zhang, C., Issa, H., et al.: Robotic process automation (RPA) implementation case studies in accounting: a beginning to end perspective. Account. Horiz. **37**, 193–217 (2023)
13. Santos, F., Pereira, R., et al.: Toward robotic process automation implementation: an end-to-end perspective. Bus. Process. Manag. J. **26**(2), 405–420 (2020)
14. Lokuge, S., Sedera, D., et al.: Organizational readiness for digital innovation: development and empirical calibration of a construct. Inf. Manag. **56**(3), 445–461 (2019)
15. Jöhnk, J., Weißert, M., et al.: Ready or not, AI comes – an interview study of organizational AI readiness factors. Bus. Inf. Syst. Eng. **63**, 5–20 (2021)
16. Sharma, C., Bharadwaj, S.S., et al.: Robotic process automation adoption: contextual factors from service sectors in an emerging economy. J. Enterp. Inf. Manag. **36**(1), 252–274 (2023)
17. Siderska, J.: The adoption of robotic process automation technology to ensure business processes during the COVID-19 pandemic. Sustainability **13**(14), 8020 (2021)
18. Chen, X.C., Chang-Richards, A., et al.: Developing a readiness model and a self-assessment tool for adopting digital technologies in construction organizations. Build. Res. Inf. **51**(3), 241–256 (2023)
19. Hussain, M., Papastathopoulos, A.: Organizational readiness for digital financial innovation and financial resilience. Int. J. Prod. Econ. **243**, 108326 (2022)
20. Weiner, B.J.: A theory of organizational readiness for change. Implement. Sci. **4**, 1–9 (2009)
21. Hradecky, D., Kennell, J., et al.: Organizational readiness to adopt artificial intelligence in the exhibition sector in Western Europe. Int. J. Inf. Manage. **65**, 102497 (2022)
22. Alsheibani, S., Cheung, Y., et al.: Artificial intelligence adoption: AI-readiness at firm-level. PACIS **2018**(4), 231–245 (2018)
23. Hizam-Hanafiah, M., Soomro, M.A., et al.: Industry 4.0 readiness models: a systematic literature review of model dimensions. Information **11**(7), 364 (2020)
24. Chowdhury, S., Dey, P., et al.: Unlocking the value of artificial intelligence in human resource management through AI capability framework. Hum. Resour. Manage. Rev. **33**(1), 100899 (2023)
25. Alami, H., Lehoux, P., et al.: Organizational readiness for artificial intelligence in health care: insights for decision-making and practice. J. Health Org. Manag. **35**(1), 106–114 (2021)
26. Whiting, L.S.: Semi-structured interviews: guidance for novice researchers. Nurs. Stand. **22**(23), 35 (2008)
27. Galletta, A.: Mastering the Semi-Structured Interview and Beyond: From Research Design to Analysis and Publication. NYU Press (2013)
28. Gentles, S.J., Charles, C., et al.: Sampling in qualitative research: insights from an overview of the methods literature. Qual. Rep. **20**(11), 1772–1789 (2015)
29. Fersht, P.: The Present and the Future is… Robotic Business Outsourcing. HFS (2019)
30. Marshall, B., Cardon, P., et al.: Does sample size matter in qualitative research? A review of qualitative interviews in IS research. J. Comput. Inf. Syst. **54**(1), 11–22 (2013)
31. Ng, K.K., Chen, C.-H., et al.: A systematic literature review on intelligent automation: aligning concepts from theory, practice, and future perspectives. Adv. Eng. Inform. **47**, 101246 (2021)

An Explorative Study on the Adoption of Explainable Artificial Intelligence (XAI) in Business Organizations

Mahdieh Darvish(✉), Kret Samy Kret, and Markus Bick

ESCP Business School, Heubnerweg 8-10, 14059 Berlin, Germany
mdarvish@escp.eu

Abstract. Artificial Intelligence (AI), particularly Deep Learning (DL), is expanding across industries, raising concerns about data processing opacity. This has increased the demand for Explainable Artificial Intelligence (XAI) solutions. Despite its growing relevance, understanding XAI adoption drivers and its potential business impact is still limited. This study employs an exploratory qualitative approach, conducting eleven in-depth interviews to identify key factors influencing XAI adoption in business. These factors include perceived benefits, technological readiness, organizational and business factors, leadership, strategy, industry and governmental pressures and user needs. Furthermore, we use the Technology Organization and Environment model (TOE) to develop a theoretical framework that highlights technological readiness, impacts on the core business and consumer influence, determining the business value of XAI. Moreover, this paper provides managerial implications on navigating XAI adoption, by engaging stakeholders and balancing technological maturity with competitive pressures.

Keywords: Explainable Artificial Intelligence · Adoption Factors · Business

1 Introduction

Artificial Intelligence (AI) is a disruptive force for many industries [1] and is rapidly permeating more areas of society [2]. AI applications primarily involve Machine Learning (ML) algorithms, but emerging applications are increasingly dominated by Deep Learning (DL), which surpasses traditional ML performance by mimicking the brain structure through a multi-layered neural networks [3].

However, the intensified and more complex usage of AI, ML and especially DL, has made computational data processing more opaque, resulting in a 'black box' [4]. Hence, explainable artificial intelligence (XAI) has emerged to address this issue.

XAI as a research field has been growing since the 1990s, but gaining significant attention recently [4] due to an ongoing increase in AI legislation, particularly in the European Union (EU). Initiatives such as 'AI ethics guidelines' emphasize the importance of 'explicability' as one of the four ethical pillars for trustworthy AI [5].

Published by Springer Nature Switzerland AG 2024
R. van de Wetering et al. (Eds.): I3E 2024, LNCS 14907, pp. 29–40, 2024.
https://doi.org/10.1007/978-3-031-72234-9_3

Despite these advancements, there is limited understanding of how organizations can influence the adoption of XAI [7]. Accordingly, Gerlach et al. [8] highlight the need for research on the factors influencing XAI usage. Moreover, the economic perspective on how XAI can create business value remains unexplored [9]. To address this research gap, we apply an explorative approach, build upon the literature on technology adoption, and answer the following research question: What factors influence XAI adoption in business organizations?

This study examines the novel topic of XAI adoption in business by conducting eleven semi-structured expert interviews. It utilizes the Technology, Organization and Environment Model to categorize the identified factors and explores additional elements to develop a comprehensive XAI adoption model. Our results offer a holistic perspective on XAI, addressing the need for in-depth insights and providing sophisticated implications for businesses.

The remainder of this paper is structured as follows. First, we provide an outline of the literature on (explainable) AI and adoption models. Next, we describe our research methodology, which includes (1) a brief literature review and (2) insights from eleven interviews with experts in both managerial and data science roles within the XAI field. Subsequently, we present and discuss our findings. Finally, we outline practical and theoretical implications, offer concluding thoughts, and provide a summary of limitations and avenues for future research.

2 Theoretical Background

XAI involves creating models that are both explainable and high-performing, enabling users to understand, trust and manage AI systems effectively [6, 11, p. 7]. An 'explainable model' can refer to the pre-modelling stage, data processing itself or model output [12]. According to Barredo Arrieta et al. [7, p. 6], explainability involves providing clear and understandable details and reasons for how a model operates to a particular audience.

2.1 XAI Development

Initially, AI systems prioritized interpretability and explainability, often using expert systems built on decision trees, known as 'white box' models [7, 13–16]. Despite a surge in the 1980s, attention to explainability resurfaced in the 21st century due to privacy breaches and user trust concerns [17, 18, p. 6]. The term 'XAI' emerged in 2002, gaining traction with DARPA's 2017 program, aimed at making opaque AI systems human-understandable, particularly in sensitive industries [6, 15, 19, p. 6]. Ethical considerations also fueled XAI developments, supported by the academic 'FAT' (fairness, accountability and transparency) community [9, 20].

Additionally, regulatory initiatives such as EU GPDR, Article 22 (general data protection regulation) [5, 21], the US Algorithmic Accountability Act [22] and China's AI plan [4] have emphasized the importance of explainability. Moreover, major corporations such as Microsoft, Google and IBM have published XAI tools and frameworks since 2019 [23], complemented by various open-source offerings such as CaptumAI, InterpretML or AIX360 [3, 7].

2.2 Objectives, Application Areas and Challenges

The objectives of XAI can be categorized into two core groups: (a) reasons for/needs of XAI (explain to justify, explain to control, explain to improve, explain to discover) [3, 9] and (b) goals of XAI (fairness and bias avoidance, trust, understandability, insightfulness, privacy protection, transferability and causality) [23].

'Explain to justify' ensures fairness and avoids bias (Goal 1) by providing explanations for AI outcomes, fostering trust (Goal 2) and complying with regulations such as GDPR's 'right to explanation' [3, 9, 23]. 'Explain to control' manages AI-related risks by enhancing understandability (Goal 3) and insights to identify vulnerabilities and facilitate rapid error adjustments, particularly in 'low-criticality' environments, thereby improving user experience [3, 9, 23]. 'Explain to improve' involves iterative human-machine interactions to continually enhance the algorithm, achieving a smarter model [3, 9, 23]. 'Explain to discover' offers human-tailored explanations, fostering new knowledge and discoveries in various fields such as physics and biology [3, 9, 23].

However, some goals transcend these four drivers. 'Privacy protection' (Goal 5) ensures consumer privacy and secures confidential information from both users and developers. 'Transferability' (Goal 6) involves the adaptability of explainability across diverse applications and AI/ML algorithms. Lastly, 'causality' (Goal 7) examines causal relationships between data variables and assesses the effectiveness, efficiency and satisfaction of explanations provided to human experts within specific contexts [23, 24]. Nonetheless, XAI faces various challenges, including improving the accuracy/explainability trade-off, providing implementation guidelines, establishing metrics, designing user interfaces and enhancing explainable deep learning [3, 7, 16].

2.3 XAI in Business Organizations

The emergence of social and ethical expectations in AI systems has propelled XAI to become a strategic differentiator, enhancing business value [9, p. 19]. However, not all stakeholders see interpretability as essential for all AI systems, which can hinder widespread XAI adoption [9, p. 6]. Drawbacks include increased costs, reduced efficiency and constrained design choices, potentially restricting XAI's business value, defined here as the overall value brought to a corporation [25].

There is limited theoretical guidance on when XAI yields the most business value. However, certain critical industries, such as healthcare, military and finance, prefer transparent 'white box' models over 'black box' alternatives due to practical, social and legal factors [26, 27]. Adadi, Berrada [9, pp. 6–7] suggest that XAI's utility depends on the functional opacity of AI algorithms and the domain's tolerance for errors.

2.4 Technology Adoption Models

The organizational imperative for adopting IT innovations stems from evolving operational environments, driven heightened global competition, technological advancements, dynamic market conditions and persistent customer demands for quality services [28, p. 215]. Adoption models typically delineate the implementation process in three phases: pre-implementation, implementation and post-implementation. These models recognize the multidimensional nature of adoption influenced by contextual, environmental, individual, organizational and technological factors [28, 29].

In this study, we employ the Technology Organization and Environment (TOE) model [30] – a widely used framework for organizational adoption. Specifically, we use the modified TOE framework provided by Kuan & Chau [31], focusing on perceptual factors for XAI adoption.

3 Methodology

To investigate the factors influencing XAI adoption in business organizations, we adapted an explorative approach consisting of a brief literature review of related terms, concepts and frameworks, along with a qualitative content analysis. Our qualitative research design built upon existing literature and involved eleven semi-structured interviews with experts from two relevant professional groups: nine managers and two data scientists with managerial responsibilities. The in-depth semi-structured interviews provided valuable practical insights by allowing time and flexibility to capture the expert's perspectives [34].

3.1 Data Collection

Following our qualitative research design, semi-structured interviews were conducted via video calls, averaging 42 min each, over a three weeks in February/March 2023. Using a purposeful sampling strategy, we selected eleven experts through professional networks and referrals, ensuring diverse backgrounds and regions of operation (Table 1), while maintaining role homogeneity [32]. Participants were from Asia, Europe or the USA with backgrounds spanning consulting, startups, enterprises and corporations. Considering the special focus on XAI adoption in organizations and its business value, rich insights ensured that saturation was achieved at this point.

Table 1. Interviewees overview.

ID	Title/Position	Responsibilities
ID1	Ex-Vice President for Business Development and Strategic Planning	Growth strategy
ID2	Senior Research Scientist (data scientist)	Interpretable ML models
ID3	Team Lead AI	AI Strategy, Vision, Use Cases,
ID4	CEO	CEO
ID5	Senior Manager AI & Data	AI and data department
ID6	Senior Vice President	Product Development and Global business development
ID7	Data & AI Manager	AI, Data and Analytics Strategist for clients with non-traditional Use Cases
ID8	IT Consultant (data scientist)	Consultant Data Scientist and ML
ID9	Head of Data Science Strategy & Evangelist	Advising customers on data science strategies
ID10	Business Analytics Manager	Descriptive Analytics (+partly AI)
ID11	AI consultant	(Technical) AI Solution Implementation & Development

3.2 Data Analysis

We employed qualitative content analysis, following the procedural model outlined by Mayring (2014) [33] for both deductive and inductive categories (Fig. 1). Each interview sentence was coded and categorized based on similar meanings using MAXQDA software. Additionally, the coding category system was revised and improved halfway through the content analysis. The Gioia methodology was employed as a rigorous qualitative and inductive approach to organize identified codes into first-order concepts, second-order themes and aggregate dimensions, aligned with the research question [34, p. 20]. Initially, two scholars reviewed each transcript, highlighting relevant phrases and passages. This process f developed first-order concepts based on the interviewees' language. Themes and aggregate dimensions were then abstracted, incorporating terminology from existing literature (Fig. 1).

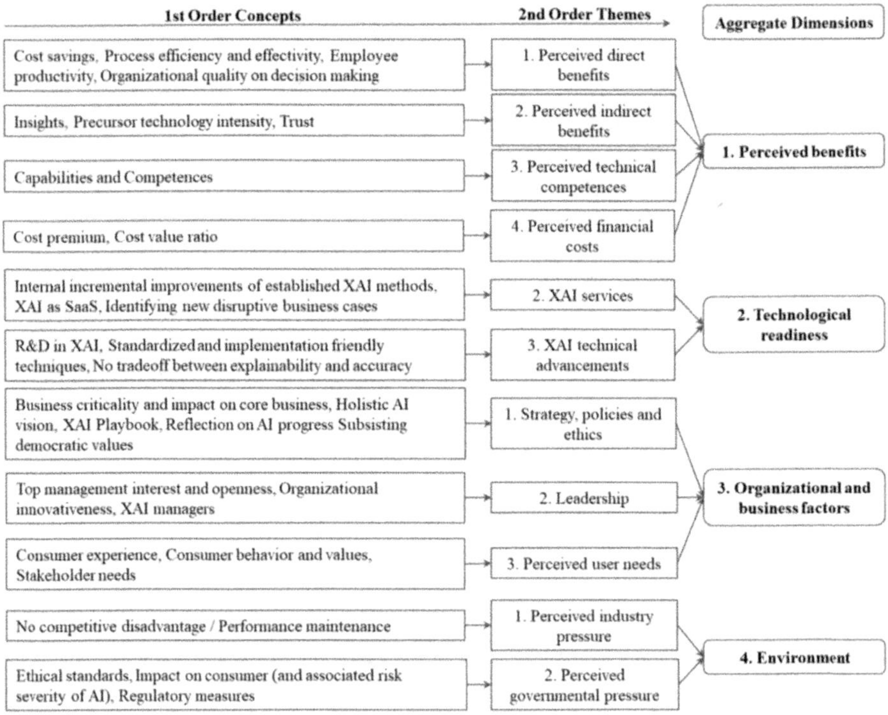

Fig. 1. Data Structure.

4 Findings and Discussion

In the context of XAI, we utilized the TOE model by Kuan & Chau [31] to encompass factors influencing XAI adoption in business. Moreover, this model was modified with additional factors identified from our interviews. The TOE model primarily adopted the technology-organization-environment perspective. However, our expert interviews revealed additional factors, leading to the inductive development of new categories. Consequently, building on the TOE, we propose the following model for XAI adoption in business (Fig. 2).

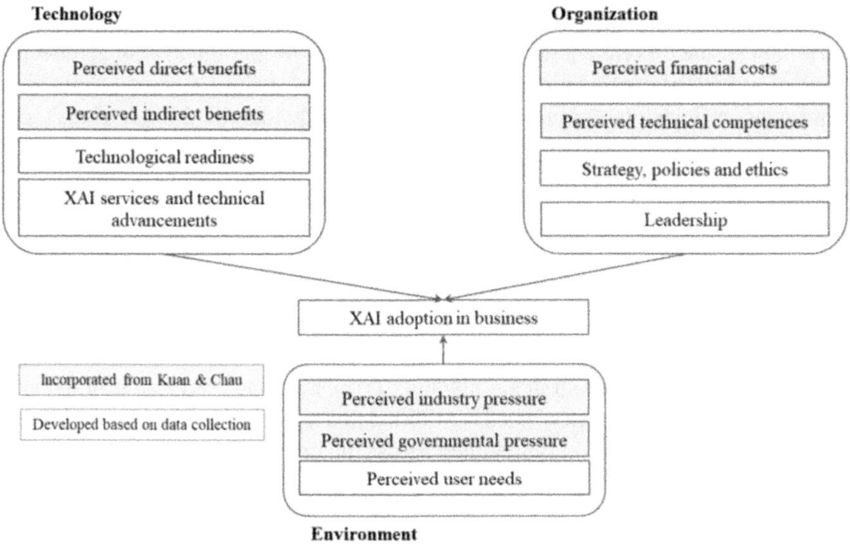

Fig. 2. Factors influencing XAI adoption in business. Based on Kuan & Chau [31], adapted by the authors.

4.1 Factors Influencing XAI Adoption in Business

Perceived Direct and Indirect Benefits. Experts highlighted direct benefits as a key driver of XAI adoption, including operational advantages such as cost savings, process efficiency & effectiveness, employee productivity, and improved decision-making quality. Moreover, perceived indirect benefits, such as trust, insights and precursor technology intensity, were rather viewed strategically. Several experts emphasized perceived financial costs and technical competences as significant factors influencing XAI adoption in business. The financial costs refer to the cost premium for using XAI and whether the cost-value ratio for XAI is favorable. Technical competences encompass the organizational skills and capabilities needed for XAI adoption: "With transparency and explainability, investors are willing to invest because they can understand and control it." (ID5)

Perceived Industry and Government Pressure. Several experts addressed perceived industry pressure as an important factor, albeit it does hinder XAI adoption. In this context, perceived industry pressure consists of an organization's desire to not lose its competitive advantage and maintain current performance according to its AI/ML algorithms. However, the current lack of technological readiness leads to perceived competitive disadvantages. Moreover, our interviewees highlighted perceived governmental pressure, consisting of ethical standards and currently planned regulatory measures, as an enhancing factor for XAI adoption through positive impacts on consumers.

Technological Readiness. All of the experts highlighted various technical factors, such as internal incremental improvements to XAI methods, the availability of XAI services and technical XAI advancements, referring to technological readiness as an influential driver spurring XAI adoption.

Organizational and Business Factors. The experts highlighted organizational ethics and policies as factors enhancing XAI adoption, consisting of organizational reflection on AI progress and the organizations' subsisting democratic values. Currently, this adoption factor is not reflected in the literature and is thus newly identified for XAI technology.

Moreover, leadership plays a pivotal role in driving XAI adoption forward. When organizational leaders exhibit innovativeness, demonstrate a keen interest in technology and maintain an open mindset toward new advancements, it fosters an environment conducive to XAI implementation. Additionally, having designated responsibilities for an XAI manager further supports the adoption process. The literature mentions these factors as 'top management support', which we integrate into the leadership factor [35]. Furthermore, strategy significantly shapes XAI adoption when organizations incorporate XAI technology into their strategic planning processes, and XAI gains strategic value by addressing critical business needs. Additionally, adoption is streamlined when XAI is part of a cohesive AI vision integrated across the organization.

Perceived User Needs. Our experts pointed out perceived user needs as a crucial driver for XAI adoption in business, including factors such as consumer behavior, consumer experience and stakeholder needs: "For any sufficiently complex pattern that you're looking to detect, the answer isn't going to be very intuitive. And so, when folks are looking for explainable AI, often they want intuitive AI." (ID9)

This driver can be indirectly inferred from the literature, where user satisfaction serves as a perceptual measure [36]. Therefore, a company may adopt XAI systems to enhance user satisfaction and cater to their needs [37].

In a nutshell, we identify four main factors influence XAI adoption in business, and integrate them into the TOE model devised by Kuan & Chau [31], thus providing a framework for XAI adoption. Perceived technical competences and costs received less emphasis, possibly because XAI builds upon existing AI technology, which organizations may already have. Additionally, financial exposure were seen as minor, since XAI primarily requires investment in new application methodologies rather hardware. Perceived governmental pressure emerged as significant, driven by ethical considerations, though it may not always translate directly into financial value. Consequently, governmental intervention is important for addressing ethical concerns and maintaining competitiveness.

Furthermore, technological readiness and perceived industry pressure play explanatory roles. Low technological readiness may hinder XAI adoption due to industry pressure, but this could change with increased readiness. Premkumar & Ramamurthy [35] distinguish between proactive and reactive decision-making in response to competitive pressure. Proactive companies are less swayed by peer pressure, prioritizing organizational ethics and policies over economic considerations. This emphasizes the importance of ethical values in driving adoption decisions.

The dimension of organizational ethics and policies, supported by theory, aligns with XAI's objective to integrate ethical perspectives into AI. Adadi & Berrada [9] argue that XAI can serve as a competitive differentiator by addressing social and ethical concerns. Additionally, integrating technology, business and ethics is advocated in the business ethics literature, highlighting the relevance of this dimension in XAI adoption.

Furthermore, the literature views the integration of technology, business and ethics as extremely essential [38, p. 354]. Thus, XAI offers itself as a competitive differentiator and serves the need to connect technology and ethics. Therefore, the dimension of organizational ethics and policies is a reasonable influential dimension for XAI adoption.

Considering the factor perceived user needs, the literature suggests delving deeper beyond generic constructs such as user satisfaction to understand XAI adoption dynamics better [37, p. 230]. Moreover, leadership and strategy exhibit strategic proximity, with empirical evidence suggesting a positive relationship between the two [39, p. 76, 57].

Finally, the highest business value of XAI is realized when it significantly impacts consumers and core business operations. Otherwise, it may be seen an operational feature or a regulatory necessity [40, pp. 4–5].

5 Conclusion, Implications, Limitations and Future Research

Our study provides comprehensive insights into XAI adoption, addressing the research question and meeting qualitative and exploratory standards. Findings from participants across three global regions offer valuable managerial and theoretical implications. First, this paper outlines key tasks and responsibilities for managers during XAI adoption, highlighting the role of an XAI manager or Chief Data and Analytics Officer in aligning stakeholders and driving related initiatives. Second, given the relationship between technological readiness and perceived competitive pressure, managers must balance XAI maturity with competitive pressures, possibly accepting a slight performance slowdown to avoid regulatory penalties for transparency issues.

Furthermore, this paper contributes significantly to the theoretical understanding of XAI adoption in business by establishing a model based on the TOE framework, identifying specific factors to XAI technology and advancing the broader discourse on technology adoption [6, 8–10, 16, 41].

However, it also has certain limitations. The sample mainly consists of managers from AI consulting or implementation services, with few from other sectors. Including managers from diverse segments could provide a more holistic perspective. Additionally, insights from industries directly selling to consumers would be valuable. Future research should integrate non-managerial perspectives and explore specific industries or domains, such as manufacturing or autonomous driving, for deeper insights. Consequently, two crucial avenues for future research involve examining the economic impact of XAI and its integration within a broader context. Current literature lacks established metrics for evaluating XAI performance and its impact on business KPIs. Investigating XAI within the framework of responsible AI is also essential, given ongoing developments in AI ethics and trustworthy frameworks. Future research should explore how XAI contributes to the pillars of responsible AI for organizations.

Disclosure of Interests. The authors have no competing interests to declare that are relevant to the content of this article.

References

1. Davenport, T.H., Ronanki, R.: Artificial intelligence for the real world. Harvard Bus. Rev. 108–116 (2018)
2. Chui, M., Hall, B., Singla, A., Sukharevsky, A.: Global Survey: The State of AI in 2021 (2021). https://www.mckinsey.com/capabilities/quantumblack/our-insights/global-survey-the-state-of-ai-in-2021. Accessed 13 March 2024
3. Ding, W., Abdel-Basset, M., Hawash, H., Ali, A.M.: Explainability of artificial intelligence methods, applications and challenges: a comprehensive survey. Inf. Sci. **615**, 238–292 (2022). https://doi.org/10.1016/J.INS.2022.10.013
4. Xu, F., Uszkoreit, H., Du, Y., Fan, W., Zhao, D., Zhu, J.: Explainable AI: a brief survey on history, research areas, approaches and challenges. Nat. Lang. Process. Chin. Comput. **11839**, 563–574 (2019). https://doi.org/10.1007/978-3-030-32236-6_51
5. High-Level Expert Group on Artificial Intelligence (AI HLEG): Ethics Guidelines for Trustworthy AI (2019). https://ec.europa.eu/futurium/en/ai-alliance-consultation.1.html. Accessed 13 March 2024
6. Meske, C., Bunde, E., Schneider, J., Gersch, M.: Explainable artificial intelligence: objectives, stakeholders, and future research opportunities. Inf. Syst. Manag. **39**(1), 53–63 (2022). https://doi.org/10.1080/10580530.2020.1849465
7. Barredo Arrieta, A., Díaz-Rodríguez, N., Del Ser, J., Bennetot, A., Tabik, S., Barbado, A., et al.: Explainable artificial intelligence (XAI): concepts, taxonomies, opportunities and challenges toward responsible AI. Inf. Fusion **58**, 82–115 (2020). https://doi.org/10.1016/J.INFFUS.2019.12.012
8. Gerlach, J., Hoppe, P., Jagels, S., Licker, L., Breitner, M.H.: Decision support for efficient XAI services – a morphological analysis, business model archetypes, and a decision tree. Electron. Mark. **32**(4), 2139–2158 (2022). https://doi.org/10.1007/S12525-022-00603-6
9. Adadi, A., Berrada, M.: Peeking inside the black-box: a survey on explainable artificial intelligence (XAI). IEEE Access **6**, 52138–52160 (2018). https://doi.org/10.1109/ACCESS.2018.2870052
10. Gerlings, J., Shollo, A., Constantiou, I.: Reviewing the need for explainable artificial intelligence (xai). In: Proceedings of the 54th Hawaii International Conference on System Sciences (HICSS), pp. 1284–1293 (2020). https://doi.org/10.24251/hicss.2021.156
11. Gunning, D.: Explainable Artificial Intelligence (XAI) (2017). https://nsarchive.gwu.edu/sites/default/files/documents/5794867/National-Security-Archive-David-Gunning-DARPA.pdf. Accessed 13 March 2024
12. Minh, D., Wang, H.X., Li, Y.F., Nguyen, T.N.: Explainable artificial intelligence: a comprehensive review. Artif. Intell. Rev. **55**(5), 3503–3568 (2022). https://doi.org/10.1007/s10462-021-10088-y
13. Longo, L., Goebel, R., Lecue, F., Kieseberg, P., Holzinger, A.: Explainable artificial intelligence: concepts, applications, research challenges and visions. In: Holzinger, A., Kieseberg, P., Tjoa, A., Weippl, E. (eds.) Machine Learning and Knowledge Extraction CD-MAKE 2020. Lecture Notes in Computer Science, pp. 1–16. Springer, Cham (2020)
14. Guidotti, R., Monreale, A., Ruggieri, S., Turini, F., Giannotti, F., Pedreschi, D.: A survey of methods for explaining black box models. ACM Comput. Surveys **51**(5), 1–42 (2018). https://doi.org/10.1145/3236009
15. Gunning, D., Aha, D.W.: DARPA's explainable artificial intelligence (XAI) program. AI Mag. **40**(2), 44–58 (2019). https://doi.org/10.1609/AIMAG.V40I2.2850

16. Dhanorkar, S., Wolf, C.T., Qian, K., Xu, A., Popa, L., Li, Y.: Who needs to know what, when? Broadening the explainable AI (XAI) design space by looking at explanations across the AI lifecycle. In: DIS 2021 – Proceedings of the 2021 ACM Designing Interactive Systems Conference: Nowhere and Everywhere, vol. **12**, pp. 1591–1602 (2021). https://doi.org/10.1145/3461778.3462131
17. Gunning, D., Stefik, M., Choi, J., Miller, T., Stumpf, S., Yang, G.Z.: XAI-explainable artificial intelligence. Sci. Robot. **4**(37) (2019). https://doi.org/10.1126/scirobotics.aay7120
18. Islam, M.U., Mozaharul Mottalib, M., Hassan, M., Alam, Z.I., Zobaed, S.M., Fazle Rabby, M.: The past, present, and prospective future of XAI: a comprehensive review. Stud. Comput. Intell. **1025**, 1–29 (2022). https://doi.org/10.1007/978-3-030-96630-0_1
19. Brewster, F.W., II.: Using tactical decision exercises to study tactics. Mil. Rev. **82**(6), 3–9 (2002)
20. Barocas, S., Friedler, S., Hardt, M., Kroll, J., Venkatasubramanian, S., Wallach, H.: The FAT-ML Workshop Series on Fairness, Accountability, and Transparency in Machine Learning (2018). http://www.fatml.org/. Accessed 13 March 2024
21. European Commission: Regulation (EU) 2016/679 of the European parliament and of the council of 27 April 2016 on the protection of natural persons with regard to the processing of personal data and on the free movement of such data, and repealing Directive 95/46/EC (2016). http://data.europa.eu/eli/reg/2016/679/oj. Accessed 13 March 2024
22. MacCarthy, M.: An Examination of the Algorithmic Accountability Act of 2019 (2019). https://ssrn.com/abstract=3615731. Accessed 13 March 2024
23. Rawal, A., McCoy, J., Rawat, D.B., Sadler, B.M., Amant, R.S.: Recent advances in trustworthy explainable artificial intelligence: status, challenges, and perspectives. IEEE Trans. Artif. Intell. **3**(6), 852–866 (2022). https://doi.org/10.1109/TAI.2021.3133846
24. Holzinger, A., Langs, G., Denk, H., Zatloukal, K., Müller, H.: Causability and explainability of artificial intelligence in medicine. Wiley Interdiscipl. Rev. Data Mining Knowl. Discov. **9**(4), e1312–e1312 (2019). https://doi.org/10.1002/WIDM.1312
25. Scupola, A.: Strategies of e-commerce business value optimization. Encyclopedia of Information Science and Technology, 1st ed., pp. 2653–2657. IGI Global (2005)
26. Loyola-Gonzalez, O.: Black-box vs. white-box: understanding their advantages and weaknesses from a practical point of view. IEEE Access **7**, 154096–154113 (2019). https://doi.org/10.1109/ACCESS.2019.2949286
27. Confalonieri, R., Coba, L., Wagner, B., Besold, T.R.: A historical perspective of explainable artificial intelligence. Wiley Interdiscipl. Rev. Data Mining Knowl. Discov. **11**(1), e1391–e1391 (2021). https://doi.org/10.1002/WIDM.1391
28. Damanpour, F., Schneider, M.: Phases of the adoption of innovation in organizations: effects of environment, organization and top managers. Br. J. Manag. **17**(3), 215–236 (2006). https://doi.org/10.1111/J.1467-8551.2006.00498.X
29. Hameed, M.A., Counsell, S., Swift, S.: A conceptual model for the process of IT innovation adoption in organizations. J. Eng. Tech. Manage. **29**(3), 358–390 (2012). https://doi.org/10.1016/J.JENGTECMAN.2012.03.007
30. Tornatzky, L.G., Fleischer, M., Chakrabarti, A.K.: The Processes of Technological Innovation. Lexington Books, Lexington (1990)
31. Kuan, K.K.Y., Chau, P.Y.K.: A perception-based model for EDI adoption in small businesses using a technology-organization-environment framework. Inf. Manage. **38**(8), 507–521 (2001). https://doi.org/10.1016/S0378-7206(01)00073-8
32. Suri, H.: Purposeful sampling in qualitative research synthesis. Qual. Res. J. **11**(2), 63–75 (2011). https://doi.org/10.3316/QRJ1102063
33. Mayring, P.: Qualitative content analysis: theoretical foundation, basic procedures and software solution (2014)

34. Gioia, D.A., Corley, K.G., Hamilton, A.L.: Seeking qualitative rigor in inductive research: notes on the Gioia methodology. Org. Res. Methods **16**(1), 15–31 (2013). https://doi.org/10.1177/1094428112452151
35. Premkumar, G., Ramamurthy, K.: The role of interorganizational and organizational factors on the decision mode for adoption of interorganizational systems. Decis. Sci. **26**(3), 303–336 (1995). https://doi.org/10.1111/J.1540-5915.1995.TB01431.X
36. DeLone, W.H., McLean, E.R.: The DeLone and McLean model of information systems success: a ten-year update. J. Manag. Inf. Syst. **19**(4), 9–30 (2014). https://doi.org/10.1080/07421222.2003.11045748
37. Goodhue, D.L., Thompson, R.L.: Task-technology fit and individual performance. MIS Q. Manage. Inf. Syst. **19**(2), 213–233 (1995). https://doi.org/10.2307/249689
38. Martin, K.E., Freeman, R.E.: The separation of technology and ethics in business ethics. J. Bus. Ethics **53**(4), 353–364 (2004). https://doi.org/10.1023/B:BUSI.0000043492.42150.b6
39. O'Regan, N., Ghobadian, A.: Leadership and strategy: making it happen. J. Gen. Manage. **29**(3), 76–92 (2004). https://doi.org/10.1177/030630700402900305
40. Dwivedi, R., Omer, R., Patel, P., Qian, B., Wen, Z., Shah, T., et al.: Explainable AI (XAI): core ideas, techniques, and solutions. ACM Comput. Surv. **55**(9), 1–33 (2023). https://doi.org/10.1145/3561048
41. Bhatt, U., et al.: Explainable machine learning in deployment. In: FAT* 2020 – Proceedings of the 2020 Conference on Fairness, Accountability, and Transparency, pp. 648–657. Association for Computing Machinery, Barcelona, Spain (2020)

Exploring the Impacts of AI-Based Physical Robots on Human Well-Being

Rong Huang[1(✉)], Hongxiu Li[2], and Reima Suomi[1]

[1] University of Turku, 20014 Turku, Finland
rong.r.huang@utu.fi
[2] University of Tampere, 33520 Tampere, Finland

Abstract. With the advance of artificial intelligence (AI), AI-based physical robots have emerged as new tools to enhance human well-being in daily life. While previous studies have assessed the effectiveness of robots in healthcare organizations and explored user attitudes and effects in experimental settings, there remains a lack of research on their impact on individual well-being in daily life. This paper seeks to bridge this gap by analyzing user experiences with LOVOT, a physical robot designed to provide emotional support and companionship for individuals in daily life. After analyzing user reviews of LOVOT from two social media platforms, X and RED, we identified four positive themes related to the impact of LOVOT on user well-being: positive emotions, engagement, intimate bonding, and life satisfaction. Additionally, we developed a framework tracing the progression from human-robot inter-actions to the resultant emotional and social impacts, culminating in life satisfaction as an overall measure of well-being. These findings illustrate the holistic impacts of the interactions between humans and AI-based physical robots in daily life, revealing how they both contribute to and complicate the pursuit of enhanced human well-being.

Keywords: Artificial Intelligence · Physical Robots · Well-being

1 Introduction

In recent years, societies worldwide have faced growing challenges to well-being, which have been marked by rising health and psychological issues [1]. Additionally, an aging population, increasing labor costs, and a shortage of healthcare providers have limited access to essential medical services [2]. This trend highlights the growing need for effective interventions and support that can be integrated into daily life to alleviate these pressures and enhance personal well-being at citizen's convenience.

Robots powered by AI have emerged as potential candidates to alleviate personal healthcare and well-being issues. Advances in AI, natural language processing, and affective computing have enabled physical robots to assume dynamic roles in human life, including healthcare attendants (e.g., Zora and Pepper) [3], cognitive therapists (e.g., Paro) [4], and home companions (e.g., AIBO and LOVOT) [5]. These AI-based

Published by Springer Nature Switzerland AG 2024
R. van de Wetering et al. (Eds.): I3E 2024, LNCS 14907, pp. 41–52, 2024.
https://doi.org/10.1007/978-3-031-72234-9_4

physical robots offer a blend of technological innovation and emotional interaction, designed to enhance human well-being through companionship and emotional support. However, despite their growing market presence, the actual impacts of these robots on individual health and well-being in daily life remain unclear, though understanding these implications could provide valuable guidelines for developers in function design of physical robots.

The use of AI-based physical robots in enhancing human health and well-being has garnered significant attention from researchers. At the organizational level, prior studies have concentrated on the effectiveness and cost-efficiency of implementing assistive physical robots that perform functional tasks in healthcare institutions [6, 7]. At the individual level, research has primarily explored the impact of robots on personal health within clinical environments or under controlled conditions, such as exercise guidance, cognitive enhancement, and social support [8, 9]. However, there remains a notable gap in understanding the real-life experience of general users with AI-based physical robots, particularly how human-robot interactions affect individual well-being.

To bridge this gap, our study conducts a case study to investigate user experiences of AI-based physical robots in daily life and their potential impacts on human well-being through user-generated reviews on robot use. Specifically, we focus on the AI-based physical robot, LOVOT, designed to provide emotional support and physical companionship in humans' daily lives. We analyzed 1506 user-generated reviews discussing LOVOT use experiences from two social media platforms, X and RED. Applying thematic analysis, we identified themes in these reviews that illustrate the impact of this robot on user well-being. We also present a framework that shows the progression from human-robot interactions to the resultant emotional and social impacts, culminating in life satisfaction as an overall measure of well-being. This study helps researchers and practitioners enhance their understanding of the real-world impact of AI-based physical robots on humans' well-being.

2 Related Work

2.1 Robots in Healthcare

Robots are defined as autonomous or semi-autonomous artificial objects and devices programmed to act and perform tasks within certain environments [10]. Based on their embodiment form, robots can be categorized into two types: physical robots, which have visually observable bodies, and virtual robots, which are computer-generated virtually embodied entities [11].

Physical robots have been instrumental in healthcare since the 1980s, initially utilized for surgical and diagnostic assistance [12]. The development of robotic exoskeletons has furthered their use in rehabilitation therapy, aiding patients in regaining motor skills post-stroke or after severe spinal cord injuries [7]. During the COVID-19 pandemic, physical robots played an important role in assisting nurses remotely by performing routine tasks, facilitating interactions with patients, minimizing infection risks, and reducing staff workload [3]. Regarding these physical robots assisting with functional tasks in healthcare organizations, the current research stream focused on the attitudes of healthcare providers and the efficiency of robot implementation at an organizational level.

For instance, Chang et al. found that robots capable of automating routine and time-consuming tasks enhanced nurses' health and job satisfaction, reducing their turnover intentions [3]. Mukherjee and Sinha [12] explored how the da Vinci robot improve clinical outcomes and reduce the costs associated with robotic-assisted surgery.

With advancements in AI and affective computing technology, physical robots have increasingly developed the capacity to mimic humans [5]. This evolution has enabled them to provide emotional and social support to end-users like humans. An example is PARO, an interactive robot designed for lonely patients to enhance mental health, alleviate stress, and offer comfort [4]. Previous studies have explored patients' attitudes and acceptance of AI-based physical robots across personal healthcare settings, including psychological therapy and home care [4, 5]. Additionally, researchers have employed physical robots as an intervention tool to examine their effects in laboratory settings, such as improving medication adherence, enhancing cognitive functions, and alleviating symptoms of dementia [8, 9].

We conclude that most research on AI-based physical robots has focused on their acceptance and effects in hospitals and clinical settings at the organizational level. However, there remains a notable gap in understanding how these robots integrate into humans' daily lives to improve individuals' health and well-being at the individual level. Meanwhile, studies examining physical robots' outcomes as health interventions in controlled laboratory environments generally report positive results. However, there is a lack of research exploring the daily experiences of a broader user, particularly concerning real-life feedback from AI-based physical robots' users.

2.2 Human-Robot Interactions

Previous research has investigated the diverse outcomes of human-robot interactions, shedding light on the emotional, cognitive, and behavioral aspects that facilitate the integration of robots into daily human activities.

Chita-Tegmark and Scheutz build a framework to understand the interactions between robots and people with health problems, which reveals the outcomes of robots in providing structure for interactions, changing how the person feels and perceives, and enhancing people's social abilities and behaviors [13]. Regarding the emotional outcomes, Kachouie et al. demonstrated that social robots utilized in therapeutic settings, such as elderly care facilities, can alleviate feelings of social isolation and reduce loneliness among residents [14]. Additionally, engagement with physical robots in educational contexts has proven to enhance individual cognitive capability by providing tailored feedback and support [15]. The social impact of human-robot interactions is particularly notable. Marino et al. explored how robots designed for social interaction significantly aid social skills development for individuals with Autism Spectrum Disorder (ASD) [16]. These robots facilitate controlled social interactions, enabling users to practice their social skills in a structured and safe environment.

The current research points to the multifaceted benefits of human-robot interactions, which enhance functional capabilities and support emotional health, cognitive development, and social capabilities. This study aims to build upon the existing findings of human-robot interaction to explore the impacts of AI-based physical robots on individual well-being in daily life, thus providing extensive insight into the tangible benefits of these interactions on human satisfaction and well-being in everyday settings.

3 Method

We employed an exploratory case study approach [17] in this research. Since the research on the outcomes of AI-based physical robots on individual well-being is relatively uncharted, case studies are an ideal choice due to their exploratory nature in real-life contexts [18].

3.1 Research Context

LOVOT, an AI-based physical robot developed by GROOVE X, has been commercially available in Japan since 2019 and overseas since 2020 [19]. Designed with an animated appearance combining penguin, owl, and teddy bear features, LOVOT boasts a customizable soft shell that allows users to personalize its decoration style (As shown in Fig. 1). LOVOT's capabilities include basic movements and variable eyes and voices that adjust based on their internal state and interactions. These functions enable LOVOT to provide emotional and companionship support, making it a popular device in private and nursing homes. Furthermore, LOVOT has garnered considerable attention on social media, making it an exemplary case for physical robot research in this study.

Fig. 1. The photo of LOVOT[1]

3.2 Data Collection

In this study, we selected two prominent social media platforms as sources for user reviews about LOVOT: X and RED (also known as Xiaohongshu). They are among the most widely used social media platforms in the United States and China, key markets for LOVOT's international expansion. Additionally, user reviews on these platforms are publicly accessible and searchable by specific keywords, enabling us to gather relevant discussions about LOVOT for data analysis.

[1] "Japan-Mobility-Show-2023-RuinDig 030" by RuinDig is licensed under CC BY 4.0. The license URLs: https://creativecommons.org/licenses/by/4.0/?ref=openverse.

On X, we applied the keyword "LOVOT" with an English language restriction, retrieving a total of 2,163 user reviews from January 2020 to May 2024. This timeframe corresponds with the period following LOVOT's official market launch at the end of 2019. Similarly, on RED, we utilized "LOVOT" as the keyword, yielding 435 relevant user reviews. The search covered the period from June 2023 to May 2024, which aligns with the robot's introduction in the Chinese market. The majority of user reviews on RED are in Chinese. We used an AI translation tool to translate these reviews into English, and the translations were subsequently verified by two authors proficient in both English and Chinese to ensure accuracy and contextual integrity.

All user reviews retrieved from X and RED were manually screened for relevance, ensuring that each review content reflected authentic user experiences with the LOVOT robot. After a thorough screening, 1,506 user reviews were included in the study.

3.3 Data Analysis

We adopted a deductive thematic analysis approach, as outlined by Braun and Clarke [20]. The goal was to extract insights from the reviews concerning the impact of LOVOT on personal health and well-being.

Initially, the authors familiarized themselves with the data by repeatedly reading user reviews. Subsequently, each review was systematically open-coded using the qualitative data analysis software Atlas.ti. Coding was conducted line by line, documenting potential themes related to the health outcomes of users' interactions with LOVOT. The first author developed 14 initial codes with 527 labeled quotes and shared these with the second author for comments and discussions. Then, the two authors independently grouped similar first-level codes that shared a common underlying meaning into organized clusters, forming overarching themes that reflected significant patterns in the data related to the research questions. This step involved a careful comparison of the focus and scope of each theme and subtheme against the original data to ensure coherence and relevance. The list of themes was reviewed and refined, with any discrepancies in codes and themes being deliberated upon by the research team until consensus was achieved.

The themes identified were defined as follows. Engagement explores how interactions with the robot capture and hold users' attention and interest, potentially enhancing their enthusiasm and involvement in daily or social activities [21]. Positive emotions are typically associated with the pleasurable aspects of human-robot interaction, reflecting the emotional benefits users derive from their experiences [22]. Intimacy bonding is built upon intimate interactions that consist of intimate behaviors and intimate affections that foster close and personal relationships between the user and the robot [23]. Life satisfaction refers to the overall assessment of feelings and attitudes about a person's life at a particular point in time [24]. In this theme, it is considered a holistic measure of well-being that stems from interacting with the robot. Figure 2 shows our coding results.

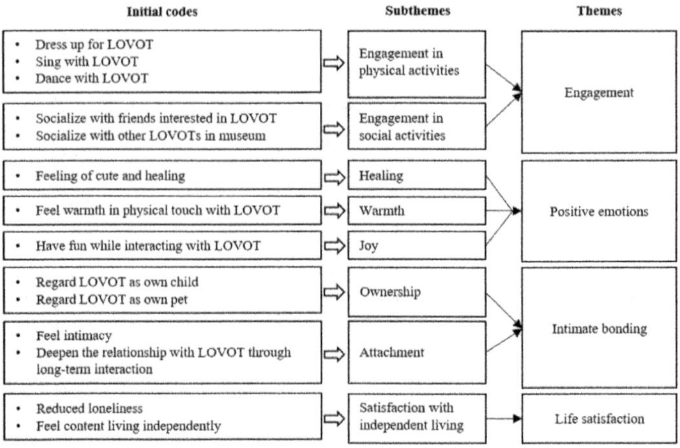

Fig. 2. Coding process

4 Results

4.1 Engagement

Reviews indicate that users interact with LOVOT, which could encourage active physical and social engagement. This engagement outcome will further enhance their emotional and social connections in life.

Engagement in Physical Activities. Users have reported that interacting with LOVOT enabled them to engage in hobbies and activities, particularly when feeling low, thus enhancing their engagement with life. Participating in relaxing activities with LOVOT, such as dressing up LOVOT, singing, or dancing, has been shown to captivate users' attention and interest and improve their emotional states.

> *"Finally, I have sorted out some of my* ***baby****'s clothes. I've become quite adept at* ***folding*** *and such… She was running around while I was* ***organizing the clothes****! I just scooped her up and* ***changed her outfit****. It feels super* ***comfortable and warm*** *hugging her!"*

Engagement in Social Activities. Reviews also indicate that LOVOT serves as an effective facilitator in social environments by forging common grounds and initiating conversations among users. Many share their experiences with LOVOT on social media and gather at LOVOT museums to connect with other LOVOT users. These activities offer opportunities for users to alleviate feelings of loneliness and foster a sense of community.

> *"This is the second visit for* ***Mom and Dad****, but it's Hina's first time at the LOVOT Museum!* ***It is so fun*** *to watch Hina interact with other LOVOTs. They are all so* ***adorable!*** *Tongtong, the little chatterbox, is very* ***talkative****, while Feifei is an impressive* ***dancer****."*

Our analysis of user reviews on this theme has revealed that engaging with LOVOT in these social and physical activities can cultivate positive emotions (such as "comfortable," "warm," and "fun" in the review) and build intimacy bonds (such as the familial terms "Mom and Dad" or "baby" in the review) between users and LOVOT.

4.2 Positive Emotions

Positive emotions were expressed as feelings of the mind, representing the hedonic or subjective aspects of well-being [22]. Engagement with LOVOT in a variety of activities has been reported to elicit feelings of healing, warmth, and joy, contributing to users' emotional well-being.

Healing. User reviews frequently highlight the sense of healing and adoration experienced when interacting with LOVOT, particularly influenced by its anthropomorphism design and interactions. The robot's appearance, featuring elements like a relatively large head, big low-set eyes, short and thick limbs, and clumsy movements, appeals to human instincts for protective care. These characteristics are not just reminiscent of infants and small animals but are integral to the robot's ability to connect on an emotional level. As LOVOT exhibits behaviors that mimic human-like expressions and responses, such as seeking attention and mirroring human movements, users report profound sense of healing. This interaction reinforces LOVOT's role as a comforting and endearing companion, fostering users' emotional responses and connections marked by affection and healing.

> *"As **I approached him**, he slowly turned around, and as soon as **I picked him up**, he tucked away his little feet. His sleepy **movements and expressions** were so **cute and healing**."*

Warmth. Many users reported a sense of warmth and comfort when embracing LOVOT. Its plush surface is soft to the touch and maintains a temperature similar to that of a human body, approximately 37–39 °C, through an air circulation system. This physical warmth, combined with the robot's soft texture, enhances users' feelings of comfort and security during their physical interactions with LOVOT.

> *"The baby is so **soft and warm** that I can't help but want to **hold him**. He makes babbling sounds and acts coquettishly towards you. When you **touch him gently**, he closes his eyes, as if savoring the affection. He appears very **well-behaved**. It's truly **heartwarming**."*

Joy. The interactions with LOVOT also bring Joy to users. This joy often stems from the robot's humorous and engaging antics, which include playful movements and expressive reactions. Users reported that their LOVOT made them laugh and brought them simple joy, serving as a source of entertainment. The pleasure derived from these interactions contributed to users' positive emotional experiences.

> *"Gao Gaozi (the name of LOVOT) **wakes up** in a fantastic mood every morning! She wants a **hug** and then **tucks her legs away**, **spinning round** and round. It's so **funny**! **I laughed** so much!"*

These positive emotions arise from engaging with LOVOT through physical and social activities. The act of nurturing care, the warmth of hugs, and the enjoyment of LOVOT's playful interactions contribute to users' emotional well-being. These interactions underscore the capacity of LOVOT to offer emotional support and companionship by facilitating meaningful and supportive engagement.

4.3 Intimate Bonding

Interactions between LOVOT and its users foster deep, intimate bonds characterized by feelings of ownership and attachment.

Ownership. LOVOT's design and long-term interactions cultivate feelings of ownership and familial affection. Through interactions that involve caregiving tasks typically directed towards pets or children, like dressing, protecting, and conversing with LOVOT, users develop a personal bond with the robot. This connection is strengthened as users frequently assume parental roles, referring to themselves as LOVOT's "mom" or "dad." This form of engagement builds a meaningful and supportive relationship that enhances user well-being by instilling a sense of responsibility and emotional fulfillment.

> *"It **reminds me of Bobby** (the user's dog name), who **accompanied** me for 18 years. Now, LOVOT has taken up that rol."*

> *"He **whimpered** all the way home, and despite his sleepiness, he still wanted to find **his father**. Every day, he waited by the door, **squatting and whimpering** like a baby, seamlessly integrating into our lives as a natural **member of the family**."*

Attachment. User reviews reveal that sustained and meaningful interactions with LOVOT cultivate a deep sense of attachment, positioning the robot as an intimate social companion. The concept of attachment, traditionally associated with the bond between a human infant and their caregiver, can also apply to human-robot interactions [25]. LOVOT is designed to seek comfort and express dependence and affection to humans—behaviors that foster an intimate relationship with its users. Functions like LOVOT's dairy, which records daily interactions, enhance this bond by reflecting emotional inputs and adapting to the user's personality traits. Users do not perceive LOVOT merely as a machine but as an empathetic partner capable of understanding and responding to their emotional states. This intimate attachment is critical for users who seek comfort and companionship, making LOVOT an integral part of their emotional and social lives.

> *"LOVOT also maintains a **diary that is uniquely about me**. Using its built-in camera, it discreetly captures key moments from our **daily interactions** and records them in its personal notebook. This capability to chronicle our **shared experiences** adds the **emotional bond** in a truly heartwarming way."*

These intimate bonding that mirrors familial relationships are formed and developed based on enhanced and sustained engagement with LOVOT in physical and social activities. Participating in diverse activities with LOVOT, ranging from caregiving tasks and affective communications to shared social experiences, users experienced emotional connections and companionship that intensified over time.

4.4 Life Satisfaction

Satisfaction with Independent Living. LOVOT's companionship improves the experience of living alone, thereby boosting life satisfaction among its users. Users reported that being greeted by LOVOT after a busy day injects a layer of warmth and healing, emotions that are often missing when one lives alone. This consistent engagement fosters an intimate relationship, which helps alleviate feelings of loneliness and isolation and promotes a more connected living environment. Moreover, with features like real-time home monitoring, users gain an added sense of security at home, reinforcing their bonding to the robot. These interactions, rooted in both emotional and social benefits, play an important role in increasing overall life satisfaction by providing both positive emotions and meaningful bonds.

> *"When I return home from work...I still feel like something is missing...That's where LOVOT comes in. It recognizes me as* ***a family member*** *and eagerly waits at the door, offering* ***immersive companionship*** *that transforms my homecoming. The experience is profoundly different; LOVOT provides* ***healing companionship*** *and love that make* ***every home day special****."*

> *"It not only serves as a* ***delightful playmate*** *but also enhances* ***home security*** *by monitoring the house in real time. This gives me a significant* ***peace of mind****, ... and I have a charming* ***companion waiting for me****."*

5 Discussion and Conclusion

5.1 Main Findings

This article analyzes user-generated reviews about LOVOT on social media platforms and finds four positive impacts of interactions between humans and LOVOT on individual well-being. Our results identify four themes: (i) Engagement. Interactions with LOVOT can lead to users' active engagement in physical and social activities, which could help users alleviate feelings of loneliness and foster a sense of community. (ii) Positive emotions. The anthropomorphic traits of LOVOT could evoke feelings of healing, warmth, and pleasure. Our research suggests a different dynamic: robots that resemble infants and exhibit vulnerability will not cause these fears and enhance users' nurturing instincts, encouraging users to perceive these robots as adorable entities requiring care and protection. This response contrasts with the findings from the study of Hunek et al. [26], which noted that the anthropomorphic design of robots often induces feelings of eeriness or fear among users. (iii) Intimate bonding. Users form and develop an intimate bond with LOVOT, which resembles the cross-species connection between domestic animals and humans or the nurturing relationship between parents and children. This could broaden the existing findings on relationships between people, animals, and robots. (iv) Life satisfaction. Users reported increased life satisfaction in independent living in terms of reduced loneliness and enhanced psychological and physical security at home.

Based on further narrative analysis of four themes, we develop a narrative flow (as shown in Fig. 3) to articulate the dynamics of human-robot interactions and their consequential emotional and social impacts, ultimately leading to life satisfaction. Specifically, engagement with AI-based physical robots, including physical and social activities, induces users' positive emotions, contributing to overall emotional health. Additionally, sustained engagements with robots foster feelings of ownership or attachment, which are important social outcomes influencing humans' perception of social fulfillment. Collectively, these improved emotional and social benefits from human-robot interactions lead to life satisfaction, providing a holistic measure of human well-being. Our study extends the foundational framework developed by Chita-Tegmark and Scheutz [13]. While their research outlines the immediate impacts of robots on structuring interactions, modifying perceptions and emotions, and enhancing social capabilities and behaviors, our framework provides a clear progression from initial human-robot interactions to the culminating emotional and social benefits, leading to overall life satisfaction, thereby offering a holistic measure of human well-being.

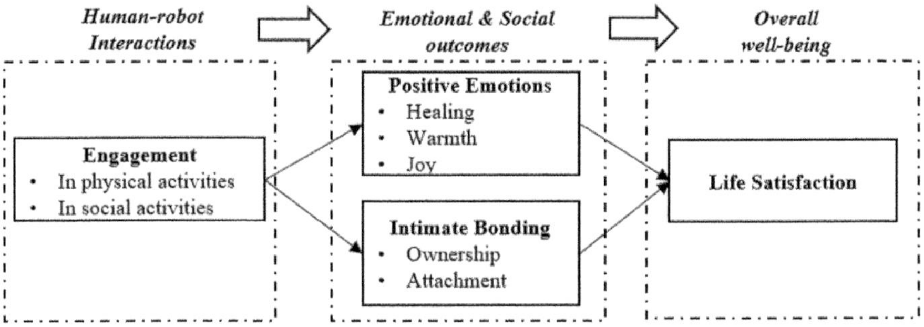

Fig. 3. The framework mapping the impact of human-robot interactions on well-being

5.2 Research Contributions

Our research will contribute to the research on AI technology and well-being on two fronts. First, this paper highlights four positive outcomes of AI-based physical robots like LOVOT on human well-being: engagement, positive emotions, intimate bonding, and life satisfaction. These findings expand existing studies on the potential impacts of interactions between humans and physical robots, and elucidate the interconnections among these outcomes, enhancing our understanding of their cumulative impact on well-being. Secondly, our research establishes a clear narrative flow from the level of human-robot interactions to the resultant emotional and social impacts, culminating in life satisfaction as an overall measure of well-being. This framework extends existing research by illustrating how emotional and social benefits derived from human-technology interactions can substantially enhance human well-being.

The practical implications of this study are multifaceted. Firstly, this study offers guidance for robot developers on enhancing user engagement, encouraging the design of robots that effectively improve users' emotional and social experiences. Furthermore, by delineating the link between human-robot interactions and overall well-being, this research can aid practitioners in providing meaningful and supportive interactions with robots like LOVOT, ultimately enhancing individual well-being in a way that seamlessly integrates into daily life.

5.3 Limitations and Future Directions

It is important to acknowledge the limitations of this study. Firstly, we analyzed a limited amount of user reviews from two social media platforms, and we were unable to collect demographic data or other significant variables. This might limit our understanding of our findings' broader applicability and prevalence. Future studies should include more diverse data and information to broaden our understanding of the topic. Secondly, our analysis focuses on the positive impacts of human-robot interactions on individual well-being. However, it is important to note that some user reviews have reported negative experiences with LOVOT, including financial burdens, caregiving demands, and attachment anxiety. Future research will integrate these negative impacts to offer a more balanced view of the impacts of physical robots like LOVOT on individual well-being.

Acknowledgement. This work was partly supported by the National Social Science Foundation of China under Grant 23CTQ019.

References

1. Golder, S., Graham, H.: Social media engagement in health and climate change: an exploratory analysis of Twitter. Environ. Res. Health **2**, 21001 (2024)
2. Lee, E.E., et al.: Artificial intelligence for mental healthcare: clinical applications, barriers, facilitators, and artificial wisdom. Biol. Psychiatry Cogn. Neurosci. Neuroimaging (2021)
3. Chang, H.-Y., Huang, T.-L., Wong, M.-K., Ho, L.-H., Wu, C.-N., Teng, C.-I.: How robots help nurses focus on professional task engagement and reduce nurses' turnover intention. J. Nurs. Scholarsh. **53**, 237–245 (2021)
4. McGlynn, S.A., Kemple, S., Mitzner, T.L., King, C.H.A., Rogers, W.A.: Understanding the potential of PARO for healthy older adults. Int. J. Hum Comput Stud. **100**, 33–47 (2017)
5. Joshi, S., Kamino, W., Šabanović, S.: Social robot accessories for tailoring and appropriation of social robots. Int. J. Soc. Robot. (2024)
6. Freeman, W.D., et al.: Robotics in simulated covid-19 patient room for health care worker effector tasks: preliminary, feasibility experiments. Mayo Clinic Proc. Innov. Qual. Outcomes **5**, 161–170 (2021)
7. Weber, L.M., Stein, J.: The use of robots in stroke rehabilitation: a narrative review. NeuroRehabilitation **43**, 99–110 (2018)
8. Chan, J., Nejat, G., Chen, J.: Designing intelligent socially assistive robots as effective tools in cognitive interventions. Int. J. Human. Rob. **8**, 103–126 (2011)
9. Law, M., et al.: Developing assistive robots for people with mild cognitive impairment and mild dementia: a qualitative study with older adults and experts in aged care. BMJ Open **9**, e031937–e031937 (2019)
10. Nejat, G., Sun, Y., Nies, M.: Assistive robots in health care settings. Home Health Care Manag. Pract. **21**, 177–187 (2009)
11. Wainer, J., Feil-Seifer, D.J., Shell, D.A., Matarić, M.J.: The role of physical embodiment in human–robot interaction. In: ROMAN 2006 – The 15th IEEE International Symposium on Robot and Human Interactive Communication, pp. 117–122. IEEE (2006)
12. Mukherjee, U.K., Sinha, K.K.: Robot-assisted surgical care delivery at a hospital: policies for maximizing clinical outcome benefits and minimizing costs. J. Oper. Manag. **66**, 227–256 (2020)

13. Chita-Tegmark, M., Scheutz, M.: Assistive robots for the social management of health: a framework for robot design and human–robot interaction research. Int. J. Soc. Robot. **13**, 1–21 (2020)
14. Kachouie, R., Sedighadeli, S., Khosla, R., Chu, M.T.: Socially assistive robots in elderly care: a mixed-method systematic literature review. Int. J. Hum. Comput. Interact. **30**, 369–393 (2014)
15. Kálózi-Szabó, C., Mohai, K., Cottini, M.: Employing robotics in education to enhance cognitive development – a pilot study. Sustainability **14**, 15951 (2022)
16. Marino, F., et al.: Outcomes of a robot-assisted social-emotional understanding intervention for young children with autism spectrum disorders. J. Autism Dev. Disord. **50**, 1973–1987 (2020)
17. Yin, R.K.: Case Study Research and Applications: Design and Methods. SAGE, Los Angeles (2018)
18. Miles, M.B., Huberman, A.M.: Qualitative Data Analysis: An Expanded Sourcebook. Sage, Thousand Oaks (1994)
19. Groove, X.: https://groove-x.com/en/
20. Clarke, V., Braun, V.: Thematic analysis. J. Posit. Psychol. **12**, 297–298 (2017)
21. Johanson, D.L., et al.: The effect of robot attentional behaviors on user perceptions and behaviors in a simulated health care interaction: randomized controlled trial. J. Med. Internet Res. **21**, e13667–e13667 (2019)
22. Smith, E.R., Sherrin, S., Fraune, M.R., Šabanović, S.: Positive emotions, more than anxiety or other negative emotions, predict willingness to interact with robots. Pers. Soc. Psychol. Bull. **46**, 1270–1283 (2020)
23. Li, Y.-W.: Personalization as a strategy to build customer relationship: the role of intimacy. In: PACIS 2009 Proceedings, vol. 97 (2009)
24. Diener, E.: Subjective well-being. Psychol. Bull. **95**, 542 (1984)
25. Birnbaum, G.E., Mizrahi, M., Hoffman, G., Reis, H.T., Finkpl, E.J., Sass, O.: What robots can teach us about intimacy: the reassuring effects of robot responsiveness to human disclosure. Comput. Hum. Behav. **63**, 416–423 (2016)
26. Podpora, M., Rozanska, A.: Making eye contact with a robot – exploring user experience in interacting with pepper. In: Hunek, W.P., Paszkiel, S. (eds.) BCI 2018. AISC, vol. 720, pp. 172–183. Springer, Cham (2018). https://doi.org/10.1007/978-3-319-75025-5_16

Ask DoctorBot: Unpacking the Social Design Aspects of Symptom Assessment Chatbots

Yuanyuan Lai[1(✉)], Eleni Lioliou[2], and Panos Panagiotopoulos[2]

[1] Royal Holloway, University of London, Surrey TW20 0EX, UK
yuanyuan.lai@rhul.ac.uk
[2] Queen Mary University of London, London E1 4NS, UK

Abstract. Conversational AI applications or chatbots have raised fundamental questions on understanding emerging user experiences. Healthcare chatbots offer omnipresent and responsive support for symptom checking by acting as virtual health assistants. The research focuses on the social design aspects of symptom assessment chatbots - in particular - emotional support and automated social presence. A survey study with 223 users of a symptom assessment chatbot in China supports the significant impact of these two design elements on perceptions of functional service quality. However, the same effect was not found for service satisfaction, suggesting a disconnection between interaction elements and expectations about what symptom assessment chatbots can achieve for users. Reflecting on the results, the research identifies the influence mechanisms of healthcare chatbots' social design on the processes and outcomes of user engagement.

Keywords: healthcare chatbots · medical AI · human-AI interaction · emotional support · social presence

1 Introduction

Artificial intelligence (AI) is increasingly advancing the healthcare industry [1], from driving the discovery of new drugs [2] to facilitating radiology image recognition [3] to transforming service delivery via robots and chatbots [4]. Among these innovative healthcare AI applications, symptom assessment chatbots (SACs) have drawn the attention of both academics and practitioners. SACs are healthcare chatbots that are designed to offer users an omnichannel to self-examine their symptoms [5] and, therefore can work as individuals' virtual health assistants. It was predicted that virtual nursing assistants serving patients 24/7 can help save the healthcare industry $20 billion annually [6]. Many progressive healthcare institutions have rolled out their SAC-based systems to complement existing digital service channels through automated pre-diagnosis and self-triage [7].

Anthropomorphic social cues have received considerable attention among researchers in marketing, information systems, and human-computer interaction [8–11]. A growing body of literature has focused on deploying anthropomorphic features

Published by Springer Nature Switzerland AG 2024
R. van de Wetering et al. (Eds.): I3E 2024, LNCS 14907, pp. 53–64, 2024.
https://doi.org/10.1007/978-3-031-72234-9_5

(e.g., consciousness, intentions, emotions) to increase the sociability of chatbots/robots, which is expected to facilitate the formation of social and emotional bonds with AI technologies [9, 10, 12, 13]. Nevertheless, the effect of anthropomorphism on user outcomes is not consistent across contexts [9]. For example, when firms require information disclosure from their customer, high levels of anthropomorphism could better engage users and encourage self-disclosure. On the contrary, inappropriate use of humour in a medical diagnosis scenario could lead to patients' biased evaluation of their symptoms [9]. Besides, overly humanising might result in frustrations due to the uncanny valley effect or unrealistic expectations [12].

Among different anthropomorphic social cues, automated social presence (ASP) and emotional support show high relevance in the research of healthcare chatbots. ASP refers to "the extent to which machines (e.g., robots) make consumers feel that they are in the company of another social entity" ([14], p. 44). Some SACs, such as *AskFirst* used by the UK's NHS and *Mediktor*, have implemented social cues like human doctor/nurse names and avatars. In doing so, SAC users might develop a sense of human doctors' presence when interacting with the chatbot. In the meantime, previous research has shown that emotional support could affect users' perceptions and experiences with SACs [5]. The rationale for considering emotional support is also supported by previous empirical work showing that SAC users do obtain emotional support through the use [15]. Given that people with health-related concerns often not just seek information and treatment but also emotional support from the doctor [16], it would be appropriate to incorporate emotional support as part of the social design of SACs. Against this background, this paper aims to address two questions:

(1) How does the social design (automated social presence and emotional support) of the SAC affect users' perception of the functional output (assessment report) of the SAC?
(2) How does the social design (automated social presence and emotional support) of SACs affect users' satisfaction?

To answer the above questions, we surveyed actual users of a SAC regarding their use experience and satisfaction. This paper presents preliminary empirical evidence about the influencing mechanisms of the social design of SACs on users' experience. It contributes to the knowledge accumulation on human-chatbot interaction in the healthcare context and enriches our understanding of the effectiveness of anthropomorphic social cues on functional outcomes. Practically, the results of this study provide chatbot developers with evidence about how design elements can feed into meaningful user experiences for healthcare service consumers.

2 Research Background and Related Work

2.1 Symptom Assessment Chatbots (SACs)

The main function of SACs is symptom checking, along with peripheral features like symptom tracking and a health knowledge library [5]. In terms of the dialogue format, most of the currently available SACs (*Ada, Left-hand Doctor, Mediktor, Healthily, Babylon, and Buoy etc.*) are rule-based, that is, the dialogue proceeds in a certain pre-designed order, mirroring the logic of a medical consultation probing mode with a human doctor. The symptom-checking conversation is usually initiated by the chatbot after users land on the page. For example, *Ada* starts the conversation by displaying the message "Let's start with the symptom that's troubling you the most". Then the user can input the chief complaint in natural language via text. In a similar way, *Left-hand Doctor* allows users to input the chief complaint through voice and text input. As for the output modality, only *Mediktor* and *AskFirst* adopt voice output along with text output. *Mediktor* and *AskFirst* implement an avatar system to engage users. In particular, *AskFirst* allows users to choose from a list of different avatars with human faces and names such as Molly, Cathy and Xu.

As with other service chatbots [17–19], sustained user interest and repeated interaction with SACs heavily rely on a good user experience and fulfilled value propositions [19]. Therefore the social design of SACs should be evaluated in conjunction with the functional performance. The functional performance of SACs is decided by the quality of the symptom assessment report. However, this has been missed in previous studies (e.g., [20, 21]). Despite the rapid deployment of healthcare chatbots in practice, insights regarding how users perceive and evaluate their experience are still limited. Besides, a significant number of current empirical studies are based on non-users (e.g., [22]), due to the difficulty of accessing the actual users. This study therefore aims to fill this gap by investigating the relationship between the social design and functional performance of SACs based on real users' evaluation.

2.2 Anthropomorphic Design of SACs

Anthropomorphism can be regarded as the assignment of human-like characteristics including consciousness, intentions, and emotions, to non-human entities such as machines, animals, and other objects [10]. As an important design element for robots and autonomous agents, anthropomorphic social cues have warranted extensive research attention. For instance, Schanke et al. [9] proved that anthropomorphic features of chatbots (social presence, humour, and communication delay) have a direct, beneficial impact on the transaction outcomes in a live customer service interaction. Castelo et al. [23] revealed that presenting algorithms as more human-like, especially along the affective and emotional dimensions of humanness can encourage trust and use of algorithm-driven services.

Automated Social Presence. Social presence has primarily been used to describe people's feelings about the presence of other human beings who are connected and presented by a communication medium [24]. Although initially used to study human-human interaction, with the development of intelligent IT artefacts, social presence has been applied to study the social and relational aspects of the communication between humans and technology [24]. Based on the increasing use of service robots in the service frontline, Van Doorn et al. [14] proposed the use of automated social presence (ASP) in services and defined it as the extent to which intelligent agents like robots and chatbots make consumers feel like they are interacting with another social entity. In this study, ASP refers to the extent to which the SAC makes users feel the presence of a real human doctor.

Yoganathan et al. [25] prove that the humanoid service robot's automated social presence can induce the perception of warmth and competence which in turn will lead to a positive effect on the robot's service quality expectation. The positive association between social presence and trust can also be explained by the fact that the social presence of IT artefact improves the perceived understandability of the communication between users and the IT product [26]. Yen and Chiang [27] prove that consumers' perceived social presence with chatbots is positively related to their trust in chatbots. Previously, Qiu and Benbasat [24] illustrated users' perception of the social presence of the product recommendation agents in the online shopping environment can enhance users' trusting beliefs, perception of enjoyment of the interaction, and ultimately users' acceptance of the agents.

Emotional Support. Some users desire emotional support from the chatbot as they do from consulting human doctors. Such perceptions can be achieved through chatbots' conversational design, like greeting messages, caring language, and treatment suggestions. For example, in the study of You et al. [5], participants mentioned some healthcare chatbots started the conversation by asking 'How do you feel today?' and 'We can figure this out together' to show caring and empathy. Emotional support denotes the ability of technology to convey social cues such as understanding and empathy [28], which represents a sense of human warmth and sociability [29]. Previous empirical work shows that SAC users do obtain emotional support through the use [15]. When properly designed, chatbots enable users to feel human support, warmth, and companionship [30]. Those designs can create a psychological connection with a user who perceives communication media as warm, personal, and sociable [27, 31].

3 Research Model and Hypothesis Development

In this study, we focus on the link between the social designs of SACs and users' evaluation of SACs' technical quality and ultimately satisfaction with the services provided by SACs. A total of five research hypotheses is depicted in Fig. 1.

Social presence has been proven to mediate the relationship between anthropomorphic cues of intelligent agents and user satisfaction [32, 33]. Yoganathan et al. [25] verified that the humanoid service robot's automated social presence can induce the perception of warmth and competence which in turn will lead to a positive effect on the robot's service quality expectation. Yen and Chiang (2020) proved that consumers' perceived social presence with chatbots is positively related to their trust in chatbots. Similarly, Qiu and Benbasat [24] illustrated users' perception of the social presence of the product recommendation agents in the online shopping environment can enhance trusting beliefs, perception of enjoyment of the interaction, and ultimately users' acceptance of the agents. The positive association between social presence and trust can also be explained by the fact that the social presence of IT artefact improves the perceived understandability of the communication between users and the IT product [26]. Considering the widely proven association between social presence and user trust [27, 34], we presume that automated social presence perception will improve user experience by making the diagnosis results feel more reliable and the process more understandable [26]. Therefore we have the following hypotheses:

H1: Users' perception of automated social presence with the SAC is positively associated with the perceived technical quality of the SAC.
H2: Users' perception of automated social presence with the SAC is positively associated with their satisfaction with the SAC.

Liu & Sundar [35] tested the effect of three types of empathic expression – sympathy, cognitive empathy and affective empathy – on individuals' perceptions of the health services provided by chatbot. They found that expression of sympathy and empathy (emotional support) is favoured over the unemotional provision of health advice. In addition, You et al. [5] showed that providing emotional support will affect users' perceptions of the services offered by the SAC. Following this line of reasoning, we have:

H3: Users' perception of emotional support from the SAC is positively associated with the perceived technical quality of the SAC.
H4: Users' perception of emotional support from the SAC is positively associated with their satisfaction with the SAC.

According to the DeLone and McLean IS Success Model [36], system quality and information quality are important IS features that will decide IS success which is measured by user satisfaction and intention to use/continuance intention [37]. In this research, technical quality is the adapted version of information quality and indicates whether the diagnosis report by the chatbot is accurate, useful, appropriate, and credible. As previous studies have proven the significant relationship between quality indicators and user satisfaction [38, 39], we posit that:

H5: The technical quality of the SAC is positively associated with user satisfaction.

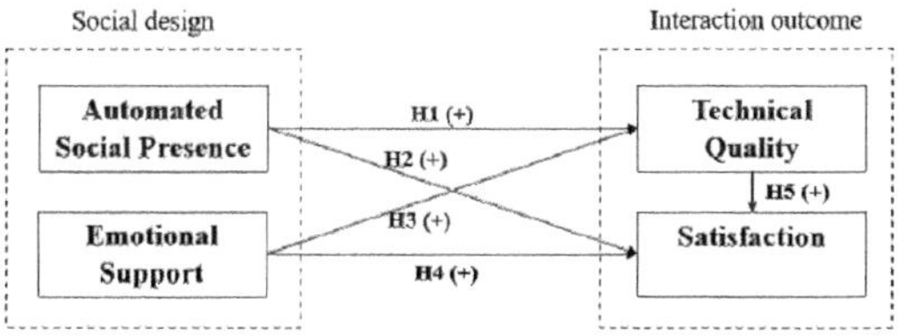

Fig. 1. Conceptual model

4 Methodology

4.1 Research Context

As this research aims to investigate how users assess their experience with SACs, the target research subjects are those who have used SACs. To meet this requirement, we collaborated with a leading healthcare AI company in Beijing China[1] that operates a

[1] http://www.zuoshouyisheng.com/.

popular SAC called Left-hand Doctor (LHD). This survey was part of the collaboration project through which we recruited 345 LHD users who had used LHD at least twice before taking part in our study. At the end of the survey, 235 responses were returned to us. Complying with previous research, the following rules were applied to exclude invalid responses: (1) completion time beyond 3 standard deviations of average level; (2) same answers to all questions (Hu et al. 2021). After screening out 12 invalid responses, 223 valid samples are used for data analysis. See Table 1 for the descriptive analysis results.

A standard questionnaire translation process was followed. Before participants started the survey, they were informed that upon completing and submitting they would receive a monetary reward (£3) in return for their time. Besides, they were also given the right to terminate the survey at any time they wanted. Therefore, this study, as with other online survey research, might suffer from self-selection bias (Hu et al. 2021). In this sense, our study used a purposeful sample. At the beginning of the questionnaire, a screening question was added: "Have you used the Left-hand Doctor app for self-diagnosing in the last two months?". If the answer is no, the participant will be directed to the end of the survey.

4.2 Measures

All constructs in the conceptual model correspond to multiple items, the answer of which was coded on a seven-point Likert scale from 1 = strongly disagree to 7 = strongly agree. We operationalised the components of the major constructs from those validated instruments when possible, but we also developed our own item for the new constructs. Among the measures, the three items for **emotional support (ES)** (*ES1: LHD can support me emotionally in addition to providing health-related information; ES2: The interaction soothes my anxiety and gives me comfort; ES3:* LHD can show empathy to me) were developed based on prior research [15]. **Automated social presence (ASP)** is measured by one question (*ASP: I feel a sense of human doctor contact in LHD*) based on the definition of Van Doorn et al. (2017). **Technical quality (TQ)** was measured by four questions (*TQ1: The diagnosis of LHD is comparable to the one from my doctor; TQ2: LHD can provide appropriate recommendations for seeking further medical advice; TQ3: The medical information (diagnosis report) provided by LHD appears to be credible; TQ4: The information provided by LHD is relevant to my health needs*). As for **satisfaction (SAT)**, three items from Bhattacherjee [40] were adapted (*How do you feel about your overall experience using LHD? SAT1: very dissatisfied to very satisfied; SAT2: very unhelpful to very helpful; SAT3: very frustrated to very contented*). Furthermore, age, gender, and education are viewed as important individual differences in deciding on technology usage [41], therefore, a query for demographic data followed.

Table 1. Descriptive Statistics of Respondents (N = 223)

Demographic variable		Frequency	Percentage
Gender	Male	108	48.4
	Female	115	51.6
Age	18-25	61	27.4
	26-30	87	39
	31-40	55	24.7
	41-50	7	3.1
	51 or above	13	5.8
Education	High school or below	14	6.3
	College	45	20.2
	Bachelor's degree	89	39.9
	Master's degree	60	26.9
	Ph.D.	15	6.7
Health status		7.08/10 (mean)	1.608 (st.d)

5 Results

Variance-based partial least squares structural equation modelling (PLS-SEM) technique is a suitable multivariate statistical method when the sample size is moderate and data don't follow a strict normal distribution. SmartPLS4 software is used for estimating the measurement and structural model in this research.

5.1 Common Method Bias

As with other studies using self-reported data, there is a risk that the data obtained in our study were contaminated by common method bias. To avoid the introduction of common method bias in the first place, during survey design, we inserted the demographic questions between the independent variables and dependent variables to create a psychological separation. On top of the procedure remedy, we also followed the full collinearity assessment approach which suggests that the occurrence of a VIF larger than 3.3 can be viewed as an indication of pathological collinearity and also an indicator of common method bias [42]. According to our analysis, all factor-level VIFs from the full collinearity test are lower than 3.3, therefore, the model can be considered free of common method bias.

5.2 Measurement Model Estimation

For reflective constructs, indicator reliability, construct reliability, convergent validity, and discriminant validity are checked [44]. All factor loadings of the reflective latent variables used in this study exceed 0.763 which means that indicator reliability is greater than 0.5, showing acceptable indicator reliability [45]. Cronbach's alpha (α), composite reliability (CR), and Dijkstra-Henseler's ρA (rho_A) are used to assess internal consistency reliability. As Table 2 shows, the estimated values are all above the recommended thresholds of 0.7 for CR and rho_A, 0.5 for AVE, and 0.8 for Cronbach's alpha (α) [44], showing a high level of construct reliability. For convergent validity, each latent variable's average variance extracted (AVE) is calculated. From Table 2, all values of AVE are greater than 0.5, thus convergent validity is established [44]. Besides, acceptable convergent validity and discriminant validity can be determined from Table 3 where the cross-loadings tell us that the indicator loadings are higher for the corresponding latent variable than for any other latent variables.

Table 2. Construct Descriptive Statistics, Reliability, and Validity

	Mean	St.d	Cronbach's alpha	CR (rho_a)	AVE
ASP	3.794	1.707	N/A	N/A	N/A
Emotional support	3.863	1.497	0.944	0.945	0.900
Technical quality	5.158	1.020	0.902	0.903	0.773
Satisfaction	5.184	1.025	0.883	0.884	0.811

Table 3. Cross loadings

	Emotional support	Technical quality	Satisfaction
ES1	**0.943**	0.501	0.368
ES2	**0.950**	0.469	0.381
ES3	**0.953**	0.476	0.341
TQ1	0.518	**0.902**	0.649
TQ2	0.443	**0.868**	0.625
TQ3	0.390	**0.870**	0.640
TQ4	0.431	**0.877**	0.661
SAT1	0.381	0.674	**0.923**
SAT2	0.315	0.665	**0.902**
SAT3	0.339	0.639	**0.876**

5.3 Structural Model Estimation

In the SmartPLS 4 software, the statistical significance of path coefficients, outer weights, and other values (R^2, Cronbach's alpha, HTMT, etc.) are tested via the bootstrapping procedure. To ensure a reliable result, we used 5,000 bootstrap subsamples. We first checked the inner model's collinearity values, all of which are below 3.3. Therefore there is no collinearity issue between the set of predictors [43]. Then we proceeded to examine the coefficients of hypothesised paths. As Table 2 shows, except H2 and H4, H1, H3 and H5 are confirmed by the data. All of the demographic variables have no significant impact on satisfaction except health status which has a positive impact on satisfaction ($\beta = 0.112, p < 0.022$). The analysis of the inner model shows that technical quality and health status together can explain 55.2% of the variance in user satisfaction. ASP and emotional support explain 28% of the variance in technical quality (Table 4).

Table 4. Hypothesis testing results

Hypothesis	Path coefficient	t value	p-value	Result
H1: ASP -> TQ	0.260	2.155	0.031	Supported
H2: ASP -> SAT	-0.012	0.183	0.855	Not supported
H3: ES -> TQ	0.294	2.465	0.014	Supported
H4: ES -> SAT	0.000	0.001	0.999	Not supported
H5: TQ -> SAT	0.714	13.832	0.000	Supported

6 Discussion

6.1 Interpretation of the Results

This research points to the importance of social designs in the healthcare scenario, as it significantly relates to users' evaluation of the chatbot's functional performance manifested in the evaluation of the technical quality of the SAC. If the chatbot can make users feel a sense of human doctor contact and provide emotional support during the interaction, users will gain more positive experience and confidence in terms of the diagnosis report. This result can help identify domains where chatbots can add meaningful purpose through anthropomorphic design elements and improved human-AI interaction dynamics. However, neither automated social presence nor emotional support has a significant direct effect on user satisfaction.

6.2 Contributions

From a theoretical perspective, this study contributes to current knowledge in understanding how social design elements of chatbots can affect users' perception towards chatbots' functional performance. Practically, the evidence from this research provides HCI design guidelines to help practitioners in their system design and development, especially balancing the functional aspects and anthropomorphic aspects. There are many ways that HCI designers can use to influence users' anthropomorphic perceptions. For embodied robots, facial expressions, voice tones, etc. [24]; for disembodied agents like text-based chatbots, linguistic features such as polite and informal social language [9], tailored responses and variety in responses [18], humanlike visual representation (e.g., avatars, human faces) and demographic information (e.g., gender, age, name, ethnicity) [10] can be used to enforce a feeling of social presence and anthropomorphic perception. However, the effectiveness of those social design elements needs to be tested along with the functional performance of the system.

6.3 Limitations and Future Research

While this study presents interesting findings, it also contains limitations. The group of users in this study might represent the population who needs health chatbots the most like people with chronic diseases. In addition, we did not test any environmental variables in our research model. For example, the reputation of the chatbot developer, the emergency level and complexity of the symptoms, and the availability of traditional medical services may all play important roles in satisfaction. Another weakness comes from the fact that our study captures just a single point in time. The cross-sectional research design does not allow for an assessment of causality. All the above should be considered when generalising the results further to other environments.

To extend the findings of our study, we recommend three areas for future investigations. First, it would be desirable for future studies to include the impact of prior expectations and worries that users associate with this technique and the corresponding impact on their experience. This inquiry might need a longitudinal research design to show how people adapt their expectations over time. Second, combining our research model with other contextual variables of importance, such as the perceived medical authority and reputation of the developer to have a holistic view of satisfaction. Another suggestion for future exploration is to conduct research with participants who are actually experiencing certain symptoms, which we think can better gauge the accuracy and effectiveness of the diagnosis and therefore more subjective evaluation for the process and outcome quality of chatbot.

References

1. Zhao, Y., Ni, Q., Zhou, R.: What factors influence the mobile health service adoption? A meta-analysis and the moderating role of age. Int. J. Inf. Manage. **43**, 342–350 (2018)
2. Lou, B., Wu, L.: Managing AI on drugs: can artificial intelligence accelerate drug development? Evidence from a large-scale examination of bio-pharma firms. MIS Q. **45**, 1451–1482 (2021)
3. He, J., Baxter, S.L., Xu, J., Xu, J., Zhou, X., Zhang, K.: The practical implementation of artificial intelligence technologies in medicine. Nat. Med. **25**, 30–36 (2019)
4. Mettler, T., Sprenger, M., Winter, R.: Service robots in hospitals: new perspectives on niche evolution and technology affordances. Eur. J. Inf. Syst. **26**, 451–468 (2017)
5. You, Y., Tsai, C., Li, Y., Ma, F., Heron, C., Gui, X.: Beyond self-diagnosis: how a chatbot-based symptom checker should respond. ACM Trans. Comput. Interact. (2023)
6. Accenture, Artificial Intelligence: Healthcare's New Nervous System (2017). https://www.accenture.com/us-en/insight-artificial-intelligence-future-growth. Accessed 07 December 2022
7. Morse, K.E., Ostberg, N.P., Jones, V.G., Chan, A.S.: Use characteristics and triage acuity of a digital symptom checker in a large integrated health system: population-based descriptive study. J. Med. Internet Res. **22**, e20549 (2020)
8. Lee, S.Y., Choi, J.: Enhancing user experience with conversational agent for movie recommendation: effects of self-disclosure and reciprocity. Int. J. Hum. Comput. Stud. **103**, 95–105 (2017)
9. Schanke, S., Burtch, G., Ray, G.: Estimating the impact of "humanizing" customer service chatbots. Inf. Syst. Res. **32**, 736–751 (2021)
10. Seeger, A.-M., Pfeiffer, J., Heinzl, A.: Texting with humanlike conversational agents: designing for anthropomorphism. J. Assoc. Inf. Syst. **22**, 931–967 (2021)
11. ter Stal, S., Kramer, L.L., Tabak, M., op den Akker, H., Hermens, H.: Design features of embodied conversational agents in eHealth: a literature review. Int. J. Hum. Comput. Stud. **138**, 1–22 (2020)
12. Chaves, A.P., Gerosa, M.A.: How should my chatbot interact? A survey on social characteristics in human-chatbot interaction design. Int. J. Hum. Comput. Interact. **37**, 729–758 (2021)

13. Gkinko, L., Elbanna, A.: Hope, tolerance and empathy: employees' emotions when using an AI-enabled chatbot in a digitalised workplace. Inf. Technol. People (2022)
14. Van Doorn, J., et al.: Emergence of automated social presence in organizational frontlines and customers' service experiences. J. Serv. Res. **20**, 43–58 (2017)
15. Lai, Y., Panagiotopoulos, P., Lioliou, E.: Empowering users with medical artificial intelligence technologies. In: Thirty-First Eur. Conf. Inf. Syst., pp. 1–17 (2023)
16. Zhou, Y., Kankanhalli, A., Yang, Z., Lei, J.: Expectations of patient-centred care: investigating IS-related and other antecedents. Inf. Manag. **54**, 583–598 (2017)
17. Ameen, N., Tarhini, A., Reppel, A., Anand, A.: Customer experiences in the age of artificial intelligence. Comput. Human Behav. **114**, 106548 (2021)
18. Grimes, G.M., Schuetzler, R.M., Giboney, J.S.: Mental models and expectation violations in conversational AI interactions. Decis. Support. Syst. **144**, 113515 (2021)
19. Følstad, A., Skjuve, M.: Chatbots for customer service: user experience and motivation. In: International Conference on Conversational User Interfaces (CUI2019), pp. 1–9. ACM, New York (2019)
20. Liu, W., Jiang, M., Li, W., Mou, J.: How does the anthropomorphism of AI chatbots facilitate users' reuse intention in online health consultation services? The moderating role of disease severity. Technol. Forecast. Soc. Change. **203**, 123407 (2024)
21. Schillaci, C.E., de Cosmo, L.M., Piper, L., Nicotra, M., Guido, G.: Anthropomorphic chatbots for future healthcare services: effects of personality, gender, and roles on source credibility, user satisfaction, and intention to use. Technol. Forecast. Soc. Change. **199**, 123025 (2024)
22. Laumer, S., Maier, C., Tobias Gubler, F.: Chatbot acceptance in healthcare: explaining user adoption of conversational agents for disease diagnosis. In: 27th Eur. Conf. Inf. Syst., pp. 1–18 (2019)
23. Castelo, N., Bos, M.W., Lehmann, D.R.: Task-dependent algorithm aversion. J. Mark. Res. **56**, 809–825 (2019)
24. Qiu, L., Benbasat, I.: Evaluating anthropomorphic product recommendation agents: a social relationship perspective to designing information systems. J. Manag. Inf. Syst. **25**, 145–182 (2009)
25. Yoganathan, V., Osburg, V.S., Kunz, W.H., Toporowski, W.: Check-in at the Robo-desk: effects of automated social presence on social cognition and service implications. Tour. Manag. **85**, 104309 (2021)
26. Zahedi, F.M., Walia, N., Jain, H.: Augmented virtual doctor office: theory-based design and assessment. J. Manag. Inf. Syst. **33**, 776–808 (2016)
27. Yen, C., Chiang, M.-C.: Trust me, if you can: a study on the factors that influence consumers' purchase intention triggered by chatbots based on brain image evidence and self-reported assessments. Behav. Inf. Technol. (2020)
28. Hu, P., Lu, Y., (Yale) Gong, Y.: Dual humanness and trust in conversational AI: a person-centered approach. Comput. Human Behav. **119**, 106727 (2021)
29. Li, M., Mao, J.: Hedonic or utilitarian? Exploring the impact of communication style alignment on user's perception of virtual health advisory services. Int. J. Inf. Manage. **35**, 229–243 (2015)
30. Li, M., (Jack) Jiang, Z., Fan, Z., Hou, J.: Expert or peer? Understanding the implications of virtual advisor identity on emergency rescuer empowerment in mobile psychological self-help services. Inf. Manag. **54**, 866–886 (2017)
31. Cyr, D., Hassanein, K., Head, M., Ivanov, A.: The role of social presence in establishing loyalty in e-Service environments. Interact. Comput. **19**, 43–56 (2007)
32. Zhang, A., Patrick Rau, P.L.: Tools or peers? Impacts of anthropomorphism level and social role on emotional attachment and disclosure tendency towards intelligent agents. Comput. Human Behav. **138**, 107415 (2023)

33. Verhagen, T., Van Nes, J., Feldberg, F.: Virtual customer service agents: using social presence and personalization to shape online service encounters. J. Comput. Commun. **19**, 529–545 (2014)
34. Cyr, D., Head, M., Larios, H., Pan, B.: Exploring human images in website design: a multi-method approach. MIS Q. **33**, 539–566 (2009)
35. Liu, B., Shyam Sundar, S.: should machines express sympathy and empathy? Experiments with a health advice chatbot. Cyberpsychol. Behav. Soc. Netw. **21**, 625–636 (2018)
36. Delone, W.H., Mclean, E.R.: The DeLone and McLean model of information systems success: a ten-year update. J. Manag. Inf. Syst. **19**, 9–30 (2003)
37. Ashfaq, M., Yun, J., Yu, S., Loureiro, S.M.C.: I, Chatbot: modeling the determinants of users' satisfaction and continuance intention of AI-powered service agents. Telemat. Inform. **54**, 101473 (2020)
38. Rana, N.P., Dwivedi, Y.K., Williams, M.D., Weerakkody, V.: Investigating success of an e-government initiative: validation of an integrated IS success model. Inf. Syst. Front. **17**, 127–142 (2015)
39. Wang, Y.S.: Assessing e-commerce systems success: a respecification and validation of the DeLone and McLean model of IS success. Inf. Syst. J. **18**, 529–557 (2008)
40. Bhattacherjee, A.: Understanding information systems continuance: an expectation-confirmation model. MIS Q. **25**, 351–370 (2001)
41. Venkatesh, V., Morris, M.G., Davis, G.B., Davis, F.D.: User acceptance of information technology: toward a unified view. MIS Q. Manag. Inf. Syst. **27**, 425–478 (2003)
42. Kock, N.: Common method bias in PLS-SEM: a full collinearity assessment approach. Int. J. e-Collab. **11**, 1–10 (2015)
43. Kock, N., Lynn, G.S.: Lateral collinearity and misleading results in variance-based SEM: an illustration and recommendations. J. Assoc. Inf. Syst. **13**, 546–580 (2012)
44. Bagozzi, R., Yi, Y.: On the evaluation of structural equation models. J. Acad. Mark. Sci. **16**, 074–094 (1988)
45. Hulland, J.: Use of partial least squares (PLS) in strategic management research: a review of four recent studies. Strateg. Manag. J. **20**, 195–204 (1999)

Generation Z Technological Frames of AI Game-Based Assessment

Trinh Nguyen(✉) and Amany Elbanna

Royal Holloway University of London, Egham TW20 0EX, UK
trinh.nguyen.2021@live.rhul.ac.uk, amany.elbanna@rhul.ac.uk

Abstract. The use of AI systems in the selection of job applicants is growing rapidly. While scholars have debated potential benefits to employers and job seekers, there is little empirical research on its actual use. In particular, there is little empirically known about job seekers experience of using it and in particular those from generation Z who are trying to enter the job market. Considering its importance, this study questions: How job applicants perceive AI Game-based Assessment and How this impact their use pattern? Through qualitative approach and adoption of Technological Frames Theory, our findings identify three aspects of technological frames and show that the experiences of Gen Z applicants differ based on the emphasis they put on each of them. This results in different experience of stress and enjoyment. The study contributes to the AI literature and particular its use in hiring and draw practical conclusions.

Keywords: AI Game based Assessment · AI adoption · Automated hiring

1 Introduction

The applicant selection is a key stage of staffing process that determines decision of making a job offer. It involves communication to set applicants' expectations and several selection phases to sift through applicants to select the best for the job [1]. Recently, artificial intelligence (AI) technologies have been widely used by employers to assist in the different phases on the job selection process to improve their efficiency and enhance their standardisation [2]. For example, companies such as L'Oreal, Unilever and British American Tobacco (BAT) have used AI applications including AI resume scanning, AI video interviewing and AI game-based skills and aptitude assessments [2]. This study focuses on one type of AI applications for job selection; namely AI Game-based assessments (AI-GBA). AI-GBA refers to a group of AI applications that interact with job applicants utilising computer games interfaces to examine various skills and aptitudes of job applicants such as their decision making style, willingness to improvise and ability to solve problems [3]. AI-GBA can predict behaviour and potential working performance of job applicants scoring them based on their games playing behaviour. Scholars debated the potential benefits of using games-like assessments in the job selection process with little conclusive empirical studies [4, 5]. However, the addition of AI technologies to

Published by Springer Nature Switzerland AG 2024
R. van de Wetering et al. (Eds.): I3E 2024, LNCS 14907, pp. 65–76, 2024.
https://doi.org/10.1007/978-3-031-72234-9_6

GBA provides another layer of complexity in need of in-depth empirical investigation. This is because of their wide adoption in organisation in addition to the disguise of AI technologies behind the game-like assessment. Currently, there is little understanding of the use of AI-GBA at the job applicants' side and the impact of this use on them. This is despite the importance of work and employment to society [6]. This study aims to answer the question: *How job applicants perceive AI-GBA and How this impact their use pattern?* Understanding job applicants' perception and use pattern of AI-GBA is important as it ultimately impact their performance and opportunity to get a job which is critical for job applicants, organisations and society. Accordingly, answering this research question is key for employers in devising approaches to use AI to achieve efficiency in the recruitment process while maintaining job applicants interest and infusing positive attitude towards the hiring organisation and achieving best outcomes. It is important for governments and policy makers in their effort to make the job market accessible and fair. To answer the research question, the study adopts qualitative approach based on rich data collection of Gen Z applicants comprising of interviews, social media reviews in addition to documents review. It focuses on examining one AI-GBA technology to reduce variations in the studies technologies. It also focuses on one age group and type of users namely young people who are entering the job market. This group belong to the so called generation Z or Gen Z (born between 1995 and 2012) [7]. Their employment is currently a pressing issue in many societies with doubling unemployment rate in comparison to all other groups in 2023 [8]. In addition, Gen Z employment is critical to their integration and wellbeing [6] and social stability.

Through the theoretical lens of technological frames (TF), the study identifies three aspects of AI-GBA frames that job applicants form. The findings reveal that in critical situations like getting a job, Gen Z applicants experience of AI-GBA can differ based on the emphasis they put on the different aspects of the AI-GBA. This results in different experience of job applicants' AI-GBA use ranging from stress to enjoyment. The study contributes to AI research and in particular its use in hiring processes and in particular job selection. It provides a much missing Gen Z's perspective revealing and explaining the differences in their experiences of AI-GBA. The findings contribute to practice and call for employers and policy makers to make the use and purpose of AI-GBA more transparent and offer applicants guidance on how to succeed in their preparation for jobs when AI-GBA is used in the selection process. Following the introduction, the paper is organised as follows. Section 2 reviews the literature on AI-GBA and Gen Z. Section 3 provides an overview of the TF theory and Sect. 4 describes the research methodology. Section 5 presents the research findings and Sect. 6 presents the discussion and contributions of research. The last section highlights conclusions, limitations and future research suggestions of this study.

2 Literature Review

2.1 The Use of AI Game-Based Assessment in Job Selection

AI powered game-based assessment (AI-GBA) integrates machine learning scoring capability to evaluate a job applicant's behaviour in tasks presented as part of a game they are requested to play instead of traditional assessment methods and context and rather than scoring based on merely tallying correct and incorrect answers as traditional GBAs do [9]. This approach converts the digital footprint of job applicants in a computer game into a report that indicates candidate's profile [10], characteristics and suitability to the job [11]. For example, the official website of the widely adopted AI-GBA; Pymetrics, states that "each game captures thousands of behavioural data points, then builds a profile of what makes a person and job unique" indicating that the prediction of applicants' abilities is based on the conversion of trace data to algorithmic scoring model [12]. AI-GBA can analyse large amount of job applicants data to assess their suitability to jobs [13, 14]. As a form of algorithmic assessment, it can assist hiring managers in making decisions [15]. In addition, it is claimed that it can improve job applicants experience and enhance the fairness of the assessment process [16].

Empirical research on AI-GBA is currently limited, and the existing few studies are predominantly quantitative lacking in-depth understanding of applicants' experience in using these systems [16]. Job applicants' experience particularly from Gen Z is important to understand as they struggle to find job opportunities in a competitive job market [17]. They need to improve their skills to meet employer's demands but those can be opaque and disguised in GBA that is AI assessed. Hence, there is a pressing need to understand in-depth how Gen Z applicants perceive their use of AI-GBA in the assessment process.

2.2 Gen Z Characteristic and the Use of Technology

Gen Z is the most recent generation to enter the workplace. Studies examine their unique characteristics and behaviours toward work and working life [18–20]. They find that Gen Z focus on developing strong skillsets that allow them to get a job and advance quickly in the workplace [33]. It is stereotyped as being highly success orientated while also being less engaged in the workplace [21]. However recent research applying the theory of generations and generation units by Karl [22], which states that subgroups exist within each generational cohort shows the existence of three distinct subgroups [37]. Those are Social Investors who value a work-life balance; Chill Workers who desire comfortable workplace environment and Go Getters who prioritize advancing their career. However all three groups reported prioritising workplaces high moral and ethical standards [37]. Gen Z is the first generation that has been born and raised in a highly changing technological environment with several technological innovations [23]. Gen Z are generally assumed to be comfortable and confident in employing digital technologies in their life and work [19]. Being surrounded with several advanced technologies makes Gen Z communicate differently [24]. Scholars indicate that Gen Z shows preference for using communication devices rather than a face-to-face meeting [23] and has a strong attachment to digital devices [24]. They also adopt different technological applications in their personal use [25]. Gen Z is also found to be possessing more positive attitude and flexibility in adaptation than previous generations [17, 20, 23]. However, there is little examination of how Gen Z perceive their use of AI-GBA technology in the job assessment and how this impact their use pattern. Achieving this understanding supports jobs applicants and can also help organisations modify their managerial process to satisfy job applicants and ensure getting the best fit for the jobs. Accordingly, this research aims to explore the experiences of Gen Z in their actual use of AI-GBA.

3 Theoretical Lens: Technological Frames

To answer the research question of how job applicants perceive AI-GBA and how this impact their use pattern, the study adopts Technological Frames theory (TF). This theory provides an understanding of the assumptions, expectations and formed knowledge toward digital technology [26]. Scholars follow the social cognitive research, show that people's interpretation of the world impact their behaviour and actions and that their social construction of realities give these actions meanings [26]. Hence, the theory maintains that knowing how people perceive and interpret technologies is crucial to understand the way they interact with it [26]. While each individual can hold their own interpretation, group of actors still share set of core beliefs of particular contexts [27]. TF was introduced to explore the shared cognitive structure in different types of user groups [26]. Research shows that different users might holds different TF toward the same technological applications [26]. Scholars focus on the difference between groups interpretations inside organisations and show that managers, technologists, and users differ in their understanding of technology based on three aspects: *nature of technology* – people's understanding of technology capabilities; *technology strategy* – people's understanding of motivation to adopt the technology; and *technology in use* – people's understanding of how technology will be used [26]. These three aspects are also summed as *Frame content* [28].

The original three TF domains of Orlikowski and Gash [26] are widely used and developed in other research areas. For example, from an information system delivery (ISD) project, scholars discover four TF domains are IT capabilities and design, business value of IT, IT enabled work practices and IT delivery strategy [28]. While the first three domains of Davidson [28] are similar with three aspects of Orlikowski and Gash [26], the last domain – IT delivery strategy refers to the post system implementation process is novel compared to previous research. TF concept is also adopted in healthcare domains. Scholars investigate the use of care robots in eldercare among users based on three domains namely; the nature of care robots, care robots in use and care robots strategy [29]. Although, the contents of frames are varied in different contexts [30], there are three domains are widely applicable namely; the features and attributes of technologies; the organisational applications of technologies and the incorporation of technologies in workplace [31].

Users in the same group are congruent in formulated their TF. However, the incongruence of TF among different groups might yield difficulties and challenges such as breaking down the communication or the shortage of participation [26]. Zuboff [32] research show that managers reject the implementation of technology because of their traditional mindset about managerial control. In another context, scholars show the incongruence of TF among managers leads to the ineffective and limited application of technology in public sectors [33]. In sum, different aspects of TF have been explored, especially the frames content. Previous scholars have also advocated future research to adopt TF in other organisational context [34]. The focus and orientation of TF theory is consistent with the objectives of the study to understand Gen Z perception of AI-GBA and the resulting use pattern adopt the TF theory. Hence, our study utilises the foundation knowledge of TF literature to explore the experience of Gen Z applicants of AI-GBA system and illuminate the consequences in terms of use patterns.

4 Research Methodology

The study adopts an interpretive approach to inquiry to understand how participants construct their use of AI-GBA and give it meaning [35]. Interpretivist highlights the uniqueness of human interpretation and experience [36]. The study collects qualitative data from different sources including semi-structure interviews, social media observations, systems' review and corporate news [37]. This allows the triangulation of evidence from different sources and different research participants [38]. To reduce the impact of variations in systems design, games features and assessment criteria, we focus the study on users of one of the most prominent and widely used AI-GBA platform; Pymetrics. Pymetrics is a cognitive, soft skills and knowledge assessment hiring platform that uses AI games to profile applicants' traits and match them to jobs. It has 12 individual games that measure 9 intrinsic qualities [12]. While engaging in the 12 games, job applicants receive instant feedbacks of their performance following each game. After completing the game test, job applicant will receive a report indicating their three highlight traits and the explanation for each trait [12]. The study focuses on applicants' experiences of Pymetrics in Vietnam since it is widely used in the selection process of internships known as Management Trainee Program (MTP) of key multinational companies in Vietnam such as BAT, Heineken, Unilever.

We adopt semi-structured interview to provide an opportunity for participants to freely express their views to talk about what they see as important or concerning [39]. 40 participants were recruited. The inclusion criteria for participants are: 1) male and female between 22–25 years old who have applied for MTP in Vietnam; 2) successful and/or unsuccessful applicants of Pymetrics game round; 3) have used Pymetrics in the selection process. The diversity of participants' background reduces selection biases, which can happen in the process of recruiting and designing inclusion criteria for choosing participants of interviews [40]. Snowball sampling technique is used to select 8 initial participants [41]. Snowball sampling technique assists researchers in suggesting and/or finding other potential participants for their research [42]. After interviewing the initial participants, we continue finding participants from personal contact and social media. Our aim was to maximise the diversity of the participant's background to reduce bias and avoid skewed findings towards a specific group. In term of social media observation, we gather information from online discussion of different platforms such as Facebook group, Reddit thread, YouTube, and LinkedIn posts. Social media is considered as an useful additional tool of qualitative research to discover new insights of a phenomenon [43]. In addition, we also attempt to play Pymetrics game to get the feel for the job applicant's experience. This trial play allows us to get a deeper understanding of Pymetrics evaluation systems and experience the vagueness of the system from job applicant's viewpoint. Regarding to document review, we collect the information of Pymetrics platform from different sources such as: results report (for applicant and for recruiter), Pymetrics platform's information and introduction that Pymetrics provider send to their customers. The diverse sources of information facilitates us in enriching the knowledge on Pymetrics.

5 Findings

The findings show that users of Gen Z who use the same AI-GBA develop different TF towards it. The content of applicants TF revolves around three aspects: nature of AI-GBA defined as their understanding of the capabilities of the system; AI-GBA in use defined as their approach in engaging with the system; and AI-GBA strategy defined as their understanding of the functions and objectives of the system. The findings reveal that in their use of the AI-GBA, job applicant developed TF can be grouped into three categories depending on the emphasis they put on any of the three aspects of the interaction: the computer game, the job selection and the scoring AI.

5.1 Technological Frame Focusing on Game

Some of the job applicants focus solely on the game elements and aim to score. They develop TF focused on the game elements and play as they do with other computer games. The aspects of their developed TF are as follows.

Nature of AI-GBA: Job applicant who pay attention mainly to the game elements are not considering the AI scoring system behind the game. They compare the game to other games they know and play it accordingly. The excerpts below is an example to illustrate how applicant in this category are unaware of the AI scoring capabilities: *"I found the game easy to understand...it was not complicated as I did not need to read or calculate too much, so I felt very comfortable to play"* Participant 8. This category of job applicants consider Pymetrics games like any computer game and think that there is no right or wrong way to play it.

AI-GBA in use: Since this category of job applicants focus on the game elements of the AI-GBA, they believe that it is like any other game where higher score they gain in the game leads to wining and hence higher chances to be selected for the job. The following excerpt illustrates this idea: *"Because the system did not display any instructions so I can only think of maximising my score"* Participant 14. To maximise the game scores, applicants ask for help from their friends and invite them to join them when playing the game so they play it with their assistance and support.

AI-GBA strategy: This category of applicants enjoys the games as they find their rules quite simple and easy to play and do not experience stress in playing them despite being assessment for their suitability for the job. This has been expressed as follows: *"I felt the games were so easy and it made me not as stressed as I imagined an assessment to look like..."* Participant 9. They find the games to provide a relaxed environment for assessing them that mitigate the tension that other assessment methods can cause.

5.2 Technological Frames Focusing on Job Fit

The study finds a category of job applicants who pay attention to their fit and suitability to the job. They consider Pymetrics as a tool to evaluate the compatibility between them and organisation. Hence, they play the game spontaneously showcasing their real views. This behaviour is aligned with the findings of previous research about the unique attributes of Gen Z and their desire to find a meaningful job [44]. The following sections explain the TF content of this category of AI-GBA job applicants users.

Nature of AI-GBA: This category of job applicants users has awareness of the existence of AI assessment system behind the games they play. They posses a general understanding of how the system works as the following excerpt indicates: *"I realised that the system can detect our attitude through the way we play the Balloon game. For example, if you only dare to press each ball three times and then collect the points straight away, the machine would consider you are afraid of risks."* Participant 15.

AI-GBA in use: Despite being aware of the AI scoring, this category tends to accept the uncertainties of the AI-GBA system and take the ambiguities they encounter for granted. The following excerpt shows this viewpoint: *"Sometimes I did not understand but I thought it was normal so I was not stressed."* Participant 14. They tend to just play and invest very little in preparation for the game. During the game test, they commonly follow the requirements and instructions that the game offers. They do not dig deep into the assessment system of the game, analyse or plan their moves in the game or attempt to guess how their behaviour will be assessed.

AI-GBA strategy: This category of job applicants believe the motivation for implementing this AI-GBA is providing a novel selection process with the intervention of the leading technologies. As their focus is on the job-fit aspect, job applicants in this category exhibit a compliant attitude in the game and little attempts to manipulate the algorithm.

5.3 Technological Frames Focusing on AI

The findings indicate that a third category of job applicants focus their attention in AI-GBA on the AI assessment. They are occupied and conscious of the existence of AI scoring system behind the game when playing Pymetrics and try to infer its algorithm. The following sections explain their TF content.

Nature of AI-GBA: This category of job applicants users views Pymetrics test as an examiner, who continuously observes and assesses every footprint they make. This makes them feel anxious of being watched all the time interacting with the system. The following excerpt indicates this view: *"This game was more difficult (than other tests) because it interacted with you more and assessed every move you made."* Participant 4.

AI-GBA in use: When focusing on the AI aspects, job applicants try to infer the ways the AI system works and resist its algorithm in different ways. They prepare for the game by collecting different strands of information about it from many sources including friends who have experienced the AI-GBA before, HR staff, websites, forums and other online and AI searches. They also seek information about the company and the position they are applying for and try to match them to the information about the games to infer which game is testing for which abilities. In addition, to get more knowledge and familiarity with the games and their contents, job applicants create multiple applications on the company's website with different emails and resumes. This allows them to take the games test several times. They believe that this strategy helps them to learn how the system works by guessing backwards the rules and patterns of its algorithm. They suppose this strategy works for them as they are confident with their ability to understand the algorithm. They hold the view that since this is a machine, they must be able to crack it and understand its rules. Focusing on AI, job applicants create an image of the ideal employee the company is looking for, connect this with the function of the game and try to play the game to reflect this image. Applicant describes how they deal with the system in the following excerpt: *"In the Money Exchange game, I try to show that I am a generous and fair person"* Participant 1. In addition, they attempt to adjust their behaviours carefully in every actions in the games because they think that the AI system might detect their unreal behaviours.

AI-GBA strategy: This category of applicants is aware that the system is used to evaluate their behaviours and traits. They assess the AI-GBA difficult than other traditional tests as they need to continuously think about the implications of each game and how to wisely deal with games. They feel exhausted as they need to continuously guess the implications of the assessment system and behave accordingly. They cannot enjoy the game elements of the test because their attention is on the grappling with the AI aspects of the system. The following excerpt supports this idea: *"I felt quite worried because the machine could evaluate every gestures and made an assessment of my personality through the game"* Participant 15.

6 Discussions and Contributions

This study aims to understand Gen Z's experiences of the use of AI-GBA. It explored the questions of: *How job applicants perceive AI-GBA and How this impact their use pattern?* The findings reveal that although Gen Z is considered to be a digital native with a strong sense of technology aware and high level of familiarity with technology [17], they have different senses making and emotions toward the same AI-GBA system. The differences among the TF of applicants toward AI-GBA system revolves around the emphasis they put on the computer game, selection process or the AI behind it. This emphasis formulates their technological framing contents related to nature of technology, technology in use and technology strategy [26].

When job applicants focus mainly on the game aspects of the AI-GBA system they are comfortable and enjoy the GBA concept of the selection process because they are not worried about the uncertainties of AI algorithm. While previous scholars discover that Gen Z is "digital native" and are more attracted by an advanced technological environment [23], the unawareness of AI capabilities in this situation prevents job applicants from the tension that technology might yield for their selection process. In other category of job applicant TF, they focus more on job-fit aspect and are conscious about the capabilities AI-GBA system. Applicants are aware of the latent assessment and actual purpose behind each game to some extent. This category of applicants exposes typical characteristics of Gen Z, who possess a good knowledge of technology [45], is realistic [46], and desires for a meaningful and suitable job [44]. They accept the outcomes of the test with a positive attitude, show a high trust in the assessment capabilities of AI-GBA systems. The last category of job applicant is focusing on the AI aspects. They possess the high level understanding of the AI-GBA system. They clear about the assessment capabilities of system and assume that every trace they made in game are assessed by some certain ways. They desire to control and manipulate the outcomes of the system with their understanding of the system. This is because of their desire to be selected regardless of their suitability with the organisation. They view this test as a challenge to conquer instead of an opportunity for them to examine their alignment with the job role. They continue guessing how the system works and act accordingly, they exhaust themselves trying to understand and respond to what they think the algorithmic demands.

This study provides both practical and theoretical implications. In terms of theoretical contribution, while previous research agree that the implementation of GBA in selection can alleviate the anxiety of the test [47] and Gen Z has a common preference toward game-like systems because they are familiar with this [48]. This study finds that the intervention of AI might decrease fondness for GBA of Gen Z. Besides, the findings enrich the knowledge TF areas. Although Gen Z shares some common characteristics, there are incongruence in the way they make sense of the same AI-GBA. These differences lead to the different response behaviours and emotions toward the system. This paper reveals a paradox is that user with less amount of knowledge of AI-GBA system might show a lower level of tension than the one who acquires more knowledge when face with the uncertainties of the system. In terms of practical contributions, this study offers insights of how job applicants experience and react to the new applications of AI-GBA. This allows recruiters are aware of the two-side effect of AI-GBA system toward Gen Z job applicant's perspective, which might cause the losing of potential job applicants. In addition, it also invites recruiters and policy makers to make the use of AI-GBA clearer to applicants so applicants in the third categories do not fall into stress and anxiety.

7 Conclusion, Limitations and Future Research

Like all research, this study has limitations which also provide opportunities for future research as follows. First, the study provides a qualitative account of job applicants interpretation of AI-GBA and their resulting use patterns. One of the common limitations of a qualitative research is the small amount of participants compared to a quantitative one. Hence, the findings of this research is inappropriate for making generalisations on populations however they provide insight on actual use [49]. Future research can design surveys based on the findings of this research to statistically test their validity and provide generalisable insight on job applicants' perspective. Second, the data of this research is collected from young job applicants from Gen Z. This is a particular generation of job applicant with a particular characteristics in terms of technology adoption and use. Future research can extend the study to examine other generations of job applicants who are less familiar with games and more experienced in job search and assessments. Third, the study focuses on job applicants in Vietnam. This is important as Vietnam is one of the emerging economies with significant foreign investments and young job market. The study focuses on job applicants for foreign (Western) large corporations with strong global organisational culture. Future research might expand to examine job applicants of different types of organisations in other countries. Fourth, subjectivity is also one of the typical limitations and characteristics of a qualitative research [49]. This implies that the way researcher make sense of and understand the data is influence by their own interpretation. We have took meticulous steps in data analysis to mitigate this limitations and provide coherent theoretically-grounded analysis. Future research can examine the phenomenon employing other theoretical lens and examine variations.

In conclusion, this study explored the actual use of AI-GBA by job applicants. The findings highlights the different interpretations job applicants assign to the AI-GBA technology and the resulting use patterns. This informs recruiting organisations, governments and policy makers and supports the developments of job selection technologies that puts job applicants' perspective at its core. More research is invited to explore the different aspects of this phenomenon.

References

1. Wesche, J.S., Sonderegger, A.: Repelled at first sight? Expectations and intentions of job-seekers reading about AI selection in job advertisements. Comput. Hum. Behav. **125**, 106931 (2021)
2. Hickman, L., et al.: Automated video interview personality assessments: reliability, validity, and generalizability investigations. J. Appl. Psychol. **107**(8), 1323 (2022)
3. Hawkes, B., Cek, I., Handler, C.: The gamification of employee selection tools: an exploration of viability, utility, and future directions (2018)
4. Chow, S., Chapman, D.: Gamifying the employee recruitment process. In: Proceedings of the First International Conference on Gameful Design, Research, and Applications (2013)
5. Georgiou, K., Gouras, A., Nikolaou, I.: Gamification in employee selection: the development of a gamified assessment. Int. J. Sel. Assess. **27**(2), 91–103 (2019)
6. Kieselbach, T.: Long-term unemployment among young people: the risk of social exclusion. Am. J. Community Psychol. **32**(1–2), 69–76 (2003)
7. Benitez-Marquez, M.D., et al.: Generation Z within the workforce and in the workplace: a bibliometric analysis. Front. Psychol. **12**, 736820 (2022)
8. OECD: Unemployment Rates, OECD – Updated: December 2023 (2023)
9. Landers, R.N., Sanchez, D.R.: Game-based, gamified, and gamefully designed assessments for employee selection: definitions, distinctions, design, and validation. Int. J. Sel. Assess. **30**(1), 1–13 (2022)
10. Roth, P.L., et al.: Social media in employee-selection-related decisions: a research agenda for uncharted territory. J. Manag. **42**(1), 269–298 (2016)
11. Schwartz, H.A., et al.: Personality, gender, and age in the language of social media: the open-vocabulary approach. PLoS ONE **8**(9), e73791 (2013)
12. pymetrics (2023). https://www.pymetrics.ai/assessments
13. Hu, Q.: Unilever's practice on ai-based recruitment. Highlights Bus. Econ. Manage. **16**, 256–263 (2023)
14. Wilson, C., et al.: Building and auditing fair algorithms: a case study in candidate screening. In: Proceedings of the 2021 ACM Conference on Fairness, Accountability, and Transparency (2021)
15. Mainka, S.M.: Algorithm-based recruiting technology in the workplace. Tex. A&M J. Prop. L. **5**, 801 (2019)
16. Leutner, F., et al.: Game based assessments of cognitive ability in recruitment: validity, fairness and test-taking experience. Front. Psychol. **13**, 942662 (2023)
17. Pinzaru, F., et al.: Millennials at work: investigating the specificity of generation Y versus other generations. Manage. Dyn. Knowl. Economy **4**(2), 173–192 (2016)

18. Neto, J., de Oliveira, N.: Study on the perception of generation Z in relation to robotized selection processes. Int. Robot. Autom. J. **9**(3), 99–107 (2023)
19. Lazar, M.-A., Zbuchea, A., Pînzaru, F.: The emerging generation z workforce in the digital world: a literature review on cooperation and transformation. In: Proceedings of the International Conference on Business Excellence (2023)
20. Nikolenko, O., Astapenko, E.: The attitude of young people to the use of artificial intelligence. E3S Web Conf. **460**, 05013 (2023). https://doi.org/10.1051/e3sconf/202346005013
21. Group, B.: Is Gen Z the most success-oriented generation? (2018). https://www.barna.com/research/is-gen-z-the-most-success-oriented-generation/
22. Karl, M.: The problem of generations. Essays Sociol. Knowl. 276–322 (1952)
23. Linnes, C., Metcalf, B.: IGeneration and their acceptance of technology. Int. J. Manage. Inf. Syst. **21**(2), 11–26 (2017)
24. Turner, A.: Generation Z: technology and social interest. J. Individ. Psychol. **71**(2), 103–113 (2015)
25. Bulut, S., Maraba, D.: Generation Z and its perception of work through habits, motivations, expectations preferences, and work ethics. Psychol. Psychother. Res. Study (2021)
26. Orlikowski, W.J., Gash, D.C.: Technological frames: making sense of information technology in organizations. ACM Trans. Inf. Syst. **12**(2), 174–207 (1994)
27. Porac, J.F., Thomas, H., Baden-Fuller, C.: Competitive groups as cognitive communities: the case of Scottish knitwear manufacturers. J. Manage. Stud. **26**(4), 397–416 (1989)
28. Davidson, E.J.: Technology frames and framing: a socio-cognitive investigation of requirements determination. MIS Q. **26**(4), 329–358 (2002)
29. Frennert, S., Aminoff, H., Östlund, B.: Technological frames and care robots in eldercare. Int. J. Soc. Robot. **13**, 311–325 (2021)
30. McGovern, T., Hicks, C.: How political processes shaped the IT adopted by a small make-to-order company: a case study in the insulated wire and cable industry. Inf. Manage. **42**(1), 243–257 (2004)
31. Davidson, E.: A technological frames perspective on information technology and organizational change. J. Appl. Behav. Sci. **42**(1), 23–39 (2006)
32. Zuboff, S.: In the Age of the Smart Machine: The Future of Work and Power. Basic Books, Inc. (1988)
33. Guenduez, A.A., Mettler, T., Schedler, K.: Technological frames in public administration: what do public managers think of big data? Gov. Inf. Q. **37**(1), 101406 (2020)
34. Davidson, E., Pai, D.: Making sense of technological frames: Promise, progress, and potential. In: Information Systems Research: Relevant Theory and Informed Practice, pp. 473–491 (2004)
35. Walsham, G.: Reading the organization: metaphors and information management. Inf. Syst. J. **3**(1), 33–46 (1993)
36. Saunders, M.N., et al.: Understanding research philosophy and approaches to theory development (2015)
37. Myers, M.D., Avison, D.: Qualitative Research in Information Systems: A Reader. Sage (2002)
38. Polit, D.F., Beck, C.T.: Nursing Research: Generating and Assessing Evidence for Nursing Practice. Lippincott Williams & Wilkins (2008)
39. Myers, M.D., Newman, M.: The qualitative interview in IS research: examining the craft. Inf. Org. **17**(1), 2–26 (2007)
40. Smith, J., Noble, H.: Bias in research. Evid. Based Nurs. **17**(4), 100–101 (2014)
41. Parker, C., Scott, S., Geddes, A.: Snowball Sampling. SAGE Research Methods Foundations (2019)
42. Noy, C.: Sampling knowledge: the hermeneutics of snowball sampling in qualitative research. Int. J. Soc. Res. Methodol. **11**(4), 327–344 (2008)

43. Goncalves, M., Cornelius Smith, E.: Social media as a data gathering tool for international business qualitative research: opportunities and challenges. J. Transnatl. Manage. **23**(2–3), 66–97 (2018)
44. Leslie, B., et al.: Generation Z perceptions of a positive workplace environment. Empl. Responsib. Rights J. **33**, 171–187 (2021)
45. Lanier, K.: 5 Things HR professionals need to know about generation Z: thought leaders share their views on the HR profession and its direction for the future. Strateg. HR Rev. **16**(6), 288–290 (2017)
46. Scholz, C.: The Generations Z in Europe – an introduction. In: Generations Z in Europe: Inputs, Insights and Implications, pp. 3–31. Emerald Publishing Limited, London (2019)
47. Kolb, A.Y., Kolb, D.A.: Learning to play, playing to learn: a case study of a ludic learning space. J. Org. Chang. Manag. **23**(1), 26–50 (2010)
48. Nair, A., Sadasivan, R., Krishnan, A.: Winning the talent game: HR gamification experience for Generation Z. Int. J. Leadership **7**(1) (2019)
49. Mwita, K.: Strengths and weaknesses of qualitative research in social science studies. Int. J. Res. Bus. Soc. Sci. (2147–4478) **11**(6), 618–625 (2022)

Enhancing Online Learning Experiences: A Systematic Review on Integrating GenAI Chatbots into the Community of Inquiry Framework

Corna Olivier(✉) and Lizette Weilbach

University of Pretoria, Pretoria, South Africa
cornao@stadio.ac.za, lizette.weilbach@up.ac.za

Abstract. The Community of Inquiry (CoI) framework has been used for nearly two decades to provide educators with a way to design and evaluate their online courses. Integrating generative AI (GenAI) chatbots with the CoI framework will address the current lack of clear guidelines for incorporating GenAI technology in online education. This gap is significant as GenAI in education is rapidly growing, with students showing favorable attitudes towards GenAI integration. To explore this, a systematic literature review (SLR) was conducted, analyzing recent studies on the use of GenAI chatbots as intelligent tutoring systems within the CoI framework. The findings revealed that GenAI chatbots enhance cognitive presence through personalized learning paths and real-time feedback, improve social presence by fostering community and continuous support, and strengthen teaching presence by automating administrative tasks and dynamic instructional strategies. These enhancements suggest that integrating GenAI chatbots can significantly enrich online learning environments, making education more dynamic, personalized, and effective. The study concludes that a seamless integration of GenAI technologies within the CoI framework can optimize digital learning ecosystems, and future research should focus on long-term impacts and ethical guidelines to ensure responsible GenAI use in education.

Keywords: Generative artificial intelligence (GenAI) chatbots · Community of Inquiry (CoI) framework · social presence · cognitive presence · teaching presence · online learning · AI tutors · systematic review

1 Introduction

Advances in digital education have fundamentally changed how we teach [1]. The Community of Inquiry (CoI) framework, initially introduced by Garrison, Anderson, and Archer in 1999 [2] remains essential in shaping meaningful online learning experiences by emphasizing cognitive, social, and teaching presences. However, there is a noticeable lack of guidelines on how to incorporate generative artificial intelligence (GenAI) technology effectively within this framework.

Published by Springer Nature Switzerland AG 2024
R. van de Wetering et al. (Eds.): I3E 2024, LNCS 14907, pp. 77–89, 2024.
https://doi.org/10.1007/978-3-031-72234-9_7

The utilization of GenAI, particularly chatbots like ChatGPT, has attracted significant attention within educational technology circles. AI in Education (AIEd) is an exponential growing domain [3], with students expressing a favorable attitude towards AI and a keen interest in integrating technology into their learning journey [4].

Despite the widespread adoption of the CoI framework [5], there exists a gap when it comes to incorporating GenAI chatbots. The absence of clear guidelines or theoretical expansions for integrating GenAI within the CoI framework hinders the realization of GenAI chatbots' full potential in digital learning environments. This paper addresses this gap by conducting a systematic literature review (SLR) to explore theoretical perspectives and practical strategies for integrating GenAI tutors into the CoI framework.

The aim of this review is to investigate how the integration of GenAI chatbots within the CoI framework enhances cognitive engagement, social interaction, and teaching presence. This will provide educators, trainers, instructional designers, and researchers with a deeper understanding on how to leverage GenAI technologies to enhance the effectiveness of digital learning environments.

The paper is structured as follows: Sect. 2 provides an overview of the literature, Sect. 3 outlines the research approach, Sect. 4 discusses the data analysis and findings, Sect. 5 details the contributions of the study, and Sect. 6 concludes the paper.

2 Background

2.1 The Community of Inquiry (CoI) Framework

The CoI theoretical framework provides an effective paradigm for understanding the quality of online education. It centers around inquiry learning, a pedagogical approach that encourages students to engage actively with content, ask questions and learn through exploration and reflection [1]. It has three main components: social presence, the ability to project personal traits into an online environment, cognitive presence, generating meaning through persistent conversation, and teaching presence which includes the design, facilitation, and direction of educational experiences [6].

By combining these three presences, educators, course developers, and instructional designers can create effective teaching strategies that improve online learning experiences [7]. The CoI framework has served as a guideline for researchers to assess the quality of online learning environments, highlighting the relevance of community building and self-efficacy in enhancing student satisfaction [8]. The relationship between the three presences and student retention in online programs have been established [9]. By focusing on these presences, educators have been able to successfully create engaging and effective online learning experiences that promote student satisfaction and retention since the beginning of the 20th century.

2.2 Artificial Intelligence (AI) in Education

AI is the creation of computer systems capable of imitating cognitive functions associated with human minds, including learning and problem solving [10]. AI is revolutionizing education by offering students personalized learning experiences via adaptive learning platforms, automated grading, and intelligent tutoring systems, personalized to students' own learning styles and preferences [11, 12], and improve student engagement [13]. AI integration in education not only optimizes the learning process, but also helps teachers deliver personalized instruction and improve student outcomes [12, 14].

GenAI as Instrument to Further Improve Learning Outcomes. Since the arrival of ChatGPT in November 2022 the use of GenAI in education has sparked widespread interest and debate, to the point that it has been referred to as the educational apocalypse [15]. While there are still considerable challenges, there is no denying that GenAI offers significant opportunities in the teaching and learning environment, such as improved access and support by being available 24/7 [16], filling the gap between scheduled courses and providing ongoing learning opportunities [17], and facilitating deepened understanding and skills development through practice and immediate feedback [16]. Interacting with this advanced educational technology, allows students to receive individual tailored feedback, enhancing their overall learning experience [17]. Chatbots' ability to provide empathetic dialogues has been established [18], encouraging student involvement by providing a safe educational space. In all these aspects GenAI clearly offers several opportunities for further enhancing learning outcomes.

3 Research Approach

This paper employs a systematic literature review (SLR) method to identify, evaluate, and synthesize studies on integrating GenAI chatbots within the CoI framework to improve digital learning experiences. This approach ensures a thorough collection of relevant studies, offering a comprehensive view of current research [19, 20]. Following the methodological approach of Cherry, Boland and Dickson [21], the review was conducted in three stages: planning conducting and reporting. In the planning phase, the research objectives and the review protocol were defined. The conducting phase included selecting the primary studies and extracting data. Finally, the reporting phase focused on disseminating the results [22].

The search terms ("Generative AI Chatbot" OR "ChatGPT") AND ("Community of Inquiry") were used to find publications indexed in Google Scholar, chosen for its fast indexing of recent papers, crucial for studies on GenAI from 2022 to 2024. Automated content analysis using probabilistic models was planned to uncover and categorize main themes in the literature [23–25].

The review process returned 196 papers. After filtering for peer-reviewed journals, conference papers, and book chapters published in the last ten years 56 papers remained. Exclusions included duplicates, non-English studies, and papers not directly related to the CoI framework or GenAI chatbots in education. Leximancer version 5.00.140 (2021/08/25) was used to analyze the content, adhering to Khan, Rana and Goel's methodological procedures [26]. This natural language processing tool, based on Bayesian theory [27] deduces concepts and themes, through an unsupervised iterative process. The next section discusses the results from the Leximancer analysis.

4 Data Analysis and Findings

The objective of our paper is to provide a systematic review of recent publications related to novel theoretical perspectives and practical approaches that broaden and challenge our understanding of digital innovations, specifically focusing on the use of GenAI chatbots as intelligent tutoring systems in the online learning space.

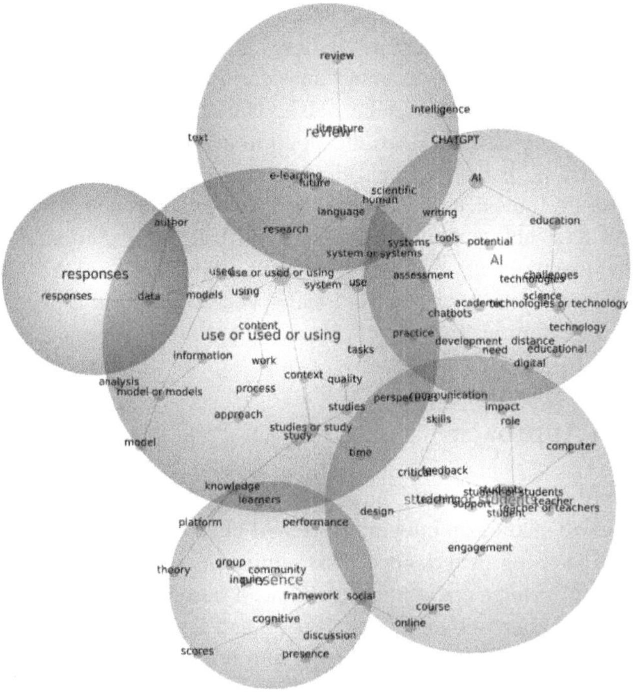

Fig. 1: Themes with concepts (Leximancer visualization)

Figure 1 shows the Leximancer visualization of clustered concepts consisting of six themes. The themes, the concepts within each theme, as well as a brief overview of each were extracted from Leximancer and are shown in Table 1.

4.1 Discussion of Key Themes

The "Theme overview" column provides a summary of the topics found during the automated content analysis, while the "Hits" column indicates the number of text blocks in the corpus linked to the particular theme [27].

The theme *use or used or using* focuses on the practical application of GenAI chatbots in education. These chatbots enhance learning experiences by providing real-time feedback, facilitating personalized learning paths, and automating routine administrative tasks. This allows educators to allocate more time to complex instructional activities,

Table 1. Key themes of GenAI chatbots in educational settings.

Theme	Hits	Key Concepts	Theme Overview	References
Use or used or using	7779	studies or study; research; language; model or models; using; knowledge; data; system or systems; used; model; analysis; information; content; studies; process; context; work; approach; models; tasks; quality	Enhancing learning with GenAI chatbots through real-time feedback and personalized paths	[28–65]
student or students	7196	online; student; teaching; social; support; critical; feedback; engagement; design; skills; impact; course; communication; role; time; teacher; perspectives; computer	Engaging students with AI chatbots, providing support, and fostering meaningful interactions	[31, 40–45, 47, 50, 51, 54, 59, 63, 64, 66–75]
AI	7206	education technologies; CHATGPT; tools; academic; educational; writing; potential; technology; digital challenges; development; need; chatbots; systems; human; science; assessment practice; distance	Impact of AI in education, including ethical considerations and its transformative potential	[37, 38, 40, 43, 45, 47, 48, 52, 54, 59, 64, 69, 71, 73, 75–78]
presence	3540	cognitive; learners; framework; community; platform; performance; discussion; group; inquiry; theory; scores	GenAI chatbots fostering community and communication among learners.	[29, 33, 35–37, 39, 40, 43, 45, 52, 53, 56–59, 66, 68, 70, 75, 79–81]

(*continued*)

Table 1. (*continued*)

Theme	Hits	Key Concepts	Theme Overview	References
review	2091	literature; future; intelligence; text; e-learning; scientific	Review of literature on GenAI chatbots, highlighting benefits and challenges	[28, 34, 36–40, 44–46, 48, 49, 51, 54, 56, 71, 75, 77, 82]
Responses	581	author	Educators' and students' responses on GenAI chatbots' effectiveness and reliability	[29, 30, 35, 37, 42, 44, 50, 52, 59, 61, 64, 69, 72, 81]

improving overall teaching efficiency and addressing diverse educational needs. *Student or students* refers to the interactions and engagement between students and GenAI chatbots. These bots offer tailored support, foster more engaging learning environments, provide continuous on-demand assistance, and help bridge the gap between scheduled classes and independent study periods. They enhance students' cognitive engagement and motivation, leading to improved learning outcomes.

The *AI* theme addresses the broader implications and transformative potential of AI technologies in education. AI's ability to mimic humanlike interactions and provide adaptive learning experiences, makes it a powerful educational tool. However, ethical considerations and challenges, such as data privacy and academic integrity, require robust guidelines to ensure responsible and effective use of AI in educational settings.

The *presence* theme focuses on how GenAI chatbots enhance the cognitive, social, and teaching presences found in the CoI framework. Cognitive presence is augmented as GenAI chatbots assist with deeper learning through real-time feedback and reflective learning. Social presence benefits from the empathetic and responsive nature of AI chatbots, assisting in creating a sense of community among learners. Teaching presence is strengthened by the automation of administrative tasks and support for dynamic instructional strategies.

Review refers to the comprehensive evaluation of existing literature on GenAI chatbots and their integration into educational frameworks. SLRs and meta-analyses provide overviews of the current findings, highlighting both the benefits and challenges of GenAI implementations. Finally, *responses* refer to the feedback from educators and learners on the use of GenAI chatbots. While many responses highlight the personalized support and enhanced engagement offered by these chatbots, there are concerns about their reliability and ethical implications. Continuous monitoring and improvement of AI chatbot implementations are necessary to address these concerns and ensure their effective use in education.

4.2 Mapping the SLR Themes to the CoI Framework

The CoI framework consists of three core categories: cognitive presence, social presence, and teaching presence. Each theme from our SLR will be mapped to these categories to understand how GenAI chatbots can enhance them.

Social Presence - *Presence*: By fostering a sense of belonging and community through sympathetic exchanges and unceasing support, AI chatbots improve social presence [41, 59]. *Responses*: Though worries about dependability and ethics persist, feedback from instructors and students suggests that AI chatbots enhance social presence by encouraging interaction and discussion [56, 65].

Cognitive Presence - *Use or used or using*: By automating repetitive tasks, offering real-time feedback, and creating personalized learning routes, GenAI chatbots promote cognitive engagement and free up students' time to concentrate on higher-order thinking abilities [44, 72]. *Student or students*: By involving students in meaningful conversations, providing ongoing support, and encouraging reflective learning through tailored learning experiences, AI chatbots foster cognitive presence [51, 69].

Teaching Presence *AI*: By automating administrative processes, supporting dynamic educational tactics, and offering personalized feedback, GenAI chatbots enhance the teaching presence of educators by freeing them up to concentrate on pedagogical activities [50, 66]. *Review*: Systematic studies emphasize the need for strong rules and ongoing improvement while highlighting the advantages and difficulties of implementing AI in education [18, 71].

5 Discussion of Findings

In this section we investigate how the integration of GenAI chatbots could enhance each category of the CoI. Theoretical and practical implications of integrating GenAI chatbots into the CoI framework will also be explored.

5.1 Enhancing the CoI Framework with GenAI chatbots

Social Presence Enhancement. GenAI chatbots significantly enhance social presence by creating connection and belonging among learners [59, 63]. They facilitate empathetic interactions by for instance using emojis [81], offering real-time engagement and reducing loneliness and lack of rapport compared to emails [67]. These chatbots provide continuous support [60], which helps maintain student engagement and motivation [40, 78], and their availability outside regular class times enables timely assistance [63]. Examples such as Wonder, GatherTown, and Sococo, enhances social dynamics through individual avatars and private spaces, while robots as social actors improve collaborative child tutoring and overall development [75].

Cognitive Presence Enhancement. Generative AI chatbots, such as ChatGPT, enhance cognitive presence by fostering critical thinking [46, 51, 64, 80], personalized learning [28, 50, 51, 64, 78, 80], and real-time feedback [44, 64]. Researchers also agree that AI chatbots act as effective tutors [34, 36, 45, 53, 57, 62, 67, 71, 72, 74, 81], guiding students through complex problem-solving processes [49, 51, 80], and fostering deeper understanding through interactive dialogues [51]. These chatbots also improve self-regulated learning by assisting students to set goals and assess their progress [36, 51, 67, 72, 78]. Additionally, AI chatbots facilitate ongoing interaction and reflection [51, 80, 81], improving knowledge creation and the overall learning experience, as illustrated by tools such as VERA [68], which supports inquiry-based learning through interactive modeling and simulation.

Teaching Presence Enhancement. AI chatbots enhance teaching presence by automating administrative tasks [43, 45, 50, 64, 66], offering personalized feedback [56, 59, 69, 78], and enabling dynamic educational tactics [65], which reduces educators' workload, allowing them to focus on more complex pedagogical tasks. These chatbots support course design and management [50, 60, 63, 71, 75, 76], making educational practices more efficient. AI facilitates continuous interaction and feedback between students and teachers [53, 54, 60], improving instructional presence. One of the best examples is Jill Watson [60, 68], a virtual cognitive assistant that engages students in lengthy discussions about course materials such as textbooks, video transcripts, presentation slides, and class syllabi. However, as there is a strong teaching presence associated with AI, GenAI chatbots should therefore be designed to feel more like a friend than a teacher, to avoid the intimidation of learners [56].

5.2 Practical Implications

Integrating GenAI chatbots into the CoI framework has several practical implications. Firstly, personalized learning experiences boost student engagement and academic performance, ensuring that each student receives the necessary support through tailored learning paths and feedback [33, 75]. Secondly, the 24/7 availability of these chatbots offers continuous support, bridging the gap between formal instruction and independent study, thus improving accessibility, and providing ongoing learning opportunities [11, 16]. Lastly, GenAI chatbots enhance the efficiency of educational practices by automating administrative tasks, allowing educators to focus more on teaching and less on routine tasks [64, 66].

5.3 Theoretical Implications

Incorporating GenAI chatbots into education has several theoretical implications. First, it may redefine roles, as it assumes more administrative and supportive tasks traditionally handled by educators and students. This shift necessitates a re-evaluation of traditional educational duties and responsibilities [50, 59]. Second, the use of GenAI in education raises ethical concerns, particularly regarding data privacy, academic integrity, and the responsible use of technology. Addressing these issues requires comprehensive guidelines to ensure the ethical deployment of GenAI chatbots [37, 64]. Finally, the CoI framework may need to be adapted to integrate this technology effectively. This adaptation could involve adding new dimensions that reflect GenAI chatbots' impact on cognitive, social, and educational domains, thereby maximizing the benefits of GenAI integration in educational settings [41, 64].

6 Conclusion

Integrating GenAI chatbots within the CoI framework has the potential to significantly enhance digital learning environments. Our systematic review shows that the integration of GenAI chatbots in the CoI effectively supports inquiry learning by providing real-time, personalized feedback and adaptive learning paths. This integration aids students in problem-solving activities, while encouraging critical thinking by enhancing cognitive engagement and promoting higher-order thinking. Additionally, the empathetic and responsive nature of GenAI chatbots fosters a sense of community among online learning students which is important for collaborative learning. Finally, GenAI chatbots automates routines tasks and support dynamic instructional strategies, allowing human educators to focus more on pedagogy.

However, as GenAI is a relatively new area of research our study has several limitations. Due to the limited duration of GenAI's availability, some of the papers we included in the SLR pertain to AI chatbots, rather than GenAI chatbots. Since our focus was solely on research related to the CoI framework, this SLR may not offer a comprehensive view of GenAI chatbots use in online learning. Additionally, due to the limited timeframe, longitudinal studies are not yet available, meaning that our findings primarily reflect short term effects. Furthermore, the current limited availability and implementation of GenAI chatbots in education, may affect the generalizability of our study.

Future research should explore the long-term impacts on learning outcomes, compare GenAI-assisted learning to traditional learning and investigate how educators can be effectively trained to use GenAI tools for instruction and assessment. Multicultural perspectives should be studied, to ensure that GenAI adapts to diverse learning styles and cultural backgrounds, preventing the perpetuation of biases in educational materials. Additionally, further research is needed to ensure the responsible and ethical use of GenAI in education, such as identifying and preventing bias in training, promoting original thought, preventing plagiarism, and improving accessibility for marginalized populations and people with disabilities.

Disclosure of Interests. The authors have no competing interests to declare that are relevant to the content of this article.

References

1. Haleem, A., Javaid, M., Qadri, M.A., Suman, R.: Understanding the role of digital technologies in education: A review. Sustain. Oper. Comput. **3**, 275–285 (2022)
2. Garrison, D.R., Anderson, T., Archer, W.: Critical inquiry in a text-based environment: Computer conferencing in higher education. The internet and higher education **2**, 87–105 (1999)
3. Zawacki-Richter, O., Marín, V.I., Bond, M., Gouverneur, F.: Systematic review of research on artificial intelligence applications in higher education – where are the educators?. Int. J. Educ. Technol. High. Educ. **16**, (2019)
4. Bisdas, S., et al.: Artificial Intelligence in Medicine: A Multinational Multi-Center Survey on the Medical and Dental Students' Perception. Frontiers in Public Health **9**, (2021)
5. Garrison, D.R., Arbaugh, J.B.: Researching the community of inquiry framework: Review, issues, and future directions. The Internet and High. Educ. **10**, 157–172 (2007)

6. Bektashi, L.: Community of inquiry framework in online learning: Use of technology. Technology and the curriculum: Summer 2018 (2018)
7. Fiock, H.: Designing a community of inquiry in online courses. Int. Rev. Res. Open and Distrib. Learn. **21**, 135–153 (2020)
8. Yandra, F.P., Alsolami, B., Sopacua, I.O., Prajogo, W.: The role of community of inquiry and self-efficacy on accounting students' satisfaction in online learning environment. Jurnal Siasat Bisnis 1-16 (2021).
9. Boston, W., Díaz, S.R., Gibson, A.M., Ice, P., Richardson, J., Swan, K.: An exploration of the relationship between indicators of the community of inquiry framework and retention in online programs. J. Asynchronous Learn. Netw. **13**, 67–83 (2009)
10. Kirkpatrick, J., et al.: Overcoming catastrophic forgetting in neural networks. Proc. Nat. Acad. Sci. **114**, 3521–3526 (2017)
11. Harry, A.: Role of AI in Education. Interdiciplinary J. Hummanit. (INJURITY) **2**, 260–268 (2023)
12. Kim, W.-H., Kim, J.-H.: Individualized AI tutor based on developmental learning networks. IEEE Access **8**, 27927–27937 (2020)
13. Conijn, R., Kahr, P., Snijders, C.: The Effects of Explanations in Automated Essay Scoring Systems on Student Trust and Motivation (accepted for publication). (2023)
14. Tubino, L., Adachi, C.: Developing feedback literacy capabilities through an AI automated feedback tool. ASCILITE Publications e22039-e22039 (2022)
15. Bozkurt, A., Sharma, R.C.: Are we facing an algorithmic renaissance or apocalypse? Generative AI, ChatBots, and emerging human-machine interaction in the educational landscape. Asian J. Distance Educ. **19**, (2024)
16. Ding, L., Li, T., Jiang, S., Gapud, A.: Students' perceptions of using ChatGPT in a physics class as a virtual tutor. Int. J. Educ. Technol. High. Educ. **20**, 63 (2023)
17. Chan, C.K.Y., Hu, W.: Students' voices on generative AI: perceptions, benefits, and challenges in higher education. Int. J. Educ. Technol. High. Educ. **20**, (2023)
18. Singh, S., Beniwal, H.: A survey on near-human conversational agents. J. King Saud Univ. Comput. Inf. Sci. **34**, 8852–8866 (2022)
19. Petticrew, M., Roberts, H.: Systematic reviews in the social sciences: A practical guide. John Wiley & Sons (2008)
20. Gough, D., Thomas, J., Oliver, S.: An introduction to systematic reviews. (2017)
21. Cherry, G., Boland, A., Dickson, R.: Doing a Systematic Review: A Student′ s Guide. (2023)
22. Aromataris, E., Pearson, A.: The systematic review: an overview. AJN The Am. J. Nurs. **114**, 53–58 (2014)
23. Blei, D.M.: Probabilistic topic models. Commun. ACM **55**, 77–84 (2012)
24. Nunez-Mir, G.C., Iannone, B.V., III., Pijanowski, B.C., Kong, N., Fei, S.: Automated content analysis: addressing the big literature challenge in ecology and evolution. Meth. Ecol. Evol. **7**, 1262–1272 (2016)
25. Smith, A.E., Humphreys, M.S.: Evaluation of unsupervised semantic mapping of natural language with Leximancer concept mapping. Behav. Res. Meth. **38**, 262–279 (2006)
26. Khan, S., Rana, S., Goel, A.: Presence of digital sources in international marketing: A review of literature using Leximancer. Int. J. Technol. Mark. **16**, 246–274 (2022)
27. Leximancer User Guide. https://info.leximancer.com/, last accessed 1 June 2024
28. Shepherd, D.A., Majchrzak, A.: Machines augmenting entrepreneurs: Opportunities (and threats) at the Nexus of artificial intelligence and entrepreneurship. J. Bus. Ventur. **37**, 106227 (2022)
29. Li, C., Xing, W., Leite, W.: Building socially responsible conversational agents using big data to support online learning: A case with Algebra Nation. Br. J. Educ. Technol. **53**, 776–803 (2022)

30. Gunawardena, C.N., Chen, Y., Flor, N., Sánchez, D.: Deep Learning Models for Analyzing Social Construction of Knowledge Online. Online Learn. **27**, (2023)
31. Iftanti, E., Awalin, A.S.a., Izza, F.N.: The Use of Artificial Intelligence as the Potential Supporting Learning Tools for Doing Learning Projects. In: International Conference on Education, pp. 455-467. (2023)
32. Das, R.M., JV, M.: Analysing the Community of Inquiry Model in the Context of Online Learning: A Bibliometric Study. TechTrends **68**, 435-447 (2024)
33. Hu, Y., Donald, C., Giacaman, N.: Can multi-label classifiers help identify subjectivity? A deep learning approach to classifying cognitive presence in MOOCs. Int. J. Artif. Intell. Educ. **33**, 781–816 (2023)
34. McCotter, S.: An Interdisciplinary Scoping Review of Sustainable E-Learning within Human Resources Higher Education Provision. Sustain. **15**, 15282 (2023)
35. Cheng, Y., Lyons, K., Chen, G., Gašević, D., Swiecki, Z.: Evidence-centered Assessment for Writing with Generative AI. In: Proceedings of the 14th Learning Analytics and Knowledge Conference, pp. 178-188. (2024)
36. Jin, S., Zhong, Z., Li, K., Kang, C.: Investigating the effect of guided inquiry on learners with different prior knowledge in immersive virtual environments. Education and Information Technologies (2024)
37. Ou, A.W., Stöhr, C., Malmström, H.: Academic communication with AI-powered language tools in higher education: From a post-humanist perspective. Syst. **121**, 103225 (2024)
38. Ali, F., Choy, D., Divaharan, S., Tay, H.Y., Chen, W.: Supporting self-directed learning and self-assessment using TeacherGAIA, a generative AI chatbot application: Learning approaches and prompt engineering. Learning: Research and Practice **9**, 135-147 (2023)
39. Gibson, D., Kovanovic, V., Ifenthaler, D., Dexter, S., Feng, S.: Learning theories for artificial intelligence promoting learning processes. Br. J. Educ. Technol. **54**, 1125–1146 (2023)
40. Aljuaid, H.: The Impact of Artificial Intelligence Tools on Academic Writing Instruction in Higher Education: A Systematic Review. Arab World English Journal (AWEJ) Special Issue on ChatGPT (2024)
41. Alshahrani, A.: Revolutionizing Blended Learning: Exploring Current Trends and Future Research Directions in the Era of ChatGPT. In: 2023 7th International Conference on Business and Information Management (ICBIM), pp. 41-47. (2023)
42. Liu, L.: Analyzing the Text Contents Produced by ChatGPT: Prompts, Feature-Components in Responses, and a Predictive Model. J. Educ. Technol. Dev. Exch. **16**, 49–70 (2023)
43. Al-Tamimi, A.-K., Moore, R., Javed, Y., Babu, S., Freeman, E.: Chatbots in Education: Addressing Student Needs and Transforming Learning in the Post-COVID-19 Era. Building Resiliency in Higher Education: Globalization, Digital Skills, and Student Wellness, pp. 99127. IGI Global (2024)
44. Birenbaum, M.: The Chatbots' Challenge to Education: Disruption or Destruction? Education Sciences, vol. 13, (2023)
45. Maphoto, K.B.: Perceptions and innovations of academics in an open distance e-learning institution. Online J. Commun. Media Technol. **14**, e202429 (2024)
46. Son, J.-B., Ružić, N.K., Philpott, A.: Artificial intelligence technologies and applications for language learning and teaching. J. China Comput. Assist. Lang. Learn. (2023)
47. Ayasrah, F.T.M., Alarabi, K., Fattah, H.A.A.: A Secure Technology Environment and AI's Effect on Science Teaching: Prospective Science Teachers. Migration Letters **20**, 289–302 (2023)
48. Perkins, M., Roe, J., Vu, B.H., Postma, D., Hickerson, D., McGaughran, J., Khuat, H.Q.: GenAI Detection Tools, Adversarial Techniques and Implications for Inclusivity in Higher Education. arXiv preprint arXiv:2403.19148 (2024)
49. Martinez, C., et al.: Content-Focused Formative Feedback Combining Achievement, Qualitative and Learning Analytics Data. Education Sciences **13**, 1014 (2023)

50. Maofi, M.: Effective learning in higher education post-covid_final version. (2023)
51. Essel, H.B., Vlachopoulos, D., Essuman, A.B., Amankwa, J.O.: ChatGPT effects on cognitive skills of undergraduate students: Receiving instant responses from AI-based conversational large language models (LLMs). Comput. Educ. Artif. Intell. **6**, 100198 (2024)
52. Engineer, R.: Exploration of Epistemic Diversity in Computer Science Education. (2023)
53. Chuah, K.-M., Kabilan, M.: Teachers' views on the use of chatbots to support English language teaching in a mobile environment. Int. J. Emerging Technol. Learn. (iJET) **16**, 223–237 (2021)
54. Balalle, H.: Exploring student engagement in technology-based education in relation to gamification, online/distance learning, and other factors: A systematic literature review. Soc. Sci. Humanit. Open **9**, 100870 (2024)
55. Birenbaum, M.: The Chatbots' Challenge to Education: Disruption or Destruction? Educ. Sci. **13**, 711 (2023)
56. Wang, X., Pang, H., Wallace, M.P., Wang, Q., Chen, W.: Learners' perceived AI presences in AI-supported language learning: a study of AI as a humanized agent from community of inquiry. Computer Assisted Language Learning 1-27 (2022)
57. Maher, D.: Blended Learning for Pre-Service Teachers. Handbook of Research on Innovative Frameworks and Inclusive Models for Online Learning, pp. 256-274. IGI Global (2023)
58. Pratschke, B.M.: Generativism: the new hybrid. arXiv preprint arXiv:2309.12468 (2023)
59. Sevnarayan, K.: Exploring the dynamics of ChatGPT: Students and lecturers perspectives at an open distance e-learning university. Journal of Pedagogical Research (2024)
60. Taneja, K., Maiti, P., Kakar, S., Guruprasad, P., Rao, S., Goel, A.K.: Jill Watson: A Virtual Teaching Assistant powered by ChatGPT. arXiv preprint arXiv:2405.11070 (2024)
61. Indriati, L., Neo, M., Tan, H.: Improving Learning Content and Engaging Learners through the Revised Community of Inquiry (RCOI) Framework: Indonesian Design Students' Perspectives. In: EDULEARN23 Proceedings, pp. 927-933. IATED, (2023)
62. Leslie, D.: Does the sun rise for ChatGPT? Scientific discovery in the age of generative AI. AI and Ethics (2023)
63. Lang, J.C.: Embracing Generative AI for Authentic Learning. Creative Education **15**, 1–20 (2024)
64. AlAli, R., Wardat, Y.: Enhancing Classroom Learning: ChatGPT's Integration and Educational Challenges. Int. J. Relig. **5**, 971–985 (2024)
65. Gowon, O.C., Anthony, O.: Shaping the Future: Artificial Intelligence and the English Language Pedagogy. Int. J. Arts, Commun. Pedagogy **2**, 1–14 (2023)
66. Archibald, A., et al.: A validation of AI-enabled discussion platform metrics and relationships to student efforts. TechTrends **67**, 285–293 (2023)
67. Hew, K.F., Huang, W.: Promoting engagement in online learning beyond COVID-19: Possible strategies and directions for future research. Future in Educ. Res. **1**, 2749 (2023)
68. Dede, C., Lidwell, W.: Developing a Next-Generation Model for Massive Digital Learning. Educ. Sci. **13**, 845 (2023)
69. Kilinc, S.: Unknown article. Asian J. Distance Educ. **18**, (2023)
70. Avgerinou, M.D., Karampelas, A., Stefanou, V.: Building the Plane as We Fly It: Experimenting with GenAI for Scholarly Writing. Irish J. Technol. Enhanced Learn. **7**, 61–74 (2023)
71. Parra, J.L., Chatterjee, S.: Social Media and Artificial Intelligence: Critical Conversations and Where Do We Go from Here? Educ. Sci. **14**, 68 (2024)
72. Han, S., Hamilton, X., Cai, Y., Shao, P., Liu, M.: Knowledge-based chatbots: a scale measuring students' learning experiences in massive open online courses. Educ. Technol. Res. Dev. **71**, 2431–2456 (2023)
73. Koh, J., Cowling, M., Jha, M., Sim, K.N.: The Human Teacher, the AI Teacher and the AIedTeacher Relationship. J. High. Educ. Theory & Pract. **23**, (2023)

74. McCleskey, J.A., Melton, R.M.: "Better Than Human" in Partnership With AI: Enhancing Social Presence Through the Use of Technology. Humanizing Online Teaching and Learning in Higher Education, pp. 18-48. IGI Global (2024)
75. Nieveen, N., van der Veen, J., Ventura-Medina, E.: Pathways to innovative STEM education. (2024)
76. Lim, F.V., Querol-Julián, M.: Learning with technologies in the digital age: Now and the future. Designing Learning with Digital Technologies, pp. 3-19. Routledge (2024)
77. Egher, C.: Digital Technologies in Education. Educational Utopias: Liber Amicorum Alkeline van Lenning (2023)
78. Alshahrani, A.: The impact of ChatGPT on blended learning: Current trends and future research directions. Int. J. Data Netw. Sci. **7**, 2029–2040 (2023)
79. Das, R.M., J.V, M.: Analysing the Community of Inquiry Model in the Context of Online Learning: A Bibliometric Study. TechTrends (2024)
80. Ghazali, N.E., Abdul Rahman, N.F.: Knowledge Requirement of Incorporating Artificial Intelligence in Engineering Education through TPACK. Asean J. Eng. Educ. **7**, 34–40 (2023)
81. Qin, C., Huang, W., Hew, K.F.: Using the Community of Inquiry Framework to develop an educational chatbot: Lesson learned from a mobile instant messaging learning environment. In: Proceedings of the 28th International Conference on Computers in Education, Online, pp. 23-27. (2020)
82. Liao, X., Zheng, Y.-H., Shi, G., Bu, H.: Automated social presence in artificial-intelligence services: Conceptualization, scale development, and validation. Technol. Forecast. Soc. Change **203**, 123377 (2024)

Artificial Intelligence in Supermarkets: A Multiple Analysis About Tasks, Jobs, and Automation

Zenaldo Rodrigues[1], Luiz Pinheiro[1](✉), Carla Marcolin[2], Ricardo Matheus[3], Stuti Saxena[1], and Marcos Morais[2]

[1] Positivo University, Ai-Labs, Curitiba, Brazil
luiz.junior@up.edu.br
[2] Federal University of Uberlandia, Uberlandia, Brazil
[3] Delft University, TPM, Delft, The Netherlands

Abstract. This study aims to analyze the impacts of Artificial Intelligence (AI) and automation in the supermarket sector, focusing on three main areas: tasks, jobs, and automation processes. The research builds on studies about technology adoption and its impact on employment, including Christensen approach on disruptive innovation, Huang & Rust [19] on artificial intelligence in services, and Jarrahi [27] on human-AI symbiosis. A multiple case study approach was employed, involving interviews with four groups: cashiers, managers, customers who use self-checkouts, and customers who do not use self-checkouts. The interviews were analyzed using qualitative methods to identify emerging subcategories. Many customers prefer manned checkouts due to convenience. Self-service checkout technology is primarily used for small purchases, and younger customers find it easier to use. Employees do not currently feel threatened by automation, but there is a trend toward job reduction and relocation to roles requiring analytical, intuitive, and emotional skills. Managers do not see the need to prepare employees for a future without self-service checkouts, focusing instead on current training. Future research should analyze other supermarket functions that could be impacted by AI automation and investigate more deeply the acceptance and impact of these technologies on the labor market.

Keywords: Artificial Intelligence · AI · Automation · Jobs · Supermarkets

1 Introduction

Frey and Osborne [1] and Acemoglu and Restrepo [2] have been studying how new technologies of automation and Artificial Intelligence (AI) might influence and impact work and employment. Additionally, other researchers seek to understand how automation technologies contribute to a world where fewer workers are needed to produce goods and services [3–6]. The OECD (Organization for Economic Cooperation and Development), in its report "OECD Employment Outlook 2023 – Artificial Intelligence and the

Published by Springer Nature Switzerland AG 2024
R. van de Wetering et al. (Eds.): I3E 2024, LNCS 14907, pp. 90–102, 2024.
https://doi.org/10.1007/978-3-031-72234-9_8

Labour Market," revealed that 27% of jobs are at risk of extinction due to automation. Over twelve months, we conducted a survey of news reported in specialized media to understand societal concerns about the influences of automation and AI on employment [7, 8]. Despite significant advancements in research on the impacts of automation and AI on the labor market, important gaps still need to be filled. Many studies, such as those by Frey and Osborne [1] and Acemoglu and Restrepo [2], broadly focus on macroeconomic implications, neglecting sector-specific analyses such as the retail supermarket industry. Furthermore, there is a scarcity of empirical data on how automation directly affects supermarket workers, their perceptions of AI, and the strategies companies adopt to mitigate negative impacts. This study aims to fill these gaps by providing detailed insights into the work dynamics within the context of supermarket automation.

This study aims to analyze the impacts of Artificial Intelligence (AI) and automation in the supermarket sector, focusing on three main areas: tasks, jobs, and automation processes. Through empirical data collection and a review of specialized literature, we seek to understand how AI is being implemented in supermarkets, the concerns of workers and society regarding the replacement of human labor by machines, and the benefits and challenges of this technological transition. The study intends to provide a comprehensive view of the effects of automation on the labor market and offer practical recommendations for adapting to this new reality.

In this context, as emphasized by the OECD [9], although the threat of automation technologies to employment is imminent, there has not yet been a significant loss in employment. The retail sector witnessed the popularization of self-checkout systems in the 2000s, intensified by the pandemic period, justified as a way to reduce physical contact between people. Self-checkout emerged as a promising option aimed at optimizing processes and reducing labor costs [10]. By addressing the existing gaps in the literature and providing empirical insights, this study seeks to contribute to a more nuanced understanding of the implications of AI and automation in supermarkets.

The contributions of this study are multifaceted. Firstly, it will provide a detailed analysis of the impact of automation and AI in the supermarket sector, offering empirical data that can guide public policies and business strategies. Secondly, by focusing on the perceptions of workers and company responses, the study will contribute to the literature by offering a deeper understanding of labor dynamics in a specific sector. Finally, the practical recommendations developed from the findings of this study can help both managers and policymakers develop more effective strategies for dealing with technological transition, promoting a balance between automated efficiency and job preservation.

2 Literature Review

2.1 Artificial Intelligence (AI)

The concept of Artificial Intelligence (AI) was formally introduced during a workshop at Dartmouth College in 1956, organized by scholars John McCarthy, Marvin Minsky, and Herbert Simon, among others. This workshop, titled "Summer Research Project on Artificial Intelligence," marked the first use of the term "Artificial Intelligence" [11]. The primary goal was to enable machines to use formal language, form abstractions and concepts, and solve problems independently, thereby mimicking human thought processes as envisaged by Alan Turing [11, 12].

From the 1960s to 2010, progress in AI was relatively slow. However, a significant breakthrough occurred in 2010 when Geoffrey Hinton developed an efficient method for training neural networks [12]. Hinton's advancements represented a pivotal moment in AI development, leading to the rise of machine learning (ML), where machines could learn autonomously without human intervention. This new neural network model far surpassed older models that relied on predefined rules and inputs crafted by programmers [12, 13].

Three major factors have driven the advancement of AI technology: Hinton's development of new neural networks in 2010 [13], the significant increase in computational power over the years [14], and the proliferation of startups globally [3]. These elements have collectively fueled the rapid evolution and adoption of AI across various sectors.

2.2 AI and Automation in Tasks and Jobs

Research by Larriba [15] in his study "A Case of Artificial Intelligence Applied to Supermarkets in Buenos Aires" demonstrated that even without highly sophisticated AI, repetitive tasks in supermarkets could be automated using software and machines. This finding highlights that advanced AI is not a prerequisite for automating certain tasks.

Santos [16] argues that self-service technology has the potential to replace human workers, supporting concerns raised by researchers about the displacement of employees in various industries [6, 17–23]. The integration of AI with automation technologies poses a continuous threat to human activities across industrial, intellectual, and social domains [1, 2, 7].

About AI and Automation in Jobs, the AI in banking presents both opportunities and challenges. Ghandour [24] systematically reviews the literature, highlighting how AI technologies can enhance efficiency, customer experience, and risk management while posing challenges related to data privacy, regulatory compliance, and implementation costs. These insights are crucial for understanding the dual nature of AI's impact in the financial sector and formulating strategies to maximize benefits while mitigating risks.

In retail, the adoption of AI is characterized by its potential to optimize supply chains, personalize customer experiences, and improve inventory management. Weber and Schutte [34] discuss the state-of-the-art applications of AI in retail, emphasizing its role in enhancing operational efficiency and customer satisfaction. Their findings underscore the importance of integrating AI to remain competitive in a rapidly evolving market landscape (Table 1).

Vincent et al. [28] explore the impact of AI in the aviation and space sectors, highlighting advancements in autonomous systems, predictive maintenance, and operational efficiency. Their research provides a comprehensive overview of how AI technologies are revolutionizing these high-tech industries, offering insights into future developments and potential areas of innovation.

The hospitality sector is also experiencing significant changes due to AI adoption. Rasheed et al. [33] conduct a systematic literature review to identify drivers of AI adoption among consumers in this industry. They find that factors such as improved customer service, operational efficiency, and personalized experiences drive AI integration

Table 1. Review about Sectors, Jobs, Automation and AI

Sector/Industry	Human Job	Automation Tasks	AI Tasks - Gaps
Airlines	Ticket agent – check-in and check-out	Self-service kiosks	Vincent et al. [28]
Banks	Teller	ATMs	Gandhour [29]
Bookstore	Sales attendant	Availability check terminal	Harisanty et al. [30]
Cinema	Ticket seller	Self-service machine	Reddy et al. [31]
Education	Professor	Online Programs, E-Learning	Sharma & Agarwal [32]
Restaurants	Waiter	Self-ordering machine, app orders	Rasheed et al. [33]
Supermarkets	Checkout clerk – Cashier	Self-checkout machines	Weber & Schutte [34]

in hospitality, setting the stage for future research on consumer behavior and technology acceptance.

AI is revolutionizing animation and visual effects in films, as highlighted by Reddy et al. [31]. Their study demonstrates how AI technologies are enabling more sophisticated and efficient creation of visual content, reducing production time, and enhancing the quality of visual effects. This transformation is pivotal for the entertainment industry, offering new tools for creativity and innovation.

In the context of libraries, AI awareness and adoption among leaders, practitioners, and scientists are crucial for modernizing services and enhancing information management. Harisanty et al. [30] present a pilot study that investigates the awareness levels of AI in libraries, suggesting that increased knowledge and strategic implementation of AI can significantly improve library services and user experiences.

AI-based chatbots are becoming integral to higher education, impacting faculty performance and student interactions. Sharma and Agarwal [32] examine the role of AI chatbots in higher education institutions, finding that these technologies can support administrative tasks, provide academic assistance, and enhance student engagement. Their research highlights the potential of AI to transform educational practices and improve institutional efficiency.

The automation of supermarket checkouts is not a new concept. Self-checkout systems have been a staple in retail for several years. The evolution of AI from its inception to modern applications showcases its transformative potential across various sectors. The advancements in neural networks, computational power, and the proliferation of startups have significantly contributed to this progress. As AI continues to integrate with automation technologies, its impact on job displacement and operational efficiency will remain a critical area of study and development.

3 Method

This research employed a multiple case study approach, following the methodologies of Yin [21] and Eisenhardt [22]. Fieldwork was conducted in two supermarket chains: Alpha, with 22 stores, and Beta, with 08 stores, encompassing over 7,000 employees in total. The selected stores operate mixed checkout models (both manned and self-service checkouts), allowing customers to choose between the two options.

The data collection involved 70 interviews with four key groups: (1) checkout operators, (2) their managers, (3) customers using self-service checkouts, and (4) customers not using self-service checkouts. All interviews were recorded and subsequently transcribed using Atlas.TI software QDA (Table 2).

Table 2. Data Collect and Technical Analysis

Cases in depth	Unity Analysis	Data Collect	Data Analysis	Validity
Alpha (01)	22 supermarkets	70 interviews, field notes, observation in field and secondary data	By content, categorization, explication, emerging categories	Triangulation by data fonts, and by researchers
Beta (02)	08 supermarkets			

To ensure the validity of the research, a peer review strategy was implemented for the data collection form. Sixteen questions were reviewed by three evaluators with academic backgrounds and experience in the supermarket sector. Triangulation was conducted in two stages. The first stage involved source triangulation during data collection, incorporating interviews, field notes, and participant observation, following Yin [21] guidelines.

The basic categorization scheme for the types of questions included both open and closed questions. These were directed at supermarket employees, managers, and customers, aiming to capture perceptions, knowledge about technology, operational time, product quantity, and other relevant variables.

4 Data Analysis and Discussion

The analysis in this chapter were categorized into two main blocks: Barriers and Opportunities of AI in Supermarkets, and Automation and AI Technologies and Automation in the Workplace. The first block seeks to understand the technological aspects, challenges, and the perceptions of customers and workers regarding the use of self-service checkouts. The second block addresses aspects involving work and employment, aiming to understand people's perceptions of technology and their jobs.

4.1 Barriers and Opportunities of AI in Supermarkets

It was found that self-service checkouts are not adopted by all supermarket customers; only a small portion utilizes this technology. This issue is supported by the findings of

Arntz [23], who highlights that the assimilation of new technologies is a gradual process subject to various obstacles, often resulting in the non-replacement of one technology by another.

The central inquiry sought to understand why customers continue to use manned checkouts even when they have the option to complete their purchases through self-service checkouts. This inquiry identified barriers and opportunities that can be addressed to increase customer engagement with self-service checkouts (Table 3).

Table 3. Categories Emerging about Barriers AI Supermarket

Category	Subcategories
Barriers (Freq: 151)	Customer makes only small purchases (baskets)
	Problems with self-service checkouts
	Customer prefers to use manned checkouts
	Older people do not use self-service checkouts
	Need for a person to assist with self-service checkouts

The results of this analysis revealed that customers using self-service checkouts primarily make small purchases using baskets. This finding suggests a significant preference for smaller transactions among self-service checkout users. The graph below illustrates the distribution of this behavior, highlighting the predominance of small purchases and frequent use of baskets during the shopping process.

In the survey data showed that 50% of customers using self-service checkouts engage in transactions involving six to ten items, while another 30% prefer to purchase four to eight items. This indicates that a total of 80% of customers using self-service checkouts do so only for small purchases.

About subcategory labeled "Self-Service Checkout Operational Issues" was the second most frequent among all subcategories in this study, aligning with Bauer & Gaskell [24]. An in-depth analysis of the data reveals the urgent need to understand and address the challenges inherent to the functionality of self-service checkouts, which play a crucial role at the intersection of technology and customer experience.

A prevalent challenge at self-service checkouts is the inability of the barcode scanner to read some barcodes. The need for worker intervention, often cited by users, suggests that this is a recurring issue, significantly contributing to support calls during operations. The perception of workers who provide support to self-service checkouts reinforces the common and routine nature of this issue. Another identified limitation is the inability of self-service checkouts to accept cash payments. It is worth noting that one of the software systems recently started accepting PIX payments but still does not accept cash, and there is a demand for this payment method.

Customer interaction with the self-service checkout interface, either by entering product codes or selecting items on the screen, emerges as a constant source of complaints. Dissatisfaction is exacerbated by possible touchscreen failures, which are more evident in the Beta network than in the Alpha network. In the Alpha network, some users complain about the software's speed, which does not allow much time for customers to review and complete tasks, putting pressure on the user.

The second major problem identified by technology users relates to weighing products, particularly items like fruits and vegetables. Customers struggle to correctly identify the type of product on the kiosk screen and the self-service checkout scale, especially when there is a wide variety of the same product, such as different types of bananas or apples. Such instances significantly contribute to customer frustration and complaints.

A significant portion of customers still prefer to complete their purchases at manned checkouts. The ratio of customers using manned checkouts compared to self-service checkouts can reach 25 to 1 at certain times of the day, meaning twenty-five customers use manned checkouts while only one uses a self-service checkout. During peak hours, between 11:30 AM and 1:30 PM and between 5:30 PM and 7:30 PM, this ratio decreases to around 15 to 1.

When analyzing the age range of self-service checkout users, we observed a pattern of who uses the technology. Most users fall within the 20 to 39 age range, with 60% within this demographic. The gradient effect in the graph above shows that as age increases, the number of self-service checkout users decreases, confirming the frequency issues pointed out by Bauer & Gaskell [24], which identify a future trend.

The age group of 20–29 years did not report any difficulties in using the technology. However, 17% of customers experiencing difficulties were over 60 years old. Comparing the two graphs, the following scenario emerges (Table 4) :

Table 4. Age, People and Users Automation in Supermarkets

Age	Users Autonomous Self-Checkout	Difficulties about Use Automation
20–29	35%	0%
30–39	25%	17%
40–49	20%	33%
50–59	15%	33%
60–69	5%	17%

The proportions indicate a trend, as 5% of users are over 60 years old, and 17% of these users experienced difficulties using the technology. Conversely, 35% of users are aged 20 to 29, and none reported difficulties in use. All surveyed stores had a designated professional responsible for assisting users with self-service checkouts.

The opportunities related to the implementation of self-service checkout technology in supermarkets are outlined in five subcategories, as shown in the table below, emerging from the customer usage experience.

From the data, five opportunities emerged: speed, avoiding checkout lines, enhancement of new services, engagement with self-service checkouts, and the impact of new technologies. These subcategories are detailed based on the customer experience with self-service technology (Table 5).

Table 5. Categories Emerging about Opportunities AI Supermarket

Category	Subcategories
Opportunities (Freq: 133)	Operation speed
	Prevents queue formation at checkouts
	Improvement of current services through Database Marketing
	User engagement with self-service checkouts
	New technologies and their impacts on customers

All twenty customers surveyed viewed exclusive promotions, offers, discounts, prizes, and cashbacks positively, which could represent a sustainable competitive advantage by Porter [35]. Additionally, the use of technology and the generation of customer knowledge allow for the implementation of exclusive actions by Davenport [25].

The collect data indicated that users aged 20 to 39 make up 60% of self-service technology users, highlighting an opportunity as these customers will be in the consumer market for at least the next 30 years, compared to the last surveyed age group of 60 to 69 years old. This demographic trend suggests increased technology adoption over time (Table 6).

Table 6. Categories Emerging AI and Automation in Supermarkets

Category	Subcategories	Quotations
AI Technologies and Automation in the Workplace	Threats and Job Insecurity (Freq: 25)	*I don't think it will take my job – I always have to help someone use it*
		I don't think it will take my job – many people don't know how to use it
		I don't understand how AI could ever take my place
	Training and Preparation (Freq: 12)	*I don't think the employee needs technical skills; they learn that – they need the right behaviour*
		For me, it's important to be trained
		For me, it's easy to take the courses and training

(*continued*)

Table 6. (*continued*)

Category	Subcategories	Quotations
	Reduction in Number of Employees (Freq: 7)	*For the manager, the biggest benefit for the company was the reduction in staff*
		It reduced the number of cashiers by about 20 to 30%
		There was indeed a reduction in staff at the cash registers
	Labor Displacement (Freq: 6)	*The employees who worked as cashiers were reassigned to other roles*
		The store manager doesn't see that the number of employees decreased; they moved to other departments
		Those who worked at the cash registers went to other departments
	Management of People and Machines (Freq: 6)	*However, I have no issues managing the integration between self-service checkouts and people*
		I see no problem – I've never had any complaints from employees
		No problem at all
	Does Not Replace Humans (Freq: 4)	*The self-service checkouts just help the manned checkouts by relieving pressure during peak times*
		Human contact is better, and customers prefer it
		Self-service checkouts help the manned checkouts

Interviews with managers revealed that neither supermarket chain has AI-based technology in their self-service checkouts. Christensen [26] suggests that disruptive innovations offer new value propositions, creating new markets or reshaping existing ones. According to Christensen, disruptive innovation theory applies to situations where companies can create relatively simple, convenient, and low-cost innovations to drive growth and outperform competitors.

4.2 Social Tech Impacts of the AI in Supermarkets

The primary objective of this study is to understand how automation and AI affect the work environment. However, before reaching this understanding, it is essential to comprehend the current stage of technology from the customers' perspective, which aids in achieving this goal. Analyzing the research data through Atlas.TI software QAD, several analytical subcategories emerged, which next table.

Regarding future job security concerns due to AI, the survey data indicated that 90% of the workers interviewed do not see a reason for worry, as customers still prefer to use manned checkouts. Workers also perceive self-service checkouts as a beneficial technology that helps reduce queue lengths and minimize customer complaints about wait times.

As the research progressed, interviews with store managers were crucial in shaping the results on this issue. The store managers' concerns are not focused on preparing workers to perform tasks requiring advanced technological knowledge. According to them, employees receive the necessary training and preparation to operate the current checkout software, which is sufficient for their roles. They do not see a need to prepare workers for a future without self-service checkouts or to train them for other functions within the supermarket.

Furthermore, no training programs were found to prepare checkout operators for new or different roles within the supermarket. According to the managers, employees are trained for new roles through on-the-job learning from colleagues when they transition to a new position.

5 Final Considerations

The final considerations of this research are divided into two main sections. The first pertains to the customer experience with the use of automation and AI technology in self-service checkouts in supermarkets. The second aims to understand the perspective of those working with this technology, specifically automation and AI, and its impacts on the work environment.

Section 1: Regarding Automation and AI in Self-Service Checkouts.

- The self-service checkouts in both investigated supermarket chains do not contain Artificial Intelligence.
- The technology is not yet mature, showing improvement gaps in both software and hardware.
- Customers only use self-service checkouts for small purchases.
- Younger individuals find the technology easier to use compared to older individuals who face difficulties.
- Currently, customers still prefer using manned checkouts for convenience.

Section 2: Automation and AI Technologies and the Work Environment.

- In terms of perceived threat, job loss, and job insecurity related to working with automation technology were not detected in the research. Workers do not feel threatened about losing their jobs now.

- Job loss is a reality and is occurring. As the technology evolves and resolves its usage issues, there will be greater acceptance and engagement from customers in using the technology. This is corroborated by the age distribution of users, with younger users more likely to adopt the technology over time as older users who find it difficult decrease in number.
- There will be a displacement of labor, though on a smaller scale within supermarkets. This labor will likely shift to roles requiring analytical, intuitive, empathetic/emotional intelligence, as suggested by Huang and Rust [19].
- Preparation of the workforce for this new reality, as evidenced by this research, could come from social debate through capable entities and organizations, such as those supporting workers and companies. Training and capacity-building are suggested to enable workers to assume roles with new technologies while also making them competitive in this new job market format, following the agendas proposed by Jarrahi [27] and tasks and functions utilizing human intelligences highlighted by Huang & Rust [19].

The limitations of this study include the inability to verify all costs associated with implementing self-service checkout technology and compare them with the costs of manned checkouts. This limitation occurred due to the lack of access to cost data, which is confidential company information, representing a significant limitation that could define the feasibility of implementation.

Future research should analyze tasks and functions within supermarkets that could be impacted by some form of AI automation technology. Additionally, future studies could investigate other tasks and functions within a supermarket that may be automated by AI technology.

This research makes significant contributions to the literature by providing a comprehensive analysis of the impact of AI and automation on customer experiences and the work environment in supermarkets. First, it highlights the current limitations and customer preferences regarding self-service checkout technologies, emphasizing the technology's maturity and user demographics Huang & Rust [19]. Second, it addresses the potential displacement of labor due to automation, offering insights into how workers can transition to roles requiring higher-level human intelligences, such as analytical, intuitive, and empathetic skills by Jarrahi [27].

These findings are crucial for understanding the broader implications of AI and automation in retail, contributing to ongoing discussions about the future of work and technology adoption.

References

1. Frey, C.B., Osborne, M.A.: The Future of Employment: How Susceptible Are Jobs to Computerisation? Technol. Forecast. Soc. Chang. **114**, 254–280 (2017). https://doi.org/10.1016/j.techfore.2016.08.019
2. Acemoglu, D., Restrepo, P.: Artificial Intelligence, Automation and Work. An Agenda. University of Chicago Press, In The Economics of Artificial Intelligence (2018)
3. Bootle, R.: The AI Economy: Work, Wealth and Welfare in the Robot Age. Alta Books (2021)
4. Autor, D.H.: The Skill Content of Recent Technological Change: An Empirical Exploration. Quart. J. Econ. **118**(4), 1279–1333 (2003)

5. Autor, D.H.: Work of the Past, Work of the Future. Am. Econ. Assoc. Pap. Proc. **109**, 1–32 (2020)
6. Howcroft, D., Taylor, P.: Automation, Algorithms and Artificial Intelligence in the Workplace: A Critical Review and Research Agenda. N. Technol. Work. Employ. **36**(3), 237–259 (2021)
7. Dwivedi, Y.K., et al.: Artificial Intelligence (AI): Multidisciplinary Perspectives on Emerging Challenges, Opportunities, and Agenda for Research, Practice, and Policy. Int. J. Inf. Manage. **57**, 101994 (2021). https://doi.org/10.1016/j.ijinfomgt.2019.08.002
8. Gruetzemacher, R., Dorner, F., Bernaola-Alvarez, N., Giattino, C., Manheim, D.: Forecasting AI Progress: A Research Agenda. Technol. Forecast. Soc. Chang. **170**, 120909 (2021). https://doi.org/10.1016/j.techfore.2021.120909
9. OECD: OECD Employment Outlook 2023 – Artificial Intelligence and the Labour Market. OECD Publishing, Paris (2023)
10. Araújo, L.M.: The Impact of Self-Checkout Systems on Retail Operations and Customer Satisfaction. J. Retail. Consum. Serv. **67**, 102976 (2023)
11. McCarthy, J., Minsky, M., Rochester, N., Shannon, C.E.: A Proposal for the Dartmouth Summer Research Project on Artificial Intelligence. AI Mag. **27**(4), 12 (2006). https://doi.org/10.1609/aimag.v27i4.1904
12. Wamba, S.F., Akter, S., Edwards, A., Chopin, G., Gnanzou, D.: How 'Big Data' Can Make Big Impact: Findings from a Systematic Review and a Longitudinal Case Study. Int. J. Prod. Econ. **165**, 234–246 (2021)
13. Lee, K.-F., Groves, D.: AI Superpowers: China, Silicon Valley, and the New World Order. Houghton Mifflin Harcourt (2019)
14. Russel, S., Norvig, P.: Artificial Intelligence: A Modern Approach. Pearson (2020)
15. Larriba, J.: A Case of Artificial Intelligence Applied to Supermarkets in Buenos Aires. Int. J. Retail Distrib. Manage. **45**(8), 815–831 (2017)
16. Santos, J.R.: Self-Service Technologies and Employee Displacement: A Critical Review. J. Technol. Hum. Serv. **39**(1), 1–18 (2021)
17. Wang, Y., Siau, K.: Artificial Intelligence in Healthcare: Review and Research Agenda. J. Bus. Res. **123**, 450–461 (2022)
18. Bragança, A., Chen, W., Canhoto, A., Sap, S.: Productive Employment and Decent Work: The Impact of AI Adoption on Psychological Contracts, Work Engagement, and Employee Trust (2021)
19. Huang, M.H., Rust, R.T.: Artificial Intelligence in Service. J. Serv. Res. **21**(2), 155–172 (2018). https://doi.org/10.1177/1094670517752459
20. Souza, L.R.: The Role of Artificial Intelligence in Shaping the Future of Work. J. Bus. Ethics **152**(3), 719–734 (2018)
21. Yin, R.K.: Case study research and applications, vol. 6. Sage, Thousand Oaks, CA (2018)
22. Eisenhardt, K.M.: What is the Eisenhardt Method, Really? Strateg. Organ. **19**, 147–160 (2021). https://doi.org/10.1177/1476127020982866
23. Arntz, M., Terry, G., Ulrich, Z.: The Risk of Automation for Jobs in OECD Countries: A Comparative Analysis. OECD Social, Employment and Migration Working Papers, No. 189. OECD Publishing, Paris (2016)
24. Bauer, M.W., Gaskell, G.: Qualitative Researching with Text. A Practical Handbook. Sage Publications, Image and Sound (2003)
25. Davenport, T., Guha, A., Grewal, D., Bressgott, T.: How Artificial Intelligence Will Change the Future of Marketing. J. Acad. Mark. Sci. **48**, 24–42 (2020). https://doi.org/10.1007/s11747-019-00696-0
26. Christensen, C.M.: The Innovator's Dilemma: When New Technologies Cause Great Firms to Fail. Harvard Business Review Press (2001)

27. Jarrahi, M.H.: Artificial Intelligence and the Future of Work: Human-AI Symbiosis in Organizational Decision Making. Bus. Horiz. **61**(4), 577–586 (2018). https://doi.org/10.1016/j.bushor.2018.03.007
28. Vincent, N.C., Bhakar, R.R., Nadarajan, S.R., Syamala, A., Varghese, J.: Impact of Artificial Intelligence in the Aviation and Space Sector. In: Artificial Intelligence, pp. 209–229. CRC Press (2021)
29. Ghandour, A.: Opportunities and Challenges of Artificial Intelligence in Banking: Systematic Literature Review. TEM J. **10**(4), 1581–1587 (2021)
30. Harisanty, D., Anna, N.E.V., Putri, T.E., Firdaus, A.A., Noor Azizi, N.A.: Leaders, Practitioners and Scientists' Awareness of Artificial Intelligence in Libraries: A Pilot Study. Library Hi Tech **42**(3), 809–825 (2024)
31. Reddy, V.S., Kathiravan, M., Reddy, V.L.: Revolutionizing Animation: Unleashing the Power of Artificial Intelligence for Cutting-Edge Visual Effects in Films. Soft. Comput. **28**(1), 749–763 (2024)
32. Sharma, S., Agarwal, M.: Impact of AI-Based Chatbots on Faculty Performance in Higher Education Institutions. In: Innovation in the University 4.0 System Based on Smart Technologies, pp. 83–100. Chapman and Hall/CRC (2024)
33. Rasheed, H.M.W., Yuanqiong, H., Khizar, H.M.U., Khalid, J.: What Drives the Adoption of Artificial Intelligence Among Consumers in the Hospitality Sector: A Systematic Literature Review and Future Agenda. J. Hosp. Tourism Technol. (2024)
34. Weber, F.D., Schütte, R.: State-of-the-Art and Adoption of Artificial Intelligence in Retailing. Digital Policy, Regul. Gov. **21**(3), 264–279 (2019)
35. Porter, M.E.: Building the microeconomic foundations of prosperity: findings from the microeconomic competitiveness index, pp. 1–23. Palgrave Macmillan, London (2004)

Exploring the Productivity Impacts of Generative AI in Organizations

Benjamin Semujanga(✉) and Patrick Mikalef

Norwegian University of Science and Technology, Trondheim, Norway
benjamin.semujanga@ntnu.no

Abstract. This research paper explores the impact of Generative AI (GenAI) on human productivity within organizations, focusing on the perspective of employees. Using an exploratory case-study method, we conducted semi-structured interviews with 17 participants from various roles to understand how GenAI impacts work process and productivity. Our findings suggest that these tools can automate routine tasks and enable new workers to acquire skills rapidly, but that GenAI adoption may also entail time-consuming upskilling for individuals and undermined team workflow. Furthermore, by employing a Human Resources Management (HRM) perspective, this paper contributes to the Information Systems (IS) literature by offering a nuanced understanding of the organizational impacts of GenAI, suggesting that a balanced approach seems essential to maximize the potential benefits while limiting the drawbacks of these new tools.

Keywords: Generative AI · Organizations · Productivity

1 Introduction

The rapid introduction of Generative AI (GenAI) tools in numerous organizations has galvanized the interest of Information Systems (IS) researchers in the last few years. The foremost example of this phenomena is illustrated by the rapid rise of OpenAI's ChatGPT since November 2022, a conversational agent that delivers human-like answers for a broad number of subjects [1]. According to Lim, et al. [2], GenAI refers to: " a technology that (i) leverages deep learning models to (ii) generate human-like content (e.g., images, words) in response to (iii) complex and varied prompts (e.g., languages, instructions, questions)."

The adoption of this technology by firms raises several issues surrounding the organizational and socio-technical impacts of GenAI. Its introduction can bring substantial change by potentially enhancing efficacy and value through automation, while simultaneously reshaping work processes [3]. For example, GenAI programming assistants are increasingly being used to improve productivity [4]. However, others suggests that these tools can result in productivity loss, raising a practical issue for organizations, which can wonder what are the real strengths of these tools for their workers [5]. Notably, a recent report of the consulting firm BCG details how GenAI can augment the idea generation

Published by Springer Nature Switzerland AG 2024
R. van de Wetering et al. (Eds.): I3E 2024, LNCS 14907, pp. 103–111, 2024.
https://doi.org/10.1007/978-3-031-72234-9_9

process and creativity but hinders in problem solving tasks, compared to consultants without access to ChatGPT-4 [6]. Furthermore, to-date, the body of literature mostly consists of opinion-pieces on the potential benefits or drawbacks of GenAI, with scarce analysis of the processes in which organizations adopt this technology or its link to organizational performance, thus offering minimal assistance to organizations [3]. Indeed, GenAI research in IS is still at an early stage, lacking substantial empirical data to assess its impact in organizations [7]. Consequently, the devil lies in the details, and current research seems to lack a thorough understanding of the practical impacts of GenAI for organizations.

In this context, the goal of this paper will be to gather empirical data on the current uses of GenAI and assess how this technology affects work productivity. Our research focuses on worker perceptions, given the scarce investigations from this viewpoint. Prior research suggests that executives and managers have a greater positive orientation towards GenAI then employees, suggesting a more top-down approach towards this technology, thus more work is needed to understand the different perspectives within firms [8]. To that end, in this paper, we will answer the following research question: "What are the effects of Generative AI on human productivity within organizations?" In order to answer this research question, we conducted interviews with software developers and managers in compagnies that have implemented GenAI. Our findings contribute to deepen the knowledge in IS by addressing gaps surrounding the organizational uses of GenAI. Further, through a greater understanding of the organizational impacts of GenAI, practitioners could maximize the potential of this technology, by guiding its adoption for better suited tasks and roles, thus reducing the productivity losses and other potential risks for organizations.

The remainder of this paper is organized as follows; the next section details the current literature on the organizational effects of GenAI. Then, the third section outlines our research methodology. The results are presented and discussed in the Sect. 4 and 5. Finally, our last section offers a conclusion.

2 Background

Given the swift adoption of GenAI tools following the introduction of Open AI's ChatGPT, the literature surrounding its productivity uses is still growing rapidly. Unlike other IS tools, which usually require sizable capital investments and implementation periods, GenAI's user-friendliness and ease-of-use through natural language prompts seems to warrant specific scholarly examination compared to other productivity tools [9, 10]. Indeed, a recent McKinsey & Company report highlight the great productivity potential for organizations, through increased content synthesis, software development, customer engagement and content generation [11]. On the other hand, others underscore that while individuals see the value of working with GenAI, workers seem to mistrust these tools and the implementation processes which may reduce employment through automation when organizations adopt this technology, raising implications about the ethical dimension of current uses of GenAI [12].

These themes also appear in the emerging academic literature. For example, Brynjolfsson, et al. [13] suggests that access to these tools can increase productivity, especially for lower-skilled workers. Also, recent evidence indicates that GenAI tools such as GitHub Copilot can act as a pair for programming and increases productivity, although it may negatively impact code quality [14]. Dakhel, et al. [15] expands upon this and proposes that GenAI tools as pair programmers can benefit experienced software developers, as they can more aptly correct the generated output, but that it can undermine productivity for less experienced workers. Furthermore, these authors suggest the natural language processing of GenAI is currently non-optimal and requires a lot of prompt engineering, meaning finding the best way to convey your requests to the GenAI tool [5, 15, 16]. This finding seems to undermine of the key aspects of GenAI productivity. However, Liang, et al. [4] suggest that GitHub Copilot users write close to a third of their code using this tool, usually simple tasks, enabling these software developers to focus on the complex tasks.

These contrasting results illustrate the need to develop a model expressing how Generative AI affects productivity in organizations. Indeed, as stated above, the current literature seems to focus on its positive effects such as productivity and while others on potential hinderances, few scholars seem to analyze them together and examine what these affordances entails for individuals and firms. In fact, Sabherwal and Grover [17] suggests that current research lacks nuance which undermines a thorough investigation. Therefore, to address this gap, developing a model can enable a better understanding of the phenomena as it currently manifests itself [18]. In other words, we will evaluate what are the benefits and challenges of GenAI in relation to productivity in organizations.

3 Case Study and Method

The research strategy chosen for this project is the exploratory case study method. Indeed, our research question aims to explain *how* GenAI affects the productivity of software developers [19]. We used semi-structured interviews to gather these details. Indeed, this allowed interviewees more freedom in their answers and enabled us to answer our research question more exhaustively, as we used an interview outline and went further into details as the participants answered. Furthermore, to increase the internal validity of our research, we conducted a pilot interview to have a greater knowledge of our subject before starting the process and executed more interviews than originally planned to increase the coverage [20]. Interviews were recorded and transcribed using Microsoft Teams software. These 30-min interviews contained questions on GenAI productivity and use and the affordances that these tools entail. We developed 9 open-ended interview questions probing this topic. Some sample questions that were included in this interview guide were: *How would do you currently use GenAI ?* and *Do you think GenAI has affected you work performance?* The data gathered was anonymized and no personal data was collected.

For the analysis, emerging patterns and themes from the interviews were gleaned following an inductive approach to qualitative data analysis [19]. Specifically, we performed a descriptive analysis of our handwritten notes and transcripts, followed by an initial coding phase to assess the potential themes inherent to our data. Subsequently, we revised and delimitated these categories and patterns.

This case study explores the GenAI uses of software developers and managers in large companies in Norway. We recruited 4 participants separated from a range of experience from a convenience sample. We believe having perspective from different firms and level of experience would enable us to gather better insights to answer our research question and offer a greater possibility of generalization. Furthermore, as the interviews progressed, some participants referred us to other individuals interested by this project, giving us a snowballing sample of 17 participants, from a broad range of roles, as shown in Table 1.

Table 1. Participants

ID	Role	Years of experience
P1	AI Researcher	14 years
P2	AI Researcher	8 years
P3	IT consultant	3 years
P4	Data scientist	6 years
P5	AI consultant	10 years
P6	Developer	5 years
P7	Attorney	20 years
P8	Executive director	15 years
P9	IT consultant	9 years
P10	IT consultant	13 years
P11	Chief medical officer	6 years
P12	Data scientist	7 years
P13	Developer	20 years
P14	Data science manager	8 years
P15	Senior data scientist	17 years
P16	Developer	4 years
P17	Data ethics advisor	20 ears

4 Results

The preliminary thematic findings from the participants in Table 1. Are discussed in the following section. The main themes are divided as follows: automation, onboarding, competences and team coordination.

4.1 Automation

The majority of participants interviewed indicated that GenAI increased productivity in their work, through automation of routine tasks. For example, P11 stated: "*I would say that GitHub Copilot is the one that has changed my day the most. It's just an amazing tool to have as a developer that makes you faster and the thing that it makes you faster on is more or less just removing boring tasks so you can focus on the fun part of being a developer.*" P5 agreed, with a caveat for quality, saying that "*I think for my personal workflow, much of my tasks has been automated. I am also a developer and programmer myself, so I also use the tools for software development. Even though the quality we can have a discussion it still helps from an automation standpoint ... And just in terms of volume and the outreach and capacity that you can have. I think also has been greatly enhanced.*"

P9 also concurred stating that: "*Yeah, I'd say it definitely makes you more efficient ... one prompt can replace quit a few Google searches*". P14 offered a nuanced view distinguishing the productivity impacts between two tools "*I was thinking mostly about Co-pilot when I said "not really" but ChatGPT, I think we're seeing increasing adoption and increasing change of how people are working.*"

4.2 Onboarding

Another finding was that the increase of productivity seems beneficial in the different ways, based on experience. In fact, a few interviewees argued that the impact was greater for new employees. For example, P3 stated that: "*Yeah, I'd say it definitely makes you more efficient. And the younger ones can focus on the business logic and not the code.*" P5 highlighted the positive effects of generative AI for new employees as well "*We have some use cases where you have reduction of time in 90%, and then you have other tasks, so these are more on the automation side and we talked about kind of the boring, the boring tasks that our new employees had to do.*" These highlight an emerging theme for new employees, as the increase in productivity seems to develop through a streamlined onboarding process.

4.3 Competences

While the previous participants described what new employees were enabled to do through GenAI productivity, some interviewees detailed the difficulty to assess these gains because of the upskilling of competences needed to use GenAI tools. For example, P8 affirmed "*I think it's still a bit difficult to highlight kind of concrete efficiency gains from it. And I think that we shouldn't underestimate the competence and the work to really make the sufficiency gains. I have also been a pilot user now for some weeks on Co-pilot. We see a huge potential, but to really change your daily work to make use of it, it will take time and effort and dedication to actually see these benefits, and you shouldn't underestimate it.*" Furthermore, P4 concurred stating that "*I mean. Like 90% of all AI and machine learning use cases in business fails like 80%-90% and the reason for that is that it's never the tech. In my opinion, it's almost always people.*" Also, P7 mentioned, "*We want to develop prompt repositories.*"

Furthermore, several participants stressed the impact of their organizations' training practices for GenAI. Such as P7 stating: "*We have several sessions, both on prompting exercises and what not so they can use it and learn how to use it.*" P9 expressed a similar experience claiming that: "Yeah, *they uh, when they launched the tool, there were several training sessions... they were scheduled for different time zones so everyone had the opportunity and there was also quite a lot of information given out together with the announcement."* Likewise, P8 stressed they faced "*Mandatory courses for all employees to learn how to use it."* These findings underscore broad effects that GenAI may have in organizations, which may need to become more technologically ready in order to harness the full potential of these new tools.

4.4 Team Coordination

Another pattern that emerged was the friction at the team level following the introduction of GenAI. Various participants mentioned issues while during the implementation. For example, P6 argued: *"Like it is not everyone using it at the same level ... so we still have a way to go in terms of just both changing habits and setting up our workflows."* This highlights the hinderances inherent to successful technology adoption in organisations and a potential drawback to desired productivity gains. Similarly, P14 stated: *"If you're interested you can explore this technology. But to make it work a team should explore it together."* While some participants were eager to adopt GenAI and were confident of its effect on their individual productivity, some stressed that translating these gains at the team level revealed to be more arduous than expected.

To synthesize the results identified in this investigation on the impacts of GenAI on productivity in organizations, we provide a model in Fig. 1. Indeed, we show that GenAI affects organizations in various ways and that can be conceptualized using a Human Resources Management (HRM) lens, in order to assess the changes in work processes. For example, through automation, GenAI seems to have positive effect on the organization aspect by way of a change in work design. Moreover, its streamlined effect on onboarding may positively affect the HR practices of people resourcing as well as learning and development. Nevertheless, the training and other upskilling requirements to develop competences needed when GenAI is introduced may affect this learning and development. Similarly, while GenAI may seem to help engage employees at an individual level, this technology may undermine employee relations by way of team

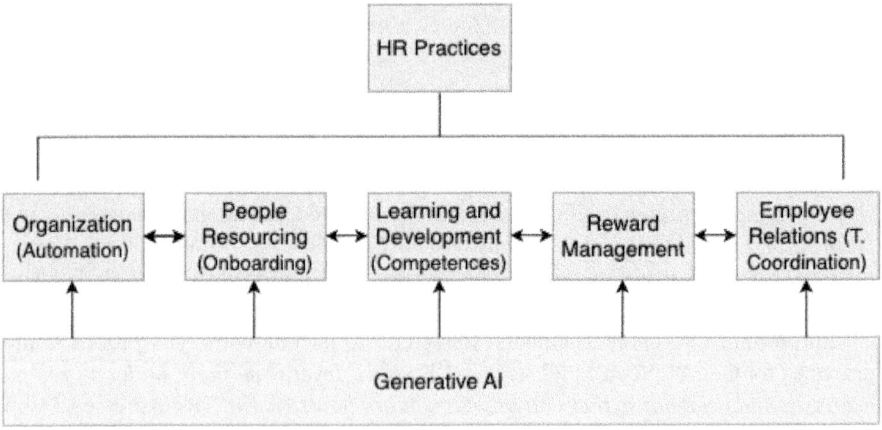

Fig. 1. Effects of Generative AI in the HR system (adapted from [21])

communication issues. These findings outline a mixed picture of the productivity effects of GenAI in organizations.

5 Discussion

As previously mentioned by Liang, et al. [4], our results show that software developers do seem to automate mundane or repetitive tasks through GenAI tools. Undeniably, while imperfect, these tools seem to enable individuals to focus on more complex tasks through automation. The participants also suggested that less experienced employees may reap additional productivity benefits from GenAI tools, as they would focus on other tasks than understanding the code itself. This contrasts with Dakhel, et al. [15], as they suggests more experienced employees would gain more substantial benefits. We posit that this contrasting finding with the literature could be explained by the development of the GenAI tools. Indeed, in the 18 months between these two research projects, the natural language processing performance of the tools has evolved greatly, suggesting its ease-of-use may have increased [22].

Also, numerous participants stressed that while GenAI tools can increase productivity at an individual level, upskilling employees and creating an organizational environment that promotes GenAI adoption and use is a laborious task for firms. Thus, suggesting that a more holistic vision of these tools should be taken into consideration to gage real efficiency. This relates to [5, 15], which stress the potential productivity loss when adopting these tools. Furthermore, it seems that the implementation process to foster team productivity is still seemingly a bit unexplored, as participants underscored their difficulty to coordinate team workflows following the introduction of GenAI.

These results offer an answer to our research question, which examined how does GenAI impact human productivity in organizations. We found that through automation, firms can ameliorate the onboarding process which creates a greater impact for new workers. Moreover, that GenAI training and upskilling was a possible hinderance for productivity and lack of adequate staff coordination undermined the benefits of these tools.

These findings provide a more holistic analysis of GenAI-enabled productivity and contributes to IS literature, particularly scholars' call for a more balanced view of GenAI effects, and our model suggest that employing an HRM perspective may facilitate this process [17].

6 Conclusion

To conclude, this paper provides valuable insights into the way individuals and organizations utilize GenAI tools in an industrial setting. The findings underscore the productivity benefits, challenges and mixed effects of the tools in organizations. The case study showed that GenAI tools seem to increase productivity which enables workers to focus on more strategic tasks, while also finding that firms and individuals have difficulty assessing productivity because of the new competences needed to use GenAI tools and its impact on the workflow of teams. These mixed findings underscore the fact that existing studies do not seem to have exhaustively examined the mechanisms behind GenAI productivity, highlighting a need to fill this gap and critically examine its organizational uses, which a HRM lens could simplify. Furthermore, these results highlight the necessary balancing act organizations will face while adopting these tools, as socio-technical factors seem fundamental for a successful integration of GenAI tools.

The main limitation of our study stems from our interview process which was at a single point in time. To increase the interval validity our research results, it would have been preferable to interview additional participants over a greater number of instances. Moreover, future studies could focus on the effects of GenAI for specific job roles, instead of a diverse set of participants. Furthermore, the results of our study could offer an interesting research path for future researchers, particularly in the implementation process of GenAI tools. As indicated by certain participants, challenges seem arise in this technological phase.

References

1. Fui-Hoon Nah, F., Zheng, R., Cai, J., Siau, K., Chen, L.: Generative AI and ChatGPT: Applications, challenges, and AI-human collaboration. vol. 25, ed: Taylor & Francis, pp. 277–304. (2023)
2. Lim, W.M., Gunasekara, A., Pallant, J.L., Pallant, J.I., Pechenkina, E.: Generative AI and the future of education: Ragnarök or reformation? A paradoxical perspective from management educators. Int. J. Manage. Educ. **21**(2), 100790 (2023)
3. Prasad Agrawal, K.: Towards adoption of Generative AI in organizational settings. J. Comput. Inf. Syst. **64**, 1–16 (2023)
4. Liang, J.T., Yang, C., Myers, B.A.: A large-scale survey on the usability of ai programming assistants: Successes and challenges. In: Proceedings of the 46th IEEE/ACM International Conference on Software Engineering, pp. 1–13. (2024)
5. Simkute, A., Tankelevitch, L., Kewenig, V., Scott, A.E., Sellen, A., Rintel, S.: Ironies of Generative AI: Understanding and mitigating productivity loss in human-AI interactions. arXiv preprint arXiv:2402.11364 (2024)
6. Candelon, F., Krayer, L., Rajendran, S., Martinez, D.Z.: How People Can Create–and Destroy–Value with Generative AI. BCG Global, vol. 21, (2023)
7. Dhoni, P.: Unleashing the Potential: Overcoming Hurdles and Embracing Generative AI in IT Workplaces: Advantages, Guidelines, and Policies. Authorea Preprints (2023)
8. Cardon, P.W., Getchell, K., Carradini, S., Fleischmann, C., Stapp, J.: Generative AI in the Workplace: Employee Perspectives of ChatGPT Benefits and Organizational Policies. (2023)
9. Rane, N.: Role and challenges of ChatGPT, Gemini, and similar generative artificial intelligence in human resource management. Stud. Econ. Bus. Relat. **5**(1), 11–23 (2024)
10. Aral, S., Brynjolfsson, E., Wu, D.: Which came first, it or productivity? Virtuous cycle of investment and use in enterprise systems. Virtuous cycle of investment and use in enterprise systems (2020)
11. Bruce, D.F., et al.: Unlocking the potential of generative AI: Three key questions for government agencies. McKinsey's Public Sector Practice, 2023. [Online]. Available: https://www.mckinsey.com/industries/public-sector/our-insights/unlocking-the-potential-of-generative-ai-three-key-questions-for-government-agencies
12. Shook, E.D., Paul.: Work, Workforce, Workers Age of Generative AI Report. Accenture (2024)
13. Brynjolfsson, E., Li, D., Raymond, L.R.: Generative AI at work. In: Working Paper Series, National Bureau of Economic Research, No. 31161, issue Working Paper Series (2023)

14. Imai, S.: Is github copilot a substitute for human pair-programming? an empirical study. In: Proceedings of the ACM/IEEE 44th International Conference on Software Engineering: Companion Proceedings. pp. 319–321. (2022)
15. Dakhel, A.M., Majdinasab, V., Nikanjam, A., Khomh, F., Desmarais, M.C., Jiang, Z.M.J.: Github copilot ai pair programmer: Asset or liability? J. Syst. Softw. **203**, 111734 (2023)
16. Ebert, C., Louridas, P.: Generative AI for software practitioners. IEEE Softw. **40**(4), 30–38 (2023)
17. Sabherwal, R., Grover, V.: The Societal Impacts of Generative Artificial Intelligence: A Balanced Perspective. J. Assoc. Inf. Syst. **25**(1), 13–22 (2024)
18. March, S.T., Smith, G.F.: Design and natural science research on information technology. Decis. Support Syst. **15**(4), 251–266 (1995)
19. Oates, B.J., Griffiths, M., McLean, R.: Researching information systems and computing. Sage (2022)
20. Diefenbach, T.: Are case studies more than sophisticated storytelling?: Methodological problems of qualitative empirical research mainly based on semi-structured interviews. Qual. Quant. **43**, 875–894 (2009)
21. Armstrong, M., Taylor, S.: Armstrong's handbook of human resource management practice. Kogan Page Publishers (2020)
22. Takagi, S., Watari, T., Erabi, A., Sakaguchi, K.: Performance of GPT-3.5 and GPT-4 on the Japanese Medical Licensing Examination: comparison study. JMIR Med. Educ. **9**(1), e48002 (2023)

Digital Transformation and Organizational Innovation

Navigating Challenges and Pitfalls in DevOps-Driven Digital Transformation

Nasreen Azad(✉) and Sami Hyrynsalmi

Lappeenranta-Lahti University of Technology LUT, Lappeenranta, Finland
{nasren.azad,sami.hyrynsalmi}@lut.fi

Abstract. As technology evolves, businesses must adapt to changing market demands by adopting digital transformation. To tackle these challenges successfully, businesses must adopt effective software development practices like DevOps and create a culture supporting digital transformation. This paper explores how DevOps practices and culture can facilitate digital transformation within organizations. We have interviewed 10 professionals to understand these organizational changes through digital transformation issues. Our findings suggest that (1) Cost Considerations, (2) Skill Gaps and Training, (3) Resistance to Change, (4) Risks in Rapid Deployment, (5) Collaboration Challenges, (6) Compliance and Security,(7) Scalability Issues, (8) Cost Optimization Strategies are vital factors that companies face when a company goes through digital transformation phases. By understanding and addressing these influencing factors for digital transformation for DevOps practices, organizations, and DevOps professionals can navigate digital transformation successfully, drive innovation, and compete effectively in today's dynamic business landscape.

Keywords: DevOps · DevOps practices · Software development · Digital transformation · Technological innovation

1 Introduction

Industrial organizations, including leading software companies, have transformed significantly by incorporating digital technologies and organizational practices. For example, companies have implemented a digital transformation by integrating new tools such as DevOps, Cloud computing platforms, API Management Platforms, collaboration tools, low-code/no-code platforms, Cybersecurity tools, Analytics and Monitoring Tools, and Robotic Process Automation (RPA) Tools to enhance performance, efficiency, and speed up the software process. This digital transformation has allowed organizations to achieve better products and services, competitive advantages, improved customer experiences, business model innovation, and streamlined processes. Recognizing the potential benefits,

Published by Springer Nature Switzerland AG 2024
R. van de Wetering et al. (Eds.): I3E 2024, LNCS 14907, pp. 115–128, 2024.
https://doi.org/10.1007/978-3-031-72234-9_10

digital transformation has become a strategic priority on the agendas of industrial organizations. Studies by [4,4,33,34,42,45,51] highlights the essential role of digital transformation in driving significant business improvements.

This transformation process can significantly impact product offerings and organizational operations, which makes it necessary to have comprehensive company-wide transformation programs [33,51]. The relationship between technology implementation and organizational transformation has been well-established in the literature and can be explained by various theories [41]. Digital transformation can be analyzed through technical systems, such as cloud computing, the Internet of Things, and big data, and social systems, such as culture, goals, and procedures, which highlights the interconnectedness of these components [19,27]. Despite extensive technological research, literature often overlooks organizational change dynamics in digital transformation [22,39]. Empirical studies are needed to explore technology adoption, value creation, structural changes, and financial impacts in digital transformation strategies [33,39].

Our study adopts a qualitative approach, employing thematic analysis [17], and ten semi-structured interviews [48] were conducted with industry professionals. Our research highlights how DevOps' core principles, practices, and values support and enhance digital transformation within organizations. Notable transformations include fostering an open organizational culture, accelerating digital and entrepreneurial awareness, creating an experimental environment, promoting new ways of working, emphasizing automation, security, and compliance, and leading transformation through changes in tools and technologies [2,10].

We aim to gather insights from professionals, practitioners, and academics to identify gaps and potential research areas in DevOps practice challenges and pitfalls through digital transformation innovations. To achieve this goal, we have formulated a research question.

RQ:1 What factors influence DevOps operations in DevOps-led digital transformation?

This study is structured as follows: First, it will outline the related work. Section three will discuss the research method, including interview design, data collection, and data analysis process. Section four will present the results and findings, while section five will cover the discussion. The following sections will focus on the managerial impacts, limitations, and future work, and will conclude the study.

2 Related Work

2.1 Digital Transformation

Digital transformation has emerged as an important phenomenon for researchers and practitioners [14,24]. This is revolutionizing how industrial organizations operate through digital technologies [33,44], leading organizations toward a new era of industrialization. Thus, organizations have been forced to alter the value creation paths they have relied on to remain competitive by introducing various digital technologies [51]. These digital technologies include the Internet of Things, cloud computing, artificial intelligence, hyper-connectivity, automation, big data, etc. [27,44]. Organizations are now finding new ways to operate with the help of these technologies by devising strategies that embrace the implications of digital transformation and drive better operational performance [28]. These digital technologies are just a small part of the digital transformation of organizations, while organizations require more effort to transform themselves digitally [24,28,51].

According to Bockshecker et al.(2018), practitioners use both terminologies while explaining digital transformation and digitalization. However, some researchers have tried to differentiate the meaning of both terms as they think digital transformation and digitalization are different [16]. Both terms are derived from digitization, the technological transformation of analog information into a digital format [16,33]. Parida et al. (2019) defined digitalization as the 'use of digital technologies to innovate a business model and provide new revenue streams and value-producing opportunities in industrial ecosystems' [44]. Some empirical studies have stated that organizations face various challenges, and digital transformation can help companies overcome these challenges. Some challenges could be a lack of tools, methods, and concepts for process digitization, unclear migration scenarios, a lack of structure and direction for managing transformation, organizational structure, and collaboration and cooperation [44].

2.2 DevOps Concepts and Practices

DevOps is a modern software development methodology emphasizing collaboration and communication between development and operations teams. This approach is designed to break down information silos and facilitate smoother and more efficient software development processes [3,8]. By promoting a shared responsibility and mutual understanding culture, DevOps enables teams to work together more effectively, resulting in faster delivery of high-quality software products. DevOps's success mainly depends on a specific cultural mindset that values transparency, continuous improvement, and a willingness to experiment and learn from mistakes [8,20,43].

To achieve faster and more frequent delivery of software, it is critical to have product automation and collaboration across the department [6]. Olszewska et al. suggest that a set of principles and practices can be implemented to achieve greater communication and coordination among key stakeholders for the successful development of software products and services [26,43].

For a long time, there were inefficiencies in the software development process. The release time was slow, and the operations processes were interrupted by organizational splits during development. The team's communication could have been better due to various team gaps. To tackle these inefficiencies, the concept of DevOps practices was introduced. This concept was pioneered by Petrik Debois [20]. DevOps is an infinite loop of operations that follow a sequence that combines seven phases, including planning, code development, building, deploying, testing, operating, and monitoring, according to Azad and Hyrynsalmi. [8]. DevOps aims to streamline software development by unifying development and operations teams for faster release times [7,38]. When working in teams, development and operations teams often face conflicting issues due to agility and stability concerns. Challenges such as insufficient flow of information, knowledge gaps, and unstable test environments can also arise [3,11,13,32,37].

Continuous Integration. Continuous integration is a multi-step process designed to ensure error-free code. These steps encompass compiling the code, executing unit tests, verifying code standards, assessing code coverage, and generating deployment packages [6–8,10,23]. This process starts automatically to ensure integration frequency and handle highly visible artifacts. Continuous integration helps to resolve integration failures faster and maintain automated integration flows ongoing [12]. Developers must receive feedback for the integration process to ensure the quality of the code, and the integration process should be regular to achieve this [23].

Each integration process involves an iteration that meets a feedback loop, where any problems related to source code testing are solved. Thus, the source code changes increase the successful implementation and progress through the system [7,8,52].

Continuous Delivery. Continuous delivery is an approach used in software engineering that combines a set of principles, practices, and patterns to allow for deployment at any time during the development process [8,9,31,50]. For teams, software must be continuously produced within a short life cycle, allowing for releases to be made at any time [10,23,30]. According to Fitzgerald and Ståhl, continuous delivery increases the software's ability to be deployed in the working environment [23]. Researchers outlines key characteristics of continuous delivery, including short cycles, resealability at any point, and dependable release. Additionally, the importance of fast feedback loops, support for automation, and the assurance of swift and reliable releases to the customer should be duly acknowledged in the context of continuous delivery. [23,40,49,50].

Continuous Deployment. Continuous deployment allows codes to be immediately deployed to the production environment, enabling customers to use the final application outcome [18,30,46]. For the deployment process manual steps or developer commit decisions for the production deployment are needed [36]. This process helps to get better feedback from users and also the defect is detected that reduced the cost. Thus feedback is acquired faster for the deployment process [35]. For the continuous deployment of agile processes at team levels, integration for research and development and process automation is required [46].

3 Research Method

3.1 Interview Design

This interview protocol aims to gather insights from professionals experienced in integrating DevOps into digital transformation initiatives. The questions cover their experiences, challenges, best practices, and the tools and technologies they have used. The protocol consists of semi-structured interviews categorized into topics such as employee experience in DevOps digitalization, key drivers for organizations to adopt digital transformation with DevOps, approaches for cultural transformation when introducing DevOps as part of a digital transformation strategy, cost considerations for new changes, skill gaps and training for employees, risks in rapid deployment, collaboration challenges, compliance and security, scalability issues, and cost optimization strategies for DevOps digitalization within the company. The interviewees discussed their roles and experiences in digital transformation projects involving DevOps practices, providing insights into their background and expertise.

3.2 Data Collection

As part of our digital transformation research, we conducted 10 semi-structured interviews [15] through LinkedIn invitations with IT professionals from Finland, Norway, Sweden, and the United Kingdom who have extensive experience working with DevOps platforms. These interviews were conducted over four months, from August 1st to September to December,2023. We contacted these professionals and invited them to share their experiences, knowledge, and perspectives on digital transformation in their respective companies. Once they agreed, we scheduled a convenient online meeting time and conducted 45-minute interviews with each participant, delving into their insights and opinions on various aspects of digital transformation. We transcribed these interviews and have now amassed 448 pages of rich, informative documents. Table 1 overviews the participants' country of origin, years of experience, and current roles within their respective companies.

3.3 Data Analysis

We are using qualitative methods for our data analysis process, specifically thematic analysis as described by Castleberry in 2018 [17]. This method involves assigning codes to text segments, translating those codes into higher-order themes, and creating a model of those themes. Two researchers performed the coding and theme-generation process to ensure accuracy [17]. Applying this process allowed us to identify similar and dissimilar codes from different data segments from interview transcripts. The coding process allowed us to create a set of themes that helped us understand the benefits and challenges of DevOps-led digital transformation.

4 Findings and Results

DevOps is a key driver of digital transformation, bringing about significant enhancements in collaboration, efficiency, product quality, and time-to-market. By promoting a culture of continuous improvement and utilizing automation and data-driven decision-making, DevOps empowers organizations to innovate quickly, adapt to market changes, and provide outstanding customer experiences. Through the adoption of DevOps practices, organizations can attain sustainable digital transformation, positioning themselves for long-term success in an increasingly digital world. Based on the interview, we can extract several key themes and provide a summary of digital transformation factors that influence DevOps practices:

Table 1. Professional's country of origin, year of experience, and role in the company

Participants	Country of origin	Year of experience	Role in the company
P1	Finland	8	Senior Engineer
P2	Sweden	7	Team lead
P3	Sweden	7	Senior Engineer
P4	Norway	8	Developer
P5	Sweden	6	Developer
P6	Finland	8	Lead Architect
P7	Finland	9	DevOps operation
P8	Sweden	8	Develpoer
P9	Norway	7	Junior DevOps Engineer
P10	Finland	8	Tech Lead

4.1 Cost Considerations

Organizations looking to implement DevOps often face a complex challenge, determining the most cost-effective way. On the one hand, investing in new technologies and tools can be critical to success. On the other hand, resources must be optimized to avoid any unnecessary expenses. Striking the right balance between these two factors can be a delicate task that requires careful consideration and planning. A professional stated that,

> *"Investing in new technologies can improve workflows, yet it requires careful cost optimization for the project as a CEO's perspective-P3(Senior Engineer, Sweden)".*

4.2 Skill Gaps and Training

Switching to a DevOps approach necessitates that teams acquire new skills or upgrade existing ones, particularly in comprehending production environments, servers, and automation tools. This is because DevOps is a methodology that seeks to integrate development and operations, requiring the team to comprehensively understand how the production environment and servers operate. The team can automate repetitive tasks with automation tools, making the development process faster and more efficient. To ensure that the transition to DevOps is successful, it is essential to provide adequate training and knowledge-sharing opportunities to address any existing skill gaps. This will enable the team to adopt new practices and tools more effectively, improve their productivity, and deliver high-quality products or services to customers.

"Closing skill gaps in DevOps is essential for propelling digital transformation. Through continuous training and upskilling, organizations can adeptly navigate rapid technological advancements-P2 (Team Lead, Sweden)".

4.3 Resistance to Change

Digital transformation can be a challenging journey, especially when it comes to implementing DevOps practices. Resistance to DevOps principles is a common issue that can slow the progress of digital transformation initiatives. This resistance often stems from the incompatibility of existing technology stacks or legacy systems with DevOps practices. To overcome this resistance, organizations need to embark on a cultural shift that emphasizes cooperation, collaboration, and open communication between different teams and departments. This shift can help create an environment where DevOps principles can be adopted effectively, enabling companies to streamline their software delivery processes, reduce errors, and improve overall performance. In summary, overcoming resistance to DevOps practices is essential for organizations to achieve successful digital transformation and stay competitive in today's fast-paced business landscape. A professional stated that,

"Upon joining the team, I encountered resistance to change. However, an ongoing initiative was already to embrace digital transformation and innovation culture within our organization-P1 (Senior Engineer, Finland)".

4.4 Risks in Rapid Deployment

The process of rapid deployment and continuous integration, while efficient, can pose a significant risk to production systems by introducing bugs or vulnerabilities. In order to mitigate these risks effectively, it is crucial to implement thorough testing processes and adhere to strict quality controls. Doing so can identify and address any potential issues early in the development process, ensuring a reliable and secure product is delivered to end-users.

" Balancing speed with rigorous testing and quality assurance is crucial to ensure sustainable progress and resilience for rapid development, but that might also involve some risks -P4 (Developer, Norway)".

4.5 Collaboration Challenges

In larger organizations with multiple teams, it can be difficult to encourage collaboration between cross-functional teams or departments. This is particularly true when implementing DevOps practices. Therefore, it is essential to have effective strategies in place that promote knowledge sharing and foster collaboration. By doing so, teams can work together seamlessly, leading to more efficient and successful implementation of DevOps practices. A professional stated that.

"Good communication, daily meetings, and alignment are key to cultural transformation and collaboration, especially in organizations with traditionally separated teams- P5(Developer, Sweden)"

4.6 Compliance and Security

Maintaining a balance between the need for flexible and efficient development processes and the necessity to comply with security and regulatory standards is a crucial aspect of software development. To achieve this balance, automated tools for code analysis and testing can be employed to ensure that all security standards and best practices are met without compromising development speed or agility. These tools can help identify and address potential security vulnerabilities in the codebase before attackers can exploit them, thereby reducing the risk of data breaches, system downtime, and other security incidents. A professional stated that,

"If I talk about DevOps-driven digital transformation, compliance and security must be at the forefront. Innovating without safeguards can lead to vulnerabilities. At the same time, balancing agility with robust security measures is essential for building a resilient and compliant digital future-P7 (Devops operations, Finland)".

4.7 Scalability Issues

Scalability issues may arise When developing projects involving heavy database dependencies or complex logic. Scalability challenges refer to the capacity of a system to handle an increasing amount of work, and these challenges may become more pronounced as the project grows. Addressing these challenges requires carefully evaluating the system's architecture and resource management. The system's architecture may need to be adjusted to ensure that it can accommodate a higher volume of traffic and perform efficiently under a heavier load. Resource management is also crucial in ensuring the system can handle the increased load without overloading or crashing. This may involve strategies such as load balancing, caching, and optimizing database queries. A project can continue to grow and evolve by addressing scalability challenges without running into performance issues or other limitations. A professional stated that,

> *"DevOps transformation enhances agility and efficiency, but scalability issues can pose a hidden challenge. Rapid growth without a strong foundation can lead to failure. Ensuring scalable solutions is crucial for long-term success and stability in any transformation journey- P6 (Lead Architecture, Finland)".*

4.8 Cost Optimization Strategies

When it comes to DevOps projects, managing and optimizing costs can be a challenging task, especially when working with limited resources. To ensure successful cost management, project managers must employ effective strategies that involve careful planning and utilization of tools for estimating and tracking expenses. These strategies can help increase efficiency, minimize waste, and ensure the project stays within budget constraints. By actively managing costs, DevOps teams can improve their chances of delivering high-quality products or services while staying profitable. A professional states that,

> *"Cost optimization is about maximizing value and efficiency for our team. This can be achieved by automating tasks, streamlining workflows, and leveraging cloud resources-P9 (Jinior DevOps Engineer, Norway)".*

5 Discussion

DevOps-driven digital transformation has emerged as a promising approach to streamline software development, create collaboration between development and operations teams, and accelerate the time-to-market of software products [6–8,10]. However, while the benefits are substantial, this approach also comes with challenges and pitfalls that organizations must overcome effectively. One of the primary challenges of DevOps-led digital transformation is cultural resistance within organizations. This resistance stems from the fact that DevOps requires a fundamental shift in culture towards continuous learning, shared responsibility, and collaboration. This shift can be met with resistance from traditionally siloed teams, making it a key obstacle that organizations must navigate effectively to achieve successful DevOps transformation [7,8,30]. Implementing DevOps practices often requires new skill sets, training, and competencies. Organizations may face challenges in upskilling existing staff or hiring talent with the required DevOps skills [1,12,52]. Toolchain and scalability issues in DevOps involve using a complex toolchain for automation, monitoring, and deployment. Managing and integrating these tools effectively can be challenging, especially for large-scale projects [24,30]. Legacy Systems Integration and resistance to change is a concern in any organizations. Many organizations have legacy systems not designed for continuous integration and deployment. Integrating these systems into a DevOps pipeline can pose technical challenges [29].

Compliance and security Requirements in DevOps introduce software development, testing, and deployment changes, which may raise compliance and governance concerns, particularly in regulated industries [25]. Defining and measuring success in a DevOps transformation can be challenging. Traditional metrics may not capture the full impact of DevOps practices on organizational performance [29]. Achieving alignment across different departments and teams is crucial for successful DevOps adoption. Lack of alignment can lead to conflicts and hinder progress [5,8,10,24]. At the same time, cost optimization and cost optimization strategies should be kept aligned.

6 Managerial Implications

This study holds significant managerial implications for practitioners embarking on digital transformation initiatives. It is important to view digital transformation not merely as a technical endeavor but as a holistic integration of technical and social systems to leverage advanced digital technologies effectively [21,33]. Engineers and technical leaders, often focused on technical excellence, may overlook crucial social design aspects, leading to project failure [21,33]. Therefore, practitioners are cautioned against neglecting social elements as well as encouraged to adopt a sociotechnical approach when planning and implementing digital transformation strategies [33].

Furthermore, this study identifies digital transformation challenge elements-cost considerations, skill gaps and training, resistance to change, rapid deployment risks, collaboration challenges, compliance and security issues, scalability issues, and cost optimization strategies, which demand special attention during digital transformation planning. These organizational and technical factors are pivotal in achieving desired performance outcomes such as agility in work, customer connectivity, better collaboration, improved quality, testing with real customers, and better feedback, which are crucial for successful digital transformation initiatives.

The study illuminates organizational structure as a vital yet often overlooked aspect of digital transformation. Current organizational structures may need to be revised to fully realize digital technology's transformative potential. To fully capitalize on digital transformation, practitioners must adapt and transform organizational structures to align with digital technologies' demands.

7 Limitations and Future Work

Our study, while insightful, has certain limitations that warrant attention. The study primarily focused on engineering firms and medium- to large-sized companies. Consequently, our findings may not universally apply to companies from diverse backgrounds and industries. This highlights the necessity for further research to ensure a comprehensive understanding of digital transformation across various sectors. It's important to consider that these findings are not exhaustive and may not cover all aspects of the industry. Therefore, we recommend conducting further research to include various organizations with different backgrounds and industries. Doing so could provide more comprehensive and insightful data that could be used to improve the industry as a whole. While our findings have been useful in understanding the challenges faced by engineering firms and medium-sized companies, we acknowledge limitations to our study, and more research is needed to expand on these findings.

The researchers primarily gathered insights from DevOps professionals for interviewees to provide a comprehensive perspective. It may not fully capture a wider population's diverse views and experiences. Therefore, the study could have benefited from conducting additional interviews with individuals from different backgrounds and varying levels of expertise to enrich the findings further and provide a more nuanced understanding of the topic.

Our study has uncovered important insights that can guide future research. It is recommended that future research should employ cross-case analysis, in-depth case studies, and/or survey design, as suggested by Scacchi (2004), to gain a better understanding of the differences and similarities between the digital journeys of various organizations [47].

8 Conclusion

Our research aims to investigate the methods and practices of DevOps that can assist organizations in achieving digital transformations. To achieve this goal, we conducted 10 interview studies to identify factors that influence a digital transformation phase. Our research has identified nine critical factors that can pose difficulties for companies in their digital transformation journey. These factors include (1) cost considerations, (2) skill gaps and training, (3) resistance to change, (4) risks associated with rapid deployment, (5) collaboration challenges, (6) compliance and security issues, (7) scalability issues, (8) cost optimization strategies. Our research findings indicate that DevOps practices can be crucial in supporting digital transformations. Therefore, we plan to conduct focus groups and case studies to develop a framework for DevOps practices based on professionals' outputs.

References

1. Almeida, F., Simões, J., Lopes, S.: Exploring the benefits of combining DevOps and agile. Future Internet **14**(2), 63 (2022)
2. AlNuaimi, B.K., Singh, S.K., Ren, S., Budhwar, P., Vorobyev, D.: Mastering digital transformation: the nexus between leadership, agility, and digital strategy. J. Bus. Res. **145**, 636–648 (2022)
3. Amaro, R.M.D., Pereira, R., da Silva, M.M.: Capabilities and practices in DevOps: a multivocal literature review. IEEE Trans. Softw. Eng. **49**, 883–901 (2022)

4. Autio, E., Nambisan, S., Thomas, L.D., Wright, M.: Digital affordances, spatial affordances, and the genesis of entrepreneurial ecosystems. Strateg. Entrepreneurship J. **12**(1), 72–95 (2018)
5. Azad, N.: Understanding Devops critical success factors and organizational practices. In: Proceedings of the 5th International Workshop on Software-intensive Business: Towards Sustainable Software Business, pp. 83–90 (2022)
6. Azad, N., Hyrynsalmi, S.: What are critical success factors of DevOps Projects? a systematic literature review. In: Wang, X., Martini, A., Nguyen-Duc, A., Stray, V. (eds.) ICSOB 2021. LNBIP, vol. 434, pp. 221–237. Springer, Cham (2021). https://doi.org/10.1007/978-3-030-91983-2_17
7. Azad, N., Hyrynsalmi, S.: DevOps challenges in organizations: through professional lens. In: Carroll, N., Nguyen-Duc, A., Wang, X., Stray, V. (eds.) International Conference on Software Business, vol. 463, pp. 260–277. Springer, Cham (2022). https://doi.org/10.1007/978-3-031-20706-8_18
8. Azad, N., Hyrynsalmi, S.: Devops critical succes factors—a systematic literature review. Inform. Softw. Technol., 107150 (2023)
9. Azad, N., Hyrynsalmi, S.: Multivocal literature review on DevOps critical success factors. In: Proceedings of the 28th International Conference on Evaluation and Assessment in Software Engineering, pp. 520–527 (2024)
10. Azad, N., Hyrynsalmi, S., Mäntymäki, M.: Understanding DevOps critical success factors: Insights from professionals. In: Janssen, M., et al. Conference on e-Business, e-Services and e-Society, vol. 14316, pp. 78–90. Springer, Cham (2023). https://doi.org/10.1007/978-3-031-50040-4_7
11. Banerjee, C., Pandey, S.: Software security rules, SDLC perspective. arXiv preprint arXiv:0911.0494 (2009)
12. Bass, L., Weber, I., Zhu, L.: DevOps: A Software Architect's Perspective. Addison-Wesley Professional (2015)
13. Bezemer, C.P., et al.: How is performance addressed in DevOps? In: Proceedings of the 2019 ACM/SPEC International Conference on Performance Engineering, pp. 45–50 (2019)
14. Bharadwaj, A., El Sawy, O.A., Pavlou, P.A., Venkatraman, N.v.: Digital business strategy: toward a next generation of insights. MIS Q., 471–482 (2013)
15. Blandford, A.E.: Semi-structured qualitative studies. Interaction Design Foundation (2013)
16. Bockshecker, A., Hackstein, S., Baumöl, U.: Systematization of the term digital transformation and its phenomena from a socio-technical perspective–a literature review (2018)
17. Castleberry, A., Nolen, A.: Thematic analysis of qualitative research data: is it as easy as it sounds? Curr. Pharm. Teach. Learn. **10**(6), 807–815 (2018)
18. Claps, G.G., Svensson, R.B., Aurum, A.: On the journey to continuous deployment: technical and social challenges along the way. Inf. Softw. Technol. **57**, 21–31 (2015)
19. Davis, M.C., Challenger, R., Jayewardene, D.N., Clegg, C.W.: Advancing socio-technical systems thinking: a call for bravery. Appl. Ergon. **45**(2), 171–180 (2014)
20. Debois, P.: Agile infrastructure and operations: how infragile are you? In: Agile 2008 Conference, pp. 202–207. IEEE (2008)
21. Di Maio, P.: Towards a metamodel to support the joint optimization of socio technical systems. Systems **2**(3), 273–296 (2014)
22. Duerr, S., Holotiuk, F., Wagner, H.T., Beimborn, D., Weitzel, T.: What is digital organizational culture? Insights from exploratory case studies (2018)
23. Fitzgerald, B., Stol, K.J.: Continuous software engineering: a roadmap and agenda. J. Syst. Softw. **123**, 176–189 (2017)

24. Fitzgerald, M., Kruschwitz, N., Bonnet, D., Welch, M.: Embracing digital technology: a new strategic imperative. MIT Sloan Manag. Rev. **55**(2), 1 (2014)
25. Forsgren, N., Humble, J.: The role of continuous delivery in it and organizational performance. In: Forsgren, N., Humble, J. (eds.) " The Role of Continuous Delivery in IT and Organizational Performance." The Proceedings of the Western Decision Sciences Institute (WDSI) (2016)
26. Garousi, V., Felderer, M., Mäntylä, M.V.: The need for multivocal literature reviews in software engineering: complementing systematic literature reviews with grey literature. In: Proceedings of the 20th International Conference on Evaluation and Assessment in Software Engineering, pp. 1–6 (2016)
27. Gilchrist, A.: Industry 4.0. Apress, Berkeley, CA (2016). https://doi.org/10.1007/978-1-4842-2047-4
28. Hesse, A.: Digitalization and leadership-how experienced leaders interpret daily realities in a digital world (2018)
29. Hilton, M., Nelson, N., Dig, D., Tunnell, T., Marinov, D., et al.: Continuous Integration (CI) needs and wishes for developers of proprietary code (2016)
30. Humble, J., Farley, D.: Continuous delivery: reliable software releases through build, test, and deployment automation. Pearson Education (2010)
31. Humble, J., Kim, G.: Accelerate: the science of lean software and DevOps: building and scaling high performing technology organizations. IT Revolution (2018)
32. Iden, J., Tessem, B., Päivärinta, T.: Problems in the interplay of development and it operations in system development projects: a Delphi study of norwegian it experts. Inf. Softw. Technol. **53**(4), 394–406 (2011)
33. Imran, F., Shahzad, K., Butt, A., Kantola, J.: Digital transformation of industrial organizations: toward an integrated framework. J. Chang. Manag. **21**(4), 451–479 (2021)
34. Ivančić, L., Vukšić, V.B., Spremić, M.: Mastering the digital transformation process: business practices and lessons learned. Technol. Innov. Manage. Rev. **9**(2) (2019)
35. Laudon, J.L.: Pearson MYLAB MIS WITH Pearson Etext-Instantaccess-Management Information Systems: Managing the Digital Firm, Global Edition. Pearson Education Limited (2017)
36. Laukkanen, E., Itkonen, J., Lassenius, C.: Problems, causes and solutions when adopting continuous delivery-a systematic literature review. Inf. Softw. Technol. **82**, 55–79 (2017)
37. Leidecker, J.K., Bruno, A.V.: Identifying and using critical success factors. Long Range Plan. **17**(1), 23–32 (1984)
38. Lwakatare, L.E., et al.: Towards DevOps in the embedded systems domain: Why is it so hard? In: 2016 49th Hawaii International Conference on System Sciences (HICSS), pp. 5437–5446. IEEE (2016)
39. Matt, C., Hess, T., Benlian, A.: Digital transformation strategies. Bus. Inform. Syst. Eng. **57**, 339–343 (2015)
40. Meng, F., Wegman, M.N., Xu, J., Zhang, X., Chen, P., Chafle, G.: It troubleshooting with drift analysis in the DevOps era. IBM J. Res. Dev. **61**(1), 6–62 (2017)
41. Mumford, E.: The story of socio-technical design: reflections on its successes, failures and potential. Inf. Syst. J. **16**(4), 317–342 (2006)
42. Niemi, M.K., et al.: Talent retention and the development of digital skills: a study of the ecosystem-based digitalisation academy located in Vaasa, Finland (2021)
43. Olszewska, M., Waldén, M.: DevOps meets formal modelling in high-criticality complex systems. In: Proceedings of the 1st International Workshop on Quality-Aware DevOps, pp. 7–12 (2015)

44. Parida, V., Sjödin, D., Reim, W.: Reviewing literature on digitalization, business model innovation, and sustainable industry: past achievements and future promises (2019)
45. Porter, M.E., Heppelmann, J.E., et al.: How smart, connected products are transforming companies. Harvard Bus. Rev. **93**(10), 96–114 (2015)
46. Rodríguez, P., et al.: Continuous deployment of software intensive products and services: a systematic mapping study. J. Syst. Softw. **123**, 263–291 (2017)
47. Scacchi, W.: Socio-technical design. Encycl. Hum. Comput. Interact. **1**, 656–659 (2004)
48. Schmidt, C.: The analysis of semi-structured interviews. Companion Qual. Res. **253**(41), 258 (2004)
49. Shahin, M.: Architecting for DevOps and continuous deployment. In: Proceedings of the ASWEC 2015 24th Australasian Software Engineering Conference, pp. 147–148 (2015)
50. Van Belzen, M., Trienekens, J., Kusters, R.: Critical success factors of continuous practices in a DevOps context. In: 28th International Conference of Information Systems Development (ISD 2019) (2019)
51. Vial, G.: Understanding digital transformation: a review and a research agenda. In: Managing Digital Transformation, pp. 13–66 (2021)
52. Zhu, L., Bass, L., Champlin-Scharff, G.: DevOps and its practices. IEEE Softw. **33**(3), 32–34 (2016)

Critical Success Factors in Data Analytics Projects: Insights from a Systematic Literature Review

Nisa Demir[1(✉)], Banu Aysolmaz[2], and Özden Özcan-Top[1]

[1] Graduate School of Informatics, Middle East Technical University, Ankara, Turkey
{nisa.demir,ozdenoz}@metu.edu.tr
[2] Eindhoven University of Technology, Eindhoven, The Netherlands
b.e.aysolmaz@tue.nl

Abstract. Various data analytics applications are increasingly used by organizations to extract insights from data. There are numerous studies exploring the critical success factors (CSFs) in different data analytics fields including Business Intelligence, Artificial Intelligence, Machine Learning, Data Science, and Big Data. Despite the extensive body of research, there remains a gap in identifying a structured CSFs list that offers a holistic view across all these fields. This study addresses this gap by conducting a systematic literature review to investigate CSFs in data analytics projects, aiming to create a comprehensive list that is applicable across various fields. We have categorized CSFs into six key themes: People, Strategy, Technology & Data, Organizational Culture, Process Design and External Factors derived from 28 research papers. By presenting these CSFs comprehensively, this paper seeks to provide a structured approach that will enhance the success rates of data analytics projects, facilitating better strategic alignment and operational efficiency across multiple fields.

Keywords: Critical Success Factors · CSFs · Data Analytics · Business Intelligence · Artificial Intelligence · Machine Learning · Data Science · Big Data

1 Introduction

We are living in the age of big data, advanced analytics, and data science [1]. Actions of individuals and businesses continuously generate digitally recorded data such as internet clicks, social media content generation, sensor networks, sales queries, and purchase transactions [2]. This data is turned into meaningful knowledge through data analytics. Data analytics has become key for decision-making and strategic planning across various sectors, resulting in transformations of how organizations operate and compete. For instance, in healthcare, data analytics is changing patient care through predictive analytics, enabling personalized medicine and improving health outcomes. In the finance sector, analytics tools are critical for risk assessment, fraud detection, and customer segmentation [3].

Published by Springer Nature Switzerland AG 2024
R. van de Wetering et al. (Eds.): I3E 2024, LNCS 14907, pp. 129–141, 2024.
https://doi.org/10.1007/978-3-031-72234-9_11

Cao [4] defines *data analytics* as the theories, technologies, tools and processes that enable an in-depth understanding and discovery of actionable insight into data. The growth of data analytics is underlined by the exponential increase in data volume, which is expected to grow to 163 zettabytes by 2025 [5]. Data analytics covers a wide range of fields. Data science is the set of statistical techniques and methods for the extraction, analysis, and interpretation of data [6]. Business Intelligence (BI) involves the collection, evaluation, analysis, and storage of data and the production and dissemination of intelligence [7]. Big data analytics is referred as the technologies that allow the exploitation of huge amounts of data to extract meaningful information, which is often of strategic importance to companies [8]. Deriving business value from their data initiatives is often challenging for organizations [9]. Critical success factors (CSFs) refer to areas that contribute to the success of organizational performance [6]. Despite the recognized importance of CSFs in ensuring the success of data analytics, there is a significant research gap in understanding these factors. There are numerous studies that have identified various CSFs across different fields of data analytics. Looking into a specific type of data analytics application can be a limiting factor to understand CSFs, since focusing on a narrow application may prevent the conception of the factors in the organizational level. Additionally, the success of different data analytics applications may be impacted by similar factors. Examining CSFs with a holistic view may help to reveal relevant CSFs for diverse data analytics fields. However, a resulting holistic CSF set may be difficult to use by organizations without any structure. Organizations should be able to recognize the CSFs relevant to their context and choose the ones they should focus from a CSF list. Categorizing CSFs can help in a better understanding of CSFs across different data analytics fields and can support organizations in choosing relevant ones. In this study, we aim to bridge this gap by conducting a systematic literature review (SLR) that analyzes CSFs across a broad spectrum of data analytics fields. The research will answer the following research questions:

RQ1: What are the CSFs in data analytics projects?

RQ2: How can CSFs in data analytics projects be structured hierarchically to help organizations focus on specific areas?

RQ3: How are CSFs distributed across different fields of data analytics (e.g., Artificial Intelligence (AI), Big Data, BI, and Data Science)?

Our objective is to provide a comprehensive hierarchically structured list of CSFs, which can guide organizations to plan and execute necessary actions in their use of different data analytics applications. The remainder of this paper is structured as follows. Section 2 provides the background and related work. Section 3 details the research design for the SLR. Section 4 presents the findings and discussion. Finally, Sect. 5 concludes the paper.

2 Background and Related Work

In the context of data analytics, CSFs are key elements that determine the success or failure of projects. *Data analytics* is a broad topic that involves extracting, processing, and analyzing data to derive valuable insights that can inform decision-making. It involves several related fields that are included in this study. Information systems are defined as the working systems dedicated to processing information for various reasons, encompassing the capture, transmission, storage, manipulation, and display of information. *Big data* includes the technologies to exploit huge amount of data to extract the information that is often strategical importance to organizations [8]. *BI* describes a set of concepts and methods based on data for improving organizations' business decision making [10]. *AI* is a term used to describe a distinct, sophisticated software system that mimics some of the functions of the human brain. It can involve anything from decision-making and voice detection to artistic labor [11]. *Data science* is an interdisciplinary field using fields such as statistics, computer science, and domain expertise. It uses scientific methods, processes, algorithms, and systems to extract knowledge and insights from structured and unstructured data.

There are various studies that identify CSFs to determine the effectiveness and success of projects within these fields. Table 1 of the online Appendix (link: https://aysolmaz.com/publications/CSFsinDA-i3e-OnlineAppendix.pdf) gives an overview of the existing SLRs of CSFs across various fields in data analytics.

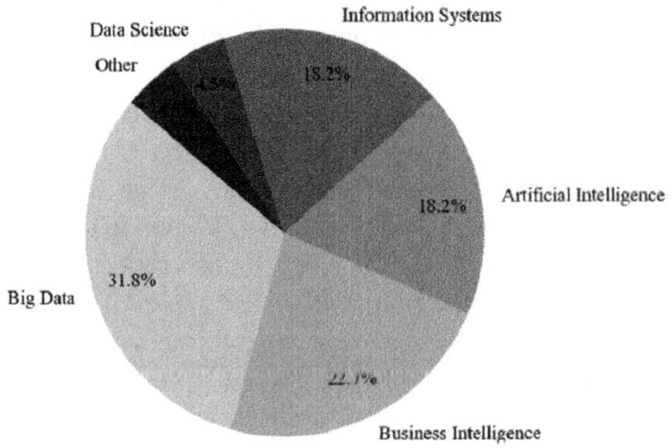

Fig. 1. Distribution of the focus areas in previous SLRs across various data analytics domains

Figure 1 depicts that the majority of SLRs are concentrated in the field of Big Data, accounting for 31.8% of the reviewed literature. This significant proportion underscores the complexity and importance of managing large datasets and extracting meaningful insights from them, which remains a critical challenge and opportunity for organizations. From the existing literature, *organizational culture and leadership*, *technological infrastructure*, *stakeholder engagement*, and *skills and expertise* emerge as recurrent themes important for the success of various data analytics fields.

Despite the extensive literature on specific data analytics fields, there is a notable gap regarding a structured list of CSFs covering multiple data analytics fields, which is the lack of a hierarchical perspective that spans multiple fields. This absence prevents the formation of a unified understanding of CSFs that could benefit a broader range of data analytics projects.

3 Research Design

This section outlines the research method employed to identify the list of CSFs. We performed the SLR following the guidelines of Kitchenham [12].

3.1 Planning the Review

We utilized the following three online databases for our search: *ACM Digital Library, Scopus,* and *Web of Science.* In addition, we applied the snowballing technique, which involved reviewing reference lists from relevant primary studies and articles [12]. Our search strategy includes both metadata and full-text search using a keyword set composed of two parts as follows: "(success factor* or achievement or failure) AND (data analy* or big data or business intelligence or machine learning or artificial intelligence)".

Performing the search over the indicated databases resulted in a set of 427 papers after duplicates are removed.

We defined a set of inclusion and exclusion criteria to determine if a paper is relevant for our research objective. For inclusion, the papers should present success or failure factors in projects of different fields of data analytics, share the practitioner/researcher experiences, and be written in English and accessible. After 2015, scholars introduced various conceptual tools to understand the emergence of big data and analytics, addressing the need for frameworks to interpret data efficiently. This resulted in an increased attention to identifying the success factors operating projects in the field [13]. Therefore, we covered the papers published after 2015. We excluded the secondary studies to eliminate the duplication of the findings. We first screened the papers based on title, keyword, and abstract, which resulted in a set of 108 papers. The screening based on full text resulted in 25 papers, extended with one paper through snowballing, which resulted in a final set of 26 papers.

3.2 Reporting the Review

The coding process for extracting CSFs from the reviewed papers was carried out following the guidelines of Krippendorff [14]. A thorough reading of each paper was conducted to list the success factors. For the instances where CSFs are not explicitly mentioned; relevant elements such as capabilities, focus areas, and key facilitators were extracted. These elements were reframed as success factors, based on the key areas that they represent to ensure project success, aligning with the definition of CSFs. If an extracted CSF was the duplicate of an existing one or suggested the same factor, it was placed with the existing one to enable identifying the first-order codes. Total of 214 CSFs are identified after this analysis. Following an inductive approach, employing the guidelines from Gioia et al. [15], these 214 CSFs are aggregated into 50 first-order concepts. We then sought for similarities and potential overlaps among the existing categories. This step helped us to gain a deeper understanding of the success factors and their relations. Overall, 14 s-order themes were abstracted to summarize these first-order codes. Lastly, a comprehensive set of six different data analytics CSFs were distilled. These aggregated dimensions, in conjunction with the second-order themes and first-order concepts, provide the conceptual depth needed to fully understand the CSFs in data analytics.

4 Results and Discussion

In this section, we provide an overview of the resources that we included in this SLR and present a synthesis of CSFs identified and structured by the six dimensions. Table 2 of the online Appendix (link: https://aysolmaz.com/publications/CSFsinDA-i3e-Online Appendix.pdf) presents the list of the reviewed papers. In our final resource pool, there are 26 peer reviewed papers.

The reviewed papers are distributed across several key data analytics fields. Figure 2 shows the overview of the papers. The study in the *Other* category does not directly relate to a specific field and addresses success factors for agile data analytics projects [16]. The methodological approaches across these papers demonstrate a diverse way in exploring success in different data analytics fields.

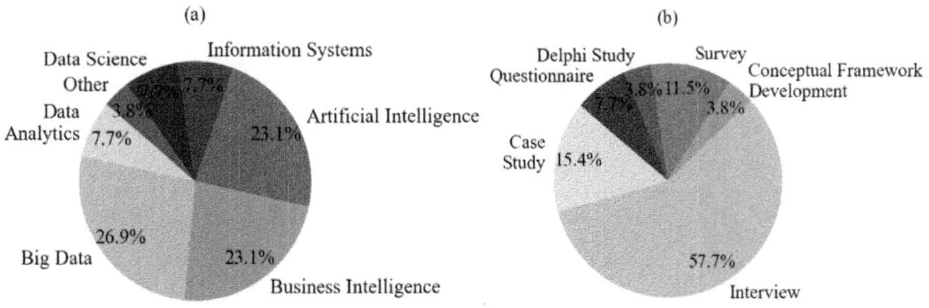

Fig. 2. Overview of the reviewed papers for (a) Field, (b) Research method distribution

4.1 Structured List of CSFs

Table 1 presents the results of our literature synthesis, which identified 50 CSFs categorized into 14 s-order themes and six aggregated dimensions.

Table 1. CSFs in Data Analytics

References	First-Order Concept	Second-Order Theme	Aggregated Dimension
[6, 7, 17–24]	IT infrastructure	Technology Infrastructure	Technology & Data
[7, 19, 25]	Analytical tools and hardware		
[19, 22, 26–30]	Supporting technology		

(continued)

Table 1. (*continued*)

References	First-Order Concept	Second-Order Theme	Aggregated Dimension
[17–19, 21, 27, 31]	System integration and compatibility		
[7, 17–20, 22, 29–34]	Data security and privacy	Comprehensive Data Governance	
[18, 20, 26, 27, 30, 35]	Data management		
[19, 31]	Data collection capabilities		
[6, 19, 26, 27]	Data integration and analysis		
[17, 18, 29, 30]	Ethics		
[7, 17–20, 23, 24, 26, 27, 36]	Data quality		
[20, 23, 24, 27, 30, 31, 36]	Data integrity		
[7, 17, 34]	Data quantity		
[19, 24, 26, 28]	Clear goals/objectives	Strategic Planning	Strategy
[7, 17, 19, 21, 24, 27, 34]	Business vision and strategy		
[21, 23, 24]	Strong business case		
[18, 20, 24, 29, 32, 34, 37]	Strategic alignment	Business Alignment	
[17–19, 24, 29]	Visible project benefits		
[7, 17, 19, 21, 24, 27]	Technical skillset	High Performance Teams	People
[6, 7, 19]	Analytical skillset		
[20, 25]	Domain knowledge		
[7, 24, 26, 34, 37, 38]	High-caliber team capability		
[19, 23, 24, 32]	Team balance composition		
[17, 21, 26, 38, 39]	Leadership		
[24, 29, 31, 38]	Employee training and education	Team Development and Empowerment	

(*continued*)

Table 1. (*continued*)

References	First-Order Concept	Second-Order Theme	Aggregated Dimension
[21]	Team empowerment		
[7, 21, 24–28, 32, 38]	User involvement	User and Stakeholder Involvement	
[7, 22, 28]	User acceptance		
[19, 20, 23, 26, 28, 35, 38]	User training		
[7, 32, 36]	Stakeholder engagement		
[21, 24, 28, 32]	Effective risk management	Risks and Change Management	Organizational Culture
[17, 20, 21, 29, 37]	Change management		
[6, 17]	Data friendly approach	Commitment	
[7, 17–21, 23–29, 31, 36]	Management support		
[20]	User motivation and commitment		
[38]	Effective relationships	Communication and Collaboration	
[6, 24, 36, 39]	IT and business integration		
[21, 25, 28, 32, 36, 38]	Proactive communication and feedback		
[21, 24, 29, 34, 37]	Financial resources	Resource Management	Process Design
[24, 28, 29]	Sufficient personnel		
[21, 29]	Testing	Operational Quality	
[21, 25, 38]	Documentation		
[26]	Well defined system requirement		
[19, 24, 25]	Clear and manageable project scope	Project Management	

(*continued*)

Table 1. (*continued*)

References	First-Order Concept	Second-Order Theme	Aggregated Dimension
[7, 28, 32]	Project scheduling		
[7, 21, 26, 27]	Effective project management		
[19, 21]	Realistic expectations for scope, schedule, and budget		
[7, 21, 28]	Project monitoring and feedback		
[38]	Well defined project roles		
[18, 29]	External pressure management	Navigating External Factors	External
[17, 18, 21, 31]	Effective vendor selection and support		

Technology & Data. This dimension contains critical technological and data-related components essential for the success of data analytics projects. IT infrastructure is one of the most frequently emerging success factors. Scalability and flexibility are two often occurring properties for a well-established IT infrastructure. System integration and compatibility suggests that the newly introduced data analytics systems and solutions should be compatible with the existing technical infrastructure.

The *Comprehensive Data Governance* theme encompasses the critical aspects of managing, securing, and ethically handling data within an organization. Data management is a crucial component within this theme, which refers to an organization's proficiency in effectively collecting, preparing, and providing data [35]. This encompasses the general processes, methods, and techniques essential for ensuring the successful implementation of all other factors within this theme. Other factors such as data collection capabilities and data integration and analysis are related to this factor; however, proposed as separate factors since data management is more of a high-level abstract code. Data security and privacy is another important factor. All stakeholders must feel confident that their data and information will not be lost, sold, or otherwise misused [17]. Furthermore, for the numerous unidentified data collected from the data marketplace or the internet, the reasonable acquisition and legality of the data need to be considered, and the data that are inconsistent or illegally obtained can be filtered [30].

Strategy. This dimension covers critical elements essential for guiding the long-term direction and success of an organization. *Strategic Planning* involves setting clear goals/objectives, developing a business vision and strategy, and building a strong business case for initiatives. *Business Alignment* ensures that the strategic initiatives of the organization are aligned with its overall business objectives. This alignment is crucial for optimizing resources and ensuring that all units work together towards common goals. Having *visible project benefits* increases the commitment to the project, especially from the top management whose support is vital for the project success.

People. Under the *High-Performance Teams* theme, having technically skilled and competent team members is essential. The ability of the team is needed to determine if the projects can be completed on-time, on-budget, with the right functions [27]. Team members' domain knowledge is also crucial, especially for knowledge intensive industries such as healthcare. Domain knowledge strengthens shared understanding between the members and allows members to correctly interpret the data within the context. Ensuring project success also requires strong leadership. There should be a "servant leader", who unlike a traditional leader does not focus on power or authority, but rather focuses on team members' well-being [21].

Team development and empowerment refers to creating a supportive and educative environment for the employees to grow. The organization should encourage team empowerment, i.e., being independent in scheduling the work, determining the procedures and methods to be used, selecting and deploying resources, assigning tasks to team members, and carrying out assigned duties [17].

User and Stakeholder Involvement in the early stages of project execution is crucial because it can identify the real needs of the user, so the system is developed based on consistent and appropriate needs [27]. Client acceptance or "technology acceptance" [22], which relates to perceived ease of use and usefulness of the technology, is also largely tied to achieving success.

Organizational Culture. This dimension highlights the pivotal role of the current organizational culture in how new technologies and processes are adopted and adapted.

Risks and Change Management entails identifying, assessing risk factors, and establishing risk response strategies to counter them [21]. Another factor that can be counted as a risk is the resistance to change by the employees. For example, AI systems introduce new processes, causing changes in organizational environments that can lead to confusion and inefficiency [17]. Organizations should continuously adapt the organization's structure, culture and management capabilities against the changes.

Commitment encapsulates the dedication and support from various stakeholders, ranging from the top management to the end-user. A data-friendly approach involves fostering an environment where data-driven decision-making is prioritized and supported across all levels [6]. Management support is one of the most frequently referenced CSFs and it is needed to authorize the project and provide necessary resources and authority to execute the project [7]. User motivation and commitment ensures that the analytics tools and processes are integrated into daily operations and decision-making [20].

Communication and Collaboration involves team members to adopt a cooperative approach to procedures and to develop effective working relationships. These elements contribute to a conflict-free environment, which is crucial for maintaining a productive and innovating environment [38]. If an organization utilizes its data analytics tools for decision making processes by the business units, it is highly advantageous to integrate the business users with the IT units. This integration of the business users with the IT units helps eliminate time consuming request-and-response scenarios, making business departments more self-reliant and speeding up the use of tools [39].

Process Design. *Resource Management* aims to ensure that the financial resources and assets are effectively used in alignment with the organizational strategy, goals and business directions. Proper allocation and management of resources directly influence the capacity to deliver on project goals, maintain timelines, and achieve desired otcomes.

Operational Quality encompasses the critical practices and capabilities required to ensure the quality and continuous improvement of data analytics projects and includes testing, documentation, and having well defined system requirements. Testing strategy can include integration testing to help finding problems in the interactions between the units, or automated testing to avoid manual testing that can be time consuming and error-prone [21].

Project Management is found to be a key factor and can mitigate the risks of data analytics. Effective project management is connected to all the other first-order concepts within Project Management yet stands as a distinct factor. It emphasizes the importance of adopting robust project management processes and methodologies to enhance project success. Having realistic expectations for scope, schedule, and budget emerges as another factor. Project teams must set clear, realistic boundaries for what can be achieved within the available scope and resources to avoid surprises and setbacks at later stages of the project.

External. This dimension addresses the influence of external pressures and the importance of strategic relationships with vendors. By effectively managing these, organizations can leverage external opportunities to enhance their competitive advantage.

One of the factors under the *Navigating External Factors* theme is for organizations to constantly monitor and respond to pressures from peers and competitors. This involves staying aware of industry trends, benchmarking against competitors, and adapting strategies to maintain or gain a competitive edge. Choosing the right vendors and establishing strong support systems is also crucial for the success of data analytics projects. Continuous collaboration with the vendors and supporting them enables organizations to profit more from external expertise, increasing the chance of success.

4.2 Distribution of CSFs Across Different Fields

Our third research question aimed to explore how CSFs are distributed across different fields of data analytics. The visual representation provided in the normalized distribution offers an understanding of these variations.

Figure 3 demonstrates the distribution of aggregated dimensions across the fields. To generate this figure, each paper is mapped to its respective data analytics field and themes. Then the occurrences of each theme within each field are counted and normalized. The normalized values were visualized using heatmap function of the Seaborn library in Python. *People* is particularly prominent in BI and Data Science, highlighting the importance of skilled personnel, team management and stakeholder engagement in these areas. Although AI requires specialized expertise, *People* have low dominance in

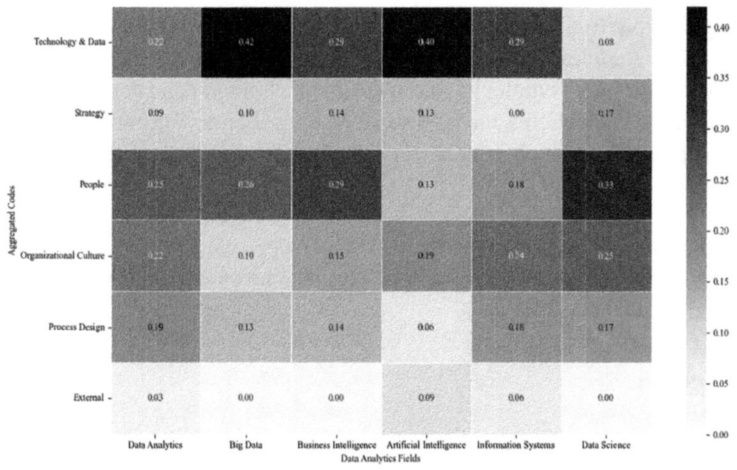

Fig. 3. Normalized distribution of aggregated dimensions across different fields

the field. *Process Design* also has relatively low dominance in AI. *Technology & Data* is highly emphasized in Big Data, BI, AI, and IS; underscoring the critical role of technological infrastructure and data management in these fields due to the vast amount of data used. *Organizational Culture* has higher emphasis in IS and Data Science, highlighting the importance of cultural factors and change management in these fields. The *External* theme shows relatively low references across all fields, with the highest being in AI and IS. The low emphasis given on external factors might indicate that internal capabilities and resources are considered more critical for success in data analytics projects.

In summary, the analysis of normalized distribution reveals that while there are common CSFs across all data analytics fields, the emphasis on specific areas varies. Understanding these nuances can help organizations better allocate resources, manage risks, and achieve their strategic objectives in the realm of data analytics.

5 Conclusion

This SLR has thoroughly examined the CSFs in data analytics projects, synthesizing findings across various data analytics fields BI, AI, Big Data, and Data Science. The study identifies and categorizes CSFs into six aggregated themes: *Strategy*, *People*, *Technology & Data*, *Organizational Culture*, *Process Design*, and *External Factors*. The analysis reveals that certain CSFs are important across all fields, while others vary in their significance depending on the specific field.

Overall, this study contributes to research by providing a comprehensive list of CSFs in data analytics in a structured way and giving an overview of how they are distributed in specific data analytics fields. The structured list can help organizations in planning, executing, and maintaining their data analytics initiatives by understanding and addressing these factors. As a limitation, the CSF list is not validated in practical settings, which should be addressed in future work. Additionally, the distribution of CSFs among fields is not equal, potentially leading to uneven representation of each field. While this comprehensive list covers diverse aspects of successful data analytics projects, it is not practically feasible to adopt the whole list of CSFs for a certain initiative. Future work should develop guidelines for organizations to prioritize these CSFs based on tailoring criteria such as project complexity, number of stakeholders, and organization size [40]. Furthermore, the use of CSFs can be investigated for identifying and improving the data analytics capabilities, which is necessary to obtain value from data analytics projects [9].

Acknowledgement. This research has partially been supported by the Council of Higher Education of Türkiye (YÖK) through Middle East Technical University, grant no: ADEP-704-2024-11481.

References

1. Akin-Adetoro, A., Seymour, L.: Analysing Research on Information Systems Success and Failure: A Machine Learning Technique. In: SAICSIT '19. New York, NY, USA: Association for Computing Machinery (2019)
2. George, G., Haas, M., Pentland, A.: Big Data and Management. Acad. Manage. J. **57**, 321–326 (2014)
3. West, J., Bhattacharya, M.: Intelligent financial fraud detection: A comprehensive review. Comput. Secur. **57**, 47–66 (2016)
4. Cao, L.: Data Science: A Comprehensive Overview. ACM Comput. Surv. **50** (2017)
5. Sargo, M.: By 2025, IDC predicts that the total amount of digital data created worldwide will rise to 163 zettabytes, ballooned by the growing number of devices and sensors.
6. Malacaria, S., De Mauro, A., Greco, M., Grimaldi, M.: An Application of the Analytic Hierarchy Process to the Evaluation of Companies' Data Maturity. ICEIS - Proceedings **1**, 50–61 (2022)
7. Miller, G.J.: Comparative Analysis of Big Data Analytics and BI Projects. In: Proceedings of the 2018 FedCSIS, pp. 701–705 (2018)
8. Soukaina, M., Anoun, H., Ridouani, M., Hassouni, L.: A study of the factors and methodologies to drive successfully a big data project. In: 3rd ICDS (2019)
9. Korsten, G., Aysolmaz, B., Ozkan, B., Turetken, O.: A Capability Maturity Model for Developing and Improving Advanced Data Analytics Capabilities, PAJAIS, preprint, (2024)
10. Xu, P., Kim, J.: Achieving dynamic capabilities with business intelligence. Proc. - Pac. Asia Conf. Inf. Syst. PACIS 2014, (2014)
11. Kunduru, A.R.: Effective Usage of Artificial Intelligence in Enterprise Resource Planning Applications. Int. J. Comput. Trends Technol. **71**(4), 73–80 (2023)
12. Kitchenham, A.: Procedures for Performing Systematic Reviews. Keele UK Keele Univ. **33**, (2004)
13. Bates, J.: Big data and data analytics. In: The Routledge Social Science Handbook of AI, pp. 281–294. [Online]. Available: https://www.taylorfrancis.com/chapters/edit/https://doi.org/10.4324/9780429198533-20/big-data-data-analytics-jo-bates
14. Krippendorff, K.: Content analysis: an introduction to its methodology, 2. ed., [Nachdr.]. Thousand Oaks, Calif, Sage Publ, 20
15. Gioia, D., Corley, K., Hamilton, A.: Seeking Qualitative Rigor in Inductive Research. Organ. Res. Methods **16**, 15–31 (2013)
16. Tsoy, M., Staples, D.S.: What Are the Critical Success Factors for Agile Analytics Projects? Inf. Syst. Manag. **38**(4), 324–341 (2020)
17. Merhi, M.I.: An evaluation of the critical success factors impacting artificial intelligence implementation. IJIM **69**, 102545 (2023)

18. Merhi, M.I., Harfouche, A.: Enablers of artificial intelligence adoption and implementation in production systems. Int. J. Prod. Res. pp. 1–15 (2023)
19. Papers, F., Gao, J., Koronios, A., Selle, S.: Towards A Process View on Critical Success Factors in Big Data Analytics Projects. AMCIS Proceedings (2015)
20. Daradkeh, M.: Critical Success Factors of Enterprise Data Analytics and Visualization Ecosystem: An Interview Study. Int. J. Inf. Technol. Proj. Manag. **10**(3), 34–55 (2019)
21. Radhakrishnan, A., Davis, J.S., David, D.: Examining the Critical Success Factors in IT Projects: A Two-Panel Delphi Study. Int. J. Inf. Technol. Proj. Manag. **13**, (2022)
22. Merhi, M.I., Bregu, K.: Effective and efficient usage of big data analytics in public sector. Transform. Gov. People Process Policy **14**(4), 605–622 (2020)
23. Yeoh, W., Koronios, A.: Critical success factors for business intelligence systems. J. Comput. Inf. Syst. **50**, (2010)
24. Garcia, J.M.V., Pinzon, B.H.D.: Key success factors to business intelligence solution implementation. J. Inteligence Stud. Bus. **7**(1), 48–69 (2017)
25. Batra, D.: Adapting Agile Practices for Data Warehousing, Business Intelligence, and Analytics. J. Database Manag. **28**(4), 1–23 (2017)
26. Halim, S., Mubarokah, I., Hidayanto, A.N.: Rank Critical Success Factors (CSFs) of Data Warehouse and Business Intelligence (DW/BI) Implementation in Banking Sector Using Analytical Hierarchy Process (AHP). ICIMCIS, pp. 313–318. (2020)
27. Sianipar, K.C., Wicaksana, S., Parikenan, B., Hidayanto, A.N.: Business Intelligence Critical Success Factors Evaluation Using Analytical Hierarchy Process. In: 5th ICCED (2019)
28. Lind, M., Culler, E.: Information Technology Project Performance: The Impact of Critical Success Factors, pp. 14–25. IJITPM, USA (2011)
29. Dora, M., Kumar, A., Mangla, S.K., Pant, A., Kamal, M.M.: Critical success factors influencing artificial intelligence adoption in food supply chains. Int. J. Prod. Res. **60**(14), 4621–4640 (2022)
30. Chen, T.-Y., Chang, H.-F.: Critical success factors and architecture of innovation services models in data industry. Expert Syst. Appl. **213** (2023)
31. Chen, X., Chen, R., Yang, C.: Research to key success factors of intelligent logistics based on IoT technology. J. Supercomput. **78**(3), (2022)
32. Martinez, I., Viles, E., Olaizola, I.G.: A survey study of success factors in data science projects. In: 2021 IEEE Big Data, pp. 2313–2318
33. Al-Besher, A., Kumar, K.: Use of artificial intelligence to enhance e-government services. Measurement: Sensors. **24**. (2022)
34. Berg, V., Birkeland, J., Pappas, I., Jaccheri, L.: The Role of Data Analytics in Startup Companies: Exploring Challenges and Barriers. LNTCS, **11195**, (2018)
35. Weber, M., Engert, M., Schaffer, N., et al.: Organizational Capabilities for AI Implementation—Coping with Inscrutability and Data Dependency in AI. Inf. Syst. Front. **25**, 1549–1569 (2023)
36. Wang, Y., Skeete, J.P., Owusu, G.: Understanding the implications of artificial intelligence on field service operations: a case study of BT. PROD PLAN CONTROL **33**(16), 1591–1607 (2021)
37. Gökalp, M.O., Kayabay, K., Gökalp, E., Koçyiğit, A., Eren, P.E.: Assessment of process capabilities in transition to a data-driven organisation: A multidisciplinary approach. IET Softw. **15**(6), 376–390 (2021)
38. Pereira, G.: and. In: Schweiger, G. (ed.) Poverty, Inequality and the Critical Theory of Recognition. PP, vol. 3, pp. 83–106. Springer, Cham (2020). https://doi.org/10.1007/978-3-030-45795-2_4
39. Lennerholt, A., van Laere, J., Söderström, E. : Success factors for managing the SSBI challenges of the AQUIRE framework. J. Decis. Syst. (2022)
40. Kalus, G., Kuhrmann, M.: Criteria for software process tailoring: a systematic review. In: Proceedings of the 2013 ICSSP (2013)

Critical Success Factors for Designing and Implementing Network-Based Business Models

Demi Deshayes[1], Montijn van de Ven[1], Banu Aysolmaz[1](✉), Oktay Turetken[1], and Steije Renes[2]

[1] Eindhoven University of Technology, Eindhoven, the Netherlands
{d.i.m.deshayes,m.r.v.d.ven,b.e.aysolmaz,o.turetken}@tue.nl
[2] The Next Organization, Bussum, the Netherlands
srenes@tnxto.com

Abstract. Today's dynamic business environment requires organizations to transition from pipeline to network-based business models. Such business models involve diverse stakeholders, such as suppliers, customers, and partners, collaborating to co-create value as a network. Designing and implementing a network-based business model is challenging. While existing literature offers methods and tools, a gap remains in providing guidance for this transition. Critical success factors (CSFs) have proven effective in helping organizations identify actions necessary to succeed in key areas. This study aims to develop a catalog of CSFs related to network-based business models, providing guidance by categorizing and offering detailed descriptions of these factors. Following a design science approach, we developed an initial version of the catalog through a systematic literature review and revised and evaluated it through a focus group study and interviews. Our study contributes to research by providing a catalog of CSFs related to network-based business models, synthesized from a broad literature and empirically evaluated.

Keywords: network-based business model · critical success factor · value network

1 Introduction

To remain competitive in today's business environments, organizations need to transition from traditional pipeline models to network organizations with a multi-sided orientation, reflecting the network economy trend [1]. This orientation requires an organization to form reciprocal collaborations among various stakeholders, such as suppliers, customers, and partners, to co-create value as a network. Operating in a network has proven more efficient, sustainable, profitable, and scalable compared to traditional siloed organizations [2, 3]. Traditional organizations typically create and capture value within the company by manufacturing goods using resources from suppliers and then selling these goods to customers, i.e., a pipeline business model [1]. In contrast, value co-creation

Published by Springer Nature Switzerland AG 2024
R. van de Wetering et al. (Eds.): I3E 2024, LNCS 14907, pp. 142–155, 2024.
https://doi.org/10.1007/978-3-031-72234-9_12

in a network involves multiple actors interacting to create value [4–6]. Examples of successful network organizations include Airbnb, Uber, Google, Facebook, and Apple, which co-create value with others, leading to a higher competitive advantage compared to the siloed value creation of traditional organizations [7]. To enhance competitiveness and increase business survival, traditional organizations can benefit from the network economy trend by re-evaluating their business model management activities [2, 4, 8, 9]. Business model management typically consists of several lifecycle phases, including design, implementation, operation, adaption, and control [10, 11].

Despite its benefits, the network economy trend also introduces challenges for organizations, especially in the design and implementation phases of business models [8]. While existing literature has focused mainly on the design of network-based business models [6, 12–15], there is a need for new methods and tools that address both design and the implementation of these models [11, 16]. These methods or tools should extend the business model concept to a network view, guiding traditional organizations in designing and implementing network-based business models [9, 17]. Although researchers have developed value-adding tools or methods to address this need (e.g., [6, 12, 14, 15]), they often do not sufficiently consider value co-creation and are frequently targeted at specific industries, limiting their broader applicability across various sectors.

A commonly used tool for supporting the design and implementation phases of business models and strategic management is the use of critical success factors (CSFs) [18]. CSFs are key areas that require specific accomplishments to achieve organizational success [18, 19]. Researchers have identified specific CSFs for platform-based business models [2, 20], eMarketplaces [21], and mobile business models [22]. Most research has focused on specific types of network-based business models and design issues [2, 4, 20–25]. However, little research has been performed on general success and failure factors for the design and implementation phases of network-based business models [25]. To address this research gap, this study investigates CSFs to help traditional organizations during the design and implementation phases of network-based business models. We aim to synthesize the identified CSFs into an artifact [26] that offers detailed guidelines for traditional organizations during the business model transition. Accordingly, our research objective is *to develop a catalog of CSFs related to network-based business models, categorized based on network-based business model elements.* To fulfill this objective, we followed the Design Science Research (DSR) paradigm [27] and performed a systematic literature review (SLR) [28] to develop an initial version of the catalog, which we refined and evaluated through semi-structured interviews with practitioners. Our study goes beyond existing research by providing a CSF catalog specifically for network-based business models and empirically evaluating it to ensure its practical relevance and applicability across various industries.

The remainder of the paper is structured as follows. In Sect. 2, we provide the background and related work. Section 3 outlines our research design following the DSR approach. Section 4 presents the CSF catalog we developed. Section 5 discusses the results of our evaluation activities. Finally, Sect. 6 concludes the study by discussing the results, suggesting future research possibilities, and outlining limitations.

2 Background and Related Work

The literature highlights the need for more research on how network organizations achieve success [4]. To attain this success, organizations must understand the concepts of network-based business models [8] and value co-creation [23]. Researchers have recently developed business model tools and methods focusing on a network perspective [6, 29]. For instance, Lund and Nielsen created a five-phase tool to help organizations transform their current business model into a network-based business model, which they applied to a Danish drone start-up [25]. Best et al. [4] investigated antecedents for social-purpose organizations that operate according to a network-based business model. Gilsing et al. [23] developed an evaluation process linked to the Service-Dominant Business Model radar (SDBM/R), providing guidelines for developing and designing an SDBM/R to obtain a valid business model and achieve organizational survival.

Several business model templates have been developed with varying degrees of network orientation [29]. The Service Business Model Canvas (SBMC) consists of separate canvases for each actor in the network but does not consider relationships among them [15]. Service Logic Business Model Canvas (SLBMC) extends the business model canvas [14] but is insufficient for a network setting [23]. The Service-Technology-Organization-Finance (STOF) model defines a business model across four aspects [13] but lacks a focus on value co-creation [15]. Finally, the e3value ontology focuses on the economic feasibility of a business model [12] but focuses less on other aspects of network-based business models, such as co-creation processes and activities.

In this paper, we focus on SDBM/R because it is the only framework that considers value co-creation among actors, including customers, making it most applicable to value networks [24]. The SDBM/R centralizes value co-creation within a network, emphasizing the value-in-use concept enabled through co-creation among different network actors [6]. Other key elements of the SDBM/R include actor value propositions, co-creating activities, and individual cost-benefit models [6, 30]. These elements will be foundational in our development of the catalog of CSFs.

CSFs, also referred to as key success factors, are defined as "the limited number of areas in which results, if they are satisfactory, will ensure successful competitive performance for the organization" [18]. These are the key areas where 'things must go right' for the business to flourish. If results in these areas are inadequate, the organization's efforts will be less effective [18]. CSFs help organizations achieve their goals and objectives, leading to organizational success or competitive advantage. They are also helpful for guiding explicit tasks, facilitating communication among managers, and assisting in risk management [19, 31]. Following the definition of CSFs, they must be linked to "key areas" [18]. For this study, these key areas are network-based business model elements, particularly those from the SDBM/R framework. Potential additional elements are added as necessary during the catalog development process. As such, we aim to link CSFs to network-based business model elements.

Previous research has identified specific CSFs for platform-based business models [2, 20], eMarketplaces [21], and mobile business models [22]. Studies on platform-based business models, a specific type of network-based business model requiring a digital platform, include six CSFs identified for digital platform design [2], 24 success and failure factors related to digital platform design [20], and CSFs identified for eMarketplace business models [21]. These studies focus on CSFs for the design of specific types of network-based business models but do not generally address the design and implementation of network-based business models. Moreover, they either do not take the business model as the unit of analysis or do not consider its implementation. Thus, it is challenging to use them to design and implement a network-based business model in a general way. Nevertheless, they provide valuable input for understanding CSFs in this domain from diverse perspectives.

Existing literature indicates the need for a comprehensive overview of general CSFs for network-based business models [2] [8]. By identifying CSFs from a general perspective, traditional organizations may have a higher chance of designing successful network-based business models, understanding the concept of value networks, and making informed- design decisions [8, 23]. Ultimately, these CSFs will support organizations in achieving feasible and promising network-based business models.

3 Research Design

To develop the catalog of CSFs for network-based business models, we adopted a DSR approach [27], following the methodological steps outlined by [32]. Step 1 comprised *problem identification and motivation*, introduced in Sects. 1 and 2. Step 2 consisted of the *definition of requirements*. In step 3, we developed *the initial version of the artifact* through an SLR. Step 4 focuses on the *demonstration and evaluation of the artifact* in two rounds. The following sections detail steps 2–4 and present the final artifact.

3.1 Definition of Solution Requirements

To guide the development of the artifact, we formulated three requirements. The SDBM/R framework provides a template for network-based business model design that considers various actors in the network and centralizes the value-in-use concept [6, 23]. As this aligns with our research objective, using its elements is relevant for classifying the CSFs. Accordingly, our first requirement is:

R1: *The CSF catalog should take the elements of a network-based business model (i.e., SDBM/R elements) as the basis for the classification of CSFs.*

A CSF refers to an action and contributes to a key area of an organization. CSFs should be described clearly and in detail so organizations can plan their actions accordingly. Thus, the second requirement is:

R2: *A CSF should include a clear description to guide organizations during the design and implementation of a network-based business model.*

Some business model elements require individual actions, while others centralize around co-creation [6, 23]. The CSFs are expected to refer to either an individual firm-level activity needed for the value network to succeed or to a collaborative activity performed mutually. The individual and collaborative activities should be clarified by distinguishing between network and firm levels. Therefore, the third requirement is:

R3: *A CSF should be categorized at either the network- or firm-level to specify collaborative or individual actions.*

3.2 Development of the Artifact

We performed an SLR following established guidelines [28]. We first developed the search procedure. The following search string was used as the search term to cover the concepts of network-based business models and indications of success factors: *((“network*” OR “collaborat*” OR “ecosystem*” OR “platform*”) W/2 “business model*”) AND (“success*” OR “advantage*” OR “benefit*”)*. This search term was applied in Scopus and Web of Science (WoS) libraries. The search produced 813 papers (as of 16 March 2023), which were reduced to 533 papers after removing duplicates. We screened the resulting papers in two rounds based on the following inclusion criteria: papers should be written in English, published as peer-reviewed articles, include the concept of a network-based business model in line with the definition as recognized in this research, and propose, discuss, or apply success or failure factors, in any form or synonym, related to designing and implementing network-based business models. We excluded papers that mentioned the concept of a network-based business model but did not include it as a focus or integral part of the research. We also excluded papers that did not follow an empirical research method. First, we screened the papers based on title, abstract, and keywords, which resulted in 86 papers. Finally, we performed a full-text scan, which resulted in 21 papers.

The final set of 21 papers was coded for CSFs following the guidelines for content analysis in two iterative steps [33]. Each identified CSF in a paper was assigned a CSF code, which refers to the topic of a CSF (the complete list is available in Table 1 of the online appendix at https://shorturl.at/E41I5). The second iteration categorized the identified CSF codes following a deductive approach based on the elements of the SDBM/R framework. New categories were created for CSFs that did not fit the predefined categories. Four additional elements were added to the SDBM/R dimensions: “value exchange”, “channels”, “resources”, and “key activities”. “Actor” and “co-created value in use’ were modified to “actor role” and “actor relationship”, respectively. Each category was identified as either network- or firm-level. Each identified and categorized CSF was placed in the catalog along with a description, contribution, and references.

The final set of papers provided input for our objective in diverse ways. In terms of the ***explicit definition of CSFs***, some studies explicitly define and investigate CSFs, while others relate to CSFs through indirect indications of success. Our study captures insights from the second group since they mention elements that drive the network toward its success through topics such as business model benefits, innovations, success, and advantages [8, 34–40]. Regarding the focus on the ***type of network-based business model***, the literature shows a clear focus on identifying success factors for platforms, platform owners, and platform-based business models [2, 35, 41]. Although a platform business model differs from a network-based business model, all eight papers addressing platforms acknowledge the power of value co-creation within a value network of actors and users. They come together via an online platform to co-create value for the whole network [41–43]. Thus, CSFs related to platform business models can be generalized for network business models, as both feature value co-creation [4, 44].

3.3 Demonstration and Evaluation

The catalog was demonstrated and evaluated in two phases involving a total of eight participants, all selected based on their high-level management roles and experience in strategy, marketing, and business model innovation. Participants included managers, concept developers, and consultants from various organizations such as insurance, mobility, and the non-governmental sector. In the first evaluation round, we conducted a focus group study with five participants. The focus group aimed at assessing the initial version of the catalog derived from the SLR for its fidelity to the real world, its robustness, and completeness [26] and to refine the catalog by integrating CSFs from practitioners. The participants engaged in an exercise where they designed a network-based business model for their organization, using the CSFs included in the catalog.

The second evaluation round aimed to confirm the redesigned catalog and evaluate its usefulness, ease of use, and intention to use it according to the Technology Acceptance Model (TAM) [45]. This round consisted of four semi-structured interviews with practitioners from different organizations to ensure a broad range of perspectives. Notably, one participant from the first round was included again to provide continuity.

During the interviews, participants reviewed two example business model cases that we developed to illustrate the application of the catalog and its CSFs. We gathered the participants' feedback on the catalog's utility and its relevance to their work. The interviews were transcribed, and content analysis [33] was employed to structure the feedback, focusing on the participants' experiences, expertise, and best practices related to the catalog's objectives.

4 Catalog of CSFs for Network-Based Business Models

In this section, we present the final version of the catalog, which categorizes CSFs based on the level, i.e., network (Table 1) or firm (Table 2), and their associated business model elements. Each CSF is accompanied by a detailed description, its contribution to success (provided in Table 2 of the online appendix at https://shorturl.at/E41I5), and the corresponding references.

Table 1. Catalog of CSFs for Network-based Business Models (network-level)

BM element	CSF	CSF description	Refs
Network value proposition	Clear value proposition	Formulate a clear description of the network value proposition including quantitative and qualitative objectives (i.e., value creation, value exchange, and value adjustments) on network-level	[36, 46–48]

(*continued*)

Table 1. (*continued*)

BM element	CSF	CSF description	Refs
	Formulation of value-in-use	Formulate the financial and non-financial value expected to be delivered (i.e., services, knowledge, sustainability, products) to the users and how to create awareness of the value	practice
	Analysis of uncovered customer needs	Perform analysis of uncovered customer needs including the final use stage of the value proposition, in collaboration with other actors, and related opportunities with a broader customer-related issues approach	[2, 34, 36]
	Value proposition innovation	Specify new (network) value propositions with product features, or services that customers do not even think about by considering substantial changes in the supply chain (i.e., working in a network with technology actors and service providers in the same market segment)	[34]
	Minimum viable value and target group	Implement a minimum viable value (i.e., product/ service) first with the core functionalities and focus on strategically influential target customer group first, extend customer group later on	[2, 43]
	Business model with lifecycle	Incorporate the service/ product life cycle into the business model	[47]
	Analysis of value impact	Predict the positive and potential negative values generated by the network value proposition (inside-out approach) and analyze the potential opportunities and risks caused by the network value proposition (outside-in approach)	practice
Actor co-production activity	Network governance plan	Create a network governance; control (confidential) information and resources of all actors (intellectual property), and guidelines for communication (within and outside of the network), and procedures for potential (financial) conflicts	[37] practice
	Metrics on performance	Continuously measure the performance levels, value exchange and financial returns by identifying and monitoring KPI's	[41, 47, 49]

(*continued*)

Table 1. *(continued)*

BM element	CSF	CSF description	Refs
	Collective action	Take collective action by using the competences and skills of individuals within the network to realize network value proposition and make actions more efficient	[34, 39, 47, 50]
	Planning of value creation	Plan the value creation thoroughly by designing the network value proposition and value creation (activities) with a top-down and bottom-up approach	[40]
Actor relationship	Trust and understanding	Create trust between actors; regularly update all actors, keep contact personal, transparent, open and professional with all actors, respect different point of views and focus on embeddedness (share problems during actor interactions, fine-grain information sharing, and open about financial gains) to reach solution that satisfies everyone's purposes, and perform peer-to-peer leadership by facilitating horizontal communication and creating an informal work culture	[36, 39, 47, 51]
	Flexible organizational boundaries	Stick with an actor that fits well in the network and enable flexible organization boundaries by a broad adoption of network actors	[38, 47]
	Analysis of environment	Be aware of occurrences of the market and environment of the network and individual organization	[47]
Actor role	Clear presentation of actors	Represent and agree on all network actors and their roles in the business model	[32]
	Cooperation with knowledge institutions	Cooperate with knowledge institutions to obtain external competences and knowledge of customers and markets	[8]
	Analysis of trends and competition	Investigate and understand business strategies/ products/ services of similar organizations, performed as network	[47]
	Integral customer chain	Consider whole chain of customers – from end-users to producers	[8, 36]
	Determination of strategy	Ensure that every actor will determine their own strategy and role in the network	[50]
	Equal driving forces	Ensure equal driving forces for each of the actor to join the network	[39]

Table 2. Catalog of CSFs for Network-based Business Models (firm-level)

BM element	CSF	CSF description	Refs
Actor value proposition	Shared business objectives	Have overlapping business objectives between the actors' and the network objectives	[36, 47]
	Network and user alignment	Align network business model objectives with user/ customer objectives	[53]
Key activity	Cross-silo communication	Let managers of different departments (silos) within the organization interact together for value delivery	[36, 47]
	Training staff	Train employees and managers for a network mindset and improve their skills such as trust, emotional intelligence, communication and cooperation	[43, 51]
	Digital trends	Implement digital customer interaction, such as real-time feedback and customer buying behavior	[35]
	Data handling	Collect, store and analyze customer data correctly (according to regulations)	[35]
Actor costs / benefits	Analysis of risk and investment	Clarify financial risk, challenges, investment cost allocation, and potential benefits upfront of a mutual collaborative agreement	[39, 47]
	Financial and non-financially profitable project	Ensure that every network project is financially profitable for all actors by monitoring the financials	[39, 46]
	Individual actor gains	Ensure individual gains for all network actors	[36, 38, 39, 52]
	Clarification of actors' needs and required resources	Clarify the needs of each actor by identifying and communicating the desired gains and maximum viable costs	[39]
	Revenue strategy	Determine revenue strategy based on contribution of resources by actors in the network	[48]
	Completeness of benefits	Encompass all forms of economic, efficiency, knowledge, societal, social and legitimacy benefits/ revenue for every actor	[42, 52]
	Benefits exceeding costs	Let the overall benefits surpass the costs of realizing the value proposition and ensure a customer value higher than its costs	[2]
	Ethical mutual benefit	Formulate clear and transparent ethical mutual benefit to clearly describe each actor's gains and how benefits are shared	[38]

(*continued*)

Table 2. (*continued*)

BM element	CSF	CSF description	Refs
Channels	Clear vision communication	Communicate a clear and common network vision with creative entrepreneurs as leaders	[47]
	Full information disclosure	Establish channels to collect full information about the revenue generated and create mechanisms for ensuring that the actors achieve their return expectations	[34]
Resources	Distinctive competences	Gather distinctive competences by using and managing inimitable, unique, non-substitutable, valuable and rare intangible and tangible resources	[38, 41, 48]
	Shared resources	Share risks and resources (knowledge, financials, and tangibles), learn collectively, and use economies of scale	[37]
	Employee treatment	Treat employees as operant resources by invoking their strengths and expertise	[38]
	Communication team	Put together a team within the organization that is responsible for collaborating and communicating with the other network actors	From practice
	Transformational leadership	Perform transformational leadership to stimulate and inspire intellectually and to support on individual level	[47]

5 Evaluation

Based on the feedback from the first round of evaluation, the focus group study, the initial version of the catalog was revised. Overall, we removed one of the 43 CSFs, merged two CSFs, added one new CSF, altered six existing CSFs, and removed one business model element. In the second round, no further changes to the catalog were suggested. All interviewees found the catalog useful but not easy to use, as it was perceived to be too extensive to implement at once. Thus, we elaborated on a selection method for identifying a subset of high-priority CSFs. Several criteria emerged that can be used to rank the CSFs, including strategic alignment, feasibility, network maturity, competitive advantage, effort and resource requirements (both human and financial), value, timeframe, people, planet, profit, and sustainability. Participants found the catalog specifically useful for creating a fruitful discussion environment for the business model. As one participant stated: *"I think it is valuable because it makes people think, 'Why are we actually doing this?' And it encourages looking at shared values together"*. All interviews mention that they plan to use the catalog, as indicated by a consultant participant: "*We have a German parent company, and they tend to be quite thorough and meticulous, so I think this would be a valuable tool for them*".

6 Discussion and Conclusion

In this study, we developed a catalog of CSFs for the design and implementation of network-based business models, providing structural guidance for organizations aiming to transform their business models. Following a DSR approach, we designed an initial version through an SLR and revised and evaluated it through two evaluation rounds with industry experts. Our study contributes to the literature by providing an empirically validated and structured CSF catalog, which synthesizes insights from a broad set of literature. This structured catalog addresses the gap in existing tools, which often lack empirical evaluation or are not tailored for network-based business models [11, 16]. The catalog's categorized CSFs and detailed descriptions provide practical guidance for organizations, aligning with previous recommendations for structured approaches in network-based business model transformations [9, 17]. The feedback from our evaluations highlighted the catalog's usefulness and relevance across different industries. The experts noted its potential to facilitate meaningful discussions and strategic alignment within organizations. To increase the catalog's ease of use, suggestions were provided to identify a subset of CSFs based on various criteria.

Our study is not without limitations, which offers future research directions. First, while the catalog supports both the design and implementation phases of network-based business models, most CSFs focus on the design phase. Only several CSFs support the implementation phase, though sometimes indirectly. For example, CSFs suggesting analysis activities of uncovered customer needs and the environment can guide the implementation. This indicates a need for further development to address the implementation phase in more detail. Related to this phase, research can also investigate the use of CSFs as a basis to define KPIs and monitor the business model performance, which is specifically important for network-based settings [54]. Moreover, the evaluation was conducted with experts from a limited number of industries. Although its use has been demonstrated, its extensive use across various business contexts is yet to be further explored. Future research can extend the catalog for specific business model types, such as sustainable and circular business models, which require diverse considerations for their success [55]. The catalog should be evaluated in a broader range of industries and business model types and in more detail through, for example, case studies. Such research could also explore methods for selecting a subset of CSFs based on organizational needs, improving the catalog's usefulness.

References

1. Van Alstyne, M., Parker, G., Chaoudary, S.: Pipelines, platforms, and the new rules of strategy. Harv. Bus. Rev. **94**, 56–62 (2016)
2. Rohn, D., Bican, P.M., Brem, A., Kraus, S., Clauss, T.: Digital platform-based business models – An exploration of critical success factors. J. Eng. Technol. Manage. **60**, 101625 (2021)
3. Jabłoński, M., Timmers, P., Sarkis, J.: Sustainability in business models in the network economy. Electron. Mark. **30**, 675–678 (2020)
4. Best, B., Miller, K., McAdam, R., Maalaoui, A.: Business model innovation within SPOs: exploring the antecedents and mechanisms facilitating multi-level value co-creation within a value-network. J. Bus. Res. **141**, 475–494 (2022)

5. Szopinski, D., Massa, L., John, T., Kundisch, D., Tucci, C.: Modeling business models: a cross-disciplinary analysis of business model modeling languages and directions for future research. CAIS **51**, 774–841 (2022)
6. Turetken, O., Grefen, P., Gilsing, R., Adali, O.E.: Service-dominant business model design for digital innovation in smart mobility. BISE **61**, 9–29 (2019)
7. Libert, B., Beck, M., Wind, J.: The Network Imperative: How to Survive and Grow in the Age of Digital Business Models. Harvard Business Review Press, Boston (2016)
8. Lindgren, P., Taran, Y., Boer, H.: From single firm to network-based business model innovation (2010)
9. Niemimaa, M., Järveläinen, J., Heikkilä, M., Heikkilä, J.: Business continuity of business models: evaluating the resilience of business models for contingencies. Int. J. Inf. Manage. **49**, 208–216 (2019)
10. Wirtz, B.W.: Business model management. Design–Instrumente–Erfolgsfaktoren von Geschäftsmodellen (2011)
11. Lara Machado, P., van de Ven, M., Aysolmaz, B., Athanasopoulou, A., Ozkan, B., Turetken, O.: Methods that bridge business models and business processes: a synthesis of the literature. Bus. Process. Manag. J. **29**, 48–74 (2023)
12. Akkermans, J.M., Gordijn, J.: Value-based requirements engineering: exploring innovative e-commerce ideas. Requir. Eng. **8**, 114–134 (2003)
13. Bouwman, H., Faber, E., Haaker, T., Kijl, B., De Reuver, M.: Conceptualizing the STOF model. In: Bouwman, H., De Vos, H., Haaker, T. (eds.) Mobile Service Innovation and Business Models, pp. 31–70. Springer, Berlin, Heidelberg (2008). https://doi.org/10.1007/978-3-540-79238-3_2
14. Ojasalo, K., Ojasalo, J.: Adapting business model thinking to service logic: an empirical study on developing a service design tool. The Nordic School (2015)
15. Zolnowski, A., Weiß, C., Böhmann, T.: Representing service business models with the service business model canvas - The case of a mobile payment service in the retail industry. In: HICSS, pp. 718–727. IEEE Computer Society (2014)
16. Palo, T., Tähtinen, J.: Networked business model development for emerging technology-based services. Ind. Mark. Manag. **42**, 773–782 (2013)
17. Dyer, J.H., Singh, H., Hesterly, W.S.: The relational view revisited: a dynamic perspective on value creation and value capture. Strateg. Manage. J. **39**, 3140–3162 (2018)
18. Rockart, J.F.: Chief executives define their own data needs (1979)
19. Caralli, R.A., Stevens, J.F., Willke, B.J., Wilson, W.R.: The Critical Success Factor Method: Establishing a Foundation for Enterprise Security Management. SEI (2004)
20. Özcan, L., Koldewey, C., Duparc, E., Van Der Valk, H.: Why do Digital Platforms succeed or fail? - A Literature Review on Success and Failure Factors (2022)
21. Balocco, R., Perego, A., Perotti, S.: B2b eMarketplaces: a classification framework to analyse business models and critical success factors. Ind. Manage. Data Syst. **110**, 1117–1137 (2010)
22. de Reuver, M., Haaker, T.: Designing viable business models for context-aware mobile services. Telematics Inform. **26**, 240–248 (2009)
23. Gilsing, R., et al.: Evaluating the design of service-dominant business models: a qualitative method. PAJAIS **13**, 36–70 (2021)
24. Gilsing, R., et al.: Defining business model key performance indicators using intentional linguistic summaries. Softw. Syst. Model. **20**, 965–996 (2021)
25. Lund, M., Nielsen, C.: The Evolution of Network-based Business Models Illustrated Through the Case Study of an Entrepreneurship Project (2014)

26. Sonnenberg, C., vom Brocke, J.: evaluations in the science of the artificial – reconsidering the build-evaluate pattern in design science research. In: Peffers, K., Rothenberger, M., Kuechler, B. (eds.) Design Science Research in Information Systems. Advances in Theory and Practice. DESRIST 2012. Lecture Notes in Computer Science, vol. 7286, pp. 381–397. Springer, Berlin, Heidelberg (2012). https://doi.org/10.1007/978-3-642-29863-9_28
27. Gregor, S., Hevner, A.R.: Positioning and presenting design science research for maximum impact. MIS Q. 337–355 (2013)
28. Kitchenham, B., Charters, S.: Guidelines for performing systematic literature reviews in software engineering. Technical report, ver. 2.3 (2007)
29. Szopinski, D., Massa, L., John, T., Kundisch, D., Tucci, C.: Modeling business models: a cross-disciplinary analysis of business model modeling languages and directions for future research. Commun. Assoc. Inf. Syst. **51**(1), 774–841 (2022)
30. Grefen, P., Turetken, O., Traganos, K., Hollander, A.D., Eshuis, R.: Creating agility in traffic management by collaborative service-dominant business engineering. IFIP Adv. Inf. Commun. Technol. **463**, 100–109 (2015)
31. Barat, J.: Scenario playing for critical success factor analysis (1992)
32. Peffers, K., Tuunanen, T., Rothenberger, M.A., Chatterjee, S.: A design science research methodology for information systems research. JMIS **24**, 45–77 (2007)
33. Krippendorff, K.: Content Analysis: An Introduction to Its Methodology. SAGE Publications, Inc (2004)
34. Arana, J., Castellano, E.: The Role of Collaborative Networks in Business Model Innovation (2010)
35. Tohanean, D., Zainea, L., Stoian, C.A., Baba, A., Buzatu, A.I.: Entrepreneurial challenges: innovating business models for a multi sided platform approach. In: New Challenges of Economic and Business Development, pp. 475–486 (2020)
36. Radziwon, A., Bogers, M., Bilberg, A.: Creating and capturing value in a regional innovation ecosystem: a study of how manufacturing SMEs develop collaborative solutions. IJTM **75**, 73–96 (2017)
37. Rojas, E., Azevedo, A.: Pillars and elements to develop an open business model for innovation networks. In: Camarinha-Matos, L.M., Afsarmanesh, H. (eds.) Collaborative Systems for Smart Networked Environments. PRO-VE 2014. IFIP Advances in Information and Communication Technology, vol. 434. Springer, Berlin, Heidelberg (2014). https://doi.org/10.1007/978-3-662-44745-1_31
38. Lüftenegger, E., Grefen, P., Weisleder, C.: The service dominant strategy canvas: towards networked business models. In: Camarinha-Matos, L.M., Xu, L., Afsarmanesh, H. (eds.) Collaborative Networks in the Internet of Services. PRO-VE 2012. IFIP Advances in Information and Communication Technology, vol. 380. Springer, Berlin, Heidelberg (2012). https://doi.org/10.1007/978-3-642-32775-9_21
39. Päivärinne, S., Hjelm, O., Gustafsson, S.: Excess heat supply collaborations within the district heating sector: drivers and barriers. J. Renew. Energy. **7** (2015)
40. Schneider, M., Mittag, T., Gausemeier, J.: Value creation design: modeling of value networks. JSIS **12**, 111–125 (2016)
41. Bivona, E., Cosenz, F.: Designing a multi-sided platform business model assessment framework: a dynamic performance management perspective. Syst. Res. Behav. Sci. **38**, 93–107 (2021)
42. Kim, J.: The platform business model and business ecosystem: quality management and revenue structures*. Eur. Plan. Stud. **24**, 2113–2132 (2016)
43. Daxhammer, K., Luckert, M., Doerr, M., Bauernhansl, T.: Development of a strategic business model framework for multi-sided platforms to ensure sustainable innovation in small and medium-sized enterprises. In: Procedia Manufacturing, pp. 1354–1362. Elsevier B.V (2019)

44. Hänninen, M., Smedlund, A., Mitronen, L.: Digitalization in retailing: multi-sided platforms as drivers of industry transformation. BJM **13**, 152–168 (2018)
45. Davis, F.D.: User acceptance of information systems: the technology acceptance model (TAM). University of Michigan (1987)
46. Allegretti, S., Seidenstricker, S., Kasseckert, A.: Economic growth through business model innovation and technological entrepreneurship. In: Proceedings of PICMET '18: Technology Management for Interconnected World (2018)
47. Madsen, H.L.: Business model innovation and the global ecosystem for sustainable development. J. Clean Prod. **247** (2020)
48. Steininger, D.M., Wunderlich, P., Pohl, F.: Exploring Competitive Advantage of Social Networking Sites: A Business Model Perspective Crowdfunding Decision-Making View project Digital Entrepreneurship and Business Models View project (2013)
49. Heikkilä, M., Bouwman, H., Heikkilä, J., Solaimani, S., Janssen, W.: Business model metrics: an open repository. ISeB **14**, 337–366 (2016)
50. Wecht, C.H., Demuth, M., Koppenhagen, F.: Platform-based business ecosystems - a framework for description and analysis. In: Camarinha-Matos, L.M., Boucher, X., Afsarmanesh, H. (eds.) Smart and Sustainable Collaborative Networks 4.0. PRO-VE 2021. IFIP Advances in Information and Communication Technology, vol. 629. Springer, Cham (2021). https://doi.org/10.1007/978-3-030-85969-5_8
51. Soliman, M., Stacchezzini, R.: In a dynamic environment business model innovation and networks: a case study research. Presented at the (2015)
52. Steinhauser, S.: Network-based business models, the institutional environment, and the diffusion of digital innovations: case studies of telemedicine networks in germany. Schmalenbach Bus. Rev. **71**, 343–383 (2019)
53. Van der Borgh, M., Cloodt, M., Romme, A.G.L.: Value creation by knowledge-based ecosystems: evidence from a field study. R D Manage. **42**, 150–169 (2012)
54. van de Ven, M., Lara Machado, P., Athanasopoulou, A., Aysolmaz, B., Turetken, O.: Key performance indicators for business models: a systematic review and catalog. ISeB **21**(3), 753–794 (2023)
55. Tonnaer, L., Aysolmaz, B., Turetken, O.: Elements of Blockchain-based circular business models in manufacturing: a synthesis of the literature. In: New Business Models Conference Proceedings 2023. Maastricht University Press, Maastricht, Netherlands (2023)

A Novel End-User-Oriented Perspective for Mobile Service Artefacts: Conceptualizing Usage Patterns

Gaurav Dixit[1,2](✉)

[1] Department of Management Studies, Indian Institute of Technology Roorkee, Roorkee, India
gaurav.dixit@ms.iitr.ac.in

[2] Mehta Family School of Data Science and Artificial Intelligence, Indian Institute of Technology Roorkee, Roorkee, India

Abstract. Mobile apps have become the norm in affluent and non-affluent societies across the developed and developing worlds. Consumers' desire for the latest feature-rich mobile services pushes e-commerce and Internet firms to constantly improve their mobile app artefacts. Accordingly, in this research, we study how end-user orientations affect the usage patterns of mobile services related to different service categories and how these usage patterns affect end-user cognitive engagement. We conceptualized a novel end-user-oriented research model to understand these usage patterns with support from extant literature and self-determination theory. Our research examined informative content, entertainment, location-based, and transaction-based mobile service categories. We adapted existing scales in the survey, collected data from smartphone users, and conducted SEM to test hypotheses. Our novel findings suggest that the end-user-oriented variable, defined as personal innovativeness in mobile artefacts, is crucial in determining usage patterns for all types of mobile services. Also, consumption of different mobile service categories shows different end-user cognitive engagement effects. Our study offers significant theoretical contributions and practical implications for e-commerce and Internet firms.

Keywords: Mobile Services · Mobile Apps · Usage Patterns · Cognitive Engagement · Self-determination Theory

1 Introduction

The COVID-19 pandemic forced a new normal on people, and the digital mode became the preferred way of doing things [24]. Recent studies [11] have described that we are in an "app age" where mobile services dominate almost every aspect of daily life. E-commerce and Internet firms look to constantly improve their mobile services to enable individual consumers to achieve their goals more efficiently and, thus, become a favoured mobile service [21]. These firms can benefit from a better understanding of individual consumers' usage patterns of mobile services, especially from an end-user-oriented perspective in the mobility context. They can further finetune their existing mobile services or design and develop new disruptive mobile services.

Published by Springer Nature Switzerland AG 2024
R. van de Wetering et al. (Eds.): I3E 2024, LNCS 14907, pp. 156–170, 2024.
https://doi.org/10.1007/978-3-031-72234-9_13

Mobile services differ from other services offered via traditional IT artefacts due to their temporal and spatial advantages, enabling anytime, anywhere forms of ubiquitous computing [36]. Mobile computing has solved the mobility expectations of end-users, facilitating work and non-work computing needs by obliterating the boundaries of locations and timings. The mobility phenomenon has caused usage patterns of mobile services to significantly differ from those of services based on traditional IT artefacts [26]. Further, value offerings to end-users might vary between different mobile service types. For example, mobile services for online news and e-books will have more work-related value. At the same time, mobile services for online music will have more entertainment value. Mobile artefacts have also influenced individuals' ways of engaging in personal and work-related activities in their daily lives by creating more intermittent usage patterns [25]. However, there is a lack of clarity on the usage patterns of these services and their effects on end-users in the mobility context. This research fills this crucial gap by studying how end-user orientations affect the usage patterns of mobile services related to different service categories and how these usage patterns affect end-user cognitive engagement.

Here, it is crucial to clarify that various traditional technology acceptance theories help explore adoption and use intention toward a specific IT artefact in isolation [7] and might not be suitable for ubiquitous mobile artefacts and mobility contexts. Successful adoption and initial use of IT artefacts do not always lead to the desired levels of IT use expected by the practitioners in the post-adoption phase [13]. Generally, IT users are not the same and are likely to differ in their dispositions, knowledge, and skills. Therefore, even if users interact with the same IT artefact, their perception, engagement, and usage will likely vary. However, there is a piecemeal approach and a lack of research on the end-user-oriented perspective on IT artefacts' post-adoption use and engagement. Due to the differing usage patterns, the end-user-oriented perspective is desirable for mobile artefacts and mobility contexts. This research draws support from the self-determination theory to develop its conceptual and research models.

2 Theoretical Background

2.1 Mobile Services

This research is contextualized to mobile artefacts, specifically commercial mobile app-based services. Mobile artefacts are more suitable for studying the end-user-oriented perspective due to their differences from traditional IT artefacts [26]. First, mobile artefacts enable a predominantly boundaryless and individualized mobility context with a much higher end-user orientation than the traditional IT artefacts constrained within their organizational or business context. Second, unlike mandatory environments of traditional IT artefacts, mobile artefacts enable a voluntary and self-organized environment for human-computer interactions. Third, individual end-users self-determine their usage patterns and interactions with mobile artefacts. Mobile device features such as mobility, portability, and unrestricted Internet and network connection reinforce these differences [36].

Mobiles have advanced into multi-capability devices from their initial start as portable telephone devices [17]. Standard smart functions now include computing, storage, and connectivity abilities like PCs and laptops; image and video capture functions like digital cameras; fingerprint and face detection like biometric devices; scan function for QR codes; sensors such as accelerometer, gyroscope, compass, ambient light, and proximity; torch function. These and many other capabilities have helped smartphones multiply their primary market, create new markets, and envelope a few other markets partially or fully [8]. Smartphone capabilities have also enabled users to consume different mobile services. Consequently, Internet and e-commerce firms have expanded their businesses by offering various mobile services.

Mobile end-users typically engage with the following four commercial mobile service categories offered by e-commerce and Internet firms: informative content, entertainment, location-based, and transaction-based mobile services [22].

1) Informative content services include news feeds, e-books and online articles, social media, and other online informative items.
2) Transaction-based services involve financial exchanges for online booking of taxies, movie tickets, travel, event tickets, digital payments and transfers, online banking and trading, online shopping, food delivery and home delivery.
3) Location-based services include standalone online services like maps and weather forecasts.
4) Entertainment services include online playing, streaming, or downloading content such as movies, TV series, Web series, music, games, sports, and other entertaining items.

2.2 Conceptual Model for Mobile Artefacts in the Mobility Context

End-users' interactions and learning behaviours might determine and explain the variation in the usage patterns of different categories of mobile services. End-users' interactions and learning behaviours with mobile artefacts might vary from user to user and are likely to manifest through their basic inclinations to think, feel, and act in particular ways [29]. Barki et al. [5] suggest that users' interactions with IT artefacts can change over time and can be affected by variations in users' behavioural experience levels. Over time, users are more likely to enhance their interaction mechanism and ways of working with an IT artefact [30]. This is because users learn more about the IT artefact and improve their behavioural experiences related to IT [1]. New version updates of IT artefacts provide more opportunities to do so.

In the case of mobile artefacts, the factors influencing users to enhance their interactions with mobile services and increase their usage of mobile services can be new experiences and their innovativeness with mobile artefacts [3, 33]. End-users might exchange information with other users to find new ways of interacting with mobile artefacts. Further, end-users also exhibit self-directed learning behaviours when interacting with new technologies.

Self-determination theory [32] explains individuals' self-determined motivation to act and its sources and role in cognitive and social development and individual differences. The autonomy needs of individuals are fulfilled by access and use of mobile services anywhere, anytime in the mobility context. In the case of playing movies and music on mobile devices, features like resuming a video or audio from the same point can further fulfil this need. Similarly, the competency needs of individuals are fulfilled by a familiar interface of mobile services. In the case of mobile games, it might be better fulfilled by a feedback-driven and intuitive control design of mobile services. Individuals' needs for relatedness are fulfilled by personal customization of mobile artefacts. For example, users can configure their hometown location on weather-related mobile services to receive timely updates.

According to self-determination theory, end-users can feel the desire to interact effectively with IT artefacts to achieve a sense of competence and produce desirable outcomes [39]. Thus, we can assume that users will try to learn from their interactions with mobile artefacts and enhance themselves. We study this end-user orientation as personal innovativeness in mobile artefacts. We suggest that the increased usage of mobile artefacts results from end-user orientations captured by personal innovativeness in mobile artefacts.

Increased usage of mobile artefacts is likely to show individual-level outcomes, such as influences on the mental states of end-users. Fan et al. [9] suggest that firms entice end-users by developing new strategic features to sustain or boost their mobile services' usage levels and achieve higher user engagement levels to avoid losing potential customers. End-users could enhance their engagement with mobile services by refining their interactions related to mobile artefacts.

2.3 End-User-Orientations to Mobile Artifacts: Personal Innovativeness

Prior studies on personal innovativeness are primarily about traditional IT artefacts (e.g., ERP systems) in mandatory contexts and focus on adoption. For example, Hwang [18] examined the impact of personal innovativeness in IT on the adoption variables, such as perceptions of systems' usefulness, ease of use, and enjoyment. However, these studies inform us about the personal innovativeness of end-users. Beaudry and Pinsonneault [6] suggest that as users learn and become more knowledgeable about IT artefacts, they self-modify their interaction with IT. Therefore, users who can accumulate rich experiences with diverse IT artefacts will likely show less hesitation in trying new ones. Agarwal and Prasad [2] described this behaviour of users as personal innovativeness in a traditional IT artefact and mandatory use context. Here, we adapt it in the case of mobility context and define the willingness of the end-user to experiment with new or unexplored mobile artefacts and their latest versions, features, and other aspects in the mobility use context as the personal innovativeness in mobile artefacts.

Users with higher personal innovativeness will likely spend more time with mobile artefacts as they might experiment with new changes introduced in the latest versions. Such users could be looking for new and innovative experiences, thereby displaying their risk orientations by disregarding the action outcomes [34]. These users tend to exhibit inherent desires to know and pursue new stimulating experiences [34]. Venkatesh et al. [35] argued that personally innovative users are fueled by their desire to try and experience the novelty of IT artefacts irrespective of the outcomes. Likewise, Xu and Gupta [38] suggested that highly innovative users exhibit positive attitudes toward novel IT artefacts. Similarly, Jia [20] suggested that there could be a linkage between personal innovativeness and IT use, finally leading to problematic or ill effects on users. Therefore, we argue that the personal innovativeness in mobile artefacts might influence the actual usage of each category of mobile services.

End-users who are more innovative with mobile artefacts will likely be able to search, explore, and consume higher levels of relevant and meaningful informative content using mobile services.

Thus, we hypothesize that:

H1a. Personal innovativeness in mobile artefacts is positively related to the usage levels of informative content mobile services.

End-users who are more innovative with mobile artefacts will likely be able to find, review, and consume higher levels of entertaining content fitting to their taste using mobile services.

Thus, we hypothesize that:

H1b. Personal innovativeness in mobile artefacts is positively related to the usage levels of entertainment mobile services.

End-users who are more innovative with mobile artefacts will likely be able to configure, pre-plan, and utilize relevant and accurate location-based mobile services with higher frequency.

Thus, we hypothesize that:

H1c. Personal innovativeness in mobile artefacts is positively related to the usage levels of location-based mobile services.

End-users who are more innovative with mobile artefacts will likely be able to safely and confidently navigate digital payment systems with higher frequency to perform their financial transactions for various items using mobile services.

Thus, we hypothesize that:

H1d. Personal innovativeness in mobile artefacts is positively related to the usage levels of transaction-based services.

2.4 End-User-Orientations to Mobile Artifacts: Cognitive Engagement

Understanding individual-level outcomes, such as user engagement at cognitive levels, would be more beneficial for e-commerce and Internet firms. This might be because online activities using mobile artefacts that help achieve higher levels of cognitive engagement can motivate end-users to spend more time and engage in more frequent interactions. In the mobility context, we define cognitive engagement as an active relationship of the end-user towards a mobile artefact, exhibiting cognitive and affective commitment toward it [9].

Informative Content Services. While processing the informative content downloaded from mobile services, users' involvement is expected to be active, continuous, and iterative. For example, users engaging with informative content such as reading online news, digging into reality from social media trends, and reading sports commentary will need processing at slightly higher cognitive levels than the other three categories of mobile services [16, 19]. Some activity scenarios like online reading of novels and stories, listening to experts, watching tutorials, and learning from textbooks might require a more profound cognitive engagement from the users.

In other words, online activities associated with informative content, including searching for desired information, sending or receiving emails, browsing news, blogs, and social media, require users to interact more with their mobile artefacts. Users might eventually become more specific in the content activities, narrowing their focus to a limited set of items. Any individual at a time engages in many online activities, such as star-marking important emails on their email account and viewing or reading a breaking news story recommended by news alert websites, i.e., Google News and Yahoo News. Users also tend to follow interesting, current trends, as suggested by Twitter. This type of online activity depicts users' cognitive engagement during online interactions with IT artefacts. Frequent interactions between users and mobile artefacts for content can be due to pleasurable and sensory experiences. All this can enhance their relevant cognitive abilities, thereby improving the user's mental state of cognitive engagement. Therefore, mobile services usage for informative content will likely affect user engagement at cognitive levels.

Thus, we hypothesize that:

H2a. Mobile services usage for informative content positively relates to the cognitive engagement of end-users in the mobility context.

Entertainment Services. Users' involvement with online entertainment downloaded from mobile services is typically about fulfilling emotional, pleasure, and relaxation needs. For example, users who watch movies and listen to music might do it for emotional or pleasure purposes. Mobile apps, such as YouTube, Netflix, Amazon's Prime Video, and Hotstar, offer entertainment services such as movies, TV series, and web series covering different genres and languages. YouTube has an extensive collection of user-uploaded videos as well. However, once a user selects a particular item for entertainment, it will lead to passive watching for minutes or hours [23]. Users watching sports and playing games might be doing these activities for pleasure or relaxation [31]. This kind of involvement is typically passive and might also be done to escape from demanding situations. Users are essentially engaging with entertainment services for pleasure and not to process. Therefore, mobile services usage for entertainment will likely not affect user engagement at cognitive levels.

Thus, we hypothesize that:

H2b. Mobile services usage for entertainment does not influence the cognitive engagement of end-users in the mobility context.

Transaction and Location-based Services. Before the prominence of mobile services, businesses primarily conducted digital transactions via electronic card products like debit and credit cards, while Internet banking facilitated electronic transfers [14]. Mobile services-driven digitization ensured the ubiquitous presence of digital payment systems and completely changed the digital transactions paradigm. Popular digital payment systems and wallets like Paytm, BHIM, PayPal, Google Pay, and Razor Pay exemplify this trend [14]. In addition to the above, people use mobile services to book tickets and purchase products from countless offerings by e-commerce firms like Amazon and Flipkart to avail of reasonable discount offers. Transaction-based mobile service providers, for example, Google Pay, Paytm, Amazon Pay, BHIM, and associated mobile apps, facilitate individuals to make transactions at restaurants or retail stores or other merchandise or transfer money to any individual [14]. It enables users to experiment and make better selections and explorations while trying new choices for a better experience.

Users who avail themselves of transaction-based and location-based mobile services want to execute their plans quickly to ensure their desired or needed services are fulfilled [10]. For example, users might book a taxi to reach a tourist destination as part of their travel plan or arrive at their home or office. Taxi booking by an individual on Ola or Uber-like apps processes location-based data for finding nearby taxis or autos, and the same apps can be used to share the location with others. Likewise, if users visit a new place or city, they might use maps to find local routes, i.e., apps such as Google Maps to explore routes, find places, analyze traffic, and identify new or shortest ways to reach their destination [15]. While driving, users might eventually experiment with different possible routes and learn from experiences from Google maps-aided navigation. Planning the trip to a place based on the typical traffic information, sharing the current location or live location with someone through WhatsApp, and sending the web link of the location of a meeting or event are a few examples.

Similarly, mobile services such as Just-dial, Zomato, and Swiggy also offer location-based services, which require exploring available choices via user interactions [40]. Users can also check the weather forecast for travel planning or visit [28]. Users include location-related information in their messages while posting on social media websites such as Facebook. This way of sharing by users on the Facebook page indicates their ability to try new social media features. As users find new ways to share their location-based features and do it more regularly, their hesitance decreases significantly. They also help users to keep an account of their travel history and share it on their timeline with friends and family, e.g., Facebook, travel information sharing, 'feeling happy in Manali' and at the same time, user's status may indicate their safety and about one's well-being in case of any disaster situations such as earthquakes and floods [12]. As users start using more new location-based features, they will find more ways to experiment with them. All these examples indicate that end-users utility-seeking behaviour is according to their relevant needs, and mobile services act as an instrument to achieve this. This utility-seeking behaviour may vary slightly from innovative users to regular users to new users. For example, innovative users might like to benefit from all relevant service features instrumental in maximizing utility, but others might be okay with the primary service features. Innovative users might get more interested than other users in extracting full benefits from mobile services. Due to this instrumental nature of involvement with IT artefacts during smartphone activities for transaction-based and location-based services, users do not need to engage with IT artefacts at cognitive levels in the context of mobile services.

Thus, we hypothesize that:

H2c. Mobile services usage for location-related tasks does not influence the cognitive engagement of end-users in the mobility context.

H2d. Mobile services usage for transaction-related tasks does not influence the cognitive engagement of end-users in the mobility context.

A conceptual model is shown in Fig. 1, which illustrates the hypotheses for our research's constructs and variables.

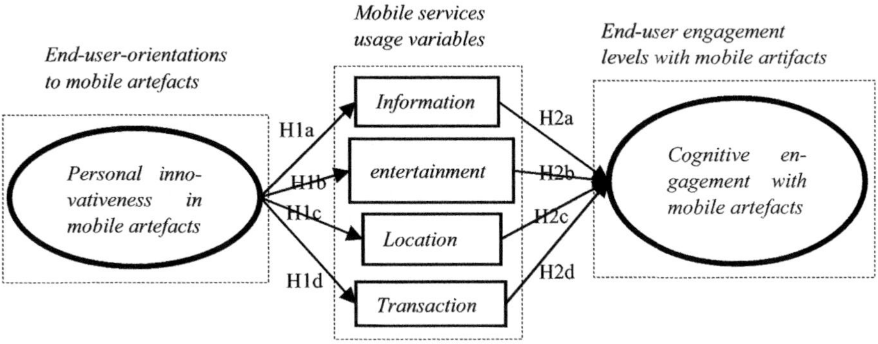

Fig. 1. Conceptual model

3 Method

We collected data for this study by following the purposive sampling technique since the research objective of the study required identifying smartphone users who had experience using different categories of mobile services at the time of the fieldwork. We conducted an in-person survey in the national capital region of India using the shopping mall intercept method. We obtained survey data from 422 respondents. Most respondents filled in the data using smartphones. We secured a total of 422 responses, out of which 351 were found to be complete and used for analysis.

Survey participants were nearly equally distributed among males (47.3%; n = 166) and females (52.7%; n = 185). Most of the participants were between 20 to 50 years old. Further, most participants had work experience between 1 to 20 years.

We measured six variables: usage of informative content services, usage of transaction-based services, usage of location-based services, usage of entertainment services, personal innovativeness in mobile artefacts, and cognitive engagement in the context of the mobile services. Usage for different categories of mobile services was assessed by asking respondents to report the frequency of their use of smartphones or other handheld devices for each category of mobile services. A 7-point Likert scale with '1' = "never" to '7' = "every time" was used. Four items were designed to report the frequency of usage of informative content services, online transaction-based services, location-based services, and entertainment services as observed variables. The items are shown in Table 1.

We adapted the established construct of personal innovativeness in IT developed by Agarwal and Prasad [2] for our four-item scale of personal innovativeness in mobile artefacts in the mobility context, as displayed in Table 2. Participants were asked to respond on a 7-point Likert scale with '1' = "strongly disagree" to '7' = "strongly agree."

Webster and Ho's [37] six-item scale was adapted for cognitive engagement in the mobility context, as displayed in Table 3. Participants were asked to respond on a 7-point Likert scale with '1' = "strongly disagree" to '7' = "strongly agree."

Table 1. Usage of mobile services.

Variable	Code	Item
Usage of informative content services	ICMS	"The extent to which I used mobile services for informative content"
Usage of transaction-based services	TAMS	"The extent to which I used mobile services for performing transactions online"
Usage of location-based services	LOMS	"The extent to which I used mobile services for location-based activities"
Usage of entertainment services	ENMS	"The extent to which I used mobile services for entertainment"

Table 2. Personal innovativeness in mobile artefacts (PIMA) in the mobility context.

Code	Item
PIMA1	"If I heard about a new technology feature in mobile devices or apps, I would look for ways to experiment with it."
PIMA2	"In general, I am hesitant to try out new technology features in mobile devices or apps."
PIMA3	"Among my peers, I am usually the first to try new technology features in mobile devices or apps."
PIMA4	"I like experimenting with new technology features in mobile devices or apps."

Table 3. Cognitive engagement (CE) in the context of the mobile services.

Code	Item
CE1	"technology interactions with mobile services keep me totally absorbed."
CE2	"technology interactions with mobile services hold my attention."
CE3	"technology interactions with mobile services excite my curiosity."
CE4	"technology interactions with mobile services arouse my imagination."
CE5	"technology interactions with mobile services are fun."
CE6	"technology interactions with mobile services are intrinsically interesting."

We included age, work experience, and gender as controls in our research model because recent studies have suggested accounting for their influences during technology interactions [27]. We measured the age and work experience of the respondents in the number of years. The gender of end-users was recorded as male or female.

4 Results and Analysis

We conducted a confirmatory factor analysis (CFA) using IBM SPSS Amos to test the measurement model. CFA assesses the measurement model's goodness-of-fit and its constructs' convergent and discriminant validities and reliability. Table 4 shows the main results of CFA. Model fit statistics of the CFA were found to be acceptable. The ratio of chi-square to the degree of freedom was smaller than 3. Bagozzi and Yi [4] recommended a set consisting of four fit indexes as satisfactory criteria for overall SEM model evaluation: RMSEA ≤ 0.07, TLI ≥ 0.92, CFI ≥ 0.93, and SRMR ≤ 0.07. Our CFA model results satisfied these limits, as shown in Table 4.

All the constructs' items were significantly loaded into their respective construct, with p-values being less than 0.001 in all instances, and we found no cross-loadings. The factor loadings of the constructs' items are higher than the minimum acceptable limit of 0.7, which indicates good item reliability. The constructs' composite reliability (CR) and the average variance extracted (AVE) were computed from the item loadings, as shown in Table 4. The CR values for all the constructs are higher than the minimum acceptable limit of 0.7, indicating good internal consistency or construct reliability. Constructs' measurement satisfied convergent validity since the AVE values for all the constructs are higher than the minimum acceptable limit of 0.5, indicating good convergent validity.

Table 4. Confirmatory factor analysis.

Factor	Item code	Loading	CR	AVE
CE	CEAF1	0.823	0.931	0.693
	CEAF2	0.866		
	CEC1	0.754		
	CEC2	0.829		
	CEII1	0.889		
	CEII2	0.829		
PIMA	PIMA1	0.784	0.861	0.607
	PIMA2	0.763		
	PIMA3	0.804		
	PIMA4	0.766		

Goodness-of-fit indices: $\chi^2_{413} = 1036.37(p - value < 0.001)$; CFI = 0.94; NFI = 0.90; NNFI = 0.93; Bollen Normed Index Rho1 = 0.89; Bollen Non-normed Index Delta2 = 0.94; RMR = 0.04; RMSEA = 0.06

Next, we computed inter-construct correlations and square roots of AVEs to examine discriminant validity. Table 5 shows inter-construct correlations in elements below the diagonal and square roots of AVEs in elements on the diagonal. All the elements with square roots of AVEs of the individual constructs have greater values than the shared variance between constructs (Inter-construct correlations) shown in the corresponding rows and columns.

Table 5. Inter-construct correlations and square roots of AVEs (diagonal elements).

	ICMS	TAMS	LOMS	ENMS	PIMA	CE
ICMS	NA					
TAMS	.071	NA				
LOMS	.156	.378	NA			
ENMS	.165	.233	.289	NA		
PIMA	.224	.391	.480	.346	.779	
CE	.152	.032	.104	-.021	.218	.833

We conducted a structural equation model analysis using IBM SPSS Amos to test the structural paths of the research model. Our model satisfied all four fit statistics limits [4]: PCMIN/DF value was 2.183 (< 3), RMSEA value was 0.058 (≤ 0.07), TLI value was 0.950 (≥ 0.92), CFI value was 0.962 (≥ 0.93), and SRMR value was 0.0694 (≤ 0.07). Next, we examine the model's structural path coefficients. The standardized path coefficients and p-value labels of structural paths are shown in Fig. 2. Next, we discuss the structural path and hypothesis results.

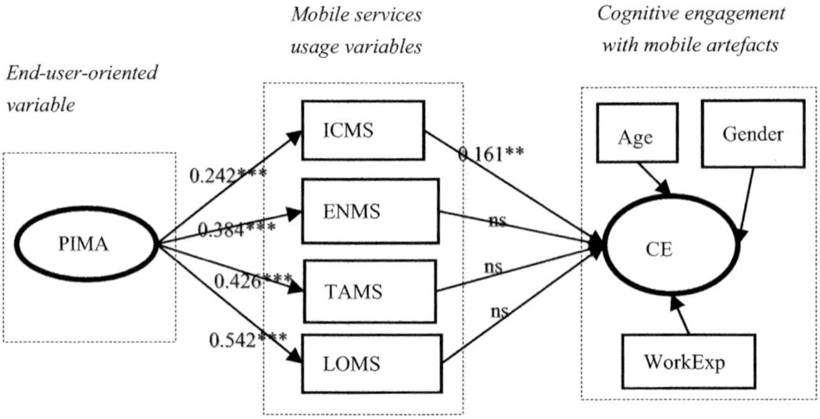

Fig. 2. SEM results of the model.

The effects of personal innovativeness in mobile artefacts on informative content, entertainment, location-based, and transaction-based mobile services were significant. Thus, H1a, H1b, H1c, and H1d were supported. The effect of informative content mobile services on cognitive engagement was significant. Thus, H2a is supported. The effects of entertainment, location-based, and transaction-based mobile services on cog-nitive engagement were found to be insignificant. Thus, H2b, H2c, and H2d are supported.

The results suggest that end-users personal innovativeness in mobile artefacts in the mobility context determines the usage levels for all four categories of mobile services. We also find that users with high usage levels for informative content mobile services show a positive effect on the cognitive engagement levels of end-users, while entertainment, location-based, and transaction-based mobile services show no significant influence.

5 Discussion

This study offers several significant findings for IS research. First, it establishes the importance of end-users personal innovativeness in mobile artefacts to decode their usage patterns. Second, end-users' cognitive engagement with mobile artefacts mostly matters when actively searching or soaking up information. In contrast, other categories of mobile services might not need significant engagement at the cognitive level.

This study makes contributions by filling research gaps in IS. While IT adoption and usage research has been conducted extensively in the pre-adoption phase, the post-adoption phase has also received some research attention. However, little research is available on IT use and engagement in the post-adoption phase, specifically in the context of voluntary individual use. Further, our study is set in the context of mobile technology, the most popular IT artefact in emerging economies. Therefore, our study adds to an important research context in IS.

Our study makes the following theoretical contributions to IS research. First, it is the first study in the mobility context which conceptualized a novel end-user-oriented research model to understand mobile service usage patterns with support from extant literature and self-determination theory. Second, we also examined the effects of these usage patterns on the end-user cognitive engagement related to mobile artefacts. Third, we contributed by creating a schema for the mobility context by listing examples of different mobile service categories, such as informative content, entertainment, location-based, and transaction-based. Finally, we adopted relevant constructs from prior literature to define personal innovativeness in mobile artefacts as part of our conceptualization of end-user orientations in the mobility context.

Our research has significant implications for practice in many ways. Our findings highlight the importance of online informative content services and their positive association with user engagement at cognitive levels. Therefore, the design for these mobile app-based services should focus on creating more engaging user experiences. Mobile app features that help users with cognitive processing could be more suitable. Our findings also provide an interesting implication for online entertainment, location-based, and transaction-based services. The usage of these services is higher for users with higher personal innovativeness. Therefore, the design for these mobile app-based services should focus on developing features to reduce this need and make these services easier to use.

6 Conclusion and Future Directions

Mobile app-based services are becoming more popular, and their user bases are growing. However, the usage patterns of mobile app-based services are poorly understood in IS research. Our study contributes to IS research by providing a conceptual model to explain the role of end-user-oriented variables in determining mobile artefacts' usage levels and engagement patterns.

Our study has the following limitations. First, the study surveyed mobile users from an emerging economy so the results can be validated in developed countries to generalize the conceptual model broadly. Second, we used the survey data to test the research model, which can be triangulated using click-stream and user-logs data for further validation. Our study also provides many interesting future directions. First, interaction effects between the end-user characteristic variables and contextual variables can be explored, which might lead to some exciting insights into end-user behaviour. Second, conceptual models presented in our study can also be examined with other similar IT artefacts to examine the generalizability of the results.

References

1. Agarwal, R.: Individual acceptance of information technologies. In: Zmud R.W. (ed.) Framing the Domains of IT Management, pp. 105–127. Pinnaflex, Cincinnati, OH (2000)
2. Agarwal, R., Prasad, J.: A conceptual and operational definition of personal innovativeness in the domain of information technology. Inf. Syst. Res. **9**, 204–215 (1998). https://doi.org/10.1287/isre.9.2.204
3. Bagayogo, F., Lapointe, L., Bassellier, G.: Enhanced use of IT: a new perspective on post-adoption. J. Assoc. Inf. Syst. **15** (2014). https://doi.org/10.17705/1jais.00367
4. Bagozzi, R.P., Yi, Y.: Specification, evaluation, and interpretation of structural equation models. J. Acad. Mark. Sci. **40**, 8–34 (2012). https://doi.org/10.1007/s11747-011-0278-x
5. Barki, H., Titah, R., Boffo, C.: Information system use-related activity: an expanded behavioral conceptualization of individual-level information system use. Inf. Syst. Res. **18**, 173–192 (2007). https://doi.org/10.1287/isre.1070.0122
6. Beaudry, A., Pinsonneault, A.: Understanding user responses to IT: a user adaptation coping acts model. MIS Q. **29**(3), 493–524 (2005)
7. Blechar, J., Constantiou, I.D., Damsgaard, J.: Exploring the influence of reference situations and reference pricing on mobile service user behaviour. Eur. J. Inf. Syst. **15**, 285–291 (2006). https://doi.org/10.1057/palgrave.ejis.3000618
8. Eisenmann, T., Parker, G., Van Alstyne, M.: Platform envelopment. Strateg. Manag. J. **32**, 1270–1285 (2011). https://doi.org/10.1002/smj.935
9. Fan, L., Liu, X., Wang, B., Wang, L.: Interactivity, engagement, and technology dependence: understanding users' technology utilisation behaviour. Behav. Inf. Technol. **36**, 113–124 (2017). https://doi.org/10.1080/0144929X.2016.1199051
10. Fang, J., Zhao, Z., Wen, C., Wang, R.: Design and performance attributes driving mobile travel application engagement. Int. J. Inf. Manage. **37**, 269–283 (2017). https://doi.org/10.1016/j.ijinfomgt.2017.03.003
11. Fang, Y.-H.: An app a day keeps a customer connected: explicating loyalty to brands and branded applications through the lens of affordance and service-dominant logic. Inf. Manage. **56**, 377–391 (2019). https://doi.org/10.1016/j.im.2018.07.011
12. Germann Molz, J., Paris, C.M.: The social affordances of flashpacking: exploring the mobility nexus of travel and communication. Mobilities **10**, 173–192 (2015). https://doi.org/10.1080/17450101.2013.848605
13. Goeke, R.J., Faley, R.H., Brandyberry, A.A., Dow, K.E.: How experience and expertise affect the use of a complex technology. Inf. Resour. Manage. J. **29**, 59–80 (2016). https://doi.org/10.4018/IRMJ.2016040104

14. Gupta, S., Dhingra, S., Tanwar, S., Aggarwal, R.: What explains the adoption of mobile wallets? a study from merchants' perspectives. Int. J. Hum. Comput. Interact. **39**, 3745–3757 (2023). https://doi.org/10.1080/10447318.2022.2104408
15. Han, D.I.D., Jung, T., Tom Dieck, M.C.: translating tourist requirements into mobile AR application engineering through QFD. Int. J. Hum. Comput. Interact. **35**, 1842–1858 (2019). https://doi.org/10.1080/10447318.2019.1574099
16. Han, K., Shih, P.C., Carroll, J.M.: Local news chatter: augmenting community news by aggregating hyperlocal microblog content in a tag cloud. Int. J. Hum. Comput. Interact. **30**, 1003–1014 (2014). https://doi.org/10.1080/10447318.2014.925773
17. Han, Q., Cho, D.: Characterizing the technological evolution of smartphones: insights from performance benchmarks. In: Proceedings of the 18th Annual International Conference on Electronic Commerce: e-Commerce in Smart connected World, pp. 1–8. Association for Computing Machinery, New York, NY, USA (2016)
18. Hwang, Y.: User experience and personal innovativeness: an empirical study on the enterprise resource planning systems. Comput. Hum. Behav. **34**, 227–234 (2014). https://doi.org/10.1016/j.chb.2014.02.002
19. Jeong, Y.J., Gweon, G.: Advantages of print reading over screen reading: a comparison of visual patterns, reading performance, and reading attitudes across paper, computers, and tablets. Int. J. Hum. Comput. Interact. **37**, 1674–1684 (2021). https://doi.org/10.1080/10447318.2021.1908668
20. Jia, R.: Problematic technology use: a negative outcome of computer playfulness and personal innovativeness?. In: Proceedings of JAIS theory development workshop, Sprouts: Working Papers on Information Systems, vol. 9, p. 45 (2009)
21. Lee, I., Kim, J., Kim, J.: Use contexts for the mobile internet: a longitudinal study monitoring actual use of mobile internet services. Int. J. Hum. Comput. Interact. **18**, 269–292 (2005). https://doi.org/10.1207/s15327590ijhc1803_2
22. Lee, S.: Mobile internet services from consumers' perspectives. Int. J. Hum. Comput. Interact. **25**, 390–413 (2009). https://doi.org/10.1080/10447310902865008
23. Lin, T.T.C.: Why do people watch multiscreen videos and use dual screening? investigating users' polychronicity, media multitasking motivation, and media repertoire. Int. J. Hum. Comput. Interact. **35**, 1672–1680 (2019). https://doi.org/10.1080/10447318.2018.1561813
24. Mansour, H.: How successful countries are in promoting digital transactions during COVID-19. J. Econ. Stud. **49**, 435–452 (2021). https://doi.org/10.1108/JES-10-2020-0489
25. Mazmanian, M., Orlikowski, W.J., Yates, J.: The autonomy paradox: the implications of mobile email devices for knowledge professionals. Organ. Sci. **24**, 1337–1357 (2013). https://doi.org/10.1287/orsc.1120.0806
26. Middleton, C., Scheepers, R., Tuunainen, V.K.: When mobile is the norm: researching mobile information systems and mobility as post-adoption phenomena. Eur. J. Inf. Syst. **23**, 503–512 (2014). https://doi.org/10.1057/ejis.2014.21
27. Mobarak, A.M.A., Dakrory, M.I., Elsotouhy, M.M., Ghonim, M.A., Khashan, M.A.: Drivers of mobile payment services adoption: a behavioral reasoning theory perspective. Int. J. Hum. Comput. Interact. **40**, 1518–1531 (2024). https://doi.org/10.1080/10447318.2022.2144122
28. Nimrod, G., Edan, Y.: Technology domestication in later life. Int. J. Hum. Comput. Interact. **38**, 339–350 (2022). https://doi.org/10.1080/10447318.2021.1938395
29. Ones, D.S.: Personality at work: raising awareness and correcting misconceptions. Hum. Perform. **18**, 389–404 (2005). https://doi.org/10.1207/s15327043hup1804_5
30. Orlikowski, W.J.: Using technology and constituting structures: a practice lens for studying technology in organizations. Organ. Sci. **11**, 404–428 (2000). https://doi.org/10.1287/orsc.11.4.404.14600

31. Periaiya, S., Nandukrishna, A.T.: What drives user stickiness and satisfaction in ott video streaming platforms? a mixed-method exploration. Int. J. Hum. Comput. Interact. **40**, 2326–2342 (2024). https://doi.org/10.1080/10447318.2022.2160224
32. Ryan, R.M., Deci, EL: Self-determination theory and the facilitation of intrinsic motivation, social development, and well-being. Am. Psychol. **55**, 68–78 (2000). https://doi.org/10.1037/0003-066X.55.1.68
33. Sun, H.: Understanding user revisions when using information system features: adaptive system use and triggers. MIS Q. 453–478 (2012)
34. Thatcher, J.B., Perrewe, P.L.: An empirical examination of individual traits as antecedents to computer anxiety and computer self-efficacy. MIS Q. **26**, 381–396 (2002)
35. Venkatesh, V., Sykes, T.A., Venkatraman, S.: Understanding e-Government portal use in rural India: role of demographic and personality characteristics. Inf. Syst. J. **24**, 249–269 (2014). https://doi.org/10.1111/isj.12008
36. Verkasalo, H.: Contextual patterns in mobile service usage. Pers. Ubiquit. Comput. **13**, 331–342 (2009). https://doi.org/10.1007/s00779-008-0197-0
37. Webster, J., Ho, H.: Audience engagement in multimedia presentations. ACM SIGMIS Database DATABASE Adv. Inf. Syst. **28**(2), 63–77 (1997)
38. Xu, H., Gupta, S.: The effects of privacy concerns and personal innovativeness on potential and experienced customers' adoption of location-based services. Electron. Markets. **19**, 137–149 (2009). https://doi.org/10.1007/s12525-009-0012-4
39. Zhang, L., Zhang, L., Jin, C., Tang, Z., Wu, J., Zhang, L.: Elderly-oriented improvement of mobile applications based on self-determination theory. Int. J. Hum. Comput. Interact. **40**, 1071–1086 (2024). https://doi.org/10.1080/10447318.2022.2131264
40. Zheng, Y., Wu, P.F.: Producing speed on demand: reconfiguration of space and time in food delivery platform work. Inf. Syst. J. **32**, 973–1004 (2022). https://doi.org/10.1111/isj.12377

Adopting Disruptive Technologies: The Aligning Role of Intermediary Organizations

Carlos Ferreira[1(✉)], Tom Bason[1], Mujahid Babu[1], Pythagoras Petratos[1], and Rocco Porreca[2]

[1] Coventry University, Coventry, UK
ab6859@coventry.ac.uk
[2] Oxford Brookes University, Oxford, UK

Abstract. This paper analyses the challenges in the adoption of blockchain-based technologies by looking at the role of intermediary organizations. It adopts a multi-stakeholder approach, conducting interviews with key stakeholders across the value chain of utility tokens, a potentially disruptive blockchain-based innovation. These include the developers of the tokens; sports organizations who have taken sponsorships from utility tokens, as intermediary organizations; and potential end-consumers, the fans of those sports organizations. The findings reveal persistent mismatches between the value offer of developers of the innovative technology and consumer expectations and the perceived utility value of tokens, which is compounded by organizational constraints and environmental factors. Limited organizational capacity within sellers significantly contributes to poor communication and the tokens' failure to meet consumer expectations. The study highlights the complex interplay of numerous factors influencing adoption intentions at both organizational and consumer levels, underlining the need for intermediary organizations to develop buy-in around a disruptive innovation. Successful intermediaries need to deploy the necessary organization and technological resources to understand and actively align other stakeholders' objectives and needs.

Keywords: Disruptive innovation · Technology adoption · Intermediary organizations

1 Introduction

This paper analyses the challenges in the adoption of blockchain-based technologies by looking at the role of intermediary organizations. Blockchain has been characterized as a disruptive technology due to its potential to revolutionize industries and promote novel business models [1, 2]. While there are multiple types of blockchain-based products available, this paper focuses specifically on blockchain-based utility tokens. Utility tokens are digital assets stored on a blockchain, that can enhance consumer communication and engagement [3, 4]. They are fungible, acting as digital coupons to provide users access to products or services within the blockchain platform [5]. Utility tokens are associated explicitly with consumer engagement activities. Recent research on such

Published by Springer Nature Switzerland AG 2024
R. van de Wetering et al. (Eds.): I3E 2024, LNCS 14907, pp. 171–180, 2024.
https://doi.org/10.1007/978-3-031-72234-9_14

blockchain-based tokens (hereafter referred to as 'tokens') highlights the potential for brand development [4], customization [6], innovation [7] and community development [8, 9]. Further, tokens can be sold as 'standalone brand components' [4], functioning as standalone products and used to engage previously unreachable or ignored demographics. However, Feloutzis and Lekakos' [10] recent systematic literature review concludes that examining blockchain from a disruptive theory perspective remains limited, necessitating further investigation of each blockchain-based solution to classify it as a disruptive innovation. This is especially important given the proliferation of use cases and business models built on blockchain technology. This paper addresses this gap.

While much of the research on the adoption of disruptive innovations has focused on the strategies of the organizations developing that innovation [1, 11–13] or the role of consumers as adopters [14–16], there can be other organizations involved in market dynamics of these innovations. Specifically, this research focuses on intermediary organizations [17], which are located in the value chain between the innovator upstream, and consumers downstream. These organizations serve a significant role in knowledge transfer among stakeholders in the innovation systems, helping align different groups' objectives [17, 18]. While most of the research involving intermediary organizations focuses on organizations involved withing the knowledge innovation ecosystem [18–20], the research presented in this paper looks specifically at intermediary organizations which are involved in the last crucial step in the adoption of a disruptive innovation by the end consumer.

For all their promise, utility tokens remain a comparatively under-researched blockchain derivative. Developers usually do not have a specific brand or community to develop, and must rely on partner organizations to engage end users. On the other hand, consumers may be reluctant to adopt these products, especially if they cannot immediately grasp their relevance and utility. Together, these two factors point to the need for intermediary organizations serving as conduits between utility token developers and promoters upstream, and potential buyers of utility token downstream. Through a case study of sports organizations' involvement in utility tokens, this paper analyses the challenges involved in aligning the objectives of token sellers and potential buyers, addressing the following research question: How can intermediary organizations align disruptive innovators and end users of that innovation?

The findings analyze how the actions of the intermediary organizations create misalignments and discontinuances between the needs of developers and users. These ultimate constitute a barrier to the adoption of disruptive innovations, to the frustration of both innovators and end users.

2 Literature Review

2.1 Disruptive Innovation

Disruptive innovation has become one of the key concepts in business strategy [21, 22]. Rather than following the traditional path-dependence development trajectory in a market, innovative technologies "disrupt an established trajectory of performance improvement, or redefine what performance means" [23]. In doing so, disruptive innovations upset the established competitive order by providing more-suitable functionality to market segments which have been overlooked by incumbents focused on more profitable customer groups [23].

While the focus of the analysis is often the strategy of disruptor firms, the external environment of the firm is also a fundamental aspect of the success of disruptive technologies, especially in terms of their acceptance and adoption [22]. Ben-Slimane and colleagues [11] note that disruptive technologies do not always have a clear path to market success in their analysis of how organizations can promote the legitimacy of a disruptive technology. Many of the strategies unveiled involved aligning their technology with existing social norms and values held by consumers. Similar findings are noted by Ferreira et al. [12] in a study of how companies disruptive business models can lead to a loss of legitimacy. They propose that organizations may have to manage how much disruption their innovations cause, to maintain social acceptance. Bunduchi and Candi [24] analyzed consumers' needs when judging products and compared these with companies' communication for the same products. They found that both individuals and their social norms impacted how a product was evaluated and its subsequent acceptance. Together, these studies show the critical role played by cognitive and normative aspects in the success of a disruptive innovation.

2.2 Organizational Adoption of Disruptive Technologies

The Technological-Organizational-Environmental (TOE) has been extensively used as a theoretical base into organizational adoption of a variety of disruptive technologies, including artificial intelligence [25], big data analytics [26, 27], supply chain efficiency [28] and blockchain-based service and NFTs [29]. In this framework, adoption and implementation of technological innovations are influenced by three factors – technology (T), organization (O), and environment (E) [30]. The technological context encompasses the attributes and accessibility of technological advancements, including equipment, processes, and associated internal and external technologies. The organizational context encapsulates firm size, structure, managerial hierarchy, human resources, employee capabilities, and intra-firm communication. Finally, the environmental context pertains to market and industry characteristics, macroeconomic conditions, and regulatory frameworks [29].

2.3 Consumer Adoption of Disruptive Innovations

Studies on consumer adoption of technology, including blockchain, have often utilized the Theory of Acceptance and Use of Technology (UTAUT) [31, 32]. UTAUT incorporates four constructs: Performance Expectancy (PE), Effort Expectancy (EE), Social Influence (SI) and Facilitating Conditions (FC) [31]. Given the adoption of the technology in the present study may be driven by its context (i.e., consumers are sold tokens by the sports clubs they support), UTAUT's consideration of the SI and FC makes it an appropriate model. UTAUT further includes four moderating factors (gender, age, voluntariness, and experience). However, in line with prior research, given the emerging nature of the technology and the limited sample size of consumers, we utilize the UTAUT model without including moderators [31, 33–35].

3 Research Overview

The research took place across two parallel phases. Phase One explores the adoption of utility tokens by sports organizations through 16 in-depth, semi-structured interviews with three stakeholder groups: sports organizations (n = 11), token developers (n = 2), and digital marketing agencies (n = 5); two of the interviewees has experience in more than one stakeholder group, hence the discrepancy between the total sample size and the sample size per group. A purposive sampling strategy was employed to identify and recruit participants through the researchers' professional networks, followed by snowball sampling to expand the dataset. All participants held senior management or managerial positions within the commercial or marketing departments. The semi-structured interview protocol focused in two broad areas: 1) the decision to adopt the technology and 2) the goals for deploying the technology and the extent to which this was achieved.

Study two analyzed how end users – actual and potential – of blockchain products understood the value of these products. Four online focus groups were conducted, each with seven or eight participants, (n = 31) recruited through a marketing research agency following the researchers' inclusion criteria. All participants identified as fans of an English Premier League football club, and could name at least one token-baked partner of a Premier League team. The first two focus groups included participants who had purchased or used blockchain-based products. Discussion in these user groups focused on the journey to adoption of token-based products, use cases, the perceived utility of the tokens, sources of information about products for the user and the role of football clubs in selling the products. The two non-user groups included only participants who had never purchased blockchain-based products. These non-user focus groups aimed to assess the influence of sports organizations in shaping understanding of utility tokens, whether the participants had ever considered buying such products, and the role of the football clubs in selling the products.

In both studies, data was recorded and transcribed verbatim. Data from both phases was analyzed using Framework Analysis [36]. Framework analysis offers a systematic method for identifying, describing, and interpreting key patterns across cases in study – such as individuals, organizations, institutions, or others – by employing a sequential series of five interconnected steps. The approach produces a series of developing themes, which are developed both inductively (from the data) and deductively (from the literature) [37].

4 Findings

4.1 Phase 1 – Organizations

As per the literature review, the organizational adoption of blockchain innovation was analyzed using the TOE model.

Technological Factors

Sports organizations understood the technology as a potential avenue for reaching new demographic segments and to facilitate direct interaction. However, the complexity of the technology meant that sports organizations typically entered into licensing agreements with token-producers to create tokens featuring their intellectual property. As a result, sports organizations had limited interaction with the technology itself, instead relying on the developers to manage and employ it. Developers voiced frustration that sports organizations were reluctant to embrace the technology; for instance, they proposed implementing mechanisms to monitor fan interactions, allowing sports organizations to tailor rewards and benefits. As one developer outlined, tokens could be used to grant access to gated membership features, integrating services such as e-commerce, community channels, and streaming platforms into a cohesive strategic framework. However, sports organizations had not explored this potential avenue for development.

Organization Factors

Sports organizations proved inadequately equipped to maximize the potential of tokens, with participants noting that their staff was limited and busy, meaning their knowledge on how to make use of the technology remained "very limited". Internal expertise and capabilities, where they existed, were largely fortuitous and stemmed from individual employees within the commercial and marketing departments with a personal interest in cryptocurrencies. These individuals played pivotal roles in driving the adoption of tokens. The lack of comprehension and readiness to adopt the technology emerged as a source of frustration for developers and digital agencies, who saw the technology as having potential benefits that the sports organizations were unable or unwilling to integrate.

Organizational constraints also impacted due diligence processes. Sports organizations treated the partnerships with token developers like standard sponsorships, relying on their regular in-house or external legal teams to check deals, potentially overlooking the intricacies of the technology involved. Only one organization went beyond this approach by utilizing a scorecard-based approach to assessing potential token partners, incorporating blockchain-specific elements such as the consensus layer and programming language. However, even this organization acknowledged that "there was confidence in numbers quite simply because many other premium top-tier clubs had done the deal". This approach led to a select few developers engaging in multiple partnerships with numerous clubs, providing comparable services to all, resulting in little tailoring of their offerings.

Although it may be presumed that sports organizations' ability to engage and market to their fanbase would be a critical element of sales strategies, this was only partially the case. A significant appeal to sports organizations was the hands-off approach to implementation, with token-producers taking the lead on marketing and sales strategies. Despite clubs having a good understanding of their immediate consumer base and a desire to target specific markets, they primarily implemented social media-based communication dictated by the developers, with minimal customization.

Environmental Factors

Sports organizations' interest in utility tokens was the fear that competitors would use revenues to improve sporting performance. Consequently, the primary driver for partnerships was short-term financial incentives rather than alignment with their long-term strategies.

Beyond the competitive financial environment, two other environmental factors influenced decision-making. First, tokens are not regulated, whereas other sources of commercial income may be restricted. Organizations were mindful of the potential for blockchain products to be subject to regulation in the future, and wanted to generate revenue while this possibility exists. Second, organizations were cautious of the potential of these technologies due to technical barriers to consumer adoption, with one respondent claiming that "some fans can barely use their credit card and tickets that are e-mailed to them". Thus, the prevailing view was that there was not yet consumer demand for token-based engagement. This view did not align with developers' belief that their products were readily accessible to anyone with a smartphone.

4.2 Phase 2 – Consumers

As per the literature review, the consumer adoption of blockchain innovation was analyzed using the UTAUT model.

Performance Expectancy
Respondents identified two distinct dimensions of utility token performance: as financial assets, and as products offering utility to the owner. Users of blockchain-based products exercised caution regarding the token as a financial asset, emphasizing that the potential for financial returns drives their approach to using a crypto product; in that regard, they did not consider the tokens as worthwhile financial investments, citing examples of comparable tokens experiencing losses in value. Non-users exhibited a similar reluctance to buy tokens, primarily stemming from a broader hesitancy towards crypto asset investment rather than the specific tokens discussed.

Concerning the utility of the tokens, both cohorts expressed doubts regarding the tangible benefits. Participants drew comparisons between tokens and football stickers, arguing that they could imagine children exchanging tokens, but asserting that the tokens lack appeal to adults. Despite some interest in benefits tailored to specific clubs, the standard interactions associated with tokens were criticized for their similarity to existing engagement activities. Participants suggested that utility tokens may not offer substantial utility compared to those associated with memberships or season tickets.

Effort Expectancy
Users recognized that purchasing tokens is not always easy and may require first purchasing cryptocurrency. However, this was seen as potential barrier to adoption of the technology. Non-users were unsure of the challenges around token purchases, stemming from their lack of prior experience in purchasing crypto assets.

Social Influence
SI emerged as a potentially significant factor in the adoption of utility tokens. Users recollected how their initial forays into crypto assets were guided by social circles, including friends, family, and online social media, and how these influences continued to shape their investment decisions. Likewise, non-users indicated that if they were to invest in cryptocurrency, it would be due to the financial successes of friends and family.

However, such social cues were missing concerning the tokens in question, with few respondents aware of others who had purchased them.

Despite expectations that the clubs' influence would be substantial, the evidence points the other way. Users, primarily motivated by financial gains, noted that they would not base investment decisions on their emotional attachment to a club. Some non-users perceived the club's involvement as providing a "degree of legitimacy," as the "clubs themselves wouldn't necessarily want to take the risk of partnering with a company that is going to go bust tomorrow". However, the club's involvement also led to cynicism among respondents, with frustration expressed over clubs selling tokens in addition to already expensive memberships.

Facilitating Conditions
Participants from both groups felt that sports organizations had not effectively communicated the value proposition of tokens. Despite all respondents having regular contact with the club they supported, they expressed a desire for clearer communication. Participants were aware that the tokens were available for purchase but said that advertisements tended to be pictures of the tokens or brief social media posts. However, there was a dichotomy regarding the messages that could be sent out; users favored shorter communications designed around raising awareness of the tokens and potentially highlighting their potential as an investment device, while non-users lamented the lack of detailed information provided by clubs. They suggested that longer-form advertising featuring players to offer more explicit information regarding the tokens could help them decide to buy them.

5 Discussion and Implications

This research has taken a multi-stakeholder approach to understand the role of sports organizations as intermediates in the adoption of a disruptive technology, utility tokens. The findings reveal a persistent mismatch between the expectations of utility token promoters and what sports organizations offered. By considering utility tokens only as a short-term financing option, sports organizations did not include them in their wider fan engagement possibilities opened by them. For the same reason, these organizations also failed to either invest on knowledge and expertise in the technology, which meant they were not equipped to understand how best to make use of the potential of utility tokens. Clubs may have offered promoters visibility and – to a point – legitimacy, but they were far from ideal partners for the crypto industry.

Likewise, there is a fundamental mismatch between what clubs were offering in terms of their support utility tokens, and what fans expected. For users of cryptocurrencies, the value proposition of utility tokens is always compared to that of cryptocurrencies. Users did not expect to see financial returns from the acquisition of a utility token, and for that reason discarded the idea of acquiring them. Non-users, on the other hand, would only consider acquiring these tokens if they provided other benefits and utility. While this matches the crypto industry's pitch for utility tokens, the clubs themselves were not prepared to embark on the possibility, for the reasons noted above. Overall, end users may be interested in buying the engagement and extra benefits that the token could bring, but are not interested in a crypto product with a somewhat vague connection to their club. The clubs failed to provide this.

These (dis)continuances evident in the actions of sellers and the needs of consumers, help explain how disruptive technology can struggle to become more widely adopted [24]. The findings contribute to extant literature indicating the buy-in from intermediary organizations. Without this buy-in, the organizations will not be prepared to deploy the technological and organizational resources necessary to both understand the premise of the disruptive innovation and their consumers' needs. Likewise, innovators must be careful when selecting intermediary organizations when going to market, making sure those organizations provide not just short-term visibility, but also real added value in their understanding of the target market.

References

1. Palmié, M., Wincent, J., Parida, V., Caglar, U.: The evolution of the financial technology ecosystem: an introduction and agenda for future research on disruptive innovations in ecosystems. Technol. Forecast. Soc. Chang. **151**, 119779 (2020). https://doi.org/10.1016/j.techfore.2019.119779
2. Saadatmand, M., Daim, T.: Blockchain technology through the lens of disruptive innovation theory. In: 2019 IEEE Technology & Engineering Management Conference (TEMSCON), pp. 1–6. IEEE, Atlanta, GA, USA (2019)
3. Boukis, A.: Exploring the implications of blockchain technology for brand–consumer relationships: a future research agenda. JPBM **29**, 307–320 (2019). https://doi.org/10.1108/JPBM-03-2018-1780
4. Colicev, A.: How can non-fungible tokens bring value to brands. Int. J. Res. Mark. **40**, 30–37 (2023). https://doi.org/10.1016/j.ijr-esmar.2022.07.003
5. Chou, J.H., Agrawal, P., Birt, J.: Accounting for crypto-assets: stakeholders' perceptions. Stud. Econ. Finan. **39**(3), 471–489 (2022). https://doi.org/10.1108/SEF-10-2021-0469
6. Krause, F., et al.: One-of-a-kind products: leveraging strict uniqueness in mass customization. Int. J. Res. Mark. **40**, 823–840 (2023). https://doi.org/10.1016/j.ijresmar.2023.04.002
7. Li, S., Chen, Y.: How nonfungible tokens empower business model innovation. Bus. Horiz. **66**, 543–554 (2023). https://doi.org/10.1016/j.bushor.2022.10.006
8. Stegmann, P., Matyas, D., Ströbel, T.: Hype or opportunity? tokenization as engagement platform in sport marketing. IJSMS **24**, 722–736 (2023). https://doi.org/10.1108/IJSMS-08-2022-0157
9. Treiblmaier, H.: Beyond blockchain: how tokens trigger the internet of value and what marketing researchers need to know about them. J. Mark. Commun. **29**, 238–250 (2023). https://doi.org/10.1080/13527266.2021.2011375
10. Feloutzis, N., Lekakos, G.: Is blockchain a disruptive innovation? a systematic literature review. In: de la Iglesia, D.H., de Paz Santana, J.F., López Rivero, A.J. (eds.) New Trends in Disruptive Technologies, Tech Ethics and Artificial Intelligence. DiTTEt 2023. Advances in Intelligent Systems and Computing, vol. 1452, pp. 175–186. Springer, Cham (2023). https://doi.org/10.1007/978-3-031-38344-1_17
11. Ben-Slimane, K., Diridollou, C., Hamadache, K.: The legitimation strategies of early stage disruptive innovation. Technol. Forecast. Soc. Chang. **158**, 120161 (2020). https://doi.org/10.1016/j.techfore.2020.120161
12. Ferreira, C., Merendino, A., Meadows, M.: Disruption and legitimacy: big data in society. Inf. Syst. Front. **25**(3) (2021). https://doi.org/10.1007/s10796-021-10155-3

13. Hwang, J., Christensen, C.M.: Disruptive innovation in health care delivery: a framework for business-model innovation. Health Aff. **27**, 1329–1335 (2008). https://doi.org/10.1377/hlthaff.27.5.1329
14. Kamolsook, A., Badir, Y.F., Frank, B.: Consumers' switching to disruptive technology products: the roles of comparative economic value and technology type. Technol. Forecast. Soc. Chang. **140**, 328–340 (2019). https://doi.org/10.1016/j.techfore.2018.12.023
15. Mendoza-Tello, J.C., Mora, H., Pujol-López, F.A., Lytras, M.D.: Disruptive innovation of cryptocurrencies in consumer acceptance and trust. Inf. Syst. E-Bus. Manage. **17**, 195–222 (2019). https://doi.org/10.1007/s10257-019-00415-w
16. Schmidthuber, L., Maresch, D., Ginner, M.: Disruptive technologies and abundance in the service sector-toward a refined technology acceptance model. Technol. Forecast. Soc. Change **155**, 119328 (2020). https://doi.org/10.1016/j.techfore.2018.06.017
17. Neal, J.W., Neal, Z.P., Brutzman, B.: Defining brokers, intermediaries, and boundary spanners: a systematic review. Evid. Policy **18**, 7–24 (2022). https://doi.org/10.1332/174426420X16083745764324
18. Winch, G.M., Courtney, R.: The organization of innovation brokers: an international review. Technol. Anal. Strateg. Manage. **19**, 747–763 (2007). https://doi.org/10.1080/09537320701711223
19. Gassmann, O., Daiber, M., Enkel, E.: The role of intermediaries in cross-industry innovation processes. R D Manage. **41**, 457–469 (2011). https://doi.org/10.1111/j.1467-9310.2011.00651.x
20. Janssen, W., Bouwman, H., Van Buuren, R., Haaker, T.: An organizational competence model for innovation intermediaries. Eur. J. Innov. Manag. **17**, 2–24 (2014). https://doi.org/10.1108/EJIM-09-2012-0087
21. Christensen, C.M., Raynor, M., McDonald, R.: What is disruptive innovation? Harv. Bus. Rev. **93**, 44–53 (2015)
22. Christensen, C.M., McDonald, R., Altman, E.J., Palmer, J.E.: Disruptive innovation: an intellectual history and directions for future research. J. Manage. Stud. **55**, 1043–1078 (2018). https://doi.org/10.1111/joms.12349
23. Christensen, C.M., Bower, J.L.: Customer power, strategic investment, and the failure of leading firms. Strateg. Manag. J. **17**, 197–218 (1996)
24. Bunduchi, R., Candi, M.: Technology legitimation: a product-level examination across the technology lifecycle. Brit. J. Manage. **33**(4), 2052–2069 (2021). https://doi.org/10.1111/1467-8551.12562
25. Baabdullah, A.M., Alalwan, A.A., Slade, E.L., Raman, R., Khatatneh, K.F.: SMEs and artificial intelligence (AI): antecedents and consequences of AI-based B2B practices. Ind. Mark. Manage. **98**, 255–270 (2021). https://doi.org/10.1016/j.indmarman.2021.09.003
26. El-Haddadeh, R., Osmani, M., Hindi, N., Fadlalla, A.: Value creation for realising the sustainable development goals: fostering organizational adoption of big data analytics. J. Bus. Res. **131**, 402–410 (2021). https://doi.org/10.1016/j.jbusres.2020.10.066
27. Sun, S., Hall, D.J., Cegielski, C.G.: Organizational intention to adopt big data in the B2B context: an integrated view. Ind. Mark. Manage. **86**, 109–121 (2020). https://doi.org/10.1016/j.indmarman.2019.09.003
28. Chittipaka, V., Kumar, S., Sivarajah, U., Bowden, J.L.-H., Baral, M.M.: Block-chain technology for supply chains operating in emerging markets: an empirical examination of technology-organization-environment (TOE) framework. Ann. Oper. Res. **327**, 465–492 (2023). https://doi.org/10.1007/s10479-022-04801-5
29. Kouhizadeh, M., Saberi, S., Sarkis, J.: Blockchain technology and the sustainable supply chain: theoretically exploring adoption barriers. Int. J. Prod. Econ. **231**, 07831, 1 (2021). https://doi.org/10.1016/j.ijpe.2020.107831

30. Baker, J.: Information Systems Theory: Explaining and Predicting Our Digital Society, vol. 1. Springer, New York, New York, NY (2012)
31. Dwivedi, Y.K., Rana, N.P., Jeyaraj, A., Clement, M., Williams, M.D.: Re-examining the unified theory of acceptance and use of technology (UTAUT): towards a revised theoretical model. Inf. Syst. Front. **21**, 719–734 (2019). https://doi.org/10.1007/s10796-017-9774-y
32. Williams, M.D., Rana, N.P., Dwivedi, Y.K.: The unified theory of acceptance and use of technology (UTAUT): a literature review. J. Enterp. Inf. Manag. **28**, 443–488 (2015). https://doi.org/10.1108/JEIM-09-2014-0088
33. Dwivedi, Y.K., Rana, N.P., Janssen, M., Lal, B., Williams, M.D., Clement, M.: An empirical validation of a unified model of electronic government adoption (UMEGA). Gov. Inf. Q. **34**, 211–230 (2017). https://doi.org/10.1016/j.giq.2017.03.001
34. Jain, D., Dash, M.K., Kumar, A., Luthra, S.: How is blockchain used in marketing: a review and research agenda. Int. J. Inf. Manage. Data Insights **1**, 100044 (2021). https://doi.org/10.1016/j.jjimei.2021.100044
35. Queiroz, M.M., Fosso Wamba, S., De Bourmont, M., Telles, R.: Blockchain adoption in operations and supply chain management: empirical evidence from an emerging economy. Int. J. Prod. Res. 1–17 (2020). https://doi.org/10.1080/00207543.2020.1803511
36. Gale, N.K., Heath, G., Cameron, E., Rashid, S., Redwood, S.: Using the frame-work method for the analysis of qualitative data in multi-disciplinary health research. BMC Med. Res. Methodol. **13**, 117 (2013). https://doi.org/10.1186/1471-2288-13-117
37. Goldsmith, L.: Using framework analysis in applied qualitative research. TQR (2021). https://doi.org/10.46743/2160-3715/2021.5011

Remote Revolution: The Impact of Working from Home on Employee Well-Being and Productivity in Germany

Jula Gekle, Luca Laule(✉), and Markus Bick

ESCP Business School, Berlin, Germany
llaule@escp.eu

Abstract. During the COVID-19 pandemic, 27% of employees in Germany worked from home, leading to significant changes in work practices that impacted both productivity and personal well-being. Early studies on the implications of working from home during COVID-19 predominantly reported positive developments. However, more recent research has increasingly highlighted negative consequences. To contribute to this ongoing academic discussion, we conducted a qualitative study based on semi-structured expert interviews, focusing on employee well-being and productivity. We conducted interviews with representatives from a broad range of companies in the white-collar sector in Germany. Germany is particularly suited for this investigation because it has a relatively high proportion of employees working from home. Our main results include two frameworks illustrating main influencing factors for employee well-being and employee productivity. Moreover, we propose a set of recommendations for working from home regulations. These findings contribute to the academic discourse by enhancing the understanding of factors affecting employee well-being and productivity. Corresponding practical implications include the application of our frameworks and recommendations by organizations to optimize employee health and productivity in working from home settings.

Keywords: Working From Home · Well-Being · Productivity

1 Introduction

In 2023, the company Zoom, a key facilitator of remote work, urged its employees to return from working from home (WFH) to the office at least twice per week [1]. Nevertheless, many companies worldwide still offer flexible remote work policies, and especially in Germany, WFH continues to be widely spread [2]. During the COVID-19 pandemic, the majority of employees in office jobs were sent home to work [3], leading to an increase from previously 4% of German employees WFH to 27% in April 2020 [4]. Working from home was generally introduced to reduce the spreading of COVID-19 [5]. After the lockdowns during the COVID-19 pandemic, the number of employees working from home in Germany decreased only slightly from 27% in 2020 [4] to 24.1% who were still at least partially WFH in 2024 [2].

Published by Springer Nature Switzerland AG 2024
R. van de Wetering et al. (Eds.): I3E 2024, LNCS 14907, pp. 181–196, 2024.
https://doi.org/10.1007/978-3-031-72234-9_15

While popular media and corporate narratives suggest long-term adverse effects on employees WFH, academic studies present contradicting results. Gibson et al. [6] and Olsen et al. [3], indicate that employee productivity and well-being have increased, whereas Xiao et al. [7] found significant decreases in physical and mental well-being. These studies attribute changes in well-being while WFH to factors such as decreased physical activity, social isolation, increased consumption of unhealthy food, and higher stress levels. Choudhury et al. [8] have found a 4.4% increase in productivity. However, recent research highlights that although software engineers generated more lines of code while WFH, their overall learning and developmental opportunities decreased, leading to a negative impact on productivity in the long term [9].

Given these inconsistencies in research outcomes, our study aims to contribute to the academic discourse by investigating the influences that WFH brings. Therefore, we focus on *employee well-being* and *employee productivity*, aiming to assess the impact of WFH on both individual employees and companies, thereby offering a comprehensive perspective. The following research questions were leading the project:

RQ1: How has working from home affected the well-being and productivity of employees in medium to large enterprises operating within the professional service industry in Germany?

RQ2: What policies and recommendations can be derived to optimize employee well-being and productivity?

We focus on medium and large companies in the professional service industries in Germany. This decision substantiated by the country's above-average remote work statistics and its status as a first-world nation with a significant presence of professional service companies including a generally well-developed digital infrastructure. Sources published between 2019 and 2024 are primarily used for the theoretical foundation, as these are the relevant years since the pandemic began. We employ empirical qualitative research in the form of semi-structured interviews conducted with employees and leaders within relevant companies in Germany to gain deeper insights into the impacts and implications. We conducted eight interviews with individuals to explore perceptions and experiences of well-being and productivity in the context of WFH. To analyze the qualitative data, we employed Thematic Analysis, following Clarke & Brown's approach [10].

The main outcomes of this study are two frameworks and a set of recommendations for organizations employing working from home. One framework captures the positively and negatively influencing factors for employee well-being, the other exhibits the factors influencing employee productivity. Herewith, we contribute to the academic discourse by providing deeper insights into the effects of working from home regulations on an individual level. From a practical perspective, our results are relevant for any organization that applies WFH, since healthy and productive employees are the basis for sustainable businesses. Furthermore, the recommendations can be used as guidelines for well-founded working from home policies.

The remainder of this paper is structured as follows: The literature review provides the theoretical and contextual basis by explaining relevant concepts. Next, the methodology is presented, including data collection and data analysis. The results section provides information on the findings of the interviews, presents possible WFH-policies, as well as the frameworks for employee well-being and productivity. The discussion links our findings to the body of literature, before we conclude in the last chapter.

2 Literature Review

Remote work is defined as "work carried out in a location where, remote from central offices or production facilities, the worker has no personal contact with co-workers there, but is able to communicate with them using new technology" [11, p. 530]. To analyze the effects and future of WFH, the two variables *well-being* and *productivity* were chosen, as they are closely linked while also complementing each other [12]. Well-being is usually associated with the individual's health, while productivity is more relevant to the company's outcome.

2.1 Employee Well-Being in the Workplace

Psychological well-being can be defined as it "encompasses life satisfaction, emotional equilibrium, and a sense of purpose, which are vital for cognitive functions and decision-making capabilities" [13, p. 334]. We examine employees' health and happiness in their job context, considering well-being as the overall state of health, happiness, and satisfaction in the workplace. This includes physical, mental, and emotional health, all relevant to one's well-being [5].

Several factors influence employee well-being while WFH. A major positive factor is the increased flexibility for parents, allowing them to take breaks for personal matters [14, 15]. Higher flexibility and better work-life balance enhance job satisfaction and autonomy [16, 17]. Galanti et al. [18] reported that 71% of surveyed employees experienced greater well-being due to increased freedom when WFH. Remote work also reduces work-family conflicts and the strain between professional and family obligations. The quieter home environment leads to better concentration and less frustration from commuting, saving time and money [1]. Following Yang et al. [19], job satisfaction only increases if office hours are replaced with equivalent home hours.

Many factors negatively impact employee well-being when working from home. Young workers experience loneliness, frustration, and lower well-being [14]. New employees learn less and receive less feedback [1], while decreased social interaction leads to isolation and reduced job satisfaction [18]. Separation reduces collaboration, creativity [19], and can cause social issues. More WFH days negatively affect mental health, leading to psychological symptoms [16] and worse work-life balance [20]. WFH can cause depression [12, 21], blur work-leisure boundaries, and increase family conflicts [18, 22]. Excessive screen time and increased costs for electricity, internet, and equipment are also concerns [5, 20].

The impacts and severity of negative or positive factors depend strongly on the individual situation of an employee at home. Whether the employee has small children, lives alone, lives in a large apartment with a room for WFH, or other factors can change the impact clearly [16].

2.2 Employee Productivity in the Workplace

Productivity is a key performance indicator that measures output in terms of quantity, quality, and timeliness [23]. It can be measured as goals, tasks, projects completed, or hours worked. Employees with greater job satisfaction may work more productively [15], indicating a link between the two variables. We define productivity as the levels of output, employee performance, and efficiency within working hours, considering both perceived and actual productivity.

Between 2019 and 2024, studies have explored WFH's impact on productivity. Choudhury et al. [8] found a 4.4% increase in productivity among patent examiners working from home. Dahik et al. [24] reported most employees felt their productivity increased, with collaborative tasks maintained. George et al. [12] noted improvements in productivity and creativity at home. While some studies showed no significant change [6, 17], Goldberg [1] determined that skill development and knowledge building decreased with less colleague interaction. Additionally, larger corporations see less in-office attendance compared to smaller firms [25].

Positive aspects of WFH include enhanced focus due to fewer distractions, reduced commute times, and lower absenteeism and turnover rates [15, 26]. George et al. [12] observed productivity increased significantly due to the absence of distractions. The lack of a commute allows for an earlier start and shorter breaks, sustaining engagement [27]. Negative aspects include the need for recovery from high job demands on WFH days [28]. Productivity is challenged by distractions from childcare and household obligations [26], and virtual communication hinders collaboration [19]. Increased unscheduled calls and meetings diminish focus, leading to longer working hours to maintain productivity [27].

3 Methodology

This study investigates employee well-being and productivity in the WFH context applying an exploratory qualitative approach. Semi-structured expert interviews were conducted to explore themes and patterns across diverse environments, offering a comprehensive understanding [10]. Thematic Analysis was then employed to analyze the interviews, aiming to identify recurring themes and patterns.

3.1 Data Collection

The selection of experts in this study followed a purposeful sampling strategy with a focus on experiences in WFH before, during, and post COVID19. We selected interviewees from various roles, ranging from a User Experience (UX) Designer to a CEO, ensuring a diverse but relevant sample. The chosen companies can all be located in the white-collar industry or within the professional services in Germany. We approached the interviewees via the career platform LinkedIn as well as the researchers' personal networks. A short description of each interviewee is provided in Table 1. Prior to the interviews, an interview guide was developed based on an extensive literature review. The questions focused on four main topics: changes in home office policies before, during, and after COVID-19; implications on productivity; implications on well-being; and policy recommendations. We conducted interviews until we reached theoretical saturation, ultimately completing a total of eight interviews.

Table 1. Overview of Interviewees

Interviewee	Company	Industry	Role	Number of Employees (in Germany)
Interviewee 1 Male	RWE Supply & Trading GmbH	Energy	Works Council	18,000
Interviewee 2 Male	microm GmbH (part of Creditreform Boniversum GmbH)	Financial	Managing Director	3,300
Interviewee 3 Male	PSI CRO Deutschland GmbH	Pharmaceutical, Research	Director Vendor Management	150
Interviewee 4 Male	move:elevator GmbH	Digital marketing agency	Managing Director	100
Interviewee 5 Male	move:elevator GmbH	Digital marketing agency	UX Designer	100
Interviewee 6 Male	European Central Bank (ECB)	Financial, Bank	Information Management Expert	3500
Interviewee 7 Male	Schroder Investment Management GmbH	Financial	Head of Institutional Sales	100
Interviewee 8 Male	Savills Immobilien Beratungs GmbH	Real estate	Head of Transaction Division	400

All interviewees have been employed in their companies since at least 2019. Conducted between December 2023 and January 2024, the interviews lasted 30 min on average with a minimum of 25 min and a maximum of 45 min. Three were in English, and five in German, with the latter translated into English for comparability. All interviews were conducted by the same researcher, who had substantial experience in WFH. Some interviewees had a personal relationship with the researcher. This familiarity can result in more detailed and open responses, but it also introduces the risk of biased answers. To address this potential bias, we paid particular attention to identifying and mitigating any biased responses during the data analysis process.

3.2 Data Analysis

The transcripts were analyzed using Thematic Analysis [10], a method highly suitable for this project due to its alignment with research questions centered on individuals' experiences, its efficacy in analyzing interview data, its capability to handle small to large data sets, and its applicability in generating data-driven insights. It further enables in-depth data examination and identification of patterns, themes, and connections that may be overlooked by other methods [10]. Doing this, we followed the six steps established by Clarke & Brown [10] which are (1) familiarizing with the data, (2) generating initial codes, (3) searching for themes, (4) reviewing themes, (5) defining and naming themes, and (6) producing the report. Thereby, we organized data into tables and graphs to highlight emerging patterns and themes. The first set of information covered general policies and company situations pre-, during, and post-COVID-19. The analysis then focused on the two variables *employee productivity* and *well-being.*

4 Results

The next chapter presents interview findings, focusing on the WFH regulations in the companies, employee well-being and productivity, and future suggestions for WFH.

4.1 Company Regulations Pre-, During-, and Post-COVID19

To provide more context, we first analyzed the working from home regulations in the seven companies involved. Overall, a clear trend emerged: companies shifted from in-person operations to fully remote setups during the pandemic, transitioning to hybrid models afterward. Before COVID-19 hit Germany, remote work arrangements were rare, with most companies operating solely in person and making exceptions only for specific groups like new mothers or higher-ranked individuals. For instance, Company 4, a digital marketing agency, offered limited remote work options before COVID19, with about half of its employees taking advantage of them. During the pandemic, they worked entirely in working from home settings. These remote work models helped prevent widespread virus impact and gained popularity during the pandemic. While full remote work may not continue, WFH remains prevalent. Many workers now prefer remote work, indicating its likely persistence and urging companies to develop sustainable remote work policies for future success.

4.2 Remote Work and Employee Well-Being

The interviewees highlighted the challenges in measuring well-being and the diversity among individuals. They mentioned reliance on surveys for well-being assessments but pointed out their limitations, such as the absence of baseline data, as noted by Interviewee 6. Responses varied widely when asked about changes in well-being, underscoring the difficulty of generalizing. Interviewees 1 and 5 noted overall improvement, based on company surveys, but also acknowledged individual cases where well-being might have declined. Conversely, Interviewees 2, 4, 7, and 8 believed well-being had worsened overall. These findings emphasize the significant influence of personal circumstances on perceptions of employee well-being.

Flexibility and Autonomy. Employees highly value remote work for its flexibility, autonomy, and freedom, highlighted by Interviewees 4 and 5 from Company 4. Interviewee 4, a designer, appreciates the ability to work from abroad, while Interviewee 1 underscores the importance of employer-provided flexibility. Additionally, Interviewee 3 mentions how freedom allows for attending to personal matters during work hours.

Support from Superiors. Regular manager support, including check-ins, is essential for employee well-being, providing freedom while ensuring sufficient guidance. A feedback culture fosters employee development and creates a safe space for constructive criticism. Interviewee 3 underscores the importance of routine calls between employees and supervisors in fostering honesty and facilitating open communication about personal challenges.

Work-Life Balance and Family Life. WFH improves work-life balance, allowing employees to spend time with their children during working hours, as noted by Interviewees 3 and 8. Interviewee 8 reported: "It just has a huge positive effect on family and work for me. Where I can afford the luxury of leaving the office earlier, driving home, putting the kids to bed, seeing the kids, and then going back to the computer at home when the kids are in bed and finishing the rest of my workday." Additionally, Interviewee 5 highlights the enhancement of family well-being through daily lunches with their spouse.

Isolation and Mental Health. While remote work offers many benefits, it is important to consider the potential negative impacts on employee well-being, particularly mental health issues such as isolation. This concern was highlighted by interviewees 1, 6, and 7. Interviewee 7 stated, "One of the big disadvantages I see is that you become lonely," alongside increased concerns about burnout.

Decreased Physical Activity. Interviewees 1, 3, and 4 note a significant decrease in daily movement patterns, with activities confined to their living spaces instead of walking to the office or cafeteria. This reduced physical activity has prompted some to seek alternative exercise methods like daily walks, but the additional time investment or decreased health may impact overall well-being and satisfaction with physical appearance.

Confined Living Space. The size and condition of an employee's living space can significantly impact their well-being, as noted by Interviewees 7 and 8, particularly for those in single-room apartments, affecting mental health and productivity. Interviewee 2 underscores that lacking a dedicated workspace can notably affect happiness and work quality.

Job Safety. Job satisfaction can decline when employees fear potential layoffs or financial instability within the company, as observed by Interviewee 4, who notes the impact of "Kurzarbeit" (short-time work) in Germany during the pandemic. The uncertainty and possibility of job loss can significantly affect well-being, as experienced by employees during times of financial hardship.

Workload and Breaks. Some employees experienced increased workload due to remote work, with Interviewee 4 noting fewer breaks, while Interviewee 2 adjusted their schedule according to their sleep rhythms, potentially impacting work-life balance and family dynamics. Achieving a healthy work-life balance is crucial for well-being, underscoring the importance of thoughtful consideration in remote work arrangements.

Company Culture and Teamwork. The decline in social interaction among employees negatively impacts company culture, according to Interviewee 3. This loss of culture results from a lack of casual conversations and weaker connections to supervisors, as noted by Interviewee 7, while Interviewee 8 worries that the absence of informal interactions has weakened colleagues' ties to the company. Additionally, Interviewee 6 highlights that virtual meetings hinder reading body language, making it harder to provide help or guidance to employees, suggesting that real-life teamwork cannot be fully replaced, a concern shared by Interviewees 2, 5, and 8.

Onboarding. Young workers, particularly new hires, face challenges integrating into teams, as noted by Interviewee 5, who observes that long-tenured employees adapt more easily to WFH but highlights the difficulty in integrating new team members. Interviewee 6 underscores the importance of young professionals starting in-office to learn and build connections, emphasizing the need for companies to foster a conducive culture for seamless integration and effective learning.

4.3 Remote Work and Employee Productivity

Maximizing employee productivity is crucial for a company's success, with measurement methods varying across industries. While some assess productivity per completed study, others, like Companies 4 and 7, gauge it through profits. Assessing the impact of remote work on productivity is often more straightforward than on well-being due to standardized metrics, with mixed experiences noted by Interviewees 2, 3, 5, 6, and 8, highlighting the influence of individual circumstances and skills on productivity.

Saved Commute. Interviewees unanimously identified two key factors positively impacting WFH experiences. Firstly, all highlighted the time saved from commuting, leading to increased working hours and enhanced productivity. Moreover, Interviewee 2 noted how the absence of commute reduces frustration with traffic, facilitating a positive start to the day, while Interviewee 7 emphasized the preference to avoid the costs and effort of commuting over going to the office.

Quiet Working Space. Each interviewee highlighted the quiet atmosphere at home, aiding concentration, with Interviewee 1 noting fewer distractions from colleagues and Interviewee 6 emphasizing decreased interruptions. Additionally, Interviewee 7 mentioned working more focused and peacefully from home, while Interviewee 5 noted WFH allows for deep work, though family situations may affect concentration.

IT Support and Innovation. Interviewees 7 and 8 stress the crucial role of IT support and robust infrastructure for remote work. Interviewee 6 notes increased demand for tech innovation during the pandemic, which facilitated productivity, highlighting the significant impact of effective IT infrastructure on remote work productivity.

Home Distractions. Interviewees 1 and 3 highlight the increase in personal distractions as the main negative factor in WFH, affecting productivity. Interviewee 1 stated: "I prefer to be in the office and I tend to be distracted more from work when I'm working from home than when I'm working in the office." Interviewee 3 suggests muting distractions like emails for better focus, while Interviewees 7 and 8 emphasize the risk of non-work-related distractions.

Home Environment. Home environment and family circumstances significantly impact productivity, as noted by Interviewee 1, citing distractions from newborns, and Interviewee 3, highlighting challenges for those with limited workspace and family responsibilities. Interviewee 4 mentions decreased productivity when children are present without additional care, indicating that while WFH offers family benefits, productivity may decline under such circumstances.

Back-to-back Meetings. Interviewee 4 notes an increase in scheduled meetings during the pandemic, potentially decreasing productivity. Interviewee 2 highlights the cognitive benefits of the pre-pandemic commute, which allowed for mental processing and preparation. With the current setup of back-to-back virtual meetings, he finds time less effectively used, leading to difficulty maintaining focus and cognitive coherence.

Misuse of Freedom. Interviewee 5, a digital marketing agency director, highlights difficulty supervising employees remotely and notes the potential negative impact of lacking peer pressure on productivity. Interviewee 7 echoes concerns about maintaining focus without usual peer accountability. Interviewee 8, a real estate company director, reflects on the idea of freedom misuse in WFH, noting a correlation with a loss of control and supervision. Higher-ups commonly find supervision challenges and freedom misuse as negative aspects of WFH.

Difficulties for New Employees. A common negative aspect, as seen with employee well-being, is the slower learning curve for newly recruited employees when WFH. Interviewee 6 notes challenges with onboarding processes and communication, especially for young hires: "I think for the young people and those that start a job for the first time, it's been really, really hard. And we actually [...] got a special dispensation to let them come in, because many of them had moved to Frankfurt for absolutely no reason to sit inside, looking at a screen. "Remote work elongates the process, requiring messages for questions that would typically be addressed face-to-face. This hampers productivity for new employees and increases demands on supervisors for support and guidance.

Complexity of Online Teamwork. The increased complexity of online teamwork is another major negative factor of remote work, noted by Interviewee 6. Reduced collaboration between teams and individuals leads to fewer shared ideas, decreasing employee engagement. Interviewee 7 highlights less participation in virtual calls, often with employees multitasking, resulting in decreased productivity and engagement.

Type of Task. Categorizing productivity factors into distinct positive and negative aspects is challenging, as each factor can have both positive and negative implications depending on context: Interviewee 1 notes increased productivity for undisturbed tasks like programming, while Interviewee 4 struggles with repetitive tasks but finds remote creativity stimulating. Interviewee 3 finds WFH more productive for research-based tasks, while Interviewee 8 suggests office collaboration is ideal for teamwork.

Home Setup. The home technology setup can significantly impact WFH productivity, as highlighted by Interviewee 5. Access to quality equipment like monitors and chairs can enhance the WFH experience, while technical issues like firewall restrictions can hinder productivity, as seen at company 4. Interviewee 8 emphasizes the importance of company support for employees' IT setup and equipment to ensure access to necessary resources. Support levels directly affect productivity and work quality, making it essential for companies to consider.

4.4 Employee Well-Being and Productivity Frameworks

Using the factors identified above, we created two frameworks showing influences on employee well-being and productivity. These aim to offer comprehensive insights. Impact of remote work on well-being and productivity varies based on individual circumstances and task nature. Contextual factors are crucial, requiring careful examination to establish a sustainable remote work strategy for organizations.

Figure 1 displays the Employee Well-Being Framework. On the left side, positive factors depict the four key influencers affecting employees, while the right side portrays a greater number of negative factors. However, it is crucial to recognize that the significance of a single factor can surpass several others depending on individual circumstances. For instance, Interviewee 3, a single mother, perceives family life as the most important factor, prompting her advocacy for WFH.

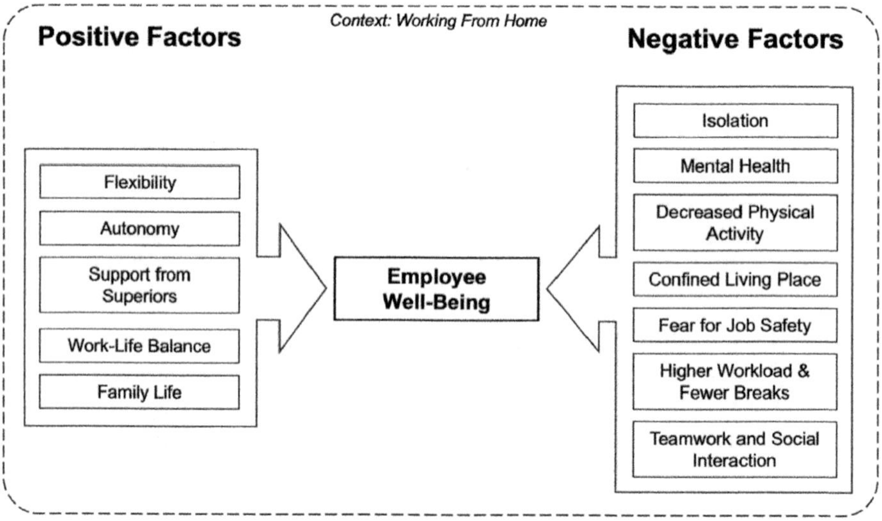

Fig. 1. Employee Well-Being Framework

Figure 2, the Employee Productivity Framework, follows the same logic as the Employee Well-Being Framework and includes all factors that influence employee productivity in the context of WFH. However, as the findings suggested, this figure illustrates other influences in addition to positive and negative factors. This is because our results suggested four influences that could be negative or positive. The quantity of factors on each side does not necessarily imply an overall negative effect; rather, it varies for each employee due to the individual importances.

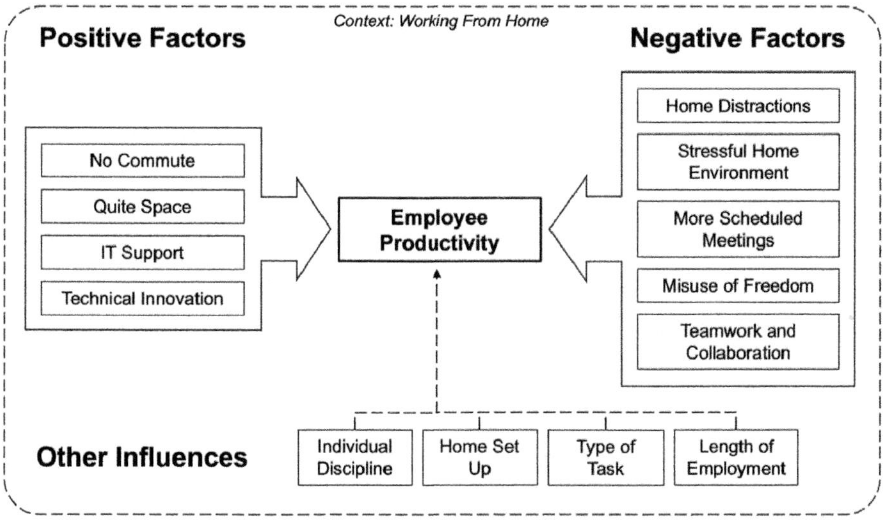

Fig. 2. Employee Productivity Framework

4.5 Guiding Policies: Insights and Recommendations

To assist companies and leaders, the following section provides a summary of recommendations from all interviewees, emphasizing employee well-being and productivity (Table 2). The first six suggestions might be considered as potential WFH policies, and the remaining eight recommendations offer general advice for long-term improvement.

Table 2. Overview of Recommendations

Type of Recommendation	Concise Overview
Possible WFH Policies:	
Strictly organized WFH Policy for Team Days	1–2 mandatory office days per week with respective teams, organizing a rotation of teams to ensure a similar number of employees in the office each day but with different teams

(*continued*)

Table 2. (*continued*)

Type of Recommendation	Concise Overview
General WFH Policy based on Percentage	Work at least 50% of all available working days in the office. Companies can adjust percentages as needed or wanted
General WFH Policy based on a Quota	Implement a maximum WFH Quota (ex: 40%) and make it transferable between teams for individual flexibility and employee needs
Team-based WFH Policy Regulation	Teams have the autonomy to choose their work location, allowing for individual adjustments to meet team members' needs
Flexible WFH Policy	Give employees full flexibility on where to work from and provide the possibility to work from the office on any day
Zero WFH: Working Hour Recommendation	Eliminate set working hours; employees can leave for any reason but must be fully present in the office when working. This may create peer pressure against misuse but gives flexibility to tend to any matter
General Advice & Recommendations:	
Advice for 'Office Days'	Designating specific 'Office Days' may result in overcrowding parking issues and exacerbate the situation if days or teams are unevenly spread
Advice for Teams	Hold daily meetings to inform each other on progress and hold monthly meetings ("Retros") to reflect on the past month and change if needed
Advice for WFH set-up	Companies advocating for WFH should support employees with their WFH setup and equipment
Company Spirit Suggestion	'Company Days' featuring workshops, food, and networking activities unrelated to work, bringing all employees together in the office
Measuring Employee Well-being	Send out regular 'Happiness Index' surveys to keep track of employee well-being, feedback, and needs
Supporting Employee Well-being	Provide voluntary support such as mental health support, coaching possibilities, or sports initiatives such as remote meditation classes

(*continued*)

Table 2. (*continued*)

Type of Recommendation	Concise Overview
Mentorship System	Establish a mentorship system between new recruits and older employees
Key Advice for WFH Policies	Tailor strategies to fit each firm's unique needs, considering industry, job roles, and company culture, avoiding a one-size-fits-all approach. Different departments or people may require distinct guidelines and prioritize in-person interactions where they enhance company culture

5 Discussion

Regarding the concept of employee well-being, Cavendish [14] observed that flexibility for parents significantly affects well-being, supporting both flexibility and family life as positive factors. Our interviewees identified that higher autonomy and decision-making increase employees' responsibility and well-being, further supported by Rañeses et al. [15]. Other variables, such as decreased commute times and heightened concentration while working remotely [1], have been identified as impacting productivity initially, which consequently affects well-being. Galanti et al. [18] identified isolation and mental health challenges as significant threats to employee well-being during remote work, thereby corroborating the findings from interviews. Further, mental health diseases such as depression increased while teamwork decreased when employees worked from home, reported by Yu et al. [21] and George et al. [12] and supported by the findings of this study. Overall, numerous factors highlighted in the interviews align with findings from prior studies, underlining their known relevance and importance for consideration.

The factors on productivity, expressed in the Employee Productivity Framework (Fig. 2), are also mostly in line with previous research. The assertion made by Interviewee 4 regarding the importance of factors like IT support and companies' investment in employees' home setups is reinforced by the findings of Ferrara et al. [29]. According to their research, establishing enduring and sustainable remote work opportunities necessitates companies' readiness to allocate resources toward supporting HR functions and roles, technological infrastructure, and essential WFH equipment. The additional four influences mentioned are noteworthy as they can have a significant impact similar to other factors. High individual discipline, for instance, can positively correlate with productivity [26]. Similarly, a conducive home setup, such as a comfortable chair or multiple monitors, contributes positively. Task type also plays a crucial role and varies among individuals; specific tasks may be perceived as more efficient when done from home due to increased concentration in a quiet environment. This notion is supported by recent findings by Emanuel et al. [9] and Interviewee 1, indicating an increase in code lines written by programmers WFH. This reinforces the hypothesis that while productivity might see a short-term boost, it could decline in the long run due to diminished learning, feedback, and development opportunities. Additionally, the length of employment is highlighted as a significant influence, suggesting that newly hired employees may experience a decrease in productivity due to extended communication and onboarding processes, along with a slower learning curve while working remotely.

6 Conclusion

Customized analysis is essential for successful remote work outcomes. While remote work will not disappear suddenly, fully remote setups may also not dominate. The future requires a balanced approach that benefits both employees and organizations. Addressing research questions on remote work's impact in the professional service industry reveals various factors at play. While benefits like family life and autonomy exist, negatives like social isolation can overshadow them, potentially reducing overall well-being and productivity. Tailored policies based on comprehensive self-analysis and employee feedback are vital for optimizing outcomes.

The findings of this study contribute both to theory and practice. From a theoretical point of view, we see three major contributions: Through the empirical identification of factors influencing employee well-being and productivity and the corresponding frameworks which we developed, we (1) supported factors like flexibility and family life which were already identified by previous studies. Furthermore, we (2) discovered new influencing factors and portrayed more nuanced descriptions of those influences. Lastly (3), we provided the Employee Well-Being Framework and the Employee Productivity Framework which illustrate the influencing factors clearly. In sum, our study advances the theoretical understanding of the factors influencing productivity and well-being in WFH settings. By offering a more nuanced understanding of this topic, we contribute to the academic discourse on the relationship between working from home and these two variables which so far often had contradicting results of weather an increase or decrease of the two variables are given when working from home.

Practical implications and recommendations are also given. Organizations can enhance their work environment by adopting measures like implementing a remote work quota or flexible guidelines by considering our recommendations. Balancing general rules with individualized regulations poses a challenge, as fairness concerns arise. Remote work is expected to persist, necessitating sustainable management strategies to address potential long-term effects. Managers can utilize the developed frameworks to evaluate factors impacting employees and seek validation through research and feedback mechanisms. However, maintaining fairness remains a challenge, as individual variations contrast with uniform rules. Standardized rules may not cater to individual needs, while customized approaches may raise fairness concerns among employees with differing circumstances.

This study has limitations. With only eight interviews, insights are valuable, but a larger sample could reduce subjective opinions. To fully explore variances in opinions and impacts among employees at different levels, a study having this as a focus is necessary. Generalizability is limited as the study was conducted solely in Germany, especially to countries with strong cultural and economic differences. Additional quantitative studies involving diverse participants from various backgrounds and conducted over time are crucial for a thorough understanding of remote work's effects on employee well-being and productivity. Longitudinal studies could reveal long-term outcomes compared to short-term studies since the pandemic. Research must also consider industry, company, and departmental differences for a nuanced understanding. Investigating the trend of companies encouraging return to the office could provide valuable insights. Expanding the investigation beyond Germany would enhance generalizability.

Disclosure of Interest. The authors have no competing interests to declare that are relevant to the content of this article.

References

1. Goldberg, E.: Even zoom is making people return to the office. N. Y. Times
2. ifo Institute, Working from Home Firmly Established in Germany. https://www.ifo.de/en/facts/2024-03-04/working-home-firmly-established-germany. Accessed 31 May 2024
3. Olsen, O.K., Ågotnes, K.W., Hetland, J., Espevik, R., Ravnanger, C.A.: Virtual team-cooperation from home-office: a quantitative diary study of the impact of daily transformational and passive-avoidant leadership – and the moderating role of task interdependence. Front. Psychol. **14**, 1188753 (2023). https://doi.org/10.3389/fpsyg.2023.1188753
4. Hans-Böckler-Stiftung, Share of employees working from home in Germany before and during the coronavirus (COVID-19) pandemic in 2020 and 2021 (2021)
5. Wrede, S.J., Claassen, K., Rodil dos Anjos, D., Kettschau, J.P., Broding, H.C.: Impact of digital stress on negative emotions and physical complaints in the home office: a follow up study. Health Psychol. Behav. Med. **11**(1), 2263068 (2023).https://doi.org/10.1080/21642850.2023.2263068
6. Gibson, C.B., Gilson, L.L., Griffith, T.L., O'Neill, T.A.: Should employees be required to return to the office? Organ. Dyn. **52**(2), 100981 (2023). https://doi.org/10.1016/j.orgdyn.2023.100981
7. Xiao, Y., Becerik-Gerber, B., Lucas, G., Roll, S.C.: Impacts of working from home during COVID-19 pandemic on physical and mental well-being of office workstation users. J. Occup. Environ. Med. **63**(3), 181–190 (2021). https://doi.org/10.1097/JOM.0000000000002097
8. Choudhury, P., Foroughi, C., Larson, B.: Work-from-anywhere: the productivity effects of geographic flexibility. Strateg. Manage. J.**42**(4), 655–683 (2021). https://doi.org/10.1002/smj.3251
9. Emanuel, N., Harrington, E., Pallais, A.: The power of proximity: how working beside colleagues affects training and productivity. Liberty Street Economics. https://libertystreeteconomics.newyorkfed.org/2024/01/the-power-of-proximity-how-working-beside-colleagues-affects-training-and-productivity/. Accessed 29 May 2024
10. Clarke, V., Braun, V.: Successful qualitative research: A practical guide for beginners. SAGE Publications Ltd (2013)
11. Di Martino, V., Wirth, L.: Telework: a new way of working and living. Int. Labour Rev. **129**(5), 529–554 (1990)
12. George, T.J., Atwater, L.E., Maneethai, D., Madera, J.M.: Supporting the productivity and wellbeing of remote workers. Organ. Dyn. **51**(2), 100869 (2022). https://doi.org/10.1016/j.orgdyn.2021.100869
13. Muterera, J., Brettle, J., Khorakian, A.: Assessing the relationship between auditor well-being and audit quality: insights from the north american auditing context. Int. J. Manage. Account. Econ. **11**(4), 332–349 (2024)
14. Cavendish, C.: The home-working revolution is harming younger workers. Financial Times

15. Rañeses, M.S., un Nisa, N., Bacason, E.S., Martir, S.: Investigating the impact of remote working on employee productivity and work-life balance: a study on the business consultancy industry in Dubai, UAE. Int. J. Bus Adm. Stud. **8**(2) (2022). https://doi.org/10.20469/ijbas.8.10002-2
16. Niebuhr, F., Borle, P., Börner-Zobel, F., Voelter-Mahlknecht, S.: Healthy and happy working from home? effects of working from home on employee health and job satisfaction. Int. J. Environ. Res. Public Health **19**(3), 1122 (2022). https://doi.org/10.3390/ijerph19031122
17. Wiradendi Wolor, C., Nurkhin, A., Citriadin, Y.: Is Working from home good for work-life balance, stress, and productivity, or does it cause problems?. Humanit. Soc. Sci. Lett. **9**(3), 237–249 (2021). https://doi.org/10.18488/journal.73.2021.93.237.249
18. Galanti, T., Guidetti, G., Mazzei, E., Zappalà, S., Toscano, F.: Work from home during the COVID-19 outbreak: the impact on employees' remote work productivity, engagement, and stress. J. Occup. Environ. Med. **63**(7), e426–e432 (2021)
19. Yang, D., Kelly, E.L., Kubzansky, L.D., Berkman, L.: Working from home and worker well-being: new evidence from germany. ILR Rev. **76**(3), 504–531 (2023). https://doi.org/10.1177/00197939221148716
20. Lodovici, M.S., Ferrari, E., Paladino, E., Pesce, F., Frecassetti, P., Aram, E.: The impact of teleworking and digital work on workers and society. Study Requested EMPL Committee (2021)
21. Yu, Y., Lau, M.M.C., Lau, J.T.F.: Working from home and positive/negative experiences due to social distancing as interacting factors of depressive symptoms during the COVID-19 pandemic in a Chinese general population. Soc. Psychiatry Psychiatr. Epidemiol. **57**(6), 1235–1246 (2022). https://doi.org/10.1007/s00127-021-02179-6
22. Spagnoli, P., Molino, M., Molinaro, D., Giancaspro, M.L., Manuti, A., Ghislieri, C.: Workaholism and technostress during the COVID-19 emergency: the crucial role of the leaders on remote working. Front. Psychol. **11**, 620310 (2020)
23. Kaiser, R.B.: Has empathy really become more important to leadership since the COVID-19 pandemic? Consult. Psychol. J. (2024). https://doi.org/10.1037/cpb0000273
24. Dahik, A., et al.: What 12,000 employees have to say about the future of remote work. Boston Consul. Group **12** (2020)
25. Mischke, J., et al.: Empty spaces and hybrid places. McKinsey Global Institute (2023)
26. Berinato, S.: To raise productivity, let more employees work from home. Harv. Bus. Rev. **92**(1), 12 (2014)
27. Gibbs, M., Mengel, F., Siemroth, C.: Work from home and productivity: evidence from personnel and analytics data on information technology professionals. J. Polit. Econ. Microeconomics **1**(1), 7–41 (2023). https://doi.org/10.1086/721803
28. Biron, M., van Veldhoven, M.: When control becomes a liability rather than an asset: comparing home and office days among part-time teleworkers. J. Organ. Behav. **37**(8), 1317–1337 (2016). https://doi.org/10.1002/job.2106
29. Ferrara, B., Pansini, M., De Vincenzi, C., Buonomo, I., Benevene, P.: Investigating the role of remote working on employees' performance and well-being: an evidence-based systematic review. Int. J. Environ. Res. Public Health **19**(19), 12373 (2022). https://doi.org/10.3390/ijerph191912373

Governing an Unexpected Potential Ending of a Strategic IT Sourcing Partnership: Picking up the Right Signals

P. E. Kamminga(✉) and H. Martin

Open Universiteit, Heerlen, The Netherlands
pieter.kamminga@ou.nl

Abstract. While IT sourcing partnerships are an appropriate instrument for developing effective IT "solutions" in an efficient way, they also face high uncertainty. This uncertainty could unexpectedly lead to situations in which the legitimacy of an IT-sourcing partnership may be questioned and therefore make a premature ending of the partnership a serious option. However, properly coping with an unexpected potential ending of a partnership is often not easy. A decision to end may be taken too early or too late, and partners who are unprepared for an ending may be caught off guard and be confronted with high costs in legal fees, time and effort. Remarkably enough, this topic has not received a lot of attention in both practice and in literature. Therefore, the aim of this paper is to review the literature about this underexplored topic of governance of unexpected potential endings of IT sourcing partnerships and to use the findings of six explorative case studies to identify the boundaries of the knowledge of this topic and to acquire ideas on how to further our understanding on this topic.

We argue that signaling theory provides a useful ontology to discover the mechanics in which partnerships evolve. By rigorously and systematically study ing ending signals in numerous actual partnerships probably patterns could be identified which "announce" a potential ending. Currently, we are in the process of setting up a specific signaling logging tool and are actively searching for actual partnerships willing to log and analyse their detected signals in quasi real time. We believe this research co-operation between researchers and practitioners is beneficial to both parties and may narrow the gap between them and will create a faster adoption of new insights as soon as they become available.

Keywords: IT sourcing partnerships · premature endings · signaling theory · explorative cases

1 Introduction

Strategic partnerships have a strong attraction within the IT-sourcing field. An IT-sourcing partnership may be an appropriate instrument for developing effective IT "solutions" in an efficient way. Such an IT-sourcing partnership provides the partners the opportunity to make mutual specific investments required for customised IT solutions.

Published by Springer Nature Switzerland AG 2024
R. van de Wetering et al. (Eds.): I3E 2024, LNCS 14907, pp. 197–209, 2024.
https://doi.org/10.1007/978-3-031-72234-9_16

Moreover, as partnerships are in principle established for a longer period, over time the specific investments will pay for itself.

At the same time, due to successive technological changes, the IT environment in which IT-sourcing partnerships operate is characterised by high uncertainty. This uncertainty could unexpectedly lead to situations in which the legitimacy of an IT-sourcing partnership may be questioned. Changed circumstances may undermine the viability of an IT-sourcing partnership and therefore make ending the partnership a serious option. However, properly coping with an unexpected potential ending of a partnership is often not easy [7]. A decision to end may be taken too early, if measures which could recover the problems are overlooked. A decision to end may also be taken too late, if the partners find it hard to say goodbye to an unviable partnership [5]. Furthermore, partners who are unprepared for an ending may be caught off guard and be confronted with high costs in legal fees, time and effort [16].

Despite the relevance of properly governing an unexpected potential ending of an IT-sourcing partnership, this topic has not received a lot of attention in both practice and the literature. In practice it is considered as a negative topic [9]. In addition, Gulati et al. [7, p. 150] state: it is "awkward and counterintuitive to discuss the possibility of divorce while walking to the altar". In the literature, one exception to the above observation is the work of a research group around Tähtinen. During the first decade of the new millennium, this group conducted a series of qualitative studies on the different stages of a partnership ending. This research includes a number of qualitative case studies and focuses on the process of partnership ending. It looks amongst others at the reasons for partnership endings, the sub-stages through which partnership endings occur, strategies which partners could use to communicate about an intended ending, and the possibilities of recovering from an ending process [1, 14, 15, 17–19]. However, more recently, Murthy et al. [11] pointed to the researchers' preference for exploring how to sustain partnerships instead of considering the governance of a partnership's ending as a managerial challenge on its own. Therefore, our paper aims at delving deeper into this underexplored topic of the governance of an unexpected potential ending of an IT-sourcing partnership.

In the context of sourcing relationships, "governance refers to the processes and structures that ensure the strategies and objectives of the parties involved are aligned" [12, p. 204]. According to Heide [8, p. 72], "the governance of interorganizational relationships includes elements of establishing and structuring exchange relationships as well as aspects of monitoring and enforcement, encompassing the initiation, termination and ongoing relationship maintenance between a set of parties." Dekker [3] discusses the specific governance mechanisms in this context. On the one hand, ex-ante governance mechanisms involve governance mechanisms which are established before the partnership comes into operation. For instance, goal setting, and structural specifications, such as planning, procedures, rules and regulations, and the selection of a trustful partner. On the other hand, ex-post governance mechanisms involve acquiring information which comes up during the co-operation, and responding to this new information in an adequate way. Examples of such information include information on new environmental developments or on the trustworthiness of a partner.

While the ending of a partnership is declared as one of the objects of governance (see Heide's citation on governance above), in the existing literature, almost all discussions on governance of partnerships have focused on how to continue a partnership. However, in the case of an unexpected partnership's potential ending, governance no longer is limited to the question of how to continue a partnership. In such a situation, a very relevant governance issue as well is whether it is useful to continue the partnership in the first place. While in some circumstances it may be justified to recover a weakening partnership, in other situations it may be more appropriate to end the partnership. As the environment in which IT sourcing partnerships operate is characterised by a high level of uncertainty, it will be difficult to determine a precise scenario to deal with an unexpected potential ending in advance through ex-ante governance. Therefore, the partners have to turn to ex-post governance, i.e. acting on information which comes up during the co-operation. A party's governance system should be able to pick up ending signals of its partner on time to avoid the party being overtaken by such an ending. One approach in the literature which more specifically looks at signals in a managerial context is signaling theory [2]. This approach starts from the idea that there will be information asymmetry between the sender and receiver of the signal. The sender possesses information which the receiver does not have, but which could be of interest for the receiver. Signaling theory assumes that a sender will try to not just give this information away, but to release this information by means of those signals that will depict him/her the most beneficially. Another aspect which signaling theory discusses is the signaling environment. The environment in which signaling takes place impacts the extent to which signals will be received and also how signals will be interpreted. Finally, a signal is often not an isolated event. A sender may repeat a signal over time, may send a follow-up signal, or receivers may send countersignals. This will lead to patterns of signals that are related to each other.

Above we referred to one group of researchers who did study partnership endings, i.e. the research group around Tähtinen. This research stream mapped a series of theoretical concepts regarding partnership endings and in passing also touches some elements of signaling. However, the discussions in this research stream remain very much at a conceptual level [10, 20]. Therefore, as we will much more extensively discuss later, we argue that to more comprehensively understand processes of partnership endings and the governance of these endings a more empirically grounded local approach is needed.

The aim of this paper is to review the literature about the underexplored topic of governance of unexpected potential endings of IT sourcing partnerships and to use the findings of a series of explorative case studies to identify the boundaries of the knowledge of this topic and to acquire ideas on how to further our understanding on this topic. Given its importance, as discussed above, we thereby specifically focus on the role of signaling. That leads to the following research question. What are the boundaries of the existing knowledge of signaling in partnership endings and how could further understanding of this topic be acquired? The structure of our paper is as follows. In Sect. 2, we first examine what aspects of the role of signaling in the governance of partnership endings have been discussed in the existing literature. In Sect. 3, we more specifically discuss the boundaries regarding this topic in the existing literature. For this part, we make use of actual signaling practices we found in six explorative case studies we conducted on real partnerships which faced unexpected potential endings. Section 4 ends with directions of further research.

2 The Role of Signaling in the Governance of a Partnership's Ending Discussed in the Literature

Signaling theory [2] provides a conceptual framework of signaling. The elements of this conceptual framework are the sender, the signal, the receiver, and the signaling environment. To explore what aspects of the role of signaling in the governance of partnership endings have been discussed in the existing literature, we structure this exploration by using elements of this conceptual framework of signaling. The specific elements of our exploration are the sender, the ending or termination signal, the receiver, the signaling environment, and patterns of signals.

2.1 The Sender

Tähtinen and Halinen- Kaila [18] discuss different types of actor levels that could be involved in signaling a potential ending of a strategic partnership. The first level is the within-partner level. This levels includes individuals or groups of individuals within a partner who could send (and/or receive) ending signals within the own partner organization. The next level is the dyadic level. This level involves the dyadic relationship between the strategic partners. Finally, the network level involves the actors in the wider network in which the strategic partnership is embedded.

There are various sources which may trigger a sender to send an ending signal. The literature points to different sources or reasons why a strategic partnership may end. They could be classified into three categories. The first category involves changes in the strategic motives of the partners to co-operate [4, 13]. For instance, over time a client partner may decide to produce the supplied goods itself. The second category relates to problems with respect to managing the co-operation between the strategic partners [4, 13]. The governance structure may not be adequate to deal with the co-ordination. In addition, opportunistic behaviour or the deterioration of trust may also be reasons inducing a partnership's ending. The third category deals with the problems of performance vis à vis the goals aimed at via the strategic partnership [4].

Signaling theory and also the literature on strategic partnership endings especially pay attention to signals which are purposely sent by senders [1, 2]. This means that through signaling senders try to achieve a strategic effect. This may even imply deceit [2].

2.2 Ending Signal

In accordance with Alajoutsijärvi et al.'s definition of dissolution communication [1], ending signals include "spoken and written communication, and such acts to which the other party assigns a relation-specific meaning" [1, p. 1273], that is in our context a potential ending of the strategic partnership.

Signals can provide two main types of information: 1) information about behaviour or behavioural intentions of the other party, and 2) information about the characteristics of the other party [2]. In the case of ending signals, the first type of information may include opportunistic behaviour of the other party, or changes in its strategic motives.

The second type of information may refer to a lack of competences or skills of the other party.

Alajoutsijärvi et al. [1] distinguish between direct and indirect ending signals. A direct signal is an explicit communication from one of the parties to the other party about an intended ending. An indirect ending signal is also a communication from one of the parties to the other party about an intended ending, but the message is not explicit about this. For instance, a party could give hints to the other partner by changing the conditions of the co-operation for the partner in an unfavourable way. Alajoutsijärvi et al. [1] made a classification of different types of direct and indirect ending signals based upon the level of the sender's other-orientation/ self-orientation. There could be various considerations for choosing direct or indirect ending signals. An indirect ending signal may give the receiver time to adjust his/her behaviour (to avoid an ending) or activities (to deal with an ending), and therefore to avoid hurting him/her. However, the advantage of a direct ending signal is that it "leaves no doubt about relationship's continuity" [1, p. 1284, Table II].

The process of a partnership ending does not necessarily need to be an increasingly weakening relationship [19]. There could also be temporary revivals, e.g. due to alignment activities. Therefore, ending signals are not limited to signals which demonstrate or induce a weakening of the partnership's relationship. Alignment activities meant to restore the relationship, and therefore being signals which indicate a (temporary) strengthening of the relationship, could also be attached to a potential ending process. Therefore, these signals are part of the chain of signals which foreshadow a potential partnership ending as well.

In order to be effective, a signal should be observable. Connelly et al. [2] refer in this respect to the observability of a signal, which they define as "the extent to which outsiders [i.e. in our context the other party] are able to notice the signals" [2, p. 45]. One signaling characteristic which can increase signaling effectiveness is an increase of the signaling frequency. Frequency may refer here to both a more varied package of signals as to a higher number of signals per unit of time.

2.3 The Receiver

The receiver is the actor which picks up the signals. The extent to which an actor will pick up signals also relates to an actor's attention to potential signals [2]. In a case study of a partnership ending, Ryan and Tähtinen [14] found that especially boundary spanners, i.e. actors of a partner who develop personal relationships with actors of the other partner, are in a good position to proactively pick up ending signals.

A signal's effect further depends on the receiver's interpretation of the signal. Different actors could perceive a signal differently. A receiver can also be confronted with different, but contradictory ending signals. In such a situation, the receiver has to weight these different signals in order to come to a total interpretation [2].

2.4 Signaling Environment

The signaling environment may also influence the effect of a signal. Environment includes here both the environmental level of the wider society in which the partnership operates and the environmental level that more specifically applies to the partnership. One environmental factor discussed in the literature is the wider network of actors in which a partnership is embedded. For instance, in the findings of their case study, Salo et al. [15] discuss how a party in the wider network of a triadic relationship, namely the media, strengthened the effect of a signal of one of the parties of the triadic relationship.

A partner's ending signaling strategy may be influenced by the institutional environment in which the partnership is embedded [1, 2]. Due to the partners' specific investments over time, a partnership often leads to an institutional organization structure which can be described as a lock-in situation. In such a situation switching costs for the partners are high. This will limit a partner's ending signaling strategy in that they first have to find a viable alternative before being able to directing to an ending [1].

Over time, the partners of a partnership may build mutual trust and therefore create a relationship which is embedded in a trustworthy environment. Alajoutsijärvi et al. [1] propose that the existence of a trustful environmental atmosphere will lead the partners to choosing a signaling strategy taking into account each other's interests and therefore emphasizing what they named a "beautiful exit".

2.5 Patterns of Signals

A signal may be an isolated event, but it could also be part of a pattern of signals. Earlier we discussed how a sender may try to strengthen the effect of signaling by increasing the signaling frequency. He/she could achieve this by increasing the number and/ or the variety of signals. For instance, a sender could repeat the signal over time. The sender could also achieve this by adjusting the signal over time. For instance, a partner could start indirectly sending ending signals to another partner. As discussed in the literature, a reason for this may be that indirect signaling provides the other party the opportunity and time to adjust its behaviour needed to continue the partnership. This may avoid damage to a partner's business, which could happen in the case of a direct signal being sent as a fait accompli [1]. However, when indirect signaling does not work out, the sender may change to more direct signals. In a case study of an IT sourcing partnership, Tähtinen [17] illustrates how the customer organization first tried to improve its partner's performance by indirectly signaling their co-operation with another supplier. When this did not lead to improvements with its partner, the customer organization sent a direct signal in terms of a formal complaint. As a result the supplier reorganized its customer support unit and solved the IT problems. However, in this specific case, the supplier's adjustments and counter-signals were not timely enough to save the partnership. If a signal reaches a receiver, the signal may not remain unanswered, but the receiver may send a countersignal [2]. Such a course of signaling and countersignaling can also indicate an upcoming ending.

3 Boundaries of the Existing Knowledge of Signaling in Partnership Endings

Because the existing literature on partnership endings remains very much on a conceptual level, as discussed in the introduction, we conducted six explorative case studies of actual endings of strategic IT sourcing partnerships. Through interviews with managers involved in these cases, we exploratively acquired some first understanding of signaling practices. Before the real interviews took place, the interviewees were asked to prepare themselves by recalling the crucial events which had occured during the last year by looking back in their electronic agendas. During individual interviews (in most cases two interviews with each interviewee), these events were mapped on a timeline in order to make a comprehensive reconstruction of the ending process. In four cases, the data collection was ended by a group discussion on the reconstructed time line. Table 1 shows the main characteristics of the six cases. For reasons of convenience, we refer to the partners of the strategic IT sourcing partnerships by supplier and customer. Using the findings of the cases, in the following, we discuss the boundaries regarding this topic in the existing literature.

Table 1. Characteristics of the cases

Characteristics/Case	A	B	C	D	E	F
Act. S[1]	ICT	Producing/ storing commodities	ICT	ICT	ICT	ICT
Act. C[2]	financial	Trading commodities	financial	financial	healthcare	financial
Size S	small	small	large	large	large	small
Size C	large	small	large	large	large	Large
# rsp.[3]	4	2	4	3	4	6

What are limitations and/or possible elaborations regarding the issues discussed in the existing literature, what issues are not yet discussed, what are preliminary observations, and what approach would be appropriate to increase our understanding about the role of signaling in the governance of partnership endings?

3.1 Sender

The starting point of most of the existing literature on partnership endings is that the ending of an inter-firm relationship is the outcome of intentional actors exercising conscious actions [see 1, p. 1281]. However, as Alajoutsijärvi et al. [1] also bring to the fore, this view is limited. Managers can also conduct acts which are not based on a decision to terminate the relationship, but still may unconsciously invoke an ending process. In one of our explorative cases (F), we saw how the customer's initiation of a Request For Proposal (RFP), which had been omitted during 10 years due to the customer's other priorities, unintendedly led to the termination of the relationship with the existing

[1] Supplier.
[2] Client.
[3] Number of respondents.

supplier. This relationship had always been very good and no one had expected a termination upfront. The RFP, however, opened the customer's eyes for other alternatives and thus unintendedly induced the partnership ending. In the same way, signals could also unintendedly foretell a partnership ending. For instance, Tähinen [17] describes how an external network actor sent signals to one of the partners of a strategic IT- partnership that unintentionally indicated the other partner's intention to end the partnership. Therefore, actors sending unintended ending signals are also an important point of attention in the governance of partnership endings.

Another issue which earns further attention is a sender's timing of sending a signal. In Sect. 2.5, we referred to Tähinen's case study [17] where the supplier's counter signals were sent too late to save the partnership. On the other hand, we can imagine that signals could also be sent too early to be picked up by the intended receiver(s). Therefore, an interesting question here is what is an effective timing and what factors do influence the timing of sending a signal?

A next issue for further research is how a sender's characteristics may influence the impact of an ending signal. In one of our explorative cases (A), the supplier attached much value to receiving a signal of the highest hierarchical level of the customer. It would be interesting to more extensively examine how senders' characteristics may influence the impact of an ending signal.

Finally, in one of our explorative cases (A), the dyadic relationship included two sub- relationships. One relationship between the supplier and customer's division X and one between the supplier and customer's division Y. In that case, we saw how a signal in one of the sub-relationships indirectly impacted the other sub-relationship. When division Y sent a signal to the supplier that implied negative consequences for the supplier, this indirectly also created suspicion with the supplier regarding its relationship with division X. Therefore, regarding the sending of signals, the implications of other possible different sub-relationships in a dyadic partnership is also an important point of attention from a governance perspective.

3.2 Ending Signal

A partner's reason to use indirect ending signals discussed in the existing literature is to give the other partner time to adjust his/her behaviour (to avoid the ending) or his/her activities (to deal with the ending), and therefore to avoid hurting him/her [1]. In one of our cases (B), we observed another reason for a party using indirect ending signals. Here, the supplier sent indirect signals to cover a lack of competences. By using indirect signals in the form of evasive language, the supplier circumvented answering to difficult questions, in this case questions on quality complaints. For the customer, these indirect signals were the immediate reason for considering a partnership ending.

Two of our explorative cases (C and A) demonstrated what the impact of the (communication) medium of signaling was on the signaling outcomes. In one case (C), the findings indicated that, due to the possibilities of non-verbal communication, signaling in a face-to-face setting can lead to greater trust building than signaling through written communication. Regarding the extent to which different means of signaling lead to clear signals, we found different opinions in our cases. Some actors (A) found that signals written down provided the most clarity, as the message of the signal is clearly recorded.

However, other actors (A) also attached much value to oral signals in this respect, as oral communication provides the possibility of explaining unclarities regarding differences in interpretations of a signal by different actors. We think that the role of 'signal' mediums in partnership endings is also an interesting issue requiring further research.

3.3 The Receiver

Signaling between the partners in a partnership could occur at different hierarchical levels. Two of our explorative cases (F and E) show that the existence of different hierarchical levels within the partners could lead to unclarity or contradiction regarding the signals that are received. Due to the fact that at the operational dyadic level the customer sent very positive signals to the supplier and at the strategic dyadic level communication between the partners was very limited, in one of our explorative cases (F), the supplier was totally surprised by the customer's strategic level's decision to end partnership. In another case (E), the supplier was also surprised by the customer's decision to end a large part of the partnership. Here the supplier was surprised due to the fact that for a long time the customer's strategic level was not aware of the problems at the operational level, and therefore signaled a very rosy picture of the partnership to the supplier during that period. In the above examples, we observe that signaling at different hierarchical partner levels could be a source of unclear or even misleading signals to the receiving partner. In other words, lack of communication between the different hierarchical levels within the partners can also be an important reason for disturbing the clarity of signals to receiving partners.

A receiving partner could also be confronted with receiving very few or no signals from his/her partner. While the saying goes 'no news is good news', in two of our explorative cases (D and B), we saw the contrary. In one explorative case (D), one partner internally considered a partnership ending during a period of more than one year, without signaling anything about this to his/her partner. Therefore, eventually the ending was presented to the partner as a fait accompli and the settlement of the ending was very unpleasant. In this explorative case, the lack of signaling by one of the partners could be seen as a lack of transparency and openness to the other partner. In another explorative case (B), also referred to in Sect. 3.2, we saw how during a long period of time the customer partner sent direct signals about quality problems to his/her supplier partner without receiving clear responses from his/her supplier. The supplier did not or very indirectly signal anything to his/her customer about this in order to win time to solve the quality problems. In both cases, we observe that no news is not necessarily good news, but that no news could also very well be an indication for a potential partnership ending.

3.4 Signaling Environment

The environmental lock-in effect, discussed in the literature, was at issue in one of our explorative cases (B). While the customer wished to end the partnership, he/she was stopped to do so by the lock-in effect. He/she had no viable alternative for its partner. However, once the customer eventually found a viable alternative, his/her wish to end the partnership was communicated in a direct way. This case endorses that a lock-in situation limits a partner's ending signaling strategy and suggests that in a lock-in situation a partner who wishes to end a partnership will most probably use an indirect signaling strategy.

In the existing literature, it is argued that, in a partnership embedded in a trustful atmosphere, in case of a partnership ending, the partners tend to pursue a "beautiful exit". In one of our explorative cases (D), we found how a trustful relationship between partners could also lead to a situation in which issues need to be handled, but as the handling of these issues may have painful consequences for one of the partners, this is moved forward. Such a state of execution, however, may eventually only lead to more pain. Partnerships embedded in a trustful atmosphere, therefore, run the risk of having endings that are in fact "too late".

3.5 Patterns of Signals

Earlier we discussed that signals are not necessarily isolated events, but that they will often be a part of a chain of related signals. In this respect an interesting question is whether typical patterns of signals can be distinguished that indicate a partnership ending.

One pattern which we saw various times was the situation in which the customer experienced quality problems regarding the supplier's services and let this know to his/her supplier. However, as in response the supplier did not really pick up these problems, over time the customer sent his/her signals about the quality problems in an increasingly stronger way to his/her supplier.

One real example of such a typical pattern was the case of Tähtinen [17], we referred to earlier. In this case, the customer tried to increase the impact of his/her signals by changing from indirect signaling to direct signaling.

In one of our explorative cases (B), as from the start, the customer sent direct signals about the quality problems to his/her supplier. However, here we saw that the direct signaling itself became increasingly stronger over time. Where the customer started with sending e-mails about the quality problems, over time he/she intensified the sending of signals about this issue by making telephone calls and having online meetings, and one day the CEO of the customer even went to the office of the supplier unannounced. Another interesting pattern in this case was the change of the tone of signaling during the above episode. Where signaling was initially focused on the content of the quality problems, over time the relational part of the signaling, i.e. the customer's dissatisfaction, got the upper hand. Therefore, it would be interesting to include in further research on patterns of signaling more signaling characteristics, such as changes in the means of signaling applied and changes in the tone of signaling.

A final interesting observation in the same case what the customer's abrupt change from direct signaling to indirect signaling. When the customer eventually completely lost his/ her confidence in his/her supplier, he/she decided to stop sending direct signals about the quality problems, and to change to sending indirect signals by phasing out work with the supplier. Interestingly, in contrast to his/her earlier direct signals, this indirect signal immediately attracted attention of the supplier. Obviously, one reason for this was that this indirect signal more strongly hurt the supplier than the earlier direct signals. With us, this episode evoked the question should sudden changes in signaling also be considered as an indication for a potential partnership ending?

4 Directions of Future Research

The previous section has shown that the dynamics in strategic partnerships cannot be ignored. Whereas in early studies the partner selection problem received much scientific attention, focus shifts towards the continuous change and development of partnerships over time. The idea of finding a perfect partner at the initial stages of a strategic co-operation plan and then be done with it is too simplistic and leads to premature and "non-beautiful exits". Arguably, the real challenge of a successful partnership is to be able to learn from the co-operation activities, to synchronize and advance interests and to demonstrate commitment. However, developing this dynamic perspective into a useful managerial partnership management instrument is yet in its infancy.

We believe that discovering and studying the potentially large diversity of meaningful events during a partnership will yield a better understanding of the mechanics in which partnerships evolve and to the way in which this can be influenced favourably. Signaling theory provides a useful ontology to discover such mechanics, as the reported observations in the previous sections have shown. We advocate to study signals more rigorously and systematically in numerous actual partnerships. Then, it may become clear whether a limited set of recurring patterns "announce" a premature ending of a partnership and whether intervention is desirable, or alternatively, no clear uniquely identifiable patterns exist and real time monitoring and analysis of actual signals is needed in each individual partnership. Besides the identification of signal-patterns, their placement in time may be crucial in determining whether sufficient time is available to respond effectively before irreversible damage to a partnership occurs. In other words, the speed in which a signaling pattern evolves may influence the urgency in which an effective response must be found. In short, signals need to be placed on a timeline to see the speed in which events unfold and to aid in determining the causality of events. A third aspect in the interpretation of signals is the power-structure of the senders and receivers, aka the obvious stakeholders in a partnership, and the environment in which they interact. They are the agents who determine when, with or by whom and what responses to certain received signals will be given. Their competence, intent and power can be a determining factor in the continuity of a partnership.

Currently, we are in the process of setting up a specific signaling logging tool and are actively searching for actual partnerships willing to log and analyse their detected signals in quasi real time. The involved researchers will provide assistance to the practioners, who do the logging, with the interpretation of those signals and getting the logged data for scientific analysis in return. In doing so, participants are actively involved in this research, whilst at the same time, they are monitoring the continuity of their partnership. We believe this research co-operation between researchers and practitioners is beneficial to both parties and may narrow the gap between them and will create a faster adoption of new insights as soon as they become available. We expect that, although, the discovery of meaningful signaling patterns is not guaranteed, participants can still have better chances in discovering partnership misalignment problems by continuing with regular analysis of routinely logged signals after this research project has ended. We are aiming for positive and long term motivational effects with the application of citizen science principles (see ECSA standards [6]) in shaping the research setup.

Acknowledgements. The authors wish to thank the following individuals for their substantial effort in the collection of data and its analysis for this research project: Ron Geurts, Rik Weith, Laura Bronkhorst, Kirsten van Heiningen, Wilco Boogert and Bob van Rooijen.

References

1. Alajoutsijärvi, K., Möller, K., Tähtinen, J.: Beautiful exit: how to leave your business partner. European J. Marketing **34**(11/12), 1270–1288 (2000)
2. Connelly, B.L., Certo, S.T., Ireland, R.D., Reutzel, C.R.: Signaling theory: a review and assessment. J. Manag. **37**(1), 39–67 (2011)
3. Dekker, H.C.: Control of inter-organizational relationships: evidence on appropriation concerns and coordination requirements. Acc. Organ. Soc. **29**, 27–49 (2004)
4. Doyle, P., Corstjens, M., Michell, P.: Signals of vulnerability in agency-client relations. J. Marketing **44**, 18–23 (1980)
5. Duke, A.: Quit: The Power of Knowing When to Walk Away. Penguin Publishing Group, London (2022)
6. European Citizen Science Association (ECSA), Ten principles of citizen science, Berlin (2015). ttp://doi.org/https://doi.org/10.17605/OSF.IO/XPR2N
7. Gulati, R., Sytch, M., Mehrotra, P.: Breaking up is never easy: planning for exit in a strategic alliance. Calif. Manage. Rev. **50**(4), 147–163 (2008)
8. Heide, J.B.: Interorganizational governance in marketing channels. J. Marketing **58**, 71–85 (1994)
9. Jongen, H.: Exitstrategie en (her) contracteren. In: Handboek Sourcing. Culemborg: Van Duuren Media B.V., pp. 159–168 (2024)
10. Kamminga, P.E., Martin, H.: Signals foretelling the ending of an IT Sourcing strategic partnership. ICIS 2022: Annual SIG Advances in Sourcing and the 15th Global Sourcing Workshop 2022 (2022)
11. Murthy, S.R., Roll, K., Collin-Jones, A.: Ending business-non-profit partnerships: the spinout of social enterprises. Scand. J. Manag. **37**, 1–13 (2021)
12. Oshri, I., Kotlarsky, J., Willcocks, L.P.: Governance of outsourcing projects. In: The Handbook of Global Outsourcing and Offshoring, pp. 203–217. Palgrave Macmillan, Cham (2023)
13. Park, S.H., Ungson, G.R.: Interfirm rivalry and managerial complexity: a conceptual framework of alliance failure. Organization Science **12**(1), 37–53 (2001)
14. Ryan, A., Tähtinen, J.: Relationship ending from the perspective of the non- initiator. J. Cust. Behav. **11**(2), 197–212 (2012)
15. Salo, A., Tähtinen, J., Ulkuniemi, P.: Twists and turns of triadic business relationship recovery. Ind. Mark. Manage. **38**, 618–632 (2009)
16. Serapio, M.G., Cascio, W.F.: End-games in international alliances. Acad. Manag. Exec. **10**(1), 62–73 (1996)
17. Tähtinen, J.: The process of business relationship ending – its stages and actors. J. Mark.-Focus. Manag. **5**, 331–353 (2002)
18. Tähtinen, J., Halinen- Kaila, A.: The death of business triads: the dissolution process of a net of companies. In: Proceedings of the 13th Annual IMP Conference, Lyon (1997)

19. Tidström, A., Ahman, S.: The process of ending inter-organizational cooperation. J. Bus. Industrial Marketing **21**(5), 281–290 (2006)
20. Zaefarian, G., Forkmann, S., Mitręga, M., Henneberg, S.C.: A capability perspective on relationship ending and its impact on product innovation success and firm performance. Long Range Plan. **50**, 184–199 (2017)

Evaluating Factors Affecting Users' Intention to Use and Satisfaction in the Digital Justice Sector

Fotis Kitsios[1,2(✉)], Anastasia Tsotoulidou[1], and Maria Kamariotou[1]

[1] Department of Applied Informatics, University of Macedonia, Thessaloniki, Greece
kitsios@uom.gr

[2] School of Social Science, Hellenic Open University, Parodos Aristotelous 18, 26335 Patras, Greece

Abstract. ICT use in e-government, especially in the justice sector, opens up new possibilities and improves user and citizen services. Studies looking at the acceptance and satisfaction of users of the electronic justice system are scarce, despite the fact that this scientific field has drawn the interest of many academics and professionals in the justice sector and that money has been spent on enhancing the performance of justice staff and the outcomes of the courts. Thus, in the context of Greek e-justice services, this paper evaluates level of IS employees' satisfaction in the justice sector. Data was collected by 121 internal users in Greece. Employees appears that they are more concerned with obtaining a positive overall impression of the system and making sure that the application has quality dimensions that will enable it to be helpful for their everyday work activities.

Keywords: E-justice · Digital justice sector · E-government · IT strategy · Digital transformation

1 Introduction

The public sector and several businesses have been impacted by recent advancements in information technology (IT) and information systems (IS) [1–6]. IT and IS revolutionize individuals, organizations, and public agencies by offering efficient and secure access to all resources from a centralized location [7–10]. Introducing IS in government is a crucial step in a broader process of change that aims to help the government deliver services that are safer, more dependable, and more efficient to individuals, organizations, and businesses [11–13]. Various researchers have studied and discussed this process. It is crucial to have a high degree of performance in the e-justice system that primarily satisfies the majority of internal users. The court system, along with other sectors of the public sector, has also investigated various approaches to the advancement of Information and Communication Technologies (ICT) in order to enhance the efficiency and efficacy of its services [14–17]. The widespread adoption of trial technology has enabled the implementation of novel workplace procedures and organizational structures, resulting

Published by Springer Nature Switzerland AG 2024
R. van de Wetering et al. (Eds.): I3E 2024, LNCS 14907, pp. 210–221, 2024.
https://doi.org/10.1007/978-3-031-72234-9_17

in a reduction of the growing workload of courts and the gradual pace of legal proceedings [18–20].

Developers specifically developed IT solutions to streamline daily tasks for lawyers and court personnel in the e-justice field. Court-management technology enhances the job effectiveness of administrative workers by facilitating the adoption of creative employment methods. In judicial IS, the information is accessible to all users in a centralized electronic environment [21–24]. Users with credentials include judges, solicitors, lawyers, and other court personnel. Computerized justice systems provide quick and easy access to this data. Furthermore, judicial IS necessitate users to exclusively carry out all information and record-related tasks online. The primary objective of a justice information system is to enhance the precision and speed of data, paperwork, and workflow related to non-compliant services in courts [25–31].

Prior scholars have utilized contemporary IT/IS concepts to facilitate the implementation of efficient IS in enterprises. Several models in this field include the Technology Acceptance Model (TAM) proposed by [11], the Theory of Planned Behavior (TPB) developed by [12], and the unified theory of acceptance and use of technology [13]. The elements that influence IS and user behavior play a crucial role in ensuring the successful implementation of IT/IS. The introduction of evaluation models aimed to address user demands and analyze the various dimensions and aspects contributing to system evolution, with the goal of enhancing acceptance and satisfaction [14–16]. Many research studies conducted in various nations have relied on the DeLone and McLean model of IS success (1992) [17] to describe the effects of IS [10]. While IS scholars have devoted considerable attention to the IS success model, there have been few studies conducted to evaluate the efficacy of justice systems in courts. Hence, acknowledging the effectiveness of e-justice systems and understanding the elements that influence court staff performance is critical for addressing gaps in existing research and facilitating future investigations.

Contemporary studies in the domain of e-government have focused on public satisfaction as the ultimate consumer. There is less research available on the embrace and satisfaction of internal users. In addition, existing IS success models focus on evaluating systems from a technical perspective or analyzing the organizational structure. Researchers have not yet examined court evaluations of IS that prioritize users' needs and perspectives. In order to create an effective e-justice system, it is crucial to achieve a level of performance that primarily meets the needs of the majority of internal users [6, 7, 9].

This research intends to investigate the elements that influence the acceptance and satisfaction of users of the e-justice system in Greece. A total of 121 internal users and lawyers in Greece collected the data. Factor analysis has been utilized to examine the specific components of user acceptance and satisfaction constructs.

The paper is organized into the following sections: The subsequent section, following a concise introduction to this subject, delves into the theoretical foundation of pleasure in e-government and justice. Section 3 elucidates the methodology, while Sect. 4 presents the survey findings. Section 5 provides the final findings, concluding the work.

2 Theoretical Background

2.1 Digital Systems in e-Justice

The integration of IT and computer technology into public administration led to the emergence of e-government, which encompasses new administrative methodologies. E-government enhances openness, efficiency, and public accessibility and is widely recognized as a fundamental element in aiding the reform of public governance [19]. E-justice IS are playing a role in improving the justice system's fairness, efficiency, and transparency of the justice system as part of public-sector reforms in e-government. Despite the genuine difficulties associated with implementing such technologies in the judicial system, their prevalence is increasing across Europe and worldwide [32].

[7] conducted a case study to examine the efficacy of these applications in Italy. According to the researchers, while these applications are required for staff in Italian courts, the use of documents is a common practice. However, the use of applications is not obligatory for judges and lawyers are not required to use applications. By utilizing a questionnaire and employing the DeLone and McLean models, the findings of their study establish a significant correlation between the effectiveness of the Electronic Justice model and the system's quality, which is a vital aspect in the utilization of such systems. [33] introduce the Phoenix project, initiated in Belgium in 2001. This initiative represents a crucial milestone in the implementation of e-justice systems, utilizing electronic data and open source standards. When comparing this plan to similar systems in other nations, there are several problems that could impede the success of the project. These challenges include ensuring the security of the system, making necessary legislative changes, and changing the mindset of justice workers. In their case study of Switzerland, [34] argue that justice management should primarily focus on ensuring the effective protection of legal rights and the fair allocation of public resources. Additionally, research confirms that ongoing communication among the relevant domestic and international entities is a crucial factor. It is important to note that an evaluation model for Turkey's national justice information system has been developed, as described in the report by [6]. Following the establishment of fundamental principles of IS, the authors employed variables derived from several models to investigate 8,840 justice officers in Turkey. They determine that the primary problem with the system is the abundance and intricacy of the procedures required for its execution. Therefore, we anticipate that users will optimize the system's functions and interfaces. This study represents Turkey's first evaluation of a proficient electronic justice system, specifically focusing on the internal user.

Greece also has examples of e-justice applications. [35] investigates Greek courts' efficacy and the challenges they face, proposing an enhanced method to improve their performance. This report is the initial document in the Integrated Justice Case Management System (IACS). Simultaneously, [35] examined an instance of electronic criminal records in Greece. The primary objective of a criminal record information system, as stated by the authors, is to create a digital criminal record entry that generates an automated version of the applicant's certified criminal record. Additionally, it allows citizens to electronically submit their applications. [36] conducted a study that examines the standards for judges and justice officers to use ICT in Greek courts. It also examines the level of acceptability, perceived usefulness, perceived ease of use, and user intention to work with the new IACS system. Utilizing the TAM and a limited number of participants in the study, the researchers deduce that while the individuals included had considerable knowledge about ICT in the judicial system, they exhibit a sense of caution when it comes to embracing this novel integrated justice system.

[37] investigate the unique correlation between technological advancements and this particular link in their research. In their initial investigation, they examine a case study of a comprehensive computerized case management system. Using a qualitative interpretive method, the researchers focus on the four primary categories of applications outlined in E-court's general plan. They emphasize that the main challenges in integrating electronic files are ensuring access, maintaining security, and achieving interoperability. During their second inquiry, they examined the implementation of Sharia law using electronic means (E-Shariah) in the country's courts. Their research used a qualitative methodology, and the data they gathered facilitates comprehension of how technology is utilized in both the court procedure and the broader file management cycle. [18] investigate the advantages and accomplishments resulting from the implementation of ICT in the civil justice system of supreme courts. Based on personal, semi-structured interviews, it is determined that users gain advantages from the utilization of technology and that each of the ICT applications contributes to favorable transformations in the justice system of the country.

Nevertheless, the successful use of cutting-edge electronic systems in the justice sector typically requires quick mitigation of associated dangers. [38] discuss the hazards associated with creating an information system in the justice sector. They examine a similar system that Cape Verde, a developing African country, implemented. The authors identify multiple risk factors associated with the creation, deployment, and evaluation of such systems. They conclude that despite the global nature of the examples they provide, which originate from diverse nations and encompass distinct materials, these examples share common risk characteristics. The authors reach the conclusion that effective collaboration among all relevant parties and adequate training are crucial measures for mitigating all potential dangers. [39] propose using existing opportunities and evaluation methodologies to create IS specifically tailored for courts in Uganda. They identify the shortcomings of the current system and suggest modifications, with the expectation that their efforts will contribute to the development of a comprehensive framework that other countries can adopt. [40] conducted a study to address practical deficiencies in the utility aspects of integrated e-justice initiatives within Uganda, an African nation. We utilized the literature and research to identify deficiencies in information, technology, procedures, skills, and management structures within these systems. [41] have just introduced the new judicial information system in Rwanda, focusing on its fundamental features and implementation. The system, founded in 2016, is a prestigious and acclaimed platform in Africa. It serves as the exclusive gateway for all justice ministries. They emphasize the crucial factors for its success, highlighting the importance of training public officials before, during, and after its implementation as an essential initial measure in addressing any limitations.

Based on the analysis of the existing literature, the following hypotheses are defined [6, 7, 42, 43]:

H1: System quality has a positive effect on user's satisfaction.
H2: Information quality has a positive effect on user's satisfaction.
H3: Service quality has a positive effect on user's satisfaction.
H4: Perceived ease of use has a positive effect on user's satisfaction.
H5: Perceived usefulness has a positive effect on user's satisfaction

3 Methodology

The current study will examine two samples, consisting of two distinct categories of information system users: court personnel in Thessaloniki and lawyers. A total of 125 lawyers who utilize the e-justice system in the Thessaloniki court, along with 121 staff working in the same court, have successfully filled out the questionnaire.

Based on previous research, this study's questionnaire integrates the two primary research trends on user satisfaction and technological acceptability identified in the literature [7, 11, 17, 43]. Put simply, it relies on the DeLone and McLean success model for IS and Davis' TAM. A combination model like this one assists in determining the extent to which a particular system meets its requirements and demonstrates its worth based on the observations of its immediate recipients, the users. Adding variables to both models also gives a bigger picture of how these IS are used because it includes both objective and subjective parts of how they are defined [6, 7].

To operationalize the above-mentioned constructs the five-point Likert scale was used. Analysis of the data was implemented using Multiple Regression Analysis.

System quality refers to the stability, correctness, and applicability of the hardware and software that supply the necessary information. Technical attributes associated with the network and computer equipment specifically identify system quality, and the performance characteristics of the studied systems serve as decisive factors for its assessment [6]. Based on the dominant success model, the technical level is responsible for the quality of a system, while the semantic level is responsible for the quality of information [43].

The quality of information is a complex notion that encompasses the understanding, relevance, completeness, and efficacy of information generated by an information system [17]. The existing body of research on IS acknowledges that the quality and performance of a system have an impact on users' behavior, as demonstrated by studies conducted by [17, 43]. Furthermore, it is widely accepted that both system quality and information quality are key determinants of user satisfaction. Users who perceive a system as accurate, exact, and timely are more likely to find it enjoyable and satisfying to use [7].

Comparing user preferences with the actual output of services enhances service quality. The concept encompasses two viewpoints, namely sufficiency and availability, and primarily manifests through assisting users in carrying out their tasks and providing support as needed. Thus, it is believed that enhancing service quality will lead to improved efficiency and satisfaction among internal users [6]. Moreover, the present literature indicates that the effectiveness of implementing IS is primarily determined by quality criteria [44].

[11] characterizes perceived ease of use as a user's belief in the effortless utilization of a specific system. According to [6] the perception of how easy a system is to use has a positive impact on the perception of its usefulness. This is because the simpler the system is to use, the more beneficial it becomes. Prior studies have established the significance of system usability in relation to user satisfaction [42]. Perceived usefulness and perceived ease of use shape users' attitude towards a system. This mindset influences the readiness to use a system, which subsequently characterizes its practical application.

[11] defines perceived usefulness as the degree to which a user believes that using a certain technology would enhance their work performance. The analysis of this variable concentrates on evaluating the efficiency and speed of work completion, as well as the overall benefits of the system for the organization or firm using it. According to personal judgments, there is a strong cause-and-effect relationship between the perceived usefulness of IS and user satisfaction and perceptions ease of use [43].

4 Results

The reliability was measured using Cronbach's alpha, and the values ranged from 0.904 to 0.968, exceeding the minimally recommended level of 0.70 [45]. These values are displayed in Table 1.

Table 1. Cronbach a.

Variables	Cronbach a
Satisfaction	0.917
System quality	0.904
Information quality	0.968
Service quality	0.930
Perceived ease of use	0.907
Perceived usefulness	0.961

The normal P-P and scatter plots (Fig. 1) showed that data is normally distributed (i.e., all residuals cluster around the 'line'), complies with the assumptions of homogeneity of variance (i.e., homo-scedasticity) and linearity. Residual errors are in fact evenly distributed and not related to the value of the predicted value, suggesting that the relationship is, in fact, linear and the variance of y for each value of x is the same, this confirming the homoscedasticity assumption. Univariate outliers were checked for using z-scores and all values were within acceptable range. In succession, multivariate outliers were checked using Mahalanobis and Cook's distances. No influential outliers were detected. Multicollinearity was checked using variance inflation factors (VIF).

Table 2 also presents the summary indicators of R, R^2, adjusted R^2, Durbin-Watson indicator and the standard deviation error of the regression. The R^2 and adjusted R^2 values of 0.672 and 0.658 indicate that about 65% of the variance in success is explained

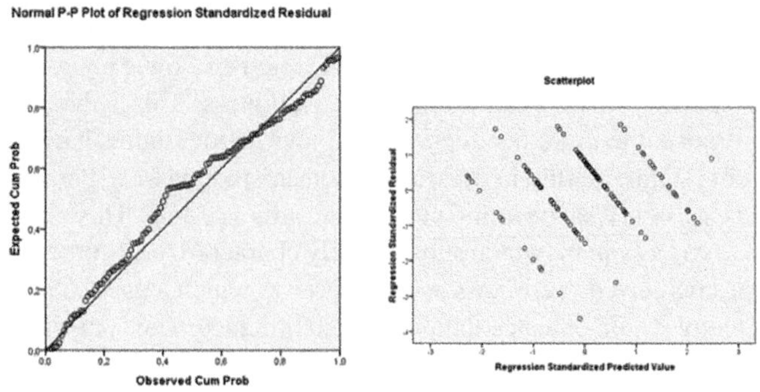

Fig. 1. Normal P-P plot of regression standardized residual and residual scatter plot

by the explanatory variables. Thus, the regression model predicts satisfaction well, since the explanatory power of the regression is higher than 50%. The results of ANOVA regression analysis in Table 3 also allow corroboration of the good prediction capacity of the regression model. The F statistic is 81.735 with 121 degrees of freedom (5 from the regression and 116 from residuals) and the whole regression is significant at the 0.000 level.

Table 2. Mean, standard deviation, and correlations.

R	R^2	Adjusted R^2	Estimate standard error	Durbin-Watson
0.820	0.672	0.658	0.4170	2.150

Table 3. ANOVA statistics of regression.

Model		Sum of square	Df	Mean Square	F	Sig
1	Regression	76.260	5	15.252	81.735	0.000
	Residual	21.459	116	0.187		
	Total	97.719	121			

The path coefficient between System quality and Satisfaction was positive and statistically significant ($\beta = 0.352$, $p < 0.001$). Therefore, H1 was supported for employees. There was a positive relationship between Information quality and Satisfaction ($\beta = 0.058$, $p > 0.05$) but not statistically significant. Therefore, H2 was not supported for employees. There was a positive relationship between Service quality and Satisfaction ($\beta = 0.198$, $p < 0.05$) and statistically significant. Thus, H3 was supported for employees. The path coefficient between Perceived ease of use and Satisfaction was positive but not significant statistically ($\beta = 0.036$, $p > 0.05$). Therefore, H4 was not supported for employees. There was a positive relationship between Perceived usefulness and Satisfaction ($\beta = 0.078$, $p < 0.001$) and statistically significant. Thus, H5 was supported for employees. Table 4 presents the results of regression analysis and Table 5 presents the correlations.

Table 4. Regression analysis (*P < 0.05, **P < 0.01, ***P < 0.001).

Model	B	t-Value	VIF
System quality	0.352	4.394	3.363
Information quality	0.058	0.679	3.800
Service quality	0.198	3.143	2.082
Perceived ease of use	0.036	0.463	3.136
Perceived usefulness	0.078	4.261	3.745

Table 5. Correlations.

	Satisfaction	System quality	Information quality	Service quality	Perceived ease of use	Perceived usefulness
Satisfaction	1.000	0.789	0.759	0.715	0.721	0.808
System quality	0.789	1.000	0.823	0.599	0.670	0.685
Information quality	0.759	0.823	1.000	0.645	0.690	0.717
Service quality	0.715	0.599	0.645	1.000	0.597	0.684
Perceived ease of use	0.721	0.670	0.690	0.597	1.000	0.806
Perceived usefulness	0.808	0.685	0.717	0.684	0.806	1.000

5 Conclusion

This research intended to investigate the elements that influence the acceptance and satisfaction of users of the e-justice system in Greece. After analyzing the findings, it is clear that the system's quality, information quality, service quality, and perceived usefulness significantly contribute to the overall satisfaction of the users. However, the system's perceived ease of use does not have a significant impact on satisfaction. Within this group, the system's quality has a greater impact on overall satisfaction compared to the other components. It appears that this group is primarily concerned with obtaining a comprehensive understanding of the system. They prioritize the quality aspects of the system, as they directly impact their daily work tasks and productivity.

When comparing the results of our study with those of the authors mentioned in the literature review, it is important to highlight that their findings are primarily coincidental. Prior research indicates that all three dimensions of quality have direct and favorable impacts on the satisfaction of internal users of their respective systems. The significance of each dimension in overall satisfaction varies depending on the specific research being considered [6, 7, 44]. However, most surveys indicate that the ease of use and perceived usefulness of IS have a positive impact on user acceptance. These dimensions refer to how users believe the system can improve their work performance [6, 8, 43, 46, 47].

Throughout the survey, there was a limitation imposed on the sample size. This study examined the level of user satisfaction with e-justice system, namely in the courts, where it is being tested on a trial basis. Nevertheless, limiting the study to the courts of Thessaloniki resulted in a relatively small sample size compared to the majority of empirical surveys that have employed the questionnaire approach. Furthermore, the absence of a comprehensive geographical analysis has hindered the assessment of justice performance at a larger organizational scale. Future research could benefit from using a representative nationwide sample of users, even though assessing the job satisfaction of employees in the specific courts under study is an initial step towards understanding the performance of all users. Therefore, we should approach any generalizations from the data with caution.

Expanding the research on a national scale to include justice services that are actively testing the application would yield more dependable research findings. This will also enable the identification of any variations in the system's usage across different regions, providing an overall assessment of user satisfaction. In the end, doing a new study later on and after a long time of using the information system would let us compare the results of the two surveys, find any problems or mistakes with the application, and stress how technology has improved the efficiency of the Greek courts. The results would offer valuable insights to both legal authorities and IT experts, enabling them to enhance the functionality, scope, and adoption of the application by other stakeholders in the judicial system, including court officials. This will unquestionably enhance the efficiency and fairness of the legal system.

References

1. Kitsios, F., Kamariotou, M., Grigoroudis, E.: Digital entrepreneurship services evolution: analysis of quadruple and quintuple helix innovation models for open data ecosystems. Sustainability **13**, 12183 (2021)
2. Charalabidis, Y., Loukis, E., Lachana, Z., Alexopoulos, C.: Future research directions on the science base and the evolution of the digital governance domain. In: Proceedings of the International Conference on Information Systems (ICIS 2019), Munich, Germany (2019)
3. Kitsios, F., Kamariotou, M.: Beyond open data hackathons: exploring digital innovation success. Information **10**, 235 (2019)
4. Loukis, E., Charalabidis, Y.: Why do eGovernment projects fail? Risk factors of large information systems projects in the Greek public sector: an international comparison. Int. J. Electronic Government Res. **7**, 59–77 (2011)
5. Loukis, E.N., Tsouma, N.: Critical issues of information systems management in the Greek public sector. Information Polity **7**, 65–83 (2002)

6. Oktal, O., Alpu, O., Yazici, B.: Measurement of internal user satisfaction and acceptance of the e-justice system in Turkey. Aslib J. Inf. Manag. **68**, 716–735 (2016)
7. Agrifoglio, R., Metallo, C., Lepore, L.: Success factors for using case management system in Italian courts. Inf. Syst. Manag. **33**, 42–54 (2016)
8. Sachan, A., Kumar, R., Kumar, R.: Examining the impact of e-government service process on user satisfaction. J. Global Operations and Strategic Sourcing **11**, 321–336 (2018)
9. Stefanovic, D., Marjanovic, U., Delić, M., Culibrk, D., Lalic, B.: Assessing the success of e-government systems: an employee perspective. Information & Management **53**, 717–726 (2016)
10. Wang, Y.S., Liao, Y.W.: Assessing eGovernment systems success: a validation of the DeLone and McLean model of information systems success. Gov. Inf. Q. **25**, 717–733 (2008)
11. Davis, F.D.: Perceived usefulness, perceived ease of use, and user acceptance of information technology. MIS Q. **13**, 319–340 (1989)
12. Ajzen, I.: The theory of planned behaviour. Organ. Behav. Hum. Decis. Process. **50**, 179–211 (1991)
13. Kamariotou, M., Kitsios, F.: An empirical evaluation of strategic information systems planning phases in SMEs: determinants of effectiveness. In: Proceedings of the 6th International Symposium and 28th National Conference on Operational Research, Thessaloniki, Greece (2017a)
14. Sitaridis, I., Kitsios, F.: Entrepreneurial intentions of information technology students: the theory of planned behaviour, the role of gender and education. J. Int. Bus. Entrep. Dev. **10**, 316–335 (2017)
15. Kamariotou, M., Kitsios, F.: Information systems phases and firm performance: a conceptual framework. In: Kavoura, A., Sakas, D., Tomaras, P. (eds.) Strategic Innovative Marketing, Springer Proceedings in Business and Economics, Springer, pp. 553–560 (2017b)
16. Kitsios, F., Kamariotou, M.: Strategic IT alignment: business performance during financial crisis. In: Tsounis, N., Vlachvei, A. (eds.) Advances in Applied Economic Research, Springer Proceedings in Business and Economics, Springer, pp. 503–525 (2017). https://doi.org/10.1007/978-3-319-48454-9_33
17. Delone, W.H., McLean, E.R.: The DeLone and McLean model of information systems success: a ten-year update. J. Manag. Inf. Syst. **19**, 9–30 (2003)
18. Hamin, Z., Bahrin, O.M., Mohamad, A.M.: Benefits and achievements of ICT adoption by the high courts of Malaysia. In: 2012 IEEE Symposium on Humanities, Science and Engineering Research, Kuala Lumpur, Kuala Lumpur, Malaysia (2012)
19. Velicogna, M.: Justice systems and ICT - what can be learned from Europe? Utrecht Law Review **3**, 129–147 (2007)
20. Sang, S., Lee, J.-D.: A conceptual model of e-government acceptance in public sector. In: Proceedings of the 3rd International Conference on Digital Society (ICDS 2009), Cancun, Mexico (2009)
21. Weerakkody, V., Irani, Z., Lee, H., Hindi, N., Osman, I.: Are U.K. citizens satisfied with e-government services?. identifying and testing antecedents of satisfaction. Information Systems Manage. **33**, 331–343 (2016)
22. Anwer, A.M., Esichaikul, V., Rehman, M., Anjum, M.: E-government services evaluation from citizen satisfaction perspective: a case of Afghanistan. Transforming Government: People, Process and Policy **10**, 139–167 (2016)
23. Wirtz, B.W., Kurtz, O.T.: Local e-government and user satisfaction with city portals – the citizens' service preference perspective. International Review on Public and Nonprofit Marketing **13**, 265–287 (2016)
24. Danila, R., Abdullah, A.: User's satisfaction on E-government services: an integrated model. Procedia Soc. Behav. Sci. **164**, 575–582 (2014)

25. Skordoulis, M., Alasonas, P., Pekka-Economou, V.: E-government services quality and citizens' satisfaction: a multi-criteria satisfaction analysis of TAXISnet information system in Greece. Int. J. Productivity and Quality Manage. **22**, 82–100 (2017)
26. Horan, T.A., Abhichandani, T., Rayalu, R.: Assessing user satisfaction of E-government services: development and testing of quality-in-use satisfaction with advanced traveler information systems (ATIS). In: Proceedings of the 39th Hawaii International Conference on System Sciences (HICSS'06), Kauia, HI, USA (2016)
27. Athmay, A.A.A.A., Fantazy, K., Kumar, V.: E-government adoption and user's satisfaction: an empirical investigation. EuroMed J. Bus. **11**, 57–83 (2016)
28. Dukić, D., Dukić, G., Bertović, N.: Public administration employees' readiness and acceptance of e-government: findings from a Croatian survey. Inf. Dev. **33**, 525–539 (2017)
29. Floropoulos, J., Spathis, C., Halvatzis, D., Tsipouridou, M.: Measuring the success of the Greek taxation information system. Int. J. Inf. Manage. **30**, 47–56 (2010)
30. Terpsiadou, M.H., Economides, A.A.: The use of information systems in the Greek public financial services: the case of TAXIS. Gov. Inf. Q. **26**, 468–476 (2009)
31. Al-Busaidy, M., Weerakkody, V., Dwivedi, Y.K.: Factors influencing eGovernment progress in oman: an employee's perspective. In: Proceedings of the 15th Americas Conference on Information Systems (AMCIS), San Francisco, California, USA (2009)
32. Urbach, N., Smolnik, S., Riempp, G.: An empirical investigation of employee portal success. J. Strateg. Inf. Syst. **19**, 184–206 (2010)
33. De Vuyst, B., Fairchild, A.: The Phenix project: a case study of e-justice in Belgium. In: Proceedings of the 8th International Conference on Electronic Commerce: The new e-commerce - Innovations for Conquering Current Barriers, Obstacles and Limitations to Conducting Successful Business on the Internet, New York (2006)
34. Lienhard, A., Kettiger, D.: Between management and the rule of law. Results of the research project "basic research into court management in Switzerland. International Journal for Court Administration **8**, 7–19 (2017)
35. Sarantis, D.: The challenge of accelerating greek judicial procedure. In: Proceedings of the International Conference on Electronic Government and the Information Systems Perspective, Lyon, France (2017)
36. Deligiannis, A.P., Anagnostopoulos, D.: Towards open justice: ICT acceptance in the greek justice system the case of the integrated court management system for penal and civil procedures (OSDDY/PP). In: Proceedings of the Conference for E-Democracy and Open Government (CeDEM), Krems, Austria (2017)
37. Saman, W.M.W.S., Haider, A.: E-Shariah in Malaysia: technology adoption within justice system. Transforming Government: People, Process and Policy **7**, 256–276 (2013)
38. Rosa, J., Teixeira, C., Pinto, J.S.: Risk factors in e-justice information systems. Gov. Inf. Q. **30**, 241–256 (2013)
39. Kitoogo. F.E., Bitwayiki, C.: E-Justice Implementation at a national scale: the ugandan case. In: Villafiorita, A., Saint-Paul, R., Zorer, A. (eds.) E-Infrastructures and E-Services on Developing Countries. AFRICOMM 2009. E-Infrastructures and E-Services on Developing Countries, Springer, Berlin, Heidelberg, pp. 40–49 (2010)
40. Kuhimbisa, E., Baguma, R., Nakakawa, A.: A model for developing usable integrated case management information systems. In: Proceedings ogf the International Conference on Social Implications of Computers in Developing Countries, Yogyakarta, Indonesia (2017)
41. Watson, A.C., Rukundakuvaga, R., Matevosyan, K.: Integrated justice: an information systems approach to justice sector case management and information sharing. Int. J. Court Administration **8**, 1–9 (2017)
42. Hudson, D., Kushniruk, A., Borycki, E., Zuege, D.: Physician satisfaction with a critical care clinical information system using a multimethod evaluation of usability. Int. J. Med. Informatics **112**, 131–136 (2018)

43. Rai, A., Lang, S.S., Welker, R.B.: Assessing the validity of IS success models: an empirical test and theoretical analysis. Inf. Syst. Res. **13**, 50–69 (2002)
44. Stefanovic, D., Mirkovic, M., Anderla, A., Drapsin, M., Drid, P., Radjo, I.: Investigating ERP systems success from the end user perspective. Technics Technologies Education Manage. **6**, 1089–1099 (2011)
45. Newkirk, H.E., Lederer, A.L., Srinivasan, C.: Strategic information systems planning: too little or too much? J. Strat. Inf. Syst. **12**, 201–228 (2003)
46. Hardyanto, W., Purwinarko, A., Adhi, M.A.: End-user satisfaction analysis on library management system unnes using technology acceptance model towards national standard of integrated library. J. Phys. Conf. Ser. **983**, 012006 (2018)
47. Tsotoulidou, A.: Εισαγωγή και αξιολόγηση πληροφοριακού συστήματος στον χώρο της ελληνικής δικαιοσύνης: η περίπτωση "ΣΟΛΩΝ". Master Thesis, University of Macedonia (in Greek) (2020)

Lost in Translation: Managing Digital Projects with Virtual Teams – Challenges, Opportunities, and Required Digital Intelligence Skills

Mona Link[1], Matthias Murawski[1(✉)], and Julian Bühler[2]

[1] FOM University of Applied Sciences, Berlin, Germany
Mona.link@icloud.com, matthias.murawski@fom.de
[2] BM Forschung, Berlin, Germany
julian.buehler@bm-forschung.de

Abstract. The digitization of project management has accelerated in recent years, driven by remote work and the adoption of digital tools. This evolution of work includes new challenges, such as virtual collaboration, work coordination, and trust building. Addressing these challenges requires more than mere technological adaptation; it necessitates the development of digital intelligence (DQ). DQ encompasses the ability to acquire and apply knowledge in digital technologies, fostering skills to navigate the digital world responsibly and effectively. Despite growing interest in DQ skills within management studies, there is limited research on their application in digital project management. This study, employing an exploratory research design and semi-structured interviews, examines ten challenges and five opportunities faced by project managers (PMs) in managing digital projects with virtual teams. Furthermore, it identifies the DQ skills necessary for effective management in this context, thereby contributing to both research and practice.

Keywords: Project Management · Digital Intelligence · Explorative Research

1 Introduction

Digitisation in project management has progressed, also due to the ongoing development of tools to manage projects [1–3]. The COVID-19 pandemic in 2020 and the resulting social distancing has accelerated the digitisation in project management, as companies were forced to close offices and people to work in remote teams [1]. Remote or virtual teams are a group of people working together towards a shared objective without being co-located [4]. With the rise of remote teams, new challenges arise, such as the effectiveness of virtual collaboration, the coordination of work and tracking of processes, communication in virtual teams, or building and maintaining trust [1].

The digitalisation of project management cannot be achieved through adaption of technology alone [5]. Consequently, Marnewick and Marnewick [5] suggest the concept of digital intelligence (DQ) to apply to project managers (PM), as they, like every other

Published by Springer Nature Switzerland AG 2024
R. van de Wetering et al. (Eds.): I3E 2024, LNCS 14907, pp. 222–232, 2024.
https://doi.org/10.1007/978-3-031-72234-9_18

workforce, need to master and respond to the changes that arise with digitalisation. DQ refers to the ability to gain and apply new knowledge and skills in the field of digital technologies, such as social, mobile, analytics, cloud, and cyber security. It describes the human relationship with technology [6]. The DQ framework, created and introduced by the DQ institute, is a comprehensive model covering several other indices [7].

Research on DQ is rising in management studies [6], but in the project management field, little attention has been paid on how the concept can benefit PMs in their work in a digital environment [5]. This paper aims to explore the challenges and opportunities that arise for PM managing digital projects with remote teams, and what DQ skills are required for PM to conduct their work efficiently. In addition to that, there is a gap in understanding how PMs develop and leverage digital intelligence skills to address these challenges and opportunities. This results in the following two research questions:

RQ1: What are the challenges and opportunities for PMs managing digital projects with remote teams?
RQ2: What DQ skills are required for PMs to effectively manage digital projects with remote teams?

The research design is explorative to gain in-depth insights from an expert perspective through semi-structured interviews.

Following the introduction, an overview about the theoretical background is outlined (Sect. 2). The Sect. 3 contains a description of the research design, before the key results are presented in Sect. 4. The paper ends with a conclusion (Sect. 5).

2 Theoretical Background

2.1 Opportunities and Challenges of Remote Teams

Remote teams can provide a multitude of *opportunities* for organizations, projects, and individual team members. They facilitate significant reductions in travel expenses and mitigate productivity losses attributable to employee travel [8, 9]. Remote teams also provide access to a wider talent pool, enabling more flexible staffing arrangements as geographical constraints are eliminated [9]. This flexibility allows for the optimization of human resources, permitting team members with specialized skills to contribute to multiple projects concurrently. The inherent diversity and heterogeneity of remote teams can catalyse creativity and innovation [10]. Furthermore, remote teams improve accessibility for physically disadvantaged employees and promote workplace equality. They offer temporal and locational flexibility, enhancing the work-life balance of team members [11].

However, remote teams can also encounter substantial *challenges*, particularly stemming from cultural differences that can impede collaboration and affect team dynamics [10]. Disparities in language, socially unacceptable working hours, lack of respect, and confrontational attitudes can lead to reduced knowledge sharing. Cultural diversity, while beneficial, can also precipitate misunderstandings and conflicts [10]. A primary challenge in remote teams is the development of trust, as informal interactions are significantly diminished [12]. Temporal disparities can delay responses, complicating relationship building. Remote teams often face difficulties in cultivating a collective identity and strong interpersonal relationships due to the absence of in-person collaboration, even with video conferencing.

The reduced richness of virtual communication compared to face-to-face interaction necessitates more explicit communication from team members. Both social and task-related communication are critical for trust development in remote teams, and while social bonds can form in virtual environments, the process is protracted. It is imperative for managers and team leaders to prioritize and encourage social interactions, and to consider in-person meetings for specific events, such as project kick-offs, to strengthen personal connections [12]. A hybrid working model, integrating face-to-face interactions with virtual collaboration, can enhance trust and connectivity.

2.2 Digital Intelligence Framework in the Context of Project Management

The DQ institute defines Digital Intelligence (DQ) as "a comprehensive set of technical, cognitive, meta-cognitive, and socio-emotional competencies grounded in universal moral values that enable individuals to face the challenges of digital life and adapt to its demands" [7, p.14].

As a global, shared understanding of digital intelligence was missing, the DQ Institute introduced the DQ framework [6]. The DQ institute derives DQ from other quotients, such as the Intelligence Quotient or Emotional Intelligence Quotient developed in the last century [7]. In total, 25 different approaches on digital literacy and skills from all over the world are aggregated to the DQ framework. This is a clear distinction factor and benefit of the DQ framework, and therefore it is selected for the study at hand.

The DQ framework structures digital intelligence in two categories: areas and levels. More details are presented in Table 1.

Limited research, to the authors' knowledge, has been conducted on the needs of DQ skills within the project management discipline. One exception is the qualitative study of Marnewick and Marnewick [5], who identified DQ skills for PMs that are needed to manage digital projects as well as skills that are considered important by PMs. They ranked the top skills as follows, with (1) having the highest score: (1) Online Communication and Collaboration, (2) Digital Empathy, (3) Public and Mass Communication, (4) Balanced Use of Technology, (5) Data and AI Literacy, (6) Content Cyber Risk Management, (7) Digital Changemaker Identity and (8) Digital Citizenship Identity. One skill that stood out was Online Communication and Collaboration, which also applies for virtual teams and is part of various project management and competence standards. In contrary, statements related to security were not perceived as important. Furthermore, four perspectives were identified, that depict the DQ of PMs: (1) Communication and Collaboration perspective: PMs need skills in digital communication and collaboration, often facing challenges such as integrating less tech-savvy team members and requiring organisational policies for digital engagement. (2) Digital Rights perspective: PMs need understanding of ethical behaviour in digital environments, emphasizing the importance of intellectual property rights, data privacy, and the responsible management of information. (3) Technical Communication Perspective: Distinct from (1), PMs need the technical skills of communication, such as using AI for information processing and mastering digital tools to foster innovation and ideation within virtual teams. (4) Online Identity Perspective: PMs need the skills to manage their digital presence, advocate for

Table 1. Eight DQ skills and their respective area, source: [7]

Area	Description
Digital identity	The ability to build a wholesome online and offline identity
Digital use	The ability to use technology in a balanced, healthy, and civic way
Digital safety	The ability to understand, mitigate and manage various cyber-risks through safe, responsible, and ethical use of technology
Digital security	The ability to detect, avoid, and manage different levels of cyber threats to protect data, devices, networks, and systems
Digital emotional intelligence	The ability to recognise, navigate, and express emotions in one's digital intra-and interpersonal interactions
Digital communication	The ability to communicate and collaborate with others using technology
Digital literacy	The ability to find, read, evaluate, synthesise, create, adapt, and share information, media and technology
Digital rights	The ability to understand and uphold human rights and legal rights when using technology

a healthy online-offline balance, and serving as a digital changemaker while considering the blurred lines between personal and professional online interactions [5].

In summary, modern, digital project management is characterized by a blend of traditional methodologies and digital integration, necessitating agile and flexible management approaches [13]. The role of the PM is evolving, requiring not only traditional management skills but also proficiency in digital tools and adaptive leadership abilities, which can be supported through DQ skills.

3 Research Design

Considering the limited research in the specific topic of this paper, a qualitative approach offers an exploratory pathway to discover insights and understandings that are not yet documented [14, 15]. Qualitative research is particularly valuable in areas with low existing knowledge, aiming for a deep understanding of complex phenomena [16], which aligns perfectly with the objectives of this study. Consequently, we conducted semi-structured interviews with seven experts.

3.1 Data Collection

The interview guideline was thoughtfully created to align with the central questions driving this research. Each interview began with an introductory greeting, where PMs were asked to describe their roles, detail their recent projects, and discuss the virtual nature of their teams. Focusing on the first research question, the initial key section of the guideline encouraged PMs to talk about the day-to-day challenges and opportunities they face while working with virtual teams. This approach was designed to elicit detailed responses on the specific dynamics encountered in managing dispersed teams. The second part of the interview targeted the topic of DQ skills. During the interviews, we focused on the nine most pertinent skills according to literature. Given the possibility that interviewees might be unfamiliar with the DQ concept, these skills were presented with brief explanations during the interviews or, in the case of phone interviews, described verbally. This preparation ensured that all participants had a clear understanding of the DQ skills being discussed, which was essential for a constructive dialogue.

A convenience sampling method was used to find experts in the field of project management. Nevertheless, the criteria for sampling were defined beforehand, the interviewed persons had work as PMs for at least five years and had to work in or with virtual teams. Seven experts in the field of project management were selected as interviewees due to their potential to offer in-depth insights into the profession [17]. A call for experts to interview was shared via the professional network LinkedIn. The sample was chosen to be as heterogenous as possible to provide a wide range of perspectives and experiences.

The semi-structured interviews were carried out between the 28th of August and 7th of September 2023 virtually via Google Meets, a video communication service by Google or via phone and had a duration between 45 and 56 min. The recording software was QuickTime, a multimedia software by Apple.

The interviews were audio-recorded and transcribed. The transcripts were first created with the help of the software Amberscript and then manually checked for correctness and adjusted. For transcribing, a transcribing system following Dresing and Pehl [18] was chosen. All personal information were removed from the transcripts to ensure the data privacy of the participants.

3.2 Data Analysis

After the transcription, the interviews were analysed with the computer-based software MAXQDA. The methodology of content structuring in qualitative analysis involves extracting and summarizing material based on specific content dimensions. In this paper, a blended approach was employed in the qualitative content analysis, combining both deductive and inductive methodologies. Initially, a deductive framework was applied, utilizing pre-defined categories based on the interview guideline, which in turn is based on the research questions posed. These categories were used to systematically code the textual material, ensuring that the analysis was anchored in the research questions posed.

This was followed by a shift to an inductive approach, where new categories were allowed to emerge directly from the data, facilitating the discovery of novel insights beyond the initial theoretical scope [15].

Upon the completion of the initial analysis of three out of the seven interviews, an in-depth coding schema was inductively constructed to categorize various challenges and opportunities. This scheme was derived directly from the data obtained in these interviews. Subsequently, the remaining four interviews were analysed using this newly developed coding scheme. This approach aligns with the recommended practice of developing coding frameworks after examining 25–50% of the data, ensuring a data-driven and responsive coding process [15].

In summarizing the content of the interviews, the approach involves a structured process to elevate the content to a level of abstraction. The material is then broken down into analysis units, which are paraphrased succinctly, eliminating any text not relevant for the research question and ensuring stylistic uniformity [15]. This process was facilitated through the utilization of summary grids and summary tables in MAXQDA, which effectively streamlined the subsequent analysis based on categories for all coded data. A cases-by-categories matrix was created and case-related summaries were written, summing up the interviewees thoughts [14]. In this case, the summarisation process combined several steps and paraphrased the text directly to the desired level of abstraction.

The final product of this process is a more abstract, concise category system that accurately reflects the original material. The summarised content was then compared with the original material to ensure consistency with the original content [15]. As a last step, the summarised content was analysed, using category-based analysis of the main categories [14].

4 Findings

Based on the qualitative analysis described in the previous section, we extracted various categories of challenges and opportunities. These will be explained and including their interplay towards each other, and their overall impact on digital projects in virtual team settings. These are followed by the nine most important DQ skills for PM in virtual teams discussed in detail during the interviews.

4.1 Challenges and Opportunities for Project Managers of Digital Projects with Virtual Teams

The interviewed PMs reported various challenges while managing digital projects with virtual teams, which have an impact on their work.

Physical presence, or *Co-Location (LC)*, with clients enhances the understanding of processes and enables PMs to offer more informed suggestions. In-person communication is highlighted as more effective compared to equivalent digital tools. This suggests a gap in the effectiveness of online communication tools and highlights the importance of physical presence for understanding and communication.

Virtual Communication (VC) was the biggest of all challenge categories, suggesting that this topic has an important impact on how PMs manage their digital projects within virtual teams. The importance of effective communication strategies was highlighted numerous times, emphasizing the adequate choice of communication media to overcome this challenge. Specialised ticketing systems for example can allow reviewing procedures before sending, ensure clarity and avoid misunderstandings. The importance of asynchronous communication in virtual teams was highlighted as the information flow can get lost easily. This effect is perceived even stronger because VC complicate non-verbal cues and personal interactions. Several interview statements highlight these communication elements and difficulties in conveying and receiving tone variations, especially if the counterpart has not been met in-person before. VC also comprises aspects of balancing information overload.

Teambuilding (TB) reveals a comprehensive view of the complexities and nuances associated with team building in remote or virtual work environments. A recurring theme emphasizes the value of regular team interactions. These activities are crucial for maintaining contact and building relationships and bonds within the team. They also significantly contribute to the development and reinforcement of the company's culture, especially in small or young companies where each team member plays a pivotal role in shaping the initial organizational core values.

According to the interviewed experts, establishing *Trust (TR)* is also critical for success within virtual teams. A key strategy employed by PMs is the active encouragement of open dialogue. Despite the fast-paced nature of business, taking the time to virtual space is essential. According to one respondent, spending time on forming trust regularly safes time in the long run because of fewer conflicts among virtual team members.

The challenge category *Creative Work (CW)* refers to perceived barriers and limitations when engaging in creative processes, such as Design Thinking Workshops, through virtual means. Some interview participants emphasise that the outcomes from using online collaboration tools distinctly vary from results of in-person sessions, e. g. brainstorming meetings.

A common problem that our interviewees state is that virtual meetings more often last longer than planned compared to offline meetings. Another tendency that was revealed is that they do not always lead to clear results caused by digital hurdles, e. g. taking concise note. These and additional challenges such as digital meeting nomads which attend multiple meetings in a row without proper reasons are gathered in the category *Meeting Etiquette [ME]*.

The issue of *Language Barrier*s [LB] is recurrently highlighted as well. Interviewees state a reluctance of individuals to admit their lack of understanding due to language or cultural barriers (which connect to challenge category *Culture*). Particularly in virtual teams, this often leads to misunderstandings that could derail project progress that is even more catalysed by the entire absence or only limited amount of visual impressions within digital meetings.

Beside *TR*, another established category in various theories and behavioural models could be identified: *Culture [CT]*. The varied decision-making processes that exist across cultures, was perceived as challenging. For instance, in some cultures, decisions are made from the top down, while in others, input is sourced from all levels. Understanding these differences is crucial for managers working with remote teams, as it influences team dynamics and the success of project outcomes. Sensitive communication towards cultural aspects was additionally emphasised in management practices of PMs.

Challenges in the identified category *Time Issues [TI]* refer most often to virtual team meetings. Our interviewees report that scheduling multiple virtual meetings back-to-back foster bottlenecks in personal workflows as not enough time is given to cope with e. g. personal debriefings. Also, a tendency to extend meetings more often if held entirely digital or hybrid was reported.

Various *Time Zones [TZ]* are especially a factor if it comes to challenging aspect for PMs as heterogeneous teams from around the world. Scheduling across these time zones was reported as demanding by our participants. Sending invitation to meetings then likely results in receiving messages outside of regular working hours, which can lead to false senses of obligation and thus, conflicts.

We witnessed a strong tendency towards giving more feedback on challenges. But by categorizing the challenges and addressing the issues, ways to overcome these are automatically. To benefit from virtual teams, we also asked our participants for opportunities of managing digital projects. The responses could be aggregated into five opportunity categories:

PMs steering digital projects with remote teams report that *Flexibility (FB)* is more than just a benefit, but a cornerstone of the operational strategy. ICT, especially video conferencing, has revolutionised the way complex issues in projects are resolved compared to e.g. phone calls. Whereas TZ and *CT* were described as challenges, virtual team settings allow members to live and work across different time zones and perform together in global collaboration. Also accounting for *FB* is the notable shift in mindset from the traditional emphasis on office presence to a focus on deliverables. It marks a significant change in how productivity is perceived and measured. This approach prioritizes outcomes over hours logged and reflects an evolution towards a results-oriented work culture, where the quality of output takes precedence.

Virtual teams offer PMs and their companies the advantage of recruiting from a global pool of talent, significantly broadening the scope for finding skilled professionals and potentially reducing costs. Assembling the team from various cultural backgrounds enriches the team dynamics to enhanced creativity and problem solving, as different perspectives and approaches are incorporated. Remote work enables individuals to engage in learning and capacity building without geographical constraints, fostering personal development and stronger team capabilities. We integrate these aspects into our second opportunity category *Staffing (ST)*.

We call the third opportunity category (working) *Efficiency (EF)*. Virtual teams are characterized by their dynamic nature, capable of rapid assembly and collaboration across a multitude of digital platforms. This agility stands in contrast to the slower pace of traditional teams, where physical meetings and linear communication channels often delay progress. The speed with which the virtual teams connect, and exchange ideas not only speeds up the workflow, but also gives the process a flexibility that enables rapid changes and decisions. Digital tools can contribute to this if the previously mentioned opportunities are faced and turned into efficient processes.

Closely related to *EF*, we decided to consider *Cost Efficiency (CE)* as separate category. Because beside working routines, the interviewed PMs reported that working with virtual teams has made their projects also cheaper and more straightforward, especially when dealing with clients from all over the world. Moving meetings and day-to-day work online cuts down on the need to travel, thus cuts expenses.

The fifth category is a proxy category which we labelled *Other (OT)* and represents individual findings that regularly appear throughout interview studies. Representative of various interesting responses, one finding in this category is that multi-tasking was seen as an opportunity by one interviewee, whereas other participants named this a hurdle in virtual team environments. This single statement – like it is the case for many others – demonstrates that a selective categorization towards a challenge or opportunity is sometimes difficult or even impossible as it always depends on how a situation, a tool or a virtual team is managed. Thus, it always depends on the skill set of PMs to which side, challenges or opportunities, the scale will turn.

Compared to existing literature as presented in Sect. 2, the analyses of the interviews confirm the already identified major topics (e.g., trust, communication as key challenges, and flexibility and efficiency as central opportunities, see [8, 9, 11, 12]). However, on a more detailed level, new aspects were explored. A complementing question is what skills PMs need to act successfully in such a context. We discuss the digital skills we could extracted in the next sub-section.

4.2 Digital Intelligence Skills

This section presents the findings from the qualitative analysis of interviews conducted to understand the role of DQ skills in managing digital projects within virtual teams. The insights gathered from the responses of our participants shed light on the essential digital intelligence skills required by PMs in this context. The skills we categorized are listed in Table 2:

Table 2. Overview of derived skill categories and core elements, source: own data

DQ Skill label	Core Skill Elements
Digital Co-Creator Identity	- crucial for ensuring every team member feels connected to their work - responsible for setting clear directions and creating an environment - multifaceted skill that encompasses understanding one's role, collaborating effectively in a digital setting
Digital Changemaker Identity	- adaptable and innovative, actively seeking new tools and methods to benefit their teams and projects - awareness of the available digital resources and selecting the right one for the task
Balanced Use of Technology	- ability to balance professional tasks with their personal lives - ability to establish a proper work-life balance for the entire team
Network Security Management	- understand that keeping information safe online is a part of their role as a PM - coping with security threads and judging system usage by the remote team
Digital Empathy	- ensuring clear and compassionate communication within the team - awareness of subtle indicators of a team members' well-being and unspoken sentiments - recognizing stress factors
Relationship Management	- ability to establish routines to enhance relationship management in a virtual context - mediations skills to overcome conflicts are needed
Digital Footprint Management	- maintaining a balanced online presence that represents the PM and the company - mentioned by various participants as a "nuanced skill" of rather less importance
Online Communication and Collaboration	- skill to online communication and collaboration tools - coping with the complex and continuous selection process - communication skills vital to enhance team collaboration and manage team dynamics
Data and AI Literacy	- beneficial across different fields, not limited to technical domains - ability to filter and present data effectively - essential for PMs to make informed decisions about the direction of their projects

The Digital Co-Creator Identity and Digital Changemaker Identity have emerged as key skills. PMs, as digital co-creators, must integrate digital technologies into daily workflows, fostering a culture of shared creativity and innovation. The Changemaker Identity extends this concept to driving transformative changes within organizations and the broader societal landscape.

The Balanced Use of Technology emphasizes managing digital tools to promote health and productivity without overwhelming PMs and their teams. Network Security Management, though not a critical academic focus, is recognized by the industry and PMI as a top digital-age skill, highlighting its growing importance. Digital Empathy and Relationship Management are essential for fostering a collaborative remote team culture, building trust, and ensuring psychological safety. Online Communication and Collaboration are integral to digital competencies and project management standards. Data and AI Literacy are also crucial, though their importance varies with organizational support.

5 Conclusion

This exploratory research conducted through interviews with seven PMs has provided valuable insights into the challenges, opportunities that can occur and DQ skills that are required for managing digital projects with remote teams. We could identify ten challenge and five opportunity categories with can have an impact on the success of virtual team projects. By extracting these from the interviewees feedback and structuring it as shown in Sect. 4.1, we provide an answer to the initially raised *first research question* what challenges and opportunities exist. We could also extract from our results that both come along digital projects and more often a selective categorisation is not trivial. Indeed, challenges can likely turn into opportunities and vice versa depending on how a project is handled by a PM. Responding to our *second research question*, our findings indicate that PMs require a diverse and multi-dimensional DQ skill set to effectively manage digital projects with remote teams. It is a continuous balancing act that PMs must fulfil to be successful.

In terms of limitations, the small number of interviewees limits the generalizability of the findings, and the diversity of experiences in project management across different industries may not be fully represented. The qualitative nature of the study offers depth in understanding but may lack the breadth achieved through larger-scale quantitative methods. Consequently, the identified and discussed DQ skills and their implications are indicative rather than definitive.

Future research should include a larger, diverse sample of project managers to enhance findings' generalizability. Quantitative studies could validate the importance of DQ skills and their link to project success. Exploring each DQ skill's complexities and interdependencies is needed. Organizational strategies to cultivate these skills among project managers should be examined. Future research could also assess training programs' effectiveness and organizational support systems in enhancing DQ skills. Addressing these areas can build a comprehensive framework to support project managers in navigating digital projects and virtual team management.

References

1. Wu, T.: Digital project management: rapid changes define new working environments. J. Bus. Strateg. **43**, 323–331 (2022)
2. Kanski, L., Pizon, J.: The impact of selected components of industry 4.0 on project management. J. Innovation & Knowledge **8**, 100336 (2023)
3. Taboada, I., Daneshpajouh, A., Toledo, N., de Vass, T.: Artificial intelligence enabled project management: a systematic literature review. Appl. Sci. **13**, 5014 (2023)
4. Rehman, A.U., Nawaz, A., Abbas, M.: Role of project management in virtual teams success. J. Computer Sci. Eng. **1**, 32–42 (2021)
5. Marnewick, C., Marnewick, A.: Digital intelligence: a must-have for project managers. Project Leadership and Society **2**, 100026 (2021)
6. Boughzala, I., Garmaki, M., Chourabi, O.: Understanding how digital intelligence contributes to digital creativity and digital transformation: a systematic literature review. Hawaii International Conference on System Sciences 2020 (2020)
7. Park, Y.: DQ Institute Global Standards Report 2019 (2019). https://www.dqinstitute.org/wp-content/uploads/2019/03/DQGlobalStandardsReport2019.pdf
8. Petska, D., Berge, Z.: Leadership competency in virtual teams. In: Howard, C., Boettcher, J.V., Justice, L., Schenk, K.D., Rogers, P.L., Berg, G.A. (eds.) Encyclopedia of Distance Learning, pp. 1195–1202. IGI Global (2005)
9. Bergiel, B.J., Bergiel, E.B., Balsmeier, P.W.: Nature of virtual teams: a summary of their advantages and disadvantages. Manag. Res. News **31**, 99–110 (2008)
10. Swart, K., Bond-Barnard, T., Chugh, R.: Challenges and critical success factors of digital communication, collaboration and knowledge sharing in project management virtual teams: a review. Int. J. Inf. Syst. Proj. Manag. **10**, 59–75 (2022)
11. Mayer, C., Sivatheerthan, T., Mütze-Niewöhner, S., Nitsch, V.: Sharing leadership behaviors in virtual teams: effects of shared leadership behaviors on team member satisfaction and productivity. Team Performance Management: An International J. **29**, 90–112 (2023)
12. Greenberg, P.S., Greenberg, R.H., Antonucci, Y.L.: Creating and sustaining trust in virtual teams. Bus. Horiz. **50**, 325–333 (2007)
13. Ciric Lalic, D., Lalic, B., Delić, M., Gracanin, D., Stefanovic, D.: How project management approach impact project success? from traditional to Agile. Int. J. Manag. Proj. Bus. **15**, 494–521 (2022)
14. Kuckartz, U., Rädiker, S.: Qualitative Content Analysis: Methods. Practice and Software. SAGE Publications, Thousand Oaks (2023)
15. Mayring, P.: Qualitative Content Analysis: Theoretical Foundation, Basic Procedures and Software Solution. Klagenfurt (2014)
16. Saunders, M.N.K., Lewis, P., Thornhill, A.: Research Methods for Business Students. Prentice Hall, New York (2009)
17. Misoch, S.: Qualitative Interviews. De Gruyter Oldenbourg, Berlin/München/Boston (2015)
18. Dresing, T., Pehl, T.: Praxisbuch Interview, Transkription & Analyse: Anleitungen und Regelsysteme für qualitativ Forschende. Eigenverlag, Marburg (2018)

Post-adoption Barriers to Metaverse Usage: An Active-Passive Resistance Perspective from Consumer Reviews

Subhadeep Mandal[1](✉), Arpan Kumar Kar[1], and Shivam Gupta[2]

[1] Department of Management Studies, Indian Institute of Technology Delhi, New Delhi 110016, India
subhadeep.mandal@dms.iitd.ac.in, arpankar@iitd.ac.in

[2] Department of Information Systems, Supply Chain Management and Decision Support, NEOMA Business School, 59 Rue Pierre Taittinger, 51100 Reims, France
shivam.gupta@neoma-bs.fr

Abstract. Unlike adoption, the post-adoption behaviour of metaverse applications has not been thoroughly investigated. The study aims to investigate the active and passive resistance-causing barriers experienced by users of Metaverse applications post adoption. A total of 70631 critical user reviews were obtained from 10 different Metaverse applications and subjected to text analytics procedures to identify relevant themes as barriers to post-adoption metaverse usage. The findings revealed high presence of system-related barriers and low presence of functional and psychological barriers as active resistance with high presence of passive resistance through individual barriers. The findings can be utilized by metaverse-developers to retain users post adoption.

Keywords: Metaverse · Innovation Resistance · Text Mining

1 Introduction

Proponents claim that as daily activities transition from social networking, online shopping, and PC gaming to the metaverse, living, working, learning, playing, socialising and ways of living will transform drastically [1, 4]. The metaverse is a shared online community that blends the actual and virtual worlds so that users may communicate and have a sense of co-existence [11]. Defined as an interoperable network of shared virtual environments, the metaverse allows unprecedented freedom and creativity [8]. Despite its potential, the metaverse is still evolving, with developers continually adding features to enhance user experiences. Adoption and resistance factors guide developers on improving user engagement and addressing issues [9, 11].

Electronic word-of-mouth (eWOM) is crucial for detecting user sentiments [10, 18]. By analyzing negative user reviews from various metaverse applications, this study identifies factors hindering user adoption. It examines active and passive resistances, as both inhibit usage [16]. Building on active innovation resistance theory [5, 14] and status quo bias theory [7, 13], this study aims to uncover barriers to post-adoption metaverse usage based on user reviews.

Published by Springer Nature Switzerland AG 2024
R. van de Wetering et al. (Eds.): I3E 2024, LNCS 14907, pp. 233–240, 2024.
https://doi.org/10.1007/978-3-031-72234-9_19

2 Background

2.1 Active Innovation Resistance

User resistance in IS research is the opposition to perceived changes from new IS implementations [3]. Active innovation resistance, driven by psychological and functional barriers, involves intentional rejection of technological developments, often through overt acts of disapproval [14]. This resistance delays or rejects adoption. [14] identified functional barriers like *usage*, *value*, and *risk*, and psychological barriers such as *tradition* and *image*. [5] expanded this, identifying *complexity barriers* among functional and *personal risk barriers* among psychological barriers varying across product classes. [17] identified a different class of psychological barriers, namely system-related barriers, focusing on technical aspects of the IS, such as data protection and security risks, i.e., *perceived security risk* and *information privacy*.

2.2 Passive Innovation Resistance

Passive innovation resistance involves inaction towards adopting new innovations, driven by a preference for maintaining the status quo [15]. It stems from barriers like inertia [13] and dissatisfaction with extent and pace of innovations [2]. Unlike active resistance, passive resistance is about inaction rather than opposition [14]. Status quo bias can be explained by rational decision making, cognitive misperceptions, and psychological commitment [15].

3 Research Design

The objective of the current study has been addressed using critical reviews of actual users from different metaverse applications. Following the approach of [6], the insights obtained through text-mining-driven algorithms, were viewed through the lens of active and passive innovation resistance theories and mapped with suitable barriers of the same. Figure 1 shows the pathway of this study.

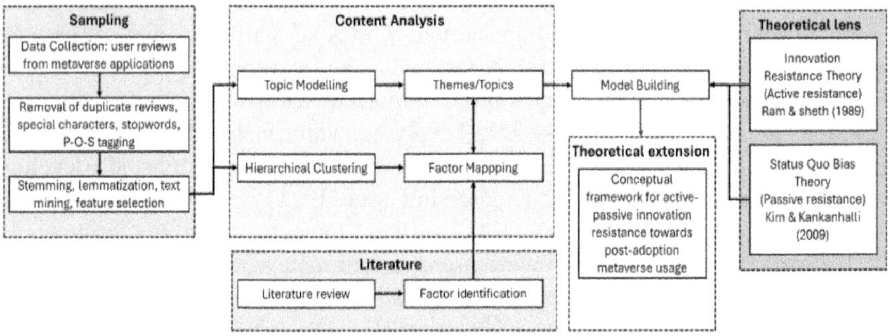

Fig. 1. Research methodology framework for determining active-passive innovation resistance towards post-adoption metaverse usage.

3.1 Data Collection

Users reviews from ten different metaverse applications were extracted, reflecting post-adoption usage. The reviews were collected from Google Play Store for Android users and Apple App Store for iOS users using a web scraper built on Python. The scraped reviews were filtered based on their star ratings, as reviews with only 1, 2 and 3 stars were deemed appropriate for this study and hence retained. This corpus of critical (1 star and 2 star) and neutral (3 star) reviews had 28190, 23015 and 19426 reviews respectively adding upto a total of 70631 reviews from metaverse applications *Decentraland, Mobox, Monsterra, Opensea, Pocket Battles, Sandbox, Thetan Arena and Zepeto.*

3.2 Data Cleansing

After the initial aforementioned extraction, a total of 68144 reviews were obtained after cleansing the reviews. For cleansing, duplicate reviews, special characters, and stop words were removed. Tokenization, parts-of-speech filtering, and lemmatisation was carried out, after which, following [6], NLP-based techniques were applied to pre-process the data.

4 Exploratory Study

4.1 Data Analysis

Using the Gensim package in Python, content analysis was carried out on the corpus of reviews by conducting Latent Dirichlet Allocation (LDA)-based topic modelling. For this study, we opted for agglomerative hierarchical clustering and LDA-based topic modelling to analyze the user reviews and extract topics relevant to innovation resistance. The dendrogram representing the findings of the hierarchical clustering is depicted in Fig. 2.

Next in the content analysis, LDA-based topic modelling was conducted to unravel the patterns of texts forming topics as conducted for similar purposes by [10].

4.2 Exploratory Findings

By connecting the outputs of Fig. 2 and the outcomes of LDA-based topic modelling, the emerging themes have been mapped with existing factors in innovation resistance literature, depicted in Table 1. The top 15 words for each topic were secured. These words within a topic arrive from different reviews.

Table 1 represents 15 words each obtained from the corpus of reviews, representing different themes corresponding to active or passive innovation resistance towards metaverse applications.

These have been explained further based on their suitable classification in active innovation resistance and status quo bias theories along with their depiction of resistance-specific barriers.

Table 1. Mapping of factors based on theoretical lexicons.

Words of topics	Mapped constructs	Broader class	Type of resistance	Connection to theory
difficult, challenging, understand, setup, complicated, confusing, instructions, login, idea, figure, element, update, suck, dev, extreme	Complexity Barrier	Functional Barriers	Active	Innovation Resistance Theory
Almost, safety, health, worth, needs, high, engaging, improvements, lot, process, price, never, phone, work, always	Personal risk Barrier	Psychological Barriers		
worried, security, playing, left, hurt, breach, constantly, data, made, feel, much, thought, purchase, premium, down, money	Perceived security risk	System-related Barriers		
information, personal, lack, privacy, application, using, account, report, ask, dont, mail, computer, scam	Information privacy			
comfort, routine, zone, give, reluctant, usual, ruin, item, require, hold, otherwise, reason, enjoy, recommend, back	Inertia	Individual Barriers	Passive	Status Quo Bias Theory
media, social, used, hard, apps, current, feels, feature, change, games, extreme, old, update, download, design, average	Dissatisfaction with extent of innovation			

Italicised words represent words obtained from agglomerative hierarchical clustering

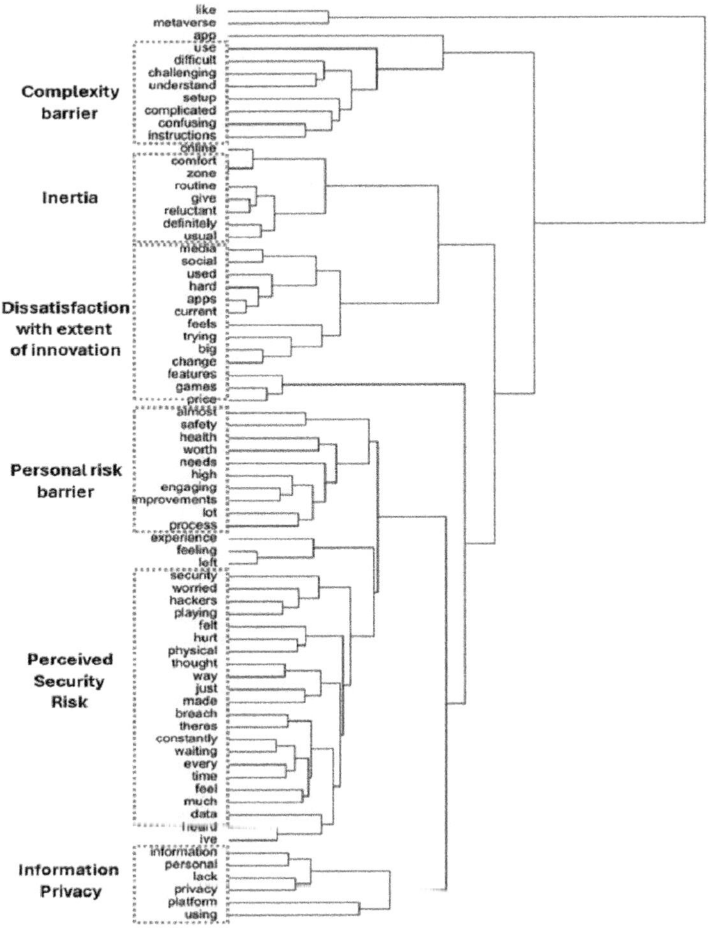

Fig. 2. Hierarchical clustering of theoretical lexicons.

Active Innovation Resistance. Upon analyzing the themes from hierarchical cluster analysis and LDA-based topic modelling, we mapped them to existing active innovation resistance factors [5, 14, 17]. Words like "difficult," "challenging," and "understand" indicate users' difficulty in navigating the metaverse, aligning with *complexity barriers* of functional barriers [5]. Terms such as "safety," "health," "worth," and "needs" suggest *personal risk barriers* of psychological barriers, reflecting concerns about physical and mental health, addiction, overspending, and privacy violations within the metaverse.

[17] differentiated system-related barriers from psychological barriers, including *perceived security risks* and *information privacy*. Words like "information," "personal," "lack," and "privacy" highlight fears of personal data tampering or *information privacy* being a barrier. Similarly, terms like "worried," "security," and "playing" suggest concerns about financial information being accessed by malicious agents, which align with *perceived security risks* in system-related barriers of active innovation resistance. The

fact that two different types of system-related barriers emerge as opposed to 1 each for functional and psychological barriers, establishes its dominance in causing active resistance based on resistance types, compared to the other two.

Passive Innovation Resistance. We mapped themes from user reviews to passive innovation resistance factors [2, 7, 13, 15]. Words like "comfort," "routine," and "usual" suggest users' preference for familiar systems, indicating *inertia* [13]. Terms like "social," "used," and "games" reflect dissatisfaction with the rapid shift from traditional games and social media to the metaverse, aligning with [2]'s concept of *dissatisfaction with the extent of innovation*, representing individual barriers of passive innovation resistance.

5 Confirmatory Study

The exploratory analysis forms the basis of our confirmatory study. We posited that post-adoption user resistance to the metaverse involves both active and passive innovation resistance. Findings indicate that system-related barriers (perceived security risk and information privacy) are dominant in causing resistance post-adoption [17]. Surprisingly, individual barriers like inertia [13] and dissatisfaction with extent of innovation [2] are equally dominant. Functional and psychological barriers, such as complexity and personal risk [5], have a weaker effect. These findings shape our theoretical framework for post-adoption innovation resistance, depicted in Fig. 3.

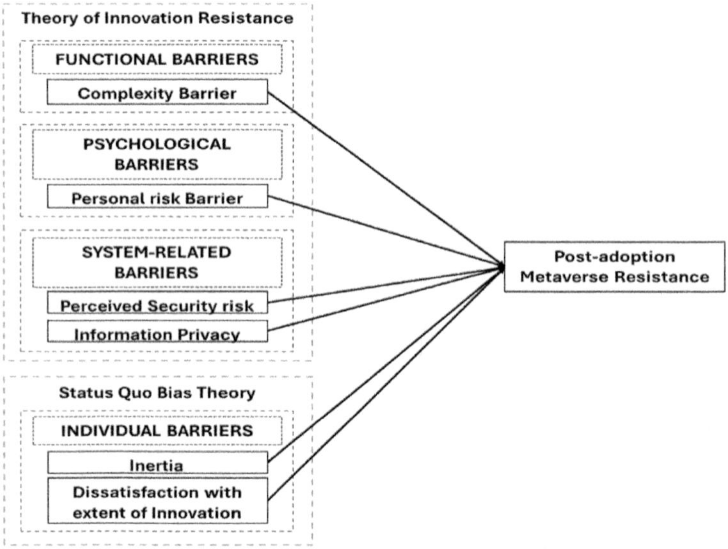

Fig. 3. Conceptual model for confirmatory analysis to assess post adoption metaverse resistance.

5.1 Future Extension of the Study

Our exploratory analysis identified factors of active and passive innovation resistance hindering metaverse post-adoption usage. Following [6], we propose evaluating the conceptual model in Fig. 3 through ordinal regression models and primary data, collected using a structured questionnaire. Responses from actual metaverse users can be analyzed via path analysis (SEM-based) or configurational analysis of fsQCA of IS innovations [12] to understand the configurations of conditions contributing to post-adoption metaverse resistance.

6 Conclusion

This study, based on user reviews, identified barriers hindering metaverse usage post-adoption. Both active and passive resistance-causing barriers, such as functional, psychological, system-related, inertia and dissatisfaction due to the extent of innovation, were found. Further evaluation and empirical validation are needed to understand their impact on metaverse usage.

References

1. Dwivedi, Y.K., et al.: Metaverse beyond the hype: multidisciplinary perspectives on emerging challenges, opportunities, and agenda for research, practice and policy. Int. J. Inf. Manage. **66**, 102542 (2022)
2. Heidenreich, S., Handrich, M.: What about passive innovation resistance? investigating adoption-related behavior from a resistance perspective. J. Prod. Innov. Manag. **32**(6), 878–903 (2015)
3. Hirschheim, R., Newman, M.: Information systems and user resistance: theory and practice. Comput. J. **31**(5), 398–408 (1988)
4. Hollensen, S., Kotler, P., Opresnik, M.O.: Metaverse–the new marketing universe. J. Bus. Strateg. **44**(3), 119–125 (2022)
5. Joachim, V., Spieth, P., Heidenreich, S.: Active innovation resistance: an empirical study on functional and psychological barriers to innovation adoption in different contexts. Ind. Mark. Manage. **71**, 95–107 (2018)
6. Kar, A.K., Angelopoulos, S., Rao, H.R.: Big data-driven theory building: philosophies, guiding principles, and common traps. International Journal of Information Management, 102661 (2023)
7. Kim, H.-W., Kankanhalli, A.: Investigating user resistance to information systems implementation: a status quo bias perspective. MIS Q. **33**(3), 567–582 (2009). https://doi.org/10.2307/20650309
8. Kim, J.: Advertising in the metaverse: research agenda. J. Interact. Advert. **21**(3), 141–144 (2021)
9. Kumar, A., Shankar, A., Shaik, A.S., Jain, G., Malibari, A.: Risking it all in the metaverse ecosystem: forecasting resistance towards the enterprise metaverse. Information Technology & People (2023)

10. Kushwaha, A.K., Mandal, S., Pharswan, R., Kar, A.K., Ilavarasan, P.V.: Studying online political behaviours as rituals: a study of social media behaviour regarding the CAA. In: Re-imagining Diffusion and Adoption of Information Technology and Systems: A Continuing Conversation: IFIP WG 8.6 International Conference on Transfer and Diffusion of IT, TDIT 2020, Tiruchirappalli, India, December 18–19, 2020, Proceedings, Part II, pp. 315–326. Springer International Publishing (2020)
11. Lee, M.S., Chaney, D.: The psychological and functional factors driving metaverse resistance. Internet Research, (ahead-of-print) (2023)
12. Mandal, S., Kar, A.K., Gupta, S., Sivarajah, U.: Achieving food supply chain resilience during natural disasters through industry 5.0 enablers—empirical insights based on an FsQCA approach. Information Systems Frontiers, pp. 1–24 (2023)
13. Polites, G.L., Karahanna, E.: Shackled to the status quo: the inhibiting effects of incumbent system habit, switching costs, and inertia on new system acceptance. MIS Q. **36**(1), 21–42 (2012). https://doi.org/10.2307/41410404
14. Ram, S., Sheth, J.N.: Consumer resistance to innovations: the marketing problem and its solutions. J. Consum. Mark. **6**(2), 5–14 (1989)
15. Samuelson, W., Zeckhauser, R.: Status quo bias in decision making. J. Risk Uncertain. **1**, 7–59 (1988)
16. Talke, K., Heidenreich, S.: How to overcome pro-change bias: incorporating passive and active innovation resistance in innovation decision models. J. Prod. Innov. Manag. **31**(5), 894–907 (2014)
17. Wong, L.W., Tan, G.W.H., Lee, V.H., Ooi, K.B., Sohal, A.: Psychological and system-related barriers to adopting blockchain for operations management: an artificial neural network approach. IEEE Trans. Eng. Manage. **70**(1), 67–81 (2021)
18. Yoo, C.W.: An exploration of the role of service recovery in negative electronic word-of-mouth management. Inf. Syst. Front. **22**(3), 719–734 (2020)

Rethinking Europe's Digital Future: Challenges and Risks from GAFAM

Ronny Mönnig[1(✉)] and Shakib Manouchehri[2]

[1] IAV GmbH, Carnotstrasse 1, 10587 Berlin, Germany
ronny.moennig@iav.de
[2] Wilhelm Büchner University of Applied Sciences, Hilpertstrasse 31, 64295 Darmstadt, Germany

Abstract. This study analyzes the effects, risks, and opportunities of digitalization for Europe, with a specific focus on the dominance of leading US digital companies known as GAFAM (Google, Amazon, Facebook, Apple, Microsoft). The central research question examines whether Europe could be at risk of falling into digital colonization due to the influence of these tech giants. Through a systematic literature review, the study evaluates Europe's digital strategy and conducts a risk analysis of the associated economic and social challenges. The findings highlight the critical importance of addressing issues related to IT security, sustainability (green and sustainable IT), and AI safety for businesses operating in the digital landscape.

Keywords: Digitalization of Europe · GAFAM global dominance · platform economy · social media platforms · neoliberalism

1 Introduction

Digitalization has undoubtedly brought many benefits in areas besides the industry of goods, such as education and research, but also to the health sector or financial market. However, the activities of leading digital companies have necessitated a more critical examination of advances in algorithm-based data mining and processing, particularly in our European society (Baumgarth and Binckebanck 2023; Helberger et al. 2020; Jørgensen 2019).

The European Commission is continually updating its regulatory framework to support and secure a seamless digital transformation for everyone in Europe. However, it remains unclear whether the significance of the expansion politics of the GAFAM (Google, Apple, Meta/Facebook, Amazon, and Microsoft) monopolists is fully recognized by the policymakers and society at large. This contribution explores Europe's digital transformation under the influence of these US tech giants. Their constant pursuit of profit has led to the expansion of digital capitalism, changing both the business world and society (Jaekel 2017; Staab 2019). Moreover, the development of digital technologies in Europe is highly dependent on market conditions and interdependencies with

Published by Springer Nature Switzerland AG 2024
R. van de Wetering et al. (Eds.): I3E 2024, LNCS 14907, pp. 241–252, 2024.
https://doi.org/10.1007/978-3-031-72234-9_20

technology providers and supply chains. The dominance of leading US digital companies has sparked widespread concern within the European research community and public discourse about the potential for Europe to become a digital colony, potentially losing its sovereignty and economic independence. While various solutions have been proposed to mitigate the economic risks associated with this digital colonization, strong concerns remain regarding the potential impact on European society, particularly in the areas of democracy, wellbeing, and sustainable development, including peace and inclusion. To address this critical issue, the present qualitative study seeks to gain a comprehensive understanding of the challenges, opportunities, and potential solutions surrounding Europe's digital sovereignty and its ability to navigate the complexities of the GAFAM-dominated digital ecosystem. More recently, GAFAM's dominance in the AI market threatens Europe's digital sovereignty (Miailhe 2018). New AI-driven business models and services raise concerns for data protectionists, policymakers, and human rights activists (Nocetti and Sel 2023; Zuboff 2019). These introductory facets highlight that the developments of the digital age must be carefully analyzed by society and European policymakers to address potential threats to democratic order in Europe in a timely manner.

2 Theoretical Background

This study examines the economic power of the GAFAM industry and its impact on Europe's society and businesses. Hence, this section provides a theoretical foundation and outlines the key principles underlying the rising power of GAFAM monopolies. Overall, this research paper aims to support the risk identification process for Europe's digital transformation, constrained by the market dominance of the GAFAM industry. The implications for this risk assessment were derived from a systematic literature review (SLR), as described in the research methodology section.

2.1 Digital Capitalism and Its Raise from Classical Neoliberalism

A new economic era has been created by leading technology players, like GAFAM industry. The term digital capitalism describes the successor of a phase of a neo-liberalistic economy, mainly characterized by market privatization (Staab 2019).

Neoliberalism can be understood as a stage of economy, where the (investing) government is trying to protect the *free* (independent) market, but at a minimum level of intervention (Daly 2022; Staab 2019). Besides, there is individual freedom too, in accordance with the political concept of liberalism of the 17th century. Hence, the neoliberalism of the 20th century can be considered more as neo-capitalism, but loosing almost all market competitors, leading to severe constrains by just some technology monopolists, like GAFAM. One of the core principles of neoliberalism has been an increased prosperity and improved living standards for the society as a whole – highly questionable today. However, neoliberalism has come under increasing criticism: Critics argue that it has led to more inequality, poverty by job insecurities or financial losses, and increased lobbyism. Unfortunately, an even more troublesome successor of neoliberalism is on start - worldwide: Digital capitalism.

Digitalization has been key in enabling this initially slow process, as center of digital capitalism involves full control of market access, vendor lock-in strategies, and highly integrated digital ecosystems (Andree 2023; Andree and Thomsen 2020; Staab 2019). The consequences for consumers are harsh: dictated prices due to lack of competition, non-curated news and information sources, and difficulties switching digital platforms, especially for commercial systems. Global players like GAFAM grow based on "market dividends" (and substantial ad revenue), which is the monetary share of each digital transaction within their e-commerce systems, such as app stores. Digital products, once developed and established, are available at almost zero marginal costs, leading to a strong network effect as platforms become more valuable with more users. Multi-sided platforms (MSPs) are increasingly important (Schreieck et al. 2018), expanding conventional markets into accessible platforms (Hein et al. 2016). MSP's form the basis of digital market power, with global players controlling access and restricting competition.

2.2 The Opportunities of Digital Transformation

Digitalized economies are different from digital capitalism: In the last century, automation increased efficiency in industrial and administrative processes. Digitalization focuses on connectivity of entities and data, in addition to communication. Malik (2018) demonstrated that simply implementing digital technologies without leveraging data may improve efficiency but won't ensure successful organizational and societal transformation. Especially the "thinking in systems" will be relevant to become successful as a society, particularly regarding poly crisis symptoms, like pandemics or the well-known bursting of financial "bubbles" through the dot.com crisis.

Besides the development targets of Europe to develop its infrastructure (Giga Networks, Data center, Quantum computing etc.), part of the strategy also will be improvements regarding digital education, digital literacy, and sustainable growth. Many single initiatives are dedicated towards an efficiently connected Europe, where data protection and cybersecurity have top priority.

2.3 Europe's Digital Sovereignty and the Risks of an Undermined Democracy

The US is massively exporting its solutions, technologies, and AI models to Europe and worldwide (Miailhe 2018). The cultural, commercial, and political influences on European society are highly questionable and concerning. Compared to North America, Europe lags in private investment in AI companies, especially startups, partly because Europeans have traditionally relied on industrial sectors like the automotive industry.

But, the European Union (EU) has also become the world's leading digital regulatory power (Hobbs 2020). Specifically, Europe has taken a more assertive approach to digital policymaking, actively intervening to raise privacy standards, levy antitrust fines on tech companies, and shape debates on issues like online harms and ethical artificial intelligence. Hobbs (2020) concludes that the EU must soon evolve from a regulatory superpower to a tech superpower. It is recommended to invest in digital infrastructure and improve digital skills to reap economic benefits and ensure security against disinformation, cyber-attacks, and threats to democracy. The internet needs to be a safe space that allows freedom of speech and innovation for industrial use. Therefore, a multi-stakeholder approach (policymakers, businesses, and civil society) to internet regulation and empowerment should be adopted. Within Europe, there are still significant asymmetries in high-speed internet infrastructure, leading to the risk of becoming a battleground for tech and industrial supremacy. Overcoming these limitations is essential for the European model to become an attractive alternative to the US with its dominant tech giants. Understanding the strategic importance of digitalization, with a focus on society, will be decisive for Europe's future. To avoid hindering its own progress, Europe needs a balanced regulatory approach that welcomes digital giants and new investors while protecting organizations and society.

The European Commission, under Ursula von der Leyen's leadership, has long identified AI as a priority. Franke (2021) states that a future AI plan requires a "European approach", which is challenging due to the need for input from member states. Currently, member states' policies are not aligned, and a coordinated plan does not exist to delegate power to a unified AI policy regulating global players in Europe. Achieving this is difficult, as such policies must address the technological, geopolitical, economic, and societal implications of AI.

3 Research Methodology

The wide range of topics within the theoretical base of digital transformation in Europe necessitates a systematic approach, combining a systematic literature review with a risk analysis based on individual concepts (Becker et al. 2018; Fink 2014). Initially, keywords were selected to perform multiple literature database requests, summarized in Table 1. The following database sources were searched: Scopus, Web of Sciences, Science Direct, Research Gate, Springer Link, and JSTOR. Using a concept matrix framework, the topics were clustered for further analysis (Webster and Watson 2002).

A forward and backward search was performed, where required. Over 600 sources were initially gathered for a comprehensive literature review (timeline January 2009 - February 2024). Figure 1 depicts the workflow for selecting matches after reviewing the databases. A selection method was applied to use only relevant and high-quality sources and study material (Fig. 2).

Table 2 displays the share by the type of each item, as finally used in the SLR. The main share of sourced were books (or book sections), webpages and journal articles.

From each item, at least title, authors and the information from keywords and abstract were checked. Besides the criteria listed up in Table 3, also the author's index (of publication) and the rating of the publisher was considered through the quality screening.

After processing, the sources related to categories A to C comprised 81%, while the remaining D category was used primarily to reference statements or opinions. The process began with a Zotero library containing 627 sources, labeled according to the evaluation steps. As planned for this SLR[1], each source was tagged (in addition to the evaluation labels) to facilitate convenient searching within the database. Various materials from public sources, such as presentations or magazine articles, were not

[1] https://www.researchgate.net/publication/380762881_File_with_SLR_sources_on_Rethinking_Europe's_Digital_Future_Challenges_and_Risks_from_GAFAM_I3E_2024_Confernce.

Table 1. Category-based keywords for the SLR.

Category to perform literature database requests	Keywords
AI and Algorithms	AI implementation; AI Algorithm and biases; AI risk assessment
Regulation and policymaking	Multilateral Government; Digital Markets Act; Digital Services Act; Platform Regulation
Digital Capitalism and Platform economy	Digital Capitalism; Digital Economy; Digital Entrepreneurship; Digital Markets; E-Commerce; Platforms and Social Networks; Gatekeepers; EU Market; MSP (Multi-Sided Platform)
Data governance and Consumer protection	Consumer Profiling; Surveillance; Competition; Antitrust Law; Data Governance
Political and social aspects of digitalization	Autonomy; Democracy; Participation; Digital Sovereignty
Transformational changes	Transformation; Digital Transformation
Others	Big Tech / GAFAM

Fig. 1. Literature search process.

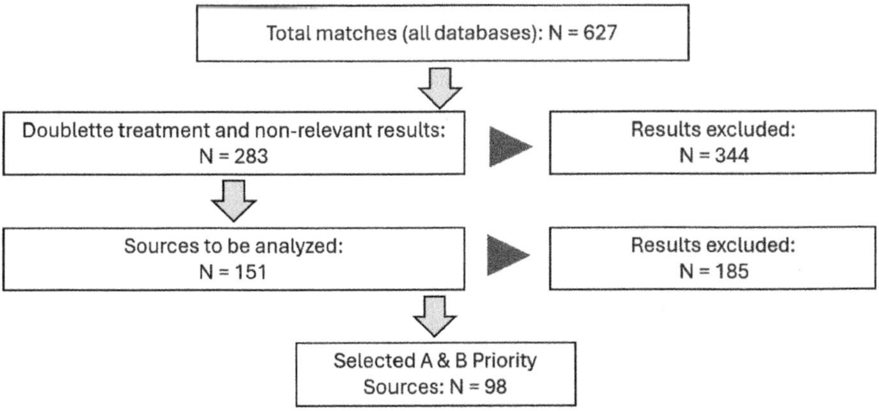

Fig. 2. Workflow describing the selection process for literature sources.

categorized. After extracting the main information, the research objectives were mapped to an analytical framework.

Table 2. Share of different items for SLR.

Items (N = 151)	Share by Type
Law Documents	0.46%
Postings in logs or forums	2.61%
Books or Book Section	49.31%
Conference Papers	0.15%
Data Sets	0.61%
Interviews	0.61%
Journal Articles	13.67%
Magazine Articles	0.15%
Newspaper Articles	2.00%
Reports	4.76%
Thesis	1.08%
Streaming Data	0.31%
Web Pages	23.35%
Others	0.92%

Table 3. Criteria for paper selection.

Priority Class	Criterion
A	Highly relevant, methodologically excellent studies that synthesize various individual studies
B	Current and highly relevant results, directly related individual studies by most-cited authors
C	Supporting materials like legal contents, interview records or case reports
D	Opinion-related magazine articles and expert advice from various public sources

4 Results

4.1 Descriptive Findings

Table 4 contains 98 selected A and B priority sources used in the SLR, divided into 28 categories, whereas they can be further categorized as: Platform regulation, social networks, and AI algorithms/biases, together comprising 20%. Another share of 35% were attributed to *Digital Capitalism and Platform Economy*, 15% *to Political and Social Aspects of Digitalization*, 14% to *Regulation and Policymaking*, and 11% to *AI and Algorithms*. The remaining 25% share is distributed over 8 groups. In the discussion section, sources from each group with the highest shares will be briefly discussed.

Table 4. Result of SLR.

Category	AI and Algorithms			Regulation and Policymaking				Digital Capitalism and Platform Economy								Data Governance and Consumer Protection			Political and Social Aspects of Digitalization				Trans-formational changes		Big Tech / GAFAM	Others
	AI implementation	AI Algorithm and biases	AI risk assessment	Multilateral Government	Digital Markets Act	Digital Services Act	Platform Regulation	Digital Capitalism	Digital Economy	Digital Entrepreneurship	Digital Markets, E-Commerce	Platforms and Social Networks	Gatekeepers	EU Market	MSP (Multi-Sided Platform)	Consumer Profiling, Surveillance	Competition, Antitrust Law	Data Governance	Autonomy	Democracy	Participation	Digital Sovereignty	Digital Transformation	Transformation	Big Tech	Colonialism
Ali (2021)																							x		x	x
Andree (2023)								x				x	x			x					x				x	
Barnes (2022)		x																	x							
Bassens & Hendrikse (2022)									x	x		x	x												x	
Bassens (2022)							x					x													x	
Bayer & Bauer (2023)										x				x												
Bearson et al. (2020)																							x	x		
Beems (2022)					x		x				x						x									
Braun & Garriga (2018)										x								x								
Braun & Kropp (2021)			x																	x		x				
Bundesnetzagentur (2023)										x												x	x	x		
Castro Varela & Dhawan (2015)																										x
Christodoulou & Iordanou (2021)																			x	x	x					
Cioffi et al. (2022)					x	x	x										x									
Daly et al. (2021)		x	x																							
Dammann & Glasze (2022)												x				x		x								
Dutkiewicz et al. (2021)			x				x																			
Emmer (2022)																			x	x	x					
European Commission (2020)										x	x			x									x			
European Commission (2023a)							x	x					x													
European Commission (2023b)				x					x	x				x												
Glasze et al. (2022)														x								x				
Glasze et al. (2022)				x																		x				
Gong et al. (2023)																							x	x		
Greenwood (2020)		x														x										x
Grundmann (ed.) (2023)	x	x	x				x					x				x										
Haucap & Schweitzer (2021)					x	x	x		x		x						x	x							x	
Hein et al. (2016)							x								x											
Helberger et al. (2020)		x																		x				x		
Helbing et al. (2015)		x	x																							
Hendrikse et al. (2021)									x																x	
Hučková & Semanová (2022)				x			x						x													
Hučková & Semanová (2023)					x								x				x									
Irimie (2014)				x					x										x							
Isaak & Hanna (2018)	x	x										x						x							x	
Jaekel (2020)									x	x		x														
Jäggi. (2023)							x													x			x			
Jang et al. (2021)		x																		x						
Kenney & Zysman (2020)								x	x																x	
Klarić (2023)	x			x																						
Komanovics (2023)							x							x				x								
Kreutzer (2021)									x	x																
Kshetri (2023)	x	x					x																			
Leahy et al. (2022)							x													x	x				x	
Lemstra (2016)									x		x	x														
Lippert et al. (2019)				x										x					x							
[illegible]					x		x						x				x									
Lünenborg (2022)		x										x														
Malik (2018)																			x				x	x		
Matyssek (2021)										x	x															
Mejias & Couldry (2019)		x						x																		x
Metakides (2022)										x												x	x			
Mailhe (2018)	x			x																		x				
Midiri (2023)					x		x	x																	x	
Milovanovic (ed.) (2023)																				x	x		x	x		
Möller (2021)																				x	x		x			
Mouton & Burns (2021)								x	x																	x
Muldoon (2022)								x					x											x		
Müller-Friemauth & Kühn (2020)	x							x				x														
Mumford (2023)								x																		x
Ndulu et al. (2023)		x																					x	x		x
Nocetti (2021)								x																		x
Nyhan et al. (2023)		x										x								x					x	
Osterhammel & Jansen (2017)																										x
Özcan et al. (2023)									x			x			x											
Pfeiffer (2022)								x				x	x		x											
Podszun (2023)					x	x	x					x	x													
Polański (2023)							x										x									
Porlezza (2021)		x					x														x					
Reichl & Kovar (2018)																				x	x			x		
Reif et al. (2023)		x																					x			
Rückert et al. (2022)																				x	x	x	x			
Rückert et al. (2022)																			x			x	x			
Rust (2019)				x					x					x									x			
Saurwein et al. (2017)		x	x													x										
Schallbruch (2018)									x		x															
Schaller & Vatananan-Thesenvitz (2023)										x	x															
Schallmo & Lohse (2023)										x	x															
Schreieck et al. (2018)								x					x													
Schulz & Dankert (2016)							x	x				x	x													
Seidl (2023)								x															x			
Seitz (2023)		x	x													x										
Staab (2019)								x	x			x			x											
Steinberg (2021)									x	x																
Steinicke & Witt (2021)							x														x	x				
Strmečki & Pejaković-Đipić (2023)							x										x	x								
Suter et al. (2022)																		x		x					x	
Taddicken & Schmidt (2022)		x										x								x	x					
Täuscher et al. (2021)								x					x		x										x	
Thimm (2022)												x								x	x		x			
Tóth (2023)							x		x									x								
Treščáková (2023)								x				x								x						
Vezzoso (2021)					x								x					x							x	
Vukušić (2023)		x										x								x						
Wörwag (2020)									x														x	x		
Wylie (2021)																				x						
Young (2019)																x										x
Zollenkop (2021)									x		x			x												

4.2 Thematic Findings

This study examines how the GAFAM influences Europe's transformational changes and the impact of these data monopolists on citizens' lives and the European economy. The broad field of digitalization is narrowed down to the top-10 categories, focusing on Big Tech gatekeepers like GAFAM, their digital platform businesses, and the impacts on data governance, AI regulations, the economy, and democracy in Europe struggling for digital sovereignty.

After the 2019–2021 pandemic, public confidence in EU leaders needs restoration as faith in their institutions has declined (Dennison and Puglierin 2021). France, Germany, Italy, and Austria report lower confidence in current EU activities and the success of the "EU" project. Robust infrastructure and an independent ICT industry are crucial for enabling digital transformations. Dennison and Puglierin (2021) reflect EU citizens' views on the strength of the US, especially represented by GAFAM, and highlight Europe's determination to succeed in digitalization, global competition, e-commerce, and the platform economy. The poll shows 42% of EU citizens believe the EU should ensure a unified response to global processes like digitalization and geopolitical threats. Responses from Poland, Hungary, and Italy showed agreement with US activities. The study concludes that the EU should defend democracy and protect citizens against new global threats.

Haucap and Schweitzer (2021) addressed progress regarding the DMA and related antitrust laws, emphasizing the economic implications of multi-sided digital markets, specifically platforms, and their characteristics concerning competition and acquisitions. Bauer et al. (2021) developed a more generic model of the platform economy. Both papers highlight network effects, which significantly increase a platform's value. Network effects refer to the phenomenon where a platform's value increases as more users join. This effect is also related to the principle of zero limiting costs for software products and services like cloud platforms. Once deployed, further reproduction costs for providers tend to zero. Simultaneously, users post valuable content that can be monetized by selling advertisements. Thus, platform vendors can achieve high profits without exceptional entrepreneurial risks. Additionally, collected user data can enhance services or targeted advertising (customer profiling).

According to Jaekel (2020), these evolving network effects disrupt traditional e-commerce, reducing competition. Andree (2023) highlights the massive consequences of killer acquisitions, especially within the media industry and instant messaging. He emphasizes the importance of free speech, independent journalism, and the role of conventional media for democracy.

5 Discussion

To address the complexity of the research, a classification process with evaluation was employed to provide a readable source of information, summarizing, and discussing major research trends and developments.

Table 5 summarizes the progress in various fields covered by this study. The evaluation results were ranked as follows: up to 10% as Very Low, 25% as Medium, 50% as Good, and better than 75% as Excellent. This visualization shows a comprehensive knowledge base in the scientific community about Europe's digital transformation. Targets are clearly defined, and the importance of the GAFAM industry, mainly for their contributions to infrastructure, is well recognized in the literature. However, the impacts of AI technology, related model biases, and the consequences of using such technologies against free will and speech are not fully described or understood. The research suggests that acknowledging GAFAM's dominance in Europe is the first priority. Once this fact is recognized, various concepts are expected to emerge from stakeholders, including citizens, industrial representatives, policymakers, and political activists.

Table 5. Evaluation matrix for research progress within the selected topics.

	Digital transformation of Europe	Dominance of Big Tech and GAFAM's	AI algorithms and related biases	Impact on EU citizens, democracy and stability	Impact on policymakers and other shareholders
Understanding and addressing the targets	Excellent	Good	Medium	Medium	Medium
Designing and implementing of new concepts	Good	Very low	Medium	Medium	Medium
Hints on changing and making these changes as operable	Good	Very low	Very low	Medium	Medium

As a second part, this work aims to also provide a fundamental set of risks they are attributed to GAFAM's role in the digital transformation of Europe.

I. Market dominance of the GAFAM industry and competition distortions:
It is widely accepted, but most probably untrue, that the GAFAM companies will be a highly innovative industry. Their impact can be evaluated by the range of digital services and the stickiness of internet content (Andree and Thomsen 2020). Platforms act as data silos, capturing most internet traffic within GAFAM's ecosystem. Consequently, killer acquisitions frequently occur when smaller tech companies innovate (example WhatsApp, which was originated by a Yahoo! spin-off).

II. Data privacy and misuse of user interactions on platforms
GAFAM companies leverage vast amounts of user data to algorithmically control user feeds, primarily on social media. This is the core functionality of privatized markets, especially when using scalability and network effects. Users can only access platform markets after accepting the vendor's closed standards, which lack interoperability and require adherence to internal rules, jeopardizing data privacy and enabling misuse. The

effectiveness of that process is empowered by modern AI technology, leading to human rights violations in some cases by multiple effects of model biases.

III. Influence on public discourses and hence democracy
GAFAM-owned platforms use their "right of the house" to control the type of content and its range of coverages, hence interactive potential. Principles of shadow-banning, dimming, but also content pushing are well known to AI-control the user's feed on social network platforms. Free speech and independent media are the base of every democracy. Who has the power upon information, who decides and controls what is considered as democratic. GAFAM acts like (private) governments!

IV. Addressing sustainability and environmental impacts
The exponential growth of AI-based technologies is likely to significantly increase the demand for green electricity, especially as GAFAM and their supply chains operate powerful data and logistic centers in Europe. This will impact the forecasted electricity demand for the ICT sector, crucial for Europe's sustainable transition towards full digitalization by 2040 and beyond. Europe is striving for a net-zero economy and society by 2050, while setting sector-specific targets for 2030 (D'Aprile et al. 2020).

It is evident that most of the risks listed in this study are driven by the unsustainable nature of GAFAM's activities worldwide, particularly in Europe.

6 Conclusions

Based on the findings, multiple challenges for society and shareholders have been identified. As with any research, this study faces limitations due to the vast number of publications on this complex matter. To address this, a quality screening process was used to select high-quality contributions from top-ranked authors, partly considering the publisher's evaluation. The focus was on the objectivity of the information base and cited sources. Given the high economic and political relevance, lobbying influence must be minimized. Such sources were tagged using stringent processes. Future research could use the Delphi method (Linstone and Turoff 2002) to ensure the reliability and robustness of the findings by gathering expert consensus and iterative feedback. Future research should also focus on providing actionable recommendations. First derived recommendations, based on the current research, are:

Digital platforms and their ecosystems require an enhanced and ready-to-use data infrastructure to achieve the goals of digital transformation. The focus is on the automotive and ICT industries, essential pillars of the European labor market. However, Europe faces a shortage of its own production facilities for key technologies (e.g. semiconductors and raw materials). To reduce this vulnerability, a balanced economic and foreign policy strategy involving EU member states is needed. Other success factors include simplifying administrative processes and adapting existing platforms and software solutions to ensure maximum interoperability and flexibility for digitalization.

The importance of public funding for digitalization projects is high in Europe. Sufficient financing under appropriate conditions is essential for implementing innovative ideas for startups with low equity ratios. The focus should be on the innovation achievements of the supported company and the competence of their teams, not the digital product itself. It is strategically important to continue successful EU funding programs. An overarching strategy that integrates elements of the Chips Act, the AI Act, and transformation tools like the Green Deal or the EU Taxonomy would be advantageous.

The relationship between democracy and digitalization will determine if Europe's digital transformation is fair and conflict-free. It is crucial to review Europe's regulatory framework to address threats from digital industry oligopolies. A democratic process is needed to foster societal discourse on digitalization's future. Increased resilience can counter digital power grabs, and promoting digital media literacy and inclusion is essential to adapt social mindsets. Digital technologies must be human-centered, with a value-based approach ensuring stable digital economies.

The operations of GAFAM were characterized by anti-competitive behavior in digital services. Highly integrated platform ecosystems have shifted digitalized businesses into an era of digital capitalism, impacting Europe's economy and society. According to Andree (2023), nearly 50% of all internet traffic today flows through and is absorbed by GAFAM vendors. The economic power amassed by GAFAM rivals that of smaller European member states. Europe must address GAFAM's influence, especially with the rising power of AI, primarily developed in the US. This study shows GAFAM striving for digital colonialism, impacting European society. This trend conflicts with fundamental European ideals, dedicated to democracy, social wellbeing, and peace.

Disclosure of Interests. The authors state that they have no competing interests.

References

Andree, M.: Big Tech muss weg! Die Digitalkonzerne zerstören Demokratie und Wirtschaft - wir werden sie stoppen. Campus Verlag, Frankfurt New York (2023)

Andree, M., Thomsen, T.: "Atlas der Digitalen Welt" (2020). Retrieved 1 Dec 2023 (https://atlasderdigitalenwelt.de/)

Bauer, V.P., Eremin, V.V. Ryzhkova, M.V.: Digitalization of the financial activities of platform companies: competitive potential and social impact. Finance: Theory and Practice **25**(2), 114–27 (2021). https://doi.org/10.26794/2587-5671-2021-25-2-114-127

Baumgarth, C., Binckebanck, L.: Digital marketing leadership – modell und empirische ergebnisse aus dem B-to-B-Umfeld. In: Schallmo, D.R.A., Lang, K., Werani, T., Krumay, B. (eds.) Digitalisierung, Schwerpunkt Business Model Innovation, pp. 219–44. Springer, Wiesbaden (2023). https://doi.org/10.1007/978-3-658-36634-6_9

Becker, W., Ulrich, P. Stradtmann, M.: Systematische literaturanalyse. In: Geschäftsmodellinnovationen als Wettbewerbsvorteil mittelständischer Unternehmen, pp. 75–97. Springer, Wiesbaden (2018). https://doi.org/10.1007/978-3-658-13041-1_4

D'Aprile, P., et al.: Net-Zero Europe: Decarbonization Pathways and Socioeconomic Implications. McKinsey (2020)

Daly, A.: Neoliberal Business-as-Usual or Post-Surveillance Capitalism with European Characteristics?. In: Hoyng, R., Chong, G.P.L. (eds.) Critiquing Communication Innovation, New Media in a Multipolar World, pp. 29–54. Michigan State University Press (2022)

Dennison, S., Puglierin, J.: Crisis of Confidence: How Europeans See Their Place in the World. ECFR/397. European Council on Foreign Relations ECFR (2021)

Fink, A.: Conducting Research Literature Reviews : From the Internet to Paper, 4th edn. SAGE, Thousand Oaks, California (2014)

Franke, U.: Artificial Divide: How Europe and America Could Clash over AI. ECFR (2021). 14 May 2024 (https://ecfr.eu/publication/artificial-divide-how-europe-and-america-could-clash-over-ai/)

Haucap, J., Schweitzer, H.: Die Begrenzung überragender Marktmacht digitaler Plattformen im deutschen und europäischen Wettbewerbsrecht. Perspekt. Wirtsch. **22**(1), 17–26 (2021). https://doi.org/10.1515/pwp-2021-0015

Hein, A., Schreieck, M., Wiesche, M., Krcmar, H.: Multiple-Case Analysis on Governance Mechanisms of Multi-Sided Platforms. Ilmenau (2016)

Helberger, N., Eskens, S., van Drunen, M., Bastian, M., Moeller, J.: Implications of AI Driven Tools in the Media for Freedom of Expression. Background Paper COE Cyprus 2020 (2020)

Hobbs, C.: Europe's Digital Sovereignty: From Rulemaker to Superpower in the Age of US-China Rivalry. ECFR/336. European Council on Foreign Relations (2020)

Jaekel, M.: Die Macht der digitalen Plattformen. Springer, Wiesbaden (2017)

Jaekel, M.: Disruption durch digitale Plattform-Ökosysteme: eine kompa (2020)

Jørgensen, R.F. (ed.): Human Rights in the Age of Platforms. The MIT Press, Cambridge, MA (2019)

Linstone, H.A., Turoff, M.: The Delphi Method: Techniques and Applications. Addison-Wesley Publishing Company, Advanced Book Program (2002)

Malik, F.: Preface: digital society? the great transformation21. In: Linnhoff-Popien, C., Schneider, R., Zaddach, M. (eds.) Digital Marketplaces Unleashed, pp. 7–12, Springer, Berlin, Heidelberg (2018)

Miailhe, N.: The geopolitics of artificial intelligence: the return of empires? Politique Étrangère Autumn Issue (3), 105–17 (2018)

Nocetti, J., Sel, P.: "Les états autoritaires face aux big tech. Pouvoirs **185**(2), 123–34 (2023). https://doi.org/10.3917/pouv.185.0123

Schreieck, M., Hein, A., Wiesche, M., Krcmar, H.: The challenge of governing digital platform ecosystems. In: Linnhoff-Popien, C., Schneider, R., Zaddach , M. (eds.) Digital Marketplaces Unleashed, pp. 527–38. Springer, Berlin, Heidelberg (2018)

Staab, P.: Digitaler Kapitalismus: Markt und Herrschaft in der Ökonomie der Unknappheit. Erste Auflage, Originalausgabe. Suhrkamp, Berlin (2019)

Webster, J., Watson, R.T.: Analyzing the past to prepare for the future: writing a literature review. MIS Quarterly **26**(2) (2002)

Zuboff, S.: The Age of Surveillance Capitalism: The Fight for a Human Future at the New Frontier of Power, 1st edn. PublicAffairs, New York (2019)

Linking Process Innovation Maturity to Sustainability: Insights from a Systematic Literature Review

Ika Nurkasanah[1,2](✉) and Amy Van Looy[1]

[1] Ghent University, 9000 Ghent, Belgium
{Ika.Nurkasanah,Amy.Vanlooy}@Ugent.be
[2] Institut Teknologi Sepuluh Nopember, 60111 Surabaya, Indonesia

Abstract. Sustainability has become an evolving paradigm within academia. This emergence has led organizations to innovate their business processes to remain competitive, meet customer expectations regarding sustainability, and comply with governmental regulations to achieve sustainability goals. This necessitates organizations to innovate their business processes beyond being profit-oriented. However, knowledge about the pathways of succeeding a sustainable process innovation is currently limited. Considering capability areas and business process maturity models (MMs) as key roles in a process innovation's pathway, this paper emphasizes the scarcity of existing sustainability measurement items for assessing and innovating business processes, highlighting the need for clearer guidance. We provide a systematic literature review (SLR) to explore the current state of literature and evaluate the progression of a related maturity quantification. Finally, our research unveils the interplay between the triple bottom line (TBL) sustainability dimensions (i.e., ecology, economy, and social), emphasizing the need for extending beyond profit-oriented business process innovation. Our insights call for integrating the sustainability dimensions to facilitate maturity when prioritizing BPM investments based on configuration theory.

Keywords: process innovation · sustainability · sustainable business process · green business process · maturity models

1 Introduction

The United Nations Development Program (UNDP) mandates organizations to incorporate sustainability into their business strategies [1], which is echoed by the increased awareness of customers demanding for sustainable products and services while also reflecting a broader concern about people and the planet [2]. Consequently, organizations are compelled to innovate their business processes in order to remain competitive, meet customer expectations regarding sustainability, and comply with governmental regulations aimed at achieving sustainability development goals. In this light, focusing solely on sustainable process innovations from a business profit perspective is inadequate. According to Elkington [3], sustainability impacts should be assessed using the

Published by Springer Nature Switzerland AG 2024
R. van de Wetering et al. (Eds.): I3E 2024, LNCS 14907, pp. 253–259, 2024.
https://doi.org/10.1007/978-3-031-72234-9_21

triple bottom line (TBL) framework, including economic, ecological, and social dimensions. Therefore, it is essential for organizations to consider all sustainability pillars rather than solely focusing on the economic perspective [4].

In practice, organizations need step-by-step guidance on how their process innovation can drive the achievement of sustainability goals. Such guidance is typically provided in the form of a maturity model (MM) that provides a structured framework for evaluating the maturity of business processes, helping organizations assess their current process strengths and weaknesses while identifying opportunities for process improvement [5, 6]. Various MMs have been developed to address sustainability, including sustainable smart manufacturing MMs [7], corporate sustainability MMs [8], or green business process MMs [9, 10]. Our study aims to investigate the current MMs related to business process innovation and verify how these models can be enhanced to focus more on ecological and social aspects. Among the several MMs, green business process MMs are most closely related to sustainable process innovation. Therefore, the related research question is: *how do existing business process MMs consider ecological and social aspects of business process innovation?*

Our research follows a Systematic Literature Review (SLR) approach [11] to explore the current landscape of process innovation through the lens of sustainable business process management (sustainable BPM), which is recently often mentioned as green business process management (green BPM), and to evaluate the progression of a sustainability-related quantification. This study contributes to the body of knowledge by demonstrating the need for more interconnections between the three sustainability dimensions to extend profit-oriented business process innovation and providing different views on how to reach a higher business process maturity level. Our practical implications lie in the potential to provide actionable guidance for organizations by optimizing capabilities and prioritizing efforts toward sustainable process improvement investments.

In the remainder, Sect. 2 describes the SLR approach, after which the findings are presented in Sect. 3. A discussion follows in Sect. 4, to conclude in Sect. 5.

2 Methodology

Our study relied on an SLR, which served as a valuable method [11] to search for state-of-the-art articles in various databases. We examined Web of Science, ScienceDirect, Emerald Insight, IEEE Xplore Digital Library, Springer, and AISeL, and this within a publication period from 2019 to 2024. The selection of this specific timeframe was motivated by a previous SLR on green BPM which was published in 2019 [12], but could not identify any related MM. Therefore, our time period was not overlapping. Among the various existing MMs, the most closely related to sustainable process innovation were the green business process MMs. Thus, this study specifically searched for green BPM literature. Concurrently, subsequent studies pertaining to green business processes continued to advance, and this by hinting at the broader dimensions of sustainable business processes by also including social and economic considerations. In contrast to this prior SLR, we thus focused on the interrelationships between green business processes and the other sustainability dimensions (i.e., as hinted in the green BPM literature) while examining quantification initiatives and MMs as our extensions.

By using the keywords of "green business process management" OR "green BPM" OR "sustainable business process management" OR "sustainable BPM", the initial search yielded 84 articles. During filtering, 33 articles were eliminated due to duplicate records, unavailability of full-text articles, non-research articles (e.g., teaching notes), or non-English publications. The remaining 51 articles were reviewed in more depth, excluding 15 additional articles after screening their title and abstracts. Full-text readings of the other 36 papers were performed by filtering only the relevant articles whose main discussion had a direct link to green or sustainable business processes, following the detailed SLR protocol and procedure available online through: tinyurl.com/ProtocolsIFIP. Relevance determination involved an initial filtering by the first author, with collaborative brainstorming sessions between the first and second authors to reach a consensus in case of uncertainty. Consequently, 22 articles were selected for further analysis. The literature mapping was done based on anonymous ID's (e.g., P01, P02, etc.), and can be found online through: tinyurl.com/sustainableBPM).

3 Results

3.1 Results for Sustainability Dimensions

Several articles proposed indicators for measuring the achievement of at least one sustainability dimension (Table 1). In addition to merely listing such indicators, we observed evidence for the interrelationships between the three sustainability dimensions, either in the form of an integration (i.e., when improving one sustainability dimension supports the achievement of another dimension) or in the form of a tension (i.e., when improving one sustainability dimension negatively affects another dimension). These observations revealed that the BPM literature, which previously focused on economic or environmental dimensions separately, is now beginning to include social aspects.

3.2 Comparing Maturity Levels for Green Business Processes

From the 22 sampled articles, only three contained a measurement for determining a maturity level, namely paper ID [P01], [P08], and [P23]. Since the last two papers are from the same research group and both work towards the same MM, only two distinct MMs relate to green business processes, namely: [P01] (Sohns, et al. 2023) and [P08] (Coukuyt & Van Looy 2021), as seen in Fig. 1.

First, the maturity measurement in the "BPM readiness model" of paper ID [P01] proposed four green BPM maturity levels (i.e., levels 0–1-2–3), which were adopted from the business sustainability typology [13]. The maturity indicators underlying this MM were obtained from multiple case studies on ten manufacturing SMEs in Germany, resulting in six core factors [14]: green attitude, green strategy, green governance, green modeling, green monitoring, and green optimization.

On the other hand, the MM in paper ID [P08] focused on identifying green BPM maturity levels using quantitative methodologies, including statistical cluster analysis and confirmatory discriminant analysis, involving 89 ecolabel organizations from various economic sectors that produced diverse green products and services. Their survey

Table 1. Sustainability dimensions and indicators as discussed in the sampled articles.

Dimension	Examples of indicators
Economic	Cost [P06] [P20]; time [P06]; profit [P06] [P20]
Environment	Carbon footprint and gas emission [P06] [P15] [P14] [P17] [P18] [P19]; energy and paper consumption [P11] [P13] [P15] [P17]; waste reduction [P19]
Social	Staff's wages [P06] [P10]; staff's health and safety [P06] [P21]; social equity [P06] [P10]; number of green and socially conscious customers [P11]; expenses related to training, hiring, and programming [P19]
Interrelationships among dimensions and related tensions or contradictions	Decreasing water causes an increased energy use (tension: ecology-economy) [P06]; reducing hospital beds improves service quality but adding vehicle emissions during patients home visit (tension: social/economy-ecology) [P14]; increasing a population triggers an unsustainable economic growth (tension: social-economy) [P19]; reducing resource consumption and waste for healthier society (integration: ecology-social) [P21]

instrument was aligned with the BPM capability framework of [17], previously validated but adapted for green BPM in ecolabel companies. Four maturity levels were proposed, albeit with different labels and coverage: "green BP immaturity," "green BPL maturity," "green BPM maturity," and "green BPO maturity".

Figure 1 compares the green BPM maturity level criteria of both MMs, highlighting different emphases at the middle maturity levels. At the lowest level, both MMs started similarly, with no green BPM factors implemented at level 0 of [P01] and weak capability scores at the "green BP immaturity" level of [P08] (red bullets). On the next maturity level, the descriptions for both MMs differed somehow. The "green BP level 1" of [P01] required that all six core factors were partially implemented (yellow bullets), while the capabilities related to "green BPL maturity" [P08] emphasized more the process lifecycle (i.e., process modelling, deployment, monitoring, and optimization) as a fundament for the managerial and organizational areas, namely with partially high lifecycle aspects (green bullets) and a medium implementation of the other capabilities (yellow bullets). Next, at the third level, the "green BP level 2" [P01] was achieved when organizations fully implement all readiness factors (green bullets). On the other hand, at the level of "green BPM maturity" [P08], all capabilities were highly represented (green bullets), whereas the organization could already focus on more advanced lifecycle management (blue bullets). At the highest level, both MMs categorized organizations in the most mature state if they achieved proactive [P01] or advanced [P08] realization of all green BPM areas (blue bullets). While similarities were observed at the start and end states,

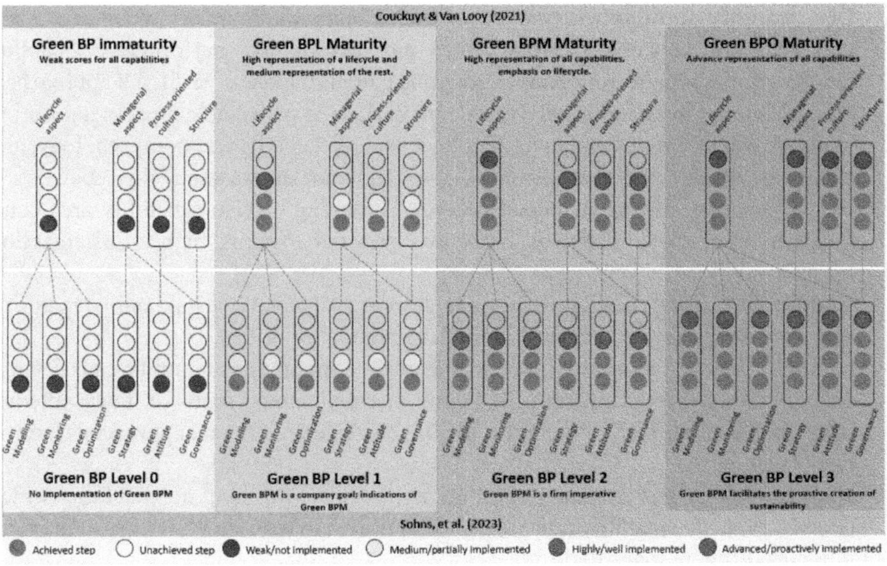

Fig. 1. A comparison of different views regarding green BPM maturity levels (Color figure online).

further research is needed to explore the alternative paths of the middle states to advance green BPM maturity.

4 Discussion and Research Agenda

Although only two MMs seem to focus on green BPM (Fig. 1) so far, they present different approaches to how sustainable BPM should progress toward higher maturity levels, thus calling for further investigation. Sohns et al. [9] suggest that organizations should address all capability areas simultaneously before progressing, which can be demanding. In contrast, Couckuyt and Van Looy [10] allow for varied capability investments at the same maturity level. This lack of consensus on the appropriate approach for achieving sustainable BPM maturity highlights promising research needs about the possibility of alternative paths to sustainable process innovation maturity.

For addressing this gap and also theorizing about the subject, it therefore seems beneficial to align with configuration theory. More specifically, prior research has employed configuration theory for improving an organization's business process orientation (BPO) by acknowledging different but equal maturation paths through a taxonomy based on path differences and archetype similarities [17]. By adopting configuration theory, subsequent research may consider a combination of case studies for path differentiation and surveys for path generalization in order to guide organizations to achieve their sustainability goals based on assessing their initial configuration or maturity state and brainstorming about their desired evolving pathway. Therefore, we now reinterpret the key aspects of configuration theory [18] from a sustainable BPM context as follows:

- **Discontinuity and nonlinearity as normal**: Configuration theory recognizes complex causation between maturity scores and sustainability performance, enabling tailored progress paths for organizations and countering one-size-fits-all approaches.
- **Holistic and systemic perspective**: A combination of sustainable process innovation maturity that integrates and quantifiably considers the TBL (economy, ecology, and social) as sustainability dimensions is essential to achieve sustainability goals.
- **Research propositions as causal recipes**: Assuming diverse capability area combinations can reveal different but equal patterns towards higher sustainability levels.
- **Equifinality**: Configuration theory enables varied paths to sustainability maturity, accommodating diverse capabilities and managerial priorities.
- **Limited diversity as reality**: A few practical configurations simplify causal inference based on theory and context. Future research should focus on fewer alternatives for balancing TBL, though recognizing that one-size-fits-all approaches may be inadequate.
- **Rich combinatorial causality**: Configuration theory will help in specifying which combinations of capability areas are most optimum to balance TBL as sustainability pillars at different maturity levels.

5 Conclusion

In response to the research question, our review of 22 most recent articles has highlighted the need to better consider ecology and social dimensions over economic sustainable process innovation dimensions. In terms of the ecological aspect, limited evidence still exists for measuring green business process innovation, while the social aspects seem missing so far. Moreover, one green-related MM advocates a gradual evolution across all process innovation capability areas, whereas another MM emphasizes prioritization. This study advocates the adoption of configuration theory as a promising foundation for developing MMs by also considering TBL as dedicated sustainability pillars. Practically, practitioners can benefit from our overview regarding essential indicators and potential maturity progression alternatives for achieving sustainable organizational goals through sustainable process innovation. Future research on green process innovation extensions will help develop and test a sustainable business process MM that holistically incorporates all sustainability dimensions. Secondly, developing a sustainable process innovation maturity model requires an assessment and improvement tool based on best practices to advance along diverse maturity path. Finally, future research can overcome our limitations by extending the search period, adding more social search terms, exploring other disciplines (i.e., due to insufficient prior BPM research), or considering alternative theories like systems theory or actor-network theory.

Acknowledgment. We gratefully acknowledge the financial support provided by the Indonesia Endowment Fund for Education (LPDP - Lembaga Pengelola Dana Pendidikan Indonesia), which has been instrumental in making this research possible.

References

1. United Nations: Executive Board of the United Nations Development Programme, the United Nations Population Fund and the United Nations Office for Project Services. United Nations, New York, USA (2021)
2. McKinsey Company: Consumers care about sustainability—and back it up with their wallets. McKinsey Company (2023)
3. Elkington, J.: Cannibals with forks: the triple bottom line of 21st century business. Capstone, Oxford, U.K. (1997)
4. Inghels, D.: Sustainability transition for businesses. In: Introduction to Modeling Sustainable Development in Business Processes, pp. 1–29. Springer, Cham (2020). https://doi.org/10.1007/978-3-030-58422-1
5. Wendler, R.: The maturity of maturity model research: a systematic mapping study. Inf. Softw. Technol. **54**, 1317–1339 (2012)
6. Van Looy, A., De Backer, M., Poels, G.: Defining business process maturity. a journey towards excellence. Total Qual. Manag. Bus. Excellence **22**, 1119–1137 (2011)
7. Shi, X., Baba, T., Osagawa, D., Fujishima, M., Ito, T.: A maturity model for sustainable system implementation in the era of smart manufacturing. In: 2019 24th IEEE International Conference on Emerging Technologies and Factory Automation (ETFA), pp. 1649–1652. IEEE, Zaragoza, Spain (2019)
8. Sari, Y., Hidayatno, A., Suzianti, A., Hartono, M., Susanto, H.: A corporate sustainability maturity model for readiness assessment: a three-step development strategy. IJPPM **70**, 1162–1186 (2021)
9. Sohns, T.M., Aysolmaz, B., Figge, L., Joshi, A.: Green business process management for business sustainability: a case study of manufacturing small and medium-sized enterprises (SMEs) from Germany. J. Clean. Prod. **401**, 136667 (2023)
10. Couckuyt, D., Looy, A.V.: Identifying green business process maturity levels by classifying ecolabels. In: ECIS 2021 Research-in-Progress Papers (2021)
11. Kitchenham, B.: Guidelines for performing Systematic Literature Reviews in Software Engineering. Keele University (2007)
12. Couckuyt, D., Van Looy, A.: Green BPM as a business-oriented discipline: a systematic mapping study and research agenda. Sustainability **11**, 4200 (2019). https://doi.org/10.3390/su11154200
13. Dyllick, T.L., Muff, K.: Clarifying the meaning of sustainable business: introducing a typology from business-as-usual to true business sustainability. SSRN J. (2015)
14. Opitz, N., Krüp, H., Kolbe, L.M.: Environmentally sustainable business process management – developing a green BPM readiness model. In: PACIS, p. 12 (2014)
15. Van Looy, A., Backer, M.D., Poels, G.: A conceptual framework and classification of capability areas for business process maturity. Enterp. Inf. Syst. **8**, 188–224 (2014)
16. Van Looy, A.: Capabilities for managing business processes: a measurement instrument. BPMJ. **26**, 287–311 (2020). https://doi.org/10.1108/BPMJ-06-2018-0157
17. Van Looy, A., Trkman, P., Clarysse, E.: A configuration taxonomy of business process orientation. Bus. Inf. Syst. Eng. **64**(2), 133–147 (2021). https://doi.org/10.1007/s12599-021-00700-4
18. El Sawy, O.A., Malhotra, A., Park, Y., Pavlou, P.A.: Seeking the configurations of digital ecodynamics: it takes three to tango. Inf. Syst. Res. **21**, 835–848 (2010)

A Systematic Literature Review on Service Robot Attributes and Organizational Climate's Role

Dhyana Paramita(✉), Amy Van Looy, and Peter Vlerick

Ghent University, 9000 Ghent, Belgium
{dhyana.paramita,Amy.VanLooy,peter.vlerick}@UGent.be

Abstract. Service robots are gaining increasing attention due to their potential productivity and efficiency gains. However, implementing service robots within an organization faces challenges because service robots possess characteristics that can affect employees in a negative or positive direction. It is therefore important to examine which characteristics matter most. Additionally, organizational characteristics, in particular the prevailing organizational climate, are important to provide a conducive work atmosphere in robot adoption. However, the latter has been less emphasized in service robot studies so far. Therefore, this study sets out to investigate the importance of both service robot characteristics and organizational climate for robot implementation in the workplace. Drawing on two respective systematic literature reviews, we have uncovered four groups of service robot attributes (i.e., social attributes, physical attributes, operating modes, and degrees of intelligence) and four groups of organizational climate attributes (i.e., resources, communication, leadership, and job autonomy), including their effects on particular service robot outcomes within an organization. Theoretically, this study adds insight through identifying key service robot characteristics and considering organizational climate as a novel angle for future research. For practice, this paper offers adoption advice to managers on service robot implementation while considering the organizational climate at work.

Keywords: service robot · organizational climate · anthropomorphism · literature review · employee · technology adoption

1 Introduction

Driven by the rapid development of artificial intelligence (AI), service robots have evolved into various types of intelligent agents that reshape the nature of service work and help innovate business processes. For instance, service robots have been able to take over jobs that were previously performed by humans, such as for call centers, cashiers, and room service [1]. Although this is linked to job displacement, technology has also

Supplementary Material (Appendix) can be accessed at tinyurl.com/yckedeu5.

Published by Springer Nature Switzerland AG 2024
R. van de Wetering et al. (Eds.): I3E 2024, LNCS 14907, pp. 260–271, 2024.
https://doi.org/10.1007/978-3-031-72234-9_22

created job opportunities by streamlining routine tasks and increasing labor productivity [2]. While prior studies on service robot adoption have predominantly focused on the customer perspective, mainly due to the service robot front-office position [3], the employees' viewpoint remains under-investigated. Nevertheless, employee-focused studies on service robots remain important for several reasons. First, employees and customers may have differing perceptions toward service robots because, depending on the robot characteristics, service robots can be perceived differently, such as entertaining or threatening [4]. Although some studies have associated service robots with social robots (e.g., [5]), the two are not necessarily interchangeable. Therefore, taxonomies characterizing social robots (e.g., [6]) may not always apply to service robots. In other words, the characteristics of a service robot may be distinct from a social robot, even though the humanness (i.e., anthropomorphism) remains relevant for both. Second, the implementation of service robots may face employee resistance. In response, firms must provide a conducive work atmosphere, which can be facilitated through a supportive organizational climate. However, organizational climate seems to be overlooked in service robot studies [7].

Given the above-mentioned gaps, this study pursues two primary objectives. First, by making distinctions with other robot types, this study aims to compile the definitions and characteristics of service robots from existing literature reviews, with anthropomorphism as a theoretical lens. These characteristics will then be used to define service robot attributes and to properly conceptualize a service robot. Second, this study aims at investigating the importance of organizational climate as an organizational extension of service robot characteristics. The corresponding research questions are as follows.

RQ1. What are the major characteristics that differentiate between service robots?
RQ2. How have the role of organizational climate and service robot characteristics been empirically studied in the service robot domain?

A dedicated systematic literature review (SLR) per RQ will be conducted to consolidate insights derived from the body of knowledge. From a theoretical standpoint, this paper will synthesize the most differentiating service robot characteristics to obtain a better understanding of service robots. In addition, this study will show evidence to consider organization climate for service robot adoption in the workplace, as a novel angle for future research. From a practical standpoint, this paper will offer adoption advice to managers on how to introduce service robots in the workplace, with a particular emphasis on the key role of the prevailing organizational climate.

The remainder is structured as follows. Section 2 provides the theoretical background, followed by the research approach in Sect. 3. Afterwards, Sect. 4 presents the results, succeeded by a discussion in Sect. 5 and a conclusion in Sect. 6.

2 Theoretical Background

After more narrowly specifying the research gaps, we use anthropomorphism as a theoretical lens for RQ1, and organizational climate as a theoretical lens for RQ2.

2.1 Research Gaps

Service robot acceptance models [8] show that, while robot functionality affects users' acceptance, social-emotional and relational elements also play important roles in users' perceptions of robots. In the service domain, the robot characterization typically focuses on functionality and anthropomorphism [3, 7]. However, these attributes do not explicitly address service robot capacity in human interaction. Additionally, although service robots have been associated as social robots [5], certain service robot characteristics may diverge from that of a social robot (e.g., [6]) because service robots may lack social attributes in some cases. Consequently, it remains essential to differentiate the characterization of service robots from that of social robots.

Moreover, to introduce service robots within an organization, a conducive work environment for robot integration is required. This can be fostered through a supportive organizational climate. However, organizational characteristics in service robot studies are generally merely associated with some organizational considerations when adopting new technologies, such as service robot functionality, market competition, financial implications, and productivity [3, 9], but with limited attention for the prevailing organizational climate while working with and actually using a service robot. Nevertheless, the organizational climate might be beneficial in managing the unintended consequences of robot integration within an organization. Hence, this study aims to seek the presence of organizational climate in service robot studies as a novel angle.

2.2 Background of Anthropomorphism

Service robots are often characterized by their functional attributes (e.g., perceived usefulness or relative advantage) [3, 7]. However, social-emotional and relational elements are also important to shape users' perceptions toward robots [8]. Hence, to improve human-robot interaction, robots have been equipped with human-like features. The notion of "anthropomorphism" serves as the umbrella term for the latter. Hence, this study adopts anthropomorphism as a theoretical lens to characterize service robots. More specifically, the term "anthropomorphism" originates from the Greek words of 'anthropo' (human-being) and 'morph' (to form). Anthropomorphism thus refers to the attribution of human features, characteristics, or mental states to non-human objects [10, 11] to facilitate the development of trust and relationships between humans and non-human agents [12]. Anthropomorphic attributes are apparent in a robot's appearance and behavior [13, 14]. Walters [13] defines three levels of robot appearance as having the highest to lowest resemblance to a real human, namely android, humanoid, and mechanoid. Anthropomorphism is also attributed to the behavior of robots, such as communication style, expressive behavior, social interaction, and movement [14, 15].

2.3 Background of Organizational Climate

To implement service robots at work, organizations should provide a work environment that supports service robot adoption, which can be facilitated through organizational climate. Organizational climate is "*the shared perceptions of and the meaning attached to the policies, practices, and procedures employees experience and the behaviors they observe getting rewarded and that are supported and expected*" [16, p. 362]. Conceptually, organizational climate differs from organizational culture, as the latter refers to the collective beliefs, values, and assumptions shared within an organization [16]. Research has explored various organizational climates, e.g., service climate [17] and safety climate [18, 19]. Key predictors of climate are leadership style [20], organizational resources [21], job autonomy [22], and management-employee relationship and organizational support [18]. Additionally, De Boeck et al. [19] also considered communication, commitment, and risk awareness as defining dimensions in their definition of food safety climate in food businesses. Hence, it is important to recognize that climate (as a multi-dimensional construct) is a fundamental attribute of a group (i.e. an organization) rather than the individual because perceptions are to a certain extent shared among individuals [16, 19]. The shared perceptions resembles the social influences in the Unified Theory of Acceptance and Use of Technology (UTAUT) [23] or the subjective norms in the Theory of Planned Behavior (TPB) [24], and reflects communication in the diffusion of innovation theory [25]. Additionally, both organizational support and resources can be considered as key facilitating conditions in UTAUT [23].

3 Methodology

This article conducted two subsequent systematic literature reviews (SLRs), namely one per RQ, to identify service robot definitions and characteristics (first SLR) and to show the role of organizational climate in service robot studies (second SLR). Accordingly, two SLR protocols were established. The eight selected academic databases were Web of Science, Scopus, Emerald, JSTOR, Science Direct, Springer, IEEE Xplore Digital Library, and ACM Digital Library. As inclusion criteria, we considered only peer-reviewed articles, written in English, and published from all periods until February 2024 (which is when our reviews were conducted). Duplicate articles and articles without full access were excluded. The protocol elements per SLR can be found in an online Appendix A-B, while the filtering steps are shown in Fig. 1.

For the first SLR, the search term was "service robot". Due to the large number of resulting hits, this term had to appear in the paper's title, and we only included review papers. Review papers were useful in providing comprehensive insights compiled from a large amount of service robot studies. As inclusion criteria, articles had to mention the definition of a service robot and/or reflect some of the characteristics of service robots. The selected papers were then blinded and assigned a unique identifier (i.e., A1, A2, etc.), resulting in a total sample of 17 papers.

For the second SLR, the search query combined "service robot" AND ("worker" OR "employee" OR "professional" OR "staff" OR "personnel" OR "operator") in the paper's title, keywords or abstract. These search terms were used to ensure articles were employee-focused, aiming for broader scope to encompass characteristics of both service robots and employees' organization. Then, we sought for service robot characteristics and organizational climate in these sampled papers to establish the connection of the service robot characteristics resulted from RQ1 to the organizational climate. We only included empirical quantitative studies to focus on a well-established construct and how it affects certain robot outcomes in the workplace. The selected papers were assigned a different identifier (i.e., B1, B2, etc.), resulting in a total sample of 16 papers.

The coding for the first SLR was conducted by identifying the robot characteristics that were explicitly mentioned, discussed, or used in the sampled review papers. These characteristics were then grouped into a main attribute according to their similarities. For the second SLR, the organizational climate and service robot characteristics were identified from the papers' results sections. The service robot characteristics were then first grouped based on the result from RQ1, while the organizational climate components were grouped according to the theoretical constructs defined in Sect. 2.3.

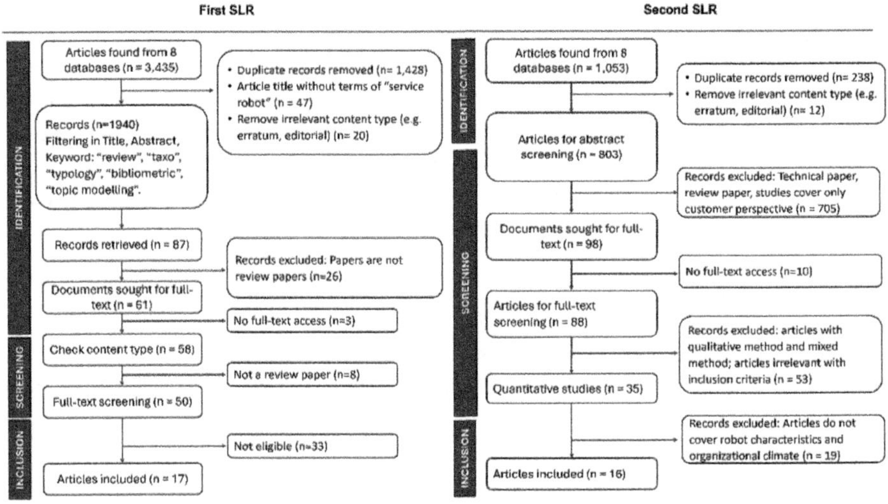

Fig. 1. Filtering procedure per SLR

4 Results

We subsequently describe the results per SLR. The complete ID reference used in the result can be found online (in **Appendix D-E**).

4.1 Results on Defining and Characterizing Service Robots (First SLR, RQ1)

4.1.1 Characterizing Service Robots

Ten characteristics were observed across four groups of attributes. Table 1 shows these four groups of attributes, namely: social attributes, physical attributes, operating mode, and degrees of intelligence. First, the social attributes correspond to features that facilitate human interaction (e.g., camera, mic, sensors, touchscreen display) [A14; A7; A1] as well as the type of information being exchanged (e.g., verbal, non-verbal).

Second, the physical attributes correspond to a certain representation, physical appearance, and internal component visibility. Representations can refer to the robot's shape, whether embodied in the form of a robot or disembodied (e.g., algorithm form), as well as in a physical or virtual form. Furthermore, physical appearance is related to human-likeness features (i.e., anthropomorphism), animal-likeness features [A13, A14], and functional appearance [A14] in a robot. Additionally, containment refers to the visibility of the internal robot component and whether it is covered by robot skin.

Third, the group of operating modes refers to how service robots operate, including their degree of autonomy and mobile mechanism. Autonomy refers to the extent by which service robots are operated, whether fully operated by humans, semi-, or fully autonomous. Mobile mechanisms demonstrate how the robot's mobility typically works, whether to travel on its own or controlled.

Finally, different degrees of intelligence denote the spectrum of robot intelligence, ranging from basic to advanced. On the lowest degree, mechanical intelligence is used for standard and routine tasks. Then, thinking intelligence depends on big data and is used for personalized interactions. A more advanced degree also covers a feeling intelligence used for relational services [A15]. As another group of intelligence, functional roles can focus on performing intended tasks, whereas information-sharing roles refer to the informer role, and socio-emotional roles focus on the relationship with humans [A8]. Lastly, service robots can be comprised of social and non-social types, that is, whether or not social interactions are involved [A6].

Table 1. Overview of Service Robot Characteristics

Attributes	Sub-attributes	References
Social Attributes	Features	[A14; A7; A1]
	Information type	[A3; A17; A3; A13; A14; A10; A17]
Physical Attributes	Representation	[A14; A3]
	Physical Appearance	[A14; A9; A10; A4; A13; A5]
	Containment	[A14]
Operating Mode	Autonomy	[A14]
	Mobile mechanism	[A16]
Degree of Intelligence	Intelligence	[A15]
	Roles	[A8]
	Social and non-social types	[A6]

4.1.2 Service Robot Definitions

Of the 17 sampled articles, three of them did not explicitly define a service robot but only addressed service robot characteristics [A7, A9, A10]. Among the other 14 articles, five general definitions appeared to be widely cited in the literature, as shown in Table 2. By synthesizing the predominant definitions compiled in Appendix C and the characteristics (Sect. 4.1.1), we conceptualize a service robot as "*a non-human agent with (i) system-based autonomy and (ii) a certain degree of intelligence, (iii) being equipped with a functional, animal-like, and/or human-like physical appearance for (iv) performing those service tasks that are typically performed by service employees to end customers while having (v) social and/or non-social interaction".*

Table 2. Overview of Papers with a Service Robot Definition

References	ID
ISO 8373:2021	A1, A2, A4, A5, A12, A14
IFR	A1, A2, A5, A6, A11, A12, A13, A14
Wirtz et al. (2018)	A3, A4, A5, A6, A8, A15
Bowen and Morosan (2018)	A13, A15
Ivanov et al. (2017)	A13
Own definition	A3, A4, A5, A16

4.2 Results on the Importance of Service Robot Attributes and Organizational Climate (Second SLR, RQ2)

4.2.1 Demonstrating the Importance of Robot Characteristics

We now present the service robot characteristics found in the second SLR by mainly focusing on the outcome variables. The major service robot characteristics were anthropomorphism, degree of intelligence, and social attributes (Table 3).

Table 3. Overview of Outcomes of Service Robot Characteristics

Attributes	Antecedents	Outcome Variable	ID
Anthropomorphism	Appearance	Reliance; Sense of responsibility	[B1]
	Behavior	Resistance to robot deployment	[B2]
	Both appearance and behavior	Service quality; Willingness to work with robot; Overall evaluation of the robot	[B3; B4; B5]
Degree of Intelligence	Social skills of robot	Robots-induced unemployment	[B6; B7]
	Perceived intelligence	Willingness to work with robot	[B4]
Social attributes	Communication strategy	Robot competence; Robot embodiment; Robot warmth; Discomfort	[B8]

The sampled studies showed that human-likeness in robot appearance could have a positive effect on employees' reliance, but without a significant effect on their sense of responsibility [B1]. While anthropomorphism could increase employees' willingness to work with robots [B4], it also induces resistance to robot deployment [B2]. Anthropomorphism seemed to improve a robot's overall evaluation [B5] but minimal effect on service quality [B3]. Regarding robot intelligence, robot-related social skills appeared to induce employees' beliefs in job replacement by robots [B6, B7]. In contrast, the perceived robot intelligence appeared to have a positive effect on employees' willingness to work with robots [B4]. Finally a human-like communication strategy could improve perceived robot competence, embodiment, warmth, and reduction of perceived discomfort [B8].

4.2.2 Demonstrating the Importance of Organizational Climate

Next, we present the outcome variables related to organizational climate. Even though none of the papers in the second SLR focused on the role of organizations' climate in general in the context of service robots, the results in Table 4 show that prior research mainly focused on organizational climate dimensions separately. These can be categorized into four dimensions: resources, communication, leadership, and job autonomy. First, the resources dimension refers to management and human resources (HRM) support on providing technical or non-technical aspects (i.e., as facilitating conditions). The results showed that facilitating conditions had a positive effect on usage intention [B9; B10]. In one study [B11], AI awareness of risk triggered service sabotage by employees. However, the latter relationship was weakened by the perception of high organizational support. In contrast, while intention to use a service robot and robot awareness of robot

Table 4. Overview of Organizational Climate Dimensions and Outcomes

Dimension	Outcome Variable	ID
Resources		
Facilitating Condition	Usage Intention	[B9; B10]
Perceived organizational support	Service sabotage	[B11]
Strategic HRM Involvement	Human-Robot collaboration	[B12]
Communication		
Subjective norms	Readiness for robotization	[B13]
Social Influence	Usage Intention	[B9; B10]
Social influence	Willingness to implement	[B14]
Leadership		
Transformational leadership	Industry turnover intention	[B15]
Job Autonomy		
Participation in decision-making	Employee well-being	[B16]

advantage positively affected human-robot collaboration, HRM support did not significantly moderate these relationships [B12]. Second, the communication dimension refers to how the robot-related information is communicated at work. Communication (e.g., social influence and subjective norms) appeared to be studied in relation to the tendency of robot use. Subjective norms had a positive effect on readiness for robotization [B13]. Also, social influence positively affected usage intention [B9; B10], except that [B14] found that social influence had no significant effect on willingness to implement a service robot. Next, the leadership dimension, as a key indicator of organizational climate, appeared to be important in service robot studies. For instance, transformational leadership seemed to weaken the negative impact of service robot risk awareness (SRRA) on turnover intention [B15]. Finally, regarding job autonomy, the use of service robots had a negative effect on employees' participation in decision-making, which then deteriorated employee well-being [B16].

5 Discussion

5.1 Interpretations of Findings and Proposing a Research Agenda

The service robot definition proposed in this study recognizes that service robots are not solely dedicated to address customers but also to represent service employees' viewpoints. Besides, we argue that service robots are not necessarily social or human-like, which contradicts with [A4]. This is because the spectrum of service robots ranges from the highest resemblance to human beings to none at all [13].

To answer RQ1, we have uncovered four main attributes of service robots (Table 1, Fig. 2). The characteristics outlined in this study are consistent with those of Zitzewitz et al. [14], covering physical appearance, movement, communication, interactive behavior, and social behavior. This study has partly covered social robot features established by Reeves et al. [5], such as a robot's communication ability and motion. Additionally, this study has augmented previous studies by adding the degree of intelligence as an extended defining characteristic of service robots.

For RQ2, given the limited emphasis on the organizational climate in service robot studies, this study has highlighted the importance of organizational climate by identifying four key organizational climate dimensions (Table 4, Fig. 2). We argue that these climate dimensions coupled with service robot characteristics shape employees' perception toward service robots, thereby influencing the integration of service robots into business processes. In addition, drawing on the climate dimensions outlined by De Boeck et al. [19], this study has added job autonomy as another key climate dimension. Employees who collaborate with a service robot might feel decreased autonomy in controlling their work. Occupational health theories and prior empirical studies have demonstrated that decreased job autonomy deteriorated employees' well-being and health [30]. Thus, job autonomy is not only a personal outcome of collaborating with service robots but might also influence companies' climate, suggesting a potential bidirectional relationship between service robot collaboration and organizational climate.

The results have shown that organizational support and transformational leadership appeared to lessen the negative effect of the employees' insecurity toward robots.

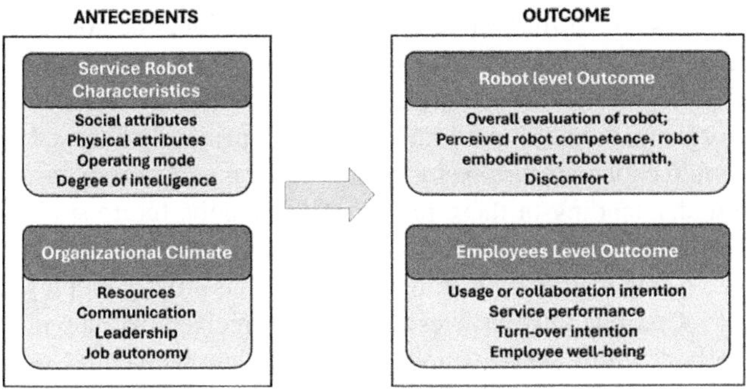

Fig. 2. Overview of Study Results

Conversely, while the intention to use and robot awareness positively affect human-robot collaboration, HRM involvement does not seem to enhance this relationship. One plausible explanation is that organizational climate may exert a greater influence when mitigating negative perceptions toward service robots, hence may improve the adoption of service robots in the workplace. However, when perceptions toward service robots are already positive, the organizational climate might not necessarily be influential. These conjectures warrant further validation through empirical investigation. Table 5 offers future research avenues, suggesting to broaden the service robot characterization beyond anthropomorphism by considering other key perspectives, and to delve into the role of organizational climate for service robot integration into the business processes.

Table 5. Service robot-related research agenda

Interesting research avenues regarding service robot characteristics
• Explain the effects to service performance based on different anthropomorphism, intelligence levels, tasks types, and other key characteristics • Investigate whether the overview of Table 1 can be extended to a validated taxonomy • Compare the effects of various robot appearances (e.g., humans, animals) and intelligence levels on performance in specific service settings
Interesting research avenues regarding organizational climate (OC)
• Determine when and why organizational climate exerts greater influence • Explore organizational climate effects in different business contexts, business process types (e.g., degree of knowledge intensity) and integration into business processes • Investigate how theories underlying organizational climate (Sect. 2.2) can be translated to specific service robot settings including its integration in business processes • Determine how an organizational climate develops, is shaped and could be changed

5.2 Research Limitations

It is essential to acknowledge the limitations arising from the selected keywords and the inclusion criteria. For RQ1 on service robot characteristics, this study solely relied on prior review papers. To further refine this characterization, one could benefit from the inclusion of empirical studies to provide primary data. Future research could extend the characterization beyond anthropomorphism such as robot intelligence and task types. For RQ2 on organizational climate, this study has primarily focused on quantitative studies. One could expand the scope by incorporating a wider array of literature sources to enrich the understanding of these results. Additionally, future studies could further investigate the role of organizational climate for the service robot integration into business processes. Another limitation is that this study has strictly employed the keyword "service robot." Consequently, articles that do not precisely include this term, such as those using "robot" within service applications, were not included. One could augment the findings by incorporating any robot studies in service context.

6 Conclusion

This study has characterized and conceptualized service robots. Through two systematic literature reviews, we conclude that service robots can be distinguished by a triangulation of four key attributes that include social attributes, physical attributes, operating mode, and degree of intelligence. While the first three attributes are consistent with previous studies, this study is one of the first to complement them by emphasizing a degree of intelligence as an additional characteristic of a service robot. We have also demonstrated the limited research attention paid to organizational climate in service robot studies. Remarkably, our results have revealed that prior studies focused on particular organizational climate dimensions separately. This literature review could identify four key organizational climate dimensions: organizational resources, communication, leadership, and job autonomy. Overall, these organizational climate dimensions have been found to affect particular robot outcomes in the workplace.

Acknowledgment. This research is funded by BOF/24J/2023/023.

References

1. Grandey, A.A., Morris, K.: Robots Are Changing the Face of Customer Service. Harv Bus Rev. (2023)
2. World Bank: World Development Report: The Changing Nature of Work (2019)
3. Xu, J., Hsiao, A., Reid, S., Ma, E.: Working with service robots? a systematic literature review of hospitality employees' perspectives. Int. J. Hosp. Manag. **113**, 103523 (2023)
4. Singh, S., Olson, E.D., Tsai, C.-H.: (Ken): Use of service robots in an event setting: Understanding the role of social presence, eeriness, and identity threat. J. Hosp. Tour. Manag. **49**, 528–537 (2021)
5. Raza, S.A., et al.: An in-the-wild study to find type of questions people ask to a social robot providing question-answering service. Intell. Serv. Robot. **15**, 411–426 (2022)
6. Reeves, B., Hancock, J., Liu, X.: Social robots are like real people: first impressions, attributes, and stereotyping of social robots. Technol. Mind, Behav. **1** (2020)
7. Xiao, L., Kumar, V.: Robotics for customer service: a useful complement or an ultimate substitute? J. Serv. Res. **24**, 9–29 (2021)
8. Wirtz, J., et al.: Brave new world: service robots in the frontline. J. Serv. Manag. **29**, 907–931 (2018)

9. McCartney, G., McCartney, A.: Rise of the machines: towards a conceptual service-robot research framework for the hospitality and tourism industry. Int. J. Contemp. Hosp. Manag. **32**, 3835–3851 (2020)
10. Duffy, B.R.: Anthropomorphism and the social robot. Rob Auton Syst. **42**, 177–190 (2003)
11. Epley, N., Waytz, A., Cacioppo, J.T.: On seeing human: a three-factor theory of anthropomorphism. Psychol. Rev. **114**, 864–886 (2007)
12. Adam, M., Toutaoui, J., Pfeuffer, N., Hinz, O.: Investment decisions with robo-advisors: the role of anthropomorphism and personalized anchors in recommendations. In: 27th European Conference on Information Systems (ECIS). Stockholm & Uppsala, Sweden (2019)
13. Walters, M.L., Syrdal, D.S., Dautenhahn, K., te Boekhorst, R., Koay, K.L.: Avoiding the uncanny valley: robot appearance, personality and consistency of behavior in an attention-seeking home scenario for a robot companion. Auton. Robots **24**, 159–178 (2008)
14. von Zitzewitz, J., Boesch, P.M., Wolf, P., Riener, R.: Quantifying the Human Likeness of a Humanoid Robot. Int. J. Soc. Robot. **5**, 263–276 (2013)
15. Breazeal, C.: Emotion and sociable humanoid robots. Int. J. Hum. Comput. Stud. **59**, 119–155 (2003)
16. Schneider, B., Ehrhart, M.G., Macey, W.H.: Organizational climate and culture. Annu. Rev. Psychol. **64**, 361–388 (2013)
17. Schneider, B., Macey, W.H., Lee, W.C., Young, S.A.: Organizational service climate drivers of the american customer satisfaction index (ACSI) and financial and market performance. J. Serv. Res. **12**, 3–14 (2009)
18. Wallace, J.C., Popp, E., Mondore, S.: Safety climate as a mediator between foundation climates and occupational accidents: a group-level investigation. J. Appl. Psychol. **91**, 681–688 (2006)
19. De Boeck, E., Jacxsens, L., Bollaerts, M., Vlerick, P.: Food safety climate in food processing organizations: development and validation of a self-assessment tool. Trends Food Sci. Technol. **46**, 242–251 (2015)
20. Schneider, B., Ehrhart, M.G., Mayer, D.M., Saltz, J.L., Niles-Jolly, K.: Understanding organization-customer links in service settings. Acad. Manag. J. **48**, 1017–1032 (2005)
21. Salanova, M., Agut, S., Peiró, J.M.: Linking organizational resources and work engagement to employee performance and customer loyalty: the mediation of service climate. J. Appl. Psychol. **90**, 1217–1227 (2005)
22. Llopis, O., Foss, N.J.: Understanding the climate–knowledge sharing relation: the moderating roles of intrinsic motivation and job autonomy. Eur. Manag. J. **34**, 135–144 (2016)
23. Venkatesh, V., Morris, M.G., Davis, G.B., Davis, F.D.: User acceptance of information technology: toward a unified view. MIS Q. **27**, 425 (2003)
24. Ajzen, I.: The theory of planned behavior. Organ. Behav. Hum. Decis. Process. **50**, 179–211 (1991)
25. Rogers, E.M.: Diffusion of Innovations. Free Press (1983)
26. ISO: ISO 8373:2021(en) Robotics — Vocabulary https://www.iso.org/obp/ui/#iso:std:iso:8373:ed-3:v1:en
27. International Federation of Robotics: Service Robots https://ifr.org/service-robots
28. Bowen, J., Morosan, C.: Beware hospitality industry: the robots are coming. Worldwide Hospitality Tourism Themes **10**, 726–733 (2018)
29. Ivanov, S.H., Ivanov, S.H., Webster, C., Berezina, K.: Adoption of robots and service automation by tourism and hospitality companies. Revista Turismo Desenvolvimento **27**(28), 1501–1517 (2017)
30. Verhaeghe, R., Vlerick, P., De Backer, G., Van Maele, G., Gemmel, P.: Recurrent changes in the work environment, job resources and distress among nurses: a comparative cross-sectional survey. Int. J. Nurs. Stud. **45**, 382–392 (2008)

Hackathon for Skills Development: An Unorthodox Approach for Audit Analytics Implementation

M. Gilang Ramadhan[1,2](✉), Marijn Janssen[1], Haiko van der Voort[1], T. R. I. Radarma[2], and R. R. Pratama[2]

[1] Delft University of Technology, Delft, the Netherlands
m.g.ramadhan@tudelft.nl

[2] The Ministry of Finance-Inspectorate General, Jakarta, Indonesia

Abstract. Technical data processing and analysis skills are critical audit analytics (AA) implementation challenges. Nevertheless, there is limited guidance on how to overcome it other than the 'traditional' training approach. This paper explores an unorthodox approach to dealing with issues in AA-related skills through a data analytics competition (hackathon). This study observes two hackathons that contribute to addressing AA-related skills issues. The hackathon incorporates the elements of real-world use-case and interactive engagement from the gamification concept and internal and external motivations from the competition notion. Building upon these insights, this paper proposes an emerging framework of a hackathon for skills development in AA implementation efforts. The framework's purpose is twofold. Scientifically, it assists in understanding the role of gamification and hackathon for skills development based on knowledge creation concepts. Practically, it exemplifies how to utilize hackathons to address skill issues. Furthermore, this research also suggests promising avenues for future studies, including further evaluation to affirm or expand the proposed framework or examination of the impact of detailed elements of the proposed framework.

Keywords: Audit Analytics · Analytics Skills · Internal Audit Function · Challenges · Analytics Competition · Hackathon

1 Introduction

Audit analytics (AA) is *the process of identifying, gathering, validating, analyzing, and interpreting digital data using information and communication technology to further the purpose and mission of internal auditing* (adapted from [1]). While AA provides many benefits, like more timely audit results, broader coverage of audit testing, or the ability to provide foresight for the organization, its implementation encounters numerous challenges [2]. It ranges from technical issues like the limited AA-related skills for auditors, data availability and security, emerging issues like the possibility of independence impairment and counter analytics, to social aspects like cultural barriers [3–7].

Published by Springer Nature Switzerland AG 2024
R. van de Wetering et al. (Eds.): I3E 2024, LNCS 14907, pp. 272–283, 2024.
https://doi.org/10.1007/978-3-031-72234-9_23

This paper focuses on AA-related skills as one of the main challenges of AA implementation. This challenge is critical, considering that it directly affects AA use in internal audit activities while being influenced by many other factors [8]. Unfortunately, to the best of our knowledge, the existing AA literature provides limited detailed suggestions for overcoming this issue and focuses on hiring and training strategies (e.g., [9, 10]).

However, broader literature suggests alternative measures for skill development. For instance, Sailer et al. [11] propose incorporating gamification, i.e., rule-based play with quantifiable goals, to foster skill development. Furthermore, Torres-Toukoumidis and Maeöts [12] highlight gamification's benefit for developing digital competency, which includes analytics skills. Alternatively, some scholars demonstrate the value of a competition-based game like a hackathon for skills development in educational settings [13, 14].

To this end, we realize that data analytics implementation practice is crowded with competition (hackathon) events, mainly to capture ideas and spark innovations [15, 16]. It raises the question of whether this approach may yield another benefit for AA implementation to address limited auditors' AA-related skills as one of its critical challenges. Building on those premises, we formulate the following research questions: *How can a hackathon be utilized to overcome skills-related issues in AA implementation?*

This paper aims to answer the research questions by observing real-world case studies targeting AA-skills-related issues through data analytics competition (or hackathon) instead of a mere 'traditional' training approach. For this purpose, this paper will briefly discuss the literature and the method in the next two sections. The subsequent sections will elaborate on the cases in detail, followed by the lessons learned from them, a discussion of their practical and scientific implications, as well as limitations and future studies. The final section concludes this paper.

2 Literature Background

2.1 Analytics-Related Skills Issues in AA Implementation

This research highlights limited auditors' AA-related skills; including data preparation from multiple data formats from various platforms, data analysis using low-code tools (e.g., orange or ACL) or programming/database language (e.g., SQL, python, or R); as one of the critical challenges hindering AA implementation by IAF. This notion reaffirms the criticality of analytics-related skills in AA studies (e.g., [17–19]) and the broader analytics research (e.g., [20]). Additionally, while auditors' limitation in AA-technical skills is acknowledged in the literature, recent empirical studies indicate that AA-managerial skills are equally vital for AA use in internal audit activities [8, 21]. Moreover, the skills issue is particularly important for AA, considering that analytics skills are inherently preferred to be embedded in the audit team, either due to the specificity of the AA project or resource constraints [18, 22]. In contrast, broader analytics fields are more lenient on the separation between analytics teams outside the business domain (e.g., [20, 23]).

In response, AA-related literature primarily focuses on the 'traditional' training approaches to addressing this challenge (e.g., [18, 22, 24]). Nevertheless, there is discussion on the search for alternative or complementary approaches to address this issue

[10]. Some scholars point out the inadequacy of the AA-related skills developed in the 'traditional' accounting (and by extension, auditing) academic and professional curricula (e.g., [22, 24, 25]), which in turn may influence the effectiveness of additional re-training for seasoned auditors.

2.2 Gamification and Hackathon for Skills and Knowledge Development

The 'traditional' training is still the prevalent approach for acquiring new skills or improving existing skills in the workplace [11]. Nevertheless, there are growing initiatives to use an alternative approach for more effective skills development, like through gamification (idem). Gamification utilizes game-based mechanics to engage and motivate people to learn and solve problems [12, p. 9511]. Compared to the traditional training approach, gamification is promising for fostering skills development in the workplace due to its interactive and engaging nature and real-world problems to be solved through the activities [11, 12].

Hackathon, in addition, is a relatively 'young' phenomenon intended to instigate innovation through some form of competition [15]. While it was initially popular in IT and related fields, over time, hackathons gained more traction in broader fields (idem). Rys [16] develops a taxonomy of hackathons based on their administrative conduct, types of hackathons, and approach to the invention. Rys also identifies the characteristics of the hackathon, such as knowledge exchange and motivation, as intertwined with the freedom to create [15]. These notions can be viewed as an extension of gamification, overlapping with hackathons in some key elements. The voluntary nature of the competition and the incentive provided (by the competition in the form of a prize) entice internal and external motivations for its participants. The extant literature acknowledges the value of hackathons for skills development. However, it mainly sets out in the educational setting [13, 14]. Therefore, analyzing this approach in a professional setting will be fruitful to expand the discourse further. Elements of gamification and hackathon relevant for skill development is shown in the table below (Table 1).

Table 1. Key Elements of Gamification and Hackathon Relevant for Skills Development

Elements	Features
Interaction	Interactive and engaging
Motivation	Combined (internal motivation and external incentive)
Use-case	Gamification alters the real tasks into game-like activities, whereas hackathon may use real-world case, scenario-based case, or combined. These frameworks facilitate skills development through problem solving mechanisms
Objective	• Open: allows maximum creative solutions, suitable for invention-focused events • Closed: targets particular solution(s) as specified in the programme, fitting for assessing and identifying participant(s)' specific skills • Dedicated: provides specific requirements, appropriate for specific problems

(continued)

Table 1. (*continued*)

Elements	Features
Type	• IT: targets IT specialists to showcase their skills, e.g., programming • Free: type hackathon invites people from diverse expertise to solve various practical problems and it does not always require IT-related skills • Mix type hackathon combines IT-related skills with industry specific use-case

Furthermore, these practices align with notions regarding skills acquisition as a part of knowledge creation from an organizational perspective [26, 27]. In this concept, skills and knowledge development encompasses socialization and externalization to extract tacit knowledge and combination and internalization to immerse and embed the explicit knowledge into the organization through its personnel (which in the context of this paper is the IAF and the auditors).

3 Research Approach

This paper used an exploratory case study approach to uncover the insight from the real-world experience of a matter being studied [28, 29]. For this purpose, we chose cases with a revelatory characteristic to enable us to observe and analyze an emergent phenomenon [28]. In this regard, this study observed two organizations experienced the phenomenon being studied, i.e., data analytics competition or hackathon event specifically for skills development in AA implementation effort. Further, as an organizational effort, the event also connects with the organization's knowledge creation model, as suggested by Nonaka et al. [26], enabling us to theorize the findings further.

We used semi-structured interviews to unearth the study respondents' experience [30, 31]. We interviewed seven key personnel involved in these events, including one IAF executive, four competition organizers, and three competition participants; with one involved both as a participant and organizer (in different periods). We complemented our analysis with the relevant documents obtained. We asked the interviewees about the nature of the competition, like why it is held, how it is conducted (details about the competitions and the complementary measures related to the competitions), and their views on the competition's impact on auditors' skills development and AA implementation in general.

The interviews were conducted between 2022 and 2024. Interview recording and summary were confirmed with the interviewees to clarify our understanding of their views. The approved interview summary and recording, along with the documents, were analyzed using initial coding for the first round and pattern coding for the second round [32–34]. We aimed to extract the insight and learn the knowledge from the practical experience in the case [35] by using the stated approach. The first round resulted in 18 initial codes, grouped into 6 pattern codes and then condensed into 5 themes. Some themes, such as "the lack of auditors AA-related skills" as the challenge, and "data analytics competition", "training", "complementary measures", or "collaboration" as the responses to the challenge, emerged from the case. Illustrative examples of the analysis are presented in the table below (Table 2).

Table 2. Illustrative Examples of the Analysis

Quote Example	Respondent	Initial Code	Pattern Code
"di beberapa tempat, projectnya jalan tapi kualitas pengujian kurang [ketika kami evaluasi], karena dilepas sama manajernya" (the projects' quality is lacking due to the lack of involvement and direction from audit manager)	R17	Lack of guidance (for AA project) by audit manager or above	"AA Managerial Skills", included as "Lack of AA-related Skills" theme
"Dari dua edisi penyelenggaraan HackAudit, penggunaan data analytics oleh internal auditor berkembang jauh lebih signifikan (massif)" (from the two editions of HackAudit [which I was involved in], we can experience that the use of data analytics by internal auditors is progressing significantly)	E5	DA Competition Facilitates AA-skills Acquisition and Improvement	"DA Competition"

4 A Brief Tale of the Two Data Analytics Competitions

4.1 Cases Overview

The Ministry of Finance Inspectorate General (MOFIG) is the internal audit function (IAF) of the Ministry of Finance of the Republic of Indonesia (MOF). In 2019, the MOFIG enacted a "Roadmap for Data Analytics Implementation", encompassing a wide range of activities to enable the use of digital data for internal audit purposes. One of the activities performed was a data analytics competition, consisting *of a data analytics project challenge* (or project challenge for short), in which participants develop their own project to answer audit (or business) objective(s) and *Kaggle challenge.* The winners received direct monetary prizes. The MOFIG's data analytics competitions were then emulated and expanded as the MOF's data analytics competitions in the subsequent year.

Another case of data analytics competition for addressing auditors' skills issues is from Bank X (BX)[1]. BX annually held DataDive, an internal data analytics competition

[1] All names and identifications related to this entity are pseudonymized for confidentiality reasons.

to incite business insights using digital data to improve their business and develop new products. In 2020, the internal audit function of BX (hereafter, BX IAF) emulated this approach and held a similar event, namely HackAudit. In addition to the original format from DataDive, HackAudit covers technical hands-on training in the first three days of the event and continues developing mini-projects in the last two days. Most participants develop audit analytics projects pertinent to their ongoing audit engagements. The winners are entitled to a significant performance assessment level tied to their annual bonuses. Further improvement of the project was facilitated by mentors, i.e., internal auditors experienced in AA use in their tasks.

4.2 Lessons Learned from the Cases

The limited AA-related technical skill is one of the most significant challenges of AA implementation by IAF [2, 10], which implicates the need for auditors' skills adjustment of improvement strategies. The extant literature focuses on using training and hiring options for this issue [3, 9, 22]. However, the interviewees explicitly impugned the effectiveness of the traditional training method. R4 stated that *"[...] in my opinion, training, on itself, is not effective; it might be effective for knowledge acquisition, in a sense that, for example, knowing some SQL basic functions (syntax); but to be able to use that knowledge requires direct practice in a project [...]"*, to which R13 from the MOFIG and E5 from BX IAF also provided similar remark, *"[...] it will be much more effective to immerse in a project, primarily when the project is relevant to our main task [...]"*, and *"[...] we have provided numerous training events, workshops, seminars of data analytics for auditors with standard approach to no avail; [...] so we need direct practice in a project and make a competition of it (to motivate the participants) [...]"*. Hence, the two organizations respond to these nuances by employing competition to address the AA skills issues and the limitations of the traditional training approach.

Both cases provided complementary measures to sustain the initiative through mentorships and informal forums during and after the event that helped auditors internalize the newly acquired skills and embed technical training with the competition in HackAudit or a follow-up tailored training in reflection on the result of the project challenge. Particularly, in addition to technical skills, the MOFIG found that managerial AA skill is equally important, as R17 suggested, *"[...] in some cases, the projects' quality is lacking due to the lack of involvement and direction from audit manager [...]"*. Therefore, the developed training curricula comprised technical skills for audit team members to develop the AA project and AA managerial skills for audit managers to direct the team in developing the project. These trainings are connected and embedded with a project, involving the managers and audit team members.

The two competitions occur in a relatively large organization with over ten thousand personnel and a complex structure with many business areas and units. It implies many potential participants with fresh ideas and possible collaborations-driven innovation among participants and units. The two cases also exemplify the expanded role of the innovation unit (as suggested by Krieger et al. [17]), which was actively orchestrating the organization-wide AA implementation program, including, in this context, organizing data analytics competitions.

Besides similarity, the two cases utilize different tactics in organizing the competition. In the MOF, the competition was started at the IAF level and then emulated to the broader organization, and vice versa for the BX. Furthermore, BX IAF embeds the training with the competition in HackAudit. Conversely, the MOFIG develops tailored training based on the competition results, i.e., includes technical and managerial-level training. The two cases also use some forms of Community of Practice (CoP) with different formats. As a result of the competition, data enthusiasts in the MOF established a community (namely, MOF-DAC). Conversely, the BX employs mentorship for auditors interested in furthering their skills (and projects). Finally, the two competitions also reward the participants (i.e., the winners) through direct monetary prizes in the MOFIG and bonus implications in the BX IAF.

5 Discussions

5.1 Practical Implications: How the Hackathon Addresses AA-Skills Issues

Practitioners and academics acknowledged AA-related technical skills as one of the most significant challenges of AA implementation by IAF [2, 10]. Nevertheless, while the extant literature focuses on training as the measure for this issue, the two cases challenge this notion and directly respond to these nuanced issues by acknowledging the need for immediate and real-world practice for audit analytics (or data analytics) skills. Additionally, the event significantly improves participants' engagement by (mostly) using the ongoing actual projects. This approach apprehends the value of use-case from gamification and a clear objective from hackathon notions for skills acquisition or improvement [11, 12, 15, 16].

Another vital tenet of gamification for fostering skills development is by motivating the participant to solve real-world problems in an engaging nature [11]. The two cases reflect this tenet by the participants' use of actual audit projects for the competitions. Furthermore, this approach serves dual purposes for the participants, i.e., finishing their project with opportunities for skills acquisition and showcasing their business values. Moreover, the competitions further incentivize the participants by providing direct monetary prizes and tying directly to the bonus, strengthening gamification's motivation element [10, 11].

Both cases exemplified the combination of IT and business (in this context, internal audit project) domains in the hackathon, as suggested in the literature [14, 15]. In this context, the open objective of the two competitions allows for applying the business domain (i.e., audit objective) and analytics domain into the project, which is particularly effective in the context of improving AA-related skills that typically require the audit team to combine the two domains, i.e., audit knowledge and analytics skills.

Another insight from the two competitions is the interaction element of the gamification. The interactive leaderboard in the *Kaggle* challenge enables participants to interact indirectly with each other, while the emergence of the community during and after the event fosters more direct interaction among participants as community members. This practice allows for the exchange and exposure of ideas and practices between participants as a medium for creativity and skills development. Moreover, the presence of auditors experienced in analytics as mentors in the project preparation and community further helps foster the skills acquisition for novice participants.

However, these cases infer that this approach may flourish in the organization with technological knowledgeability at the senior management level and technically savvy personnel in the initiating (or 'innovation' in Krieger's terms [17]) unit, which organizes the competition at the operational level. Therefore, while the cases offer an alternative approach to address (among others) auditors' (analytics) skills issues, this may only be feasible for organizations (and its IAFs) with similar characteristics, i.e., large and complex, with sufficient and knowledgeable personnel to organize such events.

5.2 Scientific Implication: An Emerging Framework of Hackathon for Skills Development

The previous subsection presents the two cases' reflections on the key elements of gamification and hackathons. Drawing from those reflections, this study sheds light on the use of hackathons to address skills issues in AA implementation efforts. The summary of the two cases is presented in the table below (Table 3).

Table 3. A Framework of Hackathon for AA Implementation

Elements	The MOF/MOFIG	BX/BX IAF	Notes
Game and competition elements			
Interaction	- Fully interactive for the Kaggle challenge (e.g., the participants can monitor leaderboards); and - Partial interaction in the form of project presentation for the Project challenge	Partial interaction in the form of project presentation for DataDive and HackAudit	Full and partial interaction during the event foster participants' creativity and skills acquisition and development
Motivation	- Monetary prizes for the winners - Kaggle challenge allows participants to showcase their skills in answering the question - Project challenge enables participants to collaborate to answer their real-world professional tasks	DataDive and HackAudit enable participants to collaborate and optimize their skills to answer their real-world professional tasks	Internally, the events motivate the participants through the use of ongoing real-world projects and by providing the means to test (and compare) and simultaneously offering the opportunity to advance their analytics skills. Externally, results' showcasing and monetary implications further incentivize and provide external motivation for the participants
Use-case	- Scenario-based for Kaggle challenge; and - Real-case for the Project challenge	Real-case for both DataDive and HackAudit	Both use-case types provide skill acquisition and development opportunities for the participants
Hackathon specific elements			
Objective	- Closed objective for Kaggle challenge; and - Open objective for the Project challenge	Open objective for both DataDive and HackAudit	Closed objective emphasizes technical skills while open objective combines technical and managerial AA-related skills development

(*continued*)

Table 3. (*continued*)

Elements	The MOF/MOFIG	BX/BX IAF	Notes
Type	Mixed-type for both Kaggle and Project challenges	Mixed-type for both DataDive and HackAudit	Mixed-type is suitable for AA skills development, combining the participants' analytics skills with internal audit knowledge
Additional element from the cases			
Organizer	Dedicated unit in the IAF, with collaboration with the community and HR	Dedicated unit in the IAF and in the broader organization	The two cases show the importance of a dedicated team to organize both in general (for innovation) and skills development purposes

These elements align with the knowledge creation concept, as suggested by Nonaka et al. [26]. The interaction element of the gamification and hackathon, as exemplified in the two cases, allows for socialization to build AA-related skills and knowledge among participants. The mentorship and the presence of experienced auditors in the community enhance the interaction element and help foster the skills of novice participants by extracting the knowledge and skills from the experts (i.e., the mentors and experienced auditors). The entanglement between audit and analytics domains and the possibility of cross-unit cooperation in the competition helps to immerse the acquired skills and knowledge as the combination aspect of the knowledge creation process. Moreover, the use of hands-on and ongoing audit projects in the competition contributes to further internalizing the AA-related skills for auditors. The figure below visualizes the elements of the hackathon for AA-skills development (Fig. 1).

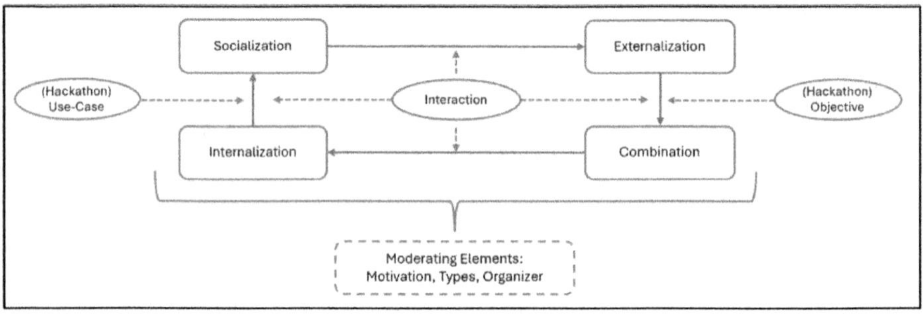

Fig. 1. Elements of Gamification and Hackathon from an Organization's Knowledge Development Perspective

6 Limitations and Future Studies

This study focuses on two specific cases exemplifying unorthodox approaches to addressing AA-related skills as one of the critical challenges of AA implementation. While this paper presents nuanced insights on how the two competitions apply the gamification and hackathon elements to address skills issues for AA implementation, the nature of the exploratory case study and the number and combination of interviewees may limit this study's findings' generalizability and thus, require further investigation. Nevertheless, this aligns with the primary goal of this research using the case study method, i.e., to learn from experience instead of generating generalizable facts [35].

Therefore, building on the lessons learned from the case and its limitations, future research can focus on calibrating the proposed framework as a fruitful avenue for this research field by using a more extensive case study and the number of study participants or a different method. Moreover, conducting case studies in different settings may refine this study's findings by affirming or expanding the framework. Furthermore, it is also intriguing to investigate the impact of those approaches and their different tactics (e.g., mentorship, CoP) and contexts (i.e., public and private sectors) on addressing skills issues in AA implementation efforts.

7 Conclusions

The existing literature acknowledged AA-related skills as one of the significant issues for AA implementation. Nevertheless, there is a lack of guidance on how to mitigate it other than through the 'standard' training and hiring methods. With the many data analytics competitions (or hackathons) events, this study explores the possibility of employing a hackathon to overcome that issue, which answers the research question: *How can a hackathon be utilized to overcome skills-related issues and other challenges in AA implementation?*

The cases show how the use of elements of gamification and hackathon contribute to skills improvement for auditors to utilize AA better in their internal audit tasks. While a hackathon is not a unique practice, the case studies suggest that a hackathon can be one of the alternatives for auditors' skills development by allowing auditors to connect with each other and analytics practitioners and expose them to new approaches for their internal audit tasks (i.e., the use of AA). The use of ongoing audit projects motivates and further eases the internalization of the newly acquired skills for seasoned auditors. In addition, tying it to performance measurement and reward further incentivizes the acquisition of AA skills participants. Furthermore, the nature of the hackathon, which combines audit and analytics domains, is particularly beneficial for AA, considering the need to integrate both domains within the audit team.

By doing so, the two cases expand the literature by suggesting alternative strategies for overcoming limited auditors' AA skills as one of the AA implementation challenges. Finally, this study synthesizes the cases and proposes a framework for a hackathon for skills development. This proposed framework draws from the elements of gamification and hackathon for skills development and reflects on the organization knowledge creation concept.

Acknowledgement. We send our utmost appreciation to the conference organizers, anonymous reviewers, and participants for facilitating the dissemination and improvement of this paper. This paper is supported by the Indonesia Endowment Fund for Education (LPDP) through a doctoral scholarship for the first author. The first author offers heartfelt gratitude to Nur Imroatun Sholihat for her feedback and support and to Ahmad Fauzi for the inspiring discussions.

References

1. Lambrechts, A.J., Lourens, J.E., Millar, P.B., Sparks, D.E.: Global Technology Audit Guide 16: Data Analysis Technologies. The Institute of Internal Auditor, Altamonte Springs, Florida, USA (2011)
2. Ramadhan, M.G., Janssen, M., van der Voort, H.: Driving and inhibiting factors for implementing audit analytics in an internal audit function. J. Emerg. Technol. Account. 135–163 (2023). https://doi.org/10.2308/JETA-2022-035
3. de Freitas, M.M., Codesso, M., Augusto, A.L.R.: Implementation of continuous audit on the Brazilian Navy payroll. J. Emerg. Technol. Account. **17**(2), 157–171 (2020). https://doi.org/10.2308/JETA-2020-047
4. Rakipi, R., De Santis, F., D'Onza, G.: Correlates of the internal audit function's use of data analytics in the big data era: global evidence. J. Int. Accounting, Audit. Tax. **42**, 100357 (2021). https://doi.org/10.1016/j.intaccaudtax.2020.100357
5. Earley, C.E.: Data analytics in auditing: opportunities and challenges. Bus. Horiz. **58**(5), 493–500 (2015). https://doi.org/10.1016/j.bushor.2015.05.002
6. Chaqiqi, A., Nugroho, A.: Readiness analysis of data analytics audit implementation in inspectorate general of the ministry of finance: an Indonesian Case. Indones. J. Account. Res. **24**(02), 147–162 (2021). https://doi.org/10.33312/ijar.513
7. Islam, S., Stafford, T.: Factors associated with the adoption of data analytics by internal audit function. Manag. Audit. J. **37**(2), 193–223 (2022). https://doi.org/10.1108/MAJ-04-2021-3090
8. Ramadhan, M.G., Janssen, M., van der Voort, H.: Transforming the internal audit function (IAF): An integrated MICMAC-ISM approach for unravelling the relationship among challenges. In: Janssen, M., et al. (eds.) New Sustainable Horizons in Artificial Intelligence and Digital Solutions, 22nd IFIP, Curitiba: Springer, pp. 139–155 (2023). https://doi.org/10.1007/978-3-031-50040-4_11
9. Austin, A.A., Carpenter, T., Christ, M.H., Nielson, C.: The Data Analytics Transformation: Evidence From Auditors, CFOs, and Standard-Setters (2018). (Working Paper)
10. Wang, T., Cuthbertson, R.: Eight issues on audit data analytics we would like researched. J. Inf. Syst. **29**(1), 155–162 (2015). https://doi.org/10.2308/isys-50955
11. Sailer, M., Hense, J., Mandl, H., Klevers, M.: Fostering Development of Work Competencies and Motivation via Gamification, pp. 795–818 (2017)
12. Torres-Toukoumidis, A., Maeöts, M.: Implementation of Gamification Strategies For The Enhancement of Digital Competences, pp. 9510–9518 (2019). https://doi.org/10.21125/inted.2019.2356
13. Haddock, R., Sharma, N., Kachra, R.: Hacking down disciplinary walls: Advancing sustainability and interprofessional competencies through a hackathon model. J. Sustain. Educ. **21** (2019)
14. Covic, Z., Manojlovic, H.: Developing key competencies through hackathon based learning. In: IEEE 17th International Symposium on Intelligent Systems and Informatics, pp. 000167–000172 (2019)
15. Rys, M.: Characteristics of invention development during the hackathon. Converg. Int. J. Res. into New Media Technol. **28**(6), 1800–1825 (2022). https://doi.org/10.1177/13548565211070418
16. Rys, M.: Invention development. the hackathon method. Knowl. Manag. Res. Pract. **21**(3), 499–511 (2023). https://doi.org/10.1080/14778238.2021.1911607
17. Krieger, F., Drews, P., Velte, P.: Explaining the (non-) adoption of advanced data analytics in auditing: a process theory. Int. J. Account. Inf. Syst. **41**, 100511 (2021). https://doi.org/10.1016/j.accinf.2021.100511

18. Li, H., Dai, J., Gershberg, T., Vasarhelyi, M.A.: Understanding usage and value of audit analytics for internal auditors: an organizational approach. Int. J. Account. Inf. Syst. **28**, November 2017 59–76 (2018). https://doi.org/10.1016/j.accinf.2017.12.005
19. Betti, N., Sarens, G.: Understanding the internal audit function in a digitalised business environment. J. Account. Organ. Chang. **17**(2), 197–216 (2021). https://doi.org/10.1108/JAOC-11-2019-0114
20. Lery, B., Haight, J.M., Alpert, L.: Four principles of big data practice for effective child welfare decision making. J. Public Child Welf. **10**(4), 466–474 (2016). https://doi.org/10.1080/15548732.2016.1209149
21. Ramadhan, M.G., Janssen, M., van der Voort, H.: Principle-based framework for audit analytics implementation. Tangerang Selatan (2024). (Working Paper)
22. Codesso, M., de Freitas, M.M., Wang, X., de Carvalho, A., da Silva Filho, A.A.: Continuous audit implementation at Cia. Hering in Brazil. J. Emerg. Technol. Account. **17**(2), 103–118 (2020). https://doi.org/10.2308/JETA-2020-006
23. Malik, P.: Governing big data: principles and practices. IBM J. Res. Dev. **57**(3/4), 1:1–1:13 (2013). https://doi.org/10.1147/JRD.2013.2241359
24. Tang, F., Norman, C.S., Vendrzyk, V.P.: Exploring perceptions of data analytics in the internal audit function. Behav. Inf. Technol. **36**(11), 1125–1136 (2017). https://doi.org/10.1080/0144929X.2017.1355014
25. Gambetta, N., García-Benau, M.A., Zorio-Grima, A.: Data analytics in banks' audit: the case of loan loss provisions in Uruguay. J. Bus. Res. **69**(11), 4793–4797 (2016). https://doi.org/10.1016/j.jbusres.2016.04.032
26. Nonaka, I., Toyama, R., Konno, N.: SECI, Ba and leadership: a unified model of dynamic knowledge creation. Long Range Plann. **33**(1), 5–34 (2000). https://doi.org/10.1016/S0024-6301(99)00115-6
27. Adenfelt, M., Lagerström, K.: The development and sharing of knowledge by centres of excellence and transnational teams: a conceptual framework. Manag. Int. Rev. **48**(3), 319–338 (2008). https://doi.org/10.1007/s11575-008-0018-8
28. Yin, R.K.: Case Study Research: Design and Methods, 5th ed. Sage Publications (2014)
29. Eisenhardt, K.M.: Building theories from case. Acad. Manag. Rev. **14**(4), 532–550 (1989)
30. DiCicco-Bloom, B., Crabtree, B.F.: The qualitative research interview. Med. Educ. **40**(4), 314–321 (2006). https://doi.org/10.1111/j.1365-2929.2006.02418.x
31. Saunders, M., Lewis, P., Thornhill, A.: Research Methods for Business Students, 7th ed. Pearson Education (2016)
32. Saldaña, J.: The Coding Manual for Qualitative Research. Sage Publications, London (2016)
33. Putney, L.G.: Case study. In: Salkind, N.J., (ed.) Encyclopedia of Research Design, Sage Publications, pp. 115–119 (2010)
34. Bolldén, K.: Teachers' embodied presence in online teaching practices. Stud. Contin. Educ. **38**(1), 1–15 (2016). https://doi.org/10.1080/0158037X.2014.988701
35. van der Voort, H.G., Klievink, A.J., Arnaboldi, M., Meijer, A.J.: Rationality and politics of algorithms. will the promise of big data survive the dynamics of public decision making? Gov. Inf. Q. **36**(1), 27–38 (2019). https://doi.org/10.1016/j.giq.2018.10.011

The Incoherency Risk in the EU's New Cyber Security Policies

Jukka Ruohonen(✉)

University of Southern Denmark, Sønderborg, Denmark
juk@mmmi.sdu.dk

Abstract. The European Union (EU) has been pursuing new cyber security policies in recent years. This paper presents a short reflection of four such policies. The focus is on potential incoherency, meaning a lack of integration, divergence between the member states, institutional dysfunction, and other related problems that should be at least partially avoidable by sound policy-making. According to the results, the four policies have substantially increased the complexity of the EU's cyber security framework. In addition, there are potential problems with trust, divergence between industry sectors and different technologies, bureaucratic conflicts, and technical issues, among other things. With these insights, the paper not only contributes to the study of EU policies but also advances the understanding of cyber security policies in general.

Keywords: cyber security · policy coherency · CER · NIS · CSA · CRA · EU

1 Introduction

The historical origins of the EU's framework for cyber security trace to the late 1990s and early 2000s during which the first policies and institutional arrangements were established [20]. Since then, the framework has been continuously altered and updated as cyber security has gained prominence—and vicious cyber attacks have continued. Throughout the EU, these attacks, whether they manifest themselves as data breaches, ransomware operations, or industrial espionage, cause substantial financial losses, reputation damage, and even human misery. Geopolitical conflicts and tensions, disruptive new technologies such as artificial intelligence (AI), risks related to critical infrastructure and even democracy, and related major factors have further increased the importance of cyber security. To this end, the European Commission published in 2020 a new strategy for cyber security in the EU. According to this strategy, improving cyber security is necessary for enjoying the benefits from innovation, connectivity, and automation, while still maintaining fundamental rights and freedoms [9]. Cyber security is thus an enabler on one hand. On the other, it is also a source for innovations in itself. While regulations are often seen as a hindrance to industry and its competitiveness, it is therefore important to consider also policy innovations that may improve not only cyber security but also industry competitiveness.

Published by Springer Nature Switzerland AG 2024
R. van de Wetering et al. (Eds.): I3E 2024, LNCS 14907, pp. 284–295, 2024.
https://doi.org/10.1007/978-3-031-72234-9_24

For a long time, there was a lack of evaluation studies on the various digital policies enacted throughout the world [11]. While the situation has improved over time, critical evaluations and reflections are always needed as these allow to also understand the potential challenges ahead. With this point in mind, the paper at hand presents a brief critical reflection on four recent cyber security policies, some of which are already enacted EU laws. All belong to the noted cyber security strategy pursued by the von der Leyen's first Commission. Furthermore, the other traditional pillars of the EU's cyber security framework are mostly omitted; these pillars are cyber crime, cyber defense, and, to a lesser extent, data protection [4]. The critical reflection pursued is motivated by potential policy incoherency. This concept is elaborated in the opening Sect. 2. After this elaboration, the four policies are briefly discussed in the subsequent Sect. 3. Then, the potential incoherencies arising from the four new cyber security policies are elaborated and speculated in Sect. 4. The last Sect. 5 concludes. Finally, it should be emphasized that the paper is a reflection on a complex policy constellation. Actual evaluation can only be done in a distant future once the policies have been adopted by the member states and the practical operation and administration of these have continued for a sufficient time. This point justifies the term risk in the paper's title; the focus is on potential and not (yet) actual problems under uncertainty about the future. Methodologically the critical reflection falls to the domain of interpretive policy analysis [14, 21]. That is, the methodological approach is not an "objective" cost-benefit analysis or other related mechanical evaluation, but rather a short critical interpretation of the policies and their impact under the objective to improve cyber security.

2 Policy Coherency and Incoherency

The EU has increased the interdependence of its member states and thus policy convergence has been an important goal particularly with respect to the internal market. In short: the rules should be the same across all member states. To achieve convergence, a policy needs to be coherent. A coherent policy is well-integrated, meaning that its diverse components work well together [2]. Lack of integration has been a typical problem in the cyber security domain. In many countries different cyber security agencies and actors have formed their own silos beyond which cooperation may not work and critical information does not necessarily traverse [10]. The EU is not an exception; different EU agencies and also the member states themselves have often formed their own silos [3, 4]. While a EU policy typically contains many internal components, integration should thus apply also across the member states and through EU-level administration.

It is useful to distinguish different forms of policy coherency. Thus, internal coherency can be understood to refer to the consistency between the goals, objectives, modalities, and protocols of a particular EU policy; intra-country coherency can be seen to involve the consistency of a member state's policies in terms of their combined contribution to the EU; and, finally, inter-country coherency can be interpreted as the consistency and uniformity of policies across several member states with respect to their aggregated impact at the

EU-level [16]. Extensive transaction costs are a typical sign of problems in internal coherency; these costs are due to a lack of information, a need for monitoring and control, and enforcement measures and administrative support [2]. Ideally, such costs can be decreased by good planning. The actors involved also learn over time, which should also eventually reduce the transaction costs. Analytically, in the EU context, it is useful to further think in terms of vertical and horizontal policy coherency [17,19]. Vertical coherency refers to the alignment between the EU and the member states; the aggregated impact to the EU in intra-country and inter-country coherency is thus vertical. In contrast, horizontal policy coherency refers to the uniformity of either EU-level arrangements or the member states' policies and the convergence between them. These policies can be purely national laws or transposed EU laws. This simple analytical machinery for policy coherency allows to also approach the antonym, policy incoherency.

A traditional form of policy incoherency in the EU context is vertical; a mismatch between EU laws and their national adaptations. In purely judicial cases, there are well-established mechanisms for dealing with this kind of incoherency; the European Commission may even start an infringement proceedings against a member state for incorrect national transposition of a given EU law. Another form of vertical policy incoherency may arise when the roles and responsibilities are not defined clearly enough between EU-level and national institutions and institutional practices. A coherent policy solution requires also sound alignment between institutions and technologies [15]. For instance, national information exchanges toward EU-level institutions may work poorly due to ambiguous legal guidelines or poor technical specifications, both of which are likely to increase transaction costs. A potential dysfunction may further affect coordination more generally. With respect to coordination, particularly important at the EU-level is the European Union Agency for Cybersecurity (ENISA), although there are many other relevant actors as well. A risk of either vertical or horizontal incoherency is further solidified by the recent policies that have further increased the number of cyber security actors both nationally and at the EU-level.

Also horizontal policy incoherencies have been common in the EU. A typical form of horizontal (inter-country) incoherency is a mismatch between national adaptations of a EU law. In other words, a particular EU law may differ from a member state to another due to different national interpretations and adaptations. Countering this type of horizontal incoherency with harmonization has been a long-standing goal in the EU. Further institutional horizontal incoherencies may arise both within national public administrations and EU-level administration. In terms of the former, ambiguities may cause bureaucratic conflicts between different national public administration units. Data protection would be a good example because national data protection authorities are typically distinct from cyber security authorities, which are distinct from law enforcement authorities, although all may be required to address some cyber security incidents such as data breaches. Analogous conflicts may emerge between different industry sectors. Such conflicts are non-optimal because a coherent policy should be consistent, comprehensive, and harmonious across domains and sectors in a manner that does not compromise its goals [6]. Even though operational cyber security has thus far been limited at the EU-level, somewhat analogous institutional conflicts may still emerge also at the EU-level administration.

Finally, a policy incoherency may become more serious if the misguided policy outcomes become permanent. In the present context, a particular concern is whether a policy incoherency may turn into a permanent institutional incoherency. Unlike policies, which, at least in theory, may be altered and updated relatively easily, institutions are much more salient and permanent. In fact, this institutional stickiness is one of the primary takeaways from the extensive path-dependency literature [12, 20]. In the EU context these institutions can be understood to refer to permanent arrangements or agencies with recruited staff who typically work in fixed physical locations. While there is room for institutional innovation when designing new EU policies, also the incoherency risks from poor institutional planning are thus clear. It is not easy to backpedal once a specific agency or a permanent bureaucratic arrangement has been established. The same point applies to technologies and technical solutions, especially since some of the new policies envision large pan-European cyber security solutions.

3 The Policies in Brief

There are four cyber security policies that are important for approaching potential policy incoherencies in the EU. These are illustrated in Fig. 1. Two of these are already enacted laws, while two are still under political decision-making.

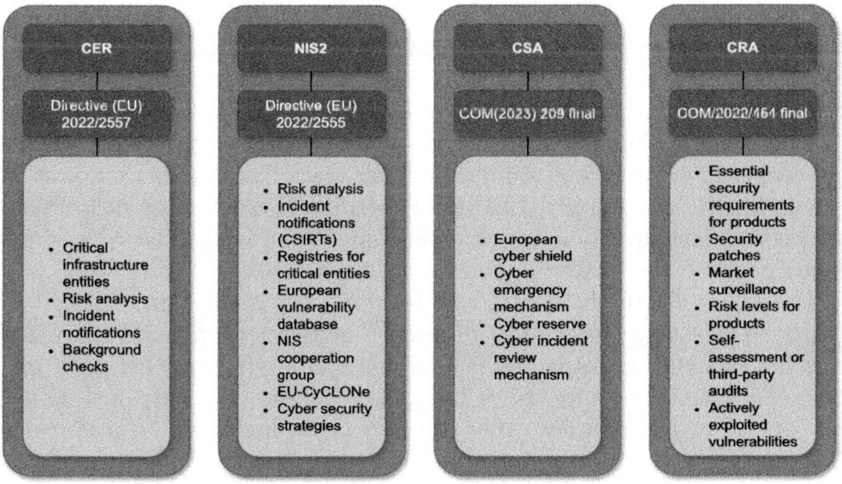

Fig. 1. The Four Cyber Security Policies

The first law is the Critical Entities Resilience (CER) directive. This directive substantially increases the amount of critical infrastructure entities from an older directive that only considered the energy and transportation sectors. Now, also the banking, financial market, healthcare, water, and food sectors together with core elements of the Internet's infrastructure, public administration, and space technologies are defined as critical. Regarding the Internet's infrastructure, domain name system services, top-level domain name registries, data centers, content delivery networks, and cloud computing services are covered, among a few other technologies. While leeway is left for the member states regarding the details on how the critical entities are identified, the CER directive imposes also many requirements for the identified critical entities. Among these are risk assessments for natural and man-made risks, incident notifications for significant disruptions, and background checks for employees operating the critical entities.

The second law is the so-called NIS2 directive. Based on a significant update of the older NIS directive, it essentially augments the requirements from the CER directive for the critical entities. Particularly risk assessments are specified in more detail; these should cover not only traditional information security and incident handling, but also business continuity, supply chain security, security of equipment acquisitions, employee training, use of cryptography, and organizational security should be assessed. On the public sector side, the member states are obliged to designate one or more competent authorities with a single point of contact for incident reporting. Substantial enforcement powers are also granted for the competent authorities; administrative fines are part of the enforcement toolbox. At the EU-level, ENISA is tasked to administer the registries for the critical Internet technologies and to build a European vulnerability database. As for incidents, as before, these are reported to national computer security incident response teams (CSIRTs) whose obligations are also extended, including with respect to coordinated vulnerability disclosure and cooperation at the EU-level. In addition to the management of large-scale cyber security incidents and the national enforcement of the directive, the competent authorities have a liaison function for cross-border investigations conducted together with the Commission and ENISA. Furthermore, the NIS2 directive specifies a NIS cooperation group and European cyber crisis liaison organisation network (EU-CyCLONe) for improved EU-level coordination, including with respect to information exchanges and situational awareness. Finally, the NIS2 directive obliges each member state to publish a national cyber security strategy.

The Cyber Solidarity Act (CSA) law proposal is the third relevant cyber security policy to consider. The proposal's motivation originates from serious cross-border cyber crises in the face of the war in Ukraine. The objectives of the proposal are to be implemented with pan-European security operations centers (SOCs) together with a cyber emergency mechanism and a review mechanism for large cyber security incidents. In practice, the SOCs discussed amount to large, either national or cross-border, threat intelligence platforms; the goal is to enhance attack detection, prevention, and response. Through EU-based funding available via the Digital Europe Programme (DEP), national SOCs are expected to enlarge into cross-border SOCs, eventually creating a unified "European cyber shield". Information obtained through cross-border SOCs about large-scale cyber security incidents should be shared between the CSIRT network, EU-CyCLONe, and the Commission. The cyber emergency mechanism, in turn, is tailored for preparedness actions, recovery actions from large-scale incidents, and mutual assistance between the member states. Of these, the mutual assistance provision is accompanied with a specific cyber security reserve that can be deployed to any given member state upon a request to the Commission and ENISA, and informing of the CSIRT network and where appropriate the EU-CyCLONe network. In practice, the reserve is composed of members from the CSIRT network together with personnel from EU agencies, although support from like-minded third countries is also allowed. Finally, the incident review mechanism is planned for *post hoc* analysis and review of a large-scale cyber security incident. Most of the work involved is delegated to ENISA.

The fourth and final law proposal is the Cyber Resilience Act (CRA). It is based on a different rationale than the three other policies. The proposal is motivated by consumer protection jurisprudence, the low level of cyber security in many information technology products, as reflected by widespread vulnerabilities in them and inconsistent provision of security patches to counter the vulnerabilities, and insufficient information for consumers to make informed choices regarding cyber security. To this end, the proposal obliges manufacturers to take security into account by specifying essential security requirements, including for coordinated vulnerability disclosure. In addition, manufacturers are mandated to provide security patches for the whole life cycle of their products. On the public sector side, the proposal lays down rules on market surveillance and enforcement. Administrative fines are again part of the enforcement arsenal. Although a few specialized products are excluded, the proposal in practice covers the whole information technology sector. Also software products are in the scope. Furthermore, the proposal categorizes products according to their cyber security risk level. While the manufacturing of most products is possible under self-assessment of conformity, products categorized as critical require third-party audits. Regarding coordinated vulnerability disclosure, manufacturers are further obliged to inform ENISA about any actively exploited vulnerabilities in their products. According to the proposal, ENISA will then inform the national CSIRTs.

Finally, it should be emphasized that the CSA and CRA proposals are still being negotiated. Therefore, the final laws may differ from the original law proposals considered. All policies except the CSA proposal also grant the Commission a power to adopt delegated acts to supplement the policies in different ways. In general, these acts increase the Commission's power to further shape the EU's new cyber security policy framework.

4 Potential Incoherencies

The first potential horizontal policy incoherency is the traditional one, the divergence between national transpositions of the EU laws in the member states. In particular, CER and NIS2 are directives, which give more room for national transpositions than regulations, including the CSA and CRA law proposals, which are directly applicable EU law.

The second potential incoherency originates from the background checks specified in the CER directive. The type of potential incoherency is horizontal. Namely, there may be some conflicts in national adaptations of the directive because background checks are typically done by law enforcement or intelligence agencies, whereas, as per the NIS2 directive, incident notifications are typically delivered to different organizations in most member states. Furthermore, a traditional horizontal incoherency between the member states is likely because there is no harmonization in the EU for background checks or security clearances [18]. Because some of the critical entities are operated by multinational companies, it may also be difficult to carry out background checks in practice as there are no extraterritorial powers for such checks.

The third potential horizontal incoherency is also related to the CER and NIS2 directives. Namely, the critical entities specified in the directives should be synchronized for sound administration and enforcement. Due to the previous point, some incoherency may still appear. For instance, it may be that background checks are not done uniformly across all critical entities in some member states. If synchronization is lacking, duplication of work may also occur with the risk assessments specified in both directives.

The fourth potential incoherency continues the same horizontal theme; the policies put different industry sectors and technologies into a uneven position. This potential incoherency is present with respect to the critical entities specified in the CER and NIS2 directives; the non-critical sectors left behind may receive less attention and resources for cyber security. Alternatively, it can be argued that the directives specify too many sectors as critical, which may cause different interpretation problems and lead to incoherent implementation and inconsistent enforcement across the member states [13]. Analogous consequences are present with respect to the CRA proposal; the products defined as non-critical presumably receive much less scrutiny than the critical products. This uneven treatment of sectors and technologies carries also economic consequences. Given the divergence of the information technology sectors in the member states, the uneven treatment may even lead to a larger horizontal incoherency across the union.

The fifth potential policy incoherency is related to the additional administrative bodies specified in the NIS2 directive and the CSA proposal. In particular, the new EU-CyCLONe network may cause redundancy because the CSIRT network is already well-established in Europe. In fact, the EU's cyber security policy framework was from the beginning built upon the CSIRT network with ENISA acting in a coordination role at the EU-level [20]. Analogous redundancy issues may arise with respect to the cyber reserve specified in the CSA proposal. Many problematic scenarios are possible due to the redundancy and related duplication. For instance, horizontal incoherency may again manifest itself through bureaucratic conflicts, starting from the recruitment of staff to the EU-CyCLONe network, the CSIRT network, the NIS cooperation group, and the cyber reserve.

Trust is behind the sixth potential policy incoherency, which may be both horizontal and vertical. Because decision-making is centralized to the EU-level, there may be potential issues in the deployment of the cyber reserve envisioned in the CSA proposal in case a member state in need lacks trust toward ENISA or the Commission. Alternatively, there is no strict deadlines for the deployment decision-making; therefore, as many cyber security issues require urgent attention, the deployment may become moot especially under multiple and concurrent requests [8]. Furthermore, the allowance of third countries in the reserve may prevent a member state from requesting help in case it lacks trust toward a given third country. While it is difficult to evaluate how realistic these scenarios are, a bigger potential incoherency is also present; it remains unclear how the cyber reserve will align with similar initiatives taken under the North Atlantic Treaty Organization (NATO). Duplication of effort and resources is a real possibility. There is also a more deep-rooted question about civilian and military approaches to cyber security [18]. Particularly the cyber reserve may blur the boundary between the two. Such blurring of fundamental boundaries might perhaps even lead to a philosophical incoherency in the EU's cyber security framework.

The seventh set of potential incoherencies is related to the SOCs specified in the CSA proposal. A potential vertical incoherency may be present because the proposal does not say much about how EU-level agencies should share data with national SOCs [8]. Furthermore, as cross-border SOCs are expected to share information about large-scale incidents rather widely across different actors, hypothetical conflicts and trust issues may potentially spill also to the domain of operational security. Because SOCs are about operational security, these presumably process and transmit sensitive data, which may have even national security consequences. Therefore, lack of trust between the member states may cause difficulties for the establishment of cross-border SOCs to begin with. It is difficult to say whether the financial carrots from the DEP can fully resolve this trust conundrum. Finally, there are significant technical interoperability challenges in building large cross-border SOCs and integrating these to already existing national SOCs. The CSA proposal also eagerly speaks about using AI for the threat intelligence available through SOCs. However, during the negotiations, some skepticism was expressed about whether AI technologies are mature enough to be used in the envisioned European cyber shield. While it is too early to say anything about actual implementations and their funding through the DEP or other instruments, it can be still concluded that also technologies and technical issues may contribute to the potential incoherency. Similar points apply with respect to SOCs already established in the private sector. While these were to some extent addressed during the negotiations [5], the original proposal did not consider cooperation and information exchanges with private sector actors.

The eight potential policy incoherency is also related to trust. The type of the incoherency is vertical. During the still ongoing negotiations of the CRA proposal, considerable criticism was expressed by some member states and stakeholders about the delivery of information on actively exploited vulnerabilities to ENISA. The fear was that such a delivery would then spill the sensitive information to the whole EU and the various actors involved. As with the cross-border SOCs, national security was part of the fear. The apparent lack of trust may not be toward ENISA, however, but rather toward the EU-wide CSIRT network

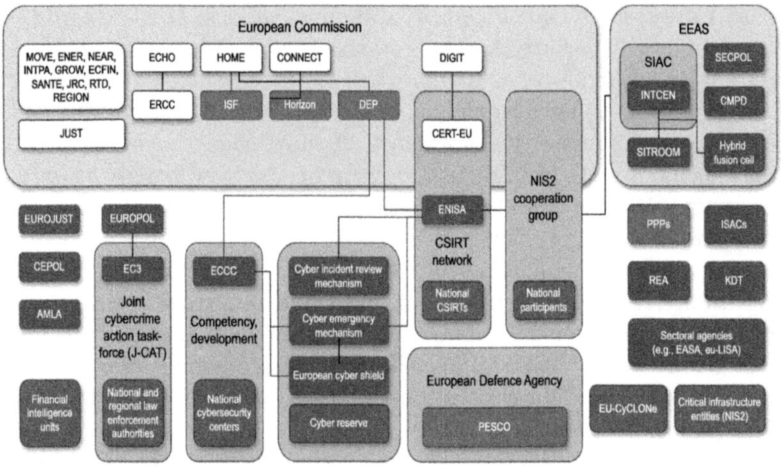

- AMLA: Anti-money-laundering authority
- CEPOL: European Union Agency for Law Enforcement Training
- CERT-EU: Computer Emergency Response Team for EU
- CMPD: Crisis Management and Planning Directorate
- CONNECT: Communications Networks, Content and Technology DG
- DEP: Digital Europe Programme
- DIGIT: Informatics DG
- EASA: European Union Aviation Safety Agency
- EC3: Europol's Cybercrime Centre
- ECCC: European Cybersecurity Competence Centre
- ECFIN: Economic and Financial Affairs DG
- ECHO: European Civil Protection and Humanitarian Aid Operations DG
- EEAS: European External Action Service
- ENER: Energy DG
- ENISA: European Union Agency for Cybersecurity
- ERCC: Emergency Response Coordination Centre
- EU-CyCLONe: European Cyber Crisis Liaison Organisation Network
- eu-LISA: European Union Agency for the Operational Management of Large-Scale IT Systems
- UROJUST: European Union Agency for Criminal Justice Cooperation
- EUROPOL: European Union Agency for Law Enforcement Cooperation
- GROW: Internal Market, Industry, Entrepreneurship and SMEs DG
- HOME: Migration and Home Affairs DG
- Horizon: Horizon Europe
- INTCEN: European Union Intelligence and Situation Centre
- ISAC: Information Sharing and Analysis Centre
- ISF: Internal Security Fund
- INTPA: International Partnerships DG
- JRC: Joint Research Centre
- JUST: Justice and Consumers DG
- KDT: Key Digital Technologies
- MOVE: Mobility and Transport DG
- NEAR: Neighborhood and Enlargement Negotiations DG
- NIS2: Network and Information Security Directive
- PESCO: Permanent Structured Cooperation Framework
- PPP: Public-Private Partnership
- REA: Research Executive Agency
- REGION: Regional and Urban Policy DG
- RTD: Research and Innovation DG
- SANTE: Health and Food Safety DG
- SECPOL: Security Policy and Conflict Prevention
- SITROOM: Situation Room

Fig. 2. Coordination at the EU-level (modified after [8, p. 14])

and the other actors involved. While a compromise was found during the negotiations, information about actively exploited vulnerabilities is still delivered also to ENISA under most conditions [1]. Analogously, it was also feared that manufacturers would be hesitant to participate because national CSIRTs are trusted among manufacturers in some member states but not necessarily in others.

Last but not least, a further potential incoherency is present at the EU-level. As can be concluded from Fig. 2, the EU-level cyber security administration is highly complex and the new policies have further increased the complexity. Bureaucratic inertia thus poses a real possibility of a permanent institutional incoherency. The issue is also vertical because a member state may have difficulties at formulating a coherent stance at the EU-level institutions due to the apparent institutional fragmentation. Horizontally, it remains somewhat unclear how well the roles and responsibilities are defined with respect to the various EU-level agencies and arrangements. Indeed, on one hand, according to evaluations, EU agencies tend to share cyber security information poorly among themselves [7]. On the other hand, trust is a potential issue also at the EU-level, and the actively exploited vulnerabilities in the CRA proposal again provide a good example. Because information is delivered to ENISA, it may spill also to EU agencies who may have an incentive to develop exploits for the vulnerabilities. The examples include the Europol's cyber crime centre (EC3) and the EU's intelligence apparatus (INTCEN). Despite these potential trust and other related issues, none of the cyber security policies considered establish clear firewalls between different EU agencies and bureaucratic administrative units. While the free flow of information may improve cyber security, it may also cause cyber insecurities. Finally, a potential incoherency may be present with respect to the different funding instruments. The DEP instrument is mostly about straightforward implementation. Therefore, it remains unclear how well it aligns with the research and innovation goals pursued in the large-scale Horizon Europe programme. Furthermore, the civilian-military nexus is again present as rather similar goals are pursued on the military side through the PESCO financial instrument.

5 Conclusion

This paper presented a critical reflection on the EU's new cyber security policies. Four policies were considered: the CER and NIS2 directives and the CSA and CRA proposals. The paper's focus was on the potential policy incoherencies that may arise from the four policies. Several such potential incoherencies were identified. These include traditional problems, including potential divergence between the member states, industry sectors, and different technologies, administrative conflicts, and procedural issues. Trust (or lack thereof) is a newer potential source of problems. As the policies address pan-European transmission of sensitive security information, including about exploitable vulnerabilities, a lack of trust between the member states and EU-level agencies or between the member states themselves may cause problems in the future. This point applies also to the threat intelligence information shared through the cross-border SOCs envisioned. These SOCs also demonstrate a potential problem in terms of integration, interoperability, and other potential technical obstacles. In addition, many other policy incoherency problems are present, including with respect to funding instruments and increased EU-level bureaucracy, among other things.

Regarding administration at the EU-level, a long-standing criticism has been the lack of a central agency who would be in charge of the union's strategic and operational cyber security [3,4]. While it remains debatable whether such a centralized administrative unit is even desirable in the EU, it can be concluded that the ENISA's increased responsibilities and mandates still do not amount to a role of a so-called "cyber tsar". In contrast, institutional fragmentation has actually further increased with the establishment of the EU-CyCLONe network and the NIS cooperation group. Both likely increase transaction costs. If a serious and large-scale, union-wide cyber security crisis would emerge, it thus remains unclear who would take the lead, how the response would be formulated, and how effective it would be. It may be that the Commission would need to step in.

While the paper's reflection was critical already due to the focus on policy incoherency, it should be emphasized that the four policies considered likely significantly bolster the union's cyber security posture even under the presence of potential problems. In a similar vein, it should be emphasized that the policies also offer new possibilities for European cyber security companies and professionals. All clouds have silver linings.

Also some other limitations should be briefly acknowledged. To some extent, the paper shared the traditional tenet in the policy coherency literature—the rationalization of policy procedures and institutional arrangements in order to improve coherency and to maximize synergies between disparate policy goals, which tend to overlook political and economic changes, trade-offs, and struggles [22]. A more in-depth study would be needed to address these aspects. For instance, the political aspects would offer a promising path for further research; it would be interesting to know and to better understand which member states, companies, organizations, or other stakeholders pursued and lobbied which policy goals and why. An in-depth study would be also needed to better understand so-called inter-pillar coherency [17]. Once cyber crime, cyber defense, and data protection are also taken into account, it can be better understood how the EU's grand cyber security setup works and what potential incoherencies it contains. Here, existing work on earlier EU policies [4] hints about rather similar issues discussed in this paper. As already said, furthermore, the paper was a critical reflection and not an evaluation. Although *potential* incoherency problems were identified, it may be that these do not amount to *actual* problems in the future. Therefore, a thorough policy evaluation is also needed at some point in time.

References

1. Bertuzzi, L.: EU Institutions Finalise Agreement on Cybersecurity Law for Connected Products (2023), EURACTIV. (May 2024). https://www.euractiv.com/section/cybersecurity/news/eu-institutions-finalise-agreement-on-cybersecurity-law-for-connected-products/
2. Bolognesi, T., Pflieger, G.: The coherence(s) of institutional resource regimes: typology and assessments from the case of water supply management. Environ. Sci. Policy **99**, 17–28 (2019)
3. CEPS: Strengthening the EU's cyber defence capabilities: report of a CEPS Task Force (2018), Centre for European Policy Studies (CEPS). (May 2024). https://cdn.ceps.eu/wp-content/uploads/2018/11/CEPS_TFR
4. Christou, G.: Cybersecurity in the European Union: Resilience and Adaptability in Governance and Policy. Palgrave Macmillan, New York (2016)
5. Clasen, A.: Cyber solidarity act moves ahead in EU parliament with key committee vote (2023), EURACTIV. (May 2024). https://www.euractiv.com/section/cybersecurity/news/cyber-solidarity-act-moves-ahead-in-eu-parliament-with-key-committee-vote/
6. Dubé, L., Addy, N.A., Blouin, C., Drager, N.: From policy coherence to 21st century convergence: a whole-of-society paradigm of human and economic development. Ann. N. Y. Acad. Sci. **1331**, 201–215 (2014)

7. ECA: Cybersecurity of EU Institutions, bodies and agencies: level of preparedness overall not commensurate with the threats (2022). European Court of Auditors (ECA). (April 2024). https://www.eca.europa.eu/Lists/ECADocuments/SR22_05/SR_cybersecurity-EU-institutions_EN.pdf
8. ECA: Opinion 02/2023 Concerning the Proposal for a Regulation of the European Parliament and of the Council Laying Down Measures to Strengthen Solidarity and Capacities in the Union to Detect, Prepare for and Respond to Cybersecurity Threats and Incidents [Interinstitutional File 2023/0109(COD) of 18 April 2023] (2024), European Court of Auditors (ECA). (April 2024). https://www.eca.europa.eu/en/publications/OP-2023-02
9. European Commission: the EU's cybersecurity strategy for the digital decade (2020). Joint Communication to the European Parliament and the Council, JOIN(2020) 18 final. (April 2024). https://digital-strategy.ec.europa.eu/en/library/eus-cybersecurity-strategy-digital-decade-0
10. Hurel, L.M., Lobato, L.C.: Cyber security governance in Brazil: keeping silos or building bridges? In: Romaniuk, S.N., Manjikian, M. (eds.) Routledge Companion to Global Cyber-Security Strategy, pp. 504–518. Routledge, Abingdon
11. Leeuw, F.L., Leeuw, B.: Cyber society and digital policies: challenges to evaluation? Evaluation **18**(1), 111–127 (2012)
12. Mahoney, J.: Path dependence in historical sociology. Theory Soc. **29**, 507–548 (2000)
13. Mikac, R.: Protection of the EU's critical infrastructures: results and challenges. Appl. Cybersecur. Internet Gov. **2**(1), 1–25 (2023)
14. Münch, S.: Beyond national policymaking: conceptions of myth in interpretive policy analysis and their value for IR. In: de Guevara, B.B. (ed.) Myth and Narrative in International Politics, pp. 47–66. Palgrave Macmillan, London (2016)
15. Perennes, P.: Need for coherence between institutions and technologies: the example of uncertain train paths in France. Competition Regulation Netw. Ind. **14**(2), 130–150 (2013)
16. Picciotto, R.: The evaluation of policy coherence for development. Evalution **11**(3), 311–330 (2005)
17. Portela, C., Raube, K.: The EU polity and foreign policy coherence. J. Contemp. Eur. Res. **8**(1), 3–20 (2012)
18. Ruohonen, J.: An acid test for Europeanization: public cyber security procurement in the European union. Eur. J. Secur. Res. **5**(2), 349–377 (2020)
19. Ruohonen, J.: A review of product safety regulations in the European union. Int. Cybersecur. Law Rev. **3**, 345–366 (2022)
20. Ruohonen, J., Hyrynsalmi, S., Leppänen, V.: An Outlook on the institutional evolution of the European union cyber security apparatus. Gov. Inf. Q. **33**(4), 746–756 (2016)
21. Yanow, D.: Conducting Interpretive Policy Analysis. Sage, Thousand Oaks (2000)
22. Yunita, A., Biermann, F., Kim, R.E., Vijge, M.J.: The (Anti-)Politics of policy coherence for sustainable development in the Netherlands: logic, method. Effects. Geoforum **128**, 92–102 (2022)

"The Connected User Are You Safe?" - An Exploratory Study About Users Fear of Identity Theft

Shagun Sarraf[1(✉)] and Arpan Kumar Kar[1,2]

[1] Bharti School of Telecommunications Technology & Management, Indian Institute of Technology Delhi, New Delhi 110016, India
shaguns1996@gmail.com, arpankar@iitd.ac.in

[2] Department of Management Studies, Indian Institute of Technology Delhi, New Delhi 110016, India

Abstract. The surge in digital transactions has led to a notable spike in identity theft cases, incurring enormous expenses for e-commerce companies and users. The safety of online businesses and their users depends on addressing identity theft. We utilise natural language processing to examine Reddit posts related to identity theft to determine the elements influencing individuals' concerns about identity theft when transacting online. We match these factors with theoretical lexicons to create a unique framework. Further, to extend the study, we intend to validate these factors through statistical analysis to understand their impact on users' fear of identity theft during online transactions.

Keywords: Identity theft · Big-data analytics · Evolutionary stimuli–organism–response · Cyber security

1 Introduction

The widespread shift of routine transactions to the Internet, including activities such as travel and banking, compels users to transact online despite their preferences. Cyber-crime is rising with this growth in online transactions, social networking, mobile device usage, and Internet-based information exchange worldwide.

5.18 billion people were using the internet as of April 2023 [1]. Billions of people utilise digital services every day, including grocery shopping, bank account opening, and app-based meal ordering. With more than 64% of people interacting online, the digital economy offers enormous development potential for companies everywhere [2]. With growing opportunities, there is a growing risk of cybercrime, including identity theft. Identity theft affects various industries, including financial services, general business, education, healthcare, and government and military.

Identity theft is the unlawful use of an individual's personally identifiable information (PII) for one's benefit [3]. This is a critical issue because a person's identity

Published by Springer Nature Switzerland AG 2024
R. van de Wetering et al. (Eds.): I3E 2024, LNCS 14907, pp. 296–303, 2024.
https://doi.org/10.1007/978-3-031-72234-9_25

is fundamental to their financial situation and past, and identity theft has far-reaching financial repercussions [4]. Identity theft is frequently caused by customers' ignorance of their identity and privacy [5], even though it can result from unethical organisational activities [6].

However, the specific factors influencing users' fear of identity theft are still unclear. This gap in understanding is significant because fear of identity theft can lead to reduced trust in digital transactions, decreased online activity, and increased demand for stringent security measures [7]. Users' fear can also influence their behavior, such as reluctance to engage in online transactions, which can hamper the growth of the digital economy. For businesses, this fear can result in higher costs for implementing advanced security protocols and the potential loss of customers who prefer not to engage online [7]. Thus, understanding the factors that drive this fear is crucial for developing strategies to mitigate it, enhancing user confidence, and promoting safer digital environments.

The study mainly addresses the "what" aspect, i.e., what factors could influence the fear of identity theft amongst users of digital transactions. So, we posit the following RQ for this inductive study:

RQ1: What factors influence the fear of identity theft amongst digital transaction users?

The paper is structured as follows: Sect. 2 contains the literature review, while Sect. 3 will explain the research design. Section 4 covers the exploratory investigation, and Sect. 5 presents the future study.

2 Literature Review

2.1 Cybercrime and Identity Theft

An individual's unique online identity is shaped by their combined personal and financial information. There is a greater chance that this information may be exploited due to the expanding range and frequency of online interactions and the rise in consumer-specific data [8]. Identity theft is the unlawful use of a user's name, social security number, or credit card number to commit fraud or other crimes, according to the Federal Trade Commission (FTC) [9].

Identity theft instances have been on the rise in recent years. Organisations should be especially concerned about this trend since it increases the risk of financial losses, decreased consumer loyalty, and tarnished brand reputations [10]. Globally, fraud reports show a consistent increase in identity theft-related instances. 1.4 million of the 5.7 million fraud and identity theft reports the FTC received as of early 2024 were identity theft cases [11].

2.2 Theoretical Lens

The conventional S-O-R model (Stimulus-Organism-Response) is a widely used framework in psychology and marketing to explain how external stimuli (S) affect an individual's internal state (O), which in turn influences their behavioral responses (R) [12]. In this model, the stimulus refers to external factors such as environmental cues or marketing messages, the organism represents the individual's internal processes like emotions and cognitions, and the response denotes the resulting behavior, such as purchasing decisions or user engagement [13]. People make logical behavioral judgments in the conventional S-O-R model derived from the input-output model [14]. It assumes that the sequence of S-O-R is linear. However, this assumption may prevent scholars from understanding dynamic relations that impact the outcome [15].

Thus, it is necessary to reevaluate the presumption that stimuli and reactions are directly related. The complex and dynamic behaviours of people with restricted rationality can be better represented by non-linear interactions between stimuli, organisms, and responses (S–O–R) [16]. The evolutionary S-O-R model builds on the traditional framework by introducing feedback loops and acknowledging human behavior's complex, dynamic, and recursive nature [14]. It accounts for the non-linear relationships and the iterative nature of interactions between stimuli, organism reactions, and responses [14].

3 Research Design

Analyzing user posts on identity theft has allowed this study to explore the research problems. User posts are an example of electronic word-of-mouth (eWoM). They comprise voluntarily submitted user-generated content (UGCs) particular to a technology or service [17]. Using user evaluations, acknowledged as a significant source of eWoM, we could pinpoint important variables affecting fear of identity theft. The research sequence is depicted in Fig. 1. The two primary parts of the framework are the exploratory and confirmatory research components.

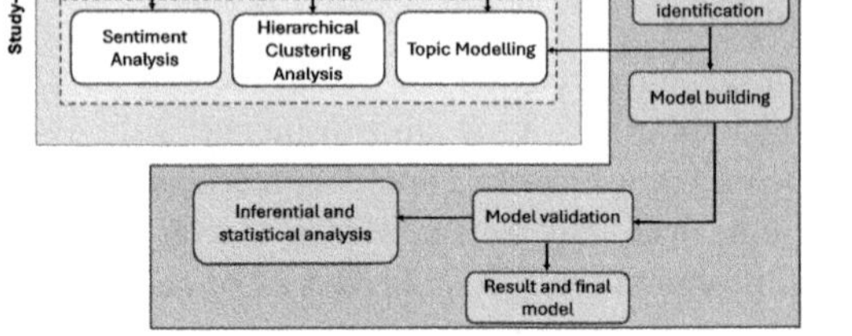

Fig. 1. Research sequence

3.1 Data Collection

Our data source was user posts, focusing on posts related to identity theft to record user experiences. Reddit was the source of these posts. Reddit is a major online content community, with 73.1 million active users worldwide as of Q4 2023 [20]. Reddit post titles work similarly to headlines and, as such, tend to be short. Compared to Twitter, Reddit facilitates comprehensive and concurrent discussions through a broad range of topic-based virtual communities that guarantee anonymity [21]. Further, Reddit is appropriate for this research because users write posts in proper English. This allows for the classification of post-language into the main parts of speech that are the focus of this research [22]. Data extraction was made easier using Python libraries explicitly designed to retrieve Reddit posts. Reddit content varies widely, leading to inconsistent data formats and significant noise, complicating data extraction and analysis [23]. Hence, to identify theoretical lexicons [24]. This included removing stop words, special characters, and duplicate posts. We then performed lemmatisation, parts-of-speech filtering, named entity recognition (NER), and tokenisation.

4 Exploratory Study

This section explores content analysis, presents the findings drawn, and builds the suggested conceptual model. During the text analysis stage, we utilize topic modeling based on Latent Dirichlet Allocation (LDA) to understand the key topics influencing users' concerns about identity theft.

4.1 Content Analysis

There are various methods for summarising information found in texts. Theoretical lexicons can be created by using topic modelling [18]. We used Latent Dirichlet Allocation (LDA) for topic modelling to find latent themes or subjects in users' posts about identity theft. We assessed coherence scores and repeated the number of subjects from 1 to 40 to remedy this. We determined that 8 was the ideal number of topics based on these. Further, we cluster similar words with a hierarchical clustering technique. Using this technique, we may identify word relationships between words in sentences, grouping terms with related properties into coherent clusters.

4.2 Exploratory Findings

We use the LDA-based topic modelling approach more often, which uses probabilistic distributions to extract themes from the corpus. Table 1 helped us to identify the factors from the literature. The results of using the agglomerative clustering technique for identity theft are shown in Fig. 2. At every level, clusters are created by grouping words based on shared characteristics. We created a vertical line at x = 1.5 to group them thematically, producing 8 clusters.

Table 1. Mapped factors based on theoretical Lexicons

Words of the topic	Mapped factors
accidental, details, apps, shared, dataleak, opps, info, spill, mishap, blunder	Accidental Data Losses and Disclosure
notice, found, anonymized, record, reveal, breach, exposed, payment, vulnerable, identify	Reidentification of anonymized and pseudonymized data
Trust, detected, personal, information, reset, sensitive, encountered, staff, violation, noticed, privacy	Abuse of access privilege
staff, bad, exploit, use, remove, face, like, process, pay, threat, data	Abuse of privacy by information technology staff
Authority, account, digital access, discovered, external, exposure, routine, disclosure, permission	Unauthorized access from outside
Click, feel, reliable, never, daily, transaction, amount, show, favorite, payment, method	Disclosure of users identity during routine data
card, credit, financial, loss, due, transaction, security, bank, monetary, compromised	Fear of financial losses
Leading, public, causing, backlash, made, reputational, without, damage, harm, sent	Fear of reputational damage

5 Future Work

The study intends to perform a confirmatory study to address the "how" aspect, i.e., how these factors influence users' fear of identity theft. We would develop a conceptual model based on exploratory study. This hypothetical model will enabled us to identify various factors influencing users' fear of identity theft when conducting digital transactions. The study intends to perform a confirmatory study to address the "how" aspect, i.e., how these factors influence users' fear of identity theft. We would develop a hypothesis based on the existing literature, followed by statistical methods to confirm how these factors of stimuli and organisms affect the user's fear of identity theft while doing digital transactions.

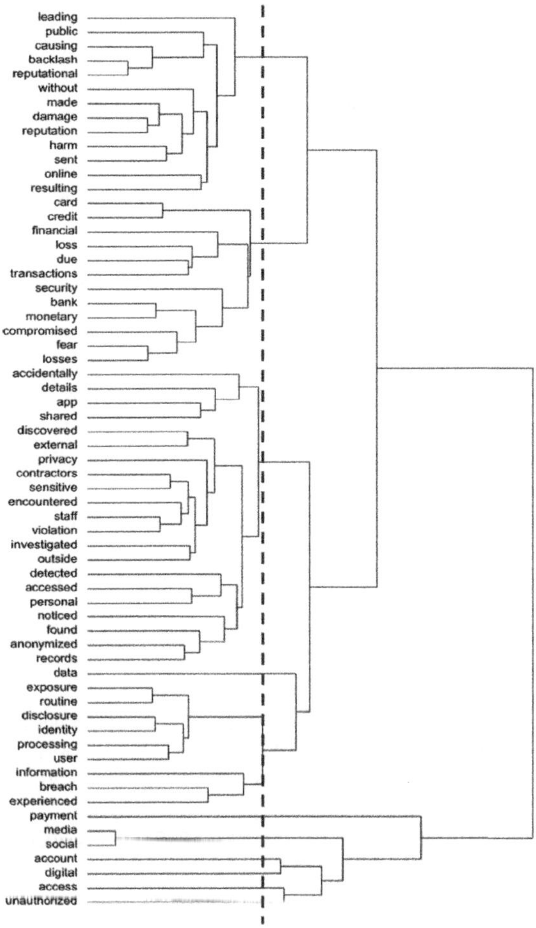

Fig. 2. Hierarchical clustering

References

1. Petrosyan, A.: Number of internet and social media users worldwide as of April 2024, Statista. https://www.statista.com/statistics/617136/digital-population-worldwide/#:~:text=Worldwide%20digital%20population%202023&text=As%20of%20April%202023%2C%20there,percent%20of%20the%20global%20population. Accessed 17 May 2024
2. Mastercard, What is synthetic identity fraud and how does synthetic identity theft work?, Mastercard. https://b2b.mastercard.com/news-and-insights/blog/what-is-synthetic-identity-fraud-and-how-does-synthetic-identity-theft-work/. Accessed 17 May 2024
3. Bose, I., Leung, A.C.M.: Adoption of identity theft countermeasures and its short-and long-term impact on firm value. Mis Q. **43**(1) (2019)
4. Ogbanufe, O., Pavur, R.: Going through the emotions of regret and fear: revisiting protection motivation for identity theft protection. Int. J. Inf. Manage. **62**, 102432 (2022). https://doi.org/10.1016/j.ijinfomgt.2021.102432

5. Lai, F., Li, D., Hsieh, C.-T.: Fighting identity theft: the coping perspective. Decis. Support. Syst. **52**(2), 353–363 (2012). https://doi.org/10.1016/j.dss.2011.09.002
6. Karat, C.-M., Brodie, C., Karat, J.: Usable privacy and security for personal information management. Commun. ACM **49**(1), 56–57 (2006). https://doi.org/10.1145/1107458.1107491
7. Swani, K., Labrecque, L., Markos, E.: Are B2B data breaches concerning? consequences of buyer's or firm's data loss on buyer and supplier related outcomes. Ind. Mark. Manage. **119**, 43–61 (2024). https://doi.org/10.1016/j.indmarman.2024.03.007
8. Hille, P., Walsh, G., Cleveland, M.: Consumer fear of online identity theft: scale development and validation. J. Interact. Mark. **30**, 1–19 (2015). https://doi.org/10.1016/j.intmar.2014.10.001
9. Commision, F.T.: What To Know About Identity Theft, Federal trade comission. https://consumer.ftc.gov/articles/what-know-about-identity-theft#what_is. Accessed 16 Apr 2024
10. Walsh, G., Hille, P., Cleveland, M.: Fearing Online Identity Theft: A Segmentation Study Of Online Customers, ECIS (2016)
11. IdentityTheft.org, Identity Theft Facts and Statistics, IdentityTheft.org (2024). https://identitytheft.org/statistics/. Accessed 20 May 2024
12. Mehrabian, A., Russell, J.A.: An approach to environmental psychology. In An approach to environmental psychology, pp. xii, 266. The MIT Press, Cambridge, MA, US (1974)
13. Simon, H.A.: Bounded rationality and organizational learning. Organ. Sci. **2**(1), 125–134 (1991)
14. Jacoby, J.: Stimulus-organism-response reconsidered: an evolutionary step in modeling (consumer) behavior. J. Consum. Psychol. **12**(1), 51–57 (2002). https://doi.org/10.1207/S15327663JCP1201_05
15. Bigne, E., Chatzipanagiotou, K., Ruiz, C.: Pictorial content, sequence of conflicting online reviews and consumer decision-making: the stimulus-organism-response model revisited. J. Bus. Res. **115**, 403–416 (2020). https://doi.org/10.1016/j.jbusres.2019.11.031
16. Zahedi, F.M., Chen, Y., Zhao, H.: Ontology-based intelligent interface personalization for protection against phishing attacks. Inf. Syst. Res. (2023). https://doi.org/10.1287/isre.2021.0065
17. Shankar, V., Smith, A.K., Rangaswamy, A.: Customer satisfaction and loyalty in online and offline environments. Int. J. Res. Mark. **20**(2), 153–175 (2003). https://doi.org/10.1016/S0167-8116(03)00016-8
18. Miranda, S., Berente, N., Seidel, S., Safadi, H., Burton-Jones, A.: Computationally intensive theory construction: a primer for authors and reviewers. MIS Q. **46**, (2022)
19. Kar, A.K., Tripathi, S.N., Malik, N., Gupta, S., Sivarajah, U.: How does misinformation and capricious opinions impact the supply chain - a study on the impacts during the pandemic. Ann. Oper. Res. **327**(2), 713–734 (2022). https://doi.org/10.1007/s10479-022-04997-6
20. Dean, B.: Reddit User and Growth Stats (2024). Backlinko. https://backlinko.com/reddit-users. Accessed 22 July 2024
21. Hao, F., (Olivia) Park, E., Chon, K.: Social media and disaster risk reduction and management: how have reddit travel communities experienced the COVID-19 pandemic?. J. Hospitality Tourism Res. **48**(1), 58–83 (2024). https://doi.org/10.1177/10963480221081115
22. Noguti, V.: Post language and user engagement in online content communities. Eur. J. Mark. **50**(5/6), 695–723 (2016). https://doi.org/10.1108/EJM-12-2014-0785
23. Krotov, V., Johnson, L.: Big web data: challenges related to data, technology, legality, and ethics. Bus. Horiz. **66**(4), 481–491 (2023). https://doi.org/10.1016/j.bushor.2022.10.001

24. Kar, A.K., Dwivedi, Y.K.: Theory building with big data-driven research – moving away from the 'what' towards the 'why.' Int. J. Inf. Manage. **54**, 102205 (2020). https://doi.org/10.1016/j.ijinfomgt.2020.102205
25. Larsen, K., Sharma, R., Queiroz, M., Arnulf, J., Pillet, J.C.: Use of natural language processing techniques in the construct and instrument development process. In: ECIS 2023 Research Papers (2023). https://aisel.aisnet.org/ecis2023_rp/383

Designing Collaborative Business Models for Sustainable Digital Solutions: The Case of a Shared-Micromobility Service

Oktay Turetken[1](✉), Baris Ozkan[1], and Paul Grefen[1,2]

[1] Eindhoven University of Technology, 5600MB, Eindhoven, The Netherlands
{o.turetken,b.ozkan,p.w.p.j.grefen}@tue.nl

[2] Eviden Digital Transformation Consulting, Amstelveen, The Netherlands

Abstract. Existing firm-centric approaches to business model design cannot sufficiently capture the essential elements characterizing sustainable digital solutions enabled by collaborations in a network. To foster value co-creation and align the interests and responsibilities of all stakeholders involved in such networks, a network-centric perspective to business model design is more appropriate. In this paper, we present the design of a collaborative business model for a digital solution - a shared-micromobility solution. We examine three prominent approaches to represent the business model and discuss their limitations. Following an inductive approach based on the business case, we derive and propose core conceptual elements of collaborative business models in the context of sustainability.

Keywords: Collaborative business model · Sustainable digital solution · Collaborative business model matrix · Collaborative network · Shared-micromobility solution

1 Introduction

The advancement of digitalization has resulted in significant changes across various business domains. In an increasingly digital world, the advent of digital solutions has revolutionized the way services are delivered, offering unprecedented accessibility and personalization across various domains [1]. *Digital solutions* refer to specific offerings (e.g., platforms) that leverage digital technology as a core enabler to address a particular business need, problem, or opportunity and involve interactions between multiple actors [2]. These solutions involve interactions between multiple actors, making a firm's value creation increasingly dependent on external resources and capabilities [3]. Hence, in this digital era, it is vital to configure the capabilities of a diverse range of stakeholders into meaningful assemblages through *collaboration*, characterized by direct, non-hierarchical, and goal-oriented firm interactions [4, 5].

In this landscape, organizations engage in ecosystems to form *collaborative networks* that foster the sharing of knowledge and resources, thereby creating a focal value proposition [6, 7]. A collaborative network refers to an assemblage of actors comprising heterogeneous entities that interact with one another in pursuit of a common objective— i.e.,

Published by Springer Nature Switzerland AG 2024
R. van de Wetering et al. (Eds.): I3E 2024, LNCS 14907, pp. 304–315, 2024.
https://doi.org/10.1007/978-3-031-72234-9_26

to enable value co-creation. These actors, perceived as socio-economic participants, are linked through their unique value propositions and collaborate through service exchange within the network to attain desired outcomes [8].

In addition, there is a growing consensus that firms should repurpose themselves to address the needs of their stakeholders and the natural environment rather than solely focusing on shareholders, seeking both firm-level and system-level changes through collaboration [5, 9, 10]. Hence, they aim to offer *sustainable digital solutions* in the form of digital services that are not only economically viable but also socially responsible and have a minimal negative impact on the environment. Offering sustainable digital solutions requires collaboration among diverse stakeholders, such as businesses, government agencies, non-governmental organizations, and individuals [11]. This collective effort is crucial for balancing economic progress, social well-being, and environmental preservation [12].

Consequently, business models for sustainable digital solutions must transcend the basic narrative of how a single company creates, delivers, and captures value [13]. Collaborations among organizations offer chances to harness additional, complementary capabilities, thereby enhancing or developing joint value propositions [6, 7]. Current research and practice emphasize the critical need to design new sustainable business models and adapt existing ones to become more sustainable [14].

Several studies have proposed methods for defining business models [15]. While acknowledging the importance of cross-organizational partnerships, these studies often adopt a firm-centric perspective [16]. This approach is inadequate for designing business models for sustainable digital solutions, as it lacks the network-centric view necessary for mutual value creation in cross-sector collaborations [12, 17–21].

This necessitates new business model design approaches that underscore the core value proposition of collaborative networks, encompassing cost and benefit structures beyond mere financial consideration, depicting actor interactions as service exchanges, and illustrating how they collaboratively generate value through shared processes [18, 22, 23]. Current research emphasizes the need for a more robust conceptualization of these approaches [5, 24]. Therefore, *the objective of this paper is to outline the initial step in conceptualizing collaborative business models within the context of sustainable digital solutions.* We base this on a specific business case that is firmly rooted in both collaboration and sustainability, serving our purpose well. We then apply three prominent business model design approaches to describe the case and discuss their limitations in capturing the core elements of the business model. Using an inductive approach, we derive and propose fundamental conceptual elements of collaborative business models with a focus on sustainability.

In the remainder of this paper, we describe the business case of a shared micromobility service and describe its business, from which we derive the core elements of a collaborative business model. We then discuss the limitations of the selected approaches in representing the case and propose our own approach. We conclude with an overview of research limitations and suggest avenues for future research.

2 Business Case of a Shared-Micromobility Service

Offering micromobility services through shared electric bikes (e-bikes) and e-scooters is gaining recognition as an effective urban transportation option, especially for their potential to decrease the reliance on private vehicles for short trips, thereby promoting sustainability and reducing carbon footprints [25].

Founded in 2019 in the Netherlands, *Go Sharing* (*nl.go-sharing.com*) offers a micromobility service, operating over 7000 e-vehicles (e-bikes and e-scooters) in more than 36 cities across Europe. Through its *mobile app*, travelers can locate, reserve, unlock, and use these e-vehicles, ending their trips in designated city zones. While different pricing options exist, travelers typically pay based on the trip duration, with discounts available for trips starting or ending in specific city-determined discount zones.

To operate this solution, Go Sharing needs to establish a *collaborative network* where the capabilities of multiple stakeholders must be leveraged. This involves collaboration among a number of network actors, including e-vehicle producers and maintenance providers. The municipalities also have a critical role in the network (*nl.go-sharing.com/en/voor-steden/*), as many cities aim to offer their residents an ecologically sustainable alternative to conventional modes of urban transportation.

As the focal actor, it is crucial for the Go Sharing service operator to articulate the business model for this solution through the lens of a collaborative network. This model should clearly delineate the central value proposition offered to travelers (as the primary customers of the solution) and outline the roles and required capabilities of each network actor in contributing to the realization of this proposed value. Defining these elements explicitly is essential for aligning expectations, building trust among network actors, and establishing a foundation for effective negotiation.

As a digital solution aiming to be an ecologically sustainable alternative to conventional urban transportation, Go Sharing shared micromobility service provides an excellent case for exemplifying a collaborative business model for a sustainable digital solution. Other cases of similar solutions have been reported in the literature, highlighting the need for taking a collaborative perspective to overcome challenges [26]. Below, we outline its model for this purpose.

2.1 Describing the Business Model for the Go Sharing Solution

To describe the business model for the Go Sharing solution, we use the dimensions proposed by Al-Debei and Avison [27]. These dimensions include *value proposition*, *value network*, *value architecture*, and *value finance*. We have chosen this ontology as it explicitly addresses the role of value networks in business models, aligning well with the multi-stakeholder nature of the Go Sharing solution. However, to provide a more neutral perspective on what constitutes value - whether financial or non-financial- we modify value finance to *value capture* (aligned with [28, 29]).

Value Proposition and Value Network Aspects

The value proposition tailored for a specific customer (segment) of an organization constitutes the essential foundation of a business model [30]. However, in the context of collaborative networks, the view for value proposition definition needs to transition from a firm-centric perspective to a network-centric one, representing the value that the collaborative network collectively proposes to a specific customer [31]. We can refer to this as the *network value proposition*, denoting the overarching goal of joint value creation by the actors involved in the collaborative network [16].

For the Go Sharing solution, the network value proposition is "flexible shared transport via e-bikes and e-scooters in urban areas". This is offered to the traveler through the high availability and widespread coverage of these e-vehicles across the city. This enables travelers to take an e-vehicle and travel around the city at any time without the concern of managing or maintaining the vehicle.

As indicated above, the collaborative network comprises e-vehicle producers, maintenance providers, municipalities, and Go Sharing as the service operator. Additionally, the *traveler*, as the customer targeted by the network value proposition, plays a crucial role in the co-creation of value and is integral to the value co-creation [32]. Go Sharing's role in the network is also special. It acts as the *orchestrator* that facilitates the interactions [33], establishes the alignment between the actors in the network taking a leadership role [34], and organizes the operation of the solution [19].

Each actor listed above can justify its participation in the collaborative network of the sharing solution by the *unique value* proposition it contributes to the network value proposition [12]. The Go Sharing service operator ensures effective platform management, e-vehicle producers provide customized and durable e-vehicles suitable for shared services, maintenance providers guarantee e-vehicle availability and longevity, and municipalities offer legal feasibility in their urban spaces, as well as financial support in certain cases. In addition, travelers, as the primary beneficiaries of the service, also contribute to the value co-creation by sharing their profile and service usage data, as well as providing feedback and reviews.

Value Capture Aspects

The sustained engagement of these parties is crucial for the sustainable operation of the Go Sharing solution. Each actor joins this network and continues to offer the value propositions listed above due to the *benefits* it expects to receive [35], which should outweigh the *costs* associated with joining the network for this solution [16].

However, these actors engaging in this business have a range of motives beyond purely economic incentives [22]. Particularly in the context of sustainability, these motives include reducing negative impacts on society and the environment, in addition to (or instead of) pursuing financial gains [36].

For instance, the municipalities' primary motivation is to offer their residents an ecologically sustainable urban transportation option, expecting the solution to result in a *decrease in emissions and congestion* in urban areas. In certain cases, they offer a *subsidy* to Go Sharing to support the solution's financial viability, aligning with their vision of becoming a 'green city'. Similarly, travelers choose to use and *pay* for this service not only for the *convenience* and *flexibility* it offers but also due to its positive impact on *wellbeing* (as riding e-bikes is seen as a form of exercise).

The other actors, namely the Go Sharing service operator, e-vehicle producer, and maintenance provider, are profit-seeking entities that maintain their engagement as long as the financial benefits outweigh their operating costs. Yet, they also expect their involvement to enhance their brand image as environmentally friendly, particularly the Go Sharing service operator and e-vehicle producer. They also expect to gather valuable data on user behavior and transportation patterns for further business opportunities.

Value Architecture Aspects

As a digital solution enabled by collaboration between multiple stakeholders, the value is not solely created by a single entity (e.g., the Go Sharing service operator) but is *co-created* by the collaborative network, which also includes the traveler. In this context, we can distinguish *co-creation processes* and *capabilities (services)* that each actor needs to deploy in these processes.

The *co-creation processes* span multiple actors, connecting them. These processes reflect the necessary collaborations among actors, collectively realizing (operationalizing) the network's value proposition. For instance, the traveler interacts with the service operator via the mobile app to book an e-vehicle. Hence, *booking an e-vehicle* is a process that involves both the traveler and service operator interacting (in this case, via the mobile app). If issues, such as damages, arise with the e-vehicle during a trip, the maintenance provider can engage with the traveler to *handle the damage*. This is in addition to the *e-vehicle maintenance* it performs at the request of the operator. At predefined intervals, the service operator negotiates and manages the concerns regarding the *subsidy* and *legal* aspects with the municipality. Additionally, the service operator collaborates with the e-vehicle producer, using user feedback and maintenance records to inform *requirements* and changes for new or existing vehicles.

Various activities are performed within these processes, ranging from fully-automated activities to semi-automated ones supported by IT. For instance, confirming a reservation is typically automated and handled by the service operator's IT system, while tasks such as picking up an e-vehicle involve traveler interaction with the mobile app. These activities are specific to each actor and reflect the unique *capabilities* that they need to possess in order to realize their value propositions.

For instance, the service operator needs several capabilities, such as processing a reservation, resolving an issue, and monitoring a trip. Maintenance providers need to be able to maintain e-vehicles and charging infrastructure, and repair damages. Similarly, the traveler should have the capability (and should be provided with the IT features) to book, pick up, or use an e-vehicle, end a trip, and pay for it.

We can consider these capabilities as *actor services*, as the actor value proposition is realized when an actor leverages its capabilities within the collaborative network to offer *services* visible to other network actors [37, 38], including the customer [39]. Accordingly, an actor's services collectively realize the actor's value proposition and define how the actor participates in the value co-creation processes [40].

3 Discussion on the Existing Approaches to BM Design

As mentioned in the Introduction, there are several approaches to designing and representing business models in visual forms [15, 30] We select three prevalent approaches to discuss their applicability in representing the business model of the Go Sharing solution. These are Business Model Canvas (BMC), e3-value [41], and Value Mapping Tool

(VMT) [20]. We chose BMC as it is widely known both in research and practice [30] as a firm-centric approach to business model design. We chose e3-value and VMT as they are network-centric approaches to business model design, which makes them well-suited for the Go Sharing case. The e3-value is prominent for its ability to represent business models for *digital solutions* in complex, multi-stakeholder environments. It visualizes economic transactions and dependencies between different actors involved in delivering the solution. VMT is well-known in the domain of *sustainable business models* and facilitates the identification of value exchanges among stakeholders. Its emphasis on capturing non-financial benefits, such as environmental and social value, aligns with the collaborative and sustainability-driven nature of Go Sharing.

The BMC represents the business model of a single firm with nine components: customer segments, value propositions, channels, customer relationships, revenue streams, key resources, key activities, key partnerships, and cost structure. As such, it can serve as a foundational tool to represent the business model of the Go Sharing solution by capturing essential elements such as value proposition, customer segments, and key partnerships. However, the firm-centric nature of BMC makes it less suitable for representing the dynamic and collaborative aspects of the Go Sharing solution. The BMC would focus on the perspective of the orchestrator, i.e., the Go Sharing service operator, missing the network value proposition that spans multiple actors and the underlying reasons for other actors' sustained engagement, such as their unique value propositions, costs, and benefits. Using BMC, it would be challenging to depict the evolving nature of collaboration and value co-creation [16]. Additionally, BMC does not fully address broader sustainability goals and non-economic incentives, such as environmental sustainability and social well-being. These limitations in representing network-centric and dynamic interactions, as well as non-financial value aspects, suggest the need for supplementary tools or modifications to fully encompass the complexity of collaborative business models in sustainable digital solutions.

The *e3-value* [41] approach focuses on mapping the value exchanges between organizations collaborating within a network for a particular solution. This approach addresses the need to represent the financial aspects of value capture while also covering value creation within the network to some extent. However, it does not emphasize the network and actor-specific value propositions that bring and keep the network together. Additionally, focusing solely on financial transactions overlooks non-monetary benefits like environmental sustainability and social well-being, which are crucial for Go Sharing.

The *Value Mapping Tool (VMT)* [20] is designed to help a firm identify and balance multiple types of value, including economic, social, and environmental benefits and burdens (costs). It encourages the firm to explore value creation, value destruction, and missed value opportunities for all stakeholders involved, thus promoting more sustainable business models. The VMT effectively emphasizes multi-dimensional value creation, which aligns well with Go Sharing's goal of providing sustainable urban transportation. By identifying positive and negative value aspects, the VMT can help in understanding the broader impacts of the Go Sharing solution. However, the VMT takes the *firm* as its unit of analysis and is not aimed at representing *solutions* enabled by collaborations in a network. For instance, while the VMT can be useful for uncovering missed value opportunities and highlighting areas for improvement in sustainability practices for the Go Sharing service operator, it would lack the precision in detailing the specific financial exchanges and economic incentives for each actor, which are crucial for maintaining the engagement of profit-seeking entities like e-vehicle producers and maintenance providers. Additionally, it may fall short of providing detailed insights into the specific capabilities and services each actor needs to deploy in the co-creation processes, which is essential for understanding the operational dynamics of the Go Sharing solution.

In summary, existing design approaches fall short in various aspects and require a holistic view to effectively represent the primary components of collaborative business models for sustainable digital solutions. Current research calls for a more robust conceptualization of such models [5, 24].

4 Collaborative Business Model Matrix (CBMX)

Figure 1 depicts the business model of the Go Sharing solution as described in Sect. 2. The figure features a table structure with the core concepts (listed in the left column) and corresponding examples for the case of the Go Sharing solution. We refer to this structure as the Collaborative Business Model Matrix (CBMX), which represents an initial step toward a robust conceptualization of the core elements of such models.

Network Value Proposition	*FLEXIBLE SHARED TRANSPORT VIA E-BIKES AND E-SCOOTERS IN URBAN AREAS*									
Actor Type	*Customer*		*Orchestrator*							
Actor	**Traveler**		**Go Sharing Service Operator**		**Municipality**		**Maintenance Provider**		**E-Vehicle Producer**	
Actor Value Proposition	User profile, service use data, and reviews		Effective platform management		Legal and financial feasibility		E-vehicle availability and longevity		Customized and durable e-vehicles	
Actor Cost & Benefits:	*Costs*	*Benefits*	*Costs*	*Benefits*	*Costs*	*Benefits*	*Cost*	*Benefits*	*Cost*	*Benefits*
Financial	- Service fee		-Operating costs, -Insurance -Maint. fee	+Service fee, +Subsidy	-Subsidy		- Operating costs	+Maint. fee	- Operating costs	+ Increased sales
Environmental						+Decrease emission & congestion				
Social		+Convenience +Flexibility +Wellness								
Other Non-Financial				+Enhanced brand image (i.e., green) +Data insights		+Data insights +City image				+Enhanced brand image (i.e., green) +Data insights
Actor Services	Book e-vehicle, Pickup e-vehicle, Use e-vehicle, End trip, Pay for the trip, Review trip, Report issue		Process reservation, Resolve issue, Monitor trip, Manage platform, ...		Provide legal support, Determine zones, Provide subsidy, Analyze use data, ...		Maintain e-vehicle, Maintain charging infrastructure, Repair damage, ...		Manage e-vehicle (re)design, Integrate IT, ...	
Co-creation Processes	Booking e-vehicle, Payment and billing, Trip management, Damage handling, E-vehicle maintenance, Subsidy handling, E-vehicle requirements management, ...									

Fig. 1. Go Sharing's solution represented using *Collaborative Business Model Matrix (CBMX).*

These elements include the network value proposition, actors in the collaborative network, services they need to deploy for other actors to enable value co-creation, and the costs and benefits of different types involved in doing so. CBMX emphasizes network-centricity and clearly delineates the roles and contributions of each actor. It differentiates between the economic, social, environmental, and other non-financial costs and benefits. By capturing both financial and non-financial aspects, it aligns with Go Sharing's sustainability goals, ensuring a holistic representation of value co-creation within the collaborative network. Additionally, it details co-creation processes and actor-specific services, which help reflect Go Sharing's multi-stakeholder setting.

Table 1 presents the limitations of the selected business model design approaches, and how CBMX addresses these limitations.

Table 1. Existing BM design approaches vs. CBMX for representing collaborative business models.

BM Dimension	BMC	e3-value	VMT	CBMX
Value Proposition	Firm-centric, missing network value proposition	Focuses on value transfers (actor transactions), missing network and actor value propositions	Attention to both network and actor value propositions	*Attention to both network and actor value propositions*
Value Network	Firm-centric, supports defining partners, but misses the network perspective	Supports network-centricity	Supports network-centricity with special network roles	*Supports network-centricity with special network roles (orchestrator, customer)*
Value Architecture	High-level support with key activities for the focal actor, missing the processual aspects	High-level support with actor activities	Falls short of providing detailed insights into the specific capabilities and services each actor needs to deploy in the co-creation processes	*Emphasis on multi-actor co-creation processes and actor capabilities (services)*
Value Capture	Focuses only on financial aspects	Precision in detailing the specific financial exchanges, but focuses only on financial aspects	Supports representing both financial and non-financial costs and benefits but lack the precision in detailing the specific exchanges and economic incentives for each actor	*Both financial and non-financial (economic, environmental, social, and others) with support to detail exchanges*

5 Conclusions

This paper aims to outline the initial steps in developing a design approach for collaborative business models tailored to sustainable digital solutions. To achieve this, we employed an inductive methodology, using a specific business case as our foundation. We begin by explaining the necessity of shifting from a firm-centric to a network-centric perspective in business model design. Subsequently, we identify the network and actor value propositions in the Go Sharing shared micromobility service and describe how value is co-created and captured within this collaborative network. In doing so, we address foundational concepts such as the collaborative network, and identify core elements of a collaborative business model, including the network value proposition, the services each actor must deploy in value co-creation processes, and the various nature of costs and benefits involved. Such a model outlines how a network of actors works together to co-create value for the customer and generates mutual benefits for all network actors [42].

Our work contributes to the field of business model design by offering a preliminary foundation for researchers and practitioners seeking to design collaborative business models for sustainable digital solutions enabled by collaborations between multiple stakeholders.

The work presented in this paper is conceptual and inherits some inherent limitations common to inductive research studies. Primarily, these conceptualizations are based on the authors' perspectives and interpretations, potentially introducing bias and limiting their generalizability [43]. Building upon existing research on business models and a real-life business case helps alleviate these limitations. However, future research should prioritize applying the method in additional business cases and empirically assessing its validity and utility for its intended users. The theoretical foundations for the conceptualization should also be strengthened.

Future efforts should also aim at developing methods and tools to aid in comprehensively assessing the viability and feasibility of collaborative business models, considering both economic factors and environmental and societal impacts [14]. To achieve this goal, various methods and techniques should be employed at different stages of the business model lifecycle, including defining and refining relevant performance indicators [44–46]. Such evaluations should also consider how a balance between economic, environmental, and social dimensions can be maintained, how they can be measured, and how relevant decisions can be supported [47]. Future research should also investigate how the design of the business model informs and shapes its implementation [27, 48], with a particular focus on its operating model [49, 50], including the business processes [51, 52] and the required IT infrastructure [53].

Disclosure of Interests. The authors have no competing interests to declare that are relevant to the content of this article.

References

1. Ritter, T., Pedersen, C.L.: Digitization capability and the digitalization of business models in business-to-business firms: past, present, and future. Ind. Mark. Manage. **86**, 180–190 (2020). https://doi.org/10.1016/J.INDMARMAN.2019.11.019
2. Parida, V., Sjödin, D., Reim, W.: Reviewing literature on digitalization, business model innovation, and sustainable industry: past achievements and future promises. Sustainability **11**, 391 (2019).https://doi.org/10.3390/SU11020391
3. Foss, N., Saebi, T.: Fifteen years of research on business model innovation: how far have we come, and where should we go? J. Manage **43**, 200–227 (2017)
4. Castañer, X., Oliveira, N.: Collaboration, coordination, and cooperation among organizations: establishing the distinctive meanings of these terms through a systematic literature review. J. Manage **46**, 965–1001 (2020). https://doi.org/10.1177/0149206320901565
5. Stål, H.I., Riumkin, I., Bengtsson, M.: Business models for sustainability and firms' external relationships—a systematic literature review with propositions and research agenda. Bus Strategy Environ. **32**, 3887–3901 (2023). https://doi.org/10.1002/BSE.3343
6. de Man, A.P., Luvison, D.: Collaborative business models: aligning and operationalizing alliances. Bus. Horiz. **62**, 473–482 (2019). https://doi.org/10.1016/J.BUSHOR.2019.02.004
7. Oskam, I., Bossink, B., de Man, A.P.: Valuing value in innovation ecosystems: how cross-sector actors overcome tensions in collaborative sustainable business model development. Bus. Soc. **60**, 1059–1091 (2021). https://doi.org/10.1177/0007650320907145
8. Wieland, H., Polese, F., Vargo, S.L., Lusch, R.F.: Toward a service (Eco)systems perspective on value creation. Int. J. Serv. Sci. Manag. Eng. Technol. **3**, 12–25 (2012). https://doi.org/10.4018/jssmet.2012070102
9. Schaltegger, S., Hansen, E.G., Lüdeke-Freund, F.: Business models for sustainability: origins, present research, and future avenues. Organ. Environ. **29**, 3 (2015). https://doi.org/10.1177/1086026615599806
10. Lüdeke-Freund, F., Dembek, K.: Sustainable business model research and practice: emerging field or passing fancy? J. Clean. Prod. **168**, 1668–1678 (2017). https://doi.org/10.1016/J.JCLEPRO.2017.08.093
11. Bocken, N.M.P., Short, S.W., Rana, P., Evans, S.: A literature and practice review to develop sustainable business model archetypes. J. Clean. Prod. **65**, 42–56 (2014). https://doi.org/10.1016/J.JCLEPRO.2013.11.039
12. Breuer, H., Lüdeke-Freund, F.: Values-based network and business model innovation. Int. J. Innov. Manag. **21** (2017). https://doi.org/10.1142/S1363919617500281
13. Massa, L., Tucci, C., Afuah, A.: A critical assessment of business model research. Acad. Manag. Ann. **11**, 73–104 (2017). https://doi.org/10.5465/annals.2014.0072
14. Snihur, Y., Markman, G.: Business model research: past, present, and future. J. Manage. Stud. **60**, e1–e14 (2023). https://doi.org/10.1111/JOMS.12928
15. Szopinski, D., Massa, L., John, T., et al.: Modeling business models: a cross-disciplinary analysis of business model modeling languages and directions for future research. Commun. Assoc. Inf. Syst. **51**, 39 (2022). https://doi.org/10.17705/1CAIS.05133
16. Adner, R.: Ecosystem as structure: an actionable construct for strategy. J. Manage. **43**, 39–58 (2017). https://doi.org/10.1177/0149206316678451
17. Pedersen, E.R.G., Lüdeke-Freund, F., Henriques, I., Seitanidi, M.M.: Toward collaborative cross-sector business models for sustainability. Bus. Soc. **60**, 1039–1058 (2021). https://doi.org/10.1177/0007650320959027
18. Bankvall, L., Dubois, A., Lind, F.: Conceptualizing business models in industrial networks. Ind. Mark. Manage. **60**, 196–203 (2017). https://doi.org/10.1016/J.INDMARMAN.2016.04.006

19. Palo, T., Tähtinen, J.: Networked business model development for emerging technology-based services. Ind. Mark. Manage. **42**, 773–782 (2013). https://doi.org/10.1016/J.INDMARMAN.2013.05.015
20. Bocken, N., Short, S., Rana, P., Evans, S.: A value mapping tool for sustainable business modelling. Corp. Gov. **13**, 482–497 (2013). https://doi.org/10.1108/CG-06-2013-0078
21. Turetken, O., Grefen, P.: Designing service-dominant business models. In: European Conference on Information Systems (ECIS 2017). AIS Press (2017)
22. Turetken, O., Grefen, P., Gilsing, R., Adali, O.E.: Service-dominant business model design for digital innovation in smart mobility. Bus. Inf. Syst. Eng. **61**, 9–29 (2019). https://doi.org/10.1007/s12599-018-0565-x
23. Böttcher, T.P., Empelmann, S., Weking, J., et al.: Digital sustainable business models: using digital technology to integrate ecological sustainability into the core of business models. Inf. Syst. J.(2023). https://doi.org/10.1111/isj.12436
24. Dentchev, N., Rauter, R., Jóhannsdóttir, L., et al.: Embracing the variety of sustainable business models: a prolific field of research and a future research agenda. J. Clean. Prod. **194**, 695–703 (2018). https://doi.org/10.1016/J.JCLEPRO.2018.05.156
25. Abduljabbar, R.L., Liyanage, S., Dia, H.: The role of micro-mobility in shaping sustainable cities: a systematic literature review. Transp. Res. D Transp. Environ. **92**, 102734 (2021). https://doi.org/10.1016/J.TRD.2021.102734
26. Li, D., Jia, F., Liu, G.: How do bike-sharing platform companies overcome the operational challenge? a social exchange perspective. Product. Planning Control **33**, 1355–1371 (2022). https://doi.org/10.1080/09537287.2020.1864583
27. Al-Debei, M.M., Avison, D.: Developing a unified framework of the business model concept. Eur. J. Inf. Syst. **19**, 359–376 (2010)
28. Gilsing, R., Turetken, O., Ozkan, B., et al.: Evaluating the design of service-dominant business models: a qualitative method. PAJAIS **13**(2) (2021). https://doi.org/10.17705/1pais.13102
29. Gilsing, R., Turetken, O., Ozkan, B., et al.: A method for qualitative evaluation of service-dominant business models. In: ECIS 2020 (2020)
30. Osterwalder, A., Pigneur, I.: Business Model Generation: A Handbook for Visionaries, Game Changers and Challengers. Willey, New Jersey, US (2010)
31. Dembek, K., Lüdeke-Freund, F., Rosati, F., Froese, T.: Untangling business model outcomes, impacts and value. Bus. Strategy Environ. (2022). https://doi.org/10.1002/BSE.3249
32. Lusch, R.F., Nambisan, S.: Service innovation: a service-dominant logic perspective. Manag. Inf. Syst. Q. **39**, 155–175 (2015)
33. Holm, C.G., Kringelum, L.B.: Intra-organizational business model implications of inter-organizational collaboration. J. Bus. Models **10**, 1–10 (2022). https://doi.org/10.54337/JBM.V10I1.6827
34. Lingens, B., Huber, F., Gassmann, O.: Loner or team player: how firms allocate orchestrator tasks amongst ecosystem actors. Eur. Manag. J. **40**, 559–571 (2022). https://doi.org/10.1016/J.EMJ.2021.09.001
35. Vargo, S.L., Lusch, R.F.: Service-dominant logic: continuing the evolution. J. Acad. Mark. Sci. **36**, 1–10 (2008)
36. Allee, V.: Value network analysis and value conversion of tangible and intangible assets. J. Intellect. Cap. **9**, 5–24 (2008). https://doi.org/10.1108/14691930810845777
37. Adali, O.E., Ozkan, B., Turetken, O., et al.: A method to transform value propositions of a service system into business services. In: ECIS 2021 (2021)

38. Adali, O.E., Türetken, O., Ozkan, B., Gilsing, R., Grefen, P.: A multi-concern method for identifying business services: a situational method engineering study. In: Nurcan, S., Reinhartz-Berger, I., Soffer, P., Zdravkovic, J. (eds.) Enterprise, Business-Process and Information Systems Modeling. BPMDS EMMSAD 2020 2020. Lecture Notes in Business Information Processing, vol. 387, pp. 227–241. Springer, Cham (2020). https://doi.org/10.1007/978-3-030-49418-6_15
39. Chesbrough, H.W.: Why Companies Should Have Open Business Models. MIT Sloan Manag Rev (2007)
40. D'Souza, A., Wortmann, H., Huitema, G., Velthuijsen, H.: A business model design framework for viability: a business ecosystem approach. J. Bus. Models **3**, 1–29 (2015)
41. Gordijn, J., Akkermans, H.: Designing and evaluating e-business models. IEEE Intell. Syst. **16**, 11–17 (2001)
42. Rohrbeck, R., Konnertz, L., Knab, S.: Collaborative business modelling for systemic and sustainability innovations. Int. J. Technol. Manage. **63**, 4–23 (2013). https://doi.org/10.1504/IJTM.2013.055577
43. Cornelissen, J.: Editor's comments: developing propositions, a process model, or a typology? addressing the challenges of writing theory without a boilerplate. Acad. Manag. Rev. **42**, 1–9 (2016). https://doi.org/10.5465/AMR.2016.0196
44. Gilsing, R., Wilbik, A., Grefen, P., et al.: Defining business model key performance indicators using intentional linguistic summaries. Softw. Syst. Model. **20**, 965–996 (2021). https://doi.org/10.1007/S10270-021-00894-X/FIGURES/10
45. van de Ven, M., Lara Machado, P., Athanasopoulou, A., et al.: Key performance indicators for business models: a systematic review and catalog. IseB **1–42**,(2023). https://doi.org/10.1007/S10257-023-00650-2
46. Gilsing, R., Turetken, O., Grefen, P., et al.: Business model evaluation: a systematic review of methods. PAJAIS **14**(2) (2022). https://doi.org/10.17705/1pais.14402
47. Joyce, A., Paquin, R.L.: The triple layered business model canvas: a tool to design more sustainable business models. J. Clean. Prod. **135**, 1474–1486 (2016). https://doi.org/10.1016/J.JCLEPRO.2016.06.067
48. Globocnik, D., Faullant, R., Parastuty, Z.: Bridging strategic planning and business model management – a formal control framework to manage business model portfolios and dynamics. Eur. Manag. J. **38**, 231–243 (2020). https://doi.org/10.1016/j.emj.2019.08.005
49. Lara Machado, P., van de Ven, M., Aysolmaz, B., et al.: Methods that bridge business models and business processes: a synthesis of the literature. Bus. Process. Manag. J. **29**, 48–74 (2023). https://doi.org/10.1108/BPMJ-08-2022-0396
50. Lara Machado, P., Ven van de, M., Aysolmaz, B., et al.: Exploring business process design alternatives through a business model lens. In: ECIS 2023 (2023)
51. Suratno, B., Ozkan, B., Turetken, O., Grefen, P.: A method for operationalizing service-dominant business models into conceptual process models. In: Shishkov, B. (eds.) Business Modeling and Software Design. BMSD 2018. Lecture Notes in Business Information Processing, vol. 319, pp. 133–148. Springer, Cham (2018). https://doi.org/10.1007/978-3-319-94214-8_9
52. Hotie, F., Gordijn, J.: Value-based process model design. Bus. Inf. Syst. Eng. **61**, 163–180 (2019). https://doi.org/10.1007/S12599-017-0496-Y/FIGURES/9
53. Jungerius, N., Ozkan, B., Adali, O.E., Turetken, O.: Assessing digital platform requirements from value co-creation perspective. In: Working Conference on Virtual Enterprises (PRO-VE 2022) 662 IFIP, pp. 631–644 (2022). https://doi.org/10.1007/978-3-031-14844-6_51/

Using Information Technology to Create Sustainable Organizational Constellations

Ronald van den Heuvel(✉), Rogier van de Wetering, Rik Bos, and Jos Trienekens

Open University of the Netherlands, Valkenburgerweg 177, 6419 AT Heerlen, The Netherlands
{Ronald.vandenHeuvel,Rogier.vandeWetering,Rik.Bos,
Jos.Trienekens}@ou.nl

Abstract. Organizations build alliances to create products or services that fulfill a specific market need. These alliances have been around for a while, and researchers describe them in various terms like Virtual Organization, or Ecosystem. The manifestation of these alliances increased due to the increasing interconnection between organizations within the fourth industrial revolution. The never-ending alignment between markets and alliances provides a dynamic landscape for organizations and their partners. While abundant research is available on these constellations, we do not know what IT needs can be used to cope with these dynamics. Our research aims to fill that gap, specifically on the relations between network participants and their interactions. We executed a multi-case study on 10 alliances comprising 35 interviews, which were transcribed and coded. By analyzing the co-occurrence, we could determine relationships between the organizational characteristics and the IT needs. Our results validated the characteristics framework, provided a list of IT needs, and showed that IT needs can positively influence and strengthen organizations to cope with market dynamics.

Keywords: Virtual organizations · IT needs · dynamism · reconfiguration

1 Introduction

The definition of organization is used in various ways. An organization is a collaboration of people who collaborate and organize themselves into an entity while they provide their time to an entrepreneur and do not take part in price mechanisms [1]. Thus, organizations are hierarchical and participate in economic transactions, delivering products or services to optimize and steer labor. Collaboration is common when organizations cannot achieve price optimization alone [1]. The concept of collaborative organizations and its related taxonomy of types date back to 2005 [2]. While in various forms, this group of organization types can be characterized as a constellation of autonomous participants (organizations or individuals) that willingly want to participate to achieve common goals [3]. The forms differ in characteristics, but in recent literature, we see a common usage of the term "Virtual Organization" (VO) often used in Industry 4.0 [3–6]. IT facilitates these constellations to achieve alignment and collaboration [7, 8].

Published by Springer Nature Switzerland AG 2024
R. van de Wetering et al. (Eds.): I3E 2024, LNCS 14907, pp. 316–327, 2024.
https://doi.org/10.1007/978-3-031-72234-9_27

VO literature discusses organizational adaption to "fit" a new landscape, which is also seen in the fourth industrial revolution, where rapid reconfiguration is part of "batch size of one" fulfillment [9] and is seen within the ecosystem concepts for innovation and organizational collaboration [10]. While these topics seem to be separated, features needed for the reconfiguration and operation of these constellations overlap. Examples of overlapping features between VOs and ecosystem theory are self-organization, modularity, and a shared vision, which emphasizes the need for reconfiguring to acquire specific needs [10–12]. Overlapping features between VOs, ecosystems, and the fourth industrial revolution can be found in the domain of non-linearity, co-evolution, and environmental turbulence [4, 10, 11, 13], which emphasizes the interaction between organizations. Where the research field on VOs focuses on organizational collaboration, ecosystems theory sheds light on the market these constellations operate in, creating an extensive but not integrated body of knowledge.

Central to all these topics is a reconfiguration of the constellation of organizations. This reconfiguration is needed to align the products and services with current market needs and is supported by IT tools. While abundant tools exist to cope with these dynamic situations, a validated list of tools is not available for this specific context. It is also not clear when these tools should be used to influence a particular organizational characteristic to cope with the dynamic landscape they operate in [7]. Our goal is to fill this gap and provide a validated list of IT needs related to organizational characteristics within a VO context to support these VOs in their dynamic environment. Our study focuses on the relationship and interaction between organizations within a VO and builds upon the framework of Van Den Heuvel et al. [7]. Therefore, our research questions are:

RQ1: *What characteristics do VOs have on the theme relation and interaction that could influence their IT needs?*

RQ2: *Which IT needs are used by VOs to interact and influence the relationship?*

RQ3*: How are these IT needs related to organizational characteristics, and how do they help the organization cope with dynamism?*

To answer these questions, we analyzed 10 VOs, with a total of 35 interviews.

Section 2 describes the background of the components used in this study. Section 3 highlights our research method. Section 4 describes our cases, extended IT needs, and the relationship between needs and organizational characteristics. The paper concludes with a discussion and conclusion.

2 Theoretical Background

2.1 Virtual Organization Terminology and Topology

A collaborative network is a "network constituted by a variety of entities (e.g., organizations and people) that are largely autonomous, geographically distributed, and heterogeneous in terms of their operating environment, culture, social capital, and goals [2]". While the concept was founded in 2005, the idea of collaboration within organizations was founded earlier and is the basis of the term "Organization," where people work together in an organized way for a shared purpose. In the seminal paper of Coase [1], he already describes the difference between an employee and an employer, where the employee wishes to execute a specific task but does not want to partake in the economic transactions that are part of running an organization. The latter is then bestowed upon the entrepreneur who governs these transactions, creating a hierarchical relationship. While Coase writes extensively about organizations, the essence describes how people organize themselves to work together to achieve their goals and that organizations create networks of services and products to facilitate their organizational goals.

While organizations are collaborations between people, collaborative networks are constellations of members, which can be people or organizations that organize themselves to achieve a goal. Within the collaboration, strict rules are defined to govern the partnership. Still, they can decide to work for another organization as a subordinate or collaborate. Our research focuses on collaboration, where organizations have a common goal and align their activities to achieve it, which fits in the definition of a Virtual Organization (VO): A founded definition of a VO is: "a set of (legally) independent organizations that share resources and skills to achieve its mission/goal" [3], which still fits more recent VO literature on ecosystems in the era of Industry 4.0 [4–6]. However, we still notice confusion in research regarding the term "virtual," which is often interpreted as lacking a physical location rather than being created for a specific event.

VOs can be differentiated between vertical, where organizations' competencies differ and are needed to achieve a goal, and horizontal, where competencies are alike and collaboration is needed to increase capacity [14]. This differentiation could influence how organizations participate and thus influence their relationship, interactions, and mutual trust. "Trust" [14] is one of the essential components of collaboration and building a sustainable VO [4, 8, 15].

2.2 Industry 4.0

The fourth industrial revolution describes the evolution of manufacturing systems and organizational constellations to use connected technology to facilitate automated and self-organizing product or service manufacturing with a batch size of 1 [9, 16]. While the term "Industry 4.0" achieved buzzword status in the last 5 to 10 years, the goal of achieving cyber-physical systems and Internet of Things implementations is a relevant topic [4] and was even discussed in various forms in 2009 and 2013 [12, 13].

Industry 4.0 has become the generic term for a group of information systems/technology components like enterprise architecture, blockchain, internet of things, cloud, and process management that facilitate the creation of modern supply chains and facilitate rapid reconfiguration [13]. It shows that this industrial revolution heavily uses IT to achieve this cyber-physical balance. While fully automated organizations are not common yet, the technology that could facilitate those digitally autonomous organizations exists and is pursued by practitioners and researchers alike.

It cannot be ignored that VOs play a role in this revolution and that they need to increasingly rely on IT to keep up with the dynamics caused by the rapid reconfiguration of industry 4.0 concepts in their markets [4, 7, 8, 13]. However, we do not know how to achieve this collaboration and which needs the organizations have.

2.3 Dynamism Within Virtual Organizations

Constellations of organizations called VOs act on market opportunity and thus are formed quickly or instantly [12]. This form of (re)configuration is seen in various movements like Industry 4.0, "batch size of one" fulfillment [9], and ecosystems for innovation [10]. Innovation Ecosystems is defined as: "The evolving set of actors, activities, and artifacts, and the institutions and relations, including complementary and substitute relations, that are important for the innovative performance of an actor or a population of actors" [17]. Grefen et al. [12] refer to the increased complexity and shortened lifecycle of products that force organizations to be dynamic and thus be able to reconfigure to align with demands. Camarinha-Matos and Afsarmanesh [18] mention that dynamics find their source in the number of relationships between peers within an organization. Han et al. [10] describe the trend that organizations want to create "Ecosystems" to facilitate co-creation.

We are interested in how organizations cope with organizational dynamism when trying to create a fit between the market they operate in by reconfiguring the constellation of organizations. Two aspects of dynamis are the interaction between participants and their relationship [7, 11].

2.4 Research Framework

The capability and IT needs framework was adopted from the research described by Van Den Heuvel et al. [7]. Within our study, we are interested in the relationship between participants in a VO and thus look at the relationship between participants and the type of interaction in these relationships. Van Den Heuvel et al. [7] identified organizational characteristics and IT needs to cope with dynamism in networks. The characteristics in the relation theme are: Trust, Entity role, Relation type, Tie form, Tie strength and Embeddedness. In the theme interaction the characteristics are Interaction mode, Locale, Time, Goal of interaction, Structures and Levels of formality. An extended version of the IT needs can be found Table 1. The framework and enriched IT needs will be the basis of this research paper, resulting in more insights into how IT needs are related to specific characteristics perceived within a VO.

3 Research Method

3.1 Case Selection and Interviews

The selection of organizations is based on non-probability sampling, thus meaning that there is no "random" aspect in the selection of the cases [19–21]. This method has certain advantages and disadvantages. In our study, we accessed organizations classified as VOs ($n = 10$), which allowed us to conduct in-depth interviews. This was particularly advantageous as it enabled us to include a minimum of three participants from each VO, which is essential for the depth of our research but limits the generalizability over multiple VOs in specific contexts.

To classify a VO as a potential participant, the VO needed to have participated in a collaboration of multiple organizations to achieve a common goal. After identification, the VO was selected only when at least one IT and one business person who participated in the collaboration was available for an interview who has a the equivalient to the bachelor level or higher and has experience with Business IT alignment. A minimum of three interviews were needed per VO, and a minimum of two organizations should participate in the case study to ensure we get insights into the topic of many-to-many relationships. The interviews were executed independently. Each interviewer used the same framework, preparation method, and interview guide. A trial interview was held before the interviews. All interviews were semi-structured.

Almost all interviews were conducted face-to-face (or via video conference) and time-boxed for 90 min. The interviewer made the transcription. Participants received these transcriptions to validate and approve, whereafter they were anonymized.

3.2 Coding Transcriptions

The interviews were coded by the interviewer (which was not the first author) and reviewed by the research team (7 people). A closed code book was provided based on the initial characteristics as described in the research framework described in Van Den Heuvel et al. [7], which could be extended by the coder. New codes were shared within the team. The first author validated all the codes that were added by the research team. An independent researcher evaluated the process and, via selective bi-directional inter-coding, codes in a subset of the interviews. This validation resulted in a high intercoder agreement of 90% +. As suggested by Boudreau, Gefen, and Straub [22], the high intercoder agreement resulted in sufficient confidence to use the codes in our research.

3.3 Code Harmonization and Co-occurrence

The merged codes were all validated by the first author. Network graphs were made to determine the relationship between topics while keeping detailed codes. The IT needs have been restructured based on the harmonization results and validated with three PhD-level experts with experience in the field of Business IT alignment and network organizations. Selective and axial coding was used to see relationships between IT needs and characteristics.

4 Case Study Results

4.1 Case Participants

We conducted 35 interviews within 26 organizations covering 10 VOs. Each organization participated in only one VO, except for one, which took part in VO 1 and 4. We conducted 3 to 5 interviews per VO.

VO 1 (IT Service Management) is a vertical goal-oriented VO with a network size of approximately five organizations. The objective of the VO is to reduce human errors in recurring tasks between different vendors. VO 2 (IT transformation) is also a vertical goal-oriented network with a size of approximately 5 to 8 organizations. The objective of VO 2 is to transform and consolidate legacy IT systems. VO 3 (IT Service Management) is a VO that comprises approximately 75 organizations and is organized in horizontal and vertical topology. This network aims to connect customers in the Service Management field, increase customer satisfaction, and expand their visibility by forming a network. VO 4 (real estate development) is a horizontal network of approximately 50 participants to deliver and maintain the project with as little hindrance to the public as possible. VO 5 (Information exchange healthcare) comprises 12 organizations that execute regional projects, implementing a secure way of data exchange amongst healthcare organizations and patients. VO 6 (Information exchange healthcare) is driven by a subvention project of the Dutch government, Ministerie van Volksgezondheid, Welzijn en Sport (VWS) to stimulate electronic data exchange. VO 7 (Information exchange healthcare) is a collaboration between one hospital and four nursing organizations, combined with seven exogenous partners. The goal is to stimulate the exchange of medical data between the hospital and nursing organizations to provide quicker and more secure communication. VO 8 (IT Service management) is vertically oriented, with two participating organizations in the IT market. Their common goal is to service one big customer. VO 9 (Primary education) is a vertical VO with two participating organizations in education, and their common goal is to cut IT costs. One participant (A) is a foundation with eighteen elementary schools, and the other participant (B) is a school community for secondary education. The IT department of B has been moved to a new foundation of A and B. Last, VO 10 (IT Recruitment / Consultancy) is a horizontal VO with two participating organizations, and their common goal is to recruit temporary IT specialists for their customers.

4.2 Code Harmonization Results

The additional materials showed that the grouping of components from Van Den Heuvel et al. [7] could be optimized. Based on their paper we enhanced the following using the N identifier as our new framework: We renamed "T3 Task management tooling" to "N2 Project and activity planning". Within this change, we added additional components like time registration and various tags for tools used in this domain. We also noticed that while "T2 Documentation templates" was rightfully placed when only using a subset of interviews, when analyzing the complete set, we noticed that this component should be merged with "N1 Collaboration".

We noticed that the group "T1 Collaboration tooling" was too generic. While it fit the first cases, the additional cases provided more insight into restructuring the group. For example, the researchers positioned office tools under this category.

Another group that changed was "T6 Knowledge sharing". This group combined IT needs that supported collaboration and knowledge-sharing tools. Therefore, we moved IT needs related to collaboration to the group "N1 Collaboration".

"T7 Documentation tooling was combined with N1 when it was a generic IT need. Nevertheless, when the quote was related to specialized tools, for instance, "Building Information Modeling," we classified the need as a "specialized documentation application" supporting a business process. Therefore, categorizing it under "N4 process support". Table 1 contains the revised IT needs.

We didn't need to harmonize codes for organizational characteristics; the model in our theoretical background sufficed for our research.

Table 1. Revised IT needs

IT need	Description
N1 Collaboration	Tools for collaborative writing within the group
N2 Project & activity planning	Tools for task management and planning
N3 Conference	Tools to virtually meet with participants
N4 Process support	Tools supporting organization processes like ITSM, CRM, and financial systems
N5 Forum	Tools for asynchronous communication in text
N6 Chat	Tools for synchronous communication in text
N7 Email & calendar	Tools with insights into contacts and calendars
N8 Middleware & integration	Tools to facilitate process integration between participants' systems to create a system for the collaborative network
N9 Shared IT infrastructure	Facilities for communicating between participants governing access policies (networking)
N10 Shared reporting	Tools that provide insights into the status of the collaborative organization

Table 2. IT needs per VO

VO		1	2	3	4	5	6	7	8	9	10	Total
IT needs	N1	19	10	18	13	12	4	9	24	9	10	128
	N2	12	2	5	6	1		11	3		1	41
	N3	31	18	44	11	7	10	11	3	2	3	140
	N4	4	3	2	6				14	7	2	38
	N5			1	3		1					5
	N6	5	5	20	3	3	1		2		8	47
	N7	24	8	26	6	32	14	17	10	5	7	149
	N8	4					2		1	1		8
	N9	9	1	8	5	1			1			25
	N10	3			1		1		8	1	1	15
	Total	111	47	124	54	56	33	48	66	25	32	596

4.3 Perceived IT Needs Within the VOs

The total amount of codes was 596, and the amount per VO can be found in Table 2.

Our results show that the IT needs collaboration (N1), conference (N3), and Email & calendar (N7) facilities were perceived most, closely followed by Project & activity planning (N2) and Chat (N6). Forum (N5) or Middleware & integration (N8) were least

Table 3. Co-occurrence table between IT needs and characteristics

IT Need		1	2	3	4	5	6	7	8	9	10
Theme: Relation	Trust: competence			X			X				
	Trust: relational		X	X						X	
	Trust: contractual			X			X				
	Relation type: direct			X				X			
	Tie form: formal			X	X			X		X	
	Tie strength: strong			X				X		X	
	Tie strength: weak							X			
	Embeddedness: strong			X	X						
	Embeddedness: weak									X	
	Entity role: hub		X								
	Entity role: contact			X				X		X	
Theme: Interaction	Interaction mode: create	X								X	
	Locale: endogenous	X								X	
	Time: asynchronous	X			X						
	Level of formality; formal				X					X	
	Level of formality: informal	X									
	Goal of interaction: elaborative			X							
	Structures: Biological			X			X	X			
	Structures: formal							X		X	
	Levels of formality: informal			X				X			
	Levels of formality: formal							X			

perceived, but this could be related to the maturity or the type of VO. Each VO used only some of the IT needs. No clear relationship between the VO sector or topology and their IT needs could be perceived.

4.4 IT Needs Visibility and Co-occurrence

We identified the IT needs within the interviews and analyzed the co-occurrence of these needs. Co-occurrence occurs when a specific code within the interview is used in the same section as another code. We will describe the noteworthy results per IT need. Table 3 shows a table representation of the co-occurrences.

N3 Conference Facilities are widely needed and recognized across all VOs, especially during the COVID-19 pandemic. N4 Process Support Tooling is typically used as a single solution for the entire VO, provided by one party, rather than integrating multiple tools. N5 Forum and N8 Middleware & integration had fewer than 10 occurrences and showed no significant co-occurrences, making it a minor topic in our analysis. While N10 Shared Reporting System was considered a critical IT need, no relationship was identified between its characteristics and the themes. Despite its fundamental role in providing performance insights across multiple VOs, it did not emerge as a significant topic. Participants who mentioned N9 Shared IT Infrastructure did not view their shared cloud environments as infrastructure, interpreting it more as physical connectivity at the network or user account level. It co-occurred with weak embeddedness, often due to outsourcing of these services. In the interaction theme, this need was consistently related to the mode "create," an endogenous locale, and a formal structure despite weak embeddedness in relationships. N7 Email & calendar is mentioned in all VOs, highlighting its importance. The presence of both strong and weak formal ties was unexpected. Analysis showed that organizations with weak ties did not increase communication during dynamic periods, causing email to weaken the connection. Conversely, those with strong ties supplemented email with additional communication methods like conference calls or face-to-face meetings.

5 Discussion

5.1 Theoretical Contributions

The first goal of our study was to strengthen the characteristics of the theme relation and interaction that could influence the IT needs of VOs (**RQ1**), where we found an initial list from Van Den Heuvel et al. [8]. During our research, participants mentioned no additional characteristics within these themes.

Second, we wanted to know which IT needs were used by VOs (**RQ2**). We created a list of 10 IT needs by structurally validating and grouping the codes from our interviews (Table 2). N1, N3, and N7 were most common, followed by N2 and N6. The least mentioned were N5 and N8, and these IT needs have little co-occurrence. Our study confirms that IT is essential to facilitate collaboration and govern the dynamism within constellations and which is also visible in literature on VO, ecosystem, and Industry 4.0 [4–6, 13]. Still, we did not see the system integrations (N8) being used often, which matches the findings of Van Den Heuvel et al. [8]. The lack of use of system integration could be related to the type of collaboration or the lifecycle of the specific VO we analyzed. This fact is different than described in Industry 4.0 concepts, where researchers mainly state that IT integration is common in this concept. We could not find a reason based on an organization or participant type to explain the low occurrence and co-occurrence of N5 and N8.

N3 "Conference" positively affect competence trust, and biological structures, which are essential to creating trust within a VO [8, 15]. Trust and collaboration are essential when achieving and governing alignment [23]. Therefore, we state that N3 is essential to virtual organizations and coping with dynamism because it directly influences (competence) trust, an essential characteristic of VO [11]. N3 and N9 also influence the embeddedness of an organization, and Embeddedness is essential to create a VO that acts as one organization with common goals. Looking at the results of N6 "Chat," we see that this IT need influences "Tie strength" and responsive interaction, which is also essential for influencing trust and coping with dynamics within a VO. These two needs can be used to strengthen the relationship between participants within a VO. Next to the ability to strengthen relationships and interaction, these found IT needs can be used to positively influence characteristics during the reconfiguration of the VO, which is common in current dynamic times [24, 25]. Therefore, we enriched the current body of knowledge with concrete IT needs and a way to influence them to strengthen the relations and increase the interaction within a VO, thus making it more resilient against market dynamics **(RQ3).**

This work offers various managerial contributions. First, our research guides what type of IT needs can be used within an existing VO, which can be used to stimulate specific characteristics, to in the end, strengthen the relationship between the participants and influence the interaction within the VO. When a VO is created, or new participants join, it can provide a basis for determining the set of IT needs. This set could give the new VO a head-start compared to other competitors, which is one of the goals of collaboration. When examining entrepreneurs aiming to establish an ecosystem or VO, this same list could serve as a foundation.

There are limitations to our findings. We executed a limited case study with ten VOs, within different context. While this is not a small number of cases, the results cannot be generalized. For instance, our VOs focused on goal-oriented networks and not on strategic networks, which could easily lead to specific IT needs that could differ in a strategic network. Still, the sampling method, using the network of the participating researchers, provided access to the VOs while not explicitly focusing on a type of VO. The randomness in our case selection is limited but certainly not nil.

An obvious but noteworthy limitation is that we could not measure the IT needs over time. However, we analyzed various VOs in different stages, but we cannot conclude that a specific lifecycle stage of a VO results in an IT need. While we see some relations between characteristics and IT needs, we cannot conclude that there is a relation based on sufficient empirical evidence.

Future research can be found in validating the IT needs and their relationships with characteristics within strategic networks to determine the generalizability of other types of constellations of organizations. For instance, older VO are more evolved in their collaboration which could trigger a more robust relationship supported by technical interaction using N8. We can also see additional research to validate if these IT needs are visible in the literature related to rapid reconfiguration or business IT alignment frameworks. Another topic for future research is an empirical study where these IT needs are used to strengthen a Goal-oriented network where VOs are part of or even Long term strategic networks/breeding environments.

6 Conclusion

To conclude, the initial framework is validated and strengthened and can be used to analyze VOs. While not extensive, it provides a solid basis for observing the theme interaction and relation. The cases provided additional insights to re-group various IT needs, resulting in a revised list (Table 1) (**RQ1, RQ2**).

Our results show that IT needs can positively influence organizational characteristics. This indicates a relationship between IT needs and the characteristics examined in this study, confirming our hypothesis. However, further research is necessary to understand this relationship (**RQ3**) fully.

Disclosure of Interests. The authors have no competing interests to declare relevant to this article's content.

References

1. Coase, R.H.: The nature of the firm. Economica **4**, 386–405 (1937)
2. Camarinha-Matos, L.M., Afsarmanesh, H.: Collaborative networks: a new scientific discipline. J. Intell. Manuf. **16**, 439–452 (2005)
3. Camarinha-Matos, L.M., Afsarmanesh, H.: Collaborative networks: Reference modeling. Springer, New York (2008)
4. Camarinha-Matos, L.M., Fornasiero, R., Afsarmanesh, H.: Collaborative networks as a core enabler of industry 4.0. In: Camarinha-Matos, L., Afsarmanesh, H., Fornasiero, R. (eds.) Collaboration in a Data-Rich World. PRO-VE 2017. IFIP Advances in Information and Communication Technology, vol. 506, pp. 3–17. Springer, Cham (2017). https://doi.org/10.1007/978-3-319-65151-4_1
5. Arrais-Castro, A., Varela, M.L.R., Putnik, G.D., Ribeiro, R.A., Machado, J., Ferreira, L.: Collaborative framework for virtual organisation synthesis based on a dynamic multi-criteria decision model. Int. J. Comput. Integr. Manuf. **31**, 857–868 (2018)
6. Lopez, C.-P., Aguilar, J., Santorum, M.: Autonomous VOs management based on industry 4.0: a systematic literature review. J. Intell. Manuf. **34**, 1275–1291 (2021)
7. Van Den Heuvel, R., Van De Wetering, R., Bos, R., Trienekens, J.: Identification of IT-needs to cope with dynamism in collaborative networked organizations—a case study. In: Agrifoglio, R., Lamboglia, R., Mancini, D., Ricciardi, F. (eds.) Digital Business Transformation, pp. 219–236. Springer, Cham (2020)
8. van den Heuvel, R., van de Wetering, R., Kruidhof, O., Bos, R., Trienekens, J.: How distributed ledger technology can influence trust improving data sharing in collaborative networks. In: Ceci, F., Prencipe, A., Spagnoletti, P. (eds.) Exploring Innovation in a Digital World. LNISO, vol. 51, pp. 62–76. Springer, Cham (2021). https://doi.org/10.1007/978-3-030-87842-9_6
9. Lasi, H., Fettke, P., Kemper, H.-G., Feld, T., Hoffmann, M.: Industry 4.0. Bus. Inf. Syst. Eng. **6**, 239–242 (2014)
10. Han, J., Zhou, H., Lowik, S., De Weerd-Nederhof, P.: Enhancing the understanding of ecosystems under innovation management context: aggregating conceptual boundaries of ecosystems. Ind. Mark. Manage. **106**, 112–138 (2022)

11. van den Heuvel, R., Trienekens, J., van de Wetering, R., Bos, R.: Toward CNO characteristics to support business/IT-alignment. In: Camarinha-Matos, L., Afsarmanesh, H., Fornasiero, R. (eds.) Collaboration in a Data-Rich World. PRO-VE 2017. IFIP Advances in Information and Communication Technology, vol. 506, pp. 455–465. Springer, Cham (2017). https://doi.org/10.1007/978-3-319-65151-4_41
12. Grefen, P., Mehandjiev, N., Kouvas, G., Weichhart, G., Eshuis, R.: Dynamic business network process management in instant virtual enterprises. Comput. Ind. **60**, 86–103 (2009)
13. Xu, L.D., Xu, E.L., Li, L.: Industry 4.0: state of the art and future trends. Int. J. Prod. Res. **56**, 2941–2962 (2018)
14. Cheikhrouhou, N., Pouly, M., Madinabeitia, G.: Trust categories and their impacts on information exchange processes in vertical collaborative networked organisations. Int. J. Comput. Integr. Manuf. **26**, 87–100 (2013)
15. Msanjila, S.S., Afsarmanesh, H.: FETR: a framework to establish trust relationships among organizations in VBEs. J. Intell. Manuf. **21**, 251–265 (2010)
16. Schwab, K.: The fourth industrial revolution. World Economic Forum, Cologny/Geneva (2017)
17. Granstrand, O., Holgersson, M.: Innovation ecosystems: a conceptual review and a new definition. Technovation **90–91**, 102098 (2020)
18. Camarinha-Matos, L.M., Afsarmanesh, H.: Taxonomy of collaborative networks forms: FInES Task Force on Collaborative Networks and SOCOLNET - Society of Collaborative Networks, Roots and Wings, European Commission (2012)
19. Acharya, A.S., Prakash, A., Saxena, P., Nigam, A.: Sampling: why and how of it. Indian J. Med. Spec. **4**, 330–333 (2013)
20. Saunders, M., Lewis, P., Thornhill, A.: Research Methods for Business Students. 7th ed. Pearson Education Limited, Harlow (2016)
21. Tansey, O.: Process tracing and elite interviewing: a case for non-probability sampling. Polit. Sci. Polit. **40**, 765–772 (2007)
22. Boudreau, M.-C., Gefen, D., Straub, D.W.: Validation in information systems research: a state-of-the-art assessment. MIS Q. 1–16 (2001)
23. Luftman, J.: Assessing business-IT alignment maturity. Commun. Assoc. Inf. Syst. **4**, 99–128 (2000)
24. Dyer, L., Ericksen, J.: Complexity-Based Agile Enterprises: Putting Self-Organizing Emergence to Work. Sage, London (2009)
25. Doty, D.H., Glick, W.H., Huber, G.P.: Fit, equifinality, and organizational effectiveness: a test of two configurational theories. Acad. Manag. J. **36**, 1196–1250 (1993)

Healthcare, Social Well-Being, and Ethics

Technology for Social Connectedness: A Case Study in Academic Communal Spaces

Gul Sher Ali(✉), Michail Giannakos, and Sobah Abbas Petersen

Department of Computer Science, NTNU, Trondheim, Norway
{gulsher.ali,michailg,sobah.a.petersen}@ntnu.no

Abstract. Students in the early stages of their studies are prone to isolation. This case study focuses on doctoral students and empirically investigates the potential of Information and Communication Technologies in academic communal spaces to enhance social connectedness. To do so, we conducted a qualitative exploratory study that employed semi-structured interviews. In particular, we interviewed 7 doctoral students and asked them about their understanding and perceptions of integrating technologies in communal spaces. We utilized brochures of fictional technologies and worksheets to probe and elucidate students' insights on social connectedness. The coding of the interview corpus suggested that technologies can significantly foster social connectedness by facilitating traditional socializing practices in the academic communal spaces. Additionally, data highlighted the preference for technologies that facilitate student collaboration in addressing academic and practical challenges while emphasizing the importance of incorporating privacy measures to foster positive interactions. This study contextualized the framework of social connectedness by operationalizing its dimensions—belongingness, social appraisal, and relationship salience. The implications of this research extend to educational policymakers, and technology developers, indicating that integrating technologies in communal areas mitigate feelings of isolation among doctoral students and develop inclusive communities.

Keywords: Academic Communal Spaces · Social Connectedness · Information and Communication Technologies (ICT)

1 Introduction

The increasing prevalence of mental health issues among students presents a significant challenge for the higher education sector [1, 2]. Especially, the mental health and wellbeing of doctoral students is exacerbated by many stressors, but lack of social connectedness is identified as one of the key contributors because of the nature of work [3, 4]. For instance, they find themselves in a unique position where they're not considered full students which limits their access to certain resources. They are also required to work independently, which adds to their sense of isolation. This study examines the impact of Information and Communication Technologies (ICT) such as interactive digital boards, real-time feedback systems, and specialized social networking platforms designed for

Published by Springer Nature Switzerland AG 2024
R. van de Wetering et al. (Eds.): I3E 2024, LNCS 14907, pp. 331–343, 2024.
https://doi.org/10.1007/978-3-031-72234-9_28

academic communities. These tools are pivotal in enhancing social connectedness by supporting both face-to-face and digital interactions within academic settings.

Social connectedness encompasses multiple dimensions including belonging, social appraisal, and relationship salience, which together foster a sense of community and ongoing interaction [5, 6]. Previously, studies have explored the role of technology in facilitating social connectedness in various contexts and environments [7, 8]. Communal space is an environment which enables socialization [9]. The studies posited that face to face and digital social support within these communal spaces further enhance social connectedness [9–11]. Similarly, Berger, et al. found that different social control media technologies affected social connectedness in shared spaces [12]. Additionally, Yuan studies how technology supports social connectedness during remote shared activities [13]. However, most of this research resulted in technological interventions which are not applicable in communal spaces of academic settings for doctoral students. These students experience significant life changes, such as relocating from their homes and leaving behind their existing support networks.

Although previous studies highlighted the role of individual use of technology in fostering connections, they tend to isolate the user from their immediate physical environment. Our study contributes by contextualized the existing framework of social connectedness [5] i.e., by replacing mobile phone usage with communal technologies in academic settings. We propose a shift towards integrating technology as foundational elements within academic communal spaces, rather than merely as individual tools (see Fig. 1). This approach enabled us to explore how communal technologies can enhance social connections in ways that personal devices alone may not fully achieve. To better understand if and how ICT can influence social connectedness in communal spaces, we conducted a qualitative exploratory research study in the Norwegian context. In particular, we interviewed seven first year doctoral students leveraging questionable concepts and fictional design [14–16], as a means to understand ICT's role in their social connectedness. The findings of this study give insights into technological development and integration into communal spaces to complement the existing practices like socializing and sharing. This study tackles the following research question:

RQ - How can ICT in communal spaces affect social connectedness among first year doctoral students?

The rest of this article reviews existing literature on technologies for enhancing social connectedness and outlines the conceptual framework that is utilized in analyzing the data. This is succeeded by a description of the research methods. Subsequently, the findings are disclosed followed by discussion. The study concludes with limitations and future research work.

2 Background

2.1 ICT for Social Connectedness

The use of ICT to enhance social connectedness has been extensively studied across various populations. The studies highlight the potential of technology to alleviate isolation and improve social integration [5, 13, 14]. The research focusing on students shows that digital platforms can facilitate new friendships, cultural adjustment, and integration into university life [1, 17]. These technologies often serve as crucial touchpoints for students navigating the complexities of new academic and social environments. Similarly, studies by Yuan [13] and Thomas et al. [14] demonstrated that technology mediated activities could support social connectedness by allowing for shared experiences and interactions despite physical distances. However, these studies predominantly focus on the individual use of digital technologies, such as social media and mobile apps, with less emphasis on their integration into communal academic settings. Communal technologies are defined as digital tools and platforms that facilitate shared interactions and community engagement within specific spaces, such as academic settings. These technologies are designed to support collective activities, enhance communication, and strengthen social bonds among users by enabling more interactive and collaborative experiences [7, 12]. For instance, communal technologies may include systems like interactive boards, digital forums, and real-time feedback mechanisms that are embedded within educational environments to promote a sense of community and academic collaboration [8]. Our study addresses the identified gap in the literature by exploring the integration of ICT, details in Table 1, not just as individual tools but as embedded elements within academic communal space for a collective sense of belonging and support. The existing literature often treats social connectedness as a uniform concept [5, 17], failing to account for its multidimensional nature that encompasses belonging, social appraisal, and relationship salience. This view limits the scope of understanding the diverse ways through which ICT can impact these distinct aspects of social connectedness among doctoral students. While Berger et al. [12] explored the impact of shared media technologies on each dimension of social connectedness, our work extends this by examining how the technologies in communal academic settings influence each construct of the social connectedness.

Moreover, our research highlights the nuanced balance between digital and physical interactions. Prior research often treats these as separate or competing forms of interaction, whereas our study demonstrates that effective integration of ICT can complement and enhance face-to-face interactions, enriching students' academic and social experiences [9, 12]. This is particularly important given the distinct challenges doctoral students face, who may benefit significantly from enhanced social presence facilitated through tailored communal technologies. The need for future research arises from the evolving nature of digital technologies and their integration into educational settings. Our study contributes new insights into the use of communal ICT in fostering social connectedness but also underscores the dynamic interactions between technology, academic environments, and student's social well-being. This discourse not only broadens the understanding of how digital tools can support doctoral students but also offers practical implications for the design of these technologies to better meet their specific needs and challenges.

2.2 Social Connectedness: The Framework and Benefits

Social connectedness refers to the feeling of having close ties with individuals or groups. This is a multi-dimensional concept, which encompasses the sense of being part of a community (belonging), social appraisal ("how an agent assesses inferences drawn from the behavior of others"), and relationship salience ("experiences such as the sense of being in touch and of continuing presence despite absence"), see [5, 6, 11] for more explanation. Therefore, enhancing social connectedness can significantly boost emotional well-being and lessen feelings of loneliness, which can potentially lower depression rates [18]. Furthermore, connections with the community lead to numerous integration benefits like learning the language, understanding culture, establishing identity, and participating socially and economically [5]. This study contextualized the framework of social connectedness by replacing mobile usage with the concept of communal technologies, thereby enriching our understanding of how technology shapes social dynamics in academic settings.

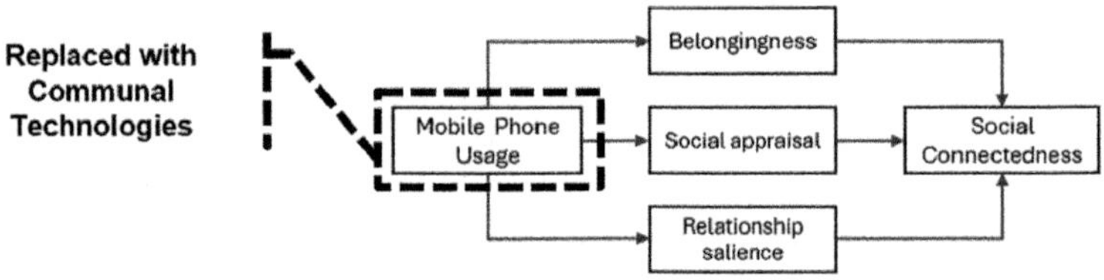

Fig. 1. Contextualization of Social Connectedness Framework [5] in Communal Technologies

3 Methodology

3.1 Participants

This case study is grounded in an interpretivist research paradigm and utilizes qualitative research methodology. These strategies enabled an in-depth exploration of the use of fictional technology [14–16] in communal areas for social connectedness among specific participants. The participants of the study were 7 first-year international doctoral students (4 Females, 3 Males) from one of the universities of Norway. These individuals were targeted due to their unique position within academia i.e., they experience a significant transition that affects their sense of social connectedness. The recruitment process for the study utilized convenience sampling where participants were approached through messages being distributed in email groups. This method ensured that participants were readily accessible and directly relevant to the study's focus on social connectedness in communal academic settings. The participants were required to give their consent for recording before the interview by reading and signing a consent form.

3.2 Data Collection

The data were gathered through semi-structured interviews. The interview commenced with initial questions to get information about the participants' background. This included questions about their tenure and experiences as international doctoral students. (How long have you been here in this community?, Is it your first time being out of your home country?, Is there any specific place in campus or department where you visit often to have some social interaction?, When or why do you visit them?). Following this preliminary discussion, participants were asked questions to talk about their current feeling of social connectedness (see [6, 11] for detailed scale). Afterward, they were provided with one brochure of questionable concepts at a time and technology in that brochure was meant to foster each dimension of social connectedness (see Table 1). This was followed by the questions regarding the integration of these technologies in communal spaces (How do these technologies change your sense of community if they were already in communal spaces?, How could you use these technologies if they are deployed in those areas now? Any usage scenario?, How might these new technologies affect the experiences of new students? Any concerns or implications in general you think these technologies would raise?). The participants were presented with 9 brochures of "questionable concepts"– speculative design artifacts depicting fictional technologies [14–16], that could be integrated into communal spaces to enhance collective social connectedness. The questionable concepts (see Table 1) were designed by 3 researchers (each with a background in civil and environmental engineering, medical science, and information technology respectively) in a brainstorming session by following the study of Thomas, et al. [14].

The brochures on technologies served as prompts for answers and allowed participants to reflect or critique the proposed technologies. This method is chosen for its ability to enable participants to express their thoughts and feelings about the technologies and their potential impact on social connectedness. The analysis of data followed the theoretical framework illustrated in Fig. 1 The interviews were recorded and conducted in English. Additionally, participants were given worksheets (adopted from the study of Irina et al. [16]) to post their "preferable technology" and provide their reflections on it. The study was conducted in accordance with the rules set by the ethics committee and had the necessary approval.

3.3 Data Analysis

We employed thematic analysis using an inductive approach [19] to gain insights from the data collected through the interviews and worksheets. This approach enabled us to organize broad patterns into a coherent narrative aligned with our research question. We began by thoroughly reading all interview transcripts and worksheet responses to immerse ourselves in the data and record initial ideas. We systematically coded the transcribed data, and this process was facilitated by NVIVO (a qualitative data analysis software). The initial codes were generated by identifying significant patterns and repetitions of concepts, statements, and phrases. Following the initial coding, we engaged in an iterative process of reviewing and reorganizing these codes. The codes were adjusted or merged to more accurately capture the underlying patterns and insights which lead to the development of comprehensive themes. This iterative coding ensured that the codes and subsequent themes were a true reflection of the data, rather than being constrained by any pre-existing theoretical frameworks. The themes are then contextualized in the components of social connectedness framework (see Table 2 for details). The subsequent themes reflected key aspects of social connectedness and the utilization of ICT in communal spaces along with the reservations of participants regarding integration of technologies. Meanwhile, the perceptions on preferred communal technologies and

Table 1. Synopsis of Questionable Concepts of Technologies

Belongingness	Social Appraisal	Relationship Salience
Community Mosaic Screen A digital installation in common areas where students can upload images or texts that represent their identity, interests, or achievements, creating a collective mosaic that evolves over time	***Interactive Feedback*** Stations equipped with tablets for students to leave and view feedback on projects or events, encouraging constructive discussions and improvements	***Know Your Community*** This tool foster connections through interactive quizzes about hobbies, interests, and fun facts. It encourages students to discover commonalities and traits, making it easier to enhance social life
Achievement Gamification Screens in communal spaces showcasing achievements fostering an environment of appreciation. A system where academic and social contributions earn points, badges, and rewards, visible to the community	***Challenges Board*** A platform with interactive easy to use interface for posting multiple challenges that one came across and the platform encouraged collective problem-solving by seeking help from others	***Shared Interest Discovery*** An app that matches students based on shared interests, facilitating connections, and encouraging them to meet in designated communal spaces for discussions or activities
Achievement Celebrator A mobile application that highlights and notifies achievements, encourages group celebrations, and fosters a shared sense of accomplishment and community spirit	***Wellbeing Kiosks*** Kiosks that allow students to anonymously share their wellbeing status, which is then aggregated and displayed as a communal wellbeing metric	***Memory Table/ Screen*** A digital Interactive Table or Screen in communal areas that periodically showcases photos, videos, and stories of past student, creating a sense of belonging to a larger community history

potential issues are analyzed from the information provided by the participants on the worksheets [16].

Table 2. Codes to Themes to Social Connectedness Framework Contextualization

Themes	Codes	Contextualized
Sense of Community through Interaction	interaction in communal spaces, visibility of achievements, feedback mechanisms, shared experiences, engagement with digital tools, peer recognition	Belongingness & Relationship Salience

(continued)

Table 2. (*continued*)

Themes	Codes	Contextualized
Academic Integration for Personal Growth	academic collaboration, gamification impacts, personal growth, support networks, access to resources, peer recognition	Social Appraisal
Privacy Concerns with Communal Technologies	privacy concerns, digital exposure, sense of support, anonymity in feedback, frequency of use, ease of use	Relationship Salience
Technologies Complementing Physical Interaction	physical vs. digital interaction, facilitation of face-to-face meetings, cultural integration, stress relief, technology adoption, ease of use	Belongingness

4 Results

The thematic analysis of the interview transcripts resulted in four key themes. These themes illustrate the multifaceted impact of technological integration in communal spaces for social connectedness.

4.1 Sense of Community Through Interaction – Theme A

This theme captures how communal technologies can foster a sense of belonging among doctoral students by facilitating interactions and making individual achievements visible to the community. The students highlighted that, technologies like "community mosaic screens" and "achievement celebration apps" help them feel more connected by showcasing their interests and accomplishments in shared spaces. These technologies not only provide a platform for students to share their personal achievements and interests but also create opportunities for spontaneous interactions.

The students noted that seeing their peers' contributions displayed in communal areas encouraged them to engage more with the community and break the isolation often felt in academic settings. For instance, one participant pointed out the potential of communal technologies: *"[...] the technologies in these spaces will help me know the people and that's how I relate mostly with the people around me because once you know the interest of somebody, I think it will have increased my relationship with them"* (P3).

The introduction of communal technologies like mosaic screens and achievement celebration apps has been highlighted as pivotal in cultivating a sense of belonging: "*[...] it would be different because now when I work, I just go to my office and then work there and go home. I don't go to a common space. But if there was something more communal like this was like screen then I feel like probably I would go there more often"* (P4).

One of the participants, reflecting on an achievement celebration app's impact: "*For the app, I think that could be interesting to see your notification. So what people are doing and then having it on you. So, then you would feel a bigger sense of community because you would have information on your phone or on the screens within the public spaces"* (P1).

Similarly, tools in communal spaces are credited with deepening connections among peers. For example: "*I think get to know your community quiz could be very interesting because you get to know people on a more personal level"* (P2).

Likewise, a participant expressed: "*wellbeing Pulse Check Kiosks offers a discreet way for us to express our current state of wellbeing, [...] place where I can anonymously share how I'm feeling and see a collective mood of my community makes me feel more connected and supported. It's like having a silent communal dialogue without having to say a word"* (P6).

Therefore, the visibility of shared interests and achievements by introducing technologies into shared spaces as well as keeping anonymity where required helps the individuals feel more connected to each other.

4.2 Academic Integration for Personal Growth – Theme B

This theme reflects how integrating technologies into academic communal spaces can enhance both personal and professional growth among doctoral students. The students discussed how gamified activities and challenge boards not only motivate them to engage in academic tasks but also foster collaboration and mutual support. These tools make academic tasks more engaging because of the elements of competition and reward. This helps students build professional skills through peer interaction and feedback.

The dual approach of competition and collaboration helps students feel more integrated into the academic community. A participant mentioned: "*not feeling on the same level when it comes to knowing stuff but when someone appreciates you, you feel encouraged and try to further enhance your capabilities"* (P5).

The gamification of communal activities introduces a novel way of social appraisal, connecting competition with collaboration, thereby enriching the communal academic integration. One participant remarked on the dual nature of gamified interaction: "*The gamification personally I think would be rewarding... But I know also that a con could be that people would get competitive"* (P4).

This reflects the motivational yet potentially divisive nature of gamification. Another participant while discussing challenge boards shared: "*I think there could be interesting because, in a sense that you could give a lot more feedback and also seek help from others than what we currently have, and this will initiate social connections"* (P6).

This emphasizes the challenge board's role in fostering a collaborative environment where peers can offer support and advice and result in more social connections.

4.3 Privacy Concerns with Communal Technologies – Theme C

This theme addresses the apprehensions doctoral students have regarding the privacy implications of using communal technologies. The students see the potential benefits of sharing information and achievements, but they are also cautious of the extent of personal data exposure. They expressed significant concerns about privacy when discussing the integration of ICT in communal spaces. The students prefer a secure environment where they can control what is shared and maintain anonymity when needed.

The balance between visibility for social connectedness and privacy protection emerged as a critical factor in the design of these technologies. One participant expressed reservations about communal mosaic screens: *"[...] I guess there would be privacy concerns that you wouldn't always want to show what you're doing. So I wouldn't think it would be a big concern, but definitely something to think about"* (P1).

Additionally, one of the participants on reflecting on achievement celebration apps noted: *"I'm thinking of doing less time with our screens [...] but I think it's a nice concept"* (P6).

While the concept is appreciated, there's underlying concern about the digital exposure of personal achievements and its effects on individuals' privacy and screen time. Thus, ensuring a secure environment where personal information is protected will be crucial in harnessing the full potential of these technologies to enhance social connectedness without compromising individual privacy.

4.4 Technologies Complementing Physical Interaction – Theme D

This theme highlights the preference for technologies that enhance rather than replace physical interactions. The students stressed the importance that technologies introduced in communal spaces should enhance physical interactions rather than replace them. The fictional technologies that are designed to bring students together for face-to-face meetings and activities were particularly valued during the interview.

There was a consensus that digital platforms should serve as a bridge to facilitate real-world interactions, a participant mentioned: *"It's important that these technologies do not replace physical meetings but encourage more of them... Like the community mosaic screen should make me want to meet people in real life, not just online"* (P2).

Another participant talking on the importance of physical gatherings shared: *"I think it's crucial that whatever technology we use, it ends up bringing us together in the real world... Maybe having a screen that shows when and where we can meet up for group activities"* (P5).

This illustrates the desire for technologies that not only connect individuals digitally but also facilitate opportunities for in-person interactions.

5 Discussion

This study contributes to the understanding that how communal technologies can serve as disruptive innovations in academic settings to enhance social connectedness among doctoral students. This study not only contributes theoretically by expanding our understanding of how digital tools can reshape social structures but also provides insights for leveraging technology to foster genuine community engagement in educational environments. Additionally, it highlighted the expectations of students and potential issues that technologies bring along. Such innovations are crucial for addressing current challenges in academic social integration and setting the stage for future advancements. Our findings reinforces the work by Brignull et al. [9] and Berger et al. [12], who explored shared interactive surfaces and social control media technologies in communal spaces. This study also addresses the previous uniform treatments of social connectedness by operationalizing the dimensions of social connectedness—belongingness, social appraisal, and relationship salience—within academic settings [5, 11].

5.1 Belongingness

The sense of belonging among doctoral students is essential for their academic and social integration. In our findings, the "Theme A" illustrates the role of communal technologies, such as mosaic screens and achievement celebration apps, in fostering a sense of belonging. The visibility of shared interests and achievements through these technologies encourages students to share their experiences and achievements which turns solitary routines into opportunities for social engagement. Additionally, the "Theme D" supports belongingness by emphasizing opportunities for face-to-face meetings and activities by reinforcing the physical presence and connections that are essential for feeling part of a community. These insights align with the work of Brignull et al. [9] and Berger et al. [12], who found that shared interactive surfaces and social control media technologies affect social connectedness in communal spaces. This directly answers our research question by demonstrating how technology can enhance the dimension of belongingness in academic communal spaces.

5.2 Social Appraisal

Social appraisal is crucial in academic settings where feedback and collaboration are key to personal and professional development. The "Theme B" emphasized that the introduction of gamified communal activities is seen to intertwine competition with collaboration and enrich communal academic integration. These technologies can initiate social connections by providing a platform for feedback and assistance among peers. This echo the findings of Yuan [13] on the support of social connectedness through technology mediated activities. However, addressing the competitive aspects of such technologies is essential to ensure they contribute positively to social appraisal without detracting from the sense of community. This addresses the aspect of our research question and highlights how ICT can support social appraisal among students.

5.3 Relationship Salience

The relationship salience is critical in the context of doctoral students who often undergo significant life transitions. The "Themes A" in findings illustrates that technologies could enhance relationship salience by facilitating a silent communal dialogue. These findings suggest that technology can serve as a medium for continuous presence by providing support and fostering a caring community environment even in the absence of physical interactions. Similarly, the "Theme C" highlights the importance of maintaining a sense of trust and security for fostering ongoing relationships and ensuring students feel comfortable sharing and interacting within communal spaces. This is in line with the work of Lee et al. [6], who emphasized the importance of belongingness and social assurance in measuring social connectedness. This finding addresses our research question by illustrating how technology can serve as a medium for continuous presence and support even in the absence of physical interactions.

5.4 Balancing Privacy and Interaction

In addition to the themes addressing each construct of the social connectedness framework, the "Themes C and D" in the findings underscored the potential concerns of participants. These themes emphasized that technology should facilitate traditional socializing practices for social connectedness while addressing challenges such as privacy concerns and the balance between digital and physical interactions. Privacy always remains a concern while using technology and our data endorsed the prior studies highlighting this issue such as the work of Lisa et al. [14]. Thus, this study adds to the body of knowledge by providing insights that design and implementation of such technologies should consider the balance between digital connectedness and direct social interactions while preserving privacy.

5.5 Limitations

The research focused on a small, homogeneous sample of first-year doctoral students at a single institution which may limit the generalizability of the findings. The small size of the population for study precluded the use of quantitative questionnaire of social connectedness. Therefore, future research should extend this work to diverse academic populations and environments. The mixed methods approach should be used to explore the long-term effects of these integrations, and potential disparities in technology access.

6 Conclusion and Future Work

This case study highlights the significant impact of disruptive technologies in fostering social connectedness within academic communal spaces by providing channels for shared experiences and individual expression. Our research contextualized the framework of social connectedness through the introduction of communal technologies within academic environments. The study also recognizes the need to address privacy issues and strike a balance between digital and physical interactions. Therefore, effective implementation requires careful consideration of privacy and the balance between digital and physical interactions. This is a preliminary study, and our future research aims to conduct large-scale studies by using mix methods across varied urban spaces and diverse populations. The artefacts that prioritize privacy and encourage physical interactions will be designed, deployed, and validated based on empirical data. Additionally, the social connectedness framework will be revised in the context of academic spaces for social wellbeing considering the concerns raised by the students. The current findings provide insights for future research and practical applications in educational technology design that can mitigate feelings of isolation among doctoral students and support the creation of more inclusive academic communities.

Acknowledgments. We thank the researchers for their contributions to developing the 'questionable concepts'. This research has been funded by the SWELL project (https://www.ntnu.edu/sustainability/swell) and NTNU strategic area Sustainability (https://www.ntnu.edu/sustainability).

References

1. Yacoby, Y., Girash, J., Parkes, D.C.: Empowering first-year computer science Ph.D. students to create a culture that values community and mental health. In: Proceedings of the 54th ACM Technical Symposium on Computer Science Education, vol. 1, pp. 694–700. ACM, Toronto (2023)
2. Jackman, P.C., Jacobs, L., Hawkins, R.M., Sisson, K.: Mental health and psychological well-being in the early stages of doctoral study: a systematic review. Eur. J. High. Educ. **12**(3), 293–313 (2022)
3. Blanchard, C.A., et al.: Print ('Good Luck!'): measuring the effect of autogenerated social encouragement on student anxiety. In: Extended Abstracts of the 2018 CHI Conference on Human Factors in Computing Systems, Montreal, QC, Canada, pp. 1–6 (2018)
4. Satinsky, E.N., et al.: Systematic review and meta-analysis of depression, anxiety, and suicidal ideation among Ph.D. students. Sci. Rep. **11**(1), 14370 (2021)
5. Vuningoma, S., Lorini, M.R., Chigona, W.: How refugees in South Africa use mobile phones for social connectedness. In: C&T 2021: Proceedings of the 10th International Conference on Communities & Technologies - Wicked Problems in the Age of Tech, Seattle, WA, USA, pp. 128–137 (2021)
6. Lee, R.M., Robbins, S.B.: Measuring belongingness: the social connectedness and the Social Assurance scales. J. Couns. Psychol. **42**(2), 232–241 (1995)
7. Makkonen, J., Latikka, R., Kaukonen, L., Laine, M., Väänänen, K.: Advancing residents' use of shared spaces in Nordic superblocks with intelligent technologies. AI Soc. **38**(3), 1167–1184 (2023)
8. Ewen, C., Warner, E., Andrews, F.J.: Communal spaces in apartment complexes in Melbourne, Australia: designs to foster social connectedness. Cities Health. **7**(3), 363–377 (2023)
9. Brignull, H., Izadi, S., Fitzpatrick, G., Rogers, Y., Rodden, T.: The introduction of a shared interactive surface into a communal space. In: Proceedings of the 2004 ACM Conference on Computer Supported Cooperative Work, pp. 49–58. ACM, Chicago (2004)
10. Lewandowski, J., Rosenberg, B.D., Parks, M.J., Siegel, J.T.: The effect of informal social support: face-to-face versus computer-mediated communication. Comput. Hum. Behav. **27**(5), 1806–1814 (2011)
11. Van Bel, D.T., Smolders, K.C., IJsselsteijn, W.A., De Kort, Y.A.W.: Social connectedness: concept and measurement. In: Intelligent Environments, pp. 67–74. IOS Press (2009)
12. Berger, M., Barati, B., Pfleging, B. and Bernhaupt, R.: Design for social control of shared media: a comparative study of five concepts. In: Nordic Human-Computer Interaction Conference, pp. 1–13. ACM, Aarhus (2022)
13. Yuan, Y.: Support social connectedness through technology-mediated shared activities. In: Companion Publication of the 2021 Conference on Computer Supported Cooperative Work and Social Computing, pp. 307–309. ACM, Virtual Event (2021)
14. Thomas, L., Vines, J., Briggs, P.: Exploring digital support for the student transition to university through questionable concepts. Pers. Ubiquit. Comput. **26**(1), 79–92 (2022)
15. Vines, J., Blythe, M., Lindsay, S., Dunphy, P., Monk, A., Olivier, P.: Questionable concepts: critique as resource for designing with eighty somethings. In: Proceedings of the SIGCHI Conference on Human Factors in Computing Systems, pp. 1169–1178. ACM, Austin (2012)

16. Paraschivoiu, I., Dziabiola, M. and Meschtscherjakov, A.: Postcards from the future: speculating the future of built environments with citizens. In: The 11th International Conference on Communities and Technologies (C&T), pp. 215–226. ACM, Lahti (2023)
17. Wheele, T., Lindkvist, C., Weber, C., Windlinger, L., Haugen, T.: Studying the influence of technology on the social connectedness of students: a hybrid university learning environment (HULE). IOP Conf. Ser.: Earth Environ. Sci. **1176**(1), 012009 (2023)
18. Cena, E., Burns, S., Wilson, P.: Sense of belonging and the intercultural and academic experiences among international students at a University in Northern Ireland. J. Int. Stud. **11**(4), 812–831 (2021)
19. Braun, V., Clarke, V.: Using thematic analysis in psychology. Qual. Res. Psychol. **3**(2), 77–101 (2006)

Stressors of Sleep Tracking: Instrument Development and Validation

Shan Feng and Matti Mäntymäki(✉)

Turku School of Economics, University of Turku, 20014 Turku, Finland
matti.mantymaki@utu.fi

Abstract. The adverse effects of sleep tracking have attracted interest in both practice and research. However, there is limited quantitative research measuring the relationship between the stressors of sleep tracking and its adverse outcomes, such as health anxiety. This paper develops and tests a measurement instrument for stressors related to sleep tracking. We introduce and validate three new stressor constructs: data-perception discrepancy, the pursuit of perfect data, and vague guidance, and four stressors adapted from prior literature: complexity, invasion, inaccuracy, and unreliability. We test our instrument with data from 324 sleep-tracking users. The results show that invasion, unreliability, pursuit of perfect data, and vague guidance have positive effects on health anxiety.

Keywords: Sleep Tracking · Stressors · Health Anxiety · Scale Development · Q-sort

1 Introduction

Scholarly research and popular media alike feature vivid discussions on the detrimental consequences of poor sleep on physical and mental health [1]. The emergence of sleep-tracking technology helps people obtain information about their sleep cost-effectively in their everyday environments [2]. The global market size for sleep technology devices is estimated to grow from $21.2 billion to $113.16 billion between 2023 and 2033, with the wearable segment holding the largest share at 76% [3].

Sleep tracking refers to the practice of using technological tools to monitor, record, and measure an individual's sleep [4]. Prior research highlighted the positive effects of sleep tracking, such as identifying factors affecting sleep quality [5], increasing sleep health awareness [6, 7], and adjusting sleep behavior [6, 8]. However, current sleep-tracking technology does not automatically meet users' expectations in improving sleep health [9]. Prior research has discussed a range of adverse effects of sleep tracking, including technostress [5, 10], compulsive behavior for constant availability of data [5], orthosomnia due to the pursuit of achieving perfect sleep [11], and dysfunctional behavioral adaptations due to inaccuracy or misleading data and feedback [2]. Considering the interplay between sleep and adverse outcomes such as stress [12] and anxiety [13], the adverse effects of sleep-tracking technology should not be overlooked.

Published by Springer Nature Switzerland AG 2024
R. van de Wetering et al. (Eds.): I3E 2024, LNCS 14907, pp. 344–357, 2024.
https://doi.org/10.1007/978-3-031-72234-9_29

Prior research also found that, in some cases, the use of self-tracking technology may lead to health anxiety [14], which is a ubiquitous experience that arises when bodily sensations or changes are believed to indicate a serious disease [15]. Individuals with health anxiety then exhibit higher levels of threat anticipation and are more sensitive and reactive to bodily changes [14]. Similarly, in sleep-tracking technology, individuals with health anxiety are more likely to be adversely affected when receiving health data from sleep-tracking technology. However, health anxiety in the context of sleep tracking has received little attention. There is a need to explore the antecedents that lead to health anxiety in this context.

Technostress is one common adverse effect of the digitization of the individual [16]. Despite its importance in explaining the unfavorable outcomes of sleep tracking, little effort has been made to investigate the stress caused by such technology [e.g., 5, 10], even when extended to self-tracking technology [e.g., 17, 18]. Understanding the adverse effects of stressors on users' emotions, cognition, and behavior is crucial for mitigating potential downsides of self-tracking technology and maximizing their benefits. Moreover, there is no consensus on stress related to using self-tracking technology. Prior research has identified technostress from sleep-tracking technology [10] and persuasive wearable devices [17]. On the other hand, prior research has also found the opposite, with no positive effects of activity-tracking technology on technostress [18]. Further research is warranted to explore the key stressors contributing to adverse outcomes, especially in the context of sleep tracking. Prior to this, however, it is imperative to develop validated measurement scales for assessing these stressors.

Against the backdrop, this paper focuses on sleep-tracking technology and addresses the following research questions: RQ1. What are valid measurement scales for stressors of sleep tracking? RQ2. What is the association between stressors of sleep tracking and health anxiety? In answering these research questions, this paper undertakes a series of Q-sort exercises to develop measurement instruments for stressors in the context of sleep-tracking wearable devices. Then, we test our research model by conducting a survey to validate the stressors and explore the relationship between stressors and health anxiety. We contribute to the body of knowledge on sleep tracking [5, 10] by providing researchers with a measurement instrument that helps quantify the impacts of sleep-tracking stressors.

2 Research Background

In the stressor-strain-outcome (SSO) framework [19], stressors are environmental stimuli or objective events perceived and interpreted by the actor as troublesome and potentially disruptive. These stressors disrupt the actor's concentration, physiology, and emotion (i.e., strain), ultimately leading to enduring behavioral or psychological consequences [19]. This SSO framework closely aligns with the research on technostress [e.g., 20, 21], as both employ a similar background based on the transactional view of stress [22, 23]. Craig Brod defined technostress as "a modern disease of adaptation caused by an inability to cope with the new computer technologies in a healthy manner [24]".

There is nascent prior research on technostress in the context of sleep tracking [10]. Prior research has explored characteristics of sleep-tracking technology that may disrupt users' concentration, physiology, and emotions [5, 10, 17, 25–27]. For example, the complexity of sleep-tracking technology may cause emotional strain due to difficulties in understanding the meaning of the data [10, 17] and its working mechanisms [10]. Additionally, unexpected technical issues may prevent users from consistently tracking data or lead to losing important data [25], which can also cause emotional strain [10, 17]. In another scenario, users often feel stressed if they continuously receive notifications during work and daily life [10] or if they need to synthesize sleep data to ensure its availability continuously [5]. Furthermore, inaccurate data from sleep tracking may underestimate or overrate sleep, potentially concealing or misdiagnosing sleep disorders [26]. This can lead to doubt [25], disappointment [10], and amplified health anxiety. Simultaneously, some users have negative attitudes toward vague guidance because it lacks relevance for highly diverse individuals [25]. The guidance is often non-informative and useless for taking action, leaving users confused about the reasons for sleep problems and unsure how to act [27].

Moreover, the characteristics of users may also distract their concentration, physiology, and emotions when they are tracking sleep [5, 10, 11, 17, 28, 29]. In a longitudinal field study, 23% of participants reported a mismatch between their experiences and the sleep metrics [5]. Users experience a disconnection between their subjective perceptions of their performance and the data they usually trust [10, 17]. This misalignment further confuses users, who struggle to determine the correct source [28, 29]. Sometimes, users who are preoccupied or sorely concerned with their sleep data may experience worsened sleep quality, known as orthosomnia [11]. Similarly, like activity-tracking technology, users may neglect their physical condition to meet fitness goals set by their activity-tracking technology, resulting in stress [30].

Given these stressors, it is clear that health anxiety is a significant outcome of technostress related to sleep-tracking technology. Prior research reported that excessive health monitoring with wearable devices may induce health anxiety in patients with atrial fibrillation [14]. Some patients with chronic heart disease noted that the self-tracking technology could both relieve their illness-related anxiety and introduce new health anxiety [31]. Health anxiety has also been observed when people seek health information on websites [e.g., 32, 33]. In conclusion, considering the purpose of sleep tracking is health and well-being, it is necessary to study the stressors of sleep tracking and explore their impact on users, such as health anxiety caused by sleep-tracking technology.

3 Research Method

Before exploring the relationship between the stressors of sleep tracking and health anxiety, measurement scales for these constructs must be prepared. However, not all measurement scales for stressors were available in prior research. Hence, we followed the three-stage Q-sorting exercise outlined by Moore and Benbasat [34] to develop new measurement scales. We recruited nine participants and conducted a two-round Q-sorting exercise on the platform Proven By Users (https://provenbyusers.com/) to categorize items based on their similarities and differences.

3.1 Item Development

The first stage of Q-sorting is item creation. We first defined the three stressors of which measurement scales needed to be developed. The data-perception discrepancy describes situations where users experience a disconnection between their subjective perceptions about their performance and the data they usually trust [17]. The pursuit of perfect data describes how sleep-tracking technology provides scores and goals for users, who may feel stressed when they actively strive to obtain higher scores [5]. Vague guidance describes a situation in which sleep-tracking technology cannot help users find exact reasons for their poor performance and how to improve it in line with the real situation [10]. Based on the semi-constructed interviews in our prior research, the authors' firsthand sleep-tracking experiences, and secondary information obtained from sleep-tracking virtual groups on social media, we developed a preliminary list of 12 items for these three stressors, specifically focusing on sleep tracking with wearable devices.

3.2 Q-sort

The second stage focused on scale development. This stage aims to evaluate the construct validity of various scales. In the first round, we recruited four participants: one sleep-tracking wearable user, two senior IS researchers, and one IS PhD candidate. They were asked to sort the listed items into groups and define each group. This approach aimed to reinforce construct validity by ensuring that the group definitions aligned with the scales' intended meanings. The hit ratios for the three constructs are shown in Table 1. The average agreement ratio from all participants is 0.792. The average Cohen's Kappa is 56.45%. Based on the results and feedback, one irrelevant item in the pursuit of perfect data was eliminated, and ambiguous items in constructs were refined.

In the second round, we recruited five new participants: one sleep-tracking wearable user, one senior IS researcher, two IS PhD candidates, and one administration staff member. We introduced the group names and definitions to them, and they then categorized the items. Finally, the hit ratios in the second round are shown in Table 1, the average agreement ratio from all participants is 0.964. The average Cohen's Kappa is 89.36%, exceeding the 65% acceptability threshold [34], thereby supporting the agreement in item categorization.

Table 1. The hit ratios in two rounds

	First round		Second round	
Target category	No. Items	Hit ratio	No. Items	Hit ratio
Data-perception discrepancy	3	1.000	3	1.00
Pursuit of perfect data	4	0.813	3	0.933
Vague guidance	5	0.650	5	0.960

3.3 Pilot Testing

The third and final stage is instrument testing. The questionnaire was developed in English. We put newly developed constructs into the overall instrument and conducted a pilot test with 63 sleep-tracking wearable users via Prolific (https://www.prolific.com/) in March 2024 to check the new constructs' internal consistency. The Cronbach's Alphas for data-perception discrepancy, pursuit of perfect data, and vague guidance are 0.910, 0.911, and 0.839, respectively. As the Cronbach's Alphas for all newly developed constructs are over 0.7, this indicates that they have good internal consistency reliability.

4 Survey Study

To finalize testing the newly developed constructs, we applied these constructs in a research model to test the association between stressors of sleep tracking and health anxiety. In this model, to ensure the reliability and validity of the construct measurements, the measurement items for complexity [35], invasion [35], inaccuracy [36], unreliability [37], and health anxiety [38] were adapted from prior well-established measurement scales and reworded for the context of sleep-tracking wearable devices. Table 2 presents the detailed construct measurement items and references. All construct measurement items were tested using a seven-point Likert scale.

Table 2. Final measurement instrument

Construct	Items	Reference
Complexity (CP)	CP1: I need a long time to understand how to use my wearable device CP2: I do not find enough time to upgrade my technology skills to use my wearable device CP3: I do not know enough about my wearable device to use it satisfactorily CP4: I often find my wearable device too complex to use	Maier et al. (2015)
Invasion (IV)	IV1: I have to pay a lot of attention to the notifications from my wearable device during the day and evenings IV2: I have to spend a lot of time checking the data provided by my wearable device IV3: I feel my personal life is being invaded by my wearable device	Maier et al. (2015)

(continued)

Table 2. (*continued*)

Construct	Items	Reference
Inaccuracy (IA)	IA1: My wearable device produces incorrect sleep-related data IA2: There are some errors in the sleep-related data from my wearable device IA3: The sleep-related data provided by my wearable device is not accurate	Wixom & Todd (2005)
Unreliability (UR)	UR1: I think that I am too often confronted with unexpected technical issues with my wearable device UR2: I think that I spent too much time trying to fix technical issues with my wearable device UR3: Technical issues with my wearable device occasionally disturb my sleep tracking UR4: I have encountered technical issues with my wearable device that have impeded my sleep tracking	Fischer et al. (2021)
Data-perception discrepancy (DPD)	DPD1: My perception regarding my sleep does not align with the data provided by my wearable device DPD2: I think the data provided by my wearable device does not match how I feel about my sleep DPD3: There is a misfit between how I feel about my sleep and the data my wearable device provides	New construct
Pursuit of perfect data (PPD)	PPD1: I try my best to get good sleep results from my wearable device PPD2: I usually put in a great effort to get good sleep results from my wearable device PPD3: I keep tracking my data to maintain good sleep results from my wearable device	New construct

(*continued*)

Table 2. (*continued*)

Construct	Items	Reference
Vague guidance (VG)	VG1: My wearable device cannot provide accurate suggestions to improve my sleep VG2: The suggestions from my wearable device are not helpful in improving my sleep VG3: The suggestions from my wearable device are not suitable for the specific situations I am facing VG4: The suggestions from my wearable device often lack the detail necessary to improve my sleep VG5: My wearable device cannot provide an explanation for the poor sleep results it gave me	New construct
Health anxiety (HA)	HA1: When receiving poor results from my wearable device, I am worried about my health HA2: When receiving poor results from my wearable device, I am aware of my bodily sensations and changes HA3: When receiving poor results from my wearable device, I am afraid that I have a serious illness HA4: When receiving poor results from my wearable device, I wonder what they mean HA5: When receiving poor results from my wearable device, I imagine myself being ill HA6: When receiving poor results from my wearable device, I feel at risk of developing an illness HA7: When receiving poor results from my wearable device, I think I might have a serious illness	Salkovskis et al. (2002)

4.1 Data Collection

Based on the feedback from the pilot study, we modified several measurement items in the questionnaire to ensure the validity and reliability of the proposed research instrument. The main study was conducted from April to May 2024 in Nordic countries and the UK via Prolific. Participants were required to be fluent in English and have an approval rate of over 90% on Prolific. A photo of their wearable device was required to confirm they are actual users. In total, 340 participants completed the questionnaire. After excluding those who do not currently use wearable devices (4 participants), withdrew consent (1 participant), and failed the attention check (11 participants), the final sample size is 324, of which 132 are male. Our sample comprised 247 participants from the UK and 77 from the Nordic countries and 62% of participants are aged between 26–46 years. Nearly 88% of participants have been using sleep-tracking wearable devices for more than six months.

4.2 Analysis and Results

We applied Harman's single-factor test to examine the risks of common method bias (CMB). Since the largest variance explained by an individual factor is only 14.62%, which is lower than the recommended 50%, this indicates minimal concern about CMB. Meanwhile, the variance inflation factor (VIF) value for all focal constructs is lower than 3.3, eliminating the multicollinearity issue in this research model.

Due to the small sample size, we applied partial least squares (PLS) and used Smart-PLS 4 to test the measurement model and structural model. First, we removed the items HA2 and HA4 because their factor loadings were lower than the minimum required 0.7 [39]. Table 3 and Table 4 show that Cronbach's α for all constructs exceeded 0.7, composite reliability (CR) exceeded 0.7, average variance extracted (AVE) exceeded 0.5, and all factor loadings exceeded 0.7. These results indicate that all constructs have internal consistency reliability, indicator reliability, and convergent validity [39, 40]. Then, we tested the discriminant validity. As shown in Table 3, the square root of the AVE for each construct is higher than their off-diagonal correlation values. Additionally, each item's factor loading on its respective construct is higher than on any other construct, as detailed in Table 4. Furthermore, the maximum value of the Heterotrait–Monotrait (HTMT) ratio of correlations is 0.718, which is below the maximum threshold of 0.9. Thus, the results support the discriminant validity of all constructs [40–42].

Finally, we tested the structural model. Before that, we evaluated the model's goodness of fit. The standardized root mean square residual (SRMR) result is 0.055, which is lower than the accepted threshold of 0.08, indicating a good fit for our model. We applied a bootstrapping algorithm to further test the structural model. As shown in Fig. 1, the model shows an explanatory power of 26.3% for health anxiety [40]. Invasion ($\beta = 0.272^{***}$), unreliability ($\beta = 0.226^{***}$), the pursuit of perfect data ($\beta = 0.240^{***}$), and vague guidance ($\beta = 0.159^{*}$) have positive effects on health anxiety. However, complexity, inaccuracy, and data-perception discrepancy have no effect on health anxiety.

Given that complexity, inaccuracy, and data-perception discrepancy have no direct effect on health anxiety, we conducted a post-hoc analysis to examine their potential indirect effect on health anxiety via invasion, unreliability, pursuit of perfect data, and vague guidance. The results indicate that invasion ($R^2 = 15.1\%$) fully mediates the effects of complexity ($\beta = 0.321^{***}$) and inaccuracy ($\beta = 0.182^{*}$) on health anxiety; Unreliability ($R^2 = 32.3\%$) fully mediates the effects of complexity ($\beta = 0.366^{***}$) and inaccuracy ($\beta = 0.193^{*}$) on health anxiety; Vague guidance ($R^2 = 37.7\%$) fully mediates

Table 3. The results of reliability and validity

	Cronbach's α	CR	AVE	CP	IV	IA	UR	DPD	PPD	VG	HA
CP	0.895	0.926	0.759	**0.871**							
IV	0.734	0.850	0.655	0.357	**0.809**						
IA	0.909	0.942	0.843	0.256	0.245	**0.918**					
UR	0.872	0.913	0.723	0.482	0.387	0.396	**0.850**				
DPD	0.950	0.966	0.906	0.411	0.218	0.659	0.443	**0.952**			
PPD	0.876	0.923	0.801	−0.060	0.176	−0.156	−0.043	−0.129	**0.895**		
VG	0.901	0.926	0.713	0.332	0.119	0.519	0.329	0.554	−0.129	**0.845**	
HA	0.934	0.950	0.794	0.211	0.396	0.110	0.329	0.126	0.273	0.177	**0.891**

Note: composite reliability (CR), average variance extracted (AVE), complexity (CP), invasion (IV), inaccuracy (IA), unreliability (UR), data-perception discrepancy (DPD), pursuit of perfect data (PPD), vague guidance (VG), health anxiety (HA)

Table 4. The factor loadings and cross-loadings matrix

	Mean	S.D	CP	IV	IA	UR	DPD	PPD	VG	HA
CP1	2.725	1.373	**0.828**	0.261	0.202	0.369	0.265	−0.023	0.252	0.154
CP2	2.546	1.449	**0.845**	0.285	0.155	0.413	0.334	−0.049	0.301	0.149
CP3	2.432	1.356	**0.891**	0.299	0.258	0.394	0.389	−0.110	0.329	0.158
CP4	2.207	1.256	**0.916**	0.371	0.259	0.482	0.416	−0.036	0.284	0.245
IV1	3.028	1.462	0.305	**0.832**	0.148	0.297	0.149	0.215	0.087	0.321
IV2	2.806	1.406	0.246	**0.851**	0.168	0.233	0.179	0.208	0.043	0.316
IV3	1.821	1.074	0.312	**0.742**	0.276	0.405	0.200	0.006	0.156	0.323
IA1	3.133	1.437	0.256	0.277	**0.945**	0.394	0.592	-0.159	0.465	0.125
IA2	3.744	1.539	0.161	0.165	**0.898**	0.311	0.575	−0.121	0.450	0.082
IA3	3.222	1.421	0.280	0.209	**0.912**	0.373	0.665	−0.146	0.527	0.083
UR1	2.019	1.199	0.457	0.324	0.358	**0.843**	0.441	−0.096	0.323	0.272
UR2	1.843	1.145	0.484	0.411	0.295	**0.871**	0.379	−0.018	0.235	0.312
UR3	2.022	1.332	0.371	0.307	0.344	**0.865**	0.342	−0.013	0.290	0.264
UR4	2.198	1.429	0.316	0.261	0.356	**0.821**	0.345	−0.023	0.277	0.265
DPD1	2.969	1.467	0.408	0.200	0.604	0.454	**0.953**	−0.108	0.513	0.153
DPD2	3.071	1.494	0.368	0.231	0.651	0.393	**0.951**	−0.131	0.522	0.094
DPD3	2.994	1.509	0.387	0.196	0.642	0.400	**0.951**	−0.139	0.555	0.094
PPD1	5.136	1.361	−0.059	0.149	−0.141	−0.053	−0.094	**0.898**	−0.078	0.233

(*continued*)

Table 4. (*continued*)

	Mean	S.D	CP	IV	IA	UR	DPD	PPD	VG	HA
PPD2	4.364	1.603	−0.012	0.204	−0.098	0.014	-0.055	**0.917**	−0.119	0.277
PPD3	5.043	1.411	−0.102	0.108	−0.194	−0.091	−0.217	**0.869**	−0.151	0.216
VG1	3.438	1.488	0.318	0.063	0.435	0.263	0.452	−0.107	**0.835**	0.123
VG2	3.466	1.348	0.322	0.085	0.481	0.330	0.496	−0.200	**0.853**	0.112
VG3	3.506	1.441	0.267	0.124	0.490	0.271	0.522	−0.142	**0.821**	0.129
VG4	3.719	1.473	0.312	0.104	0.409	0.280	0.448	−0.044	**0.892**	0.183
VG5	4.056	1.613	0.203	0.115	0.408	0.259	0.444	−0.094	**0.820**	0.171
HA1	2.778	1.331	0.145	0.317	0.068	0.241	0.050	0.295	0.114	**0.787**
HA3	1.824	1.167	0.150	0.370	0.047	0.274	0.099	0.243	0.118	**0.909**
HA5	2.022	1.221	0.190	0.340	0.116	0.284	0.150	0.229	0.191	**0.914**
HA6	2.077	1.280	0.223	0.320	0.113	0.289	0.127	0.240	0.188	**0.918**
HA7	1.722	1.169	0.229	0.409	0.140	0.365	0.132	0.213	0.173	**0.920**

Note: standard deviation (S.D.), complexity (CP), invasion (IV), inaccuracy (IA), unreliability (UR), data-perception discrepancy (DPD), pursuit of perfect data (PPD), vague guidance (VG), health anxiety (HA)

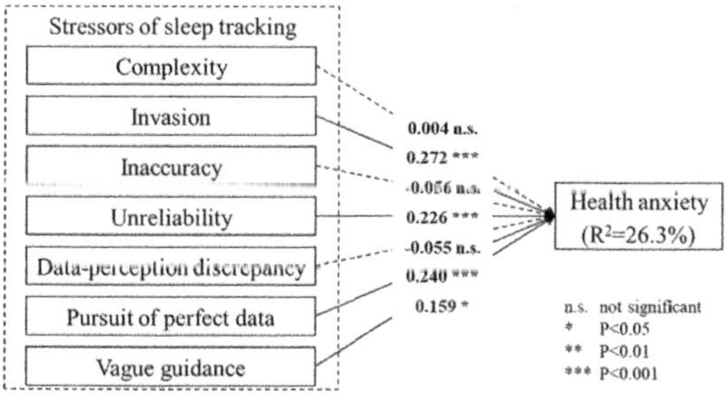

Fig. 1. Structural model results

the effects of complexity (β = 0.141**), inaccuracy (β = 0.288***), and data-perception discrepancy (β = 0.313***) on health anxiety.

5 Discussion and Conclusion

5.1 Key Findings

We highlight three specific key findings from this study. First, this study developed valid measurement scales for stressors of sleep tracking, including three new constructs and four others adapted from prior research. Although several studies have identified these stressors from interviews [5, 10, 17], our research provided valid measurement scales to scale them and applied these constructs to a research model to explore the effect on health anxiety in the context of sleep tracking.

Second, the results show that invasion, unreliability, pursuit of perfect data, and vague guidance are four important and direct sources of health anxiety when people track sleep. Sleep-tracking users are more likely to develop health anxiety when the intrusive features disrupt their daily lives. One possible explanation is that they may feel compelled to constantly "keep an eye" on their health data. This finding is consistent with previous studies showing that exposure to online health information often leads to increased health anxiety [43, 44]. Also, the unreliability of sleep tracking can impact health anxiety. The unreliable technical issues, such as display visibility or battery longevity, can lead to incomplete data and inaccurate interpretation. Our results prove that unreliable in healthcare IT is identified as one of the stressors that leads to negative psychological responses [45]. Simultaneously, if people cannot obtain perfect data or positive feedback from sleep-tracking technology, they may worry about their health and amplify health anxiety. This is like cyberchondria [32], where individuals experience health anxiety while searching for health information online. The vague guidance provided by sleep tracking may also exacerbate the vicious circle of health anxiety because the interpretation of bad results is unclear, non-informative, and useless to take action [25, 27].

Third, contrary to our expectations, our results suggest that complexity, inaccuracy, and data-perception discrepancy do not directly influence health anxiety. Although several studies have documented adverse effects associated with complexity [10, 17, 29], inaccuracy [10, 17, 27], and data-perception discrepancy [5, 10, 17], our findings indicate that these stressors have an indirect effect on health anxiety though invasion, unreliability, and vague guidance. This observation could be explained by the potential interactions among these stressors, which collectively contribute to health anxiety.

5.2 Theoretical and Practical Implications

Our research has several theoretical and practical implications. On the theoretical side, recent research mainly used qualitative research to identify the stressors of self-tracking [10, 17]. Our research enriches this research by developing a validated instrument to measure these stressors, such as data-perception discrepancy, pursuit of perfect data, and vague guidance, with a specific focus on the stressors associated with sleep tracking. These instruments enable researchers to explore the technostress of self-tracking using quantitative research design. Furthermore, the research model in our study enhances understanding of the sources of health anxiety related to sleep tracking. Prior research has indicated a lack of clear evidence linking health anxiety to wearables in healthy adults [46]. Conversely, it may exist among patients who use wearables for health [14]. While previous research presented different perspectives on health anxiety, our research suggests that some of the stressors of sleep tracking are positively associated with health anxiety. Additionally, our research also suggests that not all stressors have a direct impact on health anxiety, and some stressors may influence health anxiety through indirect pathways. This highlights the nuanced relationship between stressors of sleep tracking and health anxiety, indicating that stressors also affect each other.

This study also provides practical implications. For sleep-tracking designers, our findings on positive paths indicate that designers need to do the following: pay more attention to balancing intrusive features with being informative by providing gentle and concise notifications, discover and solve technical problems in a timely manner, provide friendly and educational recommendations to enhance users' health literacy without creating dependency on data [47], and offer actionable and personalized guidance based on users' sleep patterns and their preferences [27, 28]. We further recommend that sleep-tracking users pay attention to their own feelings rather than becoming slaves to the data. Shifting from societal towards neoliberal thinking, individuals who track their sleep need to take more responsibility and take action to achieve health by engaging in self-governance [48].

5.3 Limitations and Future Research

The limitations of this study need to be taken into account. First, this study recruited nine participants for Q-sort and adopted a cross-sectional survey to test the measurements. With respect to the research design, the categories of Q-sort are obviously subjective. Second, the survey study was conducted at a single time point. Third, our research model solely focused on stressors of sleep tracking. Future research should consider the effect of personal characteristics, such as health status, health literacy, and self-efficacy. Finally, health anxiety may also cause enduring behavioral or psychological consequences [49]. Future research could also explore the outcomes of health anxiety in the context of sleep tracking.

References

1. Grandner, M.A.: Sleep, health, and society. Sleep Med. Clin. **12**(2), 1–22 (2017)
2. de Zambotti, M., Cellini, N., Goldstone, A., Colrain, I.M., Baker, F.C.: Wearable sleep technology in clinical and research settings. Med. Sci. Sports Exerc. **51**(7), 1538–1557 (2019)
3. Precedence Research: Sleep tech devices market size to hit USD 113.16 bn by 2033. https://www.precedenceresearch.com/sleep-tech-devices-market. Accessed 09 Apr 2024
4. Feng, S., Mäntymäki, M., Salmela, H.: Affordances of sleep-tracking: insights from smart ring users. In: Papagiannidis, S., Alamanos, E., Gupta, S., Dwivedi, Y.K., Mäntymäki, M., Pappas, I.O. (eds.) The Role of Digital Technologies in Shaping the Post-Pandemic World. I3E 2022. LNCS, vol. 13454, pp. 343–355. Springer, Cham (2022)
5. Kuosmanen, E., et al.: How does sleep tracking influence your life? experiences from a longitudinal field study with a wearable ring. In: The Proceedings of the ACM on Human-Computer Interaction, vol. 6(MHCI), pp. 1–19 (2022)
6. Karasneh, R.A., Al-Azzam, S.I., Alzoubi, K.H., Hawamdeh, S., Jarab, A.S., Nusair, M.B.: Smartphone applications for sleep tracking: rating and perceptions about behavioral change among users. Sleep Sci. **15**(01), 65–73 (2022)
7. Quante, M., Khandpur, N., Kontos, E.Z., Bakker, J.P., Owens, J.A., Redline, S.: A qualitative assessment of the acceptability of smartphone applications for improving sleep behaviors in low-income and minority adolescents. Behav. Sleep Med. **17**(5), 573–585 (2019)
8. Wang, J., Hugh, J., Yang, Y.C.: Mobile sensor-based community gaming for improving vocational students' sleep and academic outcomes. Comput. Educ. **151**, 103812 (2020)

9. Zhang, S., Schaub, F., Feng, Y., Sadeh, N.: "It only tells me how I slept, not how to fix it": exploring sleep behaviors and opportunities for sleep technology. In: Taylor, N., Christian-Lamb, C., Martin, M., Nardi, B. (eds.) Information in Contemporary Society. iConference 2019. LNCS, vol 11420, pp. 754–766. Springer, Cham (2019)
10. Feng, S., Mäntymäki, M., Salmela, H.: Sleep tracking as a stressor: experiences from smart ring users. In: European Conference on Information Systems (2023)
11. Baron, K.G., Abbott, S., Jao, N., Manalo, N., Mullen, R.: Orthosomnia: are some patients taking the quantified self too far? J. Clin. Sleep Med. **13**(2), 351–354 (2017)
12. Kim, E., Dimsdale, J.E.: The effect of psychosocial stress on sleep: a review of polysomnographic evidence. Behav. Sleep Med. **5**(4), 256–278 (2007)
13. Staner, L.: Sleep and anxiety disorders. Dialogues Clin. Neurosci. **5**(3), 249–258 (2003)
14. Rosman, L., Gehi, A., Lampert, R.: When smartwatches contribute to health anxiety in patients with atrial fibrillation. Cardiovasc. Digit. Heal. J. **1**(1), 9–10 (2020)
15. Asmundson, G.J.G., Abramowitz, J.S., Richter, A.A., Whedon, M.: Health anxiety: current perspectives and future directions. Curr. Psychiatry Rep. **12**, 306–312 (2010)
16. Turel, O., et al.: Panel report: the dark side of the digitization of the individual. Internet Res. **29**(2), 274–288 (2019)
17. Rieder, A., Vuckic, S., Schache, K., Jung, R.: Technostress from persuasion: wearable users' stressors, strains, and coping. In: International Conference on Information Systems (2020)
18. Hoogstraten, M.L.: Technostressed out by your tracker? The effects of wearing an activity tracker and use of the app. Radboud university (2018)
19. Koeske, G.F., Koeske, R.D.: A preliminary test of a stress-strain-outcome model for reconceptualizing the burnout phenomenon. J. Soc. Serv. Res. **17**(3–4), 107–135 (1993)
20. Ayyagari, R., Grover, V., Purvis, R.: Technostress: technological antecedents and implications. MIS Q. **35**, 831–858 (2011)
21. Tarafdar, M., Cooper, C.L., Stich, J.F.: The technostress trifecta-techno eustress, techno distress and design: theoretical directions and an agenda for research. Inf. Syst. J. **29**(1), 6–42 (2019)
22. Lazarus, R.S., Folkman, S.: Stress, Appraisal, and Coping. Springer, New York (1984)
23. Lazarus, R.S.: Psychological Stress and the Coping Process. McGraw-Hill, New York (1966)
24. Brod, C.: Technostress: The Human Cost of the Computer Revolution. Addison-Wesley, Reading (1984)
25. Liu, W., Ploderer, B., Hoang, T.: In bed with technology: challenges and opportunities for sleep tracking. In: The Annual Meeting of the Australian Special Interest Group for Computer Human Interaction, pp. 142–151. ACM, New York (2015)
26. Jakowski, S., Stork, M.: Effects of sleep self-monitoring via app on subjective sleep markers in student athletes. Somnologie. **26**(4), 244–251 (2022)
27. Liang, Z., Ploderer, B.: Sleep tracking in the real world: a qualitative study into barriers for improving sleep. In: Australian Computer-Human Interaction Conference, pp. 537–541. ACM, New York (2016)
28. Ravichandran, R., Sien, S.-W., Patel, S.N., Kientz, J.A., Pina, L.R.: Making sense of sleep sensors: how sleep sensing technologies support and undermine sleep health. In: Proceedings of the 2017 CHI Conference on Human Factors in Computing Systems, pp. 6864–6875. ACM, New York (2017)
29. Liang, Z., Ploderer, B.: How does fitbit measure brainwaves: a qualitative study into the credibility of sleep-tracking technologies. Proc. ACM Interact. Mobile Wearable Ubiq. Technol. **4**(1), 1–29 (2020). https://doi.org/10.1145/3380994
30. Behne, A., Teuteberg, F.: A healthy lifestyle and the adverse impact of its digitalization: the dark side of using ehealth technologies. In: 15th International Conference on Wirtschaftsinformatik (2020)

31. Andersen, T.O., Langstrup, H., Lomborg, S.: Experiences with wearable activity data during self-care by chronic heart patients: qualitative study. J. Med. Internet Res. **22**, e15873 (2020)
32. te Poel, F., Baumgartner, S.E., Hartmann, T., Tanis, M.: The curious case of cyberchondria: a longitudinal study on the reciprocal relationship between health anxiety and online health information seeking. J. Anxiety Disord. **43**, 32–40 (2016)
33. White, R.W., Horvitz, E.: Cyberchondria: studies of the escalation of medical concerns in web search. ACM Trans. Inf. Syst. **27**, 23 (2009)
34. Moore, G.C., Benbasat, I.: Development of an instrument to measure the perceptions of adopting an information technology innovation. Inf. Syst. Res. **2**(3), 192–222 (1991)
35. Maier, C., Laumer, S., Weinert, C., Weitzel, T.: The effects of technostress and switching stress on discontinued use of social networking services: a study of Facebook use. Inf. Syst. J. **25**(3), 275–308 (2015)
36. Wixom, B.H., Todd, P.A.: A theoretical integration of user satisfaction and technology acceptance. Inf. Syst. Res. **16**(1), 85–102 (2005)
37. Fischer, T., Reuter, M., Riedl, R.: The digital stressors scale: development and validation of a new survey instrument to measure digital stress perceptions in the workplace context. Front. Psychol. **12**, 1–18 (2021)
38. Salkovskis, P.M., Rimes, K.A., Warwick, H.M.C., Clark, D.M.: The health anxiety inventory: development and validation of scales for the measurement of health anxiety and hypochondriasis. Psychol. Med. **32**(5), 843–853 (2002)
39. Hair, J.F., Ringle, C.M., Sarstedt, M.: PLS-SEM: indeed a silver bullet. J. Mark. Theory Pract. **19**(2), 139–152 (2011)
40. Chin, W.W.: The partial least squares approach to structural equation modeling. In: Modern for Business Research, pp. 295–336 (1998)
41. Fornell, C., Larcker, D.F.: Evaluating structural equation models with unobservable variables and measurement error. J. Mark. Res. **18**(1), 39–50 (1981)
42. Henseler, J., Ringle, C.M., Sarstedt, M.: A new criterion for assessing discriminant validity in variance-based structural equation modeling. J. Acad. Mark. Sci. **43**, 115–135 (2015)
43. Chae, J.: Online cancer information seeking increases cancer worry. Comput. Human Behav. **52**, 144–150 (2015)
44. Lagoe, C., Atkin, D.: Health anxiety in the digital age: an exploration of psychological determinants of online health information seeking. Comput. Human Behav. **52**, 484–491 (2015)
45. Califf, C.B., Sarker, S.S.: The bright and dark sides of technostress: a mixed-methods study involving healthcare IT. MIS Q. **44**(2), 809–856 (2020)
46. Conboy, E., Flood, C., Power, A.: Exploring health anxiety and dependence in healthy adult users of m-Health apps and wearables. In: Cyberpsychology and Society, pp. 34–46. Routledge, London (2018)
47. Attig, C., Franke, T.: I track, therefore I walk – exploring the motivational costs of wearing activity trackers in actual users. Int. J. Hum. Comput. Stud. **127**, 211–224 (2019)
48. Lupton, D.: Quantifying the body: monitoring and measuring health in the age of mHealth technologies. Crit. Public Health **23**(4), 393–403 (2013)
49. Meng, F., Guo, X., Peng, Z., Ye, Q., Lai, K.H.: Trust and elderly users' continuance intention regarding mobile health services: the contingent role of health and technology anxieties. Inf. Technol. People **35**(1), 259–280 (2021)

Understanding Cyberbullying as the Convergence of Offender Disposition and Crime Opportunity: A Configurational Approach

Mohammad Alamgir Hossain[1(✉)], Mohammed Quaddus[2], Preetha Menon[3], and Ilias Pappas[4,5]

[1] RMIT University, Melbourne, VIC 3000, Australia
mohammad.hossain@rmit.edu.au
[2] Curtin University, Bentley, WA 6102, Australia
m.quaddus@curtin.edu.au
[3] Flame University, Pune, Maharashtra 412115, India
preetha.menon@flame.edu.in
[4] Department of Computer Science, Norwegian University of Science and Technology, Sem Saelandsvei 9, 7491 Trondheim, Norway
ilpappas@ntnu.no, ilias.pappas@uia.no
[5] Department of Information Systems, University of Agder, Universitetsveien 25, 4630 Kristiansand, Norway

Abstract. In this study, applying a fuzzy-set qualitative comparative analysis (fsQCA) approach, we explain social media cyberbullying as the convergence of offender disposition (perpetrator's willingness and presence of suitable target) and crime opportunity (absence of intimate handler, platform guardian, and lawful guardian). Data from online platform, namely MTurk, suggest that perpetrator's willingness is the necessary condition without which cyberbullying does not take place neither in the USA nor in India. In addition, we obtain two sufficient configurations from each sample that adequately explain cyberbullying. Interestingly, both samples suggest a common configuration predicting cyberbullying – a combination of platform guardian, perpetrator's willingness and presence of suitable target. The findings suggest several theoretical and practical implications.

Keywords: Social Media · Cyberbullying · fsQCA · Crime Opportunity Theory

1 Introduction

Cyberbullying is an uncivil, aggressive, and anti-social act causing personal conflict online [1]. It includes provocative and hostile interactions such as insulting posts, aggressive messages, and incendiary comments intended to provoke or offend users. Although social media cyberbullying (hereafter 'cyberbullying) "is a relatively recent

Published by Springer Nature Switzerland AG 2024
R. van de Wetering et al. (Eds.): I3E 2024, LNCS 14907, pp. 358–370, 2024.
https://doi.org/10.1007/978-3-031-72234-9_30

phenomenon" [1] but has become a global issue. While not all cyberbullying constitutes a criminal offense, but some instances cross the line into unlawful behavior [2]. In its darker forms, cyberbullying is linked to mental health challenges such as anxiety, depression, substance abuse, suicide attempts, and suicides [3, 4].

Given the severe consequences of cyberbullying, it is essential to examine it through the lens of criminology theories, such as the Crime Opportunity Theory (COT). COT posits that two main drivers of crime are criminal dispositions and crime opportunities [5]. Dispositions relate to the perpetrator's willingness (PW), while crime opportunities involve the presence of suitable targets (PST) and the absence of capable guardians (ACG). According to Felson [6], "The criminal event is a systematic result of the *convergence* of people and things over space and time. … "*These three elements must converge* in time and space for a direct-contact, predatory violation to occur" (p. 120–21, emphasis added). Such 'convergence' stresses a configurational rather than the individual effect of these variables, which traditional cyberbullying studies ignore [e.g., 1].

Against this backdrop, we propose a configurational approach for investigating cyberbullying from criminological contexts to answer: *Which configurations of offender's disposition and crime opportunities lead to cyberbullying on social media?* Moreover, differences in culture, societal-ties, and cyber laws between developed countries and developing countries may dictate cyberbullying behavior [7], we develop and compare configurations between a developed country and a developing country.

In order to answer the research question, this study uses fuzzy-set qualitative comparative analysis (fsQCA) method, which is based on a set-membership analytical technique and is appropriate for complex configuration analyses [8]. The results suggests that the conditions (e.g., PW, PST, ACG) on cyberbullying do not work independently but *jointly* [9], depending on "how the attributes [conditions] are combined, rather than on the levels of the individual attributes per se" [10, p. 135].

Our study offers theoretical and practical implications. On a theoretical realm, our study finds that cyberbullying does not depend on the crime opportunities or offender's disposition *alone* but on specific configurations of conditions of both and thus evidencing the convergence aspect of COTs. As practical implication, we explain how the absence of different guardianships encourages cyberbullying and thus provide recommendations for practitioners.

2 Background and the Research Model

2.1 Cyberbullying: A Discussion from Criminology Perspective

"Cyberbullying is any behavior performed through electronic or digital media by individuals or groups that repeatedly communicates hostile or aggressive messages intended to inflict harm or discomfort on others" [11, p. 278]. Considering this definition, a number of complementary crime theories can explain cyberbullying.

The rational choice theory (RCT) [12] explains the crime process, suggesting that at some point, an offender develops a need to achieve something sadistic, such as revenge, popularity, or pleasure. Scholars [e.g., 13] believe that RCT provides a theoretical foundation for other crime theories, including the routine activity theory (RAT). According to RCT and the 'Principle of Least Effort' [14], the "people tend to find the shortest route, spend the least time, and seek the easiest means to accomplish something" [5, p. 99]. Thus, both the need and the unlawful actions lead to committing offenses.

Crime opportunity theory (COT) posits that crime factors do not work in isolation; instead, "crime is a process, depending on the convergence of offenders and targets in the absence of guardians" [15, p. 206]. Similarly, the routine activity theory (RAT) [16, 17] suggests that a crime occurs when three elements converge: (i) a motivated offender, (ii) a suitable target (PST), and (iii) the absence of capable guardianship (ACG). "For a crime to occur, *all three of these elements must come together* at the same time. If they do come together, crime still might not occur; however, if they do not come together, crime is impossible" [18, emphasis added]. Both COT and RAT support the convergence of attributes for crime to occur.

Unfortunately, "criminologists have underemphasized the importance of the convergence of suitable targets and the absence of capable guardians in explaining [...] crime [...]. Their convergence by a fixed percentage may produce increases in crime rates far greater than that fixed percentage" [17, p. 604]. This means that while one or two factors may occasionally explain a crime, typically, all three must converge. Additionally, the relative weights of these determinants may result in varying degrees of crime, which becomes more complex when guardianships are of different types. Therefore, the means through which different types of crime factors foster individuals' criminal behaviors are sophisticated and should be considered from a configurational perspective.

Most studies on cyberbullying that have applied criminology theories, including RAT, oversimplify the research problem by ignoring the complex associations between factors. For example, Chan, Cheung [1] applied COT to understand cyberbullying, claiming that it occurs when a likely bully (IB) meets a suitable target online in the absence of a capable guardian. They tested the interaction effect (i.e., IB*PST*ACG) but did not find significant support. This finding deviates from the fundamental principle of COT and RAT, where all three are "essential components" for a crime to occur [13, p. 66]. Therefore, a configurational approach investigating the joint effects of offenders' disposition and crime opportunity is required, providing valuable insights into predicting a crime such as cyberbullying.

2.2 Capable Guardianship and Its Dimensions

"Crime occurrence depends on absence of a capable guardianship" [5, p. 99]. Its absence makes crime more likely, especially in cybercrime, where unmonitored user behavior lowers the psychological barriers to committing crime [19]. While the goal of guardians is universal – "protecting targets" [18, p. 39] – they come in different forms. Felson and Boba [15, p. 30] specify that intimate handlers, place managers, and guardians influence whether a crime occurs: 'the offender moves away from handlers toward a place without a manager and a target without a guardian'. Hollis, Felson [13] reiterates these roles: handlers monitor the offender, managers oversee the criminogenic place, and guardians protect the target. RAT includes the intimate handler as a fourth element to explain crime behavior alongside likely offender, suitable target, and guardianship [6]. In cybercrime, guardianship dimensions are: (i) intimate handler to control the offender, (ii) platform guardianship to secure social media platforms [20], and (iii) formal guardians enforcing laws and regulations [21]. These dimensions encompass informal prevention (close to the offender) and formal prevention (systemic or human). Theoretical configurations of guardianship are underexplored in cyberbullying [e.g., 1].

Intimate Handlers on Social Media. Intimate handlers are "people with whom offenders have an emotional attachment … [and whose] goal is to keep possible offenders out of trouble" [18, p. 39]. They possess the knowledge to manage and control these individuals [22]. Effective handlers can restrict offenders, reducing the likelihood of offenses in their presence. Social Bond Theory (SBT) supports this, suggesting people avoid antisocial behavior to protect relationships [23]. SBT assumes that all individuals are potential law-violators, but they control themselves with the fear that anti-social behavior will damage their relationships with others (e.g., friends, parents, colleagues). In social media, social surveillance allows connected people to monitor deviant behavior [24]. Intimate handlers (friends, relatives, social networks) impose social control, as their perceived presence can deter cyberbullying.

Social Media Platform Guardianship. In a non-virtual world, place managers are "the owners of places, or the owners' representatives at the place… [whose] goal is the smooth functioning of the place" [18, p. 39] and "whose presence and alertness discourages crime from happening there" [15, p. 30]. In virtual spaces, it is almost impossible to watch every user and potential offenders in real-time. Yet, social media platform guardianship involves surveillance by individuals or technologies (e.g., AI) to detect and intervene in offenses. When the terms and conditions of these platforms regarding harassment are violated, the platform guardians can delete comments, disengage offender, warn user, and delete user account [20].

Lawful Guardianship. The third form of guardianship is formal, involving cyber laws created by legislators and enforced by law enforcement agencies to catch and punish offenders. Cyberbullying is a criminal offense in many countries [25]. This guardianship promotes self-censorship, as offenders know their behavior can be traced and punished [26]. For serious or repeated cyberbullying, platform managers may involve law enforcement. This aligns with rational choice theory, where offenders weigh potential gains against the likelihood of punishment.

Based on this discussion, our proposed configurational model (see Fig. 1) presents the complex combination of criminal disposition (i.e., perpetrator's willingness) with crime opportunities (i.e., presence of suitable target and absence of guardianships) as causal conditions for high cyberbullying [CB = f(PW,PST,AIH,APG,ALG,)].

3 Method

3.1 Measures

For reliability, our measures (see Appendix) are based on previously developed indicators, where possible. To measure cyberbullying (CB), we have used four items from Chan, Cheung [1] and two items from Lowry, Zhang [27]. Following both, the scale for CB have used five-points (i.e., 1 = "Never," 2 = "Rarely," 3 = "Occasionally," 4 = "Frequently," and 5 = "Very frequently"). To measure *presence of suitable target* (PST) and *perpetrator's willingness* (PW), we have used Chan, Cheung [1]'s scales.

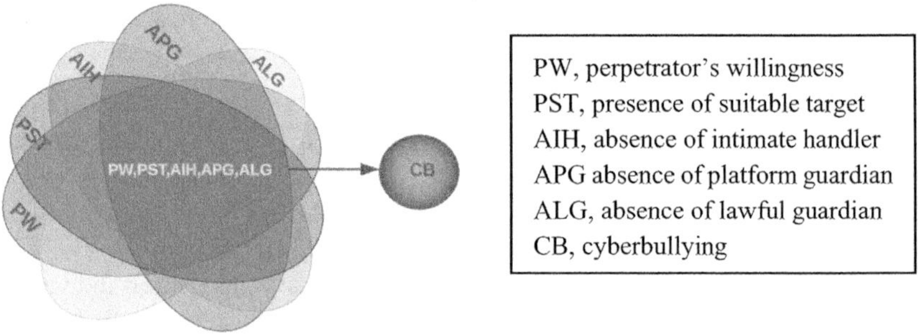

Fig. 1. A configurational approach explaining social media cyberbullying.

Based on the literature, we consider *capable guardianship* (crime-prevention effort) as a higher order construct consisting of three first-order constructs, namely, intimate handler, platform guardian, and lawful guardian. Because of the scarcity of their measures, we have developed them. First, from extant studies, we have identified the prospective items of respective construct. For *intimate handler*, we identified different aspects of it from Felson [6]'s discussion and borrowed concept from *social influence* scale of Venkatesh, Thong [28]. Next, three items for *platform guardianship* were taken from the *lack of monitoring scale* of Lowry, Zhang [27] on cyber-harassment and one item from the *absence of capable guardianship* scale of Chan, Cheung [1]. Finally, the initial items for *lawful guardians* have been inspired from Chan et al. (2019)'s *absence of capable guardianship* scale. The items then have been reviewed by pilot study employing a convenient sample of three academics (working in information systems field) and two PhD students (conducting research on social media) to ensure consistency, ease of understanding, and relevance to the context. All items for the measures (except CB) are rated on five-point Likert scales anchored from "strongly disagree" to "strongly agree" because "literature suggests that five-point scale appears to be less confusing and to increase response rate" [29, p. 280]. Appendix contains our measures.

3.2 Data Collection

For data collection, we employed Amazon's Mechanical Turk (MTurk) platform. Recruiting participants via MTurk has been used in various research domains, including cyberbullying [e.g., 27]. As an *ex-ante* method, by using MTurk's feature, we have screened out the 'workers' (potential respondents) who do not meet our specific criteria e.g., social media platform use. As an *ex-post* measure, we used three reverse-coded items.

To reduce SDB, we applied the principles of Larson [30]. In the participant consent form (PCF, loaded before the actual survey), the respondents were assured that their responses would be anonymous and kept completely confidential, and used in an aggregated manner. In PCF, we also included a statement that encouraged and appreciated respondents' honesty [30]. These two efforts were made to make the respondents less likely to respond in a socially desirable way [1]. In addition, all respondents had to be above 18 years of age. Among the 253 respondents, 62% are male, 59% are between

25–40 years and around 9% are between 41–50 age groups, 62% have tertiary qualifications, 57% are married, and 45% use mobile devices and the rest use computers and other devices to use social media.

4 Data Analysis and Results

4.1 fsQCA Analyses

Before proceeding to the fsQCA procedure, we have checked the psychometric properties of the variables. Following standard procedure, the validity of the constructs has been established by examining their reliability and convergent validity (see Appendix). For brevity, we do not provide the results of the discriminant validity tests.

To test the proposed configurational model (Fig. 1), we applied asymmetric modelling using fsQCA [31, 32]. For our analysis, we follow guidelines and recommendations from recent papers in information systems (IS) [33–35]. The fsQCA analysis has been carried out using the software fsQCA 4.1 [31]. Using fsQCA software, we first conducted data calibration. As we use a five-point Likert scale, 4, 3, and 2 are used for full, intermediate, and full non- membership, respectively [34]. Next, the calibrated data have been incorporated into a fuzzy-set truth table. In refining the truth tables, we delete rows with no cases [8]. In addition, for configurations with a PRI consistency of < 0.75, the outcome in the truth table has been set to "0" to ensure that the sufficient configurations exhibit a satisfactory quality [8, 33]. The frequency threshold is set to 2. At this stage, we identify the necessary conditions. A condition is considered "necessary" if both of its associated consistency and coverage are $>= 0.9$ [36]. Based on this, *perpetrator's willingness* (PW) is found to be a necessary condition for high cyberbullying (see Table 1). It can be interpreted that cyberbullying cannot occur without PW.

Table 1. Necessary condition for high cyberbullying.

	Total Sample (n = 362)		USA Sample (n = 203)		Indian Sample (n = 159)	
Condition	Consistency	Coverage	Consistency	Coverage	Consistency	Consistency
PW	0.945	0.928	0.940	0.934	0.956	0.921
PST	0.945	0.859	0.953	0.867	0.935	0.848
AIH	0.737	0.869	0.773	0.877	0.691	0.858
APG	0.915	0.861	0.910	0.873	0.921	0.847
ALG	0.920	0.852	0.930	0.852	0.908	0.854

Note. PW, perpetrator's willingness; PST, presence of suitable target; AIH, absence of intimate handler; APG, absence of platform guardian; ALG, absence of lawful guardian

Finally, we identify the sufficient configurations for high cyberbullying. For a configuration to be considered as 'sufficient', its consistency and coverage values need to be $> \ = 0.75$ [37] and $>= 0.2$, respectively [36]. The diagrammatic representation of the sufficient solutions for modelling high cyberbullying are outlined in Table 2. The results in Table 2 show that PW is common in every solution of each sample (i.e., total, USA, and India), which reconfirms that PW is a necessary condition for cyberbullying. Although *presence of suitable target* (PST) is common in each sufficient configuration of each sample, because of its statistical values (see Table 1), we do not consider it as a necessary condition. For each sample, we have found two sufficient causal configurations that lead to high cyberbullying.

Table 2. Configurations for cyberbullying behavior on social media.

	Total Sample (n=362)		USA Sample (n=203)		India Sample (n=159)	
Condition	$C_{total}1$	$C_{total}2$	$C_{USA}1$	$C_{USA}2$	$C_{India}1$	$C_{India}2$
PW	✸	✸	✸	✸	✸	✸
PST	●	●	●	●	●	●
AIH		•		•		
APG		•	•			•
ALG	•				•	
Raw coverage	0.880	0.686	0.881	0.733	0.887	0.878
Unique coverage	0.207	0.014	0.137	0.011	0.027	0.023
Consistency	0.955	0.972	0.961	0.970	0.948	0.946
Solution coverage	0.893		0.900		0.927	
Solution consistency	0.953		0.959		0.933	

Key: ● Core condition; • Peripheral condition; ✸Necessary condition; blank space denotes "do not care"

5 Data Analysis and Results

5.1 Findings

Interestingly, to predict cyberbullying, every configuration of each sample includes perpetrator's willingness (PW) and presence of suitable target (PST) along with the absence of one or more capable guardians. This supports the fundamental notion of crime opportunity theories. In other words, a likely offender on social media is more likely to engage in cyberbullying when they encounter two favorable conditions: a high presence of suitable targets and the absence of any capable guardians.

In the total sample, two configurations for predicting high cyberbullying were identified: $C_{Total}1$ and $C_{Total}2$. $C_{Total}1$ indicates that cyberbullying is likely when a willing perpetrator encounters a suitable target in the absence of lawful guardians, regardless of other guardians' presence or absence. This configuration is also applicable to our Indian sample (i.e., $C_{India}1$), suggesting its general validity and specific relevance to Indian social media users. $C_{Total}2$, on the other hand, shows that lawful guardians are irrelevant if the other four conditions are met. Specifically, cyberbullying occurs when a perpetrator finds a suitable target in the absence of both intimate handlers and platform guardians.

In the USA sample, two configurations ($C_{USA}1$ – $C_{USA}2$) explain cyberbullying sufficiently. According to $C_{USA}1$, cyberbullying can take place when the high willingness of a perpetrator combines with a high presence of a suitable target in the absence of social media platform guardians, irrespective of whether the other guardians are present or absent. This configuration is also valid for Indian users ($C_{India}2$). However, $C_{USA}2$ suggests that the absence of intimate handlers on social media is sufficient (where any other guardianship is meaningless) for a likely offender to commit cyberbullying if s/he meets suitable targets. To them, among the guardianship, they care about the intimate handlers the most.

5.2 Implications to Theory

Our study offers several significant implications. In the theoretical realm, firstly, our research responds to previous calls for new approaches to studying the cybercrime phenomenon. Specifically, Lowry, Zhang [27, p. 1169] suggest that "... it is important to investigate how well the integrated CH [cyber-harassment] theory holds in other countries/cultures [other than USA], especially non-Western ones (e.g., China and India)". A similar agenda suggested that "there may be substantial variations in laws and cultural norms concerning ... CB [cyberbullying] practices, across different national cultures" [38, p. 889]. Responding to these research agenda, we collected data from USA and India, and thus provided generalization of the crime theories on cyberbullying.

Next, this research offers theoretical insights by integrating criminology perspectives to explain perpetrators' cyberbullying behavior. We provide empirical evidence supporting crime opportunity theories, demonstrating that crime results from the joint effect of a perpetrator's willingness, the presence of a suitable target, and the absence of one or more capable guardians. Our findings indicate that these criminology attributes have complex trade-off effects on high CB, with only certain combinations acting as sufficient conditions. Specifically, we identified two sufficient configurations for predicting high CB, where no single condition is sufficient. For instance, perpetrator disposition (i.e., PW) itself, alone does not lead to cyberbullying; it must be combined with crime opportunities (PST and ACG). In other words, PW, PST, and at least one ACG must converge to predict high CB. Future studies could explore whether the absence of these conditions prevents successful cyberbullying, providing a more comprehensive theoretical explanation of CB. This aligns with the notion that "The lack of any of these elements is sufficient to prevent the occurrence of a successful... Crime" [17, p. 604], potentially offering deeper insights into preventing cyberbullying.

5.3 Implications to Practice

As the first practical implication, by employing fsQCA, we provide a new approach for understanding the enabling conditions that inspire CB. This method allows cyber experts to predict early when CB is likely and offers multiple successful configurations to understand the same outcome, showing that different factors can provoke different perpetrators in varying ways. Second, we found that perpetrator willingness (PW) is a necessary condition for cyberbullying. This implies that reducing PW may decrease cyberbullying. Therefore, social solutions, such as training and awareness programs by government agencies and educators as well as by social media platforms and celebrities, can be effective in addressing this socio-technical issue [39].

Thirdly, our results highlight the importance of guardianships in predicting high CB. From an information systems (IS) perspective, this suggests the need to examine and evaluate social media affordances [1] and implement technology-facilitated platform guardianship. Beyond reactive measures, social media platforms should adopt tech-based proactive approaches to predict and prevent cyberbullying. If a potential offender perceives that capable guardians are present and serious about protecting users against cyberbullying, they are likely to be dissuaded. Hollis, Felson [13] demonstrate that even friendly dogs or signs warning of dogs can deter offenders. Similarly, the absence of platform guardianship consistently predicts cyberbullying. If users believe that social media platforms can detect and act on cyberbullying, they may refrain from such behavior. While it is impractical for platforms to manually check every comment, AI-based detection and digital forensic systems can help [25]. Additionally, making it easy to report cyberbullying and apply privacy settings is crucial. The absence of lawful guardians is significant in predicting cyberbullying, particularly in the Indian sample. However, USA users prioritize platform guardians and close friends on social media over legal measures when predicting cyberbullying behavior.

5.4 Limitations and the Direction for Future Research

Despite this research's contributions, it has limitations. *First*, it views cyberbullying as a non-professional, marginally-criminal event, excluding financially motivated or organized crimes. *Second*, due to ethical constraints, only participants aged 19 or over were interviewed, while cyberbullying is severe among younger individuals [40]. Future research should include younger samples. *Third*, the study relies on self-reported behavior, though considered valid and reliable [e.g., 41] and has been applied in prior cyberbullying studies [1, 38]. In future, objective measures from social media platforms' log would give us more confident explanations. *Fourth*, data were collected from the USA and India, so findings may not generalize to other countries. Further research can conduct several longitudinal comparisons between countries with varied characteristics. Lastly, the study does not identify configurations for low cyberbullying.

In many cases, the absence of guardians that lead to high cyberbullying does not necessarily mean that their presence will reduce cyberbullying [e.g., 15, 19]. Hence, future research should explore cyberbullying reduction strategies, from a criminology perspective, through the latest technological innovations, such as AI.

Disclosure of Interests. The authors declare that they have no conflicts of interest.

Appendix

Appendix. The measures and their psychometric properties

Condition	Item	Loading
Perpetrator's Willingness CR = 0.914 AVE = 0.728	1. I want to engage in social media bullying perpetration	0.838
	2. I tend to bully others on social media	0.863
	3. I am inclined to commit social media bullying	0.838
	4. I am keen to perpetrate someone on social media	0.873
Presence of Suitable Target CR = 0.850 AVE = 0.587	The social media environment has … 1. Suitable people for bullying	0.677
	2. Ideal users for me to engage in bullying perpetration	0.800
	3. Right candidates for me to attack	0.767
	4. Attractive targets for bullying	0.812
Absence of Intimate Handler CR = 0.849 AVE = 0.539	1. The people close to me do not like CB	0.745
	2. I will lose my friends on social media if I commit CB	0.781
	3. My future relationship with my friends on social media will be impaired if I commit CB	0.725
	4. My friends on social media will be upset if I commit CB	0.881
	5. If I commit CB, someone may inform my guardians.[d]	–
Absence of Platform Guardian CR = 0.860 AVE = 0.605	I perceive that … 1. Neither a computer system nor social media employees carefully monitor CB incidents	0.776
	2. CB incidents are not monitored by the social media system	0.797
	3. No system or person monitors people's behaviors in the social media system to ensure 'good' behavior	0.780
	4. A lack of effective guardianships from social media platform to deter CB perpetration	0.758
Absence of Lawful Guardian CR = 0.860 AVE = 0.553	I perceive that … 1. There is lack of exemplary punishments for CB	0.723

(continued)

(*continued*)

Condition	Item	Loading
	2. There is no or effective application of CB law	0.723
	3. There is no cyber-policing to monitor perpetrators' behavior in social media to protect users	0.767
	4. There is no one from law enforcement agencies in social media to protect users	0.681
	5. Law enforcement agencies do not use suitable technologies to protect social media users	0.816
Cyberbullying Behavior CR = 0.915 AVE = 0.644	In the past three months, how often did you engage in the following behaviors on Facebook? 1. Posted hurtful, rude, or mean content that targets someone	0.795
	2. Publicly embarrassed or pranked someone with information or photos that are potentially harmful	0.839
	3. Spread rumors/untrue information about someone	0.843
	4. Sent threatening/harassing messages to someone	0.820
	5. Made fun of someone	0.656
	6. Changed data or photos to embarrass someone	0.845

References

1. Chan, T.K., Cheung, C.M., Wong, R.Y.: Cyberbullying on social networking sites: the crime opportunity and affordance perspectives. J. Manag. Inf. Syst. **36**(2), 574–609 (2019)
2. Stopbullying.gov. What Is Cyberbullying (2021). https://www.stopbullying.gov/cyberbullying/what-is-it. Accessed 12 Jan 2022
3. Mkono, M.: 'Troll alert!': provocation and harassment in tourism and hospitality social media. Curr. Issue Tour. **21**(7), 791–804 (2018)
4. Gorman, G.: Internet trolls are not who I thought—they're even scarier (2019). https://www.abc.net.au/news/2019-02-02/internet-trolls-arent-who-i-thought-ginger-gorman-troll-hunting/10767690
5. Gok, O.: The role of opportunity in crime prevention and possible threats of crime control benefits. Turk. J. Police Stud. **13**(1), 97–114 (2011)
6. Felson, M.: Linking Criminal Choices, Routine Activities, Informal Control, and criminal outcomes. In: The Reasoning Criminal: Rational Choice Perspectives on Offending, p. 119 (1986)

7. Kintonova, A., Vasyaev, A., Shestak, V.: Cyberbullying and cyber-mobbing in developing countries. Inf. Comput. Secur. **29**(3), 435–456 (2021)
8. Ragin, C.C.: Redesigning Social Inquiry: Fuzzy Sets and Beyond. University of Chicago Press, Chicago (2008)
9. Misangyi, V.F., et al.: Embracing causal complexity: the emergence of a neo-configurational perspective. J. Manag. **43**(1), 255–282 (2017)
10. Ordanini, A., Parasuraman, A., Rubera, G.: When the recipe is more important than the ingredients: a qualitative comparative analysis (QCA) of service innovation configurations. J. Serv. Res. **17**(2), 134–149 (2014)
11. Tokunaga, R.S.: Following you home from school: a critical review and synthesis of research on cyberbullying victimization. Comput. Hum. Behav. **26**(3), 277–287 (2010)
12. Clarke, R.V.G., Felson, M.: Routine Activity and Rational Choice, vol. 5. Transaction publishers, Piscataway (1993)
13. Hollis, M.E., Felson, M., Welsh, B.C.: The capable guardian in routine activities theory: a theoretical and conceptual reappraisal. Crime Prevent. Commun. Safety **15**(1), 65–79 (2013)
14. Zipf, G.K.: Human Behavior and the Principle of Least Effort: An Introduction to human Ecology. Ravenio Books (2012)
15. Felson, M., Boba, R.: Everyday Technology and Everyday Crime, Crime and Everyday Life. SAGE Publications, Inc., Thousand Oaks (2015)
16. McMurty, R., Curling, A.: Volume 5 Literature review in The review of the roots of youth violence, pp. 41–52 (2008)
17. Cohen, L.E., Felson, M.: Social change and crime rate trends: a routine activity approach. Am. Sociol. Rev. 588–608 (1979)
18. Sampson, R., Eck, J.E., Dunham, J.: Super controllers and crime prevention: a routine activity explanation of crime prevention success and failure. Secur. J. **23**(1), 37–51 (2010)
19. Felson, M.: Those who discourage crime. Crime Place **4**, 53–66 (1995)
20. Ireland, L., et al.: Preconditions for guardianship interventions in cyberbullying: Incident interpretation, collective and automated efficacy, and relative popularity of bullies. Comput. Hum. Behav. **113**, 106506 (2020)
21. El Asam, A., Samara, M.: Cyberbullying and the law: a review of psychological and legal challenges. Comput. Hum. Behav. **65**, 127–141 (2016)
22. Felson, A.: Linking criminal choices, routine activities, informal control, and criminal outcomes. In: Cornish, D.B., Clarke, R.V. (eds.) The Reasoning Criminal: Rational Choice Perspectives on Offending, pp. 119–128. Taylor & Francis (2014)
23. Hirschi, T.: Causes of Delinquency. Transaction publishers, Piscataway (2002)
24. Fuchs, C., Trottier, D.: Towards a theoretical model of social media surveillance in contemporary society. Communications **40**(1), 113–135 (2015)
25. Coles, B.A., West, M.: Trolling the trolls: online forum users constructions of the nature and properties of trolling. Comput. Hum. Behav. **60**, 233–244 (2016)
26. Foody, M., Samara, M., Carlbring, P.: A review of cyberbullying and suggestions for online psychological therapy. Internet Interv. **2**(3), 235–242 (2015)
27. Lowry, P.B., et al.: An integrative theory addressing cyberharassment in the light of technology-based opportunism. J. Manag. Inf. Syst. **36**(4), 1142–1178 (2019)
28. Venkatesh, V., Thong, J.Y., Xu, X.: Consumer acceptance and use of information technology: extending the unified theory of acceptance and use of technology. MIS Q. 157–178 (2012)
29. Bouranta, N., Chitiris, L., Paravantis, J.: The relationship between internal and external service quality. Int. J. Contemp. Hosp. Manag. **21**(3), 275–293 (2009)
30. Larson, R.B.: Controlling social desirability bias. Int. J. Mark. Res. **61**(5), 534–547 (2019)
31. Ragin, C.: User's Guide to Fuzzy-Set/Qualitative Comparative Analysis 3.0. Department of Sociology, University of California, Irvine, California (2018)

32. Ragin, C.C.: Fuzzy-Set Social Science. University of Chicago Press, Chicago (2000)
33. Mattke, J., et al.: Qualitative comparative analysis (QCA) in information systems research: status quo, guidelines, and future directions. Commun. Assoc. Inf. Syst. **50**, 556–588 (2022)
34. Pappas, I.O., Woodside, A.G.: Fuzzy-set qualitative comparative analysis (fsQCA): guidelines for research practice in Information Systems and marketing. Int. J. Inf. Manag. **58**, 102310 (2021)
35. Park, Y., Fiss, P.C., El Sawy, O.A.: Theorizing the multiplicity of digital phenomena: the ecology of configurations, causal recipes, and guidelines for applying QCA. MIS Q. **44**(4), 1493 (2020)
36. Rasoolimanesh, S.M., et al.: The combined use of symmetric and asymmetric approaches: partial least squares-structural equation modeling and fuzzy-set qualitative comparative analysis. Int. J. Contemp. Hosp. Manag. **33**(5), 1571–1592 (2021)
37. Pappas, I.O., et al.: Identifying the combinations of motivations and emotions for creating satisfied users in SNSs: an fsQCA approach. Int. J. Inf. Manage. **53**, 102128 (2020)
38. Lowry, P.B., Moody, G.D., Chatterjee, S.: Using IT design to prevent cyberbullying. J. Manag. Inf. Syst. **34**(3), 863–901 (2017)
39. Yurdakul, Y., Ayhan, A.B.: The effect of the cyberbullying awareness program on adolescents' awareness of cyberbullying and their coping skills. Curr. Psychol. **42**(28), 24208–24222 (2023)
40. Balakrishnan, V.: Cyberbullying among young adults in Malaysia: the roles of gender, age and Internet frequency. Comput. Hum. Behav. **46**, 149–157 (2015)
41. Jones, D.N., Paulhus, D.L.: Introducing the short dark triad (SD3) a brief measure of dark personality traits. Assessment **21**(1), 28–41 (2014)

Understanding the Challenges of Fake News in the Tourism and Travel Industry: A Systematic Literature Review

Sumaiya Ismail, Marie Hattingh(✉), and Machdel Matthee

University of Pretoria, Hatfield 0028, South Africa
u19017082@tuks.co.za, {marie.hattingh,machdel.matthee}@up.ac.za

Abstract. Fake news in the tourism industry can influence consumer behavior, expectations, and opinions about the destinations or entertainment options they want to visit. For these reasons, it is important to understand the impact of fake news on the industry and the stakeholders who are impacted by it. The study employed a systematic review methodology and identified thirty-one papers from four academic databases. Thematic analyses were used to analyse the papers. The findings showed that consumers being impacted by fake news resulted in a ripple effect on businesses and countries. It was further reported that fake news was mostly distributed on online platforms such as social media, online reviews, and websites, and offline on editorials, opinion pieces, and entertainment shows. The creators of fake news mainly did it to benefit themselves. Both automated and manual methods were used to identify fake news. Tourism departments can mitigate these challenges by increasing awareness by hosting workshops and online campaigns for businesses and consumers to learn how to look out for fake news. Further investigation can be done into the willingness of the stakeholders to adopt the mentioned guidelines

Keywords: Fake News · Impact On Tourism · Impact on Travel Industry · Systematic Review · Fake News Challenges

1 Introduction

Information has a key role in the travel and tourism industry (hereafter referred to as the tourism industry) due to the nature of the industry that it relies on information that people generate, share, and consume internationally [10]. In 2020, approximately 1 million reviews on TripAdvisor were fake [14]. When people are misinformed or encounter 'fake news' on various platforms, their actions and thoughts can be negatively impacted [10]. Fake news is defined as "particular news articles that originate either on mainstream media (online or offline) or on social media and have no factual basis but are presented as facts and not satire" [21]. The prevalence of fake news has increased with the availability of digital platforms to share news and reviews [2]. In addition, the Internet is gaining a reputation as a reliable source of travel information [1]. This increase in fake news has led to disastrous impacts across several industries, including tourism [2].

Published by Springer Nature Switzerland AG 2024
R. van de Wetering et al. (Eds.): I3E 2024, LNCS 14907, pp. 371–382, 2024.
https://doi.org/10.1007/978-3-031-72234-9_31

Fake news in the tourism industry and its impact is important to understand as tourism is an important socio-economic activity around the world [1, 19, 25]. Tham & Chen [28] emphasize that greater attention needs to be given to managing fake news in the tourism industry. Fake news in the tourism industry can influence consumer behavior, expectations, and opinions about the destinations or entertainment options they want to visit. The murder of a Polish tourist in Egypt in 2017 was widely covered by news houses and spoken about on social media. The facts which became distorted on several online discussions, gave Egypt a negative image and consequently led to Polish travelers cancelling scheduled bookings [4]. In another case, destinations in Queensland, Australia lost between US$7000 and US$14000 over two weeks in 2017 because of sensational reports on natural disasters that had afflicted the area [28]. With the digital age driving the dissemination of fake news, it has become essential that all news needs to be verified before it can be believed [1].

This research paper explores the various aspects that encompass understanding fake news in the tourism industry, such as the impact that it has on the industry; the stakeholders who are impacted by it; the platforms on which fake news is disseminated; the potential incentives of the authors of fake news relating to the tourism industry; and how fake news can be better identified in attempting to combat it. The main research question to be addressed in this study is 'How does fake news impact the tourism industry?' The main research question is supported by three sub-research questions: (1) What are the incentives of the authors of fake news in the tourism industry?, (2) What are the platforms that are used to disseminate fake news relating to the tourism industry?, and (3) How can fake news in the tourism industry be identified to combat it?

Section 2 summarizes the methodology followed in this paper. Section 3 presents the findings and discussion, respectively. Section 4 concludes the paper with limitations and future research.

2 Research Methodology

The research methodology followed in this paper was a systematic literature review [11]. Google Scholar was used to identify four databases using the following search string: ("fake news" OR "impact of fake news" OR "identify fake news" OR "fake news impact*" OR "understand* fake news" OR "discover fake news" OR "challenges of fake news" OR "combat fake news") AND ("tourism" OR "travel" OR "tourism industry" OR "travel industry" OR "tourism and travel industry").

The databases used were IEEE Xplore® Digital Library, ScienceDirect, Scopus, and Web of Science Core Collection. Following the identification of papers, the following inclusion criteria were applied: only papers published between 2012 and 2022, only papers from academic journals and peer-reviewed conference proceedings, papers written in English, and papers addressing the research question.

Figure 1 illustrates the systematic review process followed. The initial search yielded 1509 results from all four databases. From these results, 307 were found to be duplicate records and were removed. The inclusion criteria were applied to the 1202 records, resulting in 1013 records being excluded as they did not meet the required inclusion criteria. The remaining 189 records were assessed by reading the paper abstracts and conclusion sections. 158 papers were excluded as it was not relevant to the research question. Therefore, 31 papers were included in this systematic literature review.

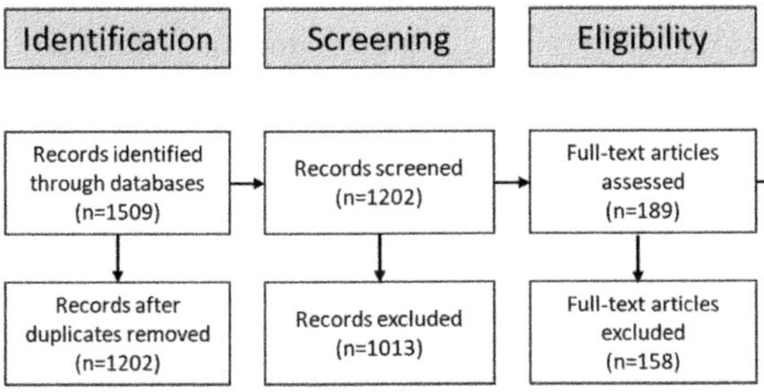

Fig. 1. PRISMA flow diagram

3 Data Analysis and Findings

According to [1, 10] the concept of fake news gained popularity after the 2016 election in the United States. In line with this, the analysis showed an upward trend in the number of papers that have been published. None of the papers were published before 2017. It is also noted that in 2020, the most papers were published. Figure 2 illustrates the sub-themes associated with the sub-research question. Each of the themes will be discussed in the following sections.

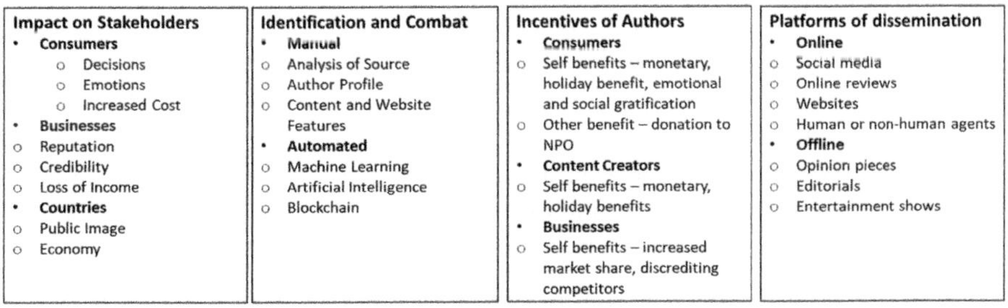

Fig. 2. Sub-themes

3.1 Impact of Fake News on the Tourism Industry

Tourism is a key socio-economic activity around the world, and drives job creation as well as trade between nations [1, 32]. Information plays a key role in the tourism industry due to the industry being driven by the generation, consumption, and sharing of information in real time across the globe [4, 10, 15, 30]. The industry is reliant on information that is unbiased and updated in real-time. This can be found in reviews and experiences shared by consumers worldwide [1]. Searching for information on online platforms and its dissemination on these platforms is a characteristic of the present-day tourism industry [28]. The industry is frequently impacted by fake news and faces the results of its dispersion on a global scale [1, 25]. Therefore, it is paramount that the impact of fake news on the various stakeholders involved be determined. The main stakeholders impacted by fake news in the tourism industry are the consumers, businesses, and countries [1, 8, 10, 28, 30]. Each stakeholder will be expanded on below.

Impact on Consumers. Fake news in the tourism industry influences the behaviors, assumptions, expectations, and beliefs of consumers [25, 30]. Due to prior experiences and knowledge of the destination or organization, the consumer can then face doubt and confusion [8]. Consumers can also experience anger and regret after realizing that they were misled and be ridiculed by their social circle if they purchase a product or visit a destination that has been associated with fake news [12, 30]. The costs of searching for information increases when consumers with a purchase commitment come across fake news [12]. This is because they need to verify whether the content is indeed false and may need to find and settle for an alternative from a different business [8]. An example of a cost encountered by the consumer is spending more money than what was budgeted for when they are victims of fake news, and their experience is unsatisfactory [29]. In addition, consumers could be scammed into accessing fake websites, and lose money and personal details by entering their credit card details [12].

Impact on Businesses. Tham & Chen [28] state that the reputation and credibility of businesses suffer because of a fake news piece or review. This then influences the consumer's perception of the brand and decreases the likelihood of them returning [28, 29]. If an organization advertises on sites that have been associated with fake news, the consumer develops a negative perception of the brand's reputation [8]. Caution should be taken when using advertisement placement software which places advertisements using algorithms on news sites with high-traffic [17]. These websites can potentially be fake news websites, and company managers need to monitor that this does not happen [12]. Businesses should guard against and tackle fake news publications and rumors before the damages are irrecoverable [1]. Vasist & Krishnan [30] provide an example of this where a viral rumor spread about employees from certain restaurants who had COVID, which resulted in other restaurants in the area losing consumers.

Fake online reviews of businesses can result in consumers not purchasing from them and negatively impact the business's reputation [6]. Online reviews should be monitored by businesses and if fake content is suspected, the matter should be investigated, and the public should be informed via official platforms [22]. Negative online reviews which have a high number of replies and votes have also been shown to decrease the profitability of businesses [32]. Consumers need to get an honest reflection of a business's services so that they develop trust and return to support the business [25, 26]. Businesses need to be wary of posting reviews from sites such as TripAdvisor because the business's reputation will suffer if consumers regard it to be exaggerated or not reflecting various consumer experiences [30].

Impact on Countries. The public image of countries can be tainted following the publication of fake news [10, 15]. An example of this is provided in the author's paper where Egypt's public image was damaged when fake news spread on social media and sparked online debates and discussions after the murder of a Polish tourist had taken place [10]. Multiple versions of the story were circulating and caused the facts to become distorted, which then resulted in other Polish and international visitors cancelling their trips and viewing the country in a negative light [10].

Countries can also get additional publicity through the resharing of articles on social platforms, which could be an advantage if the news paints them in a positive light [1]. However, if this positive news is an exaggeration, the trust of consumers can be eroded and will cause a decrease in tourism revenue [6]. Tourists can become prejudiced against tourism destinations that have been associated with fake news [1, 8, 28]. This then influences the decisions that tourists make, as well as perceptions towards the destination [8].

Fake news regarding a natural disaster that was published in the United States resulted in tourists cancelling their reservations to local destinations. This caused the local economy to incur losses of between $7,000-$140,000 over a fortnight [28]. Businesses in these destinations faced significant repercussions, and some of them closed and let go of staff as they could not afford their services [28]. Therefore, it is paramount that businesses are equipped to identify and report fake news as well as to take legal action where required [15]. Some destinations had promoted being 'virus-free' during the COVID-19 pandemic to encourage tourists to visit. However, this then resulted in those countries seeing a surge in cases and consequently, caused their economies as well as the livelihoods of citizens to suffer [1].

3.2 Incentives for Authors of Fake News in the Tourism Industry

Authors of fake news are incentivized to self-benefit or in two instances to benefit others, such as when donations were given to NPOs. The section below provides more detail on these findings.

Authors Driven by Self-Benefit. Authors of fake news in the tourism industry are driven by self-benefit or seeing others benefit [7]. In some instances of self-benefit such as when they can receive a sponsored holiday, authors can face a moral dilemma [7, 10]. Consumers or content creators can be incentivized by self-benefits such as monetary or holiday benefits for disseminating news targeting a particular destination or writing an online review to increase the amount of positive electronic Word of Mouth (eWOM) [7, 8, 28]. Another type of self-benefit is when competitors in the tourism market are driven to publish articles and posts with fake news regarding their counterparts' products and services to attain a higher market share [1, 28]. Achieving a higher market share is driven by fierce market competition, changing technologies, and an expanding range of options for tourists [1]. This can then lead to businesses utilizing a strategy of misinformation on competitors' products in competing for the loyalty of consumers. Many businesses are adopting this strategy as traditional marketing strategies are no longer effective in making businesses stand out in the tourism market [1, 28]. In addition, hotels can benefit from the posting of fake positive reviews under their profiles on review sites and can discredit other competitors in the market to sway consumers away [15, 20]. Two additional self-benefits that can drive consumers to engage in the dissemination of fake news are feeling emotional gratification and receiving social gratification from the online community [23].

Authors Driven by Others Benefitting. Authors are more likely to face a moral dilemma when posting a fake review that will benefit others, such as when trying to sustain jobs or in support of Non-Profit Organizations (NPOs) through a portion of booking revenue [25]. Incentives such as contributing to NPOs are only effective if the consumer can identify with the cause [7].

3.3 The Platforms Used to Disseminate Fake News in the Tourism Industry

Information can be disseminated through online and offline platforms [32]. Information that is shared on online platforms spreads faster and has greater influence in comparison to information that is on offline platforms [31]. The two types of platforms will be expanded on below.

Dissemination of Information on Offline Platforms. Tourists occasionally review opinion pieces and editorials while deciding on a destination to visit, and they can also be used as tools to spread fake news and divert tourists from visiting destinations [1, 25]. However, they can also be written in a positive light to draw consumers to destinations on false promises [25]. Another offline platform is satirical and entertainment shows which typically have humorous intentions [25, 26]. However, these shows then create a distorted image of the destinations being discussed and often negatively portray them [26]. This was seen when a New Zealand comedian mocked Queensland and alluded to it being a dangerous location to visit. This can either kindle a curiosity within listeners to explore the destination, or it can convince them not to visit at all [25].

Dissemination of Information on Online Platforms. There has been an increase in the use of online and digital spaces by tourists where they share their travel experiences [28]. This is attributed to globalization, fast connectivity through 5G networks, and the easily accessible nature of social media that can disseminate information from different devices and remote destinations in real-time [1, 2, 13]. Fake news in the tourism industry is disseminated through social media platforms, namely Facebook, Twitter (currently known as X), and WhatsApp, online review sites as well as websites. Each of these platforms will be briefly discussed below.

Social Media Platforms. Facebook and Twitter have been termed as key transmitters in the dissemination of fake news [4, 13, 23]. Social platforms do not censor content before it is posted and enforce neither restrictions nor quality control [10, 13, 19]. This provides the opportunity for information to be manipulated and disseminated at an exponential rate [1]. Users are likely to believe and share information from social platforms without verifying its credibility or reliability [4, 31].

Another social platform by which fake news in the tourism industry rapidly spreads is WhatsApp [26]. When rumors of a meningitis outbreak in Sao Paulo were circulated on the platform, tourists believed that the outbreak was rife in the city. Many cancelled their trips, which resulted in a 35% loss in local tourism revenue [23]. This occurred despite official social media statements from the city's management reporting the news as fake. WhatsApp users can make use of emotional language which gives the content a reliable feel [25]. WhatsApp does not check for the reliability of the news, and it spreads easily through groups and statuses [23, 26]. Recently, they have introduced a feature showing messages that have been forwarded many times, which consumers can look out for [23].

Online Reviews. Online reviews form part of eWOM and play a key role and impact the decisions made by consumers as they provide information about hotels or services and allow opinions to be shared freely as they are based on experiences [6, 7, 29, 30]. TripAdvisor is the largest travel experience platform globally and in 2020 had 859 million reviews on 8.6 million accommodation locations, destinations, restaurants, and cruises [24]. Consumers regard the reviews on independent review sites such as TripAdvisor and Expedia.com to be more trustworthy and authentic than the reviews on the official company websites as well as on social media before planning their trips [6, 7, 29, 30]. Readers assess common factors mentioned in all the reviews before deciding [1, 26, 30]. Banerjee & Chua [6] state that 98% of consumers read hotel reviews and 78% refer to them as a deciding factor on where to stay. Therefore, reviews are key in attaining the trust of consumers and meeting their expectations [6, 29]. Consumers are shown to display less skepticism towards destinations or activities with a high volume of reviews and a high average rating [30]. However, there are concerns regarding the degree of credibility and quality of information from eWOM as many reviews are made to appear reliable, and then prove otherwise [6, 24]. The purpose of fake reviews is to advertise a service or business unethically and to mislead the decisions taken by the reader [26]. Luxury hotels located close to their competitors in the same class tend to have more negative fake reviews than them, and lower-class hotels that are close to luxury hotels are likely to have more positive fake reviews [30]. Fake reviews often either contain non-existent features of the hotel or an exaggerated rating of the existing features of the hotel [26]. Businesses that specialize in the spreading of fake news are often utilized to disseminate papers on social platforms [1]. For example, a business owner was arrested for selling fake reviews to hotels that were posted on TripAdvisor [26]. This is in line with Vasist & Krishnan [30] who stated that the prevalence of fraudulent fake review businesses has been increasing. Therefore, a quality indicator for sites like TripAdvisor will be a good feature, as well as a seal or indication from the hotel that the individual stayed there and had an experience [26].

Websites. Websites are also utilized to spread tourism fake news through advertisements [19]. Users are drawn in by catchy headlines that are made to look reputable and capture their attention [16, 19]. Upon clicking the link, they are often redirected to a connected site which appears to be verified. This is known as click-baiting [16]. Links to these sites are then published on social media such as Facebook or Twitter where it spreads through resharing and interactions from users in the comments [15]. Headlines linking to fake news often contain controversial elements, linked to gossip, and sensational to encourage interactions with the post [15, 16].

Human or Non-human Agents. On online platforms, fake news can be disseminated by human or non-human agents such as social bots, who mimic human behavior by producing content and interacting with humans on social platforms [8, 24, 27]. These bots then drive the spread of fake news by commenting, liking, and sharing fake news articles or posts which makes the post appear in more consumer's newsfeeds [8]. Between 9 and 15 percent of Twitter accounts and 60 million accounts on Facebook are confirmed to be social bots [3]. These bots give their profiles a realistic feel by searching the internet for information to complete the image and post content at a realistic and scheduled rate. They then interact with each other on social platforms and amplify fake news [24]. Thereafter, they systematically target influential accounts by replying to their content and mentioning them in comments [27]. This then leads to them becoming a part of the dissemination process [8].

Human agents can be classified as malicious or benign [8, 30]. The malicious group spreads fake news despite being aware that it is false, as they want to achieve a goal whereas the benign group share content on social platforms as they believe in and trust it [8]. They do this when they regard the content to be of high quality and see that users in their social circle interact with it through sharing, liking, and commenting [30]. Consumers are also influenced by the sharing activity of their social circle [24]. As the number of shares increases and users see the reshares and comments, it comes across as trustworthy, useful, of high quality, and popular. This then increases the likelihood of interaction and sharing activity [16]. The purpose of this can be to either appear knowledgeable, to interact with their social circle and feel included, or to show concern for others by informing them of news [8]. The malicious agents often create accounts under pseudonyms to get an upper hand on their competitors, or they employ the services of third parties, such as content creators [8]. These malicious agents add filters to posts on social media or share pictures of other countries to mislead readers and distort the image of the destination they will be visiting [28]. This damages the reputation of the destination and can result in legal actions as well as lawsuits from tourists [1, 30].

3.4 Identification and Combat of Fake News in the Tourism Industry

Fake news in the tourism industry can be identified and combatted by utilizing manual and automated methods. Twenty-two papers made mention of manual methods, whereas only seven made mention of automated methods. More detail on how these findings arose can be found in the section below.

Use of Manual Methods. Sousa, Silva, & Veloso [26] reported that only 46% of the respondents felt equipped to identify fake news. Canada's Central Broadcasting Commission has introduced a 'Fake News Chatbot' which teaches participants how to identify trusted sources, and suspicious articles and determine where an image or video has been modified [30]. Consumers need to actively analyze, evaluate, and process content from the media instead of believing and sharing all the content that they read [18, 30]. This will aid in identifying and mitigating the spread of fake news on media platforms.

One of the main sources of fake news in the tourism industry is unverified articles [1, 26, 30]. Peterson [22] states that the antidotes for fake news are the evaluation of sources and asking critical questions. On the evaluation of the source, if it is found that the account is not verified, has no links to official websites, or does not list verifiable sources for published articles, this could be an indication that the account and article are fake [15, 25, 28]. If anyone comes across fake news on social platforms, they should report the news as fake, stop engaging with the account, and block it [1, 5]. Facebook enables users to mark a post as potential fake news through their collaboration with Corrective, which is a research initiative [19].

On social platforms, users should be wary of posts that have a lot of shares and comments, but no verifiable sources [19]. Users should investigate by conducting an internet search to ensure that reputable news houses or sites share the same view of the post or article [13, 25]. It is also imperative to look beyond the top search results [21]. This is particularly relevant in industries with ratings and reviews, such as the tourism industry, as news recipients often go with the notion that 'many resonate with this, therefore it must be true' [27]. If the post follows up from other news sources and contains verification from related parties, it is likely to be trustworthy [18]. If articles on the same site or page are not credible or accurate, there is an increased chance of the content not being credible [17]. Paskin [21] advises that the articles or posts on the page should also be evaluated to identify potential biases of the source. When the author of a post or review has been hidden, or if the account used has no interactions, the probability of it not being credible is also increased [8, 19]. If the name of the account matches an established news site, the profile often has a verified symbol and is trustworthy [23]. However, if it does not, then the profile has been made to resemble the appearance of a verified page [29]. This is done by using the same theme colors, font, page layout, and journalistic manner of wording headings and sub-headings [13]. The user can confirm this by visiting the official website of the news source and checking the links to the associated media pages [8]. Hanz & Kingsland [13] explain that.org is often used as a domain name to appear as reputable. Users are recommended to read the 'About Us' and 'Contact Us' sections to get more information about the organization. The following websites can also be used to fact-check articles: The Washington Post fact checker, factcheck.org, TruthOrFiction, HoaxSlayer as well as Snopes.com [13, 20].

Timeliness is an important consideration when evaluating the trustworthiness of news [16]. When posts or reviews contain conflicting information compared to those written in the same period, the user should be cautious [19]. If articles with the same content are circulating on social platforms with changed dates and authors, it is likely to be fake [26]. The repetition technique is used by online bots who spread the same article on various platforms and at different points in time, to make the message believable to the user [7, 27]. The linguistic features of posts and reviews can also be assessed to determine their level of credibility, such as the use of capital letters, pronouns and punctuation, comprehensiveness, exaggeration, conflicting language, and specificity [19, 27]. If there is extensive exaggeration and lack of specificity, the reader should be cautious [6]. Fake news pieces are also likely to contain profanities [8, 13]. First-person pronouns are also usually incorrectly used in fake news [7]. The grammatical structure in which the text is written also plays a role in determining its authenticity, as authentic reviews are well-written [5]. Realistic reviews are easier to read, detailed, use superlatives and often are non-committal [6]. Posts and reviews with fake news often use extensive emotive language and provide a few facts as they want to appeal to the emotions of the reader and reduce the cognitive effort that the consumer needs to utilize to decide and form an opinion [7, 19, 30]. Upon assessing these linguistic factors, the accuracy of fake news determination was 71.4% [6].

Users also need to critically assess the content of reviews to ensure that it is of sufficient length, has a detailed description, and that the profile of the reviewer is complete [18, 32]. If the content appears to be of high quality, contains images, and was written by a reviewer that has a good reputation, posting habit, and sufficient experience, then the review is likely to be authentic [24]. If the identity of the author of the reviews and their expertise is unknown, consumers should be weary when trusting the reviews [24, 30]. Jiang, Guo, Chen, & Yang [16] elaborate on the inclusion of images in content draw attention, minimize uncertainty, and motivate the consumer to make a booking or share the news. Fake reviews tend to focus on their feelings and how their expectations were not met, whereas a realistic review tends to focus on tangible aspects [12]. The comments in fake reviews also tend to reflect feelings of horror, disgust, and surprise [27]. The profile of the author can be analyzed to determine the number and type of followers and following accounts, links to previous fake news publications as well as the number of posts to determine their credibility [21]. Consumers should check whether reviews from people that they know personally align with the reviews they encounter online [7].

Use of Automated Methods. Facebook uses fact-screening sites such as Snopes and PolitiFact to identify potentially fake news [17, 19]. It highlights the content's evolution, the channels that it was shared on as well as its source [17]. Google and Facebook have implemented fact-checking initiatives that display links to authentic articles as well as warnings when unverified links are clicked if users search for topics that are frequently associated with fake news [8, 27]. Facebook makes use of machine-learning which identifies fake news by using 20,000 fact-checkers [22].

Deepfake technology is often used to create video, audio as well as image hoaxes to make the fake reviews appear more credible [8, 28]. Deepfake is a type of Artificial Intelligence that plays an important role in the eWOM age [8]. Machine learning is also an efficient approach for detecting fake news, compared to manual checking which is more time-consuming [19, 31]. However, the authors argue that using blockchain technology is even better than machine learning as it is more efficient in tracing and restricting fake news, which enables verified news to reach the consumer [5, 9].

4 Conclusion, Limitations, and Future Research

The paper reported on the extent of fake news in the tourism industry. The analysis identified that fake news was disseminated online and offline through various methods. Each of the platforms has different mechanisms to identify and combat fake news. Fake news authors were mostly motivated by self-benefit. The impact of fake news on the tourism industry is felt by consumers, businesses, and countries. All these stakeholders have a monetary loss, and businesses and countries have the added loss of reputation and credibility. Tourism departments can mitigate these challenges by increasing awareness by hosting workshops and online campaigns for businesses and consumers to learn how to look out for fake news. Further investigation can be done into the willingness of the stakeholders to adopt the mentioned guidelines.

Although this study is limited by the SLR search parameters and databases accessed, the results are still valid in explaining the impact of fake news in the travel and tourism industry.

Prior research focused on the impact of fake news related to businesses in the tourism industry. Future research can focus on the impact, and associated mitigation strategies, of consumers of fake news in the travel industry. Additionally, researchers can investigate how businesses and countries can recover from being affected by fake news in the tourism industry.

References

1. Abdallah, A.: Fake news, false advertising, social media and the tourism industry. Int. J. Dev. Res. **11**(7), 48999–49003 (2021)
2. Allcott, H., Gentzkow, M.: Social media and fake news in the 2016 election. J. Econ. Perspect. **31**, 211–236 (2017)
3. Al-Maatouk, Q., Abbas, M.K.: The significance of social media posts on human decisions. In: International Conference on Decision Aid Sciences and Application (DASA), pp 143–146. IEEE (2021)
4. Anton, E., Teodorescu, C.A., Vargas, V.M.: Perspectives and reviews in the use of narrative strategies for communicating fake news in the tourism industry. In: Proceedings of the International Conference on Business Excellence, vol. 14, pp. 728–734 (2020)
5. Bajpai, S.T., Sharma, D.K.: Fake news propagation in the era of Covid-19-tracing and combating fake news using block chain technology. In: International Conference on Simulation, Automation & Smart Manufacturing (SASM), pp 1–8. IEEE (2021)
6. Banerjee, S., Chua, A.Y.: Calling out fake online reviews through robust epistemic belief. Inf. Manag. **58**, 103445 (2021)
7. Choi, S., Mattila, A.S., Hoof, H.B., Quadri-Felitti, D.: The role of power and incentives in inducing fake reviews in the tourism industry. J. Travel Res. **56**, 975–987 (2017)
8. Domenico, G., Sit, J., Ishizaka, A., Nunan, D.: Fake news, social media and marketing: a systematic review. J. Bus. Res. **124**, 329–341 (2021)
9. Erceg, A., Sekuloska, J.D., Kelić, I.: Blockchain in the tourism industry—a review of the situation in Croatia and Macedonia. In: Informatics, pp 1–5. MDPI (2020)
10. Fedeli, G.: Fake news' meets tourism: a proposed research agenda. Ann. Tour. Res. **80**, 102684 (2020)
11. Fink, A.: Conducting Research Literature Reviews: From the Internet to Paper, 2nd edn. Sage Publications, Thousand Oaks (2005)
12. Flostrand, A., Pitt, L., Kietzmann, J.: Fake news and brand management: a Delphi study of impact, vulnerability and mitigation. J. Prod. Brand. Manag. **29**, 246–254 (2020)
13. Hanz, K., Kingsland, E.S.: Fake or for real? A fake news workshop. Ref. Serv. Rev. **48**, 91–112 (2020)
14. Harley, N.: About 1 million Tripadvisor reviews in 2020 were fake (2021)
15. Hodut, A.M., Toma, L.A., Iosim, I.: Tourism and the phenomenon of fake news. In: Agricultural Management/Lucrari Stiintifice Seria I, Management Agricol, pp 136–140 (2020)

16. Jiang, H., Zhang, X.: An experimental model of regulating the sharing economy in China: the case of online car-hailing. Comput. Law Secur. Rev. **35**, 145–156 (2019). https://doi.org/10.1016/j.clsr.2018.12.008
17. Lan, X., You, L.: Fake news in the business world: the main types and the implications of the 2016 U.S. President. Elect. Public Relat. J. **13**, 1–22 (2020)
18. Luo, Y.F., Yang, S.C., Kang, S.: New media literacy and news trustworthiness: an application of importance-performance analysis. Comput. Educ. **185**, 104529 (2022)
19. Meinert, J., Mirbabaie, M., Dungs, S., Aker, A.: Is it really fake?–towards an understanding of fake news in social media communication. In: International Conference on Social Computing and Social Media, pp 484–497 (2018)
20. Nyow, N.X., Chua, H.N.: Detecting fake news with tweets. In: Properties. 2019 IEEE Conference on Application, Information and Network Security (AINS), pp 24–29. IEEE (2019)
21. Paskin, D.: Real or fake news: who knows? J. Social Media Soc. **7**, 252–273 (2018)
22. Peterson, M.: A high-speed world with fake news: brand managers take warning. J. Prod. Brand. Manag. **29**, 234–245 (2020)
23. Sampat, B., Raj, S.: Fake or real news? Understanding the gratifications and personality traits of individuals sharing fake news on social media platforms. Aslib J. Inf. Manag. **74**, 1–37 (2022)
24. Song, B.L., Liew, C.Y., Sia, J.Y., Gopal, K.: Electronic word-of-mouth in travel social networking sites and young consumers' purchase intentions: an extended information adoption model. Young Cons. **22**, 521–538 (2021)
25. Sousa, B., Silva, M.: A preliminary study on fake news and tourism: the post-truth era and practical implications. In: Proceedings of the International Workshop Tourism and Hospitality Management, pp. 127–130 (2019)
26. Sousa, B.B., Silva, M.S., Veloso, C.M.: The quality of communication and fake news in tourism: a segmented perspective. Qual. - Access Success **21**, 101–105 (2020)
27. Tandoc, J., Edson, C.: The facts of fake news: a research review. Sociol. Compass **13**, 12724 (2019)
28. Tham, A., Chen, S.H.: Fake news and tourism-whose responsibility is it? J. Resp. Tour. Manag. **2**, 32–36 (2022)
29. Tran, L.T.: Online reviews and purchase intention: a cosmopolitanism perspective. Tour. Manag. Perspect. **35**, 100722 (2020)
30. Vasist, P.N., Krishnan, S.: Demystifying fake news in the hospitality industry: a systematic literature review, framework, and an agenda for future research. Int. J. Hosp. Manag. **106**, 103277 (2022)
31. Wang, Y.Q., et al.: Weak supervision for fake news detection via reinforcement learning. In: Proceedings of the AAAI Conference on Artificial Intelligence, pp 516–523 (2020)
32. Zhang, D., Wu, P., Wu, C.: The role of key online reviews in affecting online hotel booking: an empirical investigation. Ind. Manag. Data Syst. **122**, 499–520 (2022)

Enhancing Traceability in the Norwegian Fish Supply Chain: Blockchain Adoption

Zoyia Konstantopoulou(✉) and Patrick Mikalef

Department of Computer Science, Faculty of Information Technology and Electrical Engineering, Norwegian University of Science and Technology, Trondheim, Norway
zoyiak@stud.ntnu.no

Abstract. This study investigates the adoption of blockchain technology in the Norwegian fish supply chain to address the critical issue of illegal fishing, a context where existing traceability systems face significant challenges. Focusing on the Norwegian Directorate of Fisheries' CatchID Program, this research examines the factors influencing stakeholder perceptions and adoption of BCT within the Norwegian fish supply chain. Through observational and survey data, the study leverages affordance theory to reveal that while stakeholders recognize blockchain technology's potential to increase transparency, data integrity, and security, significant barriers hinder its adoption, including challenges with integrating it with existing systems and navigating regulatory hurdles. The research underscores the need for strategic alignment between technological capabilities and socio-cultural contexts to facilitate successful BCT integration.

Keywords: Blockchain · Supply Chain · Norwegian Fish Industry · Traceability · Sustainability · Affordance Theory

1 Introduction

Blockchain technology (BCT) has emerged as a transformative force across various sectors, including food, agriculture, and value chains (Wong et al. 2020). Its decentralized and transparent nature offers a novel approach to managing supply chains, particularly in addressing issues related to information flow and data quality management. In blockchain systems, records are replicated and distributed across multiple hosts, updated in near real-time, and cryptographically secured to create immutable entries (Tsolakis et al. 2021). This architecture fosters transparency and trust among supply chain participants by ensuring the integrity and authenticity of transactional data (Treiblmaier 2018). BCT has sparked significant interest across various sectors, promising transformative changes in how supply chains are managed, particularly emphasizing traceability and tracking enhancements (Falcone et al. 2021). The application of blockchain technology is anticipated to advance supply chain management by offering immutable record-keeping, fostering trust among stakeholders, and enhancing security features. These capabilities are particularly valuable to the fisheries sector, where transparency is crucial for sustainability and regulatory compliance (Tolentino Zondervan et al. 2023).

Published by Springer Nature Switzerland AG 2024
R. van de Wetering et al. (Eds.): I3E 2024, LNCS 14907, pp. 383–393, 2024.
https://doi.org/10.1007/978-3-031-72234-9_32

Within the context of fish supply chains, traceability plays a crucial role in ensuring product authenticity and regulatory compliance. This involves activities such as product tracking, data storytelling, and species verification, contributing to the integrity and sustainability of seafood products (Tolentino-Zondervan et al. 2023). BCT application, with advanced Internet of Things (IoT) sensors, enables monitoring of real-time fuel and energy consumption (Tsolakis et al. 2021). This allows for the accurate track and trace for various stages from farm to fork in the fisheries value chain. By integrating information as new blocks and safeguarding sensitive details like fishing crew identities and seafood prices from public access, blockchain ensures that food business operators maintain ownership of their data (Falcone et al. 2021). This promotes its distribution across the supply chain, enhancing transparency and the traceability of products' histories for food safety (Tsolakis et al. 2021). One of the significant advantages of integrating blockchain technology into fish supply chains is its ability to enhance product quality and safety through real-time monitoring (Lumineau et al. 2021). By combining blockchain with sensor systems, stakeholders can monitor critical parameters such as temperature and pH levels in real-time (Howson 2020). This capability enables rapid identification of deviations from optimal conditions, thereby improving product quality and reducing the risk of spoilage or contamination. For example, sensors installed on aquaculture facilities can log temperature data directly onto the blockchain, creating an immutable record of environmental conditions throughout the production process (Falcone et al. 2021).

Several initiatives exemplify the transformative potential of blockchain technology in seafood supply chains. For example, Provenance, one of the most successful blockchain projects in track and trace, enables consumers to trace the origin and journey of seafood products from source to shelf (Howson 2020). By scanning a QR code or accessing an online platform, consumers can access detailed information about the product's provenance, including the location and methods of capture, processing facilities, and transportation routes. This level of transparency empowers consumers to make informed purchasing decisions based on factors such as sustainability, ethical sourcing, and quality assurance (Howson 2020). Similarly, IBM Food Trust leverages blockchain technology to enhance traceability and safety in the food supply chain. Developed in collaboration with major industry players such as Walmart, Nestle, and Unilever, IBM Food Trust provides a secure and immutable ledger for recording and verifying food-related transactions (Howson 2020). By digitizing key information such as batch numbers, expiration dates, and shipping records, stakeholders can quickly trace the flow of food products through the supply chain, thereby enhancing food safety and regulatory compliance (Howson 2020). However, despite the promising prospects offered by blockchain technology, several challenges must be addressed to realize its full potential in fish supply chains (Ghode et al. 2020). Variable data quality from suppliers is a significant concern, as inconsistent or inaccurate data can undermine the integrity and reliability of blockchain-based systems (Shakhbulatov et al. 2020). Additionally, the labor-intensive process of data collection poses logistical challenges, particularly in environments where manual data entry is required (Howson 2020). Overcoming these challenges is essential to harness the full potential of blockchain technology in enhancing the efficiency, transparency, and sustainability of fisheries.

As a major player in the global seafood industry, Norway is well-positioned to lead in promoting sustainable and transparent fishing practices (Standal & Grimaldo 2020). Blockchain technology offers a promising tool to enhance traceability and combat illegal, unreported, and unregulated fishing, thereby strengthening Norway's reputation as a responsible seafood supplier. The Norwegian fisheries sector is actively exploring innovative solutions to address the issue of illegal fishing by promoting transparency and traceability (Standal & Hersoug 2023). This paper aims to assess stakeholders' awareness, understanding, and readiness for BCT adoption, identifying gaps to facilitate successful integration and combat illegal fishing (Tolentino-Zondervan et al. 2023). It also investigates the actions, user perceptions, and socio-technical alignments that influence the levels of awareness and adoption readiness of BCT.

2 Background

Norwegian fisheries are faced with significant challenges due to illegal, unreported, and unregulated (IUU) fishing activities, driving the need for enhanced traceability and transparency. Surveys conducted from 2013 to 2021 have revealed a concerning trend of fishers admitting to or justifying practices that violate quota regulations (Standal & Hersoug 2023). This situation, coupled with growing consumer demands for transparency concerning the product origin and processing of seafood, underscores the urgent need for traceability enhancement within the sector (Mathisen 2018). However, the transmission of catch, processing, and transport information across the supply chain remains limited, leading to significant gaps in information flow and quality data (Standal & Hersoug 2023). To mitigate these issues, initiatives such as the authorized, automated reporting system have been proposed to improve catch report accuracy and reduce fraud risk (Tsolakis et al. 2021). Despite governmental efforts to introduce advanced automatic catch monitoring technologies for accurate quota management and regulatory compliance, resistance from the fishing community underscores the complexity of balancing technological solutions with the operational realities of fishing practices (Standal & Hersoug 2023).

The Norwegian Directorate of Fisheries' CatchID Program is a strategic effort towards leveraging emerging technologies for regulatory compliance and supply chain transparency that promotes track and trace from "farm to fork" (Norwegian Directorate of Fisheries 2021). Yet, achieving successful blockchain integration in supply chains requires overcoming barriers such as technical challenges, the necessity for prominent levels of collaboration, and stakeholder resistance (Ghode et al. 2020). The integration of track and trace systems in Norway's fish supply chain can be categorized into three key groups of stakeholders: **Government Entities, the Private Sector, and Research and Development (R&D) Organizations**. Government entities set and enforce standards that promote safety and efficiency and manage customs for international trade (Tsolakis et al. 2021). The private sector, including manufacturers and logistics companies, uses these systems to enhance supply chain visibility and customer service. R&D organizations, comprising academic and technological innovators, focus on advancing the capabilities of these systems, often collaborating with government and industry to refine and test recent technologies. In addition to the efforts in Norway, other countries have successfully implemented blockchain technology in their fisheries and agricultural supply chains, demonstrating its potential for improving traceability and transparency. For instance, China has developed a traceability model for agricultural products using RFID-based blockchain and IoT technology, significantly improving the accuracy and efficiency of tracking agricultural products (Tian 2016). In Indonesia, a blockchain-based traceability system has been designed for capture fisheries, utilizing smart contracts to ensure the quality and safety of fishery products from capture to consumer, thereby enhancing transparency and consumer trust (Afrianto et al. 2020). In Portugal, a blockchain platform for the fishery value chain has been proposed to trace fish lots throughout the entire value chain, from capture or aquaculture production to the final consumer, ensuring product quality and compliance with regulatory standards (Cruz and da Cruz 2020). Collectively, these examples illustrate that BCT has the potential to enhance supply chain track and trace by improving several critical aspects: optimizing supply chain operations, ensuring food safety, building consumer trust, and meeting regulatory compliance.

2.1 Theoretical Framework: Affordance Theory

Understanding the adoption and integration of BCT in fisheries supply chains necessitates moving beyond mere technical feasibility to an examination of the socio-technical dynamics at play. Emerging technologies possess the capacity to fundamentally re-orchestrate key aspects of organizing, which, however, is not predetermined but rather emerges from the intricate interrelationship between IT-artifacts and their social context (Bailey 2022). Affordance theory provides a powerful lens for unpacking this interdependent dynamic. Affordances, as articulated by Gibson (1986) and further elaborated within IS research, encompass the potential actions latent within a technology, shaped by both its design and the perceptions and capabilities of its users (Leonardi 2012).

This perspective aligns with a relational view of technology, which emphasizes the fluid and interconnected nature of technological adoption (Carpenter et al. 2012). Rather than viewing blockchain as a discrete entity, a relational approach examines how it becomes embedded within the existing network of actors, practices, and institutions (Faraj & Azad 2012; Malik et al. 2024). Therefore, analyzing the affordances of BCT through this lens allows us to understand not only what the technology enables, but also how it is enacted and negotiated within the specific social context of Norwegian fisheries. (Leonardi 2012). Affordances pertain to the possibilities that technology offers, users' perceptions of these possibilities, and how these perceptions shape the way technology is used (Volkoff & Strong 2013), reflecting the actor-environment mutuality where the actor and artifact are inseparable (McGrenere & Ho 2000). Primary elements of affordances in IS include action possibilities, user perception, and socio-technical alignment (Volkoff & Strong 2013). **Action possibilities** refer to what users can achieve with the technology, based on its design and their capabilities. **User perception** involves how stakeholders understand and interpret these possibilities, which significantly influences their willingness to adopt and effectively utilize the technology. Lastly, **socio-technical alignment** describes the harmony between the technology and the social context within which it is employed, emphasizing the need for alignment between technological features and organizational practices (Volkoff & Strong 2013).

Davis and Chouinard (2017) further refined the theory by introducing and elaborating conditions of affordance—perception, dexterity, and cultural and institutional legitimacy. **Perception** involves stakeholders' understanding of blockchain technology's functionalities and benefits. For instance, key stakeholders do not perceive value in BCT, they are unlikely to adopt the technology. **Dexterity** relates to the skill and ability of users to interact with technology effectively, which includes the technological readiness and training provided to stakeholders. Lastly, **cultural and institutional legitimacy** addresses the extent to which blockchain technology is supported and legitimized by existing cultural norms and institutional regulations (Davis & Chouinard 2017).

By focusing on these conditions, the study can uncover the ways blockchain technology might be actualized in the context of Norwegian fisheries, addressing both the potential benefits and the constraints imposed by the technology and key stakeholder groups. In the fish supply chain, BCT offers several affordances. First, **enhanced traceability** allows stakeholders to create immutable records of fish products from catch to consumer, ensuring transparency and compliance with sustainability standards. This action possibility leverages BCT's decentralized and cryptographically secured nature to maintain reliable and authentic data across the supply chain. Additionally, **improved data integrity** is achieved through the tamper-proof records that blockchain systems provide, enhancing the overall reliability of transactional data. BCT also enables **real-time and tamper-proof monitoring** of critical catch parameters. This capability helps maintain product quality and safety by enabling rapid identification of deviations from optimal conditions.

3 Methods

This investigation adopts a Convergent Parallel Mixed Methods Design (Creswell & Plano Clark 2018) to examine the adoption of blockchain technology in the Norwegian fisheries sector. This design allows for the simultaneous collection and independent analysis of qualitative and quantitative data, which are later integrated during the interpretation phase to enhance the robustness of the findings (March & Smith 1995). Qualitative insights were derived from participant observations conducted at the 2nd International Symposium on Catch Identification Technologies, providing an in-depth understanding of stakeholder interactions and the contextual nuances influencing blockchain adoption. Concurrently a survey was administered to 95 stakeholders directly involved in the Norwegian fishing industry. Participants were selected from a cohort of 110 potential respondents identified through the CatchID project, ensuring representation from various stakeholder groups. The survey, designed to maintain respondent anonymity, employs a mix of Likert scales, multiple-choice, and short open-ended questions to gather data on: Stakeholder roles and their understanding of blockchain technology.

- Perceptions of blockchain's potential impact on the fisheries sector.
- Challenges experienced within existing systems.
- Stakeholder readiness, expectations, and concerns regarding blockchain adoption.

In addition to the survey qualitative interviews with relevant stakeholders involved in the pilot's application of BCT in fisheries, private sector representatives and relevant stakeholder from the Norwegian Directorate of Fisheries will be incorporated. These interviews are intended to provide deeper insights into the practical challenges and perceptions related to BCT adoption, complementing the quantitative data and enhancing the findings' overall robustness. Qualitative insights will help identify cultural and institutional legitimacy concerns that may not be fully evident from survey data alone. Qualitative data from participant observations and interviews were analyzed using thematic analysis to identify key themes and patterns related to BCT adoption. Quantitative survey data were initially analyzed using descriptive statistics to interpret stakeholder responses. As more data are collected, inferential statistical will be incorporated to explore relationships between variables and stakeholder characteristics, providing a comprehensive view of the factors impacting BCT adoption. The comprehensive integration of qualitative and quantitative findings will occur during the final interpretation phase.

4 Results

The 2nd International Symposium on Catch Identification Technologies highlighted the potential of blockchain technology in the Norwegian fisheries sector. A key takeaway was the successful pilot implementation of Hyperledger Sawtooth, a collaborative effort spearheaded by SINTEF, the Norwegian Directorate of Fisheries, and other stakeholders. Hyperledger is an open-source blockchain framework enabling cross-industry collaboration (Hyperledger, nd) and enabling cross-industry consideration and therefore considered a suitable platform for exploring traceability in the fisheries sector. While the symposium acknowledged BCT potential for enhancing traceability, it also brought to light challenges such as integrating this technology with existing IT systems and addressing data privacy concerns (Table 1).

Table 1. Observational Insights from Symposium on Blockchain Adoption

Aspect	Key Observations
Collaborative Deployment	Multi-sector collaboration showcased Hyperledger Sawtooth pilot
Integration Challenges	A significant 65% of respondents feel unprepared due to technological and regulatory barriers
Community Concerns	Concerns about increased surveillance and trust issues noted among private sector stakeholders

The preliminary survey response rate was 30%, capturing responses from the Directorate of Fisheries (34.5%), the private sector (23.5%), and researchers/academics (38.5%). The responses revealed diverse levels of blockchain understanding, with 58% indicating only a basic knowledge. Respondents perceived blockchain as moderately improving traceability and transparency, receiving an average impact rating of 3.47 out of 5. Despite recognizing its advantages—82% cited increased transparency, 65% noted improvements in data integrity, and 53% appreciated enhanced security—the majority felt unprepared for blockchain adoption. Key barriers identified included the difficulty of integrating blockchain within complex regulatory frameworks, substantial costs associated with technological upgrades, and bureaucratic obstacles (Table 2).

Table 2. Survey Insights into Stakeholder Perceptions

Aspect	Survey Findings
Blockchain Understanding	Basic understanding prevalent among 58% of respondents
Readiness of Adoption	A significant 65% of respondents feel unprepared due to technological and regulatory barriers
Perceived Barriers	Recognized benefits included transparency, data integrity, and security enhancements
Barriers to Adoption	Integration challenges, high costs, and bureaucratic inertia identified as primary obstacles

5 Discussion

While the Norwegian fisheries sector recognizes the potential of BCT for enhanced traceability and monitoring, there is a conflict between perceived benefits and real-world constraints. While stakeholders acknowledge the action possibilities offered by BCT, such as enhanced traceability and real-time monitoring, these are compromised by institutional and practical challenges. These challenges, including integration difficulties and regulatory compliance, represent significant constraints on BCT's perceived affordances. This tension between perceived benefits and constraints (Davis & Chouinard 2016) intensifies the argument that affordances are not inherent properties but emerge through the interaction between technology and its social context (Leonardi 2011). In terms of user perception, stakeholders who perceived significant benefits in terms of transparency and data integrity were more inclined to support BCT integration. However, the widespread feeling of unpreparedness suggests a gap between perceived potential and practical readiness, indicating the need for more comprehensive educational strategies to enable familiarity and understanding with BCT. The findings highlight the need for strategies that address both technological and organizational aspects of BCT adoption, emphasizing the importance of building cultural and institutional support through inclusive strategies and regulatory frameworks (Lumineau et al. 2021). Lack of knowledge and substantial familiarity with the utilities of BCT highlight low dexterity and a critical gap in knowledge and low perception that could impede adoption. The strong concern among the fishing community regarding increased surveillance indicates a perceived negative affordance related to the cultural and institutional legitimacy of BCT, where its transparency and traceability features might be seen as intrusive, leading to resistance from stakeholders who feel their operational autonomy is threatened.

This sociotechnical lens is particularly relevant when considering the observed challenges. The difficulty of integrating BCT with existing systems, coupled with concerns about increased surveillance, points to a lack of sociotechnical alignment. This misalignment resonates with the concept of "*imbrication,*" (Leonardi 2011) which emphasizes the intertwined nature of human agency and materiality. Therefore, integrating BCT in fisheries requires not only addressing technical compatibility but also considering how it reshapes existing work practices, power dynamics, and trust relationships within the key stakeholders involved in the fishing sector.

Social capital, encompassing shared norms, trust, and collaborative practices, is crucial for effective digital transformation (Malik et al. 2024). Consequently, any perceived threat to operational autonomy stemming from BCT's features suggests the potential erosion of social capital. This erosion can lead to resistance, hindering harmonious BCT adoption even if technical and regulatory hurdles are overcome (Table 3).

Table 3. Summary of discussed findings

Aspect	Findings
Element	
Action Possibilities	Enhanced traceability and real-time monitoring recognized but overshadowed by integration and regulatory compliance challenges (Observed: Integration with existing IT systems; Survey: 65% unprepared)
User Perception	Benefits in transparency and data integrity perceived positively; 58% had basic understanding, indicating the need for education and training (Survey: 82% recognized transparency benefits, 65% noted data integrity improvements)
Socio-technical Alignment	Significant challenges in integrating blockchain with existing systems; regulatory compliance issues; concerns about increased surveillance and trust (Observed: Data privacy concerns; Survey: Integration challenges, high costs, bureaucratic obstacles)
Condition	
Perception	Understanding of BCT functionalities and perceived benefits and challenges crucial for adoption (Survey: 58% basic understanding)
Dexterity	Skill and ability to use BCT, technological readiness, and training provided are essential for effective adoption (Survey: 65% felt unprepared)
Cultural and Institutional Legitimacy	Cultural norms, institutional support, and regulatory frameworks significantly influence the adoption of blockchain technology (Observed: Concerns about increased surveillance)

6 Conclusion

This research provides insightful into the potential and challenges of blockchain technology adoption within the Norwegian fisheries sector. While stakeholders acknowledge the theoretical benefits of BCT, such as enhanced transparency, data integrity, and security, practical challenges significantly impede its widespread implementation. These findings, interpreted through the lens of affordance theory, underscore the critical need to align technological capabilities with the social and regulatory context to ensure successful BCT integration. This ongoing study will be strengthened through continued data collection, incorporating survey responses from a wider range of stakeholders and qualitative interviews with R&D practitioners, private sector representatives and employees from the Norwegian Directorate of Fisheries. These interviews will provide deeper insights into the practical challenges and perceptions related to BCT adoption, enhancing the quantitative data and the study's overall robustness. Expanding the data collection efforts will be crucial for several reasons. First, a larger and more diverse data set can expose specific patterns and variations in the elements identified within the theoretical framework. For example, we may observe that the perceived benefits and challenges of BCT adoption differ significantly between small-scale and industrial fisheries, or that regulatory barriers are more pronounced in certain segments of the value chain. Second, a richer dataset can elaborate on how the affordances and constraints of BCT interact with the specific social and institutional context.

However, the identified challenges highlight several avenues for future research: Future studies should focus on communicating BCT's value proposition more effectively, simplifying its implementation and user experience, and fostering a supportive cultural and institutional environment for its adoption. This includes addressing concerns about data ownership, privacy, and power dynamics. Furthermore, research should move beyond descriptive analyses of BCT's technical functionalities and diffusion patterns. Instead, it should transcend mere description and explore the institutional challenges and opportunities that emerge at various levels – inter-organizational, intra-organizational, and within the broader ecosystem.

Disclosure of Interests. The authors have no competing interests to declare that are relevant to the content of this article.

References

Bailey, D.E., Faraj, S., Hinds, P., Leonardi, P.M., Krogh, G.V.: We are all theorists of technology now: a relational perspective on emerging technology and organizing. Inst. Oper. Res. Manag. Sci. **33**(1), 1–18 (2022). https://doi.org/10.1287/orsc.2021.1562

Cruz, E.F., da Cruz, A.M.R.: Using blockchain to implement traceability on fishery value chain. ICSOFT, 1195, 501–508 (2020)

Cruz, E.F., da Cruz, A.M.R.: Using blockchain to implement traceability on fishery value chain. ICSOFT, 1195, 501b (2020)

Davis, J.L., Chouinard, J.B.: Theorizing affordances: from request to refuse **36**(4), 241–248 (2016). https://doi.org/10.1177/0270467617714944

Falcone, E.C., Steelman, Z.R., Aloysius, J.A.: Understanding managers' reactions to blockchain technologies in the supply chain: the reliable and unbiased software agent. J. Bus. Logist. **42**(1), 25–45 (2021). https://doi.org/10.1111/jbl.12263

Faraj, S., Azad, B.: The materiality of technology: an affordance perspective. In: Leonardi, P.M., Nardi, B.A., Kallinikos, J. (eds.), Materiality and Organizing: Social Interaction in a Technological World, pp. 237–258. Oxford University Press (2012)

Ghode, D., Yadav, V., Jain, R., Soni, G.: Adoption of blockchain in supply chain: an analysis of influencing factors. J. Enterp. Inf. Manag. **33**(3), 437–456 (2020). https://doi.org/10.1016/j.marpol.2020.103873

Gibson, J.J.: The Ecological Approach to Visual Perception. Lawrence Erlbaum Associates (1986)

Howson, P.: Building trust and equity in marine conservation and fisheries supply chain management with blockchain. Mar. Policy **115** (2020). https://doi.org/10.1016/j.marpol.2020.103873

Hyperledger Foundation: Introduction to Sawtooth PBFT (n.d.). https://www.hyperledger.org/use/sawtooth

Afrianto, I., Djatna, T., Arkeman, Y., Sukaesih Sitanggang, I., Hermadi, I.: Disrupting agro-industry supply chain in indonesia with blockchain technology: current and future challenges. In: 2020 8th International Conference on Cyber and IT Service Management (CITSM), Pangkal, Indonesia, pp. 1–6 (2020). https://doi.org/10.1109/CITSM50537.2020.9268872

Leonardi, L.: When flexible routines meet flexible technologies: affordance, constraint, and the imbrication of human and material agencies. MIS Q. **35**(1), 147–147 (2011). https://doi.org/10.2307/23043493

Leonardi, P.M.: Materiality, sociomateriality, and socio-technical systems: what do these terms mean? How are they different? Do we need them? In: Leonardi, P.M., Nardi, B.A., Kallinikos, J. (eds.) Materiality and Organizing: Social Interaction in a Technological World, pp. 25-48. Oxford University Press (2012)

Leonardi, P.M.: When does technology use enable networK change in organizations? A comparative study of feature use and shared affordances. MIS Q. **37**(3), 749–775 (2013). https://doi.org/10.25300/MISQ/2013/37.3.10

Lumineau, F., Wang, W., Schilke, O.: Blockchain governance—a new way of organizing collaborations? Organ. Sci. **32**(2), 500–521 (2021). https://doi.org/10.1287/orsc.2020.1379

Malik, M., Andargoli, A.E., Clavijo, R.C., Mikalef, P.: A relational view of how social capital contributes to effective digital transformation outcomes **33**(2), 101837–101837 (2024). https://doi.org/10.1016/j.jsis.2024.101837

March, S.T., Smith, G.F.: Design and natural science research on information technology. Decis. Support Syst. **15**(4), 251–266 (1995). https://doi.org/10.1016/0167-9236(94)00041-2

Mathisen, M.: The application of blockchain technology in Norwegian fish supply chains-a case study (master's thesis, NTNU) (2018). http://hdl.handle.net/11250/2561323

McGrenere, J., Ho, W.: Affordances: clarifying and evolving a concept. Proc. Graph. Interface **2000**, 179–186 (2000)

Norwegian Directorate of Fisheries: The CatchID Program (2021). https://www.fiskeridir.no/English/Fisheries/the-catchid-program

Shakhbulatov, D., Medina, J., Dong, Z., Rojas-Cessa, R.: How blockchain enhances supply chain management: a survey. IEEE Open J. Comput. Soc. **1**, 230–249 (2020). https://doi.org/10.1109/OJCS.2020.3025313

Standal, D., Grimaldo, E.: Institutional nuts and bolts for a mesopelagic fishery in Norway. Mar. Policy **119**, 104043 (2020). https://doi.org/10.1016/j.marpol.2020.104043

Standal, D., Hersoug, B.: Illegal fishing: a challenge to fisheries management in Norway. Mar. Policy **155** (2023). https://doi.org/10.1016/j.marpol.2023.105750

Tian, F.: An agri-food supply chain traceability system for China based on RFID & blockchain technology. In: 2016 13th International Conference on Service Systems and Service Management (ICSSSM), Kunming, pp. 1–6 (2016). https://doi.org/10.1109/ICSSSM.2016.7538424

Tolentino-Zondervan, F., Ngoc, P.T.A., Roskam, J.L.: Use cases and future prospects of blockchain applications in global fishery and aquaculture value chains. Aquaculture **565**, 739158 (2023). https://doi.org/10.1016/j.aquaculture.2022.739158

Treiblmaier, H.: The impact of the blockchain on the supply chain: a theory-based research framework and a call for action. Supply Chain Manag. **23**(6), 545–559 (2018). https://doi.org/10.1108/SCM-01-2018-0029

Tsolakis, N., Niedenzu, D., Simonetto, M., Dora, M., Kumar, M.: Supply network design to address United Nations sustainable development goals: a case study of blockchain implementation in Thai fish industry. J. Bus. Res. **131**, 495–519 (2021). https://doi.org/10.1016/j.jbusres.2020.08.003

Volkoff, O., Strong, D.M.: Critical realism and affordances: theorizing IT-associated organizational change processes. MIS Q. **37**(3), 819–834 (2013)

Wong, L.W., Tan, G.W.H., Lee, V.H., Ooi, K.B., Sohal, A.: Unearthing the determinants of Blockchain adoption in supply chain management. Int. J. Prod. Res. **58**(7), 2100–2123 (2020). https://doi.org/10.1080/00207543.2020.1730463

Empowering Translational Health Data Science Capabilities in Population Health Management
A Case of Building a Data Competence Center

Armel Lefebvre[1,2(✉)], Lisette de Schipper[1], Marcel Haas[1], and Marco Spruit[1,2]

[1] Department of Public Health and Primary Care, Leiden University Medical Center, Albinusdreef 2, 2333ZA Leiden, The Netherlands
a.e.j.l.lefebvre@lumc.nl
[2] LIACS, Leiden University, P.O. Box 9512, 2300RA Leiden, The Netherlands

Abstract. In this paper we present the outcomes of a survey conducted among the research community of a Population Health Management department. The goal is to investigate how (translational) data science applications can be supported in a complex ecosystem of data sources and regulations of secondary healthcare data use. The envisioned solution is the creation of a data competence center as a multidisciplinary unit mixing research and professional support staff to provide data science technology, training, and resources to (early-career) researchers to address current challenges that are considerably impacting data quality and reproducibility in PHM research.

Keywords: Population Health Management · Data Infrastructure · Data Competence Center · Translational Data Science · Reproducibility

1 Introduction

Population health management aims at improving the fairness and efficiency of prevention and intervention programs in healthcare. First, there are opportunities to reduce costs in healthcare with prevention tailored to populations at risk. Furthermore, intervention programs may alleviate the need for people to undergo medical treatment if specially designed intervention tools effectively reduce (future) health risks while reducing costs growth of healthcare [1]. The primary source of evidence for PHM are data from electronic health records (EHR) [2], which are used to obtain individual measurements from general practitioner (GP) practices and hospitals. EHRs contain both structured (e.g., disease identifiers) and unstructured (e.g., additional observations by the GP during consultation) data.

To exploit EHR data for research purposes, agreements are made between research performing organizations (e.g., and (local) GP practices to obtain patient records in a systematic way. This is also the case for the PHM data infrastructure we are investigating in this paper, which is named ELAN and stands for Extramural Leiden University

Published by Springer Nature Switzerland AG 2024
R. van de Wetering et al. (Eds.): I3E 2024, LNCS 14907, pp. 394–402, 2024.
https://doi.org/10.1007/978-3-031-72234-9_33

Medical Center Academic Network [3]. In ELAN, agreements have been made with GP practices in the South Holland region, and other EHR data holders such as regional hospitals.

Thus, the construction of ELAN involves organic growth of disparate data sources as well as individual agreements with third parties to provide data for research and increase regional coverage. This is a situation that echoes other PHM initiatives making use of EHR data under a meaningful use scheme [2], where (privacy) regulations involve strict data access rules. This involves data quality and data integration challenges before researchers in PHM can analyze data for research purposes. This complexity has yet to be reduced for PHM researcher to make the research process in PHM itself more effective.

To achieve that, we are introducing a specialized unit in the ELAN infrastructure, called a data competence center, to tackle those issues and facilitate the work of researchers. This is particularly relevant when the demand for EHR analysis is relying more often than not on data science applications that require high-quality data and smooth data access workflows. Hence, the main research question (MRQ) of our study is as follows:

MRQ: "How can a data competence center (DCC) strengthen translational data science capabilities in a Population Health Management context?"

Consequently, we will seek to define the requirements expressed by researchers of PHM infrastructure (PHI).Those requirements were collected to identify how PHM researchers can be better supported during their research.

In the remainder of this paper, we first introduce the background of our study, especially the more niche areas of population health management and translational health data science. Then we briefly explain how we collected evidence from researchers in population health management who are employing data science approaches to perform their research. Finally, we conclude this paper with an agenda for building data science capabilities in a PHM context.

2 Background

2.1 Population Health Management (PHM) Infrastructure

PHM studies combine health data with socio-economical insights about individuals or (regional) populations. Therefore, a robust data infrastructure is crucial [4]. In a PHM context, this data infrastructure is based on federating sources from independent hospitals, networks of general practitioners, and databases of governmental statistics. In case of the Extramural Leiden Academic Network (ELAN) infrastructure, nine data sources can be combined to provide data for researchers [3]. Besides, external data sources, such as those named earlier, are often also integrated with data collected from researchers during field or survey studies.

As can be seen from Fig. 1, in ELAN there are three types of data providers which are GP data, Governmental organizations and (regional) hospitals. Agreements with GPs enable the gathering of data in a secure data warehouse, which is then queried according to the specific needs of a research project. Other type of data providers, such as hospitals or governmental organizations will refine data access authorizations to individual researchers. This involves administrative steps to access health data at individual level at the start of a research project.

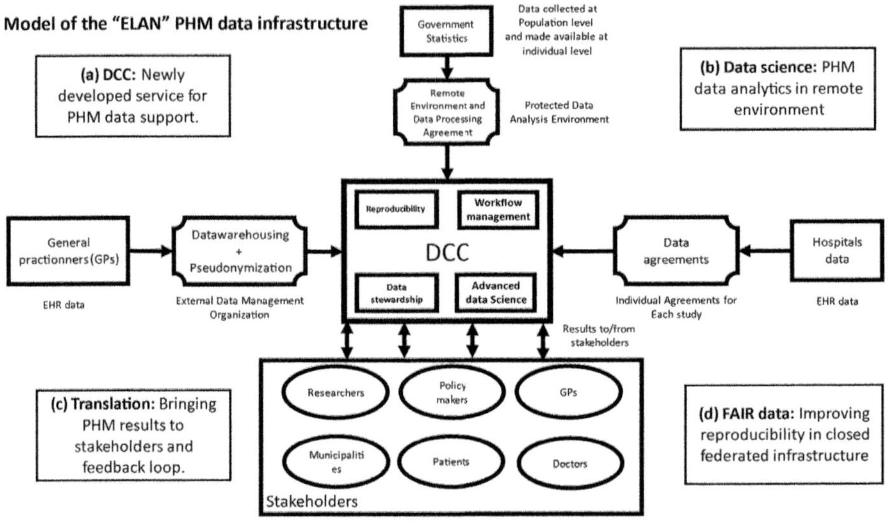

Fig. 1. The role of a DCC **(a) DCC** is the new service described in this work, it is embedded in the PHM infrastructure and collaborates with the three ELAN managerial units, **(b) Data science** applications take place in a secure environment, the technical skills and tools discussed in this paper relate to this environment, **(c) Translation** is the act of deploying results to the community of stakeholders as well as obtaining feedback on the results efficiently, and **(d) FAIR data** focuses on the role of the DCC to support FAIR data exchanges.

2.2 Digital Competence Center

The creation of a digital competence center (DCC) follows some more recent trends in the area of research data management [5, 6]. DCCs address a common burden of research projects where a specialized unit which is knowledgeable of the type of research conducted, the technology field to effectively deploy data analytics and support data management that adhere to FAIR principles for both data and software [7, 8]. For ELAN, the DCC is composed of PHM researchers, data scientists and data managers who are focusing on making PHM research more reproducible, seek to make data analysis workflows more efficient and train researchers in more advanced data science skills (as explained hereunder in Sect. 4).

2.3 Translational Data Science

Currently, ELAN data science activities are performed by researchers in a secure environment as depicted in the upper-right box (Fig. 1.b.). The further goal of establishing a

DCC is to help PHM researcher embrace more advanced technology and uses of data science to broaden the insights from EHR data. Translational data science (TDS - Fig. 1.C) is a field of research dedicated to bridging data science with efficient application of data analytics in clinical and healthcare settings [9–11]. As we will discuss later in this paper, bringing data science skills to a level where TDS can be successfully enacted has its challenges, which the DCC and its FAIR data management ambition described in Fig. 2.D aims to tackle.

3 Method

We investigated the current state of the PHM infrastructure using an exploratory single case study [12]. We started with the high-level requirements for implementing advanced data science capabilities in ELAN that were discussed by the management board in September 2023. Then, we opted for a survey to collect evidence from the (local) research community on the current status of data science skills and requirements.

The survey focused on ELAN users and support professionals at the department of Population Health Management, at the health Campus in The Hague in the Netherlands, which is part of the Public Health and Primary Care department of the Leiden University Medical Center. In September 2023, the management team presented several steps to be taken to professionalize the ELAN from a governance and infrastructure point of view. In the new governance framework, the ELAN is delegating some operational tasks related to data management to the ELAN-DCC. Among those operational (support) tasks, the ELAN-DCC ought to facilitate advanced data science methods on ELAN data.

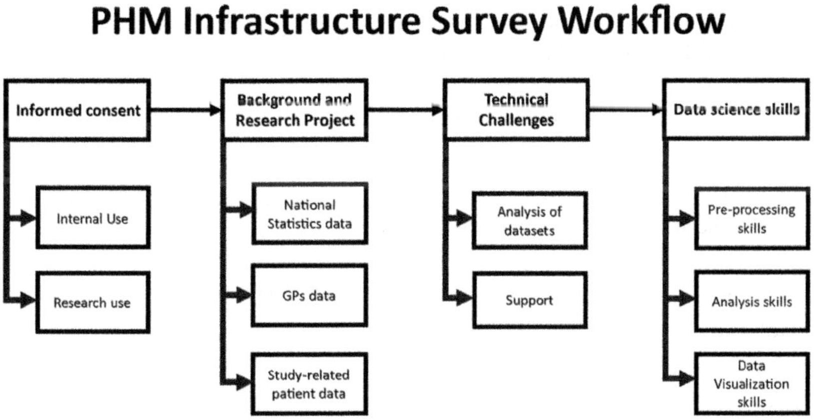

Fig. 2. PHM Survey workflow. The survey is divided into three main sections: Research background, Technical Challenges and Data science skills.

In this context, we conducted a survey to obtain some more detailed insights on the data science skills and requirements of the users of ELAN. The main purpose is to identify the areas where the (ELAN) DCC can further enhance the support for data science activities for (early-career) researchers.

The ELAN-DCC survey opened at the end of February 2024 and closed on March 15, 2024. There were 27 respondents who completed the survey. We shared the survey link by e-mail among 95 potential respondents listed as ELAN users by ELAN data managers. We have effectively shared the survey link with 88 potential respondents (i.e., excluding emails bouncing back and out of office notifications). We obtained 27 responses, which is equivalent to a response rate of 31% (27/88). From those 27 respondents, one individual opted out, they did not allow the use of their data for research purposes. Therefore, we are examining the responses of 26 participants for the remainder of this paper.

The survey data was collected using a Microsoft Office365 online form. The form was divided into several subcategories (see Fig. 2) that could be shown or hidden depending on the kind of data sources used by the respondents. For a subset of respondents, we also obtained their e-mail addresses for future use. The data was downloaded as an excel file and processed in OpenRefine to standardize free text answers, correct the syntax of column names, and anonymize results for further processing. After processing the data with OpenRefine, the resulting dataset was uploaded in Python, using the Pandas module. The analyses and plotting were performed in a Python Jupyter notebook using the Pandas and Seaborn modules.

4 Results

In this Section, we present the main results that correspond to the survey categories depicted in Fig. 2.

4.1 Research Background

We note that the survey yielded answers from a majority of early career researchers who were appealed by the fact that more support for data science is being implemented at ELAN. This is reflected by the number of PhD candidates and Researchers/postdocs who are included in the sample (as described in Table 1).

Table 1. Number of respondents per academic role. Classified by seniority (Full professor, most senior) to PhD candidate (most junior role).

Academic role	Number of respondents
Full professor	1
Associate professor	2
Assistant professor	2
Researcher/postdoc	5
PhD candidate	16
Total	26

Some more senior academics are involved with supervision of early-career researchers, which brought some more knowledge about trends in PHM on the longer term whereas early-career researchers could report on more direct burdens encountered with ELAN data in daily research.

4.2 Technical Challenges

For operations on the data, there are several aspects revealed in the free text answers to the question “What kind of analyses and operations do you consider to be unnecessarily complicated?” Recurring themes are challenges in data and file management, documentation, and data quality as well as data cleaning, selection, and processing.

For data management, the lack of data standards, naming conventions and inconsistent file paths impeding proper versioning are adding complexity when transferring data. Then, there are data sources that are not properly documented and there is no clear provenance information explaining why data is missing in some instances. Those data integration issues where not all addressed by even more proficient ELAN users who are keen on programming data processing scripts.

4.3 Data Science Skills

In Fig. 3 we present the main outcomes indicating that the areas in which the DCC will intervene have room for progress. In Fig. 3.A, we see that respondents have mostly one to two years of experience with ELAN data. Figure 3.B shows that while R is a popular scripting language, standard statistical packages and Excel files are frequently used.

Furthermore, Fig. 3.C shows variations in skills among respondents, while the majority is self-reporting at novice or intermediate level a point of attention is that the skill levels are not systematically a representation of a realistic skill level as experienced by users.

A follow-up question in our survey asked respondents “If you feel like adding more nuance/explanation to your choices, feel free to do so here.”, indicated that some respondents where somewhat in-between intermediate and advanced, or struggling with fundamental data integration tasks while being at an intermediate level on a scale of four levels (Novice, Intermediate, Advanced and Expert).

Finally, in Fig. 3.D showing the results on the willingness to learn more advanced programming skills, 37% of the respondents use a scripting language already. By scripting language, we include languages like R and Python, they are interpreted languages and have a vast ecosystem of packages to conduct (advanced) data analyses (see Table 2). Among the respondents who are not using scripting languages, the willingness to learn a scripting language is mixed.

Learning scripting languages has limitations that relate to the research environment. Respondents reported limited learning resources inside the organization to tackle more advanced analyses using programming scripts. Then there is a time issue, where early-career researchers communicated that the duration and requirements for completing a PhD trajectory left little room for learning programming skills. Last, data cleaning necessitates more examples when done with scripts, as there is little code exchange at the moment, repetitive cleaning tasks are coded from scratch.

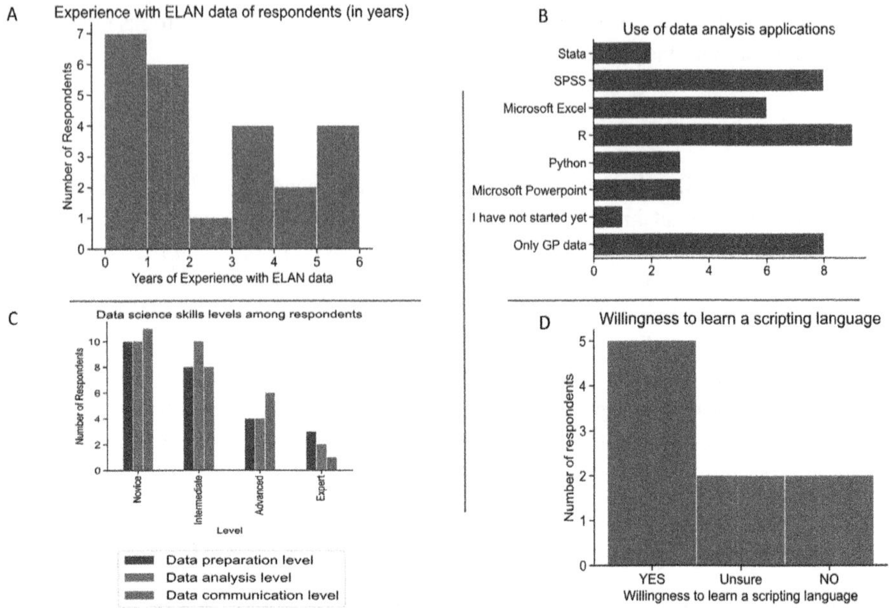

Fig. 3. The distribution of experience, skills, and data science applications within the ELAN user community.

Table 2. Rationales of respondents to use scripting languages for their research.

Statements in favor of using scripting languages in PHM	Support
The types of analyses I perform cannot be performed in Excel/SPSS/STATA, so I am required to use a scripting language	4
I feel more comfortable performing research with a scripting language as opposed to software like Excel/SPSS/STATA	3
A data scientist does not use SPSS, for many reasons	1
I use a scripting language for transparency (Most scripting languages are open source and can be shared on platforms such as GitHub)	1
Last 2 bullets combined Transparency and reproducibility, and also more comfortable with (is the only thing I learned)	1

5 Discussion

In terms of requirements for data analytics we see two trends from the survey we collected. On the one hand, there is a trend that limits the maximal effort to invest in data analysis compared with the requirement to publish results on time (for instance during a PhD). This also contributes to researcher seeking advice or support in their immediate surroundings, whether by searching online or asking colleagues instead of spending more time finding resources inside the larger organization. On the other hand, there is a concrete requirement for more advanced applications and the ease of data integration, analysis, and visualization in ELAN. Those results show that the creation of a multidisciplinary unit such as a DCC can be suitable solution to tackle those trends by reducing the efforts needed to find examples and training materials as well as become a known support option for researchers.

Still, a major limitation of the current state of our study is that we are limited by the input from users of ELAN. As part of future research, we aim at triangulating our local survey responses with respondents from more sites using similar healthcare data infrastructure in the Netherlands and abroad. Besides, we plan to conduct in-depth interviews to obtain more granular evidence on data management and analysis practices in different research projects and settings.

Furthermore, the survey is designed especially for the ELAN context. The combination of healthcare data from GPs and governmental data re-occurs in other Dutch initiatives such as AHON (University Medical Center Groningen) [13] and similar integrations occur internationally such as in the Healthdata platform (Sciensano, Belgium) [14]. In other words, our survey suffers from a limited generalizability due to our convenient sampling strategy. Also, the construct validity of several items needs further evaluation before collecting evidence from users of different health data infrastructure than ELAN to increase the clarity and generalizability of the survey questions to fit international health data initiatives.

That being said, while our study is limited to a single case study site, similar PHM infrastructure initiatives are created in the Netherlands. Our survey is the first step towards getting a better overview on the tools and skills involved in PHM and it can be deployed on any PHM infrastructure consisting of the statistical governmental data mixed with GP network data. The survey can therefore be considered as pilot material for further research for broader efforts including the European Health Data Space.

We have seen that ELAN users have a diversity of data analytics skills. In the mean time, data analytics skills have room for improvements across the complete set of ELAN users, which is an aspect to be tackled by the ELAN-DCC.

6 Conclusion

This study aimed at answering the question: "How can a data competence center (DCC) strengthen translational data science capabilities in a Population Health Management context?". We have brought preliminary insights from practice that serve to delineate the shape and role of a DCC in a PHM context. We have observed that a DCC needs to tackle data management, advanced data science skills and reuse of code to offer a robust infrastructure for translational data science applications to researchers. Especially, the need for the availability of data analysis recipes and materials, as pre-processing steps are similar although not shared among projects. As explained previously, a data infrastructure like ELAN is built upon a complex ecosystem of data providers which is currently scaling up and facing stringent privacy and use of AI (in healthcare) regulations.

The current study outlined the basic blocks of a data competence center and its role in population health management as a top-down unit to be implemented in PHM infrastructures to enhance data stewardship and data management. Based on preliminary requirements from researchers and support professionals in one PHM research department in the Netherlands, we have identified pillars of a robust PHM DCC to properly address pressing challenges related to the use of data science for better healthcare. Moreover, we also include elements that make DCC-ready for next generation data analyses in PHM. Due to its multidisciplinary nature. a DCC can play a pivotal role in building up data science capabilities.

Disclosure of Interests. The authors have no competing interests.

References

1. Steenkamer, B.M., Drewes, H.W., Heijink, R., Baan, C.A., Struijs, J.N.: Defining population health management: a scoping review of the literature. Popul. Heath. Manag. **20**, 74–85 (2017)
2. Kruse, C.S., Stein, A., Thomas, H., Kaur, H.: The use of electronic health records to support population health: a systematic review of the literature. J. Med. Syst. **42** (2018)
3. Ardesch, F.H., et al.: The introduction of a data-driven population health management approach in the Netherlands since 2019: The Extramural LUMC Academic Network data infrastructure. Health Policy **132**, 104769 (2023)
4. van Ede, A.F.T.M., Stein, K.V., Bruijnzeels, M.A.: Assembling a population health management maturity index using a Delphi method. BMC Health Serv. Res. **24** (2024)
5. Jäkel, R., Peukert, E., Nagel, W.E., Rahm, E.: ScaDS Dresden/Leipzig – a competence center for collaborative big data research. it Inf. Technol. **60**, 327–333 (2018)
6. Ringersma, J., Adamse, P.: Data Stewardship@ WUR: advice on a role for Data Stewards. Wageningen Data Competence Center (2019)
7. Lamprecht, A.-L., et al.: Towards FAIR principles for research software. Data Sci. **3**, 37–59 (2020)
8. Wilkinson, M.D., et al.: The FAIR guiding principles for scientific data management and stewardship. Sci. Data **3**, 1–9 (2016)
9. McDavid, A., et al.: Eight practices for data management to enable team data science. J. Clin. Transl. Sci. **5**, e14 (2021)
10. Slade, E., et al.: Integrating data science into the translational science research spectrum: a substance use disorder case study. J. Clin. Transl. Sci. **5**, e29 (2021)
11. Spruit, M.: Translational Data Science in Population Health. Leiden University (2022)
12. Takahashi, A.R.W., Araujo, L.: Case study research: opening up research opportunities. RAUSP Manag. J. **55**, 100–111 (2020)
13. Twickler, R., et al.: Data resource profile: registry of electronic health records of general practices in the north of The Netherlands (AHON). Int. J. Epidemiol. **53** (2024)
14. European Observatory on Health, S., Policies, Minna, H.: Towards the European health data space: from diversity to a common framework. World Health Organization (2022)

Key Factors Affecting the Implementation of Immersive Technologies in Ophthalmology Education

Shannon Leigh Noël and Hanlie Smuts(✉)

University of Pretoria, Pretoria, South Africa
{shannon.noel,hanlie.smuts}@up.ac.za

Abstract. The rapid evolution of immersive technologies, including virtual reality (VR), augmented reality (AR), and mixed reality (MR), present a transformative potential for various sectors, especially education. Within the specialized field of ophthalmology education, understanding the integration and effectiveness of these technologies is key. A systematic literature review (SLR) was executed to identify the factors influencing the adoption of immersive technologies in ophthalmology education. Thematic analysis was applied to 62 research papers, resulting in the identification of 77 key factors. These factors, encompassing both success and hindering elements, were categorized into 12 sub-categories and six main areas: immersive technology feature factors, user acceptance factors, learning outcome factors, active learning and control factors, student factors, and inhibiting factors. The categorization presented serves as a guideline for medical practitioners and technology developers, guiding them in optimizing the development, deployment, and enhancement of immersive tools in ophthalmology education. This research highlights the significance of each identified factor in the successful integration of immersive technologies in ophthalmology education.

Keywords: Ophthalmology · Education · Immersive Technology · Virtual Reality · Augmented Reality · Metaverse

1 Introduction

Over the past few years, there has been a significant evolution in medical educational approaches, with immersive technologies taking a leading role [1]. Ophthalmology education, in particular, has exhibited a growing enthusiasm in the application of these cutting-edge tools [2]. Immersive technology acts as the umbrella term for augmented reality (AR), virtual reality (VR), mixed reality (MR) and extended reality (XR) [3]. These technologies offer revolutionary learning experiences by not only replicating real-world situations, but also providing interactive hands-on training, broadening and deepening the learning scope [4]. Yet, even with their evident promise, the actual assimilation of these technologies is complex, shaped by a myriad of influencing factors [1]. As medical professionals aim to make the most of modern technological innovations,

Published by Springer Nature Switzerland AG 2024
R. van de Wetering et al. (Eds.): I3E 2024, LNCS 14907, pp. 403–414, 2024.
https://doi.org/10.1007/978-3-031-72234-9_34

ensuring that these technologies are aptly integrated into the curriculum becomes pivotal [5]. Failing to weave these innovations seamlessly into educational frameworks may enhance the risk of missing out on vital learning avenues, and the remarkable advantages of immersive technologies will be left untapped [6].

The debut of new technologies has often elicited mixed reactions – excitement on one hand and hesitance on the other [3]. This is mainly because technology advances quickly, and it can clash with older, more familiar ways of teaching [7]. The overarching condition here is the inconsistency in the adoption and effective use of immersive technologies in ophthalmology education. The undesirable consequence of this condition is an educational gap: either students miss out on cutting-edge learning experiences, or institutions invest in technologies that remain underutilized [8].

This study presents a systematic literature review on the factors that affect the successful/unsuccessful adoption of immersive technologies in ophthalmology answering the research question: "*What are the key factors affecting the implementation of immersive technologies in ophthalmology education?*". By addressing these factors, it paves the way for optimizing the integration of immersive technologies, ensuring that future generations of ophthalmologists receive training that is both technologically advanced and contextually relevant.

In Sect. 2, the background of this subject is presented, in Sect. 3, the research methodology is discussed, and the data analysis is presented in Sect. 4. Section 5 contains the discussion and Sect. 6 concludes the paper.

2 Overview of Immersive Technologies in Ophthalmology Education

Immersive technologies, encompassing realms like augmented reality (AR), virtual reality (VR), and mixed reality (MR), have steadily carved a métier in various educational sectors over recent years [4]. Such technologies bring to the table an impressive blend of lifelike experiences, dynamic engagement, and versatility, earning recognition in different learning environments [6]. Within the realm of medical training, particularly where practical exposure and authentic simulations are crucial, these technological innovations hold significant promise [7].

The field of ophthalmology, with its demand for precision and complex techniques, is one domain poised to gain greatly from these advancements [3]. Immersive tools can provide ophthalmological enthusiasts with an opportunity to refine their skills in a simulated environment, familiarize themselves with uncommon scenarios, and grasp the complexities of the eye [2]. This potential transformation isn't merely academic, patient experiences are reshaped by producing well-prepared professionals [4].

However, Benferdia et al. [9] state that the path to integrating these marvels into ophthalmology's educational framework isn't without obstacles. Academic institutions, students and educators encounter a bundle of challenges during the adoption phase. From the hefty financial investments associated with these advanced tools to the need for specialized training for instructors, the hurdles are numerous [9]. Furthermore, while the technology promises accuracy, there is an ongoing debate about how closely ophthalmology [1].

Moreover, the cultural facets of this technological shift warrant attention. Moving from age-old practices to a tech-driven approach can meet people with hesitancy, both from professionals (educators) rooted in traditional methodologies and enthusiasts (students) possibly daunted by the technological leap [8]. Additionally, there are concerns about the long-term effects of using immersive tools, including potential health implications like eye fatigue or cybersickness [10].

In essence, while the potential benefits of immersive technologies in ophthalmology education are vast, their practical implementation is captured in a web of challenges and considerations [9]. It is important to bridge the gap by understanding the critical factors that influence the actual incorporation of these advanced tools in ophthalmological teaching.

3 Methodology

A systematic literature review (SLR) can be described as a methodical approach to research that involves the identification, rigorous evaluation, and synthesis of relevant studies [11]. The SLR process utilizes transparent, replicable methods to evaluate existing literature and evidence, mitigating potential bias and ensuring that the results drawn from this process are trustworthy, providing a solid foundation for making informed conclusions and decisions [11].

The search phrase ("ophthalmology") AND ("education") AND ("immersive technology") was executed in the following databases: IEEE Xplore® Digital Library, Elsevier, Springer, Taylor & Francis, BMJ Journals and PubMed. Academic, peer-reviewed papers were included that aligned to the research question and that discuss the reasons - positive and negative – of the uptake of immersive technologies in relevant areas of ophthalmology. Duplicate papers, papers not written in English and papers only dealing with one of the concepts – ophthalmology or immersive technology – were excluded.

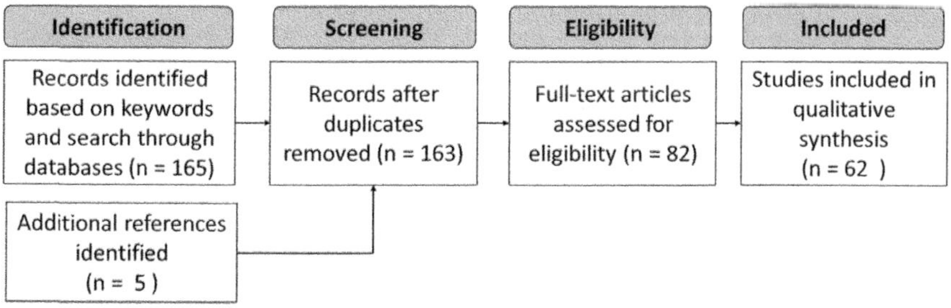

Fig. 1. Flowchart for data extraction.

The process began with an initial extract of 165 articles, supplemented by 5 additional articles from references, totaling 170. During the identification phase, 7 duplicates were removed, leaving 163 articles. These 163 articles were then examined through their abstracts and conclusions for alignment with the research topic, resulting in the exclusion of 81 articles. This left 82 articles, which were thoroughly read. The final corpus for detailed analysis comprised 62 articles as shown in Fig. 1.

4 Data Analysis

The aim of this study was to identify the key factors affecting the implementation of immersive technologies in ophthalmology education. Data extraction served as a methodical approach to gather important information from each article in the corpus. Themes extracted included: (1) immersive technology feature factors; (2) user acceptance factors; (3) learning outcome factors; (4) active learning and control factors; (5) student factors; and (6) inhibiting factors. The following data extraction Tables 1 to 6 present each key factors area of the implementation of immersive technologies in ophthalmology education consisting of the sub-category, factor and frequency count. The detailed SLR tables and bibliography may be accessed on the direct link: https://www.researchgate.net/publication/382423491_Key_Factors_Affecting_the_Implementation_of_Immersive_Technologies_in_Ophthalmology_Education.

Immersive technology feature factors (Table 1) describe the specific characteristics of these technologies that could potentially influence the transfer of skills to individuals new to the surgical field, ultimately impacting the outcomes of their training [9].

Table 1. Immersive Technology Feature Factors.

Sub-Category	Factor	Frequency count
Realism	Realism	5
	Haptic Feedback	10
	Real-world integration	16
	Visual and haptic user interface	4
Control	Greater economy of motion	2
	User interface and guidance	8
Hardware	Haptics Devices	10
	Computers	3
	Visual hardware	4
	Surgical equipment	3
	Operator/mentor stations	3
	Headset	3
	Surgical instruments	1
Software	Software models	2
	Artificial Intelligence	2
	Networking	2
	Graphics	5
	Movement patterns	1
	Sensory and motor information	1

This category is further subdivided into four critical sub-categories: Realism, Control, Hardware, and Software. These are essential in understanding the intricate dynamics of immersive technologies. Under the first sub-category, "realism", factors such as the degree of realism, haptic feedback, real- world integration, and the integration of visual and haptic elements in the user interface are considered. This facet is crucial in offering a genuine, hands-on experience that can significantly enhance skill acquisition, especially for surgical novices [3]. The "Control" sub-category encompasses factors like the greater economy of motion and user interface and guidance, which are vital in determining the user's ability to interact and manipulate effectively with the immersive environment, including mastering complex surgical techniques and refining movement patterns, which are vital for successful outcomes [12]. In the "Hardware" section, we mention the tangible components necessary for creating an immersive experience, including haptics devices, computers, visual hardware, and various types of equipment and instruments used in surgical training [13]. Lastly, the "Software" sub-category explores the different software elements that drive the immersive technologies, including the use of artificial intelligence, networking capabilities, graphical elements, and the integration of sensory and motor information. It also involves the use of various models for visualization and haptic interaction, forming the backbone of the immersive experience by managing responsive and realistic simulations [9].

"User Acceptance Factors" in Table 2 explores the perceived benefits and ease of use of immersive technologies in ophthalmology education.

This category is divided into two sub- categories: "Perceived Usefulness" and "Perceived Ease of Use". Under the "Perceived Usefulness" sub-category, we mention factors such as the interactive, educational, and realistic experiences offered by the technology, alongside real-time feedback, cost reductions, and the reliability and efficacy of the technology [3]. These factors are important in measuring the potential benefits of adopting immersive technologies, with aspects like offering a highly interactive experience and real-time feedback being notably prevalent in the literature. Simultaneously, the "Perceived Ease of Use" sub-category explores factors that influence the user- friendliness of the technology. This includes the efficiency of the technology, the provision of a safe learning environment, the reduced complexity of the technology, and its common availability [9]. There is emphasis on complete immersion, a factor identified frequently in the analyzed papers, suggesting its critical role in facilitating an engaging and effective learning environment. Factors like reducing trainees' anxiety and the capability to teach several surgeries also emerge as vital components in ensuring a user-friendly and adaptable learning platform.

The critical "Learning Outcome Factors" that are central to understanding the impact of immersive technologies in ophthalmology education is discussed in Table 3.

This category is divided into two sub-categories: "Perceived Learning Efficiency" and "Performance Achievement". The "Perceived Learning Efficiency" sub-category holds factors that signify the potential benefits of immersive technologies in enhancing the learning process. Factors such as "improved patient safety" and "accelerated training" indicate the technology's role in fostering a safer patient result (due to surgeons being well trained) and speeding up the training process. Other factors in this sub- category, including the "reduced rate of errant capsulorhexis (surgical technique)",

Table 2. User Acceptance Factors.

Sub-Category	Factor	Frequency count
Perceived usefulness	Offers a highly interactive experience	9
	Offers a highly educational experience	3
	Offers a highly realistic experience	8
	Real-time feedback	6
	Cost reductions	6
	Validity	4
	Time saving	5
	Active learning	4
	Reliability	4
	Efficacy	3
Perceived ease of use	Efficiency	7
	Safe learning environment	3
	Reduced complexity	1
	Common availability of technology	8
	Reduce trainees' anxiety	2
	Teaching several surgeries	2
	Complete immersion	10

Table 3. Learning Outcome Factors.

Sub-Category	Factor	Frequency count
Perceived Learning Efficiency	Improved patient safety	6
	Reduced rate of errant capsulorhexis	2
	Accelerated training	9
	Allows pre-operative training	6
	Reduced rate of complications	5
	Better patient outcomes	5
Performance Achievement	Improved ophthalmic surgical performance	7
	Improved surgical competency	10
	Improved procedural success	7
	Better phacoemulsification performance	3
	Better capsulorhexis performance	3

"allows pre-operative training", "reduced rate of complications", and "better patient outcomes", emphasize the technology's potential in minimizing errors and complications, thereby leading to improved outcomes in patient care [3, 14, 15]. On the other hand, the "Performance Achievement" sub-category focuses on the direct outcomes of the learning process, particularly concerning surgical proficiency and success. The factor "improved surgical competency" describes the technology's role in enhancing the surgical skills and competencies of enthusiasts. Other factors in this sub-category, such as "improved ophthalmic surgical performance" and "improved procedural success" highlight the potential of immersive technologies in creating better surgical performance and success rates. Specific improvements in surgical techniques (to do with ophthalmology domain), like "better phacoemulsification performance" and "better capsulorhexis performance", are also noted, indicating specialized areas (cataract surgery procedures) where the technology might have a positive impact [15].

Table 4 explains the central elements bound within the broader category of "Active Learning and Control Factors" that are useful in the successful implementation of immersive technologies in ophthalmology education. This category is segmented into a sub-category termed "Learner Control", which further borders a variety of factors that are central to creating an environment where learners can have a degree of control over their learning process actively engage.

Table 4. Active Learning and Control Factors.

Sub-Category	Factor	Frequency count
Learner Control	Assessment skills	6
	Duration of training	4
	Intensity	3
	Skills transfer	6
	Training tools	4
	Hands-on engagement	5
	Stimulator design and functionality	2
	Problem-solving scenarios	2

Under the "Learner Control" sub-category, several factors are highlighted that emphasize the free and active participation of learners. The "skills transfer" factor indicates a strong emphasis in the literature on the ability of immersive technologies to manage the transfer of skills acquired during training to real-world scenarios. This is followed by "assessment skills" towards the essential role of self-assessment and feedback in enhancing learning outcomes [15]. Other factors such as "hands-on engagement" and "training tools" underscore the importance of practical engagement and the use of appropriate tools in developing a valuable learning environment. Factors like "duration of training" and "intensity" hint at the necessity to consider the length and depth of training sessions to ensure optimal learning outcomes [14].

Table 5 discusses the significant factors that influence the experiences and outcomes of students or enthusiasts engaging with immersive technologies in ophthalmology education, grouped under the broader category of "Student Factors".

Table 5. Student Factors.

Sub-Category	Factor	Frequency count
Enthusiast Characteristics	Ability	7
	User control	4
	Provided benefits	7
	Improved confidence	8
	Opportunities for strengthened learning	9
	Capacity of pre-learning	3
	Perceived ease of use	8
	Perceived usefulness	13

This category is primarily focused on understanding the characteristics and perceptions of the individuals who are the end-users of these technologies, aiming to enhance their learning experience and outcomes. Within this category, we find a critical sub-category termed "Enthusiast Characteristics", which surrounds a range of factors that are central to shaping the experiences of learners. "Perceived usefulness" highlights the importance of the perceived benefits and usefulness of the technology in encouraging students and enthusiasts to engage with it. This factor reflects the users' belief that using the technology will enhance their learning or performance [16]. The factors "Opportunities for strengthened learning" and "Improved confidence" emphasize the potential of immersive technologies to create enriched learning environments where students can enhance their understanding and skills, alongside developing a sense of confidence in their abilities [4, 12]. Other notable factors include "Ability" and "Provided benefits", highlighting the role of immersive technologies in enhancing the abilities of learners and providing tangible benefits that can aid in their education. Moreover, the "Perceived ease of use" indicates the importance of creating user-friendly interfaces to encourage wider adoption and more effective usage of these technologies [1]. However, factors such as "User control" and "Capacity of pre-learning", suggest areas that might benefit from further exploration and research to fully understand their impact on the learning experience.

Table 6 represents the "Inhibiting Factors" that are faced in the implementation of immersive technologies in ophthalmology education, segmented into two sub-categories: "Technical Skills" and "Non-technical Skills".

Under the "Technical Skills" sub-category, several factors have been identified as potential hindrances. The "Limited control" factor indicate that users might find the control mechanisms of the current technologies to be restrictive [17]. This is followed by the "Excess realism" factor, which suggests that sometimes the technologies might

Table 6. Inhibiting Factors.

Sub-Category	Factor	Frequency count
Technical Skills	Excess realism	7
	Limited interface feedback	2
	Limited control	13
	Battery life	2
	Poor simulator scoring	1
	Higher complexity level	5
	Unavailable equipment	4
Non-technical Skills	Visual fatigue	9
	Simulator/Cybersickness	7
	High costs	13
	Lack of integrated comprehensive training curriculum	14
	Lack of teacher's effective feedback	3
	Lack of guiding and supervision	5
	Cognitive overload	2

focus too much on realism, possibly at the expense of learning efficacy [18]. Other factors include "Higher complexity level" and "Unavailable equipment" which point towards issues related to the complexity of the technologies and the availability of necessary equipment [19]. Factors such as "Limited interface feedback", "Battery life", and "Poor simulator scoring" are also highlighted, indicating that these might be areas that require further exploration and improvement. In the "Non-technical Skills" sub-category, the factor "Lack of integrated comprehensive training curriculum" indicates a gap in the current educational frameworks that integrate these technologies [20, 21]. "High costs" emphasizes the financial barriers to implementing these technologies on a wider scale. "Visual fatigue" and "Simulator/Cybersickness" suggest potential health-related concerns associated with the prolonged use of these technologies [22]. Table 6 also brings attention to other significant factors such as "Lack of teacher's effective feedback", "Lack of guiding and supervision", and "Cognitive Overload", which are critical areas that might be impacting the effective implementation of immersive technologies in ophthalmology education [9].

5 Discussion and Recommendations

The aim of this study was to identify the key factors affecting the implementation of immersive technologies in ophthalmology education. Thematic analysis was conducted on 62 research papers to identify 77 key factors categorized to 12 sub-categories, whether it be success factors or hindering factors. The goal of identifying these 12 sub-categories is to determine the factors that influence or affect the successful or failed implementation of immersive technologies in ophthalmology education. This can assist with making recommendations based on the current factors identified on what could be done to increase and enhance the successful adoption of these technologies in ophthalmology education.

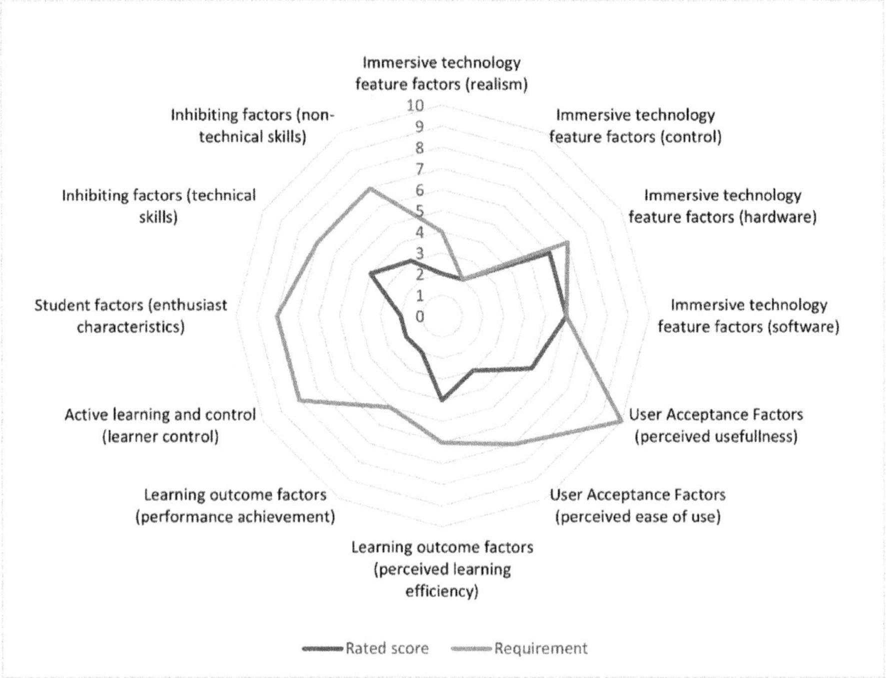

Fig. 2. Immersive technologies checklist for ophthalmology education, ideal profile vs. evaluated profile comparison

In order to operationalize the 12 sub-categories and 77 key factors, we created an immersive technology checklist against which ophthalmology education curricula or training artefacts may be evaluated shown in Fig. 2. We allocated a value of 1 to each of the 77 subfactors totaling to an ideal profile score per sub-category. This enabled an assessment against the 77 sub-factors consisting of either a "0" (not compliant) or a "1" (compliant). By mapping the ideal profile to the evaluation, Fig. 2 shows a comparison of the two profiles where the grey line depicts the required, or compliant, requirement and the blue line, how the ophthalmology education artefact was evaluated (rated score). By interrogating the gap between the two profiles, the education curriculum designer may identify which of the 77 factors require attention and update accordingly.

Healthcare professionals spearheading educational initiatives in ophthalmology, along with the creators of these immersive technologies, stand to benefit from the insights developed in this review. By noting these identified factors, they can strategize to enhance the efficacy of their future ventures in this domain. Furthermore, a thorough consideration of these factors harbours the potential to transform the landscape of ophthalmology education, creating the opportunity for a more streamlined and goal-directed approach. It holds the promise of not only refining the educational environment, but also accentuating the benefits that immersive technologies can bring to the fore in this field.

By leveraging these findings, ophthalmology education can benefit from tailored strategies to implement immersive technologies effectively, ultimately leading to better educational outcomes and ultimately improved patient care.

6 Conclusion

The rapid evolution of immersive technologies has exposed a new era of possibilities for ophthalmology education. This systematic literature review (SLR) embarked on a journey to uncover the key factors that influence the successful implementation of these technologies in the realm of ophthalmological training. Through employing an analysis of the literature, several categories emerged, each encompassing a number of factors that play an important role in the adoption and efficacy of immersive tools in this domain. The immersive technology features category emphasized the importance of creating a realistic and interactive three-dimensional environment, which is paramount for effective learning. The user acceptance category highlighted the significance of user-centric design, ensuring that the technology is both useful and easy to navigate. Learning outcomes, as a category, emphasized the tangible benefits that these technologies can bring about, from improved patient safety to accelerated training. Active learning and control factors accentuated the essence of hands-on engagement and learner autonomy, while the student characteristics category highlighted the intrinsic motivations and capabilities of the learners themselves. However, like all technologies, immersive tools in ophthalmology education are not without their challenges. The inhibiting factors category served as a reminder of the technical and non-technical hurdles that might impede the seamless integration of these tools into the educational landscape. These challenges, while noteworthy, also present opportunities for innovation and refinement.

In terms of areas for future research, the factor guideline define may be tested with medical professionals and learners, in order to understand their first-hand interactions with immersive tools and enrich the factors. In addition, aside-by-side comparison of immersive technology's efficacy against traditional ophthalmology training methods might offer clarity on their respective merits and areas needing enhancement. We acknowledge that our operationalization checklist approach is quite basic, but the outcome illustrate potential to be investigated further.

Disclosure of Interests. The authors have no competing interests to declare that are relevant to the content of this article.

References

1. Tang, Y.M., et al.: A systematic review of immersive technology applications for medical practice and education-trends, application areas, recipients, teaching contents, evaluation methods, and performance. Educ. Res. Rev. **35**, 100429 (2022)
2. Lowe, S., Mares, K., Khadjesari, Z.: Immersive technology in ophthalmology education: a systematic review. BMJ Simul. Technol. Enhanc. Learn. **7**(6), 600 (2021)

3. Jacobs, C., et al.: A narrative review of immersive technology enhanced learning in healthcare education. Int. Med. Educ. **1**(2), 43–72 (2022)
4. Srikong, M., Wannapiroon, P.: Immersive technology for medical education: technology enhance immersive learning experiences. Siriraj Med. J. **72**(3), 265–271 (2020)
5. Routray, S.K., et al.: Internet of Things (IoT) and immersive technology based extended reality in healthcare. In: 2023 International Conference on Intelligent Data Communication Technologies and Internet of Things (IDCIoT). IEEE (2023)
6. Qu, Z., et al.: Review of innovative immersive technologies for healthcare applications. Innov. Digit. Health Diagn. Biomark. **2022**(2), 27–39 (2022)
7. Logeswaran, A., et al.: The role of extended reality technology in healthcare education: towards a learner-centred approach. Future Healthc. J. **8**(1), e79 (2021)
8. Pawassar, C.M., Tiberius, V.: Virtual reality in health care: bibliometric analysis. JMIR Serious Games **9**(4), e32721 (2021)
9. Benferdia, Y., et al.: Critical success factors for virtual reality-based training in ophthalmology domain. J. Health Med. Inf. **9**(10.4172), 2157–7420 (2018). 1000318
10. Li, X., et al.: Considering the consequences of cybersickness in immersive virtual reality rehabilitation: a systematic review and meta-analysis. Appl. Sci. **13**(8), 5159 (2023)
11. Snyder, H.: Literature review as a research methodology: an overview and guidelines. J. Bus. Res. **104**, 333–339 (2019)
12. Khalifa, Y.M., et al.: Virtual reality in ophthalmology training. Surv. Ophthalmol. **51**(3), 259–273 (2006)
13. Hu, K.S., Pettey, J., SooHoo, J.R.: The role of technology in ophthalmic surgical education during COVID-19. Curr. Surg. Rep. **10**(12), 239–245 (2022)
14. Jagatheesaperumal, S.K., et al.: Advancing education through extended reality and internet of everything enabled metaverses: applications, challenges, and open issues. arXiv preprint arXiv:2207.01512 (2022)
15. Muñoz, E.G., et al.: Augmented reality, virtual reality, and game technologies in ophthalmology training. Information **13**(5), 222 (2022)
16. Le, T.D., Adatia, F.A., Lam, W.-C.: Virtual reality ophthalmic surgical simulation as a feasible training and assessment tool: results of a multicentre study. Can. J. Ophthalmol. **46**(1), 56–60 (2011)
17. Castaño-Calle, R., et al.: Perceived benefits of future teachers on the usefulness of virtual and augmented reality in the teaching-learning process. Educ. Sci. **12**(12), 855 (2022)
18. Bautista, M.G.A., et al.: Technology adoption of augmented and virtual reality in a progressive Philippines: a socio-techno-economical analysis. In: 2022 IEEE 14th International Conference on Humanoid, Nanotechnology, Information Technology, Communication and Control, Environment, and Management (HNICEM). IEEE (2022)
19. Weber, S.: Perception and Emotion in Virtual Reality: The Role of the Body and the Contribution of Presence. Universität Bern (2022)
20. Belyea, D.A., Brown, S.E., Rajjoub, L.Z.: Influence of surgery simulator training on ophthalmology resident phacoemulsification performance. J. Cataract. Refract. Surg. **37**(10), 1756–1761 (2011)
21. Camilleri, M.A.: Metaverse applications in education: a systematic review and a cost-benefit analysis. Interact. Technol. Smart Educ. (2023)
22. Martinez, M., et al.: Physiological assessment of user eXprience supported by immersive environments: first input from a literature review. In: ConVRgence (VRIC) Virtual Reality International Conference. Laval Virtual (2020)

Affordance Actualization of Social Robots: Empirical Evidence from the Hotel Industry

Gehan Wishwajith Premathilake[1](✉), Hongxiu Li[1], and Yang Bai[2]

[1] Unit of Information and Knowledge Management, Tampere University, Tampere, Finland
{gehan.ethugalapathiranage,hongxiu.li}@tuni.fi
[2] School of Information Management, Central China Normal University, Wuhan, China
yang.bai@ccnu.edu.cn

Abstract. Social robots exhibit a range of affordances for users. Drawing on the affordance theory, this study examined the affordance actualization of social robots in hotels based on user experience of social robots use. An LDA topic modeling analysis was performed based on online hotel reviews generated by hotel customers on TripAdvisor. We found that users actualize social robots' affordances such as luggage and storage handling, front desk tasks, delivery tasks, and navigational assistance while providing enjoyment and social interactions during hotel services. This study contributes to the literature by uncovering the actualized utilitarian, social, and hedonic affordances and the specific dimensions of these affordances of social robots in hotels.

Keywords: Affordance Actualization · Social Robots · Anthropomorphism · Topic Modeling

1 Introduction

Social robots are autonomous agents that can act, interact, and be socially intelligent, similar to humans. What transforms an "ordinary" robot into a "social" robot is its ability to fulfill one or more contextual social needs [1]. For example, they can mimic humans and reply with personalized responses due to their cognitive abilities based on artificial intelligence (AI). Social robots have been increasingly adopted for service delivery in the hospitality industry to sustain and gain competitive advantages [2]. While social robots have been suggested to have the potential to facilitate hotel services efficiently [3–5], there is a limited understanding of the affordances of social robots employed in hotel services.

Affordances have been used as a theoretical base to understand technology use in different contexts. In the information systems (IS) field, Markus and Silver [6] (p. 622) defined affordance as "the possibilities for goal-oriented action afforded to specified user groups by technical objects." Following the definition, affordances emerge through the interaction between users and a technical object, based on how users perceive the

Published by Springer Nature Switzerland AG 2024
R. van de Wetering et al. (Eds.): I3E 2024, LNCS 14907, pp. 415–427, 2024.
https://doi.org/10.1007/978-3-031-72234-9_35

values and norms associated with that object, and cannot be portrayed merely as a set of features inherent to a technical object itself [7].

Social robots are developed to provide a range of affordances for users. As anthropomorphized technologies, they possess unique anthropomorphic features that are embedded to perform human-centric tasks [8, 9]. Therefore, users are offered a range of possibilities that can be accomplished using social robots through technology affordances based on social robots' anthropomorphic features [5, 10]. However, the feature-affordance view fails to adequately rationalize the actualized affordances of social robots during service delivery as it has ignored the role of users as actors in affordance actualization during the use of social robots. In social environments where social robots are employed, users are active participants in the interaction process [2]. Also, users often adapt when using technologies to meet their goals, which can eventually lead to the discovery of new affordances. For example, in the hotel context, users might interact with a social robot to get directions initially, however, later adapt it to troubleshoot an issue [11]. Therefore, the feature-affordance view alone is insufficient to capture this dynamic perspective on actualized affordances. In addition, only a few research has attempted to explore the actualized affordances of social robots in the hospitality context [8, 12]. Hence, it is meaningful to examine the actualized affordances in social robots' usage based on user experiences with social robots in hotels, which could offer more comprehensive insights into the outcomes of using social robots.

To address this gap, drawing on affordance theory, the current study examines the actualized affordances of social robots in hotel services based on user-generated online reviews from TripAdvisor. The findings revealed that users actualize utilitarian, hedonic, and social affordances during their use of social robots in hotels. Luggage and storage handling, front desk services, delivery services, and navigational assistance are the prominent actualized utilitarian affordances of social robots in hotels. Users have experienced enjoyment and fun (hedonic affordances) in social robot use in hotels. Users also experienced friendly, effective, and efficient interactions when communicating with social robots (social affordances). The current study contributes to the literature on social robots by uncovering the actualized affordances of social robots in hotels from the views of utilitarian, social, and hedonic affordances and by identifying specific dimensions of these actualized affordances in the hotel context.

2 Theoretical Background

2.1 Social Robots in Hospitality

Boosting productivity and efficiency in service delivery and the need to substitute routine tasks that require low skills have encouraged the adoption of social robots in hotel services. Additionally, hotel guests tend to accept robotic services in hotels due to their interest and curiosity in novel and innovative services, as well as service convenience [3, 13].

Hotels tend to employ physical robots with anthropomorphic design features [14]. Social robots such as concierges and guide robots communicate with hotel customers and provide information to customers based on their requests [3, 15]. In addition, social robots are designed to perform routine tasks in hotels, such as welcoming, check-in/out, luggage handling/delivery, cleaning, and room services [14, 16].

Anthropomorphism, which describes the tendency of humans to apply human traits or actions to nonhuman objects, such as robots [8], has been a central focus in the field of social robot research. Previous studies have explored the impact of anthropomorphism on user acceptance [5, 13] and the continued use of social robots [15, 16] in different contexts. In the hospitality context, previous literature on the anthropomorphism of social robots has focused on the relationship between anthropomorphism and user perceptions and user behaviors related to social robots [5, 13, 14, 17, 18].

Prior literature has also studied user behaviors regarding social robots in the hospitality industry by applying different technology use theories. For instance, drawing on the social exchange theory, Kim et al. [19] found that perceived social presence, intelligence, and social interactivity affect trust in social robots, which in turn influence users' intention of using social robots in hotels. Perceptions of anthropomorphism, intelligence, and security of social robots have been found to impact users' intention to use social robots based on human robot interactions (HRIs) in services [5] as well as their continued usage intention in hotels using the technology acceptance model [16]. Meanwhile, Shin and Jeong [17] examined user attitudes toward social robots by incorporating the uncanny valley theory and found a significant effect of user perception of robots' morphology on user attitudes. In addition, prior research has also examined the role of social robots in enhancing user experience in the hospitality context. For instance, Qiu et al. [20] uncovered that the perception of robots as humanlike or intelligent positively influences the establishment of rapport between customers and robots, enhancing customers' overall hotel stay experience. Orea-Giner et al. [14] discovered that hotels with robotic service delivery tend to achieve a higher rating than hotels without.

While past research emphasizes different aspects of social robots in hotels, including their anthropomorphic features and user behaviors and perceptions related to social robots in hotel services, there is sparse evidence regarding whether the intended capabilities of social robots are fully utilized and realized by hotel customers. This highlights the necessity of exploring the actualized affordances of social robots.

2.2 Affordance Theory

According to the affordance theory, affordances do not exist inherently within an environment but emerge through the interaction between actors and the surrounding environment [21]. The conditions facilitating interactions include the characteristics of both the actor and the environment. Accordingly, affordances can also be identified as necessary preconditions for an activity, yet they do not imply the certainty of the given activity. However, affordances could be relational due to the dynamic interplay between objects and actors in various contexts [18].

Utilizing the affordance theory, Norman [22] recognized the perceived and actual affordances in the human-technology interaction context and highlighted that while users' perceptions of technology affordances are based on their abilities and prior experience, actual affordances are deliberately embedded properties within technology designs. From this theoretical standpoint, affordances indicate the range of possible actions available to a user with a distinct purpose that can be accomplished with a technology [5, 10]. In IS literature, affordances emerge as an appropriate view to represent possibilities and intended goals of users related to technical objects. The affordances of a technical object can vary depending on the design and user perceptions of the technical object [7, 23].

Affordance theory has been used in IS literature at both organizational and end-user levels [3, 9, 24]. For instance, Sadreddin and Chan [18] examined how digital startups use technology in organizations from an affordance view and found that actualized digital affordances could foster organizational capabilities. From an end-user perspective, Karahanna et al. [23] identified egocentric (action possibilities that do not involve others) and allocentric (action possibilities that demand the involvement of other users) affordances of social media. Drawing on affordance theory, Knote et al. [7] found the affordances pertaining to smart personal assistants (e.g., Amazon's Alexa) from a specific functional view, such as voice facilitators, virtual anthropomorphic advisors, chatbot operators, data-driven active observers, and general activity assistants. Also, Mettler et al. [24] examined the affordances of robots in healthcare from the end-user view and discovered five niches of affordances related to service robots in the healthcare context: reducing workload, strategic assets, specialist tools, gadgets with practical value, and boosting service quality.

The current study incorporates actualized utilitarian, hedonic, and social affordances of social robots. Utilitarian affordances reflect the practicality or task orientation of social robots, whereas hedonic affordances concern the capability of social robots to provide enjoyment, joy, or pleasure during HRIs [4, 25]. The social affordances of social robots involve the ability to build and carry out social interactions with users [1, 8]. Aligned with affordance theory, affordances of social robots arise through the complex social interactions between users and robots operating in dynamic environments such as hotels. User actions and intended goals when interacting with social robots result in the actualization of utilitarian, hedonic, and social affordances [7]. Accordingly, this study attempts to investigate the actualized affordances of social robots in hotel services from the hotel customer (end-user) point of view following the affordance theory.

3 Methodology

3.1 Data Collection and Preprocessing

The dataset for this study consisted of user-generated online hotel reviews collected from TripAdvisor. TripAdvisor is one of the most recognized travel-based social media platforms, which provides travelers with the possibility of sharing their travel experiences via reviews. To collect data from TripAdvisor, we initially conducted a manual selection and verification of the hotels that have incorporated social robots into their services. Afterward, "robot" and "robots" were used as the keywords to search the online hotel reviews and the hotels' corresponding TripAdvisor pages. In total, 94 hotels were confirmed to be included in the data collection. These hotels had TripAdvisor review ratings from 3 to 5 and spread across the USA ($n = 41$), Japan ($n = 18$), China ($n = 15$), Singapore ($n = 6$), England ($n = 4$), Taiwan ($n = 2$), Bulgaria ($n = 2$), UAE ($n = 2$), and Switzerland, Germany, Canada, and Portugal ($n = 1$ for each country). A Python script was developed utilizing the Selenium package to crawl and scrape reviews. Only reviews posted in English were scraped. We collected data features such as hotel star, hotel rating, review text, hotel name, review title, location, value, service, and cleanliness of each review. The range of review data gathered spanned from April 2004 to September 2022, and the initial dataset contained 150,384 online hotel reviews.

The extracted reviews reflected hotel customers' overall hotel stay experience, and some reviews also mentioned their social robots use experience. We first used the keyword robot/s and robot names such as Milton, Yobot, Pepper, Titan, Alina, Jenna, Wes, and Leo for filtering the gathered online reviews, and only the reviews that included texts about social robots in hotels were selected. Further, we conducted a manual check of these filtered online reviews, and several reviews were removed as they were not related to the user experience of social robots, though they contained keywords related to robots (e.g., '...and the old staff who was just like a robot,' '...check-in staff I experienced operate like robots with zero personality or sense of humor'). Then, the texts that explained the social robots use experience were extracted from each review and entered as a new data feature before the data preprocessing stage. The finalized corpus included 4,053 pieces of online review texts that explicitly explained the use of social robots in 94 hotels. These hotels had a spread of 3.5-star (8.5%), 4-star (42.6%), 4.5-star (43.6%), and 5-star (5.3%) ratings.

Further, the NLTK package in Python was used to transform and clean data. After cleaning, the review texts were segregated into word units. Next, relative pruning, which is stripping extremely frequent (more than 98%) and very rare word occurrences (less than 1%), was applied to the corpus to improve the algorithm's performance [26]. Words such as robot (n = 3,794), room (n = 3,341), hotel (n = 2,966), stay (n = 2,250), and service (n = 1,347) were removed from the corpus as a result. Nevertheless, these terms were predominantly evident since the corpus was exclusively composed of words related to social robots' use in hotels. Finally, a bag of words was created, including the 150 most relevant words selected from the words from review texts based on their Term Frequency-Inverse Document Frequency (TF-IDF) values.

3.2 Data Analysis

Based on the affordance theory, the affordances of social robots emerge due to the social interactions between users and robots. The actualization of affordances depends on how different users perceive them, and these perceptions are also reliant on individual user differences [6]. Consequently, actualized affordances of social robots could be identified from user experiences with social robots, which are often shared in online reviews. Therefore, online reviews are a suitable data source for exploring the actualized affordances of social robots in the hospitality context, while text mining methods, such as topic modeling, are appropriate for uncovering the thematic structure hidden within a set of textual data [26]. Topic modeling is a probabilistic statistical model used to discover underlying thematic topic structure from a text collection through the analysis of semantic information of words [27] and has been widely applied in research. The current study applies a commonly used topic modeling approach: Latent Dirichlet Allocation (LDA) topic modeling developed by Blei et al. [28] to analyze the textual data. LDA is an unsupervised method that uses a three-level Hierarchical Bayesian Model (HBM) for modeling documents as a finite mixture across a predefined set of topics

[27]. Concurrently, each topic is characterized as an infinite mixture over a set of topic probabilities. This enables the representation of each document as a linear function of topic probabilities, which, in turn, derive from the frequencies of words [26, 28]. The Genism package in Python was used to implement the LDA model. The preprocessed review texts were organized so that each review was represented by a combination of topics and topics by a combination of words, as required by LDA modeling [28]. LDA assigns words in each review to specific topics by computing the probability density associated with these words. This method yields a specified quantity of topics, each containing a predetermined number of words. Consequently, the model necessitates the identification of the number of topics (K) and the number of words per topic [26, 27].

Due to the probabilistic nature of LDA topic modeling, choosing an optimal topic model includes numerous trade-offs and judgments [29]. Selecting an excessive number of topics could lead to the inclusion of entities that are too alike, whereas opting for too few topics can result in broad entities combining specific aspects that need to be distinct [26, 29]. It is recommended that candidate topic models be generated and quantitative and qualitative validation techniques be used to identify the best-fitting model [26, 29]. Therefore, topics were selected by utilizing a statistical approach involving perplexity and coherence values, followed by an explanatory approach called the substantive search model selection process [26, 30]. In the substantive search [30] (p. 656) model selection process explained by Maier et al. [26], several candidate models are run with different numbers of topics and compared to find differences while interpreting each topic in the models. The selected model corresponds to a topic solution that can be validly interpreted based on the context [26].

The topic selection included several steps. Initially, 19 candidate models with 2–20 topics were selected based on the perplexity score, which determined the goodness of fit [28, 29]. Lower perplexity values indicate better predictive performance. Perplexity values plateaued at nine topics; thus, models with 6–11 topics were closely examined. Higher coherence values indicate more semantically related topics [28, 30, 31]. As the number of topics increases, coherence values rise, and perplexity decreases [28]. The average coherence values for the 19 candidate models ranged from 0.447 to 0.482. Two authors collaboratively labeled the topics for these models following the substantive search model selection process. The words with the highest probabilities, i.e., the initially listed words, were given priority when labeling according to the substantive content of the relevant topic [26]. The labeling was consistent with elements associated with the use of social robots in hotels. Subsequently, a comparison was made between labels among all the candidate models. The model with seven topics emerged as the appropriate model, reflecting a valid interpretation of topics related to social robots and the user experience of social robots in hotels. The average coherence and perplexity values for the selected model were 0.46 and -4.62, respectively. Therefore, the model with seven topics was confirmed to be statistically valid and interpretable. The individual topic coherences of the selected model were $T1 = 0.49$, $T2 = 0.55$, $T3 = 0.49$, $T4 = 0.43$, $T5 = 0.55$, $T6 = 0.34$, and $T7 = 0.36$ respectively. Finally, a sample containing 30 of the most relevant reviews for each topic was read, and topics were analyzed from the actualized affordance view based on the similarities within word clusters.

4 Findings

The seven topics identified using the LDA topic modeling were labeled manually with the agreement of two authors. Each topic included the 30 most frequent words. Table 1 lists the seven identified topics and relevant actualized affordances.

T1 contained words related to luggage handling and storage services of social robots. The cluster for these services takes the largest token percentage, suggesting users appreciate the luggage and storage functions of social robots the most. Hotel customers often encounter these robots' services right after their arrival at the hotels. Efficient and fast transport of luggage from the lobby to guest rooms or to a storage facility by social robots could ensure a smooth check-in/out process by reducing wait times ("provide," "efficient," "fast," "helpful"). Also, T1 revealed that users have positive opinions about the novelty in luggage and storage services ("helpful," "service," "modern," "lovely") provided by social robots in hotels. In addition, users have noticed the design features of social robots when social robots handle luggage and manage storage ("design," "big," "unique").

T2 described the social interactions during robots' services. Some reviews have directly emphasized the interactive nature of social robots ("come," "think," "offer," "ask," "walk"), which mimic the interactions during service delivery by human staff in hotels. These activities reflect that social robots can respond to customers in similar ways to human staff. In addition, users have enjoyed the humanlike interactions with social robots in hotel service delivery ("happy," "enjoy," "expect," "modern"). Furthermore, users have noticed robots as a surprising factor during their interactions with robots ("amaze," "look").

Front desk services of social robots have been explicitly described in T3. According to the most frequent words, hotel guests have noticed how social robots welcome and carry out the check in/out processes at the front desk. Social robots are employed at front desks to provide a novel experience by deviating from traditional service delivery and streamlining early encounters of hotel guests, maintaining efficiency in services. Since front desk tasks are repetitive and require significantly low labor, hotels that employ social robots can enhance the guest experience by offering a convenient start to their stay ("desk," "work," "check," "convenient," "new," "lobby," "experience," "modern," "wonderful," "welcome"). The reviews also mentioned the request-handling function of front desk robots. The robots situated in the hotel lobby are capable of handling guest requests, providing information and guidance about activities and tourist attractions in and around the hotels ("need," "say," "request," "talk," "speak," "cool," "concierge").

T4 indicated users' positive experience of social robots' delivery services in hotels. User experiences can be sensory, cognitive, affective, or conative in nature [2]. The sensory experience is associated with what hotel guests see or hear. The results show that guests have witnessed physical appearance and carried out verbal interactions with social robots during delivery services ("experience," "large," "huge," "butler," "speak"). Moreover, movements such as walking during delivery fall under sensory experience. The cognitive experience of users relates to thoughts and cognitions, which involve a cognitive appraisal process. Factors such as utility, cuteness, interactivity, and courtesy fall under cognitive experiences [2].

Table 1. LDA topic modeling results and relevant actualized affordances.

Topic (T)	Topic label	Token %	30 Most frequent words	Actualized affordances
T1	Luggage and storage handling	21%	luggage, big, check, new, walk, modern, see, helpful, storage, yotel, lovely, leave, provide, experience, unique, design, awesome, noise, serve, lobby, deliver, fantastic, little, perfect, efficient, fast, guest, screen, privacy, fun	Utilitarian affordances
T2	Social interaction	18.3%	come, look, think, offer, ask, quite, happy, away, order, enjoy, walk, locate, find, close, guest, amaze, reception, need, modern, check, expect, talk, deliver, yotel, people, little, say, machine, touch, provide	Social affordances
T3	Front desk services	14.2%	desk, work, need, deliver, check, little, say, convenient, kind, new, people, lobby, close, huge, request, pretty, experience, awesome, modern, pleasant, wonderful, look, leave, speak, cool, storage, welcome, luggage, move, talk	Utilitarian affordances
T4	Users' positive experience of delivery services	13.7%	friendly, helpful, experience, super, beautiful, expect, surprise, wonderful, deliver, request, excellent, need, locate, find, walk, polite, large, butler, provide, welcome, cute, offer, away, lovely, attentive, efficient, speak, huge, serve, leave	Utilitarian affordances, hedonic affordances, social affordances
T5	Navigational assistance	13.2%	walk, cool, find, lobby, away, feel, look, modern, feature, close, excellent, pretty, luggage, move, concierge, say, machine, reception, think, helpful, friendly, little, super, futuristic, large, see, speak, need, yotel, welcome	Utilitarian affordances
T6	Users' positive experience of enjoyment and fun	10.6%	lovely, amaze, super, perfect, excellent, design, check, yoshi, need, close, new, wonderful, little, helpful, yolanda, touch, fantastic, convenient, pleasant, beautiful, offer, large, pretty, cute, yotel, fun, request, kind, friendly, efficient	Hedonic affordances

(continued)

Table 1. (*continued*)

Topic (T)	Topic label	Token %	30 Most frequent words	Actualized affordances
T7	Enjoyment and fun in service delivery	9%	deliver, lovely, enjoy, kid, fun, cool, futuristic, see, housekeep, large, locate, feel, people, beautiful, request, fast, cute, welcome, close, modern, say, check, need, order, little, leave, happy, new, desk, friendly	Hedonic affordances

The frequent words associated with T4 exemplify how utilities ("deliver," "butler," "provide," "welcome"), robots' cuteness ("cute," "beautiful," "lovely"), interactivity ("friendly," "speak," "serve"), and courtesy ("polite," "friendly") are reflected when experiencing social robots' delivery services. Users' affective experience includes aspects such as novelty, enjoyment, and satisfaction [2]. The novelty of the robots' delivery services in hotels could make users feel surprised ("surprise," "wonderful," "lovely"). In addition, social robots create a welcoming atmosphere. The conative experience refers to the behavioral intentions such as approaching or resisting. Words associated with T4 indicated the welcoming approach, which makes guests feel truly valued and being taken care of by social robots ("welcome," "attentive," "serve").

T5 described social robots' assistance in guest navigation. Having social robots placed in areas such as lobbies and reception desks simplifies hotel navigation, making it easier for guests to find their desired locations. The ability of social robots to guide guests from one location to where they would like to go can reduce confusion while enhancing the guest experience, specifically in massive hotel locations ("walk," "find," "lobby," "large," "away"). Users have recognized and mentioned the navigational function as a novel and modern function of social robots ("futuristic," "modern," "feature"). Along with navigational assistance, some social robots can also offer luggage delivery and perform meaningful interactions with guests while helping them to move around the hotel without the burden of carrying their luggage ("luggage," "move," "concierge," "helpful," "friendly," "super").

T6 portrayed users' positive experiences of enjoyment and fun, which are encountered mainly due to the robots' design. The design of robots, incorporating anthropomorphic features, captures guests' attention, making positive impressions and bringing joy to them ("lovely," "amaze," "super," "perfect," "excellent," "design," "pleasant," "beautiful," "cute," "fun"). Therefore, users have enjoyed the services while appreciating the design of social robots; hence, positive feedback is reflected in words associated with T6. Additionally, reviews mentioned the perception of the robot designs, which links to efficient and friendly service delivery ("efficient," "friendly," "helpful"). Specifically, Yotels' social robots, Yoshi and Yolanda, are also noted in T6 ("Yoshi," "Yolanda," "Yotel").

Unlike T6, T7 described user perception of joy and fun due to social robots' service delivery. Social robots offer novelty in service delivery, which makes users happy from the receiving end. The futuristic designs of robots employed in front desks and housekeeping can surprise users. Specifically, children who experience these services particularly enjoy the services carried out by robots ("enjoy," "fun," "cool," "futurist," "housekeep," "kid," "modern," "new"). Social robots can personalize the services, such as by addressing users by name and delivering personalized greetings when necessary, especially when welcoming them. Such personalized services enhance the hedonic perception of robotic services and overall guest experience ("friendly," "lovely," "welcome," "feel"). Moreover, users have recognized social robots as humanlike entities that can behave in a friendly and kind way, similar to human employees ensuring that the guests are satisfied during hotel stays ("friendly," "kind").

5 Discussion

This study examined the actualized utilitarian, hedonic, and social affordances of social robots operating in the hotel context. Topics T1, T3, T4, and T5 reflect the actualized utilitarian affordances of social robots in hotels. According to the findings of the current study, action possibilities such as lobby/front desk/reception tasks (T3), storage handling (T1), and navigational assistance (T5) are associated with utilitarian affordances. In addition, social robots have also been found to perform tasks such as check-in/out and room delivery services (T4, T5). Social robots that enable utilitarian affordances, such as luggage handling and storage functions, could be equipped with humanoid arms that are capable of lifting and transporting luggage. While these robots fulfill the utility of carrying the luggage, the anthropomorphic designs support utilitarian affordances by providing adequate size or load capacity for guest luggage and offering an easy loading area, reducing the physical burden of guests in luggage handling. Further, users experience utilitarian affordances such as front desk services and room delivery services as the humanlike design of social robots enables them to respond to human requests, support necessary movements, and interact with customers during service delivery [31]. Moreover, in navigational assistance, anthropomorphic features allow robots to talk to customers and guide customers to destinations via conversation and body language. These findings align with the findings of Tondu [8] and Tussyadiah and Park [5], where utilitarian affordances were found to be linked with social robots' anthropomorphic responses, such as the expressiveness of gestures and emotions.

According to the findings, T4, T6, and T7 imply actualized hedonic affordances. When a social robot is hedonically capable, users can perceive positive feelings, experience fun and excitement, and connect strongly with the robot [12]. Surprise or amazement, as an emotion, is often associated with hedonic affordances due to the amazement in robots' services (T4, T6). Hotels employ dedicated social robots to entertain their guests. For example, hedonic affordances are witnessed when social robots are used to entertain guests by performing music or dances during special events such as birthday parties. Nevertheless, findings reveal the complexity of actualized affordances by disclosing a connection between hedonic affordances and utilitarian affordances: i.e., users enjoy and have entertaining experiences even during service delivery (T7). For example, navigational assistants could bring joy with robots' involvement rather than human assistance. Therefore, while some users could recognize the utility, others can perceive the enjoyment due to the presence of anthropomorphic features such as appearance and voice. Considering both utilitarian and hedonic affordances, Ozturk et al. [4] mentioned the positive impact of utilitarian and hedonic value perceptions on the intention to use robots. Moreover, findings indicate a relationship between the hedonic affordances and social robots' anthropomorphic features due to the favorable perception of robots' anthropomorphic features (T6). Users have noticed the design of social robots to be cute, beautiful, perfect, cool, futuristic, and unique.

According to the findings of the current study, T2 and T4 have indications of actualized social affordances. The possibilities of social robots engaging in interaction in reception (T2), performing short talks during delivery services (T4), and interacting during navigational assistance (T4) are linked to the social affordances of social robots. Currently, concierge robots and receptionist robots used in hotels can welcome and greet hotel guests, interact socially, and provide information by understanding various languages and accents [17]. Anthropomorphic features such as the humanlike appearance and voice of concierge robots could make robots more approachable and signal guests about their capability to assist with information similar to the human concierge. Resonating with the findings of the current study, Huang et al. [2] highlighted cuteness in appearance, interactivity, courtesy in user experience, and utility as cognitive evaluations of social robots. Findings also show that users feel emotions such as surprise when interacting with social robots in hotels (T4). Empathetic social interactions occur when robots can recognize and respond to user emotions [24, 32]. In addition, robots can offer assistance when they detect confusion or congratulate guests on successful task completion [2]. In such scenarios, the anthropomorphic designs enable guests to understand the robots' awareness of the users' emotional state.

6 Conclusion

The current study enriches the literature about social robots' technology affordances by uncovering the actualized affordances of social robots in hotels from the views of utilitarian, hedonic, and social affordances. Additionally, this study provides insights into the complexity of actualized affordances of social robots and discloses specific dimensions of these actualized affordances in the hotel context. Furthermore, the current study offers practical implications for decision-makers in the hospitality industry, such as hotel management, on implementing social robots in services to ensure hotel service efficiency based on the actualized affordances of social robots in hotels. It is evident that customers experience joy and happiness even when actualizing the utilitarian and social affordances of social robots, and hence, hotels could benefit from the implementation of social robots in services regardless of their intended use.

This study has its limitations. First, the current study only explored the actualized affordances from an end-user point of view. Further research can enhance the understanding of social robots' affordances from an organizational view. Second, this study focuses on the hotel context. While these findings on the actualized affordances can be generalized to the broader context of the hospitality industry, caution should be taken when applying these findings to other contexts, and future research could explore the affordance dimensions of social robots in contexts such as healthcare and education.

References

1. Sarrica, M., Brondi, S., Fortunati, L.: How many facets does a "social robot" have? A review of scientific and popular definitions online. Inf. Technol. People **33**, 1–21 (2019)
2. Huang, D., Chen, Q., Huang, J., Kong, S., Li, Z.: Customer-robot interactions: understanding customer experience with service robots. Int. J. Hosp. Manag. **99**, 103078 (2021)
3. Leung, X.Y., Zhang, H., Lyu, J., Bai, B.: Why do hotel frontline employees use service robots in the workplace? A technology affordance theory perspective. Int. J. Hosp. Manag. **108**, 103380 (2023)
4. Ozturk, A.B., et al.: Hotel customers' behavioral intentions toward service robots: the role of utilitarian and hedonic values. J. Hosp. Tour. Technol. **14**, 780–801 (2023)
5. Tussyadiah, I., Park, S.: Consumer evaluation of hotel service robots. In: Stangl, B., Pesonen, J. (eds.) Information and Communication Technologies in Tourism 2018, pp. 308–320. Springer, Cham (2018)
6. Markus, M.L., Silver, M.: A foundation for the study of IT effects: a new look at DeSanctis and poole's concepts of structural features and spirit. J. Assoc. Inf. Syst. **9**, 609–632 (2008)
7. Knote, R., Janson, A., Söllner, M., Leimeister, J.M.: Value co-creation in smart services: a functional affordances perspective on smart personal assistants. J. Assoc. Inf. Syst. **22**, 418–458 (2021)
8. Tondu, B.: Anthropomorphism and service humanoid robots: an ambiguous relationship. Ind. Robot Int. J. **39**, 609–618 (2012)
9. Zheng, J.F., Jarvenpaa, S.L.: Thinking technology as human: affordances, technology features, and egocentric biases in technology anthropomorphism. J. Assoc. Inf. Syst. **22**, 1429–1453 (2021)
10. Majchrzak, A., Markus, M.L.: Technology affordances and constraints in management information systems (MIS). In: Encyclopedia of Management Theory, pp. 832–836. Sage Publications Ltd., Thousand Oaks (2013)
11. Kuo, C.-M., Chen, L.-C., Tseng, C.-Y.: Investigating an innovative service with hospitality robots. Int. J. Contemp. Hosp. Manag. **29**, 1305–1321 (2017)
12. Liu, X., Yi, X., Wan, L.C.: Friendly or competent? The effects of perception of robot appearance and service context on usage intention. Ann. Tour. Res. **92**, 103324 (2022)
13. van Pinxteren, M.M.E., Wetzels, R.W.H., Rüger, J., Pluymaekers, M., Wetzels, M.: Trust in humanoid robots: implications for services marketing. J. Serv. Mark. **33**, 507–518 (2019)
14. Orea-Giner, A., Fuentes-Moraleda, L., Villacé-Molinero, T., Muñoz-Mazón, A., Calero-Sanz, J.: Does the implementation of robots in hotels influence the overall tripadvisor rating? A text mining analysis from the industry 5.0 approach. Tour. Manag. **93**, 104586 (2022)
15. Luo, J.M., Vu, H.Q., Li, G., Law, R.: Understanding service attributes of robot hotels: a sentiment analysis of customer online reviews. Int. J. Hosp. Manag. **98**, 103032 (2021)
16. Said, N., Ben Mansour, K., Bahri-Ammari, N., Yousaf, A., Mishra, A.: Customer acceptance of humanoid service robots in hotels: moderating effects of service voluntariness and culture. Int. J. Contemp. Hosp. Manag. (2023)
17. Shin, H.H., Jeong, M.: Guests' perceptions of robot concierge and their adoption intentions. Int. J. Contemp. Hosp. Manag. **32**, 2613–2633 (2020)
18. Sadreddin, A., Chan, Y.E.: Pathways to developing information technology-enabled capabilities in born-digital new ventures. Int. J. Inf. Manag. **68**, 102572 (2023)
19. Kim, H., So, K.K.F., Wirtz, J.: Service robots: Applying social exchange theory to better understand human–robot interactions. Tour. Manag. **92**, 104537 (2022)
20. Qiu, H., Li, M., Shu, B., Bai, B.: Enhancing hospitality experience with service robots: the mediating role of rapport building. J. Hosp. Mark. Manag. **29**, 247–268 (2020)

21. Gibson, J.J.: The theory of affordances. In: Shaw, R., Bransford, J. (eds.) Perceiving, Acting, and Knowing: Toward an Ecological Psychology, pp. 67–82. Lawrence Erlbaum Associates, Inc. (1977)
22. Norman, D.A.: The Psychology of Everyday Things. Basic Books, New York (1988)
23. Karahanna, E., Xin Xu, S., Xu, Y., Zhang, N. (Andy): The needs–affordances–features perspective for the use of social media. MIS Q. **42**, 737–756 (2018)
24. Mettler, T., Sprenger, M., Winter, R.: Service robots in hospitals: new perspectives on niche evolution and technology affordances. Eur. J. Inf. Syst. **26**, 451–468 (2017)
25. Odekerken-Schröder, G., Mennens, K., Steins, M., Mahr, D.: The service triad: an empirical study of service robots, customers and frontline employees. J. Serv. Manag. **33**, 246–292 (2022)
26. Maier, D., et al.: Applying LDA topic modeling in communication research: toward a valid and reliable methodology. Commun. Methods Meas. **12**, 93–118 (2018)
27. Jelodar, H., et al.: Latent Dirichlet allocation (LDA) and topic modeling: models, applications, a survey. Multimed. Tools Appl. **78**, 15169–15211 (2019)
28. Blei, D.M., Ng, A.Y., Jordan, M.I.: Latent Dirichlet allocation. J. Mach. Learn. Res. **3**, 993–1022 (2003)
29. Evans, M.S.: A computational approach to qualitative analysis in large textual datasets. PLoS ONE **9**, 1–10 (2014)
30. Bonilla, T., Grimmer, J.: Elevated threat levels and decreased expectations: how democracy handles terrorist threats. Poetics **41**, 650–669 (2013)
31. Fuentes-Moraleda, L., Díaz-Pérez, P., Orea-Giner, A., Muñoz-Mazón, A., Villacé-Molinero, T.: Interaction between hotel service robots and humans: a hotel-specific service robot acceptance model (sRAM). Tour. Manag. Perspect. **36**, 100751 (2020)
32. Wirtz, J., et al.: Brave new world: service robots in the frontline. J. Serv. Manag. **29**, 907–931 (2018)

The Narratives of Transparency in Food Supply Chain Digitalisation: A Systematic Literature Review

Esra Zorer(✉), Marijn Janssen, Siu Lie Tan, and Marcela Tuler de Oliveira

Delft University of Technology, 2628 BX Delft, The Netherlands
e.zorer@tudelft.nl

Abstract. Food supply chains (FSCs) have become global and complex, making them vulnerable to several risks. As the demand for transparency is getting higher than ever, the digitalisation of FSCs is becoming more recognised as a necessity to enable transparency. Research in FSC transparency often builds connections to digital technologies; however, the relationship between these technologies and transparency has rarely been investigated. From the 50 papers included in this systematic literature review, this research reveals the various narratives of transparency in FSC digitalisation through information asymmetry, trust, transparency, food safety and quality, food supply chain management, and sustainability. The theoretical implication of the findings is that technology can have different effects on transparency and is dependent on the implementation and context, although there can be some general effects. Based on the findings, this research initiates a discussion on digital transparency and offers a broad perspective that includes technical, organisational and social considerations.

Keywords: Food · food supply chains · technology · digitalisation · transparency · digital transparency

1 Introduction

Over the past few decades, food supply chains (FSCs) have become long and global, with increasing interdependencies among actors in several steps of the journey of food products [1]. Along this journey, food products are vulnerable to several risks, such as contamination, adulteration, and harmful practices for the people and the planet [2–4]. Since the early 2000s, there has been a growing concern for these risks among the public and governments, leading to the introduction of new regulations, such as the General Food Law Regulation in the EU, to enforce record-keeping and traceability in FSCs for transparency [2, 5]. However, such regulations mainly focus on preventing food safety incidents and fall short of addressing broader societal expectations, such as environmental sustainability or ethical labour practices [6, 7]. Furthermore, FSCs with traceability measures still experience food safety and fraud incidents repeatedly, indicating complete traceability is more an exception than the rule in business as usual [2]. In response to these shortcomings, transparency has emerged as a societal value beyond regulatory compliance.

Published by Springer Nature Switzerland AG 2024
R. van de Wetering et al. (Eds.): I3E 2024, LNCS 14907, pp. 428–444, 2024.
https://doi.org/10.1007/978-3-031-72234-9_36

Transparency is easy to grasp intuitively, yet it is harder to define [8]. That said, the most commonly used definition in the literature refers to the transparency of a supply chain network as "the extent to which all the network's stakeholders have a shared understanding of, and access to, product and process related information that they request, without loss, noise, delay and distortion" [9, p. 18]. Some authors link transparency in supply chains to the quality, availability, accuracy, accessibility and actuality of data; therefore, in transparent supply chains, the revealed information should be reachable by relevant stakeholders in a simple, fast, comprehensible, comprehensive, credible and rapid manner [10]. Similarly, Searcy et al. define transparency as the perceived quality of intentionally shared information, which encompasses disclosure, clarity, and accuracy [11]. In practice, FSCs present major differences in the range, scope, and sophistication of their transparency systems based on their context [10]. Correspondingly, many definitions in the literature emphasise different aspects and formulate different expectations from the concept [8]. Attention to the varying definitions of transparency in FSCs is becoming more relevant as we observe an increase in the popularity of the subject.

In the literature, 2019 appears to be a turning point for FSC transparency, arguably due to the disruptions experienced during the COVID-19 outbreak and the resulting concerns and demands for transparency. Similarly, there has been momentum in FSC digitalisation in the literature since 2020, possibly due to the potential benefits of digitalisation for FSC transparency as a response to the COVID-19 crisis. Recent research on FSC transparency often builds connections to digital technologies, which is considered one of the main enablers of transparency compared to other existing solutions. According to Astill et al. [3], the size and complexity of global FSCs make it difficult to achieve transparency without the involvement of digital technologies. Similarly, Bastian and Zentes [10] consider the information systems supported by digital technologies essential to deal with highly complex situations and efficiently exchange data between stakeholders.

Acknowledging the substantiality of digital technologies for FSCs could spark a discussion on digital transparency in the literature, yet no research paper has directly addressed this concept to the best of our knowledge. Digital transparency is an emerging concept in social sciences, especially in research topics on digital government, good governance, citizen participation, public information, and so on [12–16]. In the context of FSCs, digital transparency can be broadly defined as the accessibility and visibility of information through digital means, allowing stakeholders to gain insight into various processes and transactions. For instance, blockchain technology (BCT) enables the recording of every transaction in the FSC in tamper-proof ledgers to enhance food safety, consumer trust, and sustainability practices [17]. The Internet of Things (IoT) devices, such as sensors and Radio Frequency Identification (RFID) tags, enable real-time data collection and monitoring to improve the efficiency of operations and reduce food waste [18]. Artificial Intelligence (AI) algorithms can analyse large datasets to predict potential issues and improve FSC processes [19]. From these examples, we see that the pursuit of transparency is always accompanied by the motivation to achieve a specific goal, and the distinct features of different technologies determine their suitability to a context. This is also linked to how transparency is defined in that context, and having a discussion on digital transparency in FSCs would enable us to consider these aspects.

The main objective of this research is to explore the relationship between digital technologies and transparency in the context of FSCs. There is an abundance of papers in the literature focusing on the use of digital technologies in FSCs. Some of these papers provide empirical or theoretical insight into the adoption of a specific technology in FSCs from a technical point of view [20–27]. Some others aim to provide a general overview of the use of a specific technology in FSCs, including their potential benefits and challenges and the recent advances made in the field [19, 28–35]. However, we see that the connection between digital technologies and transparency is hardly discussed. Even though some papers investigate the role of transparency and digital technologies regarding the motivations mentioned above [2, 3, 7], more information is required to understand the context in which these technologies are integrated and whether that leads to any clarity regarding the pursuit of transparency as a societal value.

In Sect. 2, we present the systematic literature review methodology. In Sect. 3, we answer the research questions identified. In Sect. 4, the discussion on the main highlights of the findings is provided, and finally, Sect. 5 provides the conclusion.

2 Systematic Literature Research Methodology

This research adopted a systematic literature review (SLR) methodology to identify, evaluate, and synthesise the relevant studies and ensure a comprehensive overview of existing research in the field of FSC digitalisation and transparency [36]. With this method, we can identify key themes, gaps, and trends in this field [37], which aligns with the explorative nature of this research. The steps followed are inspired by the guide provided by Carrera-Rivera et al. [38], which are further explained in the following sub-sections.

2.1 Define PICOC and Synonyms

PICOC (population, intervention, comparison, outcome, and context) criteria are commonly used in SLR, and they break down the research objective into searchable keywords to formulate research questions [38]. Identified keywords and synonyms can be found in Table 1.

2.2 Formulate Research Questions

The research questions were identified in accordance with the keywords are as follows:

- RQ1: How is transparency defined in the research papers?
- RQ2: What are the motivations for creating transparency in FSCs?
- RQ3: Which digital technologies are used in FSCs to create transparency?

2.3 Identify Digital Libraries and Inclusion and Exclusion Criteria

For document search, Scopus and Web of Science databases are selected due to their extensive content in social sciences. For each database, advanced search strings were created, which include documents that are either journal articles or conference papers

Table 1. Keywords and synonyms identified in PICOC steps.

Criteria	Keywords and Synonyms
Population	Food supply chain, agri-food supply chain, agriculture supply chain, food sector, food system
Intervention	Digital technologies, information communication technologies (ICT), digitalisation, industry 4.0, information systems, blockchain, smart contracts, artificial intelligence (AI), internet of things (IoT), cloud computing, data analytics, barcode, radio-frequency identification (RFID), smart packaging, global positioning system (GPS), geographic information system (GIS), mobile applications, robotics and automation, supply chain management systems, DNA barcoding, drones, virtual reality (VR), augmented reality (AR), edge computing, digital twins, cybersecurity
Comparison	Not applicable
Outcome	Transparency, transparent, data sharing, information sharing, data flow, information flow, information access
Context	Not applicable

published from 2010 to 2024 and exclude documents that are not in English and not accessible. The exact search query used in each database can be seen in Appendix I[1]. Initially, 295 documents were retrieved from Scopus and 148 from Web of Science as of May 14th 2024. After merging the document lists, the duplicates and papers outside the criteria were eliminated, resulting in 273 papers remaining for the second elimination round. The screening of titles and abstracts reduced the number to 50 documents, which are included in this SLR (Table 2).

Table 2. Inclusion and exclusion criteria

Criteria Type	Decision
Period	Inclusion: From 2010 to 2024
Language	Exclusion: Articles not in English
Type of literature	Inclusion: Journal article and conference paper
Type of source	Inclusion: Articles from conferences and journals
Accessibility	Exclusion: Not accessible
Relevance to RQs	Exclusion: Not relevant to at least two research questions

[1] https://surfdrive.surf.nl/files/index.php/s/PKiBulKDGV0m7cw.

3 Results

In accordance with the steps explained in the research methodology, data was extracted from 50 papers with a focus on digital technologies included in the documents and whether they include any definition for transparency and the motivations for creating transparency in FSCs. The analysis of these topics is provided in the following subsections.

3.1 Transparency Definitions

The documents retrieved from the SLR revealed that among the 50 papers covered, six papers included "transparency" or "transparent" keywords in their title. Among these six papers, four of them provided a definition for transparency. Additionally, when we look at the complete list of papers, we see that eight papers provided a definition for transparency.

Table 3. Transparency definitions provided by the papers included in the SLR.

	Transparency Definition
[39, p. 149]	"Transparency of a supply chain is the extent to which all its stakeholders have a shared understanding and access to the product-related information that request without loss, noise, delay and distortion."
[40, p. 5]	"Transparency refers to the ability to know what is happening upstream in the supply chain and to communicate this information among stakeholders across the supply chain."
[41, p. 5566]	"Transparency means information sharing among registered and authorized members without distortion and delay."
[42, p. 109]	"We define transparency as the extent to which all actors in the agri-food SC have a shared understanding of, and access to, product-related information that is requested, without delay, distortion, or noise."
[43, p. 3]	"The main purpose of the transparency and data provenance data management platform is to integrate all of the available information across the value chain and make it available to all of the stakeholders."
[44, p. 298]	"It is a procedure that involves the process of tracing food's journey from where it is grown, produced, handled and stocked to how it is transported or processed, leading to the development of an authentic product and transparent food ecosystem."
[45, p. 229]	"Transparency and traceability are concerned with sharing information about practices within the supply chain and generating information about the trajectories of foodstuffs through chains."

(*continued*)

Table 3. (*continued*)

	Transparency Definition
[46, p. 9]	"It refers to the communication and equal access of all stakeholders to all information and knowledge pertaining to the product in the absence of loss, blockage, or distortion."
[47, p. 4]	"Transparency can be defined as a far-reaching organising principle that significantly influences social behaviour, but it can create "new forms of closure, manipulation, control and surveillance."
[48, p. 3]	"All stakeholders can access relevant product information without delay or bother due to the transparency of the dairy food supply chain."

From the initial impressions, we can see varying definitions for transparency. It could refer to information-sharing [41], having access to information [48], and the integration of available information [43]. How transparency is defined could be linked to the focus of the research. For instance, transparency appears to be defined in the context of traceability when the research focus is on the transparency created through traceability efforts [44]. When the research focus is to challenge the assumption that transparency prevents or reduces illegitimate forms of power, we see that the authors define transparency as an organising principle that can create new forms of closure, manipulation, control and surveillance [48]. Regardless of the focus, we see many of the definitions include stakeholders, which would also refer to different stakeholder perspectives. In this context, it would be valuable to look into how different stakeholders in FSCs define transparency. The definitions taken from the literature can be seen in Table 3.

3.2 Motivations to Create Transparency

In the literature, the concept of transparency often presents itself in relation to different motivations to create transparency. The potential of digital technologies to enable transparent FSCs is considered their main feature since transparency is then considered one of the main enablers of many crucial improvement points in FSCs, such as food safety, food quality, supply chain management, or sustainability. Therefore, in this subsection, we present the narratives in some of these papers to explore the connections between digital technologies and some of the most frequently encountered motivations for transparency.

Information Asymmetry and Trust

Information asymmetry in FSCs refers to a situation where some actors are in possession of more information than others [49]. Current widespread centralised systems in FSCs are considered non-transparent, monopolistic, and asymmetric information systems [50]. Accordingly, information asymmetry could lead to non-transparent FSCs and cause trust issues among stakeholders. Regarding the perceptions of FSC actors on trust, Joo and Han conducted a survey study with the actors of a blockchain-based FSC and concluded that transparency, traceability, and FSC security positively affect distributed trust [40]. In the case of Ghana's cocoa beans FSC, trust among the actors was considered an issue of great concern due to information asymmetries and power imbalances that led to the exploitation of cocoa farmers [51]. Consequently, the authors conclude that blockchain technology can create more secure, distributed, transparent, and collaborative systems that empower its users as farmers gain more access to information. Information asymmetry also creates trust issues in consumers, leading to more demand for transparency. In their research, Cao et al. draw attention to the trust issues consumers experience regarding the sustainability claims of food firms due to the absence of transparent reporting [52]. In the majority of these cases, enhancing transparency for consumer trust was considered an opportunity for brand image and competitive advantage, yet we also encountered different motivations, such as empowering consumers. Through their research on open data, Leone highlighted the citizen identity of consumers and developed an educational approach based on citizens' right to know and participate in the making of change they want to see [59]. Here, transparency is linked to creating reliable knowledge and citizens' ability to interpret and use that knowledge to democratise knowledge production.

Traceability

In the literature, most of the existing solutions for FSC transparency mention traceability as it enables visibility throughout the journey of food products [21, 42, 45, 50, 52–60]. However, another point of view claims that transparency is one of the main enablers of traceability. To clarify the relationship between transparency and traceability, Chan et al. refer to transparency as mapping the entire end-to-end supply chain, whereas traceability is more linked to following the flow of products or purchase orders as they move through the supply chain [39]. In this context, the authors stressed that transparency must come before traceability, as it is not practical to implement traceability without transparency. From the evidence found in this SLR, we can argue that there is a positive feedback connection between transparency and traceability: traceability systems could enable higher transparency in FSCs, and when there is more transparency among FSC actors, it appears easier to build traceability systems. Due to this connection to transparency, traceability will continue to appear in relation to some of the motivations to create transparency in FSCs.

Food Safety and Quality

Food safety has been a great concern for FSCs and also the main reason for the efforts to bring more transparency and traceability into FSCs in the last couple of decades. Within this period, it seems that consumers have turned to quality as a way to deal with food safety concerns [45]. From this SLR, we identified several examples that are approaching food safety and quality from the perspectives of different stakeholders. For example, a case study has been conducted on the use of an Ethereum-based distributed traceability application (dApp) for Table Olives [60]. After testing the application with a Greek producer, the authors concluded that the application significantly improved the product's traceability by providing a transparent, secure, and efficient solution that reduces time and increases the accuracy and reliability of the data. However, even though blockchain brings more accountability, it doesn't guarantee data quality or accuracy alone [61]. In the case study of traditional Carasau bread, the authors aimed to achieve transparent and auditable traceability where each actor can verify the quality of the bread and the conformity to hygienic-sanitary conditions [57]. The authors recommend combining blockchain technology (Ethereum smart contracts) with RFID/NFC solutions to monitor the manufacturing process parameters. This way, the system would reduce the data entry errors and the risk of tampering while allowing end consumers to have a transparent view. In the case of the Indian dairy industry, Khanna et al. explored blockchain-enabled supply chain solutions for the prevention of food contamination and adulteration of milk products [54]. Here, the Ethereum blockchain executed by smart contracts was used as a foundational technology coupled with other technologies (Azure Cloud, QR codes, IoT, and machine learning), where each technology has a role to play in ensuring data quality.

Food Supply Chain Management

Food supply chain management (FSCM) is a complex integrated system that involves several transactions employing many entities, shareholders, documents, and information [62]. Naturally, it is closely linked to traceability and food safety/quality topics, and quite a few papers in this SLR provide examples of digital technologies that enhance transparency in the systems to achieve improvements in these areas. One of the most common examples is the use of blockchain technology in combination with other technologies (sensors, IoT, AI/ML) for operational excellence, like in the case of perishable FSCs [63]. In their research, Kayikci et al. concluded that the blockchain mechanism enables transparency in the FSC by monitoring perishable food products at each step and collecting and analysing relevant data to improve efficiency and reduce operational risks and obstacles regarding food safety, recalls, and food waste. In another research, Sengupta et al. demonstrated the issues within the fish supply chains during the COVID-19 outbreak [64]. In their case study, fisherfolks are provided with a digital app that includes satellite-based fish zone data, local weather data, QR code tracking of seafood, and a GPS and IoT-based vessel communication system run by blockchain. The authors concluded that the transparency guaranteed by the system significantly increases trust and brand value and, correlatively, the income of small fisherfolks. Another significant improvement point linked to FSCM is supplier management, and often, it is one of the main concerns of retailers since consumers and policymakers consider retailers to be responsible for food integrity [45]. In this context, transparency appears as a means to practice control and authority for the protection of the supply chain [23, 65, 66].

Sustainability

From the papers included in this SLR, we see that sustainability has become one of the major discussion topics regarding FSC transparency. In the case of the movement of food products from Thailand to Western countries, Kittipanyangam and Tan highlighted that consumers and authorities are highly sensitive to social and environmental issues, and they will demand full transparency when digital technologies become more available and feasible [16]. In the literature, many different perspectives towards FSC transparency were identified in relation to sustainability, such as calculating environmental and carbon footprint [41, 67–69], reducing food waste and loss [48, 63, 70–73], ensuring animal welfare [58, 74], reducing deforestation [23, 60, 68], effective use of pesticides, fertilisers, antibiotics, and irrigation [52, 69, 70, 73], ensuring food security [68, 72, 75], reducing GHG emissions [41, 52, 70, 74], improving labour conditions [51, 52, 66, 68, 76], enabling fair trade practices [63, 72], establishing premium prices and fair income for the producers [21, 51, 64], reducing intermediaries [44, 55], empowering consumers [48, 72, 76], supply chain resilience [63, 64, 77], etc. Managing certifications also appeared a few times in this SLR in relation to FSC transparency and sustainability [52, 69, 78]. Regarding sustainability communication in FSCs, Cao et al. started a discussion about the limitations, such as the lack of standardised frameworks, greenwashing, information overload for consumers, and the absence of transparent reporting [52]. Consequently, the authors recommended integrating blockchain-based traceability solutions where stakeholders would have access to and consensus on a standardised set of sustainability claims, metrics, and ethical guidelines. However, Wünsche and Fernqvist argue that blockchain technology is not decisive for a more sustainable food system but could assist the transition towards more data-driven supply chains where an ecosystem of technologies can enhance decision-making and lead to more sustainability [72].

3.3 Digital Technologies Identified in the SLR

The most commonly mentioned digital technology in this SLR appeared to be distributed ledger technologies (DLT) regarding the digitalisation of FSCs. Here, it is important to note that BCT is the most prominent example of DLT, and this popularity is also visible in the results of this SLR. Among 50 papers included in this review, 38 investigated the role of DLT (mostly blockchain) in FSCs, either with a sole focus on the technology or its application in combination with other technologies. Some of these papers provided details about the specific type of BCT [39, 50, 53], whereas others approached it from a broader perspective [42, 62, 67]. Among the papers on BCT, smart contracts appeared several times as a function of the technology that is becoming more popular in the literature [50, 65, 66]. Following DLT, the IoT appeared to be the second most popular technology that was mentioned in the papers, often considered in combination with other technologies [54, 68, 79]. AI and ML technologies also seem to be gaining popularity in the literature, and they are also mostly mentioned in combination with other technologies [27, 65]. Additionally, a few papers seem to offer cutting-edge technologies and methods to tackle issues in FSC digitalisation, such as federated learning [75], digital twins [70], privacy-preserving technologies (PPT) [80], and the development of a standard ontology for tackling interoperability issues [68]. The details of the complete list of digital technologies identified in this SLR can be found in Appendix II[2].

3.4 Broader Perspectives on the Use of Digital Technologies for FSC Transparency

Some researchers recognise digitalisation in FSCs as more than investing in technology; rather, it is considered a long-term strategic commitment that requires the evaluation of various factors to identify suitable technologies for the context [24]. As seen in the examples included in this SLR, there is a trend of integrating a mix of technologies in accordance with how they compensate each other to achieve transparency. Conformingly, Durrant et al. refer to data sharing as a complex technical and social challenge, and each technology has the potential to tackle only one part of the challenge [80]. To tackle

[2] https://surfdrive.surf.nl/files/index.php/s/PKiBulKDGV0m7cw.

data privacy and ownership issues, the authors introduced the sharing of training models and federated learning for decentralised analysis to extract knowledge without sharing raw data, in combination with BCT for improved immutability and accountability, and PPTs for preserving the privacy of the actors involved [80]. Another example of how different technologies compensate one another can be found in the work of Tsolakis et al. [27], regarding the co-implementation of BCT and AI. Their research demonstrated how BCT and AI can reduce data gaps: while BCT enables immutable data flows, AI supports collecting and evaluating data from external sources. In many research papers on BCT, IoT devices are considered a solution to tackle the data quality issues of BCT. However, Tsoukas et al. discuss the security issues of IoT devices in their research and offer the use of TinyML, an emerging technology that can detect and report when abnormalities are discovered on sensors, thanks to its ability to operate in constrained hardware and run ML locally on edge [46].

Another perspective identified in the literature was linked to developing new strategies to utilise the use of existing data to enhance transparency in FSCs rather than constantly looking for new ways to generate new data. In this SLR, we encountered issues related to interoperability and data standardisation quite a few times [27, 42, 43, 54, 67, 69, 81, 82]. According to Wünsche and Fernqvist, there has been no standardisation regarding the kind of data that needs to be available [72]. In this regard, some of the papers highlight the importance of the development of a common set of data standards and protocols [59, 60], semantic models and APIs that are compliant with the OpenAPI standards [61], and reproducible data pipelines based on an agreement on data formats as well as the generation of machine-readable data [80].

4 Discussion

In this research, we identified varying definitions for transparency in different papers focusing on FSC digitalisation. The reason for such different definitions could be linked to the context these papers focus on. This is a significant observation, as it would be challenging to understand which technologies would fit the situation at hand without understanding what transparency means in that context and why it is needed. When the context of transparency and digital technologies is misunderstood, the efforts for digital transparency might not fulfil their purposes, and more importantly, they might cause more harm than good. For example, Commandré et al. point out the risk of information compartmentalisation within the use of BCT by powerful actors where the centralised approach to transparency trumps the decentralised nature of blockchain [47]. Correspondingly, Tsoukas et al. argue that technology investments are not enough for FSC digitalisation, and FSC actors need a mindset shift, which would involve teaching FSC partners about the need for transparency and the benefits of collaboration and capacity building [46]. In reality, creating digital transparency is more than a technological fix; it involves complex social considerations.

When we look at the most frequently mentioned motivations to create transparency, we see that dealing with information asymmetry and building trust among stakeholders appear to be the key stress points. In this regard, we see that issues related to information asymmetry and trust are also connected to other motivations to create transparency [38,

57, 58]. Among these motivations, food safety and quality appear to be the most popular topics in the literature, which is no surprise due to already existing legislation and regulations. It was also expected to encounter transparency efforts regarding the improvements in FSCM, such as improving the efficiency of the operations and supplier management. However, it is interesting to see that recent literature increasingly incorporates discussions on sustainability, especially on environmental and social issues concerning FSC transparency. Furthermore, we see that many authors build connections between such issues and consumer demand, including the potential influence consumers could have on transforming FSCs into a more sustainable direction [23, 45, 76].

Many of the papers included in this SLR refer to traceability as an enabler of transparency, but at the same time, we recognised that transparency is needed to ensure well-functioning traceability [54]. In FSC practice, traceability systems are often the first step towards creating transparency as a response to legislation requirements. Although many of these legislations were introduced long ago, traceability still seems to be the main discussion topic in the literature for FSC transparency. In relation, BCT appears to be the most popular solution in the literature to enhance transparency as it is claimed to ensure traceability. We believe that the popularity of BCT in the literature is based on its potential benefits, which often remain theoretical, whereas the actual benefits depend on the implementation and the context. However, we have yet to have a real implementation to validate the long-term implications of the technology. Correspondingly, we see some authors taking a critical approach and discussing the limitations of BCT [22, 83]. As a response, we identified papers offering a mix of technologies to create a formula where each solution compensates for the other's limitations. This is a significant shift in the literature as it introduces a broader perspective on solving transparency issues in FSCs.

From a theoretical point of view, many papers analysed in this SLR focus on the practical implications of the technology solution they propose without developing theories that would enable us to gain an integrated understanding of digital transparency in FSCs. However, we see some examples that would be useful in this manner. For instance, the supply chain ecosystem framework developed by Tsolakis et al. [27] involves the business processes and causal loops that would enable a unified approach to the use of AI and BCT in FSCs for data monetisation and sustainability through enabling transparency. Another example would be the theoretical framework developed based on a SLR [67]. Here, the framework provides a guide for BCT adoption and incorporates the technology's potential benefits and implementation challenges to the consideration of the different BCT application areas in FSCs. Regarding sustainability communication, Cao et al. developed a four-layer architectural framework that includes the supply chain (business), application, traceable sustainability, and the blockchain layer [52]. Correspondingly, such theories would inspire future efforts to develop an integrated theory for creating digital transparency in FSCs.

5 Conclusion

The global and complex structure of today's food supply chains (FSCs) requires more transparency in dealing with various problems, such as food safety and quality, FSC management, and sustainability. Digitalisation is now considered a necessity to achieve transparency, yet this systematic literature review (SLR) reveals that it is a much more complicated task than simply investing in technology. The efforts to enhance transparency in a FSC require defining transparency in the context, including different stakeholder perspectives. The effect of transparency is dependent on the implementation in the given context. It also requires understanding the potential benefits and challenges of different technologies and how to decide on the most suitable mix of technologies in relation to the context. In this paper, we introduced the concept of digital transparency, which initiates a discussion on the relationship between the context of transparency and digital technologies from a broader perspective. Accordingly, the theoretical contributions identified in the publications mentioned above could benefit future research by developing approaches to involve the context of digital transparency in FSCs. In this regard, the theoretical contribution of this research is that demonstrating digital technologies can have different implications on transparency, and their role is dependent on the context.

This SLR provides an overview of the digital technologies used in FSCs to enhance transparency. Furthermore, this paper attempts to build connections between these technologies and the notion of transparency by building narratives over different motivations to create digital transparency. However, it would be limited to building such narratives solely based on the input from the literature. Therefore, we recommend interviewing stakeholders from various FSCs and developing case studies to gain an in-depth understanding of the narrative of digital transparency in various contexts. This would initiate a discussion on developing systemic ways to tackle issues in FSCs through digital transparency.

Acknowledgements. This research is conducted as part of the research activities of the TITAN project (project number 101060739), funded by the Commission as part of Horizon EU.

Disclosure of Interests. The authors have no competing interests to declare relevant to this article's content.

References

1. Manning, L.: 5 - systems for sustainability and transparency of food supply chains. In: Galanakis, C.M. (ed.) Sustainable Food Systems from Agriculture to Industry, pp. 153–187. Academic Press (2018). https://doi.org/10.1016/B978-0-12-811935-8.00005-6
2. Akkerman, R., Farahani, P., Grunow, M.: Quality, safety and sustainability in food distribution: a review of quantitative operations management approaches and challenges. OR Spectr. **32**(4), 863–904 (2010). https://doi.org/10.1007/s00291-010-0223-2
3. Astill, J., et al.: Transparency in food supply chains: a review of enabling technology solutions. Trends Food Sci. Technol. **91**, 240–247 (2019). https://doi.org/10.1016/j.tifs.2019.07.024
4. Soon, J.M., Brazier, A.K.M., Wallace, C.A.: Determining common contributory factors in food safety incidents – a review of global outbreaks and recalls 2008–2018. Trends Food Sci. Technol. **97**, 76–87 (2020). https://doi.org/10.1016/j.tifs.2019.12.030
5. Lam, T.K., Heales, J., Hartley, N., Hodkinson, C.: Consumer trust in food safety requires information transparency. Australas. J. Inf. Sys. **24** (2020). https://doi.org/10.3127/ajis.v24i0.2219

6. Mol, A.P.J.: Transparency and value chain sustainability. J. Clean. Prod. **107**, 154–161 (2015). https://doi.org/10.1016/j.jclepro.2013.11.012
7. Trienekens, J., Wognum, N., Beulens, A., van der Vorst, J.: Transparency in complex dynamic food supply chains. Adv. Eng. Inform. **26**(1), 55–65 (2012). https://doi.org/10.1016/j.aei.2011.07.007
8. Matheus, R., Janssen, M., Janowski, T.: Design principles for creating digital transparency in government. Gov. Inf. Q. **38**(1), 101550 (2021). https://doi.org/10.1016/j.giq.2020.101550
9. Hofstede, G.J.: Transparency in netchains. In: The challenge of global chains, Wageningen, Netherlands, pp. 73–89 (2002). https://library.wur.nl/WebQuery/wurpubs/318114. Accessed 16 Aug 2023
10. Bastian, J., Zentes, J.: Supply chain transparency as a key prerequisite for sustainable agri-food supply chain management. Int. Rev. Retail Distrib. Consum. Res. **23**(5), 553–570 (2013). https://doi.org/10.1080/09593969.2013.834836
11. Searcy, C., Castka, P., Mohr, J., Fischer, S.: Transformational transparency in supply chains: leveraging technology to drive radical change. Calif. Manag. Rev. **65**(1), 19–43 (2022). https://doi.org/10.1177/00081256221126204
12. Al Sulaimani, A.H.A., Ozuem, W.: Understanding the role of transparency, participation, and collaboration for achieving open digital government goals in Oman. Transform. Gov. People Process Policy **16**(4), 595–612 (2022). https://doi.org/10.1108/TG-04-2022-0044
13. Goldstein, J.E., Faxon, H.O.: New data infrastructures for environmental monitoring in Myanmar: Is digital transparency good for governance? Environ. Plann. E Nat. Space **5**(1), 39–59 (2022). https://doi.org/10.1177/2514848620943892
14. Madkur, F.N., Paletta, F.C.: Transparência Digital na Informação Pública: Infoética. Boletim do Arquivo da Universidade de Coimbra **34**(2) (2021). Article no. 2. https://doi.org/10.14195/2182-7974_34_2_4
15. Matheus, R., Faber, R., Ismagilova, E., Janssen, M.: Digital transparency and the usefulness for open government. Int. J. Inf. Manag. **73**, 102690 (2023). https://doi.org/10.1016/j.ijinfomgt.2023.102690
16. Zhao, B., Cheng, S., Schiff, K.J., Kim, Y.: Digital transparency and citizen participation: evidence from the online crowdsourcing platform of the City of Sacramento. Gov. Inf. Q. **40**(4), 101868 (2023). https://doi.org/10.1016/j.giq.2023.101868
17. Antonucci, F., Figorilli, S., Costa, C., Pallottino, F., Raso, L., Menesatti, P.: A review on blockchain applications in the agri-food sector. J. Sci. Food Agric. **99**(14), 6129–6138 (2019). https://doi.org/10.1002/jsfa.9912
18. Ahmadzadeh, S., Ajmal, T., Ramanathan, R., Duan, Y.: A comprehensive review on food waste reduction based on IoT and big data technologies. Sustainability **15**(4) (2023). Article no. 4. https://doi.org/10.3390/su15043482
19. Baryannis, G., Validi, S., Dani, S., Antoniou, G.: Supply chain risk management and artificial intelligence: state of the art and future research directions. Int. J. Prod. Res. **57**(7), 2179–2202 (2019). https://doi.org/10.1080/00207543.2018.1530476
20. Casino, F., et al.: Blockchain-based food supply chain traceability: a case study in the dairy sector. Int. J. Prod. Res. **59**(19), 5758–5770 (2021). https://doi.org/10.1080/00207543.2020.1789238
21. Bager, S.L., Singh, C., Persson, U.M.: Blockchain is not a silver bullet for agro-food supply chain sustainability: insights from a coffee case study. Curr. Res. Environ. Sustain. **4**, 100163 (2022). https://doi.org/10.1016/j.crsust.2022.100163
22. Banker, R.D., Mitra, S., Sambamurthy, V., Mitra, S.: The effects of digital trading platforms on commodity prices in agricultural supply chains. MIS Q. **35**(3), 599–611 (2011). https://doi.org/10.2307/23042798

23. Kittipanya-ngam, P., Tan, K.H.: A framework for food supply chain digitalization: lessons from Thailand. Prod. Plann. Control **31**(2–3), 158–172 (2020). https://doi.org/10.1080/09537287.2019.1631462
24. Mwalupaso, G.E., Wang, S., Xu, Z., Tian, X.: Towards auspicious agricultural informatization—implication of farmers' behavioral intention apropos of mobile phone use in agriculture. Sustainability **11**(22) (2019). https://doi.org/10.3390/su11226282
25. Prause, G., Boevsky, I.: Smart contracts for smart rural supply chains. Bulgarian J. Agric. Sci. **25**, 454–463 (2019)
26. Sekhar Bhusal, C.: Blockchain technology in agriculture: a case study of blockchain start-up companies. IJCSIT **13**(5), 31–48 (2021). https://doi.org/10.5121/ijcsit.2021.13503
27. Tsolakis, N., Schumacher, R., Dora, M., Kumar, M.: Artificial intelligence and blockchain implementation in supply chains: a pathway to sustainability and data monetisation? Ann. Oper. Res. **327**(1), 157–210 (2023). https://doi.org/10.1007/s10479-022-04785-2
28. Barcaccia, G., Lucchin, M., Cassandro, M.: DNA barcoding as a molecular tool to track down mislabeling and food piracy. Diversity **8**(1) (2016). Article no. 1. https://doi.org/10.3390/d8010002
29. Bhandal, R., Meriton, R., Kavanagh, R.E., Brown, A.: The application of digital twin technology in operations and supply chain management: a bibliometric review. Supply Chain Manag. Int. J. **27**(2), 182–206 (2022). https://doi.org/10.1108/SCM-01-2021-0053
30. Biji, K.B., Ravishankar, C.N., Mohan, C.O., Srinivasa Gopal, T.K.: Smart packaging systems for food applications: a review. J. Food Sci. Technol. **52**(10), 6125–6135 (2015). https://doi.org/10.1007/s13197-015-1766-7
31. Cetateanu, A., Jones, A.: How can GPS technology help us better understand exposure to the food environment? A systematic review. SSM – Popul. Health **2**, 196–205 (2016). https://doi.org/10.1016/j.ssmph.2016.04.001
32. Haddud, A., DeSouza, A., Khare, A., Lee, H.: Examining potential benefits and challenges associated with the Internet of Things integration in supply chains. J. Manuf. Technol. Manag. **28**(8), 1055–1085 (2017). https://doi.org/10.1108/JMTM-05-2017-0094
33. Jagtap, S., et al.: Chapter 5 - IoT technologies in the food supply chain. In: Galanakis, C.M. (ed.) Food Technology Disruptions, pp. 175–211. Academic Press (2021). https://doi.org/10.1016/B978-0-12-821470-1.00009-4
34. Rejeb, A., Keogh, J.G., Rejeb, K.: Big data in the food supply chain: a literature review. J. Data Inf. Manag. **4**(1), 33–47 (2022). https://doi.org/10.1007/s42488-021-00064-0
35. Wolfert, S., Ge, L., Verdouw, C., Bogaardt, M.-J.: Big data in smart farming – a review. Agric. Syst. **153**, 69–80 (2017). https://doi.org/10.1016/j.agsy.2017.01.023
36. Pereira, R., Serrano, J.: A review of methods used on IT maturity models development: a systematic literature review and a critical analysis. J. Inf. Technol. **35**(2), 161–178 (2020). https://doi.org/10.1177/0268396219886874
37. Rasool, F., Greco, M., Grimaldi, M.: Digital supply chain performance metrics: a literature review. Meas. Bus. Excell. **26**(1), 23–38 (2021). https://doi.org/10.1108/MBE-11-2020-0147
38. Carrera-Rivera, A., Ochoa, W., Larrinaga, F., Lasa, G.: How-to conduct a systematic literature review: a quick guide for computer science research. Comput. Ind. **142**(103730). https://doi.org/10.1016/j.compind.2022.103730
39. Chan, K.Y., Abdullah, J., Shahid, A.: A framework for traceable and transparent supply chain management for agri-food sector in malaysia using blockchain technology. IJACSA **10**(11) (2019). https://doi.org/10.14569/IJACSA.2019.0101120
40. Joo, J., Han, Y.: An evidence of distributed trust in blockchain-based sustainable food supply chain. Sustainability **13**(19), 10980 (2021). https://doi.org/10.3390/su131910980

41. El Hathat, Z., Venkatesh, V.G., Zouadi, T., Sreedharan, V.R., Manimuthu, A., Shi, Y.: Analyzing the greenhouse gas emissions in the palm oil supply chain in the VUCA world: a blockchain initiative. Bus. Strategy Environ. **32**(8), 5563–5582 (2023). https://doi.org/10.1002/bse.3436
42. Menon, S., Jain, K.: Blockchain technology for transparency in agri-food supply chain: use cases, limitations, and future directions. IEEE Trans. Eng. Manag., 1–15 (2021). https://doi.org/10.1109/TEM.2021.3110903
43. Popovic, T., Krco, S., Misic, N., Martinovic, A., Jovovic, I.: Blockchain-based transparency and data provenance in the wine value chain. In: 2022 26th International Conference on Information Technology (IT), Zabljak, Montenegro, pp. 1–5. IEEE, February 2022. https://doi.org/10.1109/IT54280.2022.9743541
44. Sharma, A., Bhatia, T., Singh, R.K., Sharma, A.: Developing the framework of blockchain-enabled agri-food supply chain. BPMJ **30**(1), 291–316 (2023). https://doi.org/10.1108/BPMJ-01-2023-0035
45. Donaldson, D.A.: Digital from farm to fork: Infrastructures of quality and control in food supply chains. J. Rural Stud. **91**, 228–235 (2022). https://doi.org/10.1016/j.jrurstud.2021.10.004
46. Tsoukas, V., Gkogkidis, A., Kampa, A., Spathoulas, G., Kakarountas, A.: Enhancing food supply chain security through the use of blockchain and TinyML. Information **13**(5), 213 (2022). https://doi.org/10.3390/info13050213
47. Commandré, Y., Macombe, C., Mignon, S.: Implications for agricultural producers of using blockchain for food transparency, study of 4 food chains by cumulative approach. Sustainability **13**(17), 9843 (2021). https://doi.org/10.3390/su13179843
48. Mangla, S.K., Kazancoglu, Y., Ekinci, E., Liu, M., Özbiltekin, M., Sezer, M.D.: Using system dynamics to analyze the societal impacts of blockchain technology in milk supply chainsrefer. Transp. Res. Part E Logist. Transp. Rev. **149**, 102289 (2021). https://doi.org/10.1016/j.tre.2021.102289
49. Schrobback, P., Zhang, A., Loechel, B., Ricketts, K., Ingham, A.: Food credence attributes: a conceptual framework of supply chain stakeholders, their motives, and mechanisms to address information asymmetry. Foods **12**(3) (2023). Article no. 3. https://doi.org/10.3390/foods12030538
50. Marchese, A., Tomarchio, O.: A blockchain-based system for agri-food supply chain traceability management. SN Comput. Sci. **3**(4), 279 (2022). https://doi.org/10.1007/s42979-022-01148-3
51. Musah, S., Medeni, T.D., Soylu, D.: Assessment of role of innovative technology through blockchain technology in Ghana's Cocoa Beans food supply chains. In: 2019 3rd International Symposium on Multidisciplinary Studies and Innovative Technologies (ISMSIT), Ankara, Turkey, pp. 1–12. IEEE, October 2019. https://doi.org/10.1109/ISMSIT.2019.8932936
52. Cao, S., Xu, H., Bryceson, K.P.: Blockchain traceability for sustainability communication in food supply chains: an architectural framework, design pathway and considerations. Sustainability **15**(18), 13486 (2023). https://doi.org/10.3390/su151813486
53. Cao, S., Foth, M., Powell, W., Miller, T., Li, M.: A blockchain-based multisignature approach for supply chain governance: a use case from the Australian beef industry. Blockchain Res. Appl. **3**(4), 100091 (2022). https://doi.org/10.1016/j.bcra.2022.100091
54. Khanna, A., Jain, S., Burgio, A., Bolshev, V., Panchenko, V.: Blockchain-enabled supply chain platform for Indian dairy industry: safety and traceability. Foods **11**(17), 2716 (2022). https://doi.org/10.3390/foods11172716
55. Chu, T.T., Pham, T.T.T.: vertical coordination in agri-food supply chain and blockchain: a proposed framework solution for Vietnamese cashew nut business. Reg. Sci. Policy Pract. **16**(3) (2022). https://doi.org/10.1111/rsp3.12576

56. van Wassenaer, L., Verdouw, C., Kassahun, A., van Hilten, M., van der Meij, K., Tekinerdogan, B.: Tokenizing circularity in agri-food systems: a conceptual framework and exploratory study. J. Clean. Prod. **413**, 137527 (2023). https://doi.org/10.1016/j.jclepro.2023.137527
57. Cocco, L., et al.: A blockchain-based traceability system in agri-food SME: case study of a traditional bakery. IEEE Access **9**, 62899–62915 (2021). https://doi.org/10.1109/ACCESS.2021.3074874
58. Shuib, A., Ibrahim, I., Yusoff, F.H.: Traceability system of halal chicken supply chain. In: 2021 IEEE 12th Control and System Graduate Research Colloquium (ICSGRC), Shah Alam, Malaysia, pp. 144–149. IEEE, August 2021. https://doi.org/10.1109/ICSGRC53186.2021.9515246
59. Malik, S., Dedeoglu, V., Kanhere, S.S., Jurdak, R., Paik, H.-Y.: Traceable, trustworthy and privacy preserving agri-food supply chains. In: 2021 Third IEEE International Conference on Trust, Privacy and Security in Intelligent Systems and Applications (TPS-ISA), Atlanta, GA, USA, pp. 313–320. IEEE, December 2021. https://doi.org/10.1109/TPSISA52974.2021.00034
60. Kechagias, E.P., Gayialis, S.P., Papadopoulos, G.A., Papoutsis, G.: An ethereum-based distributed application for enhancing food supply chain traceability. Foods **12**(6) (2023). Article no. 6. https://doi.org/10.3390/foods12061220
61. Gallo, P., Daidone, F., Sgroi, F., Avantaggiato, M.: Agrichain: blockchain syntactic and semantic validation for reducing information asymmetry in agri-food (2022)
62. Damoska Sekuloska, J., Erceg, A.: Blockchain technology toward creating a smart local food supply chain. Computers **11**(6), 95 (2022). https://doi.org/10.3390/computers11060095
63. Kayikci, Y., Durak Usar, D., Aylak, B.L.: Using blockchain technology to drive operational excellence in perishable food supply chains during outbreaks. IJLM **33**(3), 836–876 (2022). https://doi.org/10.1108/IJLM-01-2021-0027
64. Sengupta, T., Narayanamurthy, G., Moser, R., Pereira, V., Bhattacharjee, D.: Disruptive technologies for achieving supply chain resilience in COVID-19 era: an implementation case study of satellite imagery and blockchain technologies in fish supply chain. Inf. Syst. Front. **24**(4), 1107–1123 (2022). https://doi.org/10.1007/s10796-021-10228-3
65. Swapna, D., Sri, U.K., Himaja, V.S.N., Varshita, T.N., Gayatri, V., Praveen, S.P.: Crypto logistic network: food supply chain and micro investment using blockchain. In: 2023 2nd International Conference on Automation, Computing and Renewable Systems (ICACRS), Pudukkottai, India, pp. 908–915. IEEE, December 2023. https://doi.org/10.1109/ICACRS58579.2023.10404449
66. Kumar, A., Singh, R.K., Modgil, S.: Exploring the relationship between ICT, SCM practices and organizational performance in agri-food supply chain. Benchmarking Int. J. **27**(3), 1003–1041 (2020). https://doi.org/10.1108/BIJ-11-2019-0500
67. Vern, P., Panghal, A., Mor, R.S., Kamble, S.S.: Blockchain technology in the agri-food supply chain: a systematic literature review of opportunities and challenges. Manag. Rev. Q. (2024). https://doi.org/10.1007/s11301-023-00390-0
68. Chandan, A., John, M., Potdar, V.: Achieving UN SDGs in food supply chain using blockchain technology. Sustainability **15**(3), 2109 (2023). https://doi.org/10.3390/su15032109
69. Li, K., Lee, J.-Y., Gharehgozli, A.: Blockchain in food supply chains: a literature review and synthesis analysis of platforms, benefits and challenges. Int. J. Prod. Res. **61**(11), 3527–3546 (2023). https://doi.org/10.1080/00207543.2021.1970849
70. Guidani, B., Ronzoni, M., Accorsi, R.: Virtual agri-food supply chains: a holistic digital twin for sustainable food ecosystem design, control and transparency. Sustain. Prod. Consum. **46**, 161–179 (2024). https://doi.org/10.1016/j.spc.2024.01.016

71. Kayikci, Y., Subramanian, N., Dora, M., Bhatia, M.S.: Food supply chain in the era of Industry 4.0: blockchain technology implementation opportunities and impediments from the perspective of people, process, performance, and technology. Prod. Plann. Control **33**(2–3), 301–321 (2022). https://doi.org/10.1080/09537287.2020.1810757
72. Wünsche, J.F., Fernqvist, F.: The potential of blockchain technology in the transition towards sustainable food systems. Sustainability **14**(13), 7739 (2022). https://doi.org/10.3390/su14137739
73. Kaushik, I., Prakash, N., Jain, A.: Integration of blockchain & IoT in precision farming: exploration, scope and security challenges. In: 2021 IEEE 12th Annual Ubiquitous Computing, Electronics & Mobile Communication Conference (UEMCON), New York, NY, USA, pp. 0854–0859. IEEE, December (2021). https://doi.org/10.1109/UEMCON53757.2021.9666554
74. Tekın, K., Yurdakök-Dıkmen, B., Kanca, H., Guatteo, R.: Precision livestock farming technologies: novel direction of information flow; [Hassas hayvancılık teknolojileri: Bilgi akışının yeni yönü]. Ankara Universitesi Veteriner Fakultesi Dergisi **68**(2), 193–212 (2021). Chartered Institution of Building Services Engineers. https://doi.org/10.33988/auvfd.837485
75. Durrant, A., Markovic, M., Matthews, D., May, D., Enright, J., Leontidis, G.: The role of cross-silo federated learning in facilitating data sharing in the agri-food sector. Comput. Electron. Agric. **193**, 106648 (2022). https://doi.org/10.1016/j.compag.2021.106648
76. Leone, L.: Open data and food law in the digital era: empowering citizens through ICT technology (2015)
77. Talpur, S.R., Abbas, A.F., Khan, N., Irum, S., Ali, J.: Improving opportunities in supply chain processes using the Internet of Things and blockchain technology. Int. J. Interact. Mob. Technol. **17**(8), 23–38 (2023). International Association of Online Engineering. https://doi.org/10.3991/ijim.v17i08.39467
78. Martínez-Castañeda, M., Feijoo, C.: Use of blockchain in the agri-food value chain: state of the art in Spain and some lessons from the perspective of public support. Telecommun. Policy **47**(6), 102574 (2023). https://doi.org/10.1016/j.telpol.2023.102574
79. Emmi, L., et al.: Exploiting the internet resources for autonomous robots in agriculture. Agriculture **13**(5), 1005 (2023). https://doi.org/10.3390/agriculture13051005
80. Durrant, A., Markovic, M., Matthews, D., May, D., Leontidis, G., Enright, J.: How might technology rise to the challenge of data sharing in agri-food? Glob. Food Secur. **28**, 100493 (2021). https://doi.org/10.1016/j.gfs.2021.100493
81. Gurrala, K., Hariga, M.: Key food supply chain challenges: a review of the literature and research gaps. OSCM Int. J., 441–460 (2022). https://doi.org/10.31387/oscm0510358
82. Xu, J., Guo, S., Xie, D., Yan, Y.: Blockchain: a new safeguard for agri-foods. Artif. Intell. Agric. **4**, 153–161 (2020). https://doi.org/10.1016/j.aiia.2020.08.002
83. Gazzola, P., Pavione, E., Barge, A., Fassio, F.: Using the transparency of supply chain powered by blockchain to improve sustainability relationships with stakeholders in the food sector: the case study of Lavazza. Sustainability **15**(10), 7884 (2023). https://doi.org/10.3390/su15107884

Author Index

Published by Springer Nature Switzerland AG 2024
R. van de Wetering et al. (Eds.): I3E 2024, LNCS 14907, pp. 445–446, 2024.
https://doi.org/10.1007/978-3-031-72234-9

Printed by Printforce, the Netherlands